FIREFLY
ENCYCLOPEDIA
of
TREES

FIREFLY
ENCYCLOPEDIA
of
TREES

Edited by

Steve Cafferty M.Sc.

FIREFLY BOOKS

A FIREFLY BOOK

Published by Firefly Books Ltd. 2005

First printing

Publisher Cataloging-in-Publication Data (U.S.)

Firefly encyclopedia of trees / edited by Steve Cafferty.
[288] p. : col. ill., photos. ; cm.
Includes bibliographical references and index.
Summary: Comprehensive reference to all conifer genera, major temperate
broadleaves and important tropical trees. Provides a complete profile of each
tree group, including fact panel, distribution map, list of major species, botany
and economic uses.
ISBN 1-55407-051-1
1. Trees -- Encyclopedias. I. Cafferty, Steve. II. Title.
582.16/03 22   QK475.F574 2005

Library and Archives Canada Cataloguing in Publication

Firefly Encyclopedia of trees / editor, Steve Cafferty.
Includes bibliographical references and index.
ISBN 1-55407-051-1
1. Trees--Encyclopedias. I. Cafferty, Steve II. Title: Encyclopedia of trees.
QK474.87.F56 2005   582.16'03   C2004-905514-3

Published in the United States by
Firefly Books (U.S.) Inc.
P.O. Box 1338, Ellicott Station
Buffalo, New York 14205

Published in Canada by
Firefly Books Ltd.
66 Leek Crescent
Richmond Hill, Ontario L4B 1H1

The Brown Reference Group plc.
(incorporating Andromeda Oxford Limited)
8 Chapel Place
Rivington Street
London EC2A 3DQ
www.brownreference.com

EDITORIAL DIRECTOR Lindsey Lowe
PROJECT MANAGER Graham Bateman
ART DIRECTOR Michael Whitehead
PROJECT EDITOR Stephanie Horner
TROPICAL BOTANIST & FORESTRY ADVISER Colin Pendry
HORTICULTURALIST Kay Maguire
DESIGNERS Chris Lanaway, Jane Lanaway
DTP & CARTOGRAPHIC WORK Adam Elliott, Christine Engert, Barbara Theisen
PICTURE RESEARCHER Liz Eddison
PRODUCTION DIRECTOR Alastair Gourlay
FRONT COVER PHOTOGRAPH Justin Willsmore

Printed in China

FRONTISPIECE (*page ii*) In temperate regions, deciduous broadleaf trees
visibly mark the seasons more than any aspect of the natural landscape.

THIS PAGE Following the devastation caused by the eruption of Mount
St. Helens in America's Washington state in 1980, the environment was
left to respond naturally to the disturbance. Since 1990, the most
conspicuous change has been an increase in the abundance of trees
and shrubs. Among the trees to recolonize the ash-covered slopes are
Red Alder (*Alnus rubra*), Black Cottonwood (*Populus trichocarpa*),
and Willows (*Salix* spp).

Contents

Introduction

Human beings have an affinity for trees. They inspire us, wherever we live. In cities they soften the urban landscape and help to keep us in tune with the changing seasons. Trees are an integral part of the rural environment and, even in regions where they are not, we plant them around our dwellings for shelter, fuel, timber, and their fruits.

Particular trees are identified with different areas: the Chestnuts and Elms of the northeastern United States, the Redwoods of California, the Live Oaks of the South, to the conifers of the old growth forests of the Pacific Northwest. England is synonymous with its Oak, the Mediterranean with its olive groves and cypresses. This authoritative volume gives insight into the huge diversity of trees. In fact, in the twenty-first century, we are surrounded by an unnatural diversity as numerous tree species have been introduced from around the world, greatly enriching our natural and manmade environments.

Our relationship with trees is an enduring one, though that with forests has changed since earlier generations. Where they saw the frontier wilderness of Jack London and James Fenimore Cooper, or the green hell of the unrelenting jungle, we see forests under threat from logging, pollution, or climate change. Trees now need our help to survive—but the story is by no means uniformly bleak. The Gingko, or Maidenhair Tree, the Dawn Redwood, and the Wollemi Pine are remnants of the great gymnosperm forests of the Mesozoic Era, home of the dinosaurs. Over the millennia, as new trees evolved, they dwindled to tiny populations on the edge of extinction. Rediscovered and rescued by humankind, they have been brought into cultivation, and quite literally given a new lease of life. Here the message is one of hope—if we value trees we will look after them, and their descendants will be alive for our descendants to enjoy.

COLIN PENDRY B.Sc., Ph.D.
TROPICAL FOREST BOTANIST, ROYAL BOTANIC GARDEN EDINBURGH, SCOTLAND

How the Encyclopedia is Organized

The material comprises main text, illustrations, tables to aid species identification, fact boxes for a summary of the most important genera, and a thumbnail map showing their native distribution. Species, distribution, diagnostic features of the genus, horticultural and economic importance, and any specific information relevant to that genus are detailed in the text. The tables list all the species of the genus (save in the case of larger genera where main species only are detailed) and give concise facts on common names, distribution, species diagnostic features, and details of their horticultural or economic importance. Wherever possible, the species in each table are divided into natural divisions (Subgenus, Section, Series, etc). If no such natural division is available, but species can be grouped, the general terms Group I, II, III... are used. In some cases an entire table or parts of it have been constructed in the form of a key, coded by letter. Thus the first keyed entries will be under **A**, with the alternative **AA** and even **AAA**. Further keyed items work through the alphabet: **B, BB; C, CC**, etc.

For dimensions of, for example, a leaf it is often necessary to show the normal parameters and extremes that may be found reasonably often; thus (4)5–6(6.7) in ((10)12–15(17) cm) indicates normal dimensions of 5–6 in (12–15 cm) but with common extremes of as little as 4 in (10 cm) or as much as 6.7 in (17 cm).

Many taxonomic changes have taken place over the past 20 years. New discoveries in the field, and further herbarium studies of specimens have led to the reclassification of many families and genera. To reflect these changes, the system of arrangement based on that of G.L. Stebbins in his *Flowering Plants—Evolution Above Species Level*, has largely been followed. However, where appropriate, it has been amended and updated according to the system of classification used by D.J. Mabberley in *The Plant-Book* (2nd edn), the most comprehensive modern treatment covering all groups of plants. In all but the Trees of the Tropics chapter (which is alphabetical by genus), families are arranged in evolutionary order.

Climate Zones

For each genus, and its main species, the relevant climate zone(s) in which it grows are represented at the end of the entry by the abbreviation **CZ**. The numbers link the distribution of a genus or species to the climate zone maps of North America and Europe on page 39, following the ten climate zones identified by the US Department of Agriculture. No climate zone figures are included, however, in the section "Trees of the Tropics," since all tropical regions encompass climate zones 9–10, making allowance for local variations in microclimates in tropical mountainous regions where, at altitude, local climate zones may be lower or cooler over relatively small areas.

How the Classification Works

All entries are ordered by family (with the exception of the "Trees of the Tropics" genera, which are ordered alphabetically). The example below shows how different typography is used to distinguish the names:

SALICACEAE

Salix

Willows, Salix, Osiers

The family name appears in small capital letters. Each entry is then shown by its Latin name (the genus, identified by italic type) and its common name. Most trees have a number of popular or common names of which as many alternatives as possible are included. These are shown prominently in bold type. With regard to the scientific name or binomial there should of course be just one correct name—this is shown in italic. However, it is often not quite so straightforward since historically several names have been applied to a single species. Here, the system adopted is to use the currently accepted scientific name, as far as is possible, throughout an entry but at first mention other synonyms are given, either in parentheses or by using the = sign.

Throughout this work, scientific terminology has been kept to a minimum, but inevitably some has had to be used for the sake of conciseness. For this reason there is a comprehensive Glossary at the end of the book, and the section "What is a Tree?" should be consulted for an account of the structure, reproduction, and growth of trees.

WHAT IS A TREE?

From the earliest times, plants have been classified as herbs, shrubs, or trees. Thus, the concept of a tree is extremely familiar. Our mental image of a tree is that of a perennial plant, capable of attaining considerable height, with a single, woody, selfsupporting trunk or stem that is usually unbranched for some distance above ground. Yet one of the most striking features of trees is their diversity: of forms, which is so strikingly apparent from the physiognomy of conifers, broadleaves, palms (and some bamboos, ferns, and cacti); of life histories; and of the roles played by trees in the communities of flora and fauna to which they contribute so greatly.

In the simplest of terms, there are two components to a tree: a stem (trunk) supporting, somewhere aloft, a crown of branches and foliage. Shrubs are of lower stature, the trunk is less defined, and branching is evident virtually at ground level. Yet the distinction between shrubs and trees is not always clear, and on occasion tall shrubs and low trees may intergrade. In any event, every tree must start life as a sapling, growing from a seed, or, in the rarer instances of tree-ferns, growing from a minute spore. Human influence should also be mentioned—many cultivars of true trees exist that reach only the stature of shrubs, while such practises as pruning or coppicing will also reduce a tree to the size and shape of a shrub.

Morphological Characters

Trees as isolated specimens are a common enough sight in parks, gardens, and—most notably—in arboreta, where the massing of many individuals of different species in a single collection allows comparison of the morphology or form of one species, with that of another. In such settings, it is easy to appreciate that each species is distinctive and often recognizable by a range of "morphological characters." Indeed, from an early age, most of us, in part unconsciously, make use of such characters to get to know the common kinds of tree. They include features of bark, leaves, buds, and so on, in addition to the manner of branching, which give the tree its own distinctive shape.

Notwithstanding the importance of single specimen trees—often as the result of a deliberate planting policy—trees are closely associated, in the minds of most people, with the notion of a forest or woodland. To the botanist, this embodies the science of plant sociology or ecology—what might be called the gregariousness of trees. The notion of a forest is again often derived from childhood experiences, the earliest image normally being of a habitat that is uniform in character and somewhat dark within. This simple image in fact embodies two important botanical characteristics of many forests in north temperate regions: first, the dominance of a single species

(or sometimes of two or three); and, second, the canopy-forming capacity of trees massed together, which so significantly reduces the amount of light available beneath them. Thus, there is a general form both of the individual tree and of the forest. The chief focus here is on the tree itself, though it is worth noting how very different northern temperate coniferous and deciduous forests are from the native vegetation in most parts of the humid Tropics. In northern regions, it is customary to name the forest after a single species of dominant tree, as in the oak (*Quercus* spp), beech (*Fagus* spp), pine (*Pinus* spp), or spruce (*Picea* spp) forests so widespread in North America and Europe. In the humid Tropics, by contrast, the scene is one of bewildering diversity: scores of species of widely differing height, habit, and foliage commonly play approximately equal roles in the structure of the whole. Nothing is more characteristic of tropical forest than the tall individual trees, or emergents, that protrude above the general level of the canopy.

Structural Diversity

Almost equally notable is the structural diversity of the trees themselves. One of the most astonishing is surely the Banyan Tree (*Ficus benghalensis*), a common evergreen in India. It can reach some 85 ft (26 m) in height and has long, horizontally spreading branches, which put down aerial roots at intervals; these, on reaching the ground, act as supporting pillars. Banyans probably have the biggest crowns of any trees in the world, and with their pillar or prop roots, a single tree can make a small wood. The Banyan is sacred in India, and an account of it was given as early as the fourth century B.C.E. during Alexander the Great's invasion of India at that time.

Our concern, therefore, is with this structural diversity, as seen in simple botanical terms. Yet, sturdy oak and beech, palm and pine, slender birch (*Betula* spp) and giant silk-cotton trees (*Bombax* and *Ceiba* spp) all share an essential botany that makes them all trees. In short, they exhibit structural diversity within a common plan.

ABOVE The Banyan Tree, *Ficus benghalensis*, with its downward growing aerial roots, which, once in the ground, thicken making the tree appear to be supported by pillars. The tree has religious significance to Hindus because of its longevity and is often adorned as a shrine.

FACING PAGE Pneumatophores of Bald Cypresses (*Taxodium distichum*) are produced by the roots in damp situations and stand above the ground. These giants are in the Atchafalaya Basin in Louisiana, U.S.A.

Tree Shapes

Two general forms of tree are immediately recognizable to most people—the spire-like "fir" trees and the "bushy-topped" deciduous trees. At its simplest level, this division encompasses conifers and broadleaves respectively. Two other readily discerned but less frequent forms are the fastigiate types, characterized by the Lombardy Poplar (*Populus nigra* 'Italica'), and the classic "spiky" form of the palm tree. Botanists recognize many others. Indeed, a look at deciduous trees in winter reveals the highly distinctive pattern of branching of each species. Ultimately, all features of form and branching must be related to events in the growing shoot tips where the embryonic tissues are located. All these features follow, in large measure, a program aid down in the plant's heredity but modified by environmental influences. However, they are always under precise physiological control. This points us to the first great uniformity in tree construction—the fact that within every tree, no matter what species or where it grows, lies an organized assemblage of cells and tissues. It is in terms of these cells and tissues that the wood anatomist will see the tree.

Thus, to the trained eye, each species of tree has a characteristic form, or in botanical terms, a gross morphology. This form is the outward expression of long-term events, which, though physiological in character, must reveal themselves to the observer in anatomical terms. Just as each species of tree has its own external form, its internal anatomy will likewise exhibit distinctive and sometimes unique features. For botanists, this fact opens up the immense field of the comparative study of the microscopic anatomy of wood.

The general form of any species of tree, though, is not fixed and immutable, and even the most casual observer must have met with countless everyday examples of this. Certain features are constant enough, but there is enormous variation in general habit and stature to be found within the extent of the geographical range of a single species. Nowhere is this more evident than in the Douglas Fir (*Pseudotsuga menziesii*) in different parts of its vast North American range. Or, one may contrast what we know as Lawson's Cypress (*Chamaecyparis lawsoniana*), which in cultivation is a highly variable but commonly quite low-growing ornamental tree, with the forest giants found towering to 195 ft (60 m) in western North America, where the plant is known as the Port

The Douglas Fir, *Pseudotsuga menziesii*, has extremely rapid growth, commonly putting on growth of 3 ft (1 m) in a year, sometimes 5 ft (1.5 m).

Orford Cedar. Among coniferous evergreens, such as the pines, spruces, and silver firs (*Abies* spp), much of the distinctive general form, seen from its silhouette against the skyline, of a particular species turns upon the behavior of the so-called leading shoot, and its growth in relation to that of the side shoots. Marked dominance and extremely rapid growth of the leading shoot can, over a period of years, give the very elegant spire-like habit so characteristic of the Engelmann Spruce (*Picea engelmannii*) in the Rocky Mountains. A much reduced dominance of the leader can result in the comparatively bushy-topped growth habit of certain European species of pine, such as the Umbrella Pine (*Pinus pinea*). In the Scots Pine (*P. sylvestris*), it is possible to see the profound effect on overall habit of growing trees either in close stands or as isolated individuals. Finally, as the latitudinal or altitudinal limits of a given species are approached, increasingly severely stunted and often malformed specimens are seen, scarcely recognizable as belonging to the same species as the trees that grow farther south or at a lower altitude. It is easy enough to forget that some of these gnarled and stunted specimens may be of great antiquity—possibly hundreds of years old.

It is probably true to say that few trees continue to live in a healthy state beyond four hundred or five hundred years—and this includes allegedly long-lived species such as the English Oak (*Quercus robur*)— though a small group of species is well known to live for very much longer: the Common Yew (*Taxus baccata*), for example, is known to have reached one thousand years. However, most notable are the Coast and Mountain Redwoods (*Sequoia sempervirens* and *Sequoiadendron giganteum*) of the western United States and a few other conifers; also there are well-authenticated long-lived individuals of the monocotyledonous Dragon Tree (*Dracaena draco*). In all of them, a lifespan exceeding two thousand years is attained; with isolated examples of Dragon Tree and Bristle-cone Pine (*Pinus longaeva*) living in excess of four thousand years. In practise, though, many trees have their natural lifespan cut short by demands of forest management, which call for regular felling and wood utilization, and of urban amenity forestry, where declining trees have to be felled because of the danger to the public.

Trunk and Wood Structure

Ask a child to draw a tree and he or she will start with the trunk, then add a fan or brush of branches. In short, the trunk is integral to the popular concept of a tree, yet the prominence and size of that trunk can vary enormously.

In the Tropics, trees with massive trunks and relatively little in the way of crown (due to restricted branching) are conveniently called pachycaulous (meaning thick-stemmed), while trees with relatively slender stems and a generous bushy crown from extensive branching are known as leptocaulous (slender-stemmed). In many low-growing trees, and even in some large, mature individuals of certain coniferous trees such as the Common Yew and the Old World cedars (*Cedrus* spp), a single, well-defined trunk may not always be readily recognizable, yet in normal full-grown specimens of most of our common deciduous trees, such as oaks, ashes (*Fraxinus* spp), and beeches, it is almost impossible to conceive of the tree without its trunk; and in the vast majority of conifers, this is even more emphatically the case.

The existence and continuing prominence of the trunk springs from the fact that in early life there exists a radially organized central axis extending from the young shoot tip down into the root. Initially, as in a beech

ABOVE Cottonwoods, Engelmann Spruce, and Fir trees surround Medicine Lake in the Jasper National Park, Alberta, Canada.

LEFT The Live Oak, *Quercus agrifolia*, displaying its black striped bark. Many oaks are long lived, and can survive for eight hundred years or more.

seedling in the first year of life, the line of demarcation between stem and root in this slender axis may not always be readily apparent. Yet their destinies are very different and it is the slender, already woody, stem of the sapling that is gradually transformed, over a period of years, into the trunk of the full-grown tree. Growing trees in close-set stands can inhibit the survival of lateral branches, so it is common to see stands of pine or spruce composed of trees, perhaps thirty or forty years old, in which the trunks appear to rise unbranched to an impressive height. To some extent the absence of lateral branches will have been encouraged by early "brashing" operations by foresters. Certainly, isolated individuals of the same species will present a very different picture.

Many palm species, including the Oil Palm (*Elaeis guineensis*), the Date Palm (*Phoenix dactylifera*), and the Coconut Palm (*Cocos nucifera*), are structurally quite distinct in that the trunk is in a very strict sense an unbranched stem, surmounted only by a crown of huge leaves. Palms, moreover, grow in an entirely different

manner from either hardwood or softwood (conifer) trees, and their "wood," though chemically similar and extremely tough, is in its arrangement and disposition in the stem quite unlike wood as we know it from hardwoods and softwoods. The trunks of many tropical trees are sinuous to a degree not readily matched in the trees of north temperate forests. In a mature Baobab (*Adansonia digitata*), the trunk is characteristically of immense width.

The anatomical arrangement of the cellular components of the trunk of a tree is basically similar in conifers and broadleaves, only the components themselves vary. In simple terms, a number of layers can be recognized— from the outside, the outer protective bark, the sugar-conducting phloem (or inner bark), and the inner solid core of wood (xylem) through the younger elements of which water is conducted. Between the phloem and wood there is a narrow band of actively dividing cells (vascular cambium) that produce secondary phloem to the outside and secondary xylem, or wood, to the inside.

Deconstructing Wood

To look at these layers in detail, we will start with the wood, which makes up the bulk of the trunk and is obviously the element of commercial importance. In so-called "hardwoods" or dicotyledonous (broadleaved) woody species, the wood consists, in varying proportions, of five principal components:

1. Most characteristic are the **vessels**, which are made up of many tubular cells placed end to end, with a free and open passageway between one vessel member and the next above or below it. These are the water-conducting pipelines of the plant.

2. A high proportion of most hardwoods commonly consists of the fibrous component. This is made up of a great number of long, narrow **cells** (fibers) with thick walls and tapering ends, more or less closely bound together to form a strong matrix in which the vessels are interspersed. The hardness of any particular wood will depend in considerable measure on the number of these cells and the thickness of their walls.

3. Most woods contain a certain proportion of living, fairly thin-walled cells (termed **wood parenchyma**), which are often loaded with storage starch. They run in vertical sequences among the other, thicker-walled components.

4. The living part of the whole is physiologically linked to the so-called **rays**, which are, in effect, walls consisting of a few vertically stacked layers of living (parenchymatous) cells, again commonly replete with storage starch. In a severed trunk or branch (that is, as seen in transverse section), these rays form a series of radiating lines, the broadest of which are often easily visible to the naked eye.

The Baobab (*Adansonia* spp) is often the only tree remaining leafy in times of drought in grassland Africa, owing to its large trunk of light, fleshy wood, which consists of hollow chambers that can store tens of thousands of gallons of water from wetter seasons. The tree acts as a natural reservoir, utilized by people and animals alike.

Lignin is a generalized term for a series of complex carbon compounds whose chemistry is imperfectly understood, but it is clear that there are a number of different kinds of lignin. It is interesting to note that the lignins of conifers as a group are different from those of broadleaves. The important fact for us is that these cells and their lignin confer the properties of strength and rigidity—"woodiness"—so that the thicker the lignified wall, the more completely are these properties conferred.

RIGHT Growth rings on a tree stump show the age of a tree. Each ring is simply a layer of wood produced during one tree's growing season. Rings can be narrow or wide, depending on the growing conditions— abundant rainfall increases growth, producing a wider ring. drought decreases growth, producing a narrower ring.

BELOW Superb images of natural wood structure are revealed by the electron microscope: this is Scots Pine (*Pinus sylvestris*) magnified × 500.

5. The last of the cellular components of wood are the **tracheids**. They are not often very plentiful in hardwoods, but nevertheless they make up almost the entire "woody cylinder" (apart from the rays) in all the softwoods and in a very small number of exceedingly primitive dicotyledons. Tracheids are dual-purpose elements performing at one and the same time the conducting function of a vessel member and the strengthening role of a fiber. Parts of their longitudinal walls are very freely supplied with thin sites termed pits, and it is these that allow water transfer from cell to cell.

When young and living, the walls of vessels, tracheids, and fibers become impregnated with a substance called **lignin**. When they die, this material remains so that the rigid cell shape is retained.

Thus we come to see the wood of a trunk or branch as composed of a vast interlocking plexus of microscopic cells, some of which are heavily lignified and dead at the functional maturity of the organ; interlaced with these are others (composing wood parenchyma and rays) that are still alive and in varying degrees metabolically active. All these cells originate from a cylinder of delicate meristematic (that is recurrently dividing) cells termed the **vascular cambium**, which forms the boundary line between wood and bark. Needless to say, this vascular cambium, being a meristematic or formative tissue, is of critical importance not only in the development of the tree but throughout its entire life.

Growth Rings

It is common knowledge that the rings exposed when the trunk of a tree is cut radially represent its annual growth, but how do the growth rings arise? The answer lies in the type and size of cells produced by the vascular cambium at different times of the year. Annual rings are rendered more conspicuous in many cases on account of the first-formed vessels in spring being very much larger than those that are a component of the summer wood.

English oak and ash both illustrate this feature well; such woods are known as "ring-porous." In several other woods, including beech , willow (*Salix* spp), apple (*Malus* spp), and others, there is no marked difference in vessel diameter between spring and summer wood. Such woods are known as "diffuse-porous," and in them the annual rings are often less clearly defined, though in many such examples summer wood is marked by the presence of other distinctive features apart from vessel size. In a softwood, such as Scots Pine, the tracheids formed toward the end of the growth period, in summer, are of narrower bore and have much thicker walls than those formed in spring. This fact forms the basis on which one can recognize annual growth rings in this otherwise rather uniform wood.

In the monocotyledonous angiosperms, such as palms, there is, in general, no such annual increase in girth resulting from a cylinder of vascular cambium; that is, there is no comparable secondary thickening. In a very few cases of monocotyledonous angiosperms, however, there is a peculiar form of increase in girth quite different from that which applies to the dicotyledons. A well-known example occurs in the Dragon Tree (*Dracaena draco*). Cells in its general ground tissue become meristematic—capable of division comparable with the cambial cells already described for dicotyledons (secondary meristem). However, instead of cutting off phloem cells toward the outside of the stem and xylem cells toward the center, both phloem and xylem cells are cut off toward the stem center in such a way that the increments replicate the pattern of the vascular bundles seen in the primary stem.

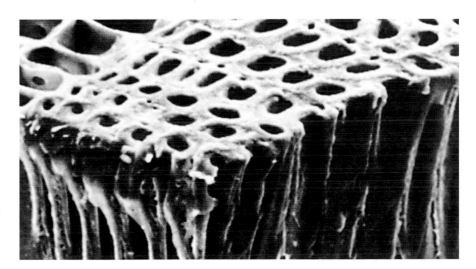

Other Diagnostic Features of Wood

The wood anatomist, wherever possible, likes to work with thin sections cut in three planes: the transverse, the radial longitudinal (as in quarter sawn wood)—in other words, parallel with a radius or diameter—and the tangential longitudinal section (as in flat sawn wood)—that is at right angles to a radius or diameter. Examined microscopically, these three preparations together provide all the information needed to identify the wood. In most cases this is possible as far as the genus, sometimes even to species, level. While a formidable array of characters becomes available through this procedure, it must not be forgotten that the wood of a tree has other diagnostic attributes, which are readily detectable without using a microscope. These include features of the fine structure as will be visible under a hand lens or with the naked eye, and such important general attributes as color and specific gravity, and the form of its bark. A consideration of color often has to take account of differences between the outer zone of living and often lighter-colored sapwood and the central core of generally nonliving and darker-hued heartwood. In commercial terms, it is the heartwood that is most valuable. To varying degrees this is impregnated with gums, resins, and other deposits that act as a natural preservative. In a limited number of woods, this heartwood has a notably distinctive color, as, for instance, in several species of ebony (*Diospyros ebenum*), where it is black, and the leguminous Logwood Tree (*Haematoxylon campechianum*), where it is purple in hue.

Woods vary greatly in specific gravity, and this important physical character is clearly linked with the uses to which particular species are put. Teak (*Tectona grandis*) is a particularly valuable timber, being a fairly heavy close-grained wood and exceptionally resistant to decay because of the deposition of resinous materials. By contrast, American balsa wood (*Ochroma* spp) is an example of a wood valued for its exceptional lightness, and the same is to some extent true of the wood of the widespread West African tree *Triplochiton scleroxylon*. In every case the usefulness of the wood is inseparably linked to its anatomical structure as revealed by a full microscopic examination. (The importance of wood from an economic or utilitarian angle is discussed on pages 32–39.)

FACING PAGE Timber-producing trees can be categorized into two distinct groups, conifers (e.g. pines) which yield the softwoods of commerce, and broadleaves or angiosperms (e.g. oaks) which yield the hardwoods. The trunk is formed of several living and nonliving layers. The outmost layer is the cork which protects the tree from damage, lowers water loss and insulates against cold and heat. New layers of cork are produced by the cork cambium, these two layers collectively form the outer bark. Below this is the phloem (inner bark or bast). This layer conducts essential food materials round the tree; as it dies it contributes further tissues to the outer bark. The vascular cambium is usually just one cell thick but is the life-giving zone of the trunk; by divisions it produces new phloem cells to the outside and new wood cells to the inside. The bulk of the tree is the true wood (xylem). The outermost layer (sapwood) is formed of tubular cells that conduct water from the roots to the leaves; a new ring of sapwood cells (the growth rings) is added annually by the vascular cambium. Over a period of years the sapwood loses its water-conducting function, and becomes the tree's "trashcan," all waste products of metabolism (particularly lignin) being deposited in the cells. Thus a central cylinder of heartwood is formed which acts as a strength-giving backbone of the tree.

LEFT The wood of the tree is here shown cut for lumber, except for the outer round-sided "slabs" which are "chipped" and processed into chipboard. The outer portion of the wood has few knots and is usually cut into planks, while the central core has more knots and is cut into thick planks or beams. Alternatively, the trunk may be "peeled" to produce plywood or processed for papermaking.

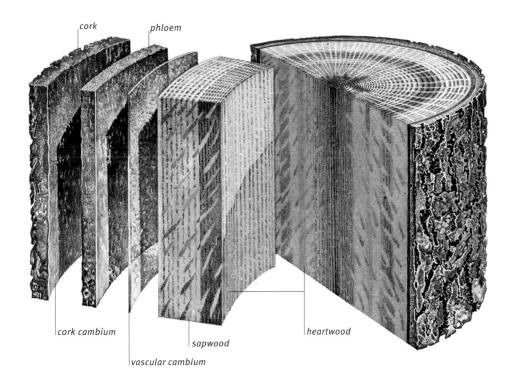

cork   phloem

cork cambium

vascular cambium

sapwood

heartwood

Pine (*Pinus* sp)   Oak (*Quercus* sp)

BELOW Light micrographs of transverse sections of three types of wood (x 75) show that density of the wood is clearly related to intensity of staining, hence thickness of the walls and quantity of cell contents. *Left* Balsa, an extremely light timber. The wood has very thin-walled fibers and the vessels are large and widely spaced. *Center* Boxwood, a dense, compact timber. The fiber tracheids have a tendency to be thick-walled and the vessels are small and evenly spaced throughout the early and late wood—a feature of diffuse porous wood. *Right* Ebony, an extremely heavy timber. The wood has very thick-walled fibers and the vessels are small, widely spaced and frequently blocked by deposits of gum.

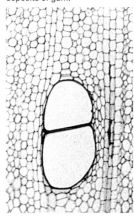

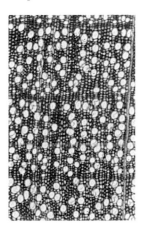

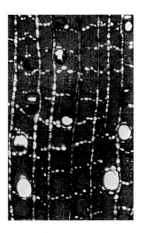

Bark

Without its bark or rind, the living tree would be very incomplete. In botanical terms, bark is defined as "all those tissues lying external to the vascular cambium," and as such it includes a diversity of components. In more detail, bark may be divided into an "inner bark" or "bast" formed from the vascular cambium and an "outer bark" formed largely from the cork cambium (*see* the illustration on page 16). Formerly, anatomists sometimes distinguished two fractions of inner bark: "hard" bast, which is composed of fibers, and "soft" bast or the living elements of the phloem. To the layperson, "bark" often means only these rough outer layers; yet the living phloem elements are indeed vital components of the tree, since their function is to conduct sugars and other organic products of metabolism from one part of the plant to another.

The outer bark is protective, but it is not uncommon to see trees that have become the victims of browsing animals and have had their bark more or less stripped down to the wood. Some species have evolved measures to reduce such attacks, including stinging hairs (*Ficus* spp) and long thorns on their stems (*Acacia* spp), and may even have entered symbiotic relationships with fauna—particularly insects—which live on the host tree and can help to protect it from the ravages of large herbivores by swarming over the trunk and branches and stinging the grazing animals. Protective measures are useful, for where this "bark ringing" results in a complete ring of phloem being removed, death of the tree will ensue because the transfer of organic products from the leaves down to the roots has been fatally impeded.

Scientists know that phloem carries organic products about the plant with great speed and efficiency, but even now the mechanism of this process is still not fully understood. The phloem of a tree, however, is predominantly of secondary origin, meaning it has been formed, like the secondary wood (or xylem), from the activity of the vascular cambium. Also, in trees, certain of the derivatives of the vascular cambium mature into fibers constituting the "hard bast" fraction of the inner bark, while yet others form ordinary living (parenchymatous) tissues. Thus, this secondary phloem is, like secondary xylem (or wood), a complex tissue and one that is renewed year after year. The rays, too, extend out into the phloem, often expanding there so sharply as to present a characteristic trumpet-like form in transverse section.

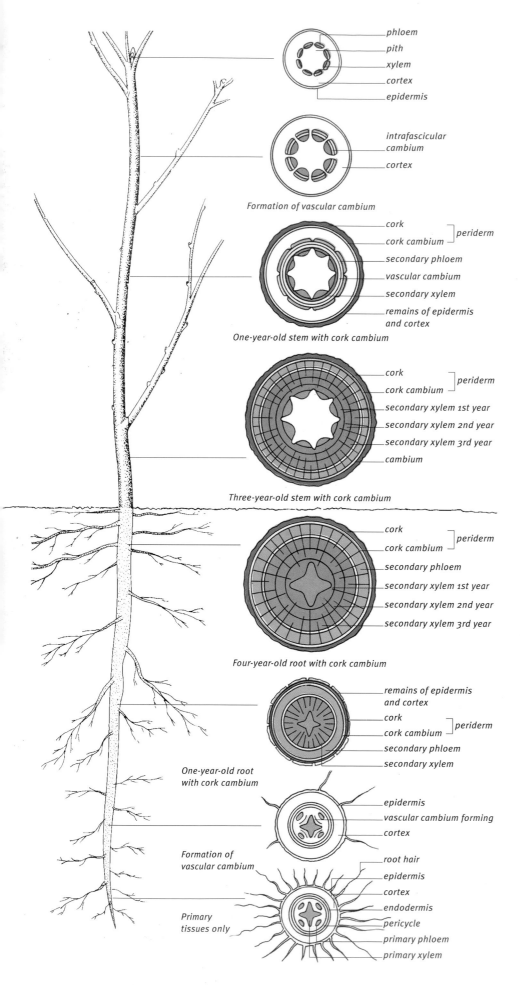

phloem
pith
xylem
cortex
epidermis

intrafascicular cambium
cortex

Formation of vascular cambium

cork
cork cambium] periderm
secondary phloem
vascular cambium
secondary xylem
remains of epidermis and cortex

One-year-old stem with cork cambium

cork
cork cambium] periderm
secondary xylem 1st year
secondary xylem 2nd year
secondary xylem 3rd year
cambium

Three-year-old stem with cork cambium

cork
cork cambium] periderm
secondary phloem
secondary xylem 1st year
secondary xylem 2nd year
secondary xylem 3rd year

Four-year-old root with cork cambium

remains of epidermis and cortex
cork
cork cambium] periderm
secondary phloem
secondary xylem

One-year-old root with cork cambium

epidermis
vascular cambium forming
cortex

Formation of vascular cambium

root hair
epidermis
cortex
endodermis
pericycle
primary phloem
primary xylem

Primary tissues only

External to this elaborately constructed inner bark, in the early life of a woody stem or branch, lies the green cortex, bounded on the outside by the original "skin tissue" or epidermis. Such an arrangement, however, cannot accommodate any marked expansion in girth unless a mechanism exists for the epidermis and cortex to keep pace by cell division or cell expansion (or both); and this is only rather rarely the case. Normally, a special new growing zone, or secondary meristem, has to arise; this is called the cork cambium or phellogen. Once formed, it can make provision for the entire protective-tissue requirement of trunk or branch and at the same time solve the girth problem. Seriated layers of corky tissues interrupted only by scattered breathing pores termed lenticels provide the protective skin. The girth problem is solved in various ways but often by periodic renewal of the cork cambium in increasingly deep tissues. When a young branch or sapling trunk that is green in its first season abruptly turns brown or grayish in hue, this color change is almost invariably correlated with the appearance of the first layers of cork. Commonly, of course, the superficial cork amounts to only a thin skin but in rare cases, as in the Cork Oak (*Quercus suber*), much thicker layers are formed.

Thus, bark is functionally very important to the tree, being both the locus of conduction (translocation) of organic substances (inner bark) and the provider of the tree's outer protective skin (outer bark). Other components include nests of exceedingly hard, thick-walled cells, which are aptly termed stone-cells. The bark of many trees is a commercial source of tannins and various crystalline deposits and in many, including the Para Rubber Tree (*Hevea brasiliensis*), there are special vessels, the lacticifers, that can be tapped to collect a latex for conversion to (natural) rubber.

Perhaps the main interest of bark to the layperson and botanist alike lies in the variety and diagnostic value of its external features. Even the most casual observer can see at a glance the differences between the rugged, fissured bark of oaks, the fibrous "stringy" bark of false acacias (*Robinia* spp), the scaly bark of planes (*Platanus* spp) with their "jig-saw puzzle" surface pattern, and the almost papery texture of the silver-white bark clothing the upper regions of trunk and branches in several species of birch (*Betula* spp). Though most conifers have a bark that is in varying degrees scaly in texture, some are highly distinctive, such as the Sierra Redwood or Wellingtonia (*Sequoiadendron giganteum*), in which the texture is so softly spongy that it can be punched without detriment to the aggressive fist!

Indigenous peoples down the centuries have come to know the marks of recognition in the barks of a great many species of trees, and botanists now recognize the importance of pursuing this study on a scientific basis.

The Root System

Absorption and anchorage are the two chief functions of a root system. Examination of a broadleaf tree seedling will show two deep green cotyledons (seed leaves) well clear of ground level. Below them the stem (hypocotylar) region passes almost imperceptibly into the crown of the young primary root (radicle) below ground level. At first it is a simple structure, "programed" to grow down into the soil (positively geotropic), but soon becomes branched, through the origin of numerous lateral roots. These arise at a deep level in the tissues of the parent root and well back from the apex. Immediately behind the apex, most roots display a fur of microscopically small root hairs—the root's principal water-absorbing components.

In most tree species, the process of secondary thickening (production of wood and phloem through cambial activity) sets in at a remarkably early stage. Thus, though the young root begins life with a different arrangement of vascular tissues from the stem, it will not be long before they bear a considerable resemblance to one another, at least when examined in transverse section—a central core of wood surrounded by the vascular cambium and bark.

Internal similarities at tissue level are, however, overshadowed by differences in gross morphology that are plainly evident. Roots never bear leaves and are not a normal site of bud production. Moreover, roots are not green (in all typical cases) and, as mentioned, they branch in a manner peculiar to themselves. The tip of a young root, as it makes its way through the soil, is protected by a root cap, which is continually renewed from behind as it gets pushed off by the progress of the root through the soil. The root cap also has no parallel in the shoot apex.

Minute anatomical details concern us less here than a consideration of the tree's root system seen as a whole, its general character, depth, and extent of spread in the soil. These are the features that vary greatly from one tree species to another. Many coniferous species, for example, are relatively shallowrooted, hence easily storm-blown. It should be borne in mind, however, that an uprooted tree reveals a mere fraction of its total root system, the lateral spread of which may far exceed that of the leafy crown. Calculating the sum of the lengths of the multiplicity of fine branch roots that go to make up an entire root system reveals prodigious overall figures. The apparent "free space" beneath and around a tree is in a very full sense "occupied" by its root system, and competition between root systems in a forest soil is intense and unrelenting.

A Symbiotic Relationship

The relationship between a tree's root system, the surrounding soil, and its varied microflora is inevitably a complex one. Many factors—physical, chemical, and biological—have to be taken into consideration. The study of this so-called rhizosphere is even now only in its infancy. Sufficient is known, however, to make it clear that the relationship between a tree's roots and soil microorganisms can be both complex and important; and to some extent the same may hold for the root systems of adjacent trees.

Perhaps the best-known and most fully investigated of these symbiotic relationships is that between tree root and mycorrhiza—the soil fungus that often plays an interactive role between the leaf litter layer and the soil, and the roots of trees. This relationship shows itself in the form of a mantle of fungal threads or hyphae (singular: hypha), collectively known as the mycelium, which encases many of the young rootlets and invades the intercellular space system of the root's cortex. The rootlets, stimulated by the fungal invasion to branch freely, are often conspicuous for their coralloid form. Scots Pine (*Pinus sylvestris*) and European Beech (*Fagus sylvatica*) are well-known examples, but the phenomenon is very widespread in tree root systems. It seems that both fungus and host tree draw benefit, the latter especially through improved capacity for absorption of certain nutrients conferred by the presence of the mycorrhizal fungus.

The roots of alders (*Alnus* spp) present another interesting association. Here the root system has associated with it nitrogen-fixing microorganisms, the exact nature of which is not yet certain because, so far, it has not been possible to grow them in pure culture. At present there are several species referred to the genus *Frankia* and believed to be related to the filamentous bacteria sometimes known as ray fungi (actinomycetes). A similar relationship is known in some other, quite unrelated trees. Perhaps the best-known root nodules are those on roots of the members of the pea family (Leguminosae or Fabaceae) where the microorganisms involved are bacterial species belonging to the genus *Rhizobium*.

Modified Roots

A number of distinct forms of modified roots occur in trees. Around the bases of tropical trees, surface roots are often extended vertically upward as plank-like triangles of wood serving as buttresses to the trunk. In other cases, for example screw pines (*Pandanus* spp) and some mangrove species, roots arising from stems above the soil strike obliquely downward and form props or stilts; similar aerial roots occur in figs (*Ficus* spp), where they do not always reach the soil but hang below branches as aerial breathing roots. Tree roots originating underground can also assume respiratory functions, as is the case with the Swamp Cypress (*Taxodium distichum*).

ABOVE Buttress roots of the Chataignier Tree (*Sloanea curlbea*) provide additional support to this rainforest tree.

FACING PAGE Line diagram showing the formation of various secondary tissues of the stem and root that increase the girth of these organs. In both stems and roots two types of cambia arise, which by divisions form secondary tissues: the vascular cambium produces secondary xylem (the water-conducting tissue—wood) and secondary phloem (the food-conducting tissue), while the cork cambium produces protective tissues (cork) that effectively replace the epidermis of the young organs.

Acuminate   Acute   Apiculate

Aristate   Cuspidate   Emarginate

Mucronate   Obcordate   Obtuse

Retuse   Truncate

ABOVE Leaf tips.

BELOW Leaf margins.

Ciliate   Crenate   Dentate

Entire   Incised   Laciniate

Runcinate   Serrate   Serrulate

Sinuate   Spiny   Undulate

RIGHT Young shoot and leaves of European Beech (*Fagus sylvatica*) showing the main elements.

FAR RIGHT A "typical" broadleaved leaf in cross-section, showing the anatomical arrangement of the various tissues. The palisade mesophyll with its numerous chloroplasts is the main power center where photosynthetic activity occurs.

BELOW Leaf arrangement and attachment.

Alternate   Amplexicaul   Decurrent

Opposite   Perfoliate   Petoliate

Sessile   Sheathing   Stipulate

Leaves

The leaves of trees are almost infinitely diverse in size and form. Some, which are minute and scale-like, the layperson might scarcely deem to be leaves at all. Examples are provided by the she-oaks (*Casuarina* spp) and some conifers. The botanist sees them as leaves, recognizing a more or less constant relationship between stem, leaf, and the bud or branch in its axil. Seeking out the axillary bud, the botanist designates as compound the leaves of walnuts (*Juglans* spp), ashes, and sumacs (*Rhus* spp), in all of which the leaf is composed of numerous leaflets, by contrast with such trees as oaks, elms (*Ulmus* spp), beeches, and limes (*Tilia* spp), where the leaves are all "simple," though differing in shape. In short, there has arisen a considerable terminology in the descriptive morphology of leaves. The outcome is that, reading such a technical description, another botanist can form instantly a clear mental image of the precise shape and character of the leaf in question. Some tropical trees bear extraordinarily large leaves, for example *Anthocleista* spp, a well-known genus of forest trees in tropical West Africa, in which the leaves can exceed 3 ft (1 m) in length and be proportionately broad. The same holds good in many monocotyledons; one has only to think of bananas and the related plantains and, of course, the compound leaves of palms.

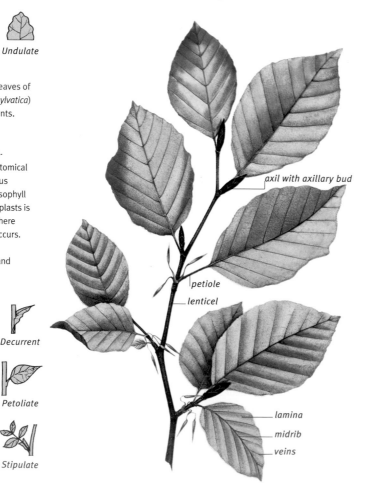

axil with axillary bud

petiole

lenticel

lamina

midrib

veins

The Function of Leaves

More interesting than purely descriptive aspects, however, is the functional view of leaves, namely their general structural features as seen in relation to their functioning as the primary food factories of the tree. In early summer a score of different tree species will display as many subtly different shades of green in their foliage. All normal leaves indeed show a remarkable compromise between the need, on the one hand, for maximum exposure of surface to the light and for freedom of entry of the carbon dioxide essential for carbon assimilation (photosynthesis) and, on the other, to include adequate safeguards against excessive water loss through the process of transpiration. These considerations explain the broad expanse of leaf blade (lamina), the presence often of long leaf stalks or petioles allowing leaf blades to take up advantageous positions, the presence (most frequently on the undersurface) of countless microscopic openings, the stomata (singular: stoma), and, finally, an adequate protective skin or cuticle. The venation system provides both a skeleton and conducting tissues continuous with those of the stem.

The basic anatomical plan of leaves is uniform, though the variations on this plan are numerous. In all leaves the epidermis forms the outermost layer of living cells. This is normally one cell thick and is bounded on the outside by the impermeable cuticle, which is interrupted only by the actual pores of the stomata (shown on the illustration below). The internal tissues or mesophyll are the powerhouse of the leaf, each cell containing numerous green chloroplasts in which photosynthesis occurs. In most leaves two types of mesophyll cell can be found. The upper or palisade mesophyll comprises columnar cells that are separated from one another by numerous narrow air channels. The lower or spongy mesophyll consists of irregularly shaped cells with large air spaces between them. Most of the chloroplasts occur in the palisade cells.

Each leaf of a tree can thus be seen as a delicately adjusted piece of machinery attuned to a functional life of immense importance—the synthesis of organic compounds such as sugars and starch from two simple raw materials: water and carbon dioxide.

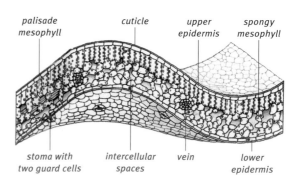

palisade mesophyll   cuticle   upper epidermis   spongy mesophyll

stoma with two guard cells   intercellular spaces   vein   lower epidermis

LEFT Species of Swamp Cypress (*Taxodium* spp) are part of the warm temperate forests of Reelfoot Lake National Wildlife Refuge, Tennessee, U.S.A. They are unusual among conifers in that they lose their leaves—either annually or at irregular intervals.

BELOW Leaf shapes.

Acicular   Auriculate   Cordate

Cuneate   Deltate   Digitate

Elliptic   Ensiform   Falcate

Hastate   Lanceolate   Linear

Obcordate   Oblanceolate   Oblique

Oblong   Obovate   Orbicular

Oval   Ovate   Palmately lobed

Palmatifid   Palmatisect   Pedate

Peltate   Pinnate   Bipinnate

Pinnatifid   Pinnatisect   Bipinnatifid

Reniform   Sagittate   Spathulate

Pectinate   Trifoliolate

Climatic and Seasonal Responses

In different climates very different stresses will be brought to bear on leaves. In the humid Tropics there is less emphasis on the protective, water-retaining, cuticle, while tree species of semi-arid regions are often of the type known as sclerophylls—characterized by leaves that are stiff and hard in texture, limited in size, and with a pronounced thick cuticle—indicating that they have adapted to resist drought. Accepting the differences between climatic zones, quite astonishing diversity can prevail within a single climatic regime, as a glance at the composition of forests in the Tropics will indicate. Tropical diversity is bewildering, but even trees presenting such diversified leaf morphology as oak, beech, and ash can all be components of a single temperate woodland.

We still know far too little of the individual economies of different species of tree, but one familiar aspect is that of leaf drop, which is a feature of fall in north temperate lands, and is also often related to the onset of a dry season in hot countries with a markedly seasonal climate. Leaf drop can be seen as a form of economy measure, enabling a tree to shut down activity, and take a rest, in a particularly unfavorable season of any kind. It is extremely widespread among dicotyledonous trees and rare in conifers, though occurring in the larches (*Larix* spp) and swamp cypresses (*Taxodium* spp), for example. The so-called evergreens always display green foliage, but they too have their times of leaf fall, albeit more unobtrusively. Individual leaves rarely last for more than a few seasons.

It goes without saying that leaves supply a considerable range of characters usable by taxonomic botanists. Indeed, though allowance has to be made for variation (seen, for example, in marked degree in mulberries (*Morus* spp)), species can often be recognized by their leaves, especially if we take into account microscopic features of leaf anatomy, important among which is the hair covering or indumentum, when present. Even so, caution is advised, for strikingly close resemblances can be found between the leaves of quite unrelated plants (maples (*Acer* spp) and true planes (*Platanus* spp) provide a case in point) while in the Tropics trees of a great many quite unrelated species have in common more or less ovate, smallish, short-stalked leaves. Only in rare cases, say the fan-shaped leaves of the Maidenhair Tree (*Ginkgo biloba*) or the distinctively fourlobed leaves of the tulip trees (*Liriodendron* spp), is leaf form instantly diagnostic. The winter buds of deciduous species can also lead to instant recognition. Such features are a boon to paleobotanists attempting to identify the trees of the past.

Space does not permit us to make more than a passing reference to the foliage of trees as a habitat for other organisms. Clearly, they are the habitat of an almost limitless diversity of colonists and feeders, perhaps most notably in the world of the insects and the birds. However, their utilization by other organisms is always to some extent bound up with their importance as a principal primary builder of the world's organic matter. Their all-round ecological significance, therefore, needs no further stressing.

Flowers and Fruits

In botanical terms, flowers are often described as consisting of "essential organs," surrounded by "floral envelopes." The latter—petals and sepals—constitute the most conspicuous features of most flowers, including those of many trees. Numerous kinds of tree, however, including all the catkin-bearing species, are without conspicuous floral envelopes, their essential organs being associated only with relatively inconspicuous, scale-like structures termed bracts. The most colorful feature of many flowers is the corolla (comprising the petals), but this is not necessarily so.

Pollination and Fertilization

The cones of coniferous trees constitute a type of flower, for in common with other flowers they are concerned with the transference of microspores (or pollen) to the receptive female parts. In most cases, an initially soft female cone gives rise, eventually, to an ultimately hard-scaled cone as seen in the pines. Quite different are the "berry-like" seeds found in junipers (*Juniperus* spp) and in the Common Yew (*Taxus baccata*).

In conifers, the male cones (staminate flowers) in season produce myriad tiny pollen grains, which in due course germinate by way of a pollen tube from which the microscopic sex cells or male gametes are finally released. At the "receiving end" of the wind-dispersed pollen grains are the familiar female cones (ovulate flowers), which are still young and soft, with scales open. Each such female cone represents one or more so-called "naked ovules" set among scales. Each ovule is a giant spore (megaspore) with protective "wrappings" in the form of spore container and integuments, and concealed within it lies the female gamete—the egg cell (ovum). In time, fertilization takes place, giving rise to a "naked seed" (whence the term gymnosperm = naked seed). In some conifers pollination is separated from fertilization by as much as a year.

In flowering plants or angiosperms—in this context the hardwood or broadleaved trees—we find more elaborately constructed and more varied flowers, most of which show the familiar components: calyx (sepals), corolla (petals), and, internal to these, the pollen-producing stamens, and the ovary or ovaries containing the ovules. It is the ovary that characterizes the angiosperms, enclosing as it does, right from the outset, the young and developing ovules and finally the seeds, so that they are at no time "naked." This enclosing organ means that a special receptive area (stigma) and conducting region (style) become essential adjuncts to the ovary. Pollen is transferred by wind, water, insect, or other animals to the stigma, where it germinates, producing a pollen tube, which grows down through the style, eventually coming into close contact with the ovule via a minute opening termed the micropyle. The pollen tube

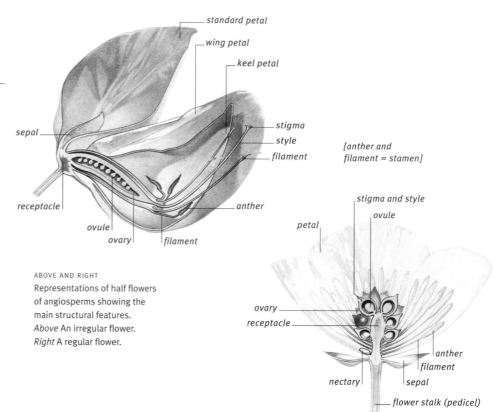

[anther and filament = stamen]

ABOVE AND RIGHT
Representations of half flowers of angiosperms showing the main structural features.
Above An irregular flower.
Right A regular flower.

ruptures and two male gametes are discharged. One will fuse with the egg, thus setting a seed. As with gymnosperms, pollination and fertilization are separate events, though the lag between them is shorter than for conifers.

It appears as if the entire evolutionary history of flowers has been geared to pollen transference, or pollination, and the pollinating agency has profoundly modified floral form, in trees as in other flowering plants. Thus, among tree species, we can recognize on sight as wind-pollinated the bulk of catkin-bearing trees, including the hazels (*Corylus* spp), birches (*Betula* spp), and poplars (*Populus* spp), for in all of them there is an abundance of loose pollen, no nectar, and no conspicuous insect-attracting feature. Willows (*Salix* spp), with their large nectaries, constitute an exception and are insect-pollinated.

In marked contrast stand those trees with large and colorful flowers—the only ones indeed that many laypeople would recognize as "flowering trees" at all. The great majority of these are adapted to a range of insect vectors of pollen, but quite numerous species, especially in the Tropics, are adapted for pollination by birds. These tend to have exceptionally strongly constructed flowers, often scarlet or multi-colored. A few trees, in various parts of the world, have bat-pollinated flowers. Such flowers, which characteristically open in the evening, are often large, somber in color, and capable of emitting characteristic musty odors. Examples occur in a number of families, including the Leguminosae, Myrtaceae, and Cactaceae.

The expression "flowering tree" is apt to conjure up a picture of cherries and almonds (*Prunus* spp), crab apples (*Malus* spp), and others grown for their blossoms in parks or gardens. The reality is very different, for all broadleaf

BELOW Cone structure. Details of the structure of the cone-scales of mature or fruiting cones of conifers, showing the position of the bract-scale (1), the ovuliferous-scale (2), and the seeds (3)—the latter having developed from the fertilized ovules. (a) and (b), Douglas Fir (*Pseudotsuga* sp) showing that the scales are distinct from each other. (c) and (d), Arbor-vitae (*Thuja* sp) showing that the bract- and ovuliferous-scales are fused to form a single cone-scale (4). (a) and (c), sectional view from side; (b) and (d), view from above. The term cone-scale is often loosely applied to the scale that contributes most to the fruiting cone irrespective of origin.

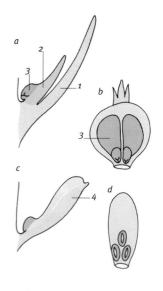

trees are potentially "flowering" at some stage in their lives, otherwise reproduction could not occur, except very locally by sucker growth. The diversity of floral form will be apparent from the tree entries in the main sections of the book. In the humid Tropics there is often a steady succession of flowers, of different species, throughout the year. Each must be geared to the season of availability of its principal pollinator; but still too little is known about the precise range of pollinators utilized by many tropical trees. In north temperate regions, where spring and summer are the seasons of flowering, bees of various kinds must surely rank as the most important group of pollinating organisms.

Flowering is but the prelude to fruit production; and just as a fruit (botanically) is a ripened or mature ovary, so a seed is a matured fertilized ovule, carrying deep within it the embryo plant of the new generation. It is important to appreciate that if cross-pollination has been achieved this new embryo will possess, in varying degree, a new genetic constitution. This is of immense significance both for the evolutionary process and for the "improvement" of trees for use by human agency.

It is possible to look at the fruits of trees from the angle of the botanist, who classifies such structures in a manner that is convenient for descriptive purposes. Thus, there are "dry" fruits (capsules) that open or dehisce, thereby shedding their seeds; and there are "fleshy" fruits of many kinds. Some species—Elderberry (*Sambucus nigra*) for one—have their seeds lodged in compartments of a wholly fleshy fruit wall, while others, including plums and cherries, have a fruit wall (or pericarp) that is itself made up of an outer skin, a middle fleshy portion, and an innermost stony layer. The seed in such a case exists as the "kernel" within the stone. Thus, the botanist distinguishes the berry from the stone fruit or drupe.

Seed Dispersal

Fruit structure, however, cannot be viewed in any complete way without reference to its vital ecological implications, especially in connection with seed dispersal. In this context we can contrast the dry, dehiscent capsules of willows, which release their tiny seeds equipped with tufts of hairs to be dispersed by wind, with the great range of drupe and berry fruits that have in every case a built-in food store that will attract a dispersal agent, most often some species of bird. Young elderberry saplings lodged in unlikely places are sometimes eloquent testimony to the efficiency of a dispersal mechanism that allows the seeds to be voided in a viable state after the fleshy substance surrounding them has been digested.

Clearly, both mechanisms can lead readily to long-distance dispersal, an important consideration in the successful distribution of tree species in nature. It is less easy to see how this can be achieved in the case of trees where both fruit and seed are bulky, as in the Horse Chestnut (*Aesculus* spp), and not obviously attractive to animal dispersal agents. Even the ingenious winged fruitlets of the various species of *Acer* (sycamores and maples) seem unlikely to carry the new plantlet far from the parent tree, and the same can almost certainly be said of the explosive fruits of the tropical American Sandbox Tree (*Hura crepitans*). The light, winged fruitlets of ashes and pines, and the winged seeds that abound among the tree species of the tropical family Bignoniaceae, will surely fare better. The fruit of the Coconut Palm (*Cocos nucifera*) is exceptional among heavy fruits in that there is considerable evidence for its long-distance dispersal by ocean currents.

Germination

When the seed germinates and the new plant begins to grow, a range of controlling factors immediately becomes operative. Soil reaction, available nutrients, moisture supply, and temperature must all be right if the plant is to survive. Most decisive of all, perhaps, is the inevitable factor, or complex of factors, entailed by the term competition. This relates not only to pressures exerted by countless other plants in the immediate vicinity but also to the influences exerted by various members of the animal kingdom, not least by human agency. The first mowing of a lawn in spring is often the occasion for "elimination by decapitation" of innumerable seedlings of sycamore or maple, and sometimes other species. Though all normal seeds carry, either free or within their cotyledons, a food reserve, it must frequently happen that this supply is exhausted before successful establishment has been achieved. Once established, in the face of all competitors, the young tree is free to grow.

ABOVE The fruits of the Norway Maple, *Acer platanoides*, are distinctive boomerang-shaped keys. These consist of two samaras (fruits), each of which has a single wing and seed, and can fly quite a distance. BELOW *Pinus* cones, shown here at various stages of maturity, are the fertilized female reproductive organs. Once fully developed, the overlapping scales open to discharge their seed in early fall.

The resting buds of temperate woody plants, such as those of the Horse Chestnut (*Aesculus hippocastanium*), are surrounded by a layer of sticky scale leaves which protect the following season's embryonic leaves and flowers. During spring, in response to the warmer temperatures, they unfold and the leaves and flowers rapidly expand, provided they have been exposed to a period of winter chilling. If maintained in warm conditions throughout the winter, however, the buds remain dormant.

The Growth of Trees

The growth of trees is a large, complex subject, and only the barest essentials can be touched upon here. Whole treatises have been written on the growth of many of the economically important trees, and successful growth of introduced species must always be a primary concern of the forester. Often this entails fitting a particular exotic species into a type of environment that especially suits it. At other times successful growth has to be coaxed from a species by appropriate treatment of an essentially unfavorable environment, as with the vast plantations of Sitka Spruce (*Picea sitchensis*) on the peat moors of northern Europe. In natural forest communities it is probably reasonable to assume a strong correlation between the component species and the character of the substratum. We think of beech on chalk, oak on heavy clays, pine and birch on nutrient-poor sands and gravels, and alder along the banks of rivers. Thus, the successful growth of each appears linked to a given environment; yet the ecological amplitude of most common native trees is certainly wider than such a generalization would indicate. Competition remains operative.

Growth will tend at all times to be closely dependent on adequate water and nutrient supplies, and on temperature, the latter often a limiting factor. The seasonal character of tree growth in north temperate latitudes, so familiar almost to pass without comment, reflects this correlation with temperature, but it must not be forgotten that there are also important links with two aspects of the light factor—day length and absolute light intensity. The student of growth phenomena in trees is often faced with the difficult task of elucidating the relative significance of several quite distinct factors in the environment, each of which is known to be operative in a general way. These the student endeavors to study in relation to the demonstrable overall growth increment, as shown by suitable measurements, and resulting in a figure for "net assimilation rate," or "productivity." The mechanisms by which trees achieve this are beyond the scope of this brief introduction. Suffice it to say that the reactivation of the cambium in spring (*see* pages 15–16) is brought about through the production and mobilization of plant growth hormones (auxins) in the expanding buds. Meanwhile, during the upsurge of activity in the primary apical meristems, stored food is used up and energy released, sufficient to allow cell division and cell enlargement to go on apace. The reactivated vascular cambium loses no time in forming new tissues (xylem and phloem), that will facilitate rapid transport of raw materials and mobilized storage products. There is an intense level of chemical activity within the individual cells, and as this entails respiration, photosynthesis, protein-building, the fashioning of new cell walls, and other processes, it is easy to appreciate something of its hidden complexities.

The outward manifestation of all this internal activity (at cellular level) is the burgeoning of new leaves on trees in spring. When we bear in mind that a single mature foliage leaf will commonly comprise some fifteen million cells, we begin to glimpse something of the unimaginable scale of cell production, each spring, in a single forest tree. Nevertheless, this particular manifestation of growth is there for all to see. Opening buds, new leaves, elongating twigs, these cannot pass unnoticed, but not so the scarcely perceptible increments in girth and stature of the older trees. Fast-growing species, birches for example, illustrate how rapidly height increases in the early years following successful establishment and how markedly it slows down later. Yet some increments will take place, however slight, in every spring for the duration of the tree's life. With few exceptions, at least in temperate regions, the increase in girth of a tree at breast height (5 ft/1.5 m) is very close to 1 in (2.5 cm) a year. This figure is for trees growing under conditions where their crowns are not inhibited from full development by overcrowding, and is useful for estimating a tree's age. Thus, with a breast-height girth of 8 ft (2.5 m) the tree will be about one hundred years old.

Some exceptions to this general rule are:
• Wellingtonia (*Sequoiadendron giganteum*)
• Coast Redwood (*Sequoia sempervirens*)
• Cedar of Lebanon (*Cedrus libani*)

Illustration showing the lifecycle of the Douglas Fir (*Pseudotsuga menziesii*) with details of the management and cropping of these trees. Commercially each tree is harvested while still healthy and not allowed to deteriorate with age.

(a) Young trees (8–9 years old) are thinned out and usually sold as Christmas trees. (b) At 30–40 years the lower branches start to drop off; the tree can be harvested for pulping. (c) At 50–60 years the timber may be pulped and straight trunks used as poles. (d) At 100 years the trunk can be cut for use as construction timber or "peeled" for plywood. (e) Growth slows after 100 years but the trunk is still used for timber. A mature tree may reach 330 ft (100 m). (f) After several centuries the tree starts to decline—the branches fall, the bark peels, and the trunk begins to rot. (g) Even the upper branches die in the end and the rotten trunk is so weak that ... (h) ... it topples to the ground.

- Douglas Fir (*Pseudotsuga menziesii*)
- Southern beeches (*Nothofagus* spp)
- Turkey Oak (*Quercus cerris*)
- Tulip Tree (*Liriodendron tulipifera*) and
- London Plane (*Platanus* × *acerifolia*), all of which increase girth at 2–3 in (5–7.5 cm) a year;
- Scots Pine (*Pinus sylvestris*)
- Horse Chestnut (*Aesculus hippocastanum*) and
- Common Lime (*Tilia* × *europaea*), which increase girth at less than 1 in (2.5 cm) a year.

In other climates very different conditions of growth prevail. In the humid Tropics two years of more or less uninterrupted growth activity can easily result in a tree many feet high. On the fringe of the great deserts of the world, notwithstanding the high temperatures, water shortage makes the trees of the specialized genera that grow there among the most slow-growing of all. In the high Arctic, temperature imposes comparably severe restrictions. On wind-exposed coastal stations both wind velocity and salt spray can play a part in restricting the height and distorting the growth of trees. Even so, for certain species at least, life itself may be retained with tenacity, in the face of all obstacles. Thus, the shock is the greater when a single virulent fungus such as *Ceratocystis ulmi* (the cause of Dutch Elm Disease) can bring about the death of up to ten million elms in Great Britain in the course of a few seasons. Our knowledge of the botany of trees often appears powerless to arrest this devastation—though the use of native, disease-resistant species and better silvicultural practises can help. It is equally powerless to check the havoc wreaked from time to time by forest fires on the tinder-dry, oil-rich, evergreen eucalyptus forests of Australia. Our remedy must be to grow more native trees.

a   b   c   d   e   f   g   h

FORESTS

Forests and woods currently occupy some 30 percent of the world's land surface, from the Tropics to high latitudes (about 70° in the northern hemisphere), from sea level to about 12,500 ft (3,800 m). Where the climate is too dry, too cold, or too exposed, forest gives way to grassland, bogs, tundra, or desert scrub, in which trees are of little or no importance.

Within those parameters, forests occur where there is a reasonably long growing season with mean temperatures not much below 50°F (10°C), a reliable supply of ground moisture, and shelter from winds.

with herbs and mosses on the ground. In deciduous forests there are large differences in the environment depending on the presence or absence of leaves, and many herbaceous species are adapted to these seasonal differences.

The Forest Ecosystem

Forests depend on suitable environmental conditions prevailing in a region, but are themselves important in modifying the environment, and create a series of micro-environments that profoundly influence the occurrence of plants and animals in forest communities. The canopy reflects or absorbs up to 99 percent of incident sunlight, so the forest floor is generally cooler than outside the forest and may be rather dimly lit. Winds are greatly slowed by tree cover, giving damper conditions and providing shelter to plants and animals that could not tolerate exposed conditions. The soil too is modified by the dominant trees, both by their extraction of water and by the physical and chemical effects of the leaf litter they shed. Leaf litter supplies the humus, which sustains the clay humus complex of the soils and contains the reserves of soluble nutrients. Leaves with abundant organic acids or very woody tissues such as pine needles decompose slowly to give a thin, nutrient-poor, acid soil; leaves with less acid organic matter are quickly broken down to give deeper, more fertile soils. Mycorrhiza (*see page 17*) can provide the tree with nutrients derived from saprophytic fungi, making the tree less dependent on soil fertility. Most of the nutrients in a forest are held in the tissues of the organisms that make up the ecosystem, and in virgin forest the level of nutrients is maintained relatively constant by recycling through food chains. Deforestation interrupts this cycle and the nutrients are dissipated. The destruction of forest by humans has not only removed the habitats that result from tree cover, it has also greatly reduced the fertility levels of many regions.

Foresters and ecologists distinguish several layers within a forest. The most obvious is the canopy, which is composed of the crowns of the tallest trees. Occasionally there is a further stratum of light-demanding, giant emergent trees protruding above it, as in lowland tropical rainforest. Below the canopy is a layer of understory trees; beneath that shade-tolerant shrubs form another stratum,

Forest Dynamics

In global terms, species composition of a forest is dependent on the prevailing climate, while on a regional scale there are variations according to soil conditions. At the finest scale further variation arises from the dynamics of a forest. A mature closed canopy casts dense shade, and only plants adapted to conditions of low light and high root competition can grow beneath it. Trees with seedlings that can develop under a closed canopy are known as shade bearers, and generally have large seeds. Species requiring high light conditions are known as light demanders and can grow only in the gaps left by tree falls, fires, or landslides. Their seeds are often small, wind-dispersed, and produced in huge numbers. As the seedlings always colonize gaps, they are referred to as pioneer species. In practise there is a spectrum of types from obligate shade bearers to strict pioneers. In the temperate deciduous forest of North America, pioneers *Pinus strobus*, *Quercus* spp, and *Castanea* spp tend to be replaced in the absence of catastrophic forest destruction by shade bearers *Acer* spp, *Tsuga* spp, and *Fagus* spp. *Shorea*, the principal timber species of Indo-Malaysia, are near-pioneers, favored by mild but not total forest disturbance. Pioneers occur in large gaps as even-age stands, and a coarse mosaic of large patches of different age develops.

Shade bearers succeed pioneers, replacing themselves or each other on smaller areas so that ultimately a mixed-age stand develops with a fine-scale mosaic of gap, building phase, and high mature forest. This dynamic aspect of forest composition, with different species adapted to different temporal niches in the growth cycle, has major ecological and commercial implications, and the science of silviculture is based on understanding and manipulating it.

ABOVE Seedlings of shade bearers can grow in conditions of low light and high root competition.

FACING PAGE The fall colors of Maple, Birch, and Beech light up a hillside, Cape Breton Highlands National Park, Canada.

It is doubtful whether there is ever an equilibrium state, or constant species composition; a catastrophe, or indeed climatic change, sooner or later intervenes to cause gross alteration. Many tree species are still making slow migrations poleward from their Ice Age refuges in response to the sudden increases in temperature when the last Ice Age ended ten thousand years ago. It must be remembered that the forests we see today are merely a snapshot of the earth's ever-shifting patterns of diversity, with each species reacting differently to changing climates. Many species that are common today were rare during the Ice Ages, while others have been driven to extinction by these climatic shifts.

Forests of the World

Forests are the climax vegetation over about 20 million square miles (50 million km²) of the world's land masses, though human activity has substantially altered them— or entirely removed them from vast areas, including much of western Europe. Biogeographers have divided the world into "biomes" or climatic zones, which support types of vegetation that are structurally and functionally similar, though they may be separated by large distances and composed of quite different species. The biomes in which forests are the climax vegetation are discussed here.

Richest of all the world's forest types is the tropical rainforest. The high temperatures and constant humidity mean that an unmatched number of species flourish in this biome. Paradoxically, the apparent fertility is not sustainable if the natural tree cover is removed: nutrients are rapidly leached from the soil by the frequent—often heavy—rainfall, making the land unsuitable for agriculture or grazing other than in the short term.

PRINCIPAL FOREST TYPES OF THE WORLD

The main areas of the world occupied by natural forest before interference by Man.

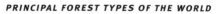

- evergreen tropical rainforest
- sclerophyllous (Mediterranean)
- temperate rainforest
- temperate deciduous
- boreal coniferous forest
- seasonally dry (monsoon) tropical forest

Tropical Rainforest

Tropical rainforest occurs between 25° north and south and covers 7 million square miles (18 million km²), in three great blocks centered on Amazonia, the Guinea-Congo region of Africa, and Southeast Asia, from the Western Ghats of India to the islands of the western Pacific. There are also smaller zones in coastal Brazil, Central America and the Caribbean, east Madagascar, and the Mascarenes. It is found in areas where the mean annual temperature is greater than 70°F (20°C), which receive in excess of 80 in (2,000 mm) of rain per year and have at least 4 in (100 mm) of rain in the driest month. The soils of such forests are deep and weathered and are typically strongly leached and low in nutrients.

This is the most diverse and luxuriant of forests; 307 species of tree have been found in 2.4 acres (1 ha) of forest on the eastern flank of the Andes. There are thought to be well over 100,000 species of plants in this biome, and new species, even large trees, are still being discovered. All three rainforest regions have abundant Leguminosae, Myrtaceae, and Euphorbiacae, while Southeast Asian forests are dominated by the Dipterocarpaceae and South American forests have numerous Lecythicidaceae.

Lowland tropical rainforests are structurally the most complex of forests, with a main canopy at 100–165 ft (30–50 m) and emergents to 195 or even 260 ft (60–80 m). Below are many smaller trees, palms, and, in wetter areas, tree ferns. Tree seedlings are numerous, but at ground level the vegetation is rarely dense except at the forest margins or in forest that is regrowing after clearance (secondary forest). Woody climbers (lianas) are common, and buttresses frequently support the tall trees, which are relatively slender, given their enormous heights. Epiphytes, mainly orchids, ferns, and—in the Americas—bromeliads and Cactaceae, are common in areas of high rainfall, where they may festoon the branches of the larger trees.

There are three other types of wet tropical forest, distinct from lowland rainforest, that merit special attention. **Heath forests** occur on freely draining, nutrient-poor, acidic, sandy soils and have a great many densely growing small trees. In extreme cases the canopy may be as low as 16 ft (5 m). The tough, leathery (sclerophyllous) leaves are generally very small and often have a high reflectivity (albedo). They decay slowly, and there is often a deep litter layer. Heath forests are structurally distinct from lowland rainforest, are much less diverse, and contain many unique species of trees.

Emergent layer
165 ft (50 m)

130 ft (40 m)

Canopy
100 ft (30 m)

66 ft (20 m)

33 ft (10 m)
Understory

Profile diagram of a climax African tropical forest showing the three layers typical of such forests. The main canopy is very dense so that the understory must cope with low light intensity and high humidity. The trees of the canopy normally have long slender trunks, much of the support coming from the association of the trees in the massed canopy, but those in the emergent layer lack this material support and often have well-developed buttress roots to help hold up the trunk.

Upper montane rainforest (also called **cloud forest** or **elfin woodland**) grows above the cloud level on tropical mountains. The cloud level may be as low as 2,000 ft (600 m) or as high as 10,000 ft (3,000 m), depending on local conditions. This type of rainforest has the low, dense canopy of tiny, sclerophyllous leaves that characterizes heath forest, and there are intriguing suggestions that the trees are under similar pressures, in spite of their very different climates. Unlike heath forest, however, both trees and the ground surface of the upper montane type are thickly swathed in mosses and epiphytes, including many rare orchids. The soil is waterlogged for much of the time, and deep layers of peat often develop.

Mangrove forests occur on muddy tidal shores where they may form dense belts several miles across. Typically, the trees are evergreen with thick, leathery leaves and have many physiological adaptations to this extreme environment, including viviparous seeds, which develop into seedlings on the parent tree and are able to establish themselves rapidly on the unstable muddy substrate. Various types of prop and aerial root are another characteristic of these trees, as are breathing roots or pneumatophores, which enable the root system to respire in the anerobic mud.

Exploitation of tropical rainforests remained relatively light until some fifty years ago. Since then, population growth—combined with advances in technology—have threatened these fragile ecosystems, in particular through wide-scale logging, mining, and the building of dams and highways. Worldwide, already about 40 percent of lowland tropical rainforest has disappeared, with some formerly timber-producing countries now needing to import timber.

A forest fire is lit by rangers in the warm temperate forest of Yosemite National Park, California, U.S.A., in order to provide clear ground for the germination of new trees.

A field of *Quercus ilex*, the Holm Oak, survives the arid conditions of the Extramadura, Spain, despite entire forests being denuded in the Mediterranean between the sixteenth and nineteenth centuries.

rainforest, dry forests are shorter, with the canopy rarely reaching 100 ft (30 m), and usually very much smaller. Emergents are rare, lianas are much less frequent, and epiphytes are also much rarer. The trees of dry forests are closely related to those of rainforests, but overall their diversity is lower by far.

Dry forests are found in the same climatic zones as savanna grasslands, but on more fertile soils. All savanna tree species are adapted to frequent fires, and burning of dry forests can convert them into savannas. Dry forests have suffered far greater impact from humans than the rainforests because they grow on fertile soils, have more agreeable climates, are more suitable for intensive agriculture, and are easier to clear since they contain less biomass and have a long dry season during which they can be burned. As a result, little dry forest now remains worldwide; for example, only 2 percent of the original dry forest of Central America is intact, compared with some 85 percent of the Amazonian rainforest.

Mediterranean Biome

This biome is characterized by winter rains, and covers some 700,000 square miles (1.8 million km²) in narrow strips of land along the Mediterranean, the southeastern coasts of Africa, Australia, and South America, and the coast of California. The summers are hot and dry, the winters warm and wet, and annual rainfall is between 20 and 40 in (500–1,000 mm) but irregular, and there are prolonged periods of water deficit. Spring is the main growing and flowering season. The vegetation is typically a mosaic of valley forests, open woodlands, shrublands, and grasslands. *Quercus* spp. dominate in both the Mediterranean and in California, *Eucalyptus* in Australia, *Nothofagus* and *Acacia* in Chile, and *Olea*, *Sideroxlyon*, and *Rhus* in South Africa. Many species possess sclerophyllous leaves, which minimize water loss during dry periods but allow the trees to take advantage of the occasional rain that falls outside the wet season. Diversity in this biome is huge, in spite of the small area it occupies.

The Mediterranean Basin has been a center of civilizations from ancient times, and deforestation and soil erosion have destroyed most of the original forest, leaving variously degraded communities. Originally the forest was dominated by a canopy of Holm Oak (*Quercus ilex*) 50–60 ft (15–18 m) tall, with shrubs and herbs beneath, but this has largely been replaced by a dense shrub vegetation called *maquis*. This is very rich in species, but subject to periodic fires and becomes degraded by excessive grazing and burning to shorter, more open *garrigue*. These shrublands have their equivalent in other continents—and are known as chaparral in California, matorral in Chile, and fynbos in South Africa.

Seasonally Dry Tropical Forests

Seasonally dry tropical forests occur as broad bands to the north and south of the tropical rainforest biome, and may be found as far north as 30° in India. The total area of this biome is approximately 3 million square miles (7.5 million km²). Mean annual temperatures range from 70 to 85°F (20 to 30°C) with annual rainfall averaging 60–100 in (1,500–2,500 mm). However, it is the seasonal variability in rainfall that distinguishes it from rainforest, with a winter dry season of between four and seven months. During the winter many trees lose their leaves, and even those that keep them become dormant until moist conditions are restored. Flowering generally occurs just before the leaves emerge, and the forests may be spectacularly beautiful at these times. In comparison with

Temperate Deciduous Forests

For many people in the West, temperate deciduous are the most familiar of forests, being the natural vegetation of extensive areas of eastern North America, Europe, southern South America, southeastern Australia, and New Zealand, covering a total of some 2.7 million square miles (7 million km²). Their mean annual temperature is 40–70°F (5–20°C) and average annual rainfall is between 20 and 100 in (500–2,500 mm), though distribution during the year varies greatly among the different regions. Winter frosts are characteristic and some areas have long, cold winters.

Temperate deciduous forests are dominated by broadleaved trees such as *Quercus*, *Fagus*, *Acer*, and *Ulmus* in the northern hemisphere, *Nothofagus* in South America and New Zealand, and *Eucalyptus* in Australia. The deciduous forests of eastern North America occupy a wide latitudinal range extending from Florida to Canada, and they are subdivided into a number of associations, depending on the species present. The European forests are the least diverse, because the southward migrations of temperate species during the Ice Ages were blocked by the Mediterranean, and many species were eliminated from the area.

Across their ranges these forests are structurally similar, with a canopy between 65 and 100 ft (20–30 m) high, an understory of smaller trees such as *Corylus* or *Cornus*, and an extensive layer of seedlings, herbs, and ferns at ground level. Because the deciduous canopy is less dense, a greater proportion of light reaches the forest floor than in tropical rainforest (dominated by evergreen species), and consequently the ground flora is more extensive.

Loss of leaves at the onset of winter is a response to cold, which stops photosynthesis. The removal of chlorophyll before leaf fall exposes anthocyanins and other pigments, causing the leaves to turn spectacular shades of red and yellow. Many species of tree delay the growth of new leaves in the spring until there has been a prolonged period of warm weather, so that leaves do not emerge during a winter warm spell. For the deciduous strategy to be successful, the summer growth period needs to be long and sufficiently warm to produce a new crop of leaves, form the following year's buds, and lay down carbohydrate reserves to sustain the plant during its winter dormancy until the new leaves are fully functional.

Forests in Europe have been very fragmented by centuries of human activity and those in North America suffered extensive deforestation during the eighteenth and nineteenth centuries. Now considerable recuperation is taking place as it is no longer economic to farm previously forested sites, and extensive new growth forests have become established.

Altitude, as well as latitude, determines forest type. The Aspen, *Populus tremula*, which forms "montain" boreal forest in Colorado, is one deciduous species that thrives in cool, temperate areas of the U.S.A.

Temperate Rainforests

This is a very small and scattered biome, with the largest areas found on the Pacific coast of North America from northern California to southern Alaska and smaller areas in southeastern Australia, Tasmania, New Zealand, and Chile. Annual rainfall exceeds 80 in (2,000 mm) and occurs throughout the year. All areas have mild, oceanic climates, and temperatures barely drop below freezing.

On the Californian coast, rainforest extends into the Mediterranean biome because of summer fogs, whose moisture sustains the Coastal Redwoods (*Sequoia sempervirens*), the tallest trees in the world, reaching 370 ft (110 m), which are the most prominent feature of these forests. Indeed, this biome is dominated by evergreen trees; other species prominent in North America include the Douglas firs (*Pseudotsuga*), Red Cedar (*Thuja plicata*), spruces (*Picea*), and firs (*Abies*). Many of these trees are enormous and long-lived. In Australia dominants include the Karri (*Eucalyptus diversicolor*) and other eucalypts; in Tasmania *Nothofagus* and *Dacrydium* dominate, while in Chile *Nothofagus* dominates with *Fitzroya*. Overall, however, species diversity in these temperate rainforests is lower than in temperate deciduous forests.

The canopy of this biome is generally between 130 and 200 ft (40–60 m), and the trunks may reach 65 ft (20 m) in circumference. Light penetration is often limited, and the litter quite acidic, so the ground layer is limited to saplings of the canopy trees, along with herbs and ferns.

With their huge trees, these forests are very attractive to commercial loggers, and in North America they have often been clear felled, endangering mammals and birds such as the Spotted Owl that rely on old-growth forests. Ongoing battles are being fought between loggers and conservationists.

Boreal Forests

Boreal forests—known as *taiga* in Eurasia—stretch in a broad band centered around latitude 60° north, from Norway to the Pacific coast of Russia and from coastal Alaska to Newfoundland. Smaller areas at lower latitudes are found on high mountain ranges, including the Appalachians, the Alps, and parts of the Himalaya. There is no equivalent forest in the southern hemisphere because there are no large land masses at the corresponding latitude.

This biome covers some 4.6–5.8 million square miles (12–15 million km²). Mean annual temperature is between 25 and 40°F (–5 to 5°C), and mean annual rainfall between 8 and 80 in (200–2,000 mm). Summers are mild, with mean July temperatures of 50–70°F (10–20°C), but winters are very cold, and can be as low as –60°F (–50°C) in central Siberia.

These forests are structurally very simple, with a dense canopy to 100–130 ft (30–40 m), though this is much lower and more open at the biome's altitudinal and latitudinal limits. These evergreen forests are dominated by *Pinus*, *Picea*, and *Abies*, and in the coldest regions of Siberia by *Larix* spp. Below the canopy is a layer of evergreen shrubs such as junipers and various Ericaceae. Deciduous shrubs such as willows and alders may also be present. There is often very little regeneration under the dense canopies, and the ground cover there may be very sparse and consist of little more than moss, so that eventually thick layers of peat may develop.

Fire is the most common agent of disturbance, with 90 percent caused by lightning. The trees possess numerous adaptations to fire; many species have thick bark to protect the trunk, and some have cones that open after fire to allow their light-demanding seedlings to take advantage of temporarily open habitats. Boreal forest consists of a mosaic of regrowing forest, and old-growth forests are rare. Most of the boreal forest was relatively undisturbed until comparatively recently, but it is now increasingly being exploited for timber.

A snow-covered forest of *Pinus*, *Picea*, and *Abies* growing near the treeline in Swamp Canyon, Bryce Canyon National Park, Utah, U.S.A.

TREES AND MANKIND

Throughout the ages, people have exploited the wood from forests for fuel, implements, shelter and housing, furniture, and fencing. Only in modern times has a concept of management of forests been developed for the perpetuation of their products, and only very recently has the full scope and range of the resource begun to be realized.

In spite of significant depletion, forests occupy almost 30 percent of the earth's land surface. They are of immense variety, from dwarf trees with imperceptible growth in the Arctic regions, to species-rich, structurally varied equatorial rainforest; from vast areas of closely stocked coniferous forest in North America and northern Europe, to open savanna with a low stocking of trees that covers extensive areas in the Tropics and subtropics.

Forestry

The growing stock of trees is estimated to be 13,600 billion cubic ft (386 billion m³) of which two-thirds is hardwood and one-third softwood. Total annual production is some 120,000 million cubic ft (3,400 million m³), 36 percent of it coniferous. Over half of all wood removed is used as fuel.

For millennia the immense wealth of forests has been exploited by mankind, whose activities have reduced their area to less than half their greatest extent. Since ancient times natural forest has been cleared for crops, for protection against wild beasts or human enemies, and to obtain its products. At the onset of the Iron Age most of western Europe, for example, was clad in forest—spruces, pines, and birches in Scandinavia; pines, firs, beeches, and oaks in central Europe; oaks, birches, and pines in the British Isles. Early man took such timber as he required to satisfy his simple needs, used wood as charcoal, and cleared trees for pastures and crop production. The main instruments of destruction have been fire and the grazing of domestic stock, supplemented at times by the deliberate release of nonindigenous species of herbivores. This history of depletion is far from over: the net area of forest in the world is still decreasing by almost 25 million acres (10 million hectares) per annum, principally by logging, and also by shifting cultivation in South America, Africa, and parts of Asia. There were, however, some increases in the area of temperate and boreal forests during the 1990s.

Forest Management

Today's industrial needs generate an increasing range of uses, often involving the breakdown of the structure of raw wood, and its reconstitution into paper or board, or its combination with plastics into new materials. With the inexorable rise in world population, and thus an increase in world consumption of wood, a continual increase in the supply of wood is required from a dwindling area of forest. The need for management is evident.

Forests fulfill a wide variety of functions essential to our well-being. They counter soil-erosion and reduce flooding; they protect agriculture and modify local climatic extremes; they ensure regular water supplies and prevent pollution; they provide habitats for a vast array of plants and animals—in itself a resource. Forests, woodlands, and trees are essential parts of attractive landscapes and an important recreational facility for urban populations.

The modern forester therefore faces a dilemma: how to increase the sustained supply of wood as rapidly and economically as possible and protect the forest ecosystem to maintain all the other benefits (often not economically quantifiable) derived from the forest. This challenge must be met within the economic framework of individual governments. The approach is to select practical patterns of action, supported by scientific findings, in order to achieve a balance between efficient husbanding and safeguarding the environment.

Silviculture is the art of creating and then tending a forest. It involves the application of detailed knowledge of the life history and general characteristics of trees, with particular reference to environmental factors. Each tree species differs in its requirements and its reactions to site conditions, in its pattern of growth, and in its ability to withstand extremes of climate or terrain. By understanding these factors for all the trees within the climatic range, silviculturalists control the development of the forests under their care.

Once a forest is established, it needs continuous tending to maturity, and periodical thinning to give more room for the best trunks, which are selected to remain. As maturity approaches, measures must be taken to nurture the next generation. These include natural seeding, replanting after clearing with the same or another species, or planting under the shelter of the existing stand. Various silvicultural systems have been evolved to secure the regeneration of forests in different conditions, and the more diverse the structure, the more complex the system. The simplest system (not necessarily the best) is clearcutting followed by replanting. The most complicated selection system is

ABOVE The fire-tolerant Longleaf Pine, *Pinus palustris*, is given a chance to survive after the forest it inhabits, in Pensacola, Florida, U.S.A., is subjected to a prescribed burn, which removes non-indigenous brush. *Pinus palustris* remains standing and its seedlings sprout from the fertile ash.

FACING PAGE Planted trees enrich the urban landscape, especially when they are in proportion and harmony with the surrounding built environment, here on the University of Minnesota campus, Minneapolis, U.S.A.

Afforestation is the creation of new areas of forest in areas where trees have been lost due to industry, farming, or climate deterioration.

that in which single scattered mature trees are removed periodically to encourage continuous natural regeneration and the maintenance of a permanent uneven-aged structure, normally of mixed species. This system is often used in mountain regions to prevent erosion.

Afforestation is the creation of new areas of forest or woodland on sites that have been without tree cover for a long period—often hundreds of years or longer. Such sites may have been farmed and allowed to deteriorate or they may have changed because of climatic factors, as in the case of sand-dune invasion or as a result of industrial dereliction such as slag heaps in a mining area. In nearly all cases afforestation is in fact restoration of tree cover after a long interval and in totally different conditions.

The purpose of afforestation is often to satisfy the growing demand for industrial wood, but other objectives, such as flood control, shelter, prevention of erosion, or the amelioration of the climate (particularly in arid countries), are also important. The current rate of increase in newly created forest is 12 million acres (5 million ha) each year, but with losses of some 37 million acres (15 million ha) the net loss is of the order of 25 million acres (10 million ha) annually. Large afforestation programs have been carried out in many countries; the Tennessee Valley scheme, which restored the "dust-bowl" to fertility in the 1930s, was one early success, and in the countries of the European Union some 2.47 million acres (1 million ha) of surplus farm land has been reafforested since the early 1990s. China, India, Russia, and the United States had the largest areas of plantation at the start of the new millennium.

The techniques required for afforestation differ from those used to regenerate existing forests. Conditions are nearly always harsh, soils impoverished, exposure to wind or sun severe, and the risk of damage by animals and pests much greater than in the more stable forest ecosystem. In wet uplands the land must be drained and impacted soils broken up by some form of cultivation to enable the tree roots to penetrate. On arid slopes in hot climates terracing may be needed to conserve any rainfall, and in rocky terrain it is sometimes essential to import soil to establish new trees. Fertilization of the soil, particularly with phosphates, is nearly always necessary.

The species selected for afforestation are not always the same as those of the indigenous forests. Industrial needs demand fast-growing species, which must also be hardy to withstand the rigorous conditions as pioneers. This normally means that conifers (often introduced or exotic species) form the bulk of the planting. The Monterey Pine (*Pinus radiata*) from California is the main species used in Australia and New Zealand; the Cuban Pine (*P. caribaea*) from the southeast United States is much used in South Africa; and Sitka Spruce (*Picea sitchensis*), a native of North America, is the principal species used to afforest the wet uplands in Britain.

In some countries where conditions permit, the initial planting may include broadleaves such as oaks, alder, poplars, eucalypts, and birches; the more rigorous the conditions, however, the less chance of successfully establishing a diverse crop in the original planting. Afforestation must be viewed as the pioneer stage in the restoration of a forest ecosystem that may take fifty or a hundred years to re-establish. Nevertheless, even a monoculture of a pioneer coniferous species can bring great environmental gain to the site. Protection from grazing, disturbance, wind, and erosion, and the conservation of moisture, start the chain of events in the development of the site from plantation to forest with its diversity of composition and structure, flora and fauna.

Improvement of Existing Forests

The need to conserve natural forest systems for their environmental value, rather than replace them with man-made forest, and at the same time increase their potential production of utilizable wood, now receives increasing attention from foresters. Tropical rainforests, exploited for their timbers and degraded by shifting cultivation, pose many silvicultural problems. Natural regeneration is difficult to ensure and the introduction of exotic species only adds to the progressive destruction of the ecosystem.

In the past, the need for a country to formulate a national policy was mainly dependent on the need for a sustained or increased yield from its forests to supply established wood-using industries. Developing countries tended simply to exploit the forest to obtain capital for other purposes or land for agriculture. Today the situation is changing: increasing pressure on dwindling natural resources demands strong commitment to manage existing resources and develop new ones.

In this context a number of essential components are required of a national forestry policy. Efficiency of production and harvesting must be balanced against conservation measures and safeguarding the environment against pollution. The dominant use in multiple-use forests must be defined. This may be protective rather than productive—as in the creation of national parks and wilderness areas. There is a need to define how forests are to fulfill national aims and there must be investment in the form of trained experts and capital to gain a continuing output in raw materials while remaining sensitive to the needs of local people, without whose cooperation long-term management will fail. Genetic research is particularly important; improvements in this field could contribute to increases in yields of plantations and managed forests, lowering pressures on the remaining natural forests. Forest managers at all levels must be trained in the scientific basis for the application of forestry techniques, which will result in greater yields of wood with reduced damage to the environment.

Forest Products

Forests provide one of the world's most vital renewable resources. The forests themselves are the habitat of many plants and animals and the home of many peoples, who depend on their environment for food, clothes, building materials, fuel, and other supplies. In global terms, forests are the source of a wide range of raw materials for major forest industries and for minor forest products.

From the wealth of statistics associated with forestry and forest products, perhaps the most remarkable fact to emerge is that about half the world's annual forest crop is used as fuel (either as firewood or as charcoal) and that three billion people depend on it.

The major forest industries are concerned with timber and timber products, plywood, wood chips, wood pulp, and paper. Minor forest products include: leaf fodder and litter; bark for use as cork or tanstuffs; ornamental trees and shrubs; medicinal plants; edible fruits, seed, and other plant parts; naval stores (see below); oils, fats, resins, turpentine, gums, latex, dyestuffs, and sap sugar; fibers, yarns, and flosses; osiers, canes, bamboos, reeds, rushes, and thatching materials. Plants have also given rise to mineral products in the form of peat, lignite, and coal.

Major Forest Products

Forest industries are based on the utilization of part or all of the forest tree. Mature trees are felled, the branches removed, and the trunk sawn into logs from which solid timber components are cut. The world is consuming ever-greater quantities of wood. The F.A.O. (Food and Agriculture Organization) estimated that in 2002 about 120,000 million cubic ft (3,400 million m^3) of wood were consumed, a 50 percent increase from the early 1970s. Industry uses 47 percent of timber production, and 53 percent is used as fuel. Of the wood used in industry, about two-thirds is currently used for timber (beams, posts, railway sleepers, and so on) and woodbased panels (plywood, particle board, etc.) in the ratio of about three to one. The remaining third of the wood used industrially is made into pulp, which is the basis of the paper industry, but is also used by the chemical industry to create products as diverse as synthetic fibers, cellulose-based plastic materials, lacquers, and explosives, and in the processes of tanning and distillation. About half of the paper produced globally is used for wrapping and packaging, a third is used for high-quality writing and printing papers, and the rest, about a seventh, is used for newsprint.

At a time when world consumption of wood and is increasing, large areas of forest in many countries are being turned over to agriculture each year, and many of the present exporters of timber are aiming to meet not more than their own needs in the long-term future.

Moreover, much of the world's forest area is situated in very remote areas and its utilization is likely to become increasingly costly. Planted forest to date amounts to only about 5 percent of the total exploitable forest area, so the vast majority of the wood cut at present is being "mined" from forests not planted by people and in which little or no capital has been invested before the harvesting operation. Thus there is a strong likelihood that wood—especially higher quality timber required for joinery, furniture, and other uses—will become increasingly scarce and costly. The best, usually hardwood, takes longer to produce and requires more care in growing than, say, wood grown to produce paper. Wood for fuel is easier still to grow: high-quality teak, for instance, is harvested at 60 years, spruce, for paper, can be cropped as thinnings at 10 years, whereas cottonwood can be cut for fuel at just 5 years.

Minor Forest Products

The many and varied products of the forest have served to provide for many of our needs since earliest recorded times. The relative importance of so-called minor forest products has changed over the years with industrialization and technological development. Naval stores provide a good example. The term first appears in England in the sixteenth century and covers the very important group of shipbuilding materials (pitch, tar, and timber) derived from pine species. These commodities have always been of vital importance for the building and caulking of wooden ships and waterproofing their associated ropes, rigging,

In planted conifer forests, mature trees are selectively felled and the branches removed when they reach an appropriate size for logging.

RIGHT Rubber is tapped from *Hevea brasiliensis*, the major source of the commercial rubber used for car tires, shoe soles, and elastic in clothes.

and cordage. Much naval strategy of seafaring nations from the sixteenth through nineteenth centuries was based on a regular and reliable supply of these materials.

Naval stores now form part of the silvichemical industry, which is concerned with the production of chemicals from trees. The industry covers a wide range of materials, such as lignin derivatives, vanillin, essential oils, maple syrup, oleoresins, alkaloids, tannins, rubber, true gums, ethanol, acetic acid, vitamins, and waxes. The natural dyestuffs indigo and logwood are important locally, though synthetic dyes have largely taken over the world market.

Of the forest plants that are edible or produce edible fruits and seeds, cocoa, coconut, coffee, tea, bananas, and spices are all major commodities. Latex and rubber are tapped both from forest trees and from plantation-grown crops. Chicle, the basis of chewing gum, is a natural product from a forest tree and is obtained by tapping the tree every five years to collect the exudate.

Several species of forest trees produce extracts that have valuable medicinal properties. In tropical forests *Cinchona* spp are a source of quinine; *Carapa* spp growing in America and Africa provide medicinal materials from both the bark and seeds; *Strychnos* spp give rise to a number of alkaloids, which combine medicinal properties with the deadly poisons strychnine, brucine, and curarine. These three examples demonstrate that it is critical to conserve the genetic diversity of our forest species, since there are undoubtedly other "minor" products that have yet to be discovered for the benefit of future generations.

Forests and Society

From earliest times trees have been venerated, used in religious symbolism and for esthetic purposes. The yggdrasil of Norse mythology, a huge spreading ash tree, was the very pillar of the world, binding together earth, heaven, and hell. Trees and groves were sacred to the Greeks, often being associated with particular deities: the oak with Zeus, the olive with Athena, the laurel with Apollo. Such veneration did not prevent trees being felled, but when virgin forest was cleared individual trees or clumps would be left as holy relics—a custom worthy of resurrection today. Transplanting of trees is known to have been practised as early as 1500 B.C.E. in Egypt, and in classical times Theophrastus and Pliny recorded methods of tree care. The regard that societies have had for trees is reflected in countless placenames that owe their origin to the trees that grew in the vicinity, while tree imagery in poetry, prose, and song is found in every language.

With the growing sophistication of society in the Middle Ages, demands on the forest estates of the developing countries of the world increased to provide the raw materials for manufacturing.

BELOW The Coconut Palm, *Cocos nucifera*, provides many things for the millions of people in the Tropics. The wood is used for housebuilding, the woven fronds for walls and thatch, and the fibrous husk for rope. The nut provides food and drink and its shells are used as cups and vessels. From the sap, toddy is extracted and enjoyed as an alcoholic beverage.

Up to the thirteenth and fourteenth centuries, the administration and exploitation of Europe's natural forests was often controlled by royal authority. Many forests provided hunting grounds for their majesty's pleasure. However, this patronage waned concurrently with an increased demand for forest resources in the form of naval stores and fuel for the early iron-smelting industries. The "gaps" produced by such exploitation were soon filled by increasingly sophisticated agricultural demands and practises. The result was the loss throughout Europe of vast tracts of natural forest that were never replaced. Concern over the depletion of European forests was constantly being voiced. For example, legislation was enacted in 1581 to try to control the destruction of the oak forests to the south of London, which were being exploited for the production of charcoal for the iron-smelting industry.

From the view of what is termed amenity forestry there was, however, one clear benefit from this age. The period from the fifteenth through nineteenth centuries was a time of naval powers, colonization, and exploration—all made possible because of the forest resources of the homelands. With the opening up of new lands, thousands of new and curious plants were discovered, including trees. This supply of unusual plants was further stimulated by their becoming fashionable among the new upper classes. The age of the landscape garden in which trees formed a primary part began. Specimen tree collections in the form of arboreta and artificial landscapes began to appear in earnest during the eighteenth century, especially around the family residences of estates in Great Britain and in France. Amenity planting reached its peak in the nineteenth century, and many magnificent specimen trees still stand in testimony to the endeavors of estate foresters a century or more ago.

Trees in the Urban Landscape

The ravages of two world wars necessitated the landscape of Europe to be rejuvenated and its towns and cities rebuilt. With increasing appreciation of town planning and the contribution that trees make to the quality of life, local and central government authorities in a number of countries made resources available for the planting and maintenance of trees in both urban and rural areas. New towns were built in which provision was made for new plantings while at the same time preserving the existing tree population, especially where they formed essential features of the landscape. Professional associations lobbied legislatures to enact regulations to provide for due consideration to the preservation and conservation of treed landscapes that were threatened by development. Fragile areas were given special status, preservation orders provided, and tree-planting grants to private individuals and organizations were made available from government-sponsored agencies.

In spite of increased public awareness and protective legislation in many countries, the destruction of trees continues, and not only in those forests and woodlands that are harvested for the timber they produce. The emphasis on road transport, the provision of by-passes, out-of-town shopping centers, and parking lots has been responsible for the loss of many elegant trees in cities and their environs. Vandalism contributes to pointless casualties, especially in new landscapes. Many authorities prefer to record their tree-planting progress by the number of trees planted instead of those that become successfully established. Indeed, far too many cases new trees end up merely as supports for their stakes because there are not sufficient funds to allow for aftercare.

Far greater loss and mutilation of trees occur in the name of progress. Those people involved with the development or use of land must carry a large portion of blame. Urban society requires more houses, factories, and roads. It is only when loud local protests have been mounted that, for example, highway planners have been forced to realign routes that were initially carved through irreplaceable trees and wooded areas. An awareness of the landscape blight that highway construction can cause has resulted in many fine planting schemes financed by central governments. But trees are more than simply ornamental additions: lining a road with trees can give protection from wind turbulence, thereby increasing highway safety. Other benefits include reduction in noise levels (for example the rustle of leaves can mask traffic roar) and the alleviation of glare caused by modern buildings.

Housing developments consume large numbers of trees despite the conditions placed by planning authorities on their retention and protection. The alteration of the water table following disruption of the soil during building work, the laying down of hard surfaces and the excavation and infilling that alter the configuration of the land, deprive existing trees of their sources of moisture to the extent that they are placed under stress at a time when they are attempting to adjust to the changed environment in which they find themselves. A tree has no option but to die when its environment changes for the worse. The provision of utility services involves digging trenches to lay down pipes for power supply, and when major roots are cut, not only is the stability and nutrient source of the tree in jeopardy but fungal disease can gain entry into the cut surfaces.

Individual owners of trees must also take a share of the blame for the mutilation of trees and their destruction. Many people resort to the practise of lopping or pollarding in the mistaken belief that pruning reduces the thickness of the branches or will stop, for example, the drip of honeydew from limes and sycamores, which ruins the protective paint of cars. On new developments an inappropriate choice of trees to enhance a property results in the trees overtaking the limited space available.

The average suburban property is not large enough to support a tree of forest proportions and therefore it is wiser to plant the smaller type tree—birches (*Betula* spp), rowans (*Sorbus* spp), hickories (*Carya*), or some of the smaller maples, for example *Acer griseum* or *A. hersii*, rather than beeches, oaks, or monkey puzzles.

Trees are under threat in rural contexts, too. In Europe, hedgerows have been the traditional site for trees since the loss of the true forest cover and are, in effect, linear nature reserves. The effects of diseases, such as the devastating effect of Dutch Elm Disease on the English Elm, and the overall reduction of hedges as field sizes grow as agriculture becomes more mechanized, continue to alter the landscape. The arable farmer complains that trees reduce his cropping areas or that the roots damage expensive machinery. While these are valid complaints, every farm will have areas that cannot be cropped and where groups of trees could be planted to form spinneys and copses. Stock requires shade—protection in the summer and in the winter—and therefore good cattle husbandry includes the provision of trees in pastures. Having provided protection and shelter, these same trees can produce timber for use in the estate or farm in the centuries to come.

Specimen trees and banks of flowers in the one hundred year old gardens of Butchart Gardens, the landscaped site of an abandoned quarry on Canada's Saanich Peninsula, British Columbia.

An established tree left standing in the wasteland of a new factory development may still struggle to survive in its altered environment.

Amenity or Urban Forestry

With the greater mobility of city populations of the Western world, their demand for recreational areas has introduced the amenity woodland—areas of trees set aside for their aesthetic and recreational value as opposed to their timber production potential. The proximity of these woodlands to population centers dictates how frequently they are used. Their management, usually the responsibility of local authorities, has to take into account the pressures that visitors place on the delicate balance of a woodland ecosystem. The concept of so-called "urban forestry" has been with us for four decades. The concept, first developed in Canada, has been defined as a practise that "does not deal entirely with city trees or with single tree management but rather with tree management in the entire area influenced and utilized by the urban population." By definition, a forest or plantation managed for the production of timber comes within the above definition of the urban forest, and many government forest departments have now realized the recreational value of the commercial forest. In Holland, forests are opened for recreational purposes once the initial establishment stage has been completed, and in Great Britain forest walks are now to be found in all the large afforested areas. Even private forests have been opened to the public by provision of, for example, nature trails. In North America, vast tracts of forest are accessible for recreation purposes, including, for instance, long sections of the Applachian Trail stretching from Georgia to Maine.

Amenity woodlands and commercial forests therefore require the same approach. Because the landscape of Europe has been manipulated by humans to the extent that natural forest is virtually nonexistent, management of woodlands for amenity is essential. The forester aims at what is termed a sustained yield and hence income. For the amenity forester the value of woodlands is expressed in terms of social benefit, meaning that external finance is required. However, there is no reason why woodland areas cannot be managed at two levels—the income from the true forestry used to subsidize the amenity facilities. In an amenity woodland, trees have to be replaced, and therefore silvicultural practises are demanded just as they are in the commercial forest.

NATURAL AND PLANTED FOREST IN THE US AND EUROPE	
Country	**Percentage of land forested (2000)**
United States	24.7
Europe	46.0
Germany	30.7
France	27.9
Belgium	22.2
Great Britain	11.6
Netherlands	11.1
Denmark	10.7
Ireland	9.6

Source: F.A.O.

Trees have been referred to as the furniture of the landscape, and all members of society must share responsibility for their survival. It is irresponsible for the public to expect conservation measures from public authorities and unrestricted access to woodlands. The compaction of the soil by many feet and the dumping of litter caused by open access, for example, will only hinder conservation measures. The task of maintaining a national heritage as represented by the country's rural and urban landscape is enormous and initiative rests with all, not just a few, if the inheritance is to be passed on to future generations.

The extent of the forest clearing since early days can be seen from the table below in which the area of forest, including plantations, is given as a percentage of the total area of land—for most of these countries the "natural" forest cover should be over 80 percent.

Climate: the Deciding Factor

Despite the significant human impact on the extent of the world's forests, which may include the present concern that industrialization and the burning of fossil fuels is quickening the pace of global warming, the present world distribution of tree species is a reflection of their climatic requirements and, in particular, a minimum temperature, below which they cannot grow.

The United States Department of Agriculture (U.S.D.A.) has identified ten climate zones for the North American continent, based on mean annual minimum temperature, ranging from Zone 1 (Arctic: below -50°F/-45°C) through Zone 10 (tropical: 30–40°F/ -1–5°C). These zones are shown on the map opposite of North America and have become the standard reference for botanists and other workers in the field of plant geography. For comparative purposes, the same system has been adopted to show Europe's climate zones (except that Zone 10 does not apply), with an adjustment made for the oceanic climate of the British Isles, tempered as it is by the influence of the Gulf Stream passing up the Atlantic on the west side of the country, so that in Britain Zone 8 equates to Zone 9 in the United States or continental Europe.

In the following chapter, these climate zones (abbreviated to **cz**) are shown as a range for all genera, and specifically for all species where the information is available. This is common practise in horticultural works, because in instances where certain species are not widely grown, it is impossible to attribute them with any confidence to a specific zone. In addition, many (though by no means all) hybrids and cultivars are not allocated to any climate zones because often they are either not relevant or difficult to determine owing to the mixed parentage of the hybrid or cultivar.

CLIMATE ZONES: NORTH AMERICA

Source: U.S.D.A.

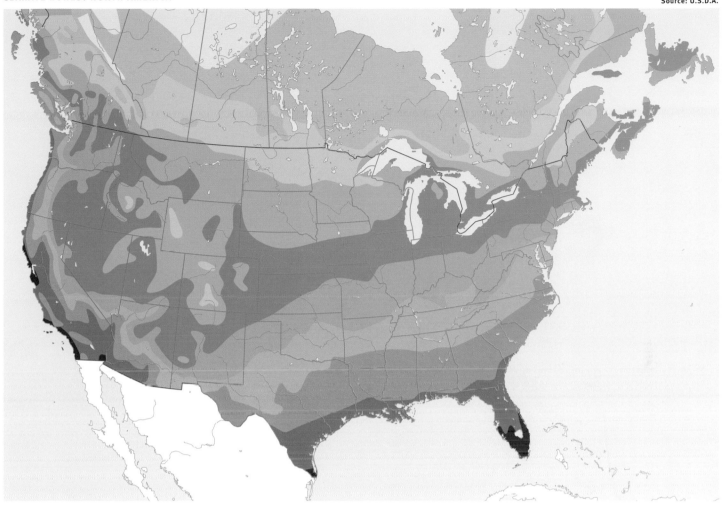

CLIMATE ZONES: EUROPE

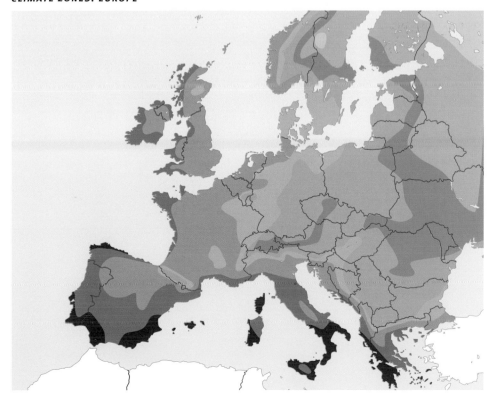

HARDINESS ZONES: NORTH AMERICA

°F	ZONE	°C
below -50	1	below -45
-50 to -40	2	-45 to -40
-40 to -30	3	-40 to -34
-30 to -20	4	-34 to -29
-20 to -10	5	-29 to -23
-10 to 0	6	-23 to -17
0 to 10	7	-17 to -12
10 to 20	8	-12 to -7
20 to 30	9	-7 to -1
30 to 40	10	-1 to 5

HARDINESS ZONES: EUROPE

°F	ZONE	°C
below -50	1	below -45
-50 to -40	2	-45 to -40
-40 to -30	3	-40 to -34
-30 to -20	4	-34 to -29
-20 to -10	5	-29 to -23
-10 to 0	6	-23 to -17
0 to 10	7	-17 to -12
10 to 20	8	-12 to -7
20 to 30	9	-7 to -1
30 to 40	10	-1 to 5

TREES OF EVERY KIND

Three main types of trees are popularly recognized in terms of a single character—the leaf. They are the conifers, with basically needle- and scale-like leaves; the broadleaves, which primarily have flattened simple or compound leaves that are generally smaller than those of the third group—the monocotyledon trees such as the palms—in which the leaves are also flattened but mainly fanlike or fernlike in appearance.

There is no doubt that the broadleaves are the dominant natural tree-form throughout the modern world, except in the more extreme cooler climates, where conifers prevail. Particularly in temperate and warm temperate areas, forestry policy is often to replace natural broadleaved forest or grassland with conifer monoculture under which conditions these trees thrive.

The palms are mainly tropical, with only a few of the 2,650 species found in subtropical and temperate regions. They are an ancient group and there is some evidence that their distribution was once wider—even in the Tropics.

Today, the conifers are the only gymnosperms that occur in any quantity. Their history extends back some 300 million years, but currently they dominate only the cooler and cold areas of the world, such as the vast boreal region of the northern hemisphere and mountain habitats worldwide. Their continuing success compared with other gymnosperm groups is probably due in part to the evolution of drought-resistant features, such as the needle- and scale-like leaves. Other gymnosperms with a tree form are represented by two quite differing groups: the cycads and the Maidenhair Tree (*Ginkgo biloba*). Both are the barest relicts of a flora that dominated the world during Mesozoic times, 225 to about 64 million years ago, though their evolutionary history extends back at least as far as that of the conifers.

The only other primitive tree-like forms found today are the so-called tree-ferns, which represent but a small proportion of the 10,000 species of all ferns. Though the fossil record of tree-ferns extends back only about 190 million years, the record of all ferns goes back 350 million years. It is interesting to observe the similarity in gross form between tree-ferns, cycads, and palms, all groups that have evolved at quite different times and along vastly different lines, not the least in forms of reproduction.

The last group of tree-like species included here are the "tree cacti," which are adapted to harsh desert climates. In botanical terms, they could be deemed broadleaves, as they are dicotyledonous angiosperms, but because most lack true leaves, having spines instead, and because, at least in the young stage, mechanical support is given by the water storage tissue of the photosynthetic tissues not the wood, tree cacti bear little resemblance to a conventional broadleaf.

Conifers, broadleaves, monocotyledon trees, and tree cacti clearly take up the greatest space in this chapter, but tree-ferns, cycads, and the Maidenhair Tree all have comprehensive coverage for their size. The conifers section includes all genera found the world over, despite the fact that many Asian and southern hemisphere genera occur in temperate northern hemisphere cultivation only as shrubs, rockery, or alpine subjects. The dominant status, and consequent great variety, of the broadleaves makes it impossible to cover all genera to the same detail. Therefore coverage is restricted to those genera native to or cultivated in the cool, temperate, and warm-temperate Mediterranean- type climates; broadleaved trees of the Tropics appear in "Trees of the Tropics." Selection of genera is difficult since many comprise mostly shrubs but some trees. Such genera are included when they contain important trees even if the majority are shrubs or smaller. Once selected, coverage of species is comprehensive in that all important species are considered, whether trees or not. Thus, included under "Willows," are shrubby sallows and osiers and even the Arctic Willow, which grows to a height of only a few inches. The monocotyledons, palms, and tree cacti are found within the Temperate Broadleaves or Trees of the Tropics sections, as is appropriate.

FACING PAGE Beech are dominant or codominant in temperate forests throughout the northern hemisphere. Several species are cultivated for their handsome spreading shape and foliage.

BELOW The Arctic Willow, *Salix arctica*, is a shrub that never exceeds 2 ft (60 cm) in height and grows in clumps that form dense mats on the tundra in North America, Europe, and Asia. The minute, wind-pollinated flowers are borne in dense, erect catkins. Male and female catkins are found on separate plants.

Tree-Ferns

Unlike other tree species, tree-ferns are true ferns of the Class Filicopsida, related to the common Male Fern (*Dryopteris filix-mas*) and Bracken (*Pteridium aquilinum*). In most ferns, however, the stem is reduced to a compact rootstock, as in the Male Fern, or elongated, as in the rhizome of Bracken. In both cases, the aerial foliage, both sterile and fertile leaves (or fronds as they are often called in ferns), arises, even in Bracken, at ground level direct from that stem.

"Tree-fern" is the name given to members of the families Cyatheaceae and Dicksoniaceae in which the rhizome is erect and stout and forming a trunk, with a crown of leaves at its apex. This arborescent growth is also developed in *Sadleria*, a genus of the Blechnaceae, and occasionally in other *Blechnum* species, for example *B. gibbum*. It is only in the Cyatheaceae and Dicksoniaceae, however, that the plants reach any size and ecological importance. This account is confined to those species.

The gross morphology of the tree-fern stem differs considerably from that of the angiosperm tree trunk. First, the tree-fern rarely branches; when it does, the stem divides dichotomously into two equal branches. Occasionally side branches may form, as for instance in *Cyathea mexicana*, from adventitious buds at the base of old petioles. Second, the tree-fern is without a true bark layer, though its outer surface is roughened by leaf-stalk remains and often covered with lichens, mosses, and other epiphytes, in common with other trees of the tropical forest. Third, there is no massive root system as in true trees; the lower part of the stem has many adventitious roots, which become entangled and form a tough covering often doubling the thickness of the trunk, thus supporting it. Tree-ferns may grow up to 80 ft (25 m) but at this height they are usually supported by surrounding vegetation.

The internal organization of tissues of the tree-fern is less advanced than in true trees, though, at the cellular level, xylem (water-transporting cells) and phloem (sugar-transporting cells) are present and perform the same functions as in higher plants but, unlike conifers and broadleaved trees, there is no secondary tissue and the fern trunk cannot increase in girth. The xylem and phloem are associated in vascular bundles (meristeles), which are embedded in an often corrugated cylinder of lignified fibers (sclerenchyma) collectively called a dictyostele.

The leaves are arranged in a spiral arrangement around the stem and form a rosette at its apex, which is protected by scales or hairs. The number of mature leaves in the crown varies with the species, being from five or six, as in *C. contaminans*, to as many as forty, as in *C. atrox*. In some species, as the leaf dies and falls it leaves a characteristic scar on the trunk surface; in others, the petiole remains as a persistent covering for many years, for example *Dicksonia antarctica* and *Cyathea pseudomuelleri*. The leaf architecture is that of a typical fern, usually being twice to four times divided. The midrib (rhachis) and petiole (or stipe) may be covered in scales or thorns (as in *Cyathea*) or stiff bristles (as in *Dicksonia*). Anatomically, the leaf-blade tissue is similar to angiosperms but there is less ecological variation in thickness or adaptation to drought. Along each side of the petiole are peg-like outgrowths called pneumathodes; on the young leaf they act as respiratory or water-control organs.

Like most ferns, reproduction is by spores formed on the backs of normal green leaves. In some species, such as *Cyathea lurida*, the fertile leaves are morphologically distinct, being reduced in area. The spores are produced in sporangia growing in clusters called sori, which are protected when young (or in some species until the spores ripen) by a membranous flap or cover called an indusium. Spores give rise to the sexual generation, which is a small wedge-shaped platelet of green cells (gametophyte), in which the sexual organs are embedded. On fertilization of the female egg-cell by the motile male sperm, a new tree-fern (sporophyte) plant develops, which may not reach maturity for ten to fifteen years.

Dicksonia antarctica, displaying generally very large and multiple pinnate fronds that are typical of tree-ferns. They are produced in a crown with the leaves arranged in a spiral pattern. Tree-ferns are slow growers, growing at a rate of about 1–2 in (2.5–5 cm) per year. Spores are produced on the underside of the leaves.

Tree-ferns are currently recognized as comprising two distinct families. Cyatheaceae contains the genera *Cyathea* and *Cremidaria,* though the latter is often included within the former. Dicksoniaceae includes all other genera, *Dicksonia, Cystodium, Culcita, Thyrsopteris, Cibotium,* and *Calochlaena.* Two allied families, Lophosoriaceae and Metaxya, are not included here.

The main differences between Cyatheaceae and Dicksoniaceae can be summarized as follows. Cyatheaceae have scales on the stem apex, petiole, midrib, and veins; the sori are in the middle rather than the edge of the leaf; they may lack indusia or (more likely) have a saucer- or cup-like one that may, in some species, enclose an entire sorus. Dicksoniaceae, on the other hand, have stiff hairs or bristles and sori on the edges of the leaf, which are protected by thin flap-like indusia on their inner face and the reflexed margin of the leaf on the outside.

The twenty-five species of *Dicksonia* are distributed in the southern hemisphere. In New Zealand they grow from sea level to 2,000 ft (600 m) in the *Nothofagus–Podocarpus–Dacrydium* forests. In the southernmost latitudes *Dicksonia squarrosa* regularly withstands frost. In southeast Australia and Tasmania, *D. antarctica* is an important constituent in the *Nothofagus* forest, where it forms a layer 10 ft (3 m) high under the dense canopy, because the young tree-ferns are able to grow when receiving only 1 percent of the total light. Dense hairs protect the growing tips of dicksonias, enabling them to survive forest fires. *Dicksonia* spreads into the tropical areas of New Guinea and the Malesian archipelago, reaching Sumatra and Luzon (*D. blumei*), where they grow in mid-montane rainforest. Eight species are found in the Americas reaching as far north as Mexico (*D. cicutaria*). The genus is not found in Africa, but one endemic species (*D. arborescens*) is found on the island of St. Helena. Fossil tree-ferns have been found from as far back as the Jurassic period, and one, identified as *Coniopteris hymenophylloides,* most resembles *Dicksonia.*

Dicksonia fibrosa, called "Whekiponga" by the Maoris of New Zealand, is used in the building of their huts and fences, since the trunks last well in the ground and there is a belief that rats cannot gnaw their way through such tough material. It is also used both structurally and decoratively in ceremonial houses (runaga-houses), where the outer surface is shaved off to accentuate the gray and black pattern left by the leaf-scars.

Cyathea contains over 600 species, spread throughout the Tropics, north to the Himalaya and Japan's north Honshu island (*C. spinulosa*), south to Tasmania (*C. australis*) and the southern tip of New Zealand, where *C. smithii* grows in the *Metrosideros lucida* forest within a few feet of the ice of Franz Josef glacier. Elsewhere in South and Southeast Asia tree-ferns are common throughout the everwet rainforest and are a significant component in the mid- and upper-montane forest, particularly where clouds regularly rest. They are a conspicuous member of open grassland species above the treeline, about 10,000 ft (3,000 m) in New Guinea, Sumatra, and Sulawesi. Surprisingly, though each plant must produce many grams of spores, germination or dispersal is low and species are not wide ranging, and almost every mountain range has its endemics, as in the case, for instance of *C. pseudomuelleri* of Mt. Wilhelmina. A few species are widespread and common in secondary forest and near rivers throughout mainland and island Southeast Asia, for example *C. contaminans.*

The genus is less dominant in Africa, where one savanna species, *C. dregei,* can withstand periodic burning. In America the genus has its center of speciation in tropical South America, here too mainly as a forest species, reaching Mexico in the north and Paraguay in the south.

Cyathea species are used for house building by native peoples throughout its range, and living trees are often left for this purpose when forest is cleared for gardens. Maoris make jugs and vases from *C. dealbata* (called Ponga—hence Ponga ware) and other New Zealand species. When shaved, the vascular tissue and leaf-gaps make an attractive pattern. The Maoris also use the pith from the upper part of the trunk as a type of sago, and they, as do indigenous people in New Guinea, Borneo, Indonesia, and elsewhere, eat the young unfurling fronds as a vegetable. Dried fronds are also used for bedding by Maoris. In Sabah, hollowed tree-fern stems are used as bee-hives.

The masses of adventitious roots at the bases of *Cyathea* trunks are used in orchid culture, either as sawn solid slabs or broken in potting mixtures. Trade in all species of *Dicksonia* and *Cyathea* is prohibited by the Convention of International Trade in Endangered Species (C.I.T.E.S), except with special license.

Tree-ferns are cultivated as ornamentals in parks in warm temperate and tropical areas, for example several *Dicksonia* species and *C. medullaris.* Propagation from spores is slow and germination rate low, though once established they require very little management. *D. antarctica* is grown in conservatories in Europe and is often established outside in the more oceanic areas. The slowness of growth is a deterrent to short-term landscapers.

Tree ferns are ferns that grow with a trunk elevating the fronds above ground level. However, they do not form new woody tissue in their trunks. The trunk is supported by a fibrous mass of roots that expands as the tree-fern grows. A tree-fern can often be transplanted by cutting it off at the base of the trunk and replanting it. It will grow a new root system so long as it is kept moist. Shown here *Dicksonia antarctica.*

The Maidenhair Tree

The Maidenhair Tree (*Ginkgo biloba*) is the only living representative of a large ancient Order of conifer-like trees. *Ginkgo* is named for the Japanese word for the plant or its nuts.

The Maidenhair Tree is sacred according to the Buddhist religion and has been cultivated for many centuries in China and Japan, especially in the grounds of temples. It became known to Western science in the eighteenth century when the first specimens were planted in Europe. For some time it was believed that the species may have been saved from extinction only by cultivation in the Far East, but there is now good evidence for believing that it occurs in a truly wild state at the borders of Chekiang and Anhwei provinces in eastern China. Over the last 235 years the tree has been planted widely and grown successfully under many different conditions of soil and climate. It is also remarkably free of disease and resistant to pests and air pollution.

The Order Ginkgoales flourished mainly during the Mesozoic era, especially during the Jurassic period (about 150 million years ago) when dinosaurs dominated the fauna. The genus *Ginkgo* itself probably extends back to this period, but the group was very rich in species and some of them certainly represent distinct genera. *Ginkgo* enjoyed a worldwide distribution and the species were no doubt important constituents of the flora. Fossil leaf remains are often found abundantly in deltaic sediments laid down during Mesozoic times. *Ginkgo* declined toward the end of the Mesozoic era, and this continued during the Tertiary until today only the one species remains.

Ginkgo forms a massive tree, and old specimens—some more than one thousand years old—attain a very large size. In the young tree there is usually a strong leader, which forms the main trunk. The branches are somewhat straggly and these give the tree its rather distinctive appearance in the winter leafless condition. The leaves are especially interesting, with a wedge-shaped leaf blade borne on a long stalk (petiole); the venation is an open forking system without any vein fusions. It is the delicate fern-like foliage and the shape of the lamina that account for the tree's English popular name of Maidenhair Tree. In the fall the foliage turns a brilliant shade of yellow.

There are separate male and female trees. It appears that most of the earlier specimens planted in Europe were male, the first female one being recorded near Geneva in 1814. Some trees in cultivation have had branches of the opposite sex grafted onto them.

The pollen-bearing cones are not especially distinctive, being similar in a general way to the male cones of conifers. Seeds are usually borne in pairs but sometimes on stalks that appear to be equivalent morphologically to the male cones. Both are carried on leafy dwarf-shoots. Thus, there is no female cone in *Ginkgo* comparable with that in conifers.

One of the most remarkable features of the reproductive cycle in *Ginkgo* is the presence of swimming male cells (sperm) similar to those found in cycads. Indeed, there are several features of seed development that are similar in cycads and *Ginkgo*. It is believed that these do not indicate any close relationship, rather that they are primitive features that have been retained by these extraordinary ancient and primitive plants.

Ginkgos grow well in most temperate regions except the cold northern regions. They seem impartial to soil type, so long as it is fertile, and grow best in sunny positions. They make imposing specimen trees but are also often planted in avenues; they are tolerant of pollution and so make useful trees for industrial areas. Cultivars available include 'Fastigiata,' a columnar form with semierect branches, 'Pendula' with weeping branches, and 'Tremonia,' which has a conical form.

The mature seed has a soft outer fleshy layer, which has the unpleasant odor of rancid butter. For this reason male trees are usually preferred for avenue planting. In the Orient, the white seed kernel is regarded as a delicacy.

BELOW AND FACING PAGE
The Maidenhair Tree (*Ginkgo biloba*)is easily distinguishable by its fanshaped and bilobed leaves which grow alternately on the branches. They grow slowly in clusters and produce a long shoot with scattered leaves. Leaves also have distinctive, slightly raised veins which give a ribbed appearance to the foliage.

Cycads

The cycads, comprising ten or perhaps eleven living genera, are a group of very primitive woody plants that look like palms, though they are not at all closely related to this group. They represent the second largest order of living gymnosperms. They are distinguished from the conifers by a number of important characters, most conspicuously by their palm-like habit and large pinnately compound leaves, but also by quite numerous structural and reproductive characters.

Perhaps more than any other group of plants (except the Maidenhair Tree, *see* page 44), the cycads deserve to be called "living fossils," for the group reached its climax of evolutionary development in the Mesozoic era (about 200 million years ago) and since then has apparently declined without undergoing any appreciable evolutionary change. The earliest fossil cycads are known from the Permian period of the late Paleozoic (about 240 million years ago) and these, in the form of their seedbearing organs and in other characters, were very like the living genus *Cycas*. In the succeeding Triassic and Jurassic periods, cycads had a widespread distribution and, judging from the number of fossilized leaves in deltaic sediments laid down during these periods, the plants were often abundant. As fossil plants are nearly always preserved in a dismembered state—and cycads are no exception—few Mesozoic forms have yet been reconstructed, but those that have show surprisingly little difference from some of the living representatives.

The geographical distribution of the living genera suggests that they are of ancient origin. *Cycas*, with about 17 species, is distributed most widely: it extends from Polynesia through Madagascar and northward to Japan; *Stangeria*, with only a single species, is confined to South Africa; *Encephalartos* (about 46 species) is more widely distributed in tropical and southern Africa. *Bowenia*, with only 2 species, is in northern Australia. *Macrozamia* (15 species) and *Lepidozamia* (2 species), which is sometimes included within *Macrozamia*, are also Australian. *Ceratozamia* (10 species) and *Dioon* (10 species) are found in Mexico and Central America. *Microcycas* (1 species) is confined to Cuba, and *Zamia* (40 species) is more widely distributed in tropical America. This pattern of distribution is usually interpreted to mean that the cycad genera are relict and happen to have survived in these relatively confined areas.

As cycads are very ancient plants it is not surprising that they exhibit many peculiar features, some of which may be of a truly primitive nature. Most are rather palm-like with an unbranched erect stem bearing a crown of leaves. It is not known if this is a truly primitive condition or whether it may represent a

Cycads are of real scientific
interest but little economic
value. They are more appreciated
for their lush tropical form.

reduction from something more elaborate, since it
is difficult to ascertain the habit of the fossil forms.
Macrozamia hopei, a native of Queensland, Australia,
is reputed to be the tallest of the cycads, growing to
about 65 ft (20 m). Some living cycads have only a short
subterranean stem; this is likely to be a modified and
reduced condition. They are extremely slow-growing and
long-lived plants, and it has been estimated that some
living specimens may be over one thousand years old.
They produce new leaves at rather prolonged intervals
and may sometimes enter a dormant phase when no new
growth occurs for several years.

Like all other contemporary gymnosperms, cycads are
woody plants but their wood is peculiarly spongy. The
leaflets of the pinnately compound leaves in most cycads
have a system of forking veins running more or less
parallel, but in *Cycas* there is only a single mid-vein and
in *Stangeria* the leaflets have a fern-like venation with a
mid-vein and forking laterals.

The root system is not without peculiarities. Some
roots grow up to the soil surface and branch profusely to
form coralloid masses. These roots contain microscopic
blue-green alga (cyanobacteria) in a special layer of cells
in the outer tissues. The cycad is believed to benefit from
atmospheric nitrogen fixed by the algae.

Cycads have separate male and female plants. In all
but the female of *Cycas*, the reproductive structures are
borne in massive cones (usually terminally on the stem),
growth of the stem then being continued from a bud near
the cone base. In the female of *Cycas* there are no cones;
instead the seed-bearing megasporophylls, which
resemble the vegetative leaves to some extent, are borne
in place of ordinary leaves and the stem therefore goes
on growing and producing new leaves beyond.

There are several exceptional characteristics of the
reproductive process but perhaps the most interesting is
the production of swimming sperm. Two are produced in
each germinated pollen grain after pollination of the
ovules (young seeds). In only one other seed plant—the
Maidenhair Tree—are motile sperm produced.

Cycads are sometimes called sago palms because the
soft, starch-rich tissues of the stem in some species, for
example *C. circinalis* and *C. revoluta*, can be used to
prepare a kind of sago. The large seed kernels can also
be eaten but they may be poisonous unless prepared in a
certain way. Cycads, especially *Cycas* species, are
cultivated as greenhouse ornamentals in temperate
countries or outdoors in tropical gardens. The one most
commonly grown as an ornamental is *C. revoluta*.

Conifers

Conifers are an ancient group, their fossil history extending back to the late Carboniferous period (300 million years ago); several families are represented only by fossils. The living families themselves are mostly ancient: the monkey puzzle family (Araucariaceae) and redwood family (Taxodiaceae) extend back to the Jurassic period (95 million years ago) and the pine family (Pinaceae) at least to the Lower Cretaceous (135 million years ago).

The living conifers and taxads (yews) comprise some seventy genera divided among nine families. They are the only numerically and economically important groups of gymnosperms; the other groups containing tree forms are the Maidenhair Tree (*Ginkgo biloba*) and the cycads.

Conifers are sharply divided into northern hemisphere and southern hemisphere groups—a telling distribution that probably has extremely early origins and may relate to the time when there were two major land masses separated by the east-west–running Tethys Sea, though it is certain other factors are involved. For example, there has undoubtedly been much extinction, since there is fossil evidence that in the Jurassic and Cretaceous eras members of the Araucariaceae grew in Europe and other areas of the northern hemisphere. Many conifer genera now confined to relatively small areas once enjoyed a very much wider distribution. Coast Redwood (*Sequoia sempervirens*), now confined to western North America, was in earlier geological times widespread in the northern hemisphere. Several Far Eastern genera were once more widely distributed, too. Two million years ago the Pleistocene glaciations pushed many genera south, a contraction from which not all have fully recovered.

Most conifers are trees of cooler climates (either high latitude or high altitudes). Few occur in tropical or subtropical lowlands. Large areas in higher latitudes are still naturally dominated by conifer forest, though all but the most inaccessible have been exploited for timber. Many conifers of particular value as timber trees have been planted extensively well beyond their areas of natural distribution. Monterey Pine (*Pinus radiata*), native to a limited area of California, has been planted in many areas of Australia, New Zealand, and South Africa, where it has become a very important timber tree.

The "softwoods" of commerce are by definition the timbers produced by conifers. The term is not altogether appropriate, for the softest woods are in fact obtained from broadleaved trees, and some conifer woods are fairly hard, for example Yew (*Taxus baccata*). Softwoods, however, have a greater homogeneity than hardwoods (the broadleaves) for they lack the same differentiation of their elements (*see* What is a Tree?, page 8). Softwoods are a major constructional material, and used in various manufacturing industries (paper, textiles, synthetic board, packing materials, and chemicals). Resins from conifers are the source of turpentine and other substances for the paint, pharmaceutical, and perfumery industries. The seed kernels of some pines are eaten, especially the Stone Pine or Umbrella Pine (*Pinus pinea*). As a source of food, though, conifers have little use.

In horticultural terms, conifers are highly valued. Numerous varieties have special ornamental merits. Some members of the cypress and pine families (Cupressaceae and Pinaceae) are particularly rich in named horticultural varieties, many of them of dwarf form and prized for "alpine" gardens. Intergeneric hybrids among conifers have arisen in cultivation. The best-known hybrid is the remarkably vigorous × *Cupressocyparis leylandii,* a cross between *Chamaecyparis nootkatensis* and *Cupressus macrocarpa,* now widely grown as a hedge plant and screen-forming tree.

Conifer Taxonomy

The conifers are generally considered to represent a Class Pinopsida within the gymnosperms. Living conifers (including yews) comprise nine families, which are shown in the accompanying table, together with their genera. Taxaceae is included within the conifers, but some botanists would regard these as representing a separate Order. One reason for this is that their seeds are not borne in cones in the manner of typical conifers. In this, the Taxaceae is not alone—typical cones are not formed in the Southern Pine Family (Podocarpaceae) or in the Cow's Tail Pine Family (Cephalotaxaceae). These three families, together with Phyllocladaceae, which lack the typical (female) cones, are commonly and conveniently referred to as "taxoids" to distinguish them from the remaining five families, which have recognizable cones and are correspondingly known as "pinoids." The inclusion of the junipers (Juniperus—Cupressaceae) may, at first glance, seem exceptional as a "pinoid"; the fruiting cone is fleshy and commonly known as a "berry." Closer examination, however, soon reveals the characteristic cone structure—it is merely the fleshy scales that are misleading.

In biological terms, the distinction between "pinoids" and "taxoids" is significant because the former group is adapted to wind dispersal of its seeds (except *Juniperus*) and the latter (including *Juniperus*) to animal dispersal.

Some texts refer to the "taxoids" as having "imperfect cones" and the "pinoids" as having "perfect cones." This raises the question of the term to be used for the female reproductive structure. The term cone is quite acceptable for the "pinoids" but not for the "taxoids" for the reason already given. Traditionally the term female flower has been used for both "pinoids" and "taxoids" and is still used by some taxonomists, but others would restrict the term "flower" to the angiosperms (flowering plants) only, though even here the word has to be severely stretched to cover all cases. In this book, the practise is to use the words male cone for the male reproductive structures of both "pinoids" and "taxoids" and female cone for the female reproductive structures of the "pinoids." "female cone" (within inverted commas) has been adopted for the female structures of the "taxoids." In other words, cone = perfect cone, and "cone" = imperfect cone, to use the other current expressions for the female structures.

FACING PAGE Old growth mixed conifer forest, Olympic National Forest, Washington, U.S.A., showing the conical growth habit typical of many conifers.

Diagnostic Features
of the Conifer Families

Pinaceae—the Pine Family

Leaves needle-like and, as are the cone-scales, spirally arranged but sometimes, by twisting, appearing two-ranked; buds scaly; male and female cones on the same plant (monoecious); cone-scales of two kinds—bract-scales and ovuliferous-scales, the latter separate from and borne in the axils of the bract-scales and bearing two inverted ovules on the upper surface, these giving rise to a distinctive type of seed with a membranous wing extending from the base; micro-sporophylls (stamens) of male cone with two pollen sacs; pollen grains with two bladder-like wings except in *Larix*, *Pseudotsuga*, and *Tsuga*. Widespread in the northern hemisphere. Twelve genera: *Abies* (firs), *Cathaya*, *Cedrus* (true cedars), *Hesperospeuce*, *Keteleeria*, *Larix* (larches), *Nothotsuga*, *Picea* (spruces), *Pinus* (pines), *Pseudolarix* (Japanese Golden Larch), *Pseudotsuga* (Douglas firs), and *Tsuga* (hemlocks or hemlock spruces). (*Cathaya* is a Chinese genus but as yet no material or data are available in the West.)

* The word cone-scale is used here to mean the main contributor to the mature cone and may be the ovuliferous-scale, as in the Pinaceae, or the (supposed) fused bract- and ovuliferous-scale in the Cupressaceae, Taxodiaceae, and Araucariaceae. Unless otherwise qualified, the word cone refers to the female (ovulate) structure.

Taxodiaceae—the Redwood Family

Leaves linear to awl-shaped and, like the cone-scales, spirally arranged (except *Metasequoia*, where they are opposite); buds not scaly; monoecious; cone-scales not distinct as bract- and ovuliferous-scales, these being almost completely united to form a virtually single structure and each bearing

two or more erect or inverted ovules; these give rise to seeds, which, in some genera, have marginal wings. Microsporophylls with 2–9 pollen sacs; pollen without wings. Nine genera, eight in the northern hemisphere, but *Athrotaxis* is southern hemisphere: *Athrotaxis* (Tasmanian cedars), *Cryptomeria*, *Cunninghamia*, *Glyptostrobus*, *Metasequoia* (Dawn Redwood), *Sequoia* (Coast Redwood), *Sequoiadendron* (Big Tree, Giant Sequoia, or Sierra Redwood), *Taiwania*, *Taxodium* (swamp cypresses).

Sciadopityaceae

Formerly included in Taxodiaceae, the single genus *Sciadopitys* (Japanese Umbrella Pine) is now considered sufficiently distinct to merit placement in its own family.

Evergreen monecious tree. Scale leaves closely adpressed to shoot and scale-like. Needle leaves in spiral whorls at ends of branches. Male cones sub-terminal and consisting of spirally arranged scales with two pollen sacs per scale. Female cones sub-terminal and solitary with fertile scales spirally arranged and with 5–9 ovules.

Araucariaceae—the Monkey Puzzle Family

Leaves narrow to broad with parallel veins, and, as are the cone-scales, spirally arranged; monoecious or dioecious; bract- and ovuliferous-scales not distinct, but fused into a single structure and each bearing a single ovule, the subsequent seed being shed with the cone-scale. Male cone relatively large; microsporophylls with up to about twelve pollen sacs; pollen without wings. Three genera, mainly southern hemisphere: *Agathis* (kauri or kauri pines), *Araucaria* (monkey puzzles), *Wollemia*.

The original forests of Scots Pine (*Pinus sylvestris*), which once dominated large tracts of the uplands of Scotland, survive only as scattered remnants, in which widely spaced individual trees have branched trunks and a broad canopy (cf. the image on the facing page).

Cupressaceae—the Cypress Family

Adult leaves mostly small and scale-like (juvenile leaves
sometimes needle-like) typically in opposite pairs, rarely in
whorls of three; monoecious or dioecious; cones more or less
globose, small, 0.8–1.2 in (2–3 cm) diameter, the scales in pairs
and either peltate or flattened and imbricate, at least finally
more or less woody (berry-like in *Juniperus*), the fertile scales
with one to numerous erect ovules; seeds winged or not. In
Juniperus the (ovulate) cone is much reduced to a single pair
(or whorl of 3–8,) fertile scales which coalesce and become
fleshy. In the typical cone of this family the scale is commonly
interpreted as resulting from the complete fusion of a bract-
and an ovuliferous-scale. Twenty genera: *Actinostrobus,
Austrocedrus, Callitris, Calocedrus, Chamaecyparis* (false
cypresses), *Cupressus* (cypresses), *Diselma, Fitzroya, Fokienia,
Juniperus* (junipers), *Libocedrus, Microbiota, Neocallitropsis,
Papuacedrus, Pilgerodendron, Platycladus, Tetraclinis, Thuja*
(arbor-vitae), *Thujopsis, Widdringtonia.*

Podocarpaceae—the Southern Pine Family

Leaves spirally arranged in all except *Microcachrys* and either
scale-like or needle-like; monoecious or dioecious; cones
much reduced to a few scales and maturing to contain only
one seed (from an inverted ovule), which may be surrounded
or embedded in a fleshy structure known as the epimatium—
of doubtful homology, but commonly interpreted as an
ovuliferous-scale; cones may be borne on a fleshy stalk or
"foot" (hence "podocarp"); pollen grains mostly winged.
The family is virtually confined to the southern hemisphere.
Only a few species extending north of the Equator. Seventeen
genera: *Acmopyle, Afrocarpus, Dacrycarpus, Dacrydium,
Falcatifolium, Halocarpus, Lagarostrobus, Lepidothamnus,
Microcachrys, Microstrobus, Nageia, Parasitaxus, Podocarpus*
(podocarps), *Prumnopitys, Retrophyllum, Saxegothaea,
Sundacarpus.*

Phyllocladaceae

Once included in Podocarpaceae, the single genus *Phyllocladus*
is considered sufficiently distinct to merit placement in its
own family.

Monoecious or dioecious evergreen trees. Shoots with a
terminal bud and leaf-like shoots (phylloclades). Leaves radial
subtending phylloclades and scale-like. Male cones, cylindrical
catkins, clustered at the ends of branches. Female cones
solitary in axils of leaves or on margins of phylloclades.

Cephalotaxaceae—Cow's Tail Pine Family

Leaves spirally arranged on main shoots, but appearing
as in two opposite ranks on laterals; pollen sacs 3–5; usually
dioecious; cones much reduced comprising a few decussate
pairs of simple bracts each subtending two ovules, but there
is generally only one seed in the whole cone when it
reaches maturity; the nature "cone" is relatively large,
protrudes beyond the original cones, and has an outer

fleshy layer (aril) with a thin inner woody layer. *Amentotaxus*
and *Cephalotaxus* are the genera, the ten species all being
natives of the northern hemisphere.

Taxaceae—the Yew Family

Regarded by some authorities as a separate Class (Taxopsida)
and Order (Taxales) of its own, Taxaceae is the only family. One
reason is that the seeds are borne terminally on short axillary
shoots, which bear a few scales at the base; typically conifers
have seeds borne *laterally*. Evergreen trees or shrubs; leaves
more or less linear, often appearing two-ranked, spirally
arranged; normally dioecious; 3–8 (or 9) microsporophylls
with pollen sacs; pollen grains wingless. "Cones" axillary,
comprising a single ovule without subtending bract, the
seed finally surrounded by a colored fleshy aril. No resin
ducts in wood. Four genera, three in the northern hemisphere,
but *Austrotaxus* is southern hemisphere: *Austrotaxus,
Pseudotaxus, Taxus* (yews), *Torreya.*

Close stands of Scots Pine
(*Pinus sylvestris*) make good
shelter belts. When planted
close together each tree has a
narrow canopy, and the trunks
are therefore ideal for timber.

Pinus nigra var *maritima*

The Monterey Pine (*Pinus radiata*) is much at home on shorelines, and thrives along North America's warm, wet Pacific Coast.

Pinus

Pines

The true pines (genus *Pinus*) are a group of evergreen conifers found almost exclusively in the north temperate regions of the Old and New Worlds. They range from just south of the Equator in the Malay Archipelago, South and Central America, and northward to the limit of the northern coniferous forests on the edge of the Arctic Circle.

Pines are predominantly trees of broadly pyramidal habit, but a few shrubs occur. The leaves in adult plants are of two types: bracts and adult leaves. The bracts are scale-like and are borne spirally, usually on lower parts of young shoots ("long shoots"). They are normally deciduous and bear in their axils so-called undeveloped or "short shoots." It is on these short shoots that the adult leaves (needles) arise. These are borne in clusters of 2–5 (usually two, three, or five, but at

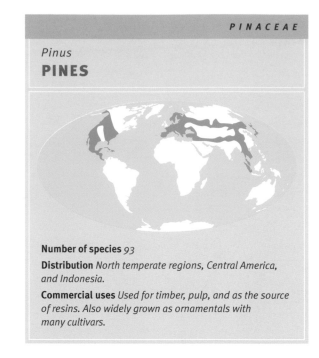

PINACEAE

Pinus
PINES

Number of species 93

Distribution *North temperate regions, Central America, and Indonesia.*

Commercial uses *Used for timber, pulp, and as the source of resins. Also widely grown as ornamentals with many cultivars.*

times up to eight or reduced to one). The needles spring from a basal sheath of between eight and twelve bud scales. These adult leaves persist for up to five years or more.

The male and female cones are separate but on the same tree. The male cones are short and cylindrical, and are catkin-like. The female cones have a central axis bearing spirally arranged bract-scales, in the axils of which eventually arise the cone-scales (ovuliferous or fertile scales), each bearing two ovules on the lower surface. The apex of these cone-scales becomes enlarged and this enlargement (apophysis) may bear a more or less central spine or prickle. Part of the apophysis may be raised and differentiated to form what is called an umbo and this may bear a spine or prickle. The cones may be erect, inclined, or pendulous.

Pollination

Pollination is by wind and pollen is often so abundantly produced that it may be visible. Dispersal of pollen is aided by each grain having two bladder-like wings. At least a year elapses between pollination in the spring and fertilization, during which time the female cone remains small. After fertilization it grows rapidly to adult size, at first green becoming brown, and seeds are commonly ripe by about the following fall. Some species, however, require an extra year. The seeds in most species are winged, the wing almost always being longer than the seed.

The Bristle-cone Pine (*Pinus longaeva*) is one of the most remarkable species. It grows in the Rocky Mountains of Colorado, Utah, Nevada, and Arizona. In these high-altitude conditions it grows extremely slowly, becoming gnarled and stunted with much dead wood. Some specimens are reckoned to be the oldest living things on earth today, reaching ages of up to 6,000 years.

PLANTS WITH THE COMMON FALSE NAME "PINE"

Common Name	Species	Family
Black Pine	*Callitris calcarata*	Cupressaceae
Brazilian Pine (Parana Pine)	*Araucaria angustifolia*	Araucariaceae
Celery Pine	*Phyllocladus trichomanoides*	Phyllocladaceae
Chile Pine	*Araucaria araucana*	Araucariaceae
Cypress Pine	*Callitris* spp	Cupressaceae
Ground Pine	*Ajuga chamaepitys*	Labiatae
Hoop Pine (Moreton Bay Pine)	*Araucaria cunninghamii*	Araucariaceae
Huon Pine	*Lagarostrobus franklinii*	Podocarpaceae
Japanese Umbrella Pine (Parasol Pine)	*Sciadopitys verticillata*	Sciadopityaceae
Kauri Pine	*Agathis* spp (especially *A. australis*)	Araucariaceae
King William Pine	*Athrotaxis selaginoides*	Taxodiaceae
Needle Pine	*Hakea leucoptera*	Proteaceae
Norfolk Island Pine	*Araucaria heterophylla*	Araucariaceae
Parana Pine	*Araucaria angustifolia*	Araucariaceae
Red Pine	*Dacrydium cupressinum*	Podocarpaceae
Rubber Pine	*Landolphia klrkll*	Apocynaceae
Screw Pine	*Pandanus* spp	Pandanaceae
She Pine (White Pine)	*Podocarpus elatus*	Podocarpaceae
White Cypress Pine	*Callitris glaucophylla*	Cupressaceae
White Pine	*Podocarpus elatus*	Podocarpaceae

Pinus wallichiana

The Significance of Pines

The timber of pines is the most important of all the softwoods. The most widely planted forest species are the Scots Pine (*P. sylvestris*), Monterey Pine (*P. radiata*), and Corsican Pine (*P. nigra* spp *salzmanii*). The timber is utilized in every kind of constructional work and carpentry. The resin helps to preserve the wood considerably and when coated with creosote it is ideal for outdoor use as telegraph poles, railroad sleepers, and road blocks. The wood of the Scots Pine is known as yellow deal; its resin, obtained by tapping the trees, is distilled to give turpentine and rosin. Destructive distillation in closed (air-absent) vessels yields tar and pitch. Pine oils are obtained by distillation of leaves and shoots.

TOP LEFT Opportunist Lodgepole Pines (*Pinus contorta* ssp *latifolia*) eke out an existence on the bleak rock columns known as hoodoos that form the landscape in Bryce Canyon National Park, Utah, U.S.A. This species is distinguished by its thinner bark and longer, generally wider, yellow green leaves. A native of the Rocky Mountains, it only releases the bulk of its seed after forest fires.

Pines are also planted extensively for ornament, either singly or in groups for landscaping, and as shelter trees. Notable tall ornamentals are the Lodgepole Pine (*P. contorta* ssp *latifolia*), Cluster Pine (*P. pinaster*), Stone Pine (*P. pinea*), and Weymouth Pine (*P. strobus*). Dwarf forms include the Lacebark Pine (*P. bungeana*), the Dwarf Mountain Pine (*P. mugo* 'Pumilo'), and *P. sylvestris* 'Beuvronensis.'

The Monterey Pine (*P. radiata*) is outstanding as a windbreak, especially on sea coasts; these trees also remove salt from the atmosphere. It is very extensively planted in New Zealand especially on poor soils. The seeds or kernels of the Stone Pine (*P. pinea*), which are large and soon lose their vestigial wing, are eaten as a delicacy in the Mediterranean region, where they are known as *pignons*.

Propagation is usually from seed in the spring and is timed so as to avoid frost damage to the young seedlings. Cultivars are grafted. Young seedlings are transplanted about every two years to stimulate development of abundant fibrous roots. Most species are tolerant of a wide range of soils, provided they are well drained, but some species are more or less calcicole, meaning they require a distinctly lime-rich soil.

The common name "pine" has been applied to many pine-like trees that do not belong to the genus *Pinus*—indeed some are not even conifers. The table above indicates some examples. **CZ2–4**

The Main Species of *Pinus*

Subgenus *Strobus* – the Soft Pines
Leaves with one vascular bundle. Sheaths of short shoots (those bearing leaf clusters) deciduous. Base of scale leaves not decurrent. The wood contains little resin and the timber is soft.

A *Leaves in clusters of 5.*
B *Margin of leaves (lens) serrulate.*

P. cembra **Swiss Stone Pine or Arolla Pine.** Alps of C Europe, NE USSR, and America. Tree 33–82(130) ft (10–25(40) m). Shoots tomentose with thick brown hairs. Leaves dark green, 2–5 in (5–12 cm), lacking conspicuous white lines on the back. Mature cones 2–3 in (5–8 cm) with unarmed terminal umbo; seeds without wings. **CZ5**
‘Aureovariegata’ A form with yellow-tinged leaves.
‘Stricta’ A columnar form with ascending branches.

P. lambertiana **Sugar Pine.** N. America. Tree 165–330 ft (50–100 m). Shoots tomentose. Leaves 2.8–4 in (7–10 cm) with conspicuous white lines on back. Mature cones (10)12–20 in ((25)30–50 cm); seeds with wings longer than themselves. **CZ7**

P. peuce **Macedonian Pine.** Balkan Mountains. Tree 33–66 ft (10–20 m). Shoots greenish, hairless and without bloom. Leaves 2.8–5 in (7–12 cm). Mature cones more or less cylindrical, 3–6 in (8–15 cm); apophysis much swollen; seeds 0.3–0.4 in (8–10 mm) with longer wings. **CZ5**

P. strobus **Weymouth Pine or White Pine.** N. America. Tree 82–165 ft (25–50 m). Shoots hairless, without bloom. Leaves 2.4–5.5 in (6–14 cm), soft and flexible. Mature cones often curved, 3–8 in (8–20 cm) with flat apophysis; seeds mottled, 0.24–0.28 in (6–7 mm) long with longer wings. **CZ3**
‘Compacta’ A slow-growing dwarf form with a dense habit.
‘Contorta’ A form with twisted branches and leaves.
‘Fastigiata’ A form with erect branches and columnar habit.
‘Prostrata’ A prostrate form with flat or slightly ascending branches.

P. wallichiana (*P. griffithii, P. excelsa*) **Himalayan or Bhutan Pine.** Himalaya and westward to Afghanistan. Tree usually about 115 ft (35 m), but sometimes 165 ft (50 m). Shoots hairless with evident bloom. Leaves 5–8 in (12–20 cm). Mature cones 6–10 in (15–25 cm) with convex apophysis, its umbo touching the scale below; seeds 0.3–0.35 in (8–9 mm) with longer wings. **CZ7**

BB *Margin of leaves (lens) entire.*

P. aristata **Hickory or Bristle-cone Pine.** SW U.S. Usually a bushy tree reaching 50 ft (15 m). Shoots pale orange, soon hairless. Leaves 0.8–1.6 in (2–4 cm). Mature cones 1.6–3.5 in (4–9 cm), the terminal umbo with a slender curved spine 0.24–0.32 in (6–8 mm) long. **CZ6**

AA *Leaves in clusters of 1–4.*

P. wallichiana

P. bungeana **Lacebark Pine.** NW China. Tree 66–100 ft (20–30 m). Shoots hairless. Leaves 2–4 in (5–10 cm) with entire (smooth) margins (lens); in clusters of 3. Mature cones 2–2.8 in (5–7 cm); apophysis with an umbo bearing a broad-based recurved spine; seeds 0.3–0.5 in (8–12 mm) with short wings. The popular name derives from the exfoliating bark exposing striking multicolored areas of bare trunk. **CZ7**

P. cembroides **Mexican Stone Pine.** Arizona to Mexico. Tree 20–23 ft (6–7 m). Shoots dark orange, soon hairless. Leaves 0.8–2 in (2–5 cm) with serrulate margin (lens), in clusters of 1–4. Mature cones almost globose, 1–2 in (2.5–5 cm) with a broad umbo; seeds 0.6–1.2 in (1.5–3 cm), with unusually narrow wings. **CZ7–8**

Subgenus *Pinus* – the Hard Pines
Leaves with 2 vascular bundles. Sheaths of short shoots persisting. Base of scale-leaves decurrent. The wood contains significant amounts of resin and the timber is relatively hard.

C *Leaves in clusters of 3 (exceptionally otherwise, e.g .*
P. halepensis, P. radiata, *leaves in twos).*
D *Leaves not exceeding 6 in (15 cm) in length.*

P. halepensis **Aleppo Pine.** Mediterranean region and W Asia. Tree 33–50 ft (10–15 m). Leaves 2.4–6 in (6–15 cm), sometimes in clusters of 2. Mature cones 3–5 in (8–12 cm), the apophysis more or less flattened, the umbo obtuse and unarmed (ie with no prickle or spine). **CZ8–9**

P. radiata **Monterey Pine.** California. Tree 82–100 ft (25–30 m). Leaves 4–6 in (10–15 cm), occasionally in clusters of 2. Mature cones 2.8–5.5 in (7–14 cm), stout, asymmetric, sessile, and reflexed, the apophysis rounded with a minute prickle. **CZ4**

P. rigida **Pitch Pine or Easter Pine.** E U.S. Tree 33–50(82) ft (10–15(25) m). Leaves firm, 2.8–5.5 in (7–14 cm). Mature cones symmetrical 1.2–2.8 in (3–7 cm), umbo prominent with a sharp, slender, recurved prickle. **CZ4**

DD *Leaves more than 6 in (15 cm).*

P. coulteri **Coulter or Big-cone Pine.** S California and S Mexico. Tree to 82 ft (25 m). Shoots with bloom. Leaves 6–12 in (15–30 cm). Mature cones massive, 10–13.5 in (25–35 cm), the raised apophysis with a large umbo forming a stout, curved spine; wings thick and twice the length of the seeds. **CZ8**

P. strobus

P. contorta

P. sylvestris

Pine leaves are nearly always produced in clusters or bundles of two to five, with each bundle bearing at the base a sheath followed by the leaves. Each bundle of leaves forms a slender cylinder. Individual leaves are long and narrow with conspicuous rows of white stomata.

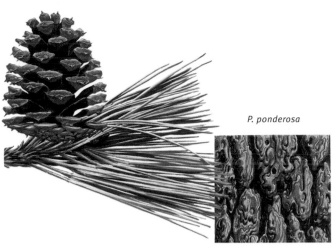

P. ponderosa

P. halepensis

P. radiata

P. pinaster

P. nigra var *maritima*

P. palustris Longleaf or Pitch Pine. E U.S. Tree to 130 ft (40 m). Bud scales white fringed. Shoots not bloomed. Leaves 8–17.5 in (20–45 cm). Mature cones 6–8 in (15–20 cm), almost without stalk, the umbo with a short reflexed prickle; seed wings membranous, about twice the length of seeds. **CZ8–9**

P. ponderosa Western Yellow Pine. W N. America. Tree 165–245 ft (50–75 m). Shoots without bloom. Leaves 5(6)–10 in (12(15)–25 cm). Leaf clusters sometimes 2, 4, or 5. Mature cones yellowish-green, almost without stalks, 3–6 in (8–15 cm), the umbo with a stout, recurved prickle. **CZ4**

P. jeffreyi Jeffrey's Pine. W N. America. Tree similar to *P. ponderosa* but shoots with bloom. Mature cones larger and resin with a characteristic citronella-like smell. **CZ6**

P. taeda Loblolly Pine. E and SE U.S. Tree 66–100(165) ft (20–30(50) m). Shoots without bloom. Leaves (5)6–10 in ((12)15–25 cm), bright blue-green. Mature cones sessile, 2.4–5 in (6–12 cm), the umbo projected as a stout triangular somewhat recurved spine; seeds 0.25–0.28 in (6–7 mm) with wings about 1 in (2.5 cm). **CZ7**

CC *Leaves in clusters of 2.*
E *Leaves not exceeding 3 in (8 cm).*

P. sylvestris Scots Pine or Scotch Fir. N and C Europe and W Asia. Tree 66–130 ft (20–40 m). Upper part of the trunk smooth and reddish. Leaves 0.8–2.8 in (2–7 cm), blue-green, often twisted. Mature cones 1.2–2.8 in (3–7 cm), the umbo almost symmetrical with a minute prickle. The subspecies *scotica* is broad-topped and native only in the highlands of N England and Scotland. **CZ2**

P. mugo Mountain Pine. Mountains of C Europe. Very similar to *P. sylvestris* but usually a shrub with leaves a brighter green. Very variable. **CZ2**

P. contorta Shore Pine. Coastal areas of W N. America. Tree to 33 ft (10 m). Leaves 1.2–2 in (3–5 cm), firm and twisted. Mature cones very oblique, 0.8–2 in (2–5 cm); prickles of the umbo prominent but fragile. The ssp *latifolia* (Lodgepole Pine) is the inland representative. **CZ7**

EE *Leaves predominantly more than 3 in (8 cm).*

P. pinea Stone Pine or Umbrella Pine. Mediterranean region. Mushroom-shaped tree 50–82 ft (15–25 m). Leaves 4–8 in (10–20 cm). Mature cones almost globular, 2.4–3.5 in (6–9 cm). The species is known by its seeds, which are 0.5–0.7 in (12–18 mm) long, the wing only 0.25–0.28 in (6–7 mm) and quickly falling off. **CZ8–9**

P. halepensis Aleppo Pine. Leaves also in threes—see earlier description, under Leaves in clusters of 3. **CZ8–9**

P. radiata Monterey Pine. Leaves mainly in threes—see earlier description, under Leaves in clusters of 3. **CZ8–9**

P. thunbergii Japanese Black Pine. Japan. Tree to 100 ft (30 m). Winter buds grayish-white, not resinous, with fimbriate scales free at the tips. Leaves (2.4)3–4 in ((6)8–11 cm), the basal leaf-sheath terminated by 2 long filaments. Mature cones 1.6–2.4 in (4–6 cm), the umbo with a prickle or not. **CZ5–6**

P. pinaster Cluster Pine. W Mediterranean region. Tree to 100 ft (30 m). Winter buds not resinous. Leaves 4–8 in (10–20 cm), firm; basal leaf-sheath without terminal filaments. Mature cones symmetrical, in clusters, 3.5–7 in (9–18 cm), the umbo with a prominent prickle. **CZ8**

P. nigra Austrian or Black Pine. Austria and eastward to the Balkan Peninsula. Tree 66–130(165) ft (20–40(50) m). Bark characteristically dark gray and fissured into scaly plates. Leaves 3.5–6.3 in (9–16 cm) and firm. Mature cones symmetrical, 2–3 in (5–8 cm), the umbo usually with a short prickle. The variety *maritima* is the Corsican Pine, with lighter green, twisted leaves 5–7 in (12–18 cm). **CZ4**

The somewhat somber color of the Monterey Pine (*Pinus radiata*) is enlivened in the spring when the new shoots and cones emerge.

Picea

Spruces

The genus *Picea* comprises some forty species of evergreen trees and is widely distributed over the cooler areas of the northern hemisphere of both Old and New Worlds, from the Arctic Circle to the high mountains of the more southerly warm temperate latitudes of the tropic of Cancer.

Spruces form trees of more or less conical outline with irregularly branched horizontal to pendulous branches and reddish-brown furrowed bark. The branchlets are characterized by woody peg-like decurrent leaf bases, which are continuous with cushion-like structures (pulvini) surrounding the shoots, separated from each other by grooves. Winter buds may be resinous or not. The leaves are needle-like, appearing either more or less radially arranged around the lateral shoots (leading shoots are less constant) or somewhat parted laterally beneath (pectinate), that is the lower ranks of leaves at least are in two horizontal rows, one row on each side of the shoot. The leaves are of two types: diamond-shaped quadrangular with the width about equal to the height, or flattened with the width much greater than the height, so that there are essentially only two sides—an upper and a lower. Each leaf has typically two marginal resin ducts, sometimes one or rarely none.

Male and female cones are borne separately on the same tree, the male ones axillary in yellow or crimson catkin-like clusters, the female terminal. Young female cones are green or purple, each cone with numerous scales and each scale with two ovules at the base on the underside. Once fertilized, the cones ripen within the year and are pendulous and do not break up when ripe. The seeds are winged and more or less compressed.

The cool, wet climate of coastal Oregon ideally suits the Sitka Spruce (*Picea sitchensis*) and other species of the genus. Where sufficient light penetrates, individual trees can develop a horizontally branching habit and support moisture-loving mosses and lichens. A typical characteristic is the retention of inner branches and twigs after they are dead.

Most species of *Picea* succeed in wet and cold soils, although in shallow soils they may not withstand much wind; otherwise they tolerate a lot of exposure and when firmly rooted can serve as windbreaks.

Three North American species are of great economic importance: Red Spruce (*P. rubens*), Black Spruce (*P. mariana*), and White Spruce (*P. glauca*), all three being widely used in the paper pulp industry. In Norway and the British Isles the Norway Spruce (*P. abies*) is widely planted for afforestation, and likewise the Sitka Spruce (*P. sitchensis*), which has proved particularly successful as it can tolerate a very wide range of poor soils from sandy to cold, wet, and boggy. Each of these species occupies not far short of 10 percent of the total productive forest in the two countries.

Spruce wood is soft and without odor, is easy to work and takes a good finish. It is used in general carpentry, for propping poles, packing cases, and sounding boards—and also for stringed instruments. The timber is also extensively turned into wood pulp for use in the manufacture of paper and rayon. The resin of the Norway Spruce is purified to yield Burgundy pitch and the leaves and shoots are distilled to give Swiss turpentine. Extracts of shoots and leaves (also of *P. abies*) mixed with various sugary substances can be fermented to make spruce beer. The bark of *P. abies* is also used commercially in the tanning of leather.

Various conifers are sold as Christmas trees, though the Norway Spruce is the most commonly chosen. Other spruces are extensively planted as ornamentals, notably cultivars of Colorado Spruce (*P. pungens*) and Englemann Spruce (*P. engelmannii*). There are a number of dwarf spruces that have proved popular for planting in rock gardens, including *P. glauca* 'Albertina Conica' and *P. abies* 'Clanbrassiliana,' 'Nidiformis,' and 'Pumila.' **CZ2–9**

P. pungens

P. omorika

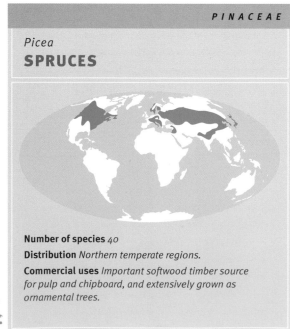

PINACEAE

Picea
SPRUCES

Number of species *40*

Distribution *Northern temperate regions.*

Commercial uses *Important softwood timber source for pulp and chipboard, and extensively grown as ornamental trees.*

P. sitchensis

P. omorika

P. abies

The Main Species of *Picea*

Group I: Leaves flattened (showing virtually only 2 surfaces) with 2 white stomatic bands on the apparent lower surface (facing down on horizontal branches), the apparent upper surface green, rarely with a broken stomatic line.

A *First-year lateral shoots hairy.*

P. omorika **Serbian Spruce.** Europe, especially the former Yugoslavia. Tree to 100 ft (30 m). Leaves on horizontal branches more or less parted below and exposing shoot (pectinate), thin, keeled on both surfaces, (0.3)0.5–0.7 × 0.08 in ((8)12–18 × 2 mm); abruptly pointed. Mature cones 1.2–2.4 in (3–6 cm), ovoid-oblong. **CZ5**

P. brewerana **Brewer's or Siskiyou Spruce.** W U.S. Tree to 130 ft (40 m). Leaves radially spreading on pendulous shoots, 0.8–1(1.2) in (2–2.5(3) cm), slightly convex on both surfaces; apex pointed. Mature cones 2.4–5 in (6–12 cm), cylindrical-oblong; cone-scales entire. **CZ6**

AA *First-year lateral shoots hairless. Leaves pectinate on lower surface of shoot. Cone-scale with jagged margin.*

P. jezoensis **Yeddo Spruce.** NE Asia, Japan. Tree to 165 ft (50 m). Leaves 0.4–0.8 in (1–2 cm), the apex pointed but not horny and pricking. Mature cones 1.6–3 in (4–8 cm), cylindrical-oblong. Variety *hondoensis,* with shorter leaves, often does better when cultivated than the type. **CZ5**

P. sitchensis **Sitka Spruce.** Coastal regions of W U.S. Tree to 195 ft (60 m). Leaves 0.6–1 in (1.5–2.5 cm) with sharp, horny, pricking apical point; convex, slightly keeled on both surfaces. Mature cones 2.4–4 in (6–10 cm), cylindrical-oblong. **CZ7**

Group II: Leaves 4-sided and quadrangular diamond-shaped in cross-section, the width equal to or slightly less than the height; each side with (2)3–5(6) white (not banded) stomatic lines.

B *First-year lateral shoots hairless (but sometimes hairy in* Picea abies *and* P. asperata*) and at least the upper ranks of leaves bent forward over the shoot.*

C *Lower ranks of leaves parted laterally into two more or less horizontal sets (pectinate), those above overlapping.*

P. abies (*P. excelsa*) **Norway or Common Spruce.** C and N Europe. Tree to 165 ft (50 m). Leaves 0.4–0.8(1) in (1–2(2.5) cm), green. Mature cones cylindrical, 4–6 in (10–15 cm). Occasionally has faint pubescence on shoots. About 150 cultivars including many named dwarf forms. **CZ5**

P. glauca **White Spruce.** N U.S. (Alaska) and Canada. Tree to 100 ft (30 m). Leaves 0.3–0.7 in (8–18mm), glaucous (blue-green), with a rank smell when bruised. Mature cones cylindrical-oblong, 1.4–2 in (3.5–5 cm). **CZ3**

CC *Lower ranks of leaves not parted underneath but more or less pointed downward (radially arranged).*

P. smithiana **Himalayan Spruce.** The Himalaya. Tree 100–165 ft (30–50 m). Winter buds more or less resinous. Leaves 0.08–0.16(0.2) × 0.04 in (2–4(5) × 1 mm); apex acute. Mature cones 5–6(7) in (12–15(18) cm), cylindrical. **CZ9**

P. asperata **Chinese or Dragon Spruce.** W China. Tree to 82 ft (25 m). Winter buds more or less resinous. Shoots yellowish-brown, sometimes hairy. Leaves subradially arranged, 0.4–0.7 in (1–1.8 cm), sometimes curved; apex acute. Mature cones 3–4 in (8–10 cm), cylindrical-oblong. **CZ6**

P. schrenkiana **Schrenk's Spruce.** C Asia. Tree to 115 ft (35 m). Winter buds not resinous. Shoots gray. Leaves radially arranged, 0.8–1.4 in (2–3.5 cm), sometimes curved; apex pointed. Mature cones 2.8–4 in (7–10 cm), cylindrical-oblong; cone-scales entire. **CZ6**

Developing female cones of the Sitka Spruce (*Picea sitchensis*), are distinguished by their clustering habit and pale red color. Male cones are pale yellow in color.

P. pungens

P. smithiana

BB *First-year lateral shoots hairless but all ranks of leaves more or less spreading outward, radially or subradially at 45° to almost 90°, the upper ranks not bent forward over the shoot. Mature cones more than 2 in (5 cm).*

P. polita **Tiger-tail Spruce.** Japan. Tree to 130 ft (40 m). Leaves 0.6–0.8 in (1.5–2 cm), curved, very rigid, with sharp pricking point; shiny deep green. Mature cones 3–4 in (8–10 cm). **CZ6**

P. pungens (glaucous cultivar) **Colorado Spruce.** SW U.S. Tree to 165 ft (50 m) with horizontal branches. Leaves 0.6–1 in (1.5–2.5 cm), somewhat incurved, glaucous on all sides with waxy bloom obscuring the stomatic lines; rigid and stiff with sharp, prickly point, more leaves on upper than lower half of shoot. Mature cones 2.4–4 in (6–10 cm), cylindrical-oblong. The description covers the cultivar 'Glauca' (Blue Spruce) with horizontal branches and 'Koster' with pendulous branches, both of which are commonly planted. **CZ3**

BBB *First-year lateral shoots hairy and lower leaves parted laterally into 2 horizontal sets (pectinate), those above overlapping. (In* P. asperata *and* P. mariana *the leaves are more or less radially arranged.)*

D *Terminal bud with basal ring of awl-shaped (acicular) scales; cones less than 2 in (5 cm).*

P. mariana **Black Spruce.** NW N. America. Tree 66–100 ft (20–30 m). Young shoots glandular, hairy. Leaves 0.28–0.6 in (7–15 mm), somewhat glaucous with stomatic lines on the sides next to the shoot; apex blunt. Mature cones ovoid. **CZ3**

P. rubens **Red Spruce.** Canada and south to N Carolina. Leaves 0.4–0.6 in (1–1.5 cm), abruptly acute, deep to bright green, about twice as many stomatic lines on the side next to the shoot. Mature cones 1.2–1.6(2) in (3–4(5) cm), oblong. **CZ3**

DD *Terminal bud without basal ring of awl-shaped (acicular) scales. Cones more than 2 in (5 cm).*

P. engelmannii **Engelmann Spruce.** W N. America. Tree 66–165 ft (20–50 m). First-year shoots yellowish-gray with glandular pubescence. Leaves 0.6–1 in (1.5–2.5 cm) with acute apex, upper ranks bent forward over shoot; rank smell on bruising. Mature cones up to 3 in (8 cm). Rare in cultivation. **CZ3**

P. obovata **Siberian Spruce.** N Europe, N Asia. Tree to 165 ft (50 m). First-year shoots brown, pubescence fine. Leaves 0.4–0.7 in (1–1.8 cm), apex acute. Mature cones 2.4–3 in (6–8 cm), cylindrical-ovoid; scales entire. **CZ2**

P. orientalis **Oriental Spruce.** Asia Minor and Caucasus. Leaves dark green, shining, 0.25–0.3 in (occasionally 0.5 in) (6–8 mm (occasionally 12 mm)), with blunt apex. Mature cones 2.4–3.5 in (6–9 cm), cylindrical-ovoid. **CZ5**

Group III: Leaves pectinately arranged and quadrangular but somewhat compressed from above down, thus, in cross-section, the width is greater than the height. Twice as many stomatal lines on the 2 sides next to the shoot (upper side) as on the other 2 (lower) sides (lens). Cones more than 2 in (5 cm).

P. alcoquiana **Alcock Spruce.** Japan. Tree to 82 ft (25 m). Primary shoots hairy, lateral ones not; terminal bud lacking awl-shaped (acicular) scales at base. Leaves 0.4–0.8 in (1–2 cm), with 5–6 stomatic lines on each upper side and 2 on each lower side. Mature cones 2.4–5 in (6–12 cm), cylindrical-oblong. **CZ6**

P. glehnii **Sakhalin Spruce.** Japan. Tree to 130 ft (40 m). Shoots reddish-brown, terminal bud with awl-shaped (acicular) scales at the base. Leaves 0.25–0.5 in (6–12 mm) with 2 white stomata bands above and 1 or 2 broken lines on each lower side; apex obtuse or acute. Mature cones 2–3 in (5–8 cm), cylindrical-oblong. **CZ6**

P. likiangensis **Likiany Spruce.** W China. Tree to 100 ft (30 m). Shoots grayish-yellow. Upper 2 ranks of leaves imbricate and bent forward more or less parallel with the shoot. Leaves 0.3–0.6 in (8–15 mm), with 2 white bands above and 1–2 (3, 4) broken stomata lines on each lower side; apex acute, horny pointed. Mature cones 2–3 in (5–8 cm), cylindrical-oblong. **CZ6**

Abies

Firs

Abies is a genus of evergreen trees comprising some forty to fifty species widely distributed in the mountainous regions of the northern hemisphere: in central and southern Europe (southern Spain and the facing region of North Africa), in Asia northward from and including the Himalaya, as well as Japan, and extensive areas of North America. The generic name occurs in classical Latin, referring to some kind of fir tree, though not necessarily a species of *Abies*. However, in the English language the word "fir" is now restricted to species of this genus, except that Douglas Fir is the traditional name for species of the genus *Pseudotsuga* and Scotch Fir is a name commonly given to the Scots Pine (*Pinus sylvestris*). Some authorities use the name silver firs for members of the genus *Abies* to separate them from other firs.

It is not difficult to distinguish the genus *Abies*. The identifying combination of characters is: erect cone breaking up at maturity, needles occurring singly, and a rounded disk-like needle scar that is not raised above the level of the bark, thus giving a virtually smooth branchlet.

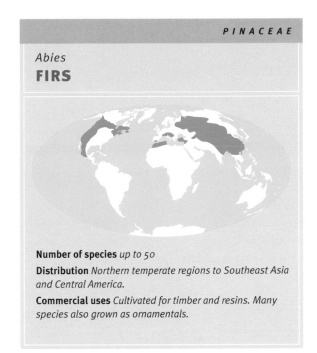

PINACEAE

Abies
FIRS

Number of species *up to 50*
Distribution *Northern temperate regions to Southeast Asia and Central America.*
Commercial uses *Cultivated for timber and resins. Many species also grown as ornamentals.*

Some thirty species are planted outside their native regions but more for their fine and lofty appearance than as a commercial undertaking. The Common Silver Fir (*Abies alba*), Grand Fir (*A. grandis*), Noble Fir (*A. procera*), and Caucasian Fir (*A. nordmanniana*) are the commonest firs grown for ornament in parks and gardens, the first three also having some value on a limited scale as plantation trees. They require a moist, preferably deep soil, a damp climate, and clean air—their susceptibility to atmospheric pollution rendering them unsuitable in or near industrial areas. Fraser's Balsam Fir (*A. fraseri*) and the Balsam Fir (*A. balsamea*) are used as Christmas trees in the United States and Canada.

Firs are subject to attack by insects, aphid species of the genus *Adelges* being particularly serious. The extent of injury varies with the region. Thus, *Adelges piceae* has little more than nuisance value in Europe, whereas in Canada it can destroy trees of *Abies balsamea* at all stages. *Abies* wood is sold as (white) deal and varies from white to yellowish or reddish-brown with no obvious distinction between heartwood and sapwood. Resin canals are normally absent.

This soft wood is easily worked, yielding a good surface, which readily accepts paint and polish. Its main use is for indoor work, but treated with a preservative it has been used outdoors, for telegraph poles, for example. As the wood has no noticeable smell it has also been used for crating grocery and dairy products that might otherwise be tainted.

In certain American firs, the bark of young trees bears "resin blisters." Steam distillation removes turpentine, the residual solid being rosin, which is used in the manufacture of products such as plastics, soaps, and varnishes. Canada balsam, extensively used as a permanent mounting medium in microscopical preparations, and in pharmacy, is obtained from the Balsam Fir and other North American species. **CZ2–9**

BELOW New growth of *Abies balsamea* 'Prostrata' forms lime-green tips before darkening to the usual glaucous (bluish-green) tinge of the mature needles.

LEFT As an ornamental specimen tree, the Noble Fir (*Abies procera*), cannot fail to impress for its height and bearing. Growth is rapid after a number of years and it can reach heights of 200 ft (60 m) in its native environment.

The Main Species of *Abies*

Group I: Needles all arranged in one plane or at least some of them widely parted above (pectinate). Needles flat unless otherwise indicated.

A. alba (*A. pectinata*) **Common Silver Fir.** Mountains of C and S Europe. Tree to 165 ft (50 m). Branchlets hairy, not grooved; winter buds not resinous. Leaves 0.6–1.2 in (1.5–3 cm), notched at apex with 2 white stomatal bands on lower surface. Resin canals lateral. **CZ5**

A. balsamea **Balsam Fir. Balm of Gilead.** Widespread in N. America, extending to Arctic Circle. A source of the resin Canada balsam. Tree to 82 ft (25 m). Branchlets hairy, not grooved; winter buds resinous. Leaves 0.6–1 in (1.5–2.5 cm), notched at apex with 4–9 lines of whitish stomatal bands on lower surface only. Resin canals median. **CZ3**

A. concolor **Colorado or White Fir.** Mountains of Colorado to S California, New Mexico, Arizona, and Mexico. Tree to 130 ft (40 m). Branchlets minutely hairy or hairless; winter buds resinous. Leaves 1.6–2.4 in (4–6 cm) with white stomatal lines on both surfaces; not notched at apex. Resin canals lateral. **CZ5**

A. grandis **Grand or Giant Fir.** W N. America. Tree to 330 ft (100 m); does well in cultivation, but then reaches only some 165 ft (50 m). Practically free from injury by disease or insect attacks and resistant to frost. Branchlets olive-greenish, minutely hairy to almost hairless; winter buds resinous. Leaves 1.2–2.4 in (3–6 cm), notched at apex; white stomatal bands only on lower surface. Resin canals lateral. **CZ6**

A. magnifica **Red Fir.** Oregon through California. Tree to 230 ft (70 m). Branchlets minutely rusty pubescent; winter buds resinous. Leaves 1–1.6 in (2.5–4 cm), quadrangular in section, not notched at apex; stomatal bands on all sides. Resin canals lateral. **CZ6**

A. procera (*A. nobilis*) **Noble Fir.** Cascade Mountains, Washington to N California. Tree to 260 ft (80 m). Commonly planted under forestry conditions where it may reach 165 ft (50 m), but sometimes suffers serious aphid attack. Branchlets minutely rusty pubescent; winter buds resinous. Leaves 1–1.4 in (2.5–3.5 cm), flat or grooved above, not or slightly notched at apex; stomatal bands on both surfaces. Resin canals lateral. **CZ6**

A. spectabilis **Himalayan Fir.** NW Himalaya. Tree to 165 ft (50 m). Branchlets reddish-brown with pubescence in grooves; winter buds resinous. Leaves 1–2.4 in (2.5–6 cm), notched at apex; stomatal bands only on lower surface. Resin canals lateral. **CZ8**

Group II: Needles not pectinate as in Group I, but densely overlapping above. Branchlets hairy. Needles flat.

A. amabilis **Red Silver Fir.** Mountains of British Columbia, Alberta, and Oregon through Washington. Tree to 260 ft (80 m), but only about 100 ft (30 m) in cultivation and subject to aphid attack; winter buds resinous. Leaves 0.8–1.2 in (2–3 cm), truncate or notched at apex; stomatal bands white, only on lower surface. Resin canals lateral. **CZ6**

A. cilicica **Cilician Fir.** Mountains of Asia Minor, N Syria, and Antitaurus. Tree to 100 ft (30 m). Winter buds with a few scales free at the tips, not or only slightly resinous. Leaves 0.8–1.2 in (2–3 cm), slightly notched at apex; stomatal bands whitish, only on lower surface. Resin canals lateral. Cone with hidden bracts. **CZ6**

A. nordmanniana **Nordmann or Caucasian Fir.** N Caucasus, Asia Minor. Tree to 165 ft (50 m). Very similar to *A. cilicica*, but winter bud scales not free and cone with exserted (protruding) and reflexed bracts. **CZ5**

Group III: Needles neither overlapping nor pectinate but directed upward and outward; flat.

A. koreana **Korean Fir.** Korea. Tree to 60 ft (18 m) sometimes shrubby in cultivation. Winter buds slightly resinous. Leaves 0.4–0.8 in (1–2 cm), usually tapering downward with whitish stomatal bands only on lower surface. Resin canals median. **CZ6**

Group IV: Needles radially arranged around branchlets.

A. cephalonica **Greek Fir.** Mountains of Greece. Tree to 100 ft (30 m). Winter buds resinous. Leaves flattened, 0.8–1.2 in (2–3 cm), apex sharply pointed; white stomatal bands on lower surface only. Resin canals lateral. **CZ6**

A. pinsapo **Spanish Fir or Hedgehog Fir.** S Spain. Tree to 82 ft (25 m). Tolerant of lime. Winter buds resinous. Leaves 0.6–0.8 in (1.5–2 cm), thick rigid, apex not sharp-pointed. Resin canals median. **CZ7**

A. koreana

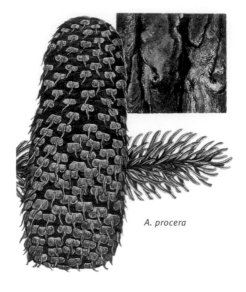

A. procera

A. magnifica

A. pinsapo

A. alba

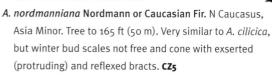

A. nordmanniana

A. procera

A. koreana

A. nordmanniana

Tsuga

Hemlocks or Hemlock Spruces

Tsuga is a genus of about fourteen evergreen trees (sometimes bushes) native to North America, Japan, China, Taiwan, and the Himalaya. In habit they are broadly pyramidal, the branches horizontal to somewhat pendulous. The leaves are flat, short-stalked (petiolate), and spirally inserted but appearing in two horizontal ranks by twisting of the petiole; the stalk is borne on a projecting decurrent leaf-base. The leaves persist for several years, finally falling off to leave a semicircular scar on the leaf-base.

Spruces (*Picea*) are distinguished from *Tsuga* by the leaves being sessile (without stalks), with more prominent roughly diamond-shaped leaf-scars, and cones more than 1 in (2.5 cm) long, except that *T. mertensiana* and the closely related supposed hybrid *T. × jeffreyi* have cones to 2.8 in (7 cm) long. The male cones are minute, up to 0.2 in (5 mm), sometimes yellowish-white, but more often a shade of red. The female cones are typically small, rarely exceeding 1 in (2.5 cm). They are pendulous and ripen in the first year but will persist for several years after shedding their seeds, which are small and winged, two occurring under each cone-scale.

Hemlocks like good, fairly well-drained soil. Propagation is usually by seed, the varieties and forms by shoot cuttings or by grafting. In addition to the numerous varieties and forms, mostly of the species *T. canadensis* (Common or Canada Hemlock), there are a number of intergeneric hybrids, namely *Tsuga × Picea* (= *Tsugo-Picea*); *Picea × (Tsugo-Picea)*; *Tsuga × (Tsugo-Picea)*; *Keteleeria × Tsuga*.

The horizontal-pendulous branching habit of the Western Hemlock (*Tsuga heterophylla*) is an identifiable feature of members of the *Tsuga* genus. The foliage has a distinctive aromatic smell when crushed.

The wood of the Common Hemlock is used for building construction generally and for ladder making. The resin is also useful and is known commercially as Canada pitch. The bark contains tannin, which is extracted for tanning leather etc. Western Hemlock (*T. heterophylla*), the species most frequently cultivated as an ornamental, is also being found in forestry plantations—particularly under hardwood crops. **CZ5–9**

PINACEAE

Tsuga
HEMLOCKS

Number of species *14*
Distribution *Temperate North America and East Asia.*
Commercial uses *Grown as ornamentals and also cultivated for timber and some medicinal uses.*

The Main Species of *Tsuga*

Leaves essentially in one plane (pectinate), flat above and grooved. Cones 0.8–1.2 in (2–3 cm).

T. sieboldii **Japanese Hemlock.** S Japan. Tree to 100 ft (30 m) in its native habitat, about half as tall in Europe, where it is often little more than a large bush. Branchlets hairless (glabrous), leaves notched, margin entire. Cones pendulous, ovoid, 0.9 × 0.5 in (2.3 × 1.2 cm), with flat-topped scales and dark brown when mature. Bark pink-gray, at first smooth with horizontal folds, later cracking into squares and becoming flaky. **CZ6**

T. canadensis **Common or Canada Hemlock.** E N. America. Tree to 82–100 ft (25–30 m). Branchlets covered in fine hairs (pubescent). Leaves with serrulate margins, distinct stomata lines beneath and with distinct green edges. Cones numerous on side shoots, ovoid, 0.8 × 0.4 in (2 × 1 cm), coffee-brown when ripe. Bark orange-brown on young trees, dark purplish gray-brown when mature. Many forms and varieties in cultivation. **CZ5**

T. heterophylla **Western Hemlock.** Coastal regions of W N. America. Tree 100–196 ft (30–60 m). Branchlets pubescent. Leaves with serrulate margins, indistinct stomata lines beneath and edges not obviously different. Cones pendulous and numerous on side shoots, blunt, ovoid, 0.8–1.2 in (2–3 cm), green to purplish when young, becoming light brown. Bark gray-green and smooth when young, russet-brown and narrowly fissured when mature. **CZ6**

T. diversifolia **Northern Japanese Hemlock.** Japan. Tree to 82 ft (25 m) in its natural habitat, but often a large shrub in cultivation. Branchlets pubescent all round. Leaves with entire margins, 0.3–0.6 in (8–15 mm), notched at apex. Cone cylindrical ovoid, 0.8–1.1 in (2–2.8 cm), dark shiny brown. Bark orange-brown with pink fissures. **CZ5**

T. chinensis **Chinese Hemlock.** W China. Tree to 167 ft (50 m). Branchlets pubescent. Leaves with entire margins, up to 1 in (2.5 cm), notched at apex sometimes with a few marginal serrulations. Cone long-ovoid, 1.2 × 0.5 in (3 × 1.3 cm), green turning to red-brown. Bark with curving patterns of dark gray-green scales becoming very flaky and fissured dark brown and gray. **CZ6**

T. caroliniana **Carolina Hemlock.** Mountains of SE U.S. Tree to 50 ft (15 m) occasionally to 82 ft (25 m). Branchlets pubescent. Leaves with entire margins, 0.3–0.6 in (8–18 mm), not or scarcely notched at apex with conspicuously white stomata bands below. Cone long-ovoid, 1 × 0.6 in (2.5 × 1.5 cm), orange-brown. Bark dark red-brown with yellow pores, becoming fissured and purple-gray. **CZ6**

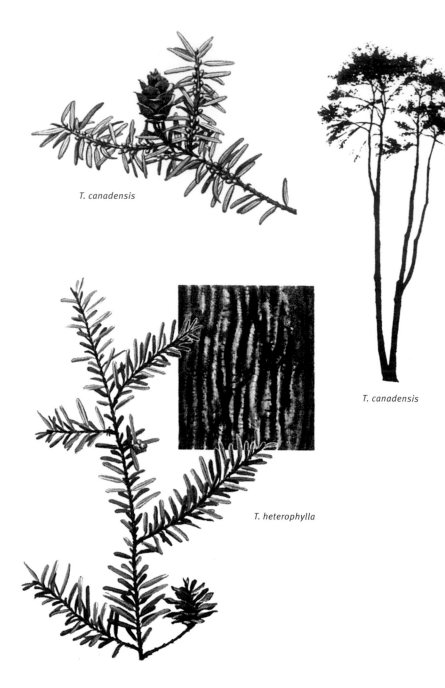

T. canadensis

T. heterophylla

T. canadensis

Nothotsuga

A genus of a single species, *Nothotsuga longibracteata,* native to China, formerly treated as belonging to the genus *Tsuga*. To 33 ft (10 m) tall with light green glossy linear leaves with stomata on both surfaces. Not widely cultivated. **CZ8**

Hesperopeuce

The genus *Hesperopeuce* comprises a single species from western North America. *Hesperopeuce mertensiana* (Mountain Hemlock) was formerly placed in the genus *Tsuga* but is now differentiated on account of the radial arrangement of the blue-green leaves. Tree usually to about 100 ft (30 m), but up to 167 ft (50 m) in its native habitat. Cones spruce-like in clusters on shoot tip, 2.8–1.4 in (7 × 3.5 cm), green when young, turning deep red-brown when mature. Bark brownish-orange with fine vertical fissures. **CZ5**

Pseudotsuga
Douglas Firs

Some twenty types of Douglas Fir have been described but only four are recognized as "good" species. They are natives of western North America, China, Japan, and Taiwan, and succeed on a wide range of soils but flourish in a damp climate on a moist, well-drained soil.

Douglas Firs are evergreen trees, generally pyramidal in the early stages, finally somewhat widely spreading. The winter buds are characteristically spindle-shaped, not unlike those of the beech. The branchlets have slightly raised oval leaf-scars and the leaves are needle-like, grooved above, and spirally arranged. They have two white stomatic lines on the lower side and appear to be in one plane because the leaf-base is twisted (except in *Pseudotsuga japonica*). Each leaf has two marginal resin canals and one vascular strand. Male and female cones are separate but borne on the same tree. The male cones are short and catkin-like comprising numerous pollen sacs; the females are terminal, consisting of numerous persistent cone-scales, each scale with two ovules beneath. The mature cone is pendulous with the bract-scale prominently exserted (protruding), its apex being three-lobed. The seeds are winged.

The generic name *Pseudotsuga* (literally "false hemlock") suggests a relationship with *Tsuga*, but Douglas Firs are easily distinguished by the plainly visible trifid exserted bract-scales of the mature cones and by the leaf-bases being not, or scarcely, decurrent. The genus *Abies*, in which the Douglas Firs were once placed, is distinct in its erect mature cones whose scales fall away from a persistent axis. In *Abies*, moreover, there is no exserted trifid bract-scale and the leaf-scars are circular and flat and level with the branchlet surface.

The timber of *P. menziesii* is in great demand and is the premier wood of North America. Though constituting half the standing timber of the western forests, its exploitation without replacement is a cause of concern. Individual trees provide an immense quantity of timber which is, however, very variable in strength and grain, and requires careful grading to ensure reasonable uniformity. It is used for practically every type of construction work—houses, bridges, and boats, for general carpentry, rolling stock, and all kinds of poles and posts including commemorative flagstaffs. A mature Douglas Fir is also a fine sight as an ornamental tree, especially when cleared of the lower and dead branches. Single subjects are therefore extensively planted in rural areas and parks, while some dense stands can be found in forested areas. **CZ6–8**

Pseudotsuga menziesii, a species of Douglas Fir, named for the Scottish botanist David Douglas (1798–1834), has been widely exploited for its timber in the forests of western North America. The lower branches can mar its esthetic value and so are often cleared on specimen trees planted for ornamental purposes.

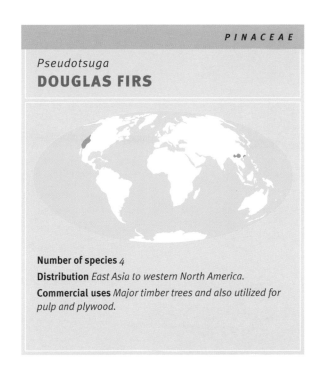

PINACEAE

Pseudotsuga
DOUGLAS FIRS

Number of species 4
Distribution *East Asia to western North America.*
Commercial uses *Major timber trees and also utilized for pulp and plywood.*

P. menziesii

The Main Species of *Pseudotsuga*

Group I: Leaf apices acutely pointed, or, if somewhat blunt, then not broadly rounded or notched. Cones 2–7 in (5–18 cm).

P. menziesii (*P. douglasii, P. raxifolia*) **Oregon or Gray Douglas Fir.** W N. America extending to N Mexico. Tree to 330 ft (100 m). Branchlets pubescent, rarely glabrous. Leaves 0.8–1.2 in (2–3 cm), acute or blunt, dark green or bluish-green above. Cones 2–4 in (5–10 cm), the trifid bract-scales usually erect, occasionally reflexed. The crushed leaves have a characteristic pleasant citronella-like smell. **CZ8**

var *glauca* E Rocky Mountains from Montana to Mexico. Tree to about 130 ft (40 m). Leaves shorter and thicker than the type, bluntly pointed, glaucous, smelling of turpentine when crushed. Cones 2.4–3 in (6–7.5 cm), the bracts usually with reflexed tips. Typical specimens are distinctive and known locally as Colorado Douglas Fir, but a continuous chain of intermediates connects it with the type. **CZ8** Planted for its decorative value only since it has no commercial potential.

P. macrocarpa **Large-coned Douglas Fir.** SW California. Tree 40–52(82) ft (12–16(25) m). Leaves 1–1.4 in (2.5–3.5 cm), light green. Cones 4–7 in (10–18 cm), the bract-scales less exserted than in *P. menziesii*. The size of the cone at once distinguishes this species from all others. **CZ8**

Group II: Leaf apices broadly rounded or notched. Cones 1.2–2.4 in (3–6 cm).

P. japonica **Japanese Douglas Fir.** SE Japan. Tree 50–100 ft (15–30 m). Branchlets glabrous. Leaves notched, directed forward but spreading in all directions, not obviously arranged in one plane, pale grayish-green. Cones 1.2–2 in (3–5 cm), few-scaled (15–20). **CZ6**

P. sinensis **Chinese Douglas Fir.** W China. Tree to about 66 ft (20 m). Branchlets hairy, reddish-brown. Leaves 1–1.2 in (2.5–3 cm), arranged in one plane. Cones 2–2.4 in (5–6 cm). **CZ8**

P. japonica

P. macrocarpa

P. macrocarpa

P. menziesii (male cones)

Unusually among the conifers, all *Larix* species are deciduous and can produce striking fall colors before the needles drop.

L. decidua

L. kaempferi

Larix

Larches

Larix is a genus of about nine species of deciduous, commonly fast-growing trees, native to the cooler mountainous regions of the northern hemisphere.

Larches are more or less pyramidal trees with spreading irregularly whorled branches. The leaves are borne spirally on the long shoots, but are most conspicuous as dense clusters on the very short shoots. The female cones are finally erect and are very attractive when young, with crimson bract-scales ("larch noses"). The cones mature within a year, becoming pale brown, but persist after the shedding of seeds. There are two seeds under each ovuliferous- or cone-scale, each seed having a thin, well-developed wing. Mature cones are essential for species determination. In the young cone and at the time of pollination the bract-scale much exceeds the ovuliferous-scale, but at maturity the bract-scale may or may not be hidden by the ovuliferous-scale.

Larches do best on well-drained light or gravelly loams and are intolerant of low-lying areas where water is liable to accumulate and which are subject to frost. The wood is strong and durable and used for posts, pit-props, barges, etc. The relatively rapid rate of growth of most species is also an advantage when a quick return on investment is being sought. A disadvantage of larch cultivation, however, is that many are susceptible to a number of diseases.

The bark has been used for tanning and dyeing and has medicinal properties (mainly in veterinary practise, for example the use of Venice or Larch turpentine). In summer the leaves exude a whitish and sweet substance known as briancon larch manna, which was also once used in medicine. It contains the unusual trisaccharide sugar melecitose. **CZ1–8**

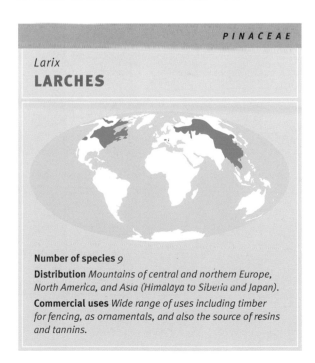

PINACEAE

Larix
LARCHES

Number of species 9
Distribution *Mountains of central and northern Europe, North America, and Asia (Himalaya to Siberia and Japan).*
Commercial uses *Wide range of uses including timber for fencing, as ornamentals, and also the source of resins and tannins.*

L. × eurolepis

L. decidua

L. kaempferi

L. laricina

The Main Species of *Larix*

Unless otherwise stated, all species below have an almost concealed bract-scale that does not project beyond the cone-scale (= ovuliferous-scale).

Group I: Leaves with 2 distinct white or greenish-white bands on underside.

L. kaempferi (L. leptolepis) **Japanese Larch.** Japan. Tree to 100 ft (30 m). Leaves 0.8–1.4 in (2–3.5 cm), each white band beneath comprising 5 rows of stomata. Cones up to 1.4 in (3.5 cm) with tips of cone-scales recurved, reddish-brown, and scaly sometimes with flakes that break away. Makes rapid growth and is much planted. **CZ1–7**

L. griffithiana **Sikkim Larch.** E Nepal, Sikkim, Tibet. Tree to 66 ft (20 m). Leaves 1.2–1.6 in (3–4 cm) with greenish-white bands beneath. Cones erect, cylindrical, abundant, purple-brown, 2.4–4.5 in (6–11 cm); bract-scales protruding as fine points, some depressed against cone. Bark reddish-brown with scales. Grows best in mild climates. **CZ7**

Group II: Leaves without white bands beneath.

L. laricina **Tamarack, Eastern Larch.** N. America. Tree to 66 ft (20 m). Leaves 1.2 in (3 cm). Branchlets hairless (glabrous). Cones 0.6 × 0.4 in (1.5 × 1 cm) with 12–15(16) scales, glabrous on outside and shining, with erect or slightly incurved tips. Bark dull pink or pinkish-brown, finely flaking but with no fissures. Tolerates wet peaty soils. **CZ1–4**

L. gmelini **Dahurian Larch.** NE Asia. Tree to 100 ft (30 m). Leaves 1.2 in (3 cm). Branchlets usually covered in fine hairs. Cones 0.8–1 in (2–2.5 cm) with 20–40(50) scales, glabrous on outside and shining, with erect or slightly incurved tips. Bark reddish-brown and scaly. **CZ1–4**

L. decidua (L. europaea) **European Larch.** N and C Europe and Siberia. Tree to 115 ft (35 m). Leaves 0.8–1.2 in (2–3 cm). Cone-scales 40–50 straight not incurved at apex and pubescent to shortly tormentose (downy) outside; bract-scales about half length of cone-scales. Bark greenish gray-brown and smooth when young, later becoming fissured vertically. **CZ2**

L. russica (L. sibirica) **Siberian Larch.** E Russia and Siberia. Tree to 100 ft (30 m). Leaves 0.6–1.2 in (1.5–3 cm). Cone-scales slightly incurved at apex and pubescent to shortly tomentose outside; bract-scales about one-third length of cone-scales. **CZ2**

L. × eurolepis **Dunkeld Larch.** A vigorous natural hybrid between *L. decidua* and *L. kaempferi*, pollen being supplied by the first species. What might be called typical specimens are intermediate between the parents, but seedlings from the hybrid itself show a wide range of variation between the original parents. Bark reddish-brown. Shows greater resistance to insect and fungal pests than other species. **CZ5**

L. occidentalis **Western Larch.** N. America (British Columbia, Oregon, Washington, Idaho). Tree 140–180 ft (43–55 m). Leaves 1.2–2 in (3–5 cm). Cones tall, ovoid, 1.2–2 in (3–5 cm), purple-brown when ripe; bract-scales protrude as long spreading or down-curved points. Bark purplish-gray with deep wide fissures with flaky edges. **CZ5**

L. gmelini

ABOVE AND RIGHT *Larix* species have pendulous branchlets of two kinds: slender, elongated ones which bear leaves singly and spirally, and short, spurlike ones which bear 20–40 leaves crowded in a terminal tuft. The trees are quite bare in winter.

Pseudolarix

Golden Larch

The Golden Larch (*Pseudolarix amabilis* = *P. kaempferi*) is a splendid deciduous tree, reaching 130 ft (40 m). Its leaves turn a rich, golden-yellow in fall, whence the Chinese name "chin-lo-sung," Golden Deciduous Pine, is derived. *Pseudolarix amabilis* is the only confirmed species of the genus and is native to east China (Chekiang and Kiangsi provinces). A second species, *P. pourieli*, from central China has been proposed but this is known only from vegetative material; it has small quantitative differences from *P. amabilis* and may be the juvenile state of this species.

The leaves of *Pseudolarix* are needle-like, about 1.6–2.6 in (4–6.5 cm) × 0.08–0.12 in (2–3 mm); they are produced either singly and spirally arranged on long shoots, which are rough with persistent bases of shed leaves or in umbrella-like clusters on short shoots that are characteristically club-shaped and curved with persistent scales and distinct close-set, annual rings separated by constrictions. The cones are not unlike those of *Larix*, the males clustered in catkins about 1 in (2.5 cm) across, the females on the same tree about 2 × 0.4 in (5 × 1 cm) comprising thick, acuminate, woody scales that break up at maturity, releasing the seeds.

The Golden Larch differs from *Larix* (in which genus it was once placed) in having more robust leaves, curved short shoots, more or less pointed cone-scales (not blunt-rounded), and the cone breaking up at maturity (it remains intact in *Larix*). *Pseudolarix* is quite hardy in the warmer parts of temperate regions but slow growing. It requires a good, deep, well-drained soil but is intolerant of lime. **CZ6**

LEFT The underside of Golden Larch (*Pseudolarix amabilis*) etched against the light shows a number of short shoots, with the distinctive annual rings apparent. The whorls of leaves are beginning to show their end of season colors.

ABOVE *Cedrus atlantica*, the Atlas Cedar, forms a showy tree with a generous, spreading branching habit.

LEFT Barrel-shaped immature male cones of *Cedrus atlantica* var *glauca* are held erect from the silvery-blue tinged needles.

Cedrus

Cedars

Cedrus is a genus of stately evergreens commonly regarded as comprising four species: *C. atlantica*, *C. brevifolia*, *C. deodara*, and *C. libani*. Some authorities consider them all to be geographical infraspecific taxa of a single species. This is probably true, but long-standing horticultural practise and convenience keeps them at the species level. They have a wide but discontinuous distribution in the Old World.

All species have long and short shoots, the latter with clusters of needle-like leaves, 0.25–2 in (0.5–5 cm), according to species. Male cones are erect, ovoid, or conic, up to 2 in (5 cm), opening September–November. Female cones are erect, up to 0.4 in (1 cm), and borne terminally on short shoots. The fruiting cones, which take two or three years to mature, are oval-oblong, rounded at the apex and about 2–4 in (5–10 cm); the numerous flattened scales are finally deciduous from a central axis. On average, trees do not bear cones until they are 40 or 50 years old.

Cedars grow best in a well-drained rich loam or sandy clay. Propagation is from seed. Mature cones should be gathered in the spring and kept in a warm place. The cone-scales break away and free the seeds, which are then ready for germination; the seedlings are planted out in the following spring. Apart from *C. brevifolia*, which is little cultivated, all the species have numerous forms. Probably the best known is the Blue Cedar *(C. atlantica* var *glauca)*, which is prized for specimen planting and is probably the best colored of all "blue" forms of conifer.

The wood of *Cedrus* is soft but durable and is widely used in building construction and for furniture. The resin has been used for embalming. **CZ7–8**

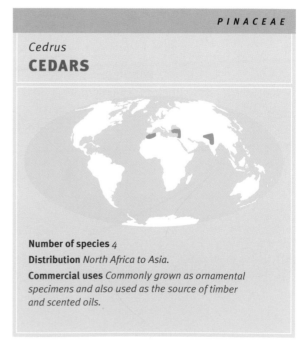

PINACEAE

Cedrus
CEDARS

Number of species 4
Distribution *North Africa to Asia.*
Commercial uses *Commonly grown as ornamental specimens and also used as the source of timber and scented oils.*

TREES HAVING THE COMMON NAME "CEDAR"

Common Name	Species
African Cedar	*Juniperus procera*
Alaska Cedar	*Chamaecyparis nootkatensis*
Atlantic or Atlas Cedar	*Cedrus atlantica*
Australian Red Cedar	*Toona* spp
Bastard Cedar	*Soymida febrifuga, Chukrasia tabularis*
Bermuda Cedar	*Juniperus bermudiana*
Black Cedar	*Nectandra pisi*
Blue Cedar	*Cedrus atlantica* var *glauca*
Cedar Elm	*Ulmus crassifolia*
Cedar of Goa	*Cupressus lusitanica*
Cedar of Lebanon	*Cedrus libani*
Cyprus Cedar	*Cedrus brevifolia*
Eastern Red Cedar	*Juniperus virginiana*
Himalayan Black Cedar	*Alnus nitida*
Himalayan or Indian Cedar	*Cedrus deodara*
Himalayan Pencil Cedar	*Juniperus oxycedrus* spp *macrocarpa*
Incense Cedar	*Calocedrus decurrens*
Japanese Cedar	*Cryptomeria* spp
Mahogany Cedar	*Entandrophragma candolei, E. cylindricum*
Mlanje Cedar	*Widdringtonia nodiflora*
Oregon Cedar	*Chamaecyparis lawsoniana*
Pencil Cedar	*Juniperus* spp (especially *J. virginiana*)
Prickly Cedar	*Styphelia acerosa*
Red Cedar	*Juniperus* spp (especially *J. virginiana*)
Sharp Cedar	*Juniperus oxycedrus*
Siberian Cedar	*Pinus cembra*
Southern White Cedar	*Chamaecyparis thyoides*
Stinking Cedar	*Torreya taxifolia*
Western Red Cedar	*Thuja plicata*
West Indian Cedar	*Cedrela* spp
White Cedar	*Melia azederach*
Yellow Cedar	*Chamaecyparis* spp

C. libani

C. libani

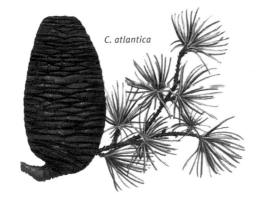

C. atlantica

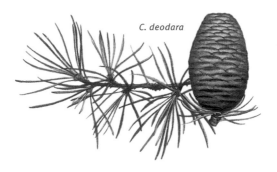

C. deodara

The Species of *Cedrus*

C. atlantica Atlas or Atlantic Cedar. N. Africa
(Algeria). A pyramidal tree up to 130 ft (40 m)
with an upright leading shoot and lateral
branches ascending, but not becoming horizontal.
Needles 1 in (2.5 cm). Cones 2–2.8 × 1.6 in
(5–7 × 4 cm), with a flat or slightly depressed
apex. Var *glauca* (Blue Cedar) has light blue or
waxy leaves. **CZ7**

C. brevifolia Cyprus Cedar. Mountains of Cyprus. A
broad dome-shaped tree up to 40 ft (12 m) with
spreading to recurved leading shoots. Needles
0.2–0.25 in (5–6 mm). Cones 2.8 × 1.6 in (7 × 4 cm)
with a depressed apex and short umbo. **CZ7**

C. deodara Himalayan or Indian Cedar, Deodar.

W Himalaya. A pyramidal tree when young, though
irregular when mature, growing up to 196 ft (60 m)
with a pendulous leading shoot and slightly
drooping lateral branches with pendulous tips.
Needles 1–2 in (2.5–5 cm) with an apical spine.
Cones 2.8–4 × 2–2.4 in (7–10 × 5–6 cm), barrel-
shaped with a rounded apex. **CZ8**

C. *libani* Cedar of Lebanon. Lebanon, Taurus
Mountains, Syria. A dome-shaped tree up to 130 ft
(40 m) with an upright to spreading leading shoot
and characteristic tiers of lateral branches
ascending for a few feet then becoming horizontal.
Needles 1–1.25 in (2.5–3 cm). Cones 3–4 × 1.8 in
(8–10 × 4.6 cm) with a flat or depressed apex. **CZ7**

Keteleeria

Keteleeria

Keteleeria contains about four "good" species, but segregates from these, according to some authorities, raise this number to nine. It is similar to *Abies* in its upright (not pendulous or reflexed) cones, and differs mainly by the cone falling in one piece, whereas in *Abies* the cone-scales are deciduous from their axis. The leaves of *Keteleeria* are keeled above and (mostly) below, the undersurface is pale yellowish-green as in yews (*Taxus* spp) and there are no whitish stomatal bands on the undersurface, as in *Abies*.

Keteleerias are evergreen trees native to southeast, central, and western China extending to Indochina and Taiwan. In form they are pyramidal to finally more or less dome-shaped with spreading branches in whorls. The leaves are needle-like, linear to slightly tapering, solitary, spirally inserted but are mostly twisted so as to lie in one plane (pectinate). When mature, the large, upright cones ripen in the first year. Each cone consists of numerous persistent broad woody scales, each in the axil of a forked bract-scale about half the cone-scale length. The seeds are winged and similar to those in *Abies*—two are produced for each cone-scale.

Keteleerias are only marginally hardy in temperate regions and thus distinctly rare in cultivation and even then only two of the species are represented: *K. davidiana* (central and west China, Taiwan) and *K. fortunei* (east China). The former is the most hardy of this generally "unhardy" genus but the latter has survived in cultivation in Italy. **CZ7–10**

Metasequoia, Sequoiadendron, Sequoia

Redwoods

The redwoods comprise three genera of living coniferous trees: *Metasequoia* (one living species; some ten fossil representatives), *Sequoia*, and *Sequoiadendron* (each with a single living species). Though *Metasequoia* is placed in the family Taxodiaceae, some Chinese authorities have suggested that all its species should be separated out as a separate family—Metasequoiaceae. *Metasequoia* is unusual in that it is deciduous.

The **Dawn Redwood** (*Metasequoia glyptostroboides*) was originally described from fossil material in 1941 and appears to have been widely distributed in the northern hemisphere back to the Cretaceous period (136 million years ago) and extending through to the early and middle parts of the Tertiary (down to about 26 million years ago). The living tree was described in 1945 from Hupeh and Szechuan provinces of China. It was introduced into cultivation in 1948 from seed received at the Arnold Arboretum in Boston, U.S.A., and is now widely grown in temperate regions. It has proved quite hardy. In Great Britain, examples grow to 66 ft (20 m) and though female cones are produced they do not appear to set seed, possibly because of failure of the male cones to produce fertile pollen. Its possibility as a forestry tree is being considered as it is a fast grower—3 ft (1 m) a year in the first ten years, but then slowing down. In cultivation, *Metasequoia* favors well-drained sloping ground but is equally at home on moist land near a lake or stream or even in an average garden soil.

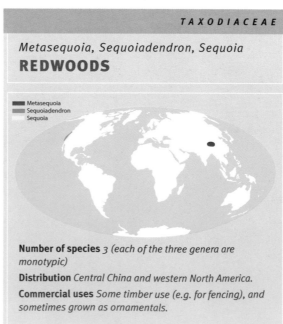

Metasequoia, Sequoiadendron, Sequoia
REDWOODS

■ Metasequoia
■ Sequoiadendron
□ Sequoia

Number of species *3 (each of the three genera are monotypic)*
Distribution *Central China and western North America.*
Commercial uses *Some timber use (e.g. for fencing), and sometimes grown as ornamentals.*

Sequoiadendron giganteum

ABOVE LEFT The foliage of *Keteleeria davidiana*, the leaves at the top clearly showing their twisted bases, which causes them to lie in one plane.

FACING PAGE The immense trunk of a Coast Redwood (*Sequoia sempervirens*) dwarfs its neighboring trees.

The Giant Sequoia (*Sequoiadendron giganteum*) known as General Grant in California's Sequoia National Park, at over 275 ft (84 m), is not the tallest tree in the world but probably the most massive.

Supplies of Sierra Redwood timber are limited but when available it is used mainly for farm buildings, posts, and stakes since the wood is durable, especially in contact with soil. Though straight-grained, light, and soft, the wood is not particularly easy to work.

This vigorous and long-lived tree is much grown in parks and gardens, either as specimen trees or, in particularly imposing fashion, lining roads and avenues. 'Aureum' is a slower-growing cultivar with a dense upswept crown and pale gold young foliage; 'Pendulum' has a weeping form with downswept side branches. Adult *Sequoiadendron* and certain specimens have so captured the American imagination that they have been assigned personal individual names. The General Sherman Tree, for example, which stands in the Sequoia National Park, is alleged to be more than 3,000 years old and is claimed, at 2,000 tons, to be the most massive (though not the tallest) tree in the world.

The Coast Redwood (*Sequoia sempervirens*) is now the only extant member of the genus *Sequoia*. Native specimens are immense and stately, more or less columnar, evergreen trees, found wild only on the narrow coastal "fog belt" on the Pacific coast of North America from southwestern Oregon through northern and central California to south of Monterey. It rarely extends inland for more than about 25 miles (40 km) and will not grow at altitudes of more than 3,500 ft (1,000 m). Trees of this species are probably the tallest in the world, the maximum height being about 400 ft (120 m); the diameter of the trunk at ground level may reach 30 ft (10 m). The Coast Redwood may live for nearly 1,000 years, the average lifespan being between 400 and 800 years.

The tree is at its best on a good, moist but well-aerated soil with considerable atmospheric moisture. On the California seaboard it has successfully grown under such ideal conditions that it forms pure forest, with the enormous trunks unusually close to one another. The *Sequoia* can also grow (but less impressively) in thin soil on rocky slopes. It is unusual among conifers in that it suckers freely and thus can readily regenerate by sprouts from the bases of felled trees. This is important because, though seeds are readily formed, the successful germination rate is low and, moreover, the seedlings are intolerant of shade.

The wood of *Sequoia* is in great demand, being soft, fine-grained, easy to work, and it takes a good polish. Extremely long lengths are obtainable of up to 6 ft (2 m) wide without defects. It is used in building construction and carpentry generally, also for paneling, railway sleepers, telegraph poles, road blocks, fence poles, etc. Excessive demand has denuded many of the original forests but some have been preserved by conservation efforts.

As with the Giant Sequoia, the Coast Redwood is an outstanding tree for single specimen planting in parks and large gardens. 'Adpressa' is a smaller-leaved cultivar that has creamy-white young foliage. **CZ5–8**

In its general appearance and especially its deciduous habit, the Dawn Redwood resembles the Swamp Cypress (*Taxodium distichum*) but the Dawn Redwood has the leaves and shoots opposite, not alternate. Diseases and pests are not yet established.

The **Sierra Redwood** (*Sequoiadendron giganteum*) is a native of the western slopes of California's Sierra Nevada. It was formerly placed in the genus *Sequoia* along with *S. sempervirens* with which it shares the characteristic thick, spongy bark. It is sometimes confused with the Japanese Red Cedar (*Cryptomeria japonica*) but this tree has leaves 0.4–0.6 in (1–1.5 cm) with incurved points, whereas the leaves of *Sequoiadendron* are less than 0.4 in (1 cm), awl-shaped, with straight tips.

Propagation is best from imported seeds, but cuttings can be used toward the end of summer. Erect shoots are best, but if side shoots are used, these should, after rooting, be cut back when dormant buds will be stimulated to give leading shoots. Cuttings can be struck in sandy soil and should root by spring.

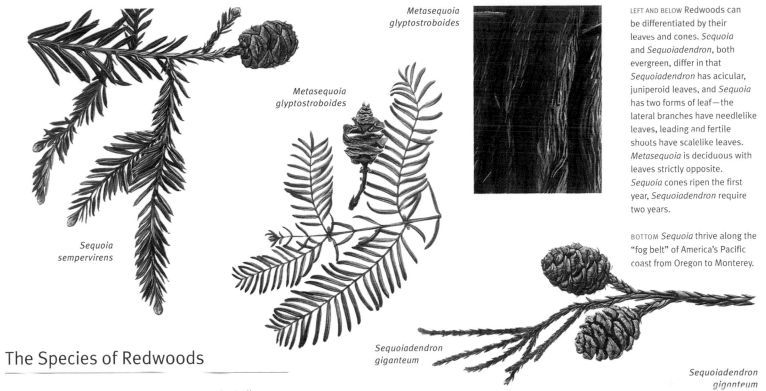

*Sequoia
sempervirens*

*Metasequoia
glyptostroboides*

*Metasequoia
glyptostroboides*

LEFT AND BELOW Redwoods can
be differentiated by their
leaves and cones. *Sequoia*
and *Sequoiadendron*, both
evergreen, differ in that
Sequoiadendron has acicular,
juniperoid leaves, and *Sequoia*
has two forms of leaf—the
lateral branches have needlelike
leaves, leading and fertile
shoots have scalelike leaves.
Metasequoia is deciduous with
leaves strictly opposite.
Sequoia cones ripen the first
year, *Sequoiadendron* require
two years.

BOTTOM *Sequoia* thrive along the
"fog belt" of America's Pacific
coast from Oregon to Monterey.

*Sequoiadendron
giganteum*

*Sequoiadendron
giganteum*

The Species of Redwoods

Single-sex coniferous trees with woody cones of spirally
arranged compound scales (the bract-scale is not distinct,
but fused with the ovuliferous-scale). Leaves arise singly
or in pairs and are evergreen, needle, or awl-shaped, and
either alternately (spirally) arranged or deciduous, needle-
shaped, opposite (as are the leafy dwarf shoots), and
in the same plane.

Metasequoia glyptostroboides Dawn Redwood. Hupeh and
  Szechwan Provinces, China. Tree, in its native habitat, to
  about 130 ft (40 m) tall but in cultivation, since its
  introduction, to no more than 66 ft (20 m). Crown conical.
  Young bark usually orange-brown, flaking; older bark more
  brownish and somewhat furrowed. Leaves deciduous
  yellowish-green, all in one plane (pectinate) in opposite
  pairs along the shoots, flat and linear, 0.08–0.16 × 0.08
  in (2–4 × 2 mm). Male cones grouped in small ovoid clusters,
  2–5 at base of leaves; female cones more or less cylindrical
  to 1 in (2.5 cm) on stalk to 2 in (5 cm), each composed
  of about 12 green scales, somewhat swollen at the tips,
  seeds winged. **CZ5**

Sequoiadendron giganteum Sierra Redwood, Big Tree, Giant
  Redwood, Giant Sequoia, Mammoth Tree, Wellingtonia.
  California. Tree to 330 ft (100 m). Crown conical. Bark light
  brown, thick, soft, fibrous, deeply furrowed. Leaves
  evergreen, alternate, of one sort, ovate to lanceolate,
  0.12–0.3 in (3–7 mm), sometimes to 0.5 in (12 mm). Male
  cones sessile, 0.16–0.3 in (4–8 mm), yellow when mature in
  spring; female cones ellipsoidal, 2–3 × 1.6–2.2 in (5–8 ×
  4–5.5 cm), very woody, finally pendulous, the scales
  flattened, diamond-shaped, each with 3–9 seeds and with
  slender spine when young; ripening second year. Seeds
  0.12–0.25 in (3–6 mm), pale brown, winged. **CZ7**

Sequoia sempervirens Coast Redwood. S California. Tree to
  394 ft (120 m). Crown conical. Bark brown, thick, soft, fibrous,
  furrowed. Leaves evergreen, dark green, alternate, of two
  sorts (dimorphic): on leading shoots more or less spirally
  arranged, ovate-oblong to 0.2 in (6 mm), tip incurved, while
  on lateral shoots more or less in two ranks, needlelike and
  often falcate, 0.2–0.7 in (6–18 mm). Minute male cones to
  0.06 in (1.5 mm); female cones ovoid to 1 in (2.5 cm), finally
  pendulous, scales slightly flattened obliquely, ridged, often
  deciduous, each scale bearing 2–5 winged seeds. **CZ8**

Taxodium

Swamp Cypress

Taxodium is a genus of two closely related species of deciduous or more or less evergreen trees, popularly known as swamp cypresses. They are natives of the southeastern United States and Mexico. The shoots (branchlets) are either persistent with axillary buds near the end of each year's growth or deciduous without buds and falling within the current year or at irregular intervals. The leaves are pale green, flattened, or awl-shaped, arranged essentially in one plane on the deciduous shoots or radially on the persistent shoots. Male and female cones are present on the same plants, the male in pendulous panicles. The female cones ripen in one year and when mature are globular, 1 in (2.5 cm) in diameter, comprising numerous peltate scales, which are irregularly foursided on the outside. Each scale bears two angular three-winged seeds.

The most commonly cultivated species, *T. distichum* (Swamp or Bald Cypress), is a tall handsome tree whose pale green foliage gives it a delicate feathery appearance. It favors swamps and streams, but grows equally well on drained soil. In swamps the roots produce upright protuberances or "knees," which rise above the level of the water to assist in root aeration. These "knees" are comparable to the specialized roots of mangroves and other tropical swamp inhabitants.

Taxodium mucronatum (Montezuma or Mexican Cypress) is less hardy than *T. distichum* and so less cultivated. The former is evergreen in its native Mexico but becomes deciduous in cooler climates. In the Mexican village of Santa Maria del Tule near the city of Oaxaca, one specimen, named El Gigante, has become a historic landmark. The Spanish conquistador Hernán Cortés wrote about this same

T. ascendens

T. distichum

T. mucronatum

T. ascendens

ABOVE RIGHT **The Swamp Cypress** *Taxodium distichum* has distinctive feathery foliage and fissured bark. The "knees" the species produces to aid root aeration are apparent in this clump of swamp cypresses which flourish in South Carolina, U.S.A.

tree, which he saw during his expedition of the 1520s. For a long time this tree was believed to have the thickest trunk in the world; in fact, its massive size was the result of three trees having grown and fused together.

The timber most used is from *T. distichum*; it is soft and does not shrink, resists insect attack, and is little affected by damp. These qualities make it a suitable packaging material and useful for piping, ventilators, fencing, and garden furniture. **CZ7–9**

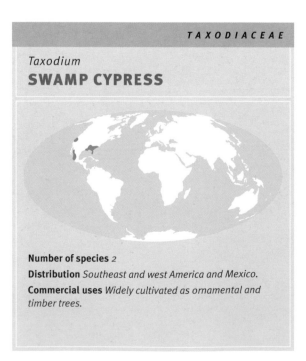

TAXODIACEAE

Taxodium
SWAMP CYPRESS

Number of species *2*
Distribution *Southeast and west America and Mexico.*
Commercial uses *Widely cultivated as ornamental and timber trees.*

T. distichum

The Species of *Taxodium*

T. distichum **Swamp or Bald Cypress.** SE U.S. and westward to Illinois and Missouri; Arizona. Tree to 100–165 ft (30–50 m). Branches more or less horizontal, conical at first becoming roundheaded at maturity. Leaves spreading, characteristically delicate pale green, 0.3–0.7 in (8–18 mm), spirally arranged but twisted at the base and, as a result, appearing in one plane; reddish-brown at the end of the season and falling separately or with the deciduous branchlets. **CZ7**

T. mucronatum **Montezuma or Mexican Cypress.** Mexico. Tree much the same size as *T. distichum* but not well known outside its native Mexico. It differs from *T. distichum* in being half- to fully-evergreen with longer male cones, the pollen sacs opening in the fall and not in spring as in the other species. **CZ9**

Cunninghamia

Chinese Firs

Cunninghamia (Chinese or China firs) is a genus of two, perhaps three, species native to China and Taiwan. The Chinese Fir (*C. lanceolata*) is infrequently found in cultivation but in its native China it is an important timber tree. These are evergreen trees with spreading branches. The leaves are stiff, decurrent, linear-lanceolate with serrulate margins, white-banded beneath, and spread in two ranks, but arise spirally. Male cones are oblong, borne in terminal clusters. Females occur on the same tree as the males and are subglobose, comprising rather thin, leathery, overlapping, serrate, pointed scales without distinct bract-scales. There are three inverted ovules per scale, each maturing to a narrowly winged seed.

Chinese firs are not particularly hardy except in the milder/warmer parts of temperate regions, hence are little seen in cultivation, and then only in sheltered positions on a good soil. They will regenerate from stumps of felled trees. Propagation is best from seed, but cuttings from erect shoots may be used.

Two species have been positively identified. *Cunninghamia lanceolata* (south and west China) grows to 82 ft (25 m) and has leaves 1.2–2.4 × 0.08–0.25 in (3–6 cm × 2–6 mm) with two broad, white stomatal lines beneath. The mature cones are 1–2 in (2.5–5 cm) long. The timber is much used for coffins. *Cunninghamia konishii* (Taiwan) reaches the same height or more and differs from the former species by having smaller and narrower leaves, 0.7–1.1 × 0.08 in (1.8–2.8 cm × 2 mm); stomatal bands are absent or not clearly marked. The mature cones are up to 1 in (2.5 cm) long. The doubtful species is *C. kawakamii*, also from Taiwan, which is intermediate in form between the two previous species and is probably a variety of *C. konishii*. **CZ8–9**

ABOVE The Chinese Fir *Cunninghamia lanceolata* has a somewhat untidy habit which makes it less useful as an ornamental, though it is valued for its timber in China.

BELOW The foliage of *Cunninghamia konishii* is distinguished from *C. lanceolata* by its smaller, narrower leaves, which are said to persist on the branches for eight years rather than five, as in *C. lanceolata*.

Athrotaxis

Tasmanian Cedars

Athrotaxis comprises three species of evergreen trees or shrubs, all from the mountains of Tasmania. The leaves are spirally arranged and scale- or awl-like. Cones are unisexual, the females woody, ripe within one year, more or less globose and comprising 5–20(25) spirally arranged scales, each subtending a bract, which is fused with its scale except at the tip. The scales are swollen at their free (outer) end, tapering to the base at the point of attachment. The seeds are winged.

The Smooth Tasmanian Cedar (*A. cupressoides*) is a tree to 20–40 ft (6–12 m) in its native mountain habitat in central and western Tasmania, where it grows at altitudes in excess of 3,300 ft (1,000 m), though it reaches no more than about half this height in cultivation. The branchlets are rounded and concealed by the densely packed adpressed, decussate scale-like leaves, about 0.12 in (3 mm) long, which are rhombic in outline, with a translucent, finely serrated margin. The leaf bases overlap and on bigger branches the leaves are larger. Female cones are finally about 0.5 in (12 mm) across, comprising five or six scales, the free tip of each bract-scale projecting as a short, spiny point. *Arthrotaxis cupressoides* is distinguished from the other two species by having scale-leaves closely adpressed along their entire length to the branchlets and by the absence of stomatal bands on the ventral surface.

The King William Pine (*A. selaginoides*) can attain heights of over 100 ft (33 m) in its native western Tasmanian habitat. The leaves are 0.28–0.5 in (7–12 mm) long, lanceolate to awl-shaped, curved toward but free of the branchlet, and pointing forward at about an angle of 30 degrees. They are much less densely arranged than in the previous species from which *A. selaginoides* is also distinct in having two stomatal bands on the ventral surface of the leaf and lacking translucent margins.

Variety *japonica* is commonly favored as an ornamental forming a bright green narrowly conical crown with a rounded apex. It is fully hardy, growing best in cool, damp areas with good, deep alluvial soil. Propagation is by seeds or cuttings. There are numerous cultivars; 'Elegans' is often planted but despite its name is sometimes an untidy sight. Its leaves are 0.8–1.2 in (2–3 cm) long and of the juvenile type; they are of a fine green color in summer changing to reddish-bronze as winter approaches. Cones are rarely produced in this cultivar.

In Japan about one-third of the area under afforestation is devoted to var *japonica*. The tree is planted by temples and lines many celebrated avenues to which it has contributed much of their fame. The wood is durable, easy to work, and resistant to insects. It is much used in construction and for furniture, and the bark is valuable as a roofing material. **CZ7**

LEFT *Athrotaxis selaginoides*, despite the common names Tasmanian Cedar and King William Pine, is neither a cedar nor a pine.

The Summit Cedar (*A. laxifolia*) is intermediate in form between the former species, growing to a height of 33 ft (10 m) in the mountains of western Tasmania. Its leaves are slightly spreading, 0.16–0.25 in (4–6 mm) long, the margin translucent and entire; two stomatal bands are present on the upper (ventral) surface.

The wood of Tasmanian cedars has some value in cabinetmaking and lighter types of carpentry. All three species are marginally hardy in temperate zones. **CZ9**

Cryptomeria
Japanese Red Cedar

The Japanese Red Cedar (*Cryptomeria japonica*) is the only member of its genus but exists in two distinct, geographically isolated varieties. The one seen most frequently found in cultivation is var *japonica* from Japan, while var *sinensis* is native to China. Cryptomerias are evergreen trees with reddish-brown bark that detaches in longish shreds. The leaves are spirally arranged in five ranks and more or less awl-shaped, 0.25–0.5 in (6–12 mm) long, the base decurrent on the shoot. Male and female cones occur on the same branch, the male in short spike-like clusters, each with numerous pollen sacs, the female solitary and maturing in one year into a woody, erect, stalked cone 0.8–1.2 in (2–3 cm) across comprising twenty to thirty wedge-shaped composite scales. The outer edge of each composite scale (cone-scale) is disc-like and has a more or less central recurved spine, with the upper margin bearing three to five short rigid processes.

Variety *japonica* is of more compact appearance, the branches more spreading and the leaves stouter; the female cones comprise some thirty scales, each fertile scale maturing to bear five seeds. In var *sinensis* the habit is more open, with the ultimate branchlets tending to droop; the female cones rarely have more than twenty scales, each fertile scale maturing to bear two seeds.

Glyptostrobus
Chinese Swamp Cypress

The Chinese Swamp Cypress or Chinese Water Pine (*Glyptostrobus lineatus* = *G. pensilis*) is a small deciduous tree native to south China where it appears to be mainly a cultivated tree, possibly because it is believed to bring luck to the home and rice crops. It is scarcely hardy in temperate regions, hence rarely seen in cultivation outside China. Like the Swamp Cypress (*Taxodium distichum*), in its natural habitat it is characteristic of damp places.

Glyptostrobus is closely related to *Taxodium*, differing in its pear-shaped, stalked female cones comprising thin, elongated nonpeltate scales, which are coarsely toothed at their apices; the seeds are oval-oblong with a single wing and not, as in *Taxodium*, three-angled and appearing as if bearing three thick wings. The shoots are hairless and of two types: either persistent (usually terminal) and spirally arranged with axillary buds, or deciduous, falling with the leaves and without axillary buds. The leaves on

RIGHT *Cryptomeria japonica* has attractive red bark which makes up for its somewhat untidy form.

persistent shoots are scale-like, 0.08–0.12 in (2–3 mm) long, spirally arranged, and overlapping; those on deciduous shoots are more or less needle-like, 0.3–0.5 in (8–12 mm) long and about 0.04 in (1 mm) wide, and arranged in the same plane, one row on each side of the shoot (pectinate) and falling with the shoot in the fall. The sexes are separate but on the same tree, the male cones in hanging clusters, the females finally about 0.7 in (18 mm) long on a 0.5–0.7 in (12–18 mm) long stalk. **CZ9**

Taiwania

Taiwania

The genus *Taiwania* has three very closely related species of evergreen trees, which may in fact be geographical subspecies of a single species: *T. cryptomenoides*. They are native to north Myanmar, southwest China, Taiwan, and Manchuria.

Taiwania cryptomenoides is a tree to about 200 ft (60 m) but rarely reaches more than 50–52 ft (15–16 m) in cultivation. Its leaves are of two types: on juvenile and sterile shoots they are awl-shaped, 0.5–0.8 in (12–18 mm) long, curved, and much like those of *Cryptomeria*, with a broad glaucous stomatal band on each surface; on adult and fertile shoots the leaves are scale-like, smaller to about 0.25 in (6 mm) long, triangular, and overlapping with stomatal lines on all surfaces. The female cones are sub-globose, and 0.4–0.45(0.6) in (10–11(15) mm) long, comprising numerous rounded and mucronate scales. Each scale bears two ovules, which mature into winged seeds.

(*Taiwania* is related to *Cunninghamia*, but the latter bears three ovules per scale.)

Taiwania cryptomenoides is scarcely hardy in temperate regions, but has survived with winter shelter. **CZ9**

SCIADOPITYACEAE

Sciadopitys

Japanese Umbrella Pine

The Japanese Umbrella Pine or Parasol Pine (*Sciadopitys verticillata*) is an evergreen pyramidal tree that can attain heights of 130 ft (40 m) in its native habitat of central Japan, where it sometimes forms forests up to an altitude of 3,300 ft (1,000 m).

The bark is almost smooth but separates into thin shreds. The leaves are of two types. The main ones are in whorls of (10)20–30 paired leaves 3–5 × 0.08–0.12 in (8–12 × 2–3 mm), with each pair united along their whole length by their sides; stomata are found only over a small area in the groove on the lower surface. The appearance of each whorl is very much like that of the stays of an open umbrella. Along the internodes between these whorls are triangular, somewhat overlapping, scale-like leaves, which are green at first, becoming brown in the second year.

The male cones are in terminal clusters, each cone with spirally arranged pollen sacs. The female cones are solitary, occurring on same tree as the males, each comprising numerous (ovuliferous) scales, which, in the young state, are much smaller than the subtending bract-scales, but greatly exceed them in the mature cone when they become woody and more or less wedge- or fan-shaped. Each scale bears seven to nine seeds in the second year, the cone then becomes ovoid and 3–5 × 1.4–2 in (8–12 × 3.5–5 cm), the upper margin of each scale being slightly recurved. Seeds are compressed ovoid, 0.5 in (12 mm), and narrowly winged.

This species is a slow grower and hardy in temperate regions, where it readily produces seed by which it is propagated. However, it is uncommon in cultivation and grown only for its unique appearance—quite unlike any other conifer. The wood is durable and water resistant, which makes it useful for boatbuilding. **CZ6**

LEFT *Glyptostrobus pensilis* is related to the swamp cypresses *Taxodium*, but differs in its habit as it does not have the upright protuberances that characterize *Taxodium* species.

BELOW *Taiwania cryptomenoides* towers above many conifers in cultivation.

Araucaria
Monkey Puzzle

Araucaria is a genus of evergreen coniferous trees, all of which are confined to the southern hemisphere, notably South America, Australasia, and the islands of the South Pacific. It includes the well-known Monkey Puzzle Tree or Chile Pine (*A. araucana* = *A. imbricata*), the Norfolk Island Pine (*A. heterophylla* = *A. excelsa*), and the Parana Pine or Candelabra Tree (*A. angustifolia*). The genus is very closely related to the kauri pines (*Agathis*), but an essential difference is that the seeds are free from the cone-scale in *Agathis* and not adnate as in *Araucaria*.

Members of *Araucaria* are tall imposing trees with branches in regular whorls. The bark of the old trees may be ridged with the remains of old leaf-bases or rough and peeling. The leaves persist for many years and are flat and broad or awl-shaped and curved; some species have awl-shaped juvenile leaves. Male and female cones are usually borne on different trees but may sometimes occur on separate branches of the same tree. The male cones grow in large cylindrical terminal or subterminal clusters, each with numerous pollen sacs. The females mature in two to three years, often as very large globose or ovoid cones of woody overlapping scales, which break up when the seeds are ripe. There is one seed on each scale and adnate to it, with a marginal wing on all edges in most species.

The wood of *Araucaria* is resinous, straight-grained, and easy to work. *Araucaria araucana*, *A. bidwillii* (Bunya-Bunya), and *A. cunninghamii* (Moreton Bay Pine or

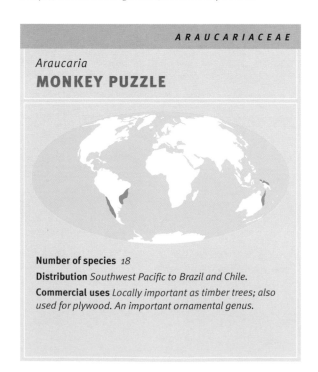

ARAUCARIACEAE

Araucaria
MONKEY PUZZLE

Number of species *18*
Distribution *Southwest Pacific to Brazil and Chile.*
Commercial uses *Locally important as timber trees; also used for plywood. An important ornamental genus.*

Hoop Pine) are the most important timber trees. The timber is mainly used for general indoor joinery and carpentry and for boxes and masts as well as pulp for papermaking. For all practical purposes it can be used as a substitute for the Scots Pine (*Pinus sylvestris*).

The striking appearance of the Monkey Puzzle Tree has made it a popular subject for cultivation in parks and gardens. It was most popular during the late nineteenth century and is not frequently planted these days. The tree was introduced to Britain by Archibald Menzies in 1795, who apparently removed some of the edible seeds when dining with the Viceroy of Chile. It became popular after a good supply of seed was sent back by William Lobb in 1844. Its fascinating habit led to much planting in highly unsuitable places, especially suburban gardens where it rarely does well, looks out of place, and is generally bedraggled and unhappy through loss of the lower branches at an early stage—a response to poor soils and atmospheric pollution. It thrives on moist but adequately drained soils in a humid and clean atmosphere. It is, and looks, at its best in arboreta and parks especially when in pure stands rather than randomly distributed among other trees.

In addition to *A. araucana*, the seeds of *A. bidwillii* are important in the diet of indigenous people. For this reason there are government restrictions on felling in certain areas.

The Norfolk Island Pine is, among others, commonly grown as an indoor plant and does well when planted in a large tub with a good fibrous loam—leafmold and sand mixture. There is, however, one fine specimen of this plant growing outdoors in the famous subtropical gardens at Tresco, one of the Isles of Scilly, about 30 miles (50 km) west of Land's End in Cornwall, England. **CZ8–9**

The distinctive candelabra-like form of *Araucaria araucana* is an unmistakable feature of the vegetation of the volcanic lake district of southern Chile.

A. araucana

The Main Species of *Araucaria*

Group I: Leaves broad and flat, about 0.75 in (1.8 cm). Cone-scales without or with only vestigial wings.

A. araucana (*A. imbricata*) **Chile Pine or Monkey Puzzle Tree.** Chile and W Argentina. Tree 100–165 ft (30–50 m) with spreading, stout, upwardly curved branches of striking appearance. Leaves 1–2 × 1 in (2.5–5 × 2.5 cm), densely imbricated, ovate-lanceolate but with a broad base, firm and with a sharp, pointed apex. Male cones in catkin-like clusters, cylindrical, 3.1–5 in (8–12 cm); mature cones more or less globose up to 6(8) in (15(20) cm) across; seeds somewhat compressed, 1–1.5 in (2.5–3.5 cm), adnate to scale, each with recurved apical appendage. **CZ8**

A. bidwillii **Bunya-Bunya.** Coastal Queensland, Australia. Tree to 165 ft (50 m) and fast-growing. Main branches horizontal, younger branchlets pendulous. Leaves on sterile shoots 0.7–1 × 0.16–0.4 in (18–25 × 4–11 mm), lanceolate, with a narrow base, the apex tapering to a long stiff point; leaves on fertile shoots (and the upper branches) stiffer and incurved, 0.6–1 in (1.5–2.5 cm). Sexes usually on separate plants, the male in clusters, 6–7 × 0.7 in (15–18 × 1.3 cm), cylindrical, and catkin-like; mature cones elliptical, up to 12 × 9 in (30 × 23 cm), and weighing up to 11 lb (5 kg); scales large with a long recurved point, seeds large, pear-shaped, up to 2.4 × 1 in (6.5 × 2.5 cm) with a rudimentary wing. **CZ9**

A. angustifolia **Parana Pine or Candelabra Tree.** Brazil and Argentina. Tree to 115 ft (35 m) with a flat crown, the branches in whorls of 4–8. Leaves with long points, stiff and leathery, the stomata on lower surface; leaves of sterile branches 1.2–2.4 × 0.2 in (3–6 × 0.5 cm) and appearing opposite, those of fertile branches shorter and arranged spirally. Cones 7 in (17 cm) across, 5 in (12 cm) high, each scale with a recurved, stiff appendage; seeds 2 × 0.8 in (5 × 2 cm), light brown. Allied to *A. araucana* but differs in the leaves being softer and less crowded. The wood is soft and commercially valuable. **CZ9**

Group II: Leaves either more or less awl-shaped to broadly ovate or less than 0.5 in (1 cm). Cone-scales obviously winged.

A. heterophylla (*A. excelsa*) **Norfolk Island Pine.** Restricted to Norfolk Island in the South Pacific. Handsome tree to 230 ft (70 m), main branches horizontal, lateral branches sometimes pendulous. Leaves on young lateral and sterile shoots 0.4–0.5(0.6) in (8–13(15) mm), spreading, not crowded, and those on older and fertile shoots incurved, crowded, overlapping, 0.25–0.3 in (6–7 mm) with incurved horny point, the midrib hardly visible. Male cones in clusters, 1.4–2 in (3.5–5 cm) and catkin-like; mature cones more or less globose, about 4–5 in (10–12 cm) across; seeds with well-developed wings, the adnate scales each with a flat triangular incurved spine. Much cultivated as an ornamental tree in the Mediterranean area and places of similar climate. Many cultivars. **CZ9**

A. heterophylla

A. araucana

The whorled leaf arrangement of the Norfolk Island Pine, *Araucaria heterophylla*, is much appreciated as an ornamental in warm temperate regions.

A. cunninghamii **Moreton Bay Pine or Hoop Pine.** Mainly in New South Wales and Queensland, Australia; also in New Guinea. Tree 200–230 ft (60–70 m). Bark characteristically cracking into horizontal hoops or bands, peeling. Branches horizontal, the branchlets mostly concentrated at the ends. Leaves on sterile lateral branches and on young trees in general lanceolate, 0.3–0.6(0.75) in (8–15(19) mm), straight and spreading with a sharp, pointed apex; on older trees and on fertile branches, leaves more crowded, shorter, incurved with a short pointed apex. Male cones in clusters, 2–3 in (5–7.5 cm) and catkin-like; mature cones broadly ellipsoidal about 6 × 3 in (10 × 7.5 cm) with exserted stiff, recurved apices of the cone-scales; seeds with narrow membranous wings. **CZ9**

A. columnaris **New Caledonian Pine.** New Caledonia and Polynesia. Tree closely allied to *A. heterophylla* under which name it often appears. Fertile and older branchlets with densely overlapping, incurved leaves, each with a distinct midrib, giving a characteristic and distinctive whip-cord appearance; leaves on sterile and young branchlets triangular or lanceolate. **CZ9**

A. balansae **New Caledonia.** Tree 40–60 ft (12–18 m), the branches more or less horizontal and turning down at the ends. Leaves densely crowded, broadly awl-shaped, about 0.12 in (3 mm), with stomata on inner surface. Mature cones at the apex of short shoots, oval, 2.4 × 2 2.6 in (6 7.5 × 5–6.5 cm), each scale with a hard bristle 0.3 in (8 mm). Close to *A. columnaris,* which has larger leaves. Of little or no commercial value. **CZ9**

A. heterophylla

Agathis

Kauri Pines

The kauri or kauri pines are the most tropical genus of all the
conifers. Some twenty species have been described but five
(or more) may be, at most, subspecies. Representatives are
found in the wettest tropical rainforests of the Malay
archipelago, Sumatra, the Philippines, and Fiji, with outliers
in the subtropical forests of Queensland in Australia and
northernmost New Zealand.

Kauri pines are imposing evergreen trees with massive
columnar trunks and large spreading crowns. Male and
female cones are borne on separate trees. Kauri pines differ
from *Araucaria* by the seed being free from the (ovuliferous)
scale and not adnate to it, the leaves being larger and broad
and flat rather than more or less awl-shaped or lanceolate,
and the seeds being mostly unequally winged whereas in
Araucaria they are wingless or about equally winged.

Agathis timber is one of the most valuable softwoods
in the world and is highly prized for boatbuilding, as a
decorative veneer, and for household utensils and drawing

One of the most tropical of
conifers, the Kauri *Agathis
australis* is economically prized
both for its high quality timber
and its resin.

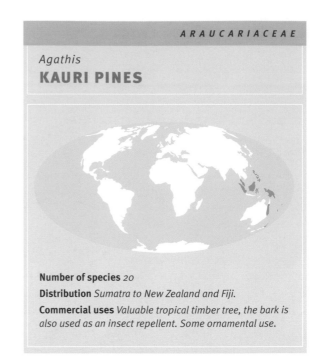

ARAUCARIACEAE

Agathis
KAURI PINES

Number of species *20*
Distribution *Sumatra to New Zealand and Fiji.*
Commercial uses *Valuable tropical timber tree, the bark is
also used as an insect repellent. Some ornamental use.*

boards. The wood of most species is strong, durable, and
of excellent quality and because of the shedding of lower
branches in young specimens, is remarkably free from knots.

All parts contain a resin (kauri gum), which in several
species exudes spontaneously and from injuries,
accumulating on branches, trunks, and at the base of trees.
It has been extensively used in the manufacture of varnishes,
linoleum, and paints, being also known as an animé and
more specifically as copal, damar, or dammar, these last two
a reference to *A. dammara*, formerly known as *Dammara
alba* and *Agathis alba*. Other sources are from *A. robusta* and
the highly important *A. australis*, the Kauri (or Cowdie) Pine
from the North Island of New Zealand. In addition to the
freshly exuded resin, there are large quantities of fossil resin
preserved in peat bogs where kauri pines no longer grow.
This supply is even more highly esteemed, sought after, and
commercially exploited. The preserving peat has also been
distilled to yield a petroleum spirit and turpentine.

Kauri pines have been so over-exploited for their products
that government action was required to conserve them. Most
Agathis timber now comes from small groves or isolated trees
scattered through primary forest, but the plantations on Java
promise to be a major timber source when the virgin
rainforests have disappeared. **CZ9**

Wollemia

Wollemia

A genus of a single, very rare, species—*Wollemia nobilis*—
only discovered in the 1990s in New South Wales, Australia,
with characteristic trimorphic leaves and a spongy bark,
related to the genus *Agathis*. In cultivation from 2005. **CZ9**

Cupressus

Cypresses

Cupressus—the true cypresses—is a genus comprising, as now understood, about thirteen species. Cypresses are widely distributed in the New and Old Worlds, from Oregon to Mexico, the Mediterranean area, western Asia, the western Himalaya, and China.

The cypresses are evergreen trees, rarely shrubs; the branchlets are densely clothed with small overlapping scale-like decussate leaves with minute denticulate-fringed margins (lens). On older branches the leaves are more awl-shaped, larger, and spreading. Male and female cones are terminal and solitary on separate branches of the same tree. Mature female cones are globose to broadly elliptic, mostly more than 0.4 in (1 cm) across, with six to twelve finally woody, peltate scales, each bearing six to twelve (sometimes as many as twenty) more or less winged seeds, which may be smooth or beset with a few resinous tubercles. The cones require eighteen months to mature.

The limits of the modern genus have been reduced by the transfer of a number of species to *Chamaecyparis*, commonly known as false cypresses. In almost all cases trees and shrubs of both genera are easily distinguished. In *Chamaecyparis* the ultimate branchlets are usually flattened in one plane, and these flattened foliar-like sprays (phyllomorphs) are commonly horizontally (though sometimes more or less vertically) disposed. In *Cupressus* the ultimate branchlets are generally less flattened but diverge in various directions so no phyllomorphs are evident. The *Chamaecyparis* species tend

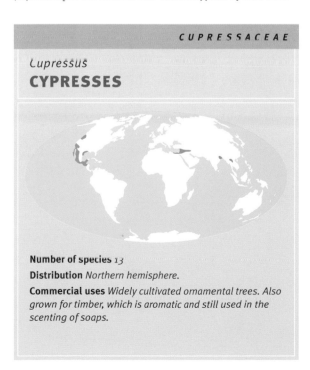

CUPRESSACEAE

Cupressus
CYPRESSES

Number of species *13*
Distribution *Northern hemisphere.*
Commercial uses *Widely cultivated ornamental trees. Also grown for timber, which is aromatic and still used in the scenting of soaps.*

to be much more hardy than those of *Cupressus*, which, in much of northern Europe at least, are regarded as "semi-tender." There is no doubt that the two genera are closely related and this is borne out by the existence of the inter-generic hybrid × *Cupressocyparis*.

In suitable climatic conditions, including reasonably clean air, cypresses are not particular as to soil type, succeeding on light to heavy loams and even on a highly sandy soil, provided adequate moisture is maintained. This is true of *Cupressus macrocarpa* (Monterey Cypress), the most commonly planted species in the British Isles, which does well by the sea in the southwest, where the high relative humidity no doubt significantly reduces transpiration and thus equally the demand for water. Propagation of species is mainly by seeds and the cultivars by cuttings and sometimes by grafts on the appropriate stock.

Despite cypresses being susceptible to bacterial and fungal diseases, the wood of many species is commercially valuable, being durable and easily worked. It is used in general building construction, carpentry, and for posts and poles, but not for packing cases since the often spicy odor of the wood may contaminate susceptible contents. The most commonly used timbers are those of *C. macrocarpa* and *C. sempervirens*. These two species are also widely planted as ornamentals but their "semi-tenderness" restricts them to the mildest areas of their range and they are likely to suffer in anything approaching a severe frost. In more subtropical areas of the world, plantations, especially of *C. macrocarpa*, have been established. This species is also increasing in popularity as a screening or hedging plant. **CZ6–9**

Cupressus sempervirens, the classic cypress of the Mediterranean region, extends as far as the mountains of northern Iran. Cypresses occur in mixed evergreen forests or as standards, but are now widely distributed as semi-tender species throughout the northern hemisphere.

The Main Species of *Cupressus*

Group I: Leaves conspicuously resinous and glandular on the back, the ultimate branchlets typically diverging at all angles and not flattened into one plane as phyllomorphs.

C. macnabiana **Macnab Cypress.** Mainly N California. Shrub or small tree to about 40 ft (12 m). Branchlets compressed dorsiventrally; leaves rich green or glaucous, about 0.04 in (1 mm), densely set; apices enlarged and blunt. Mature cones 0.5–0.75 in (12–19 mm) across with 6–8 scales. **CZ8**

C. arizonica **Rough-barked Arizona Cypress.** Arizona, Mexico, and New Mexico. Tree 50–82 ft (15–25 m). Bark rough reddish-brown, graying, not exfoliating. Branchlets not compressed; leaves acute, deep green to grayish-green, about 0.08 in (2 mm), the margin (lens) finely toothed. Mature cones 0.5–1 in (12–25 mm) across with 6–8 scales. **CZ6–8**

C. glabra **Smooth Arizona Cypress.** C Arizona. Tree 23–60 ft (7–18 m). Bark cherry-red, smooth, and exfoliating each year. Branchlets not compressed. Leaves 0.06–0.08 in (1.5–2 mm) long, white-spotted with resin, acute, finely toothed margin (use lens), gray to grayish-green, keeled. Mature cones 0.8–1 in (2–2.5 cm) across, with usually 8(5–10) scales, each with a prominent umbo. Tolerates calcareous soils and is drought-resistant. **CZ7**

Group II: Leaves not conspicuously resinous or glandular on the back, but sometimes with a faint nonresinous "slit" or "pit," and then ultimate branchlets flattened in one plane.

A *Ultimate branchlets flattened in one plane (phyllomorphs), more or less horizontally disposed. Cones subglobose, 0.3–0.6 in (8–16 mm) across.*

C. lusitanica var *benthamii* **Mexican Cypress, Cedar of Goa.** Mexico. Tree to about 108 ft (33 m). Leaves shining, dark green, with central dorsal "pit" and acute apex. Mature cones about 0.5–0.6 in (12–15 mm) across with 6–8 scales, each scale with a prominent umbo, slightly, or not reflexed; seeds smooth. **CZ8**

C. torulosa **Bhutan or Himalayan Cypress.** W Himalaya and Szechwan, China. Tree to 165 ft (50 m). Ultimate branches more or less flattened, curved, and characteristically whiplike. Leaves about 0.06 in (1.5 mm), somewhat blunt at the apex, usually with a dorsal, central "pit." Mature cones about 0.4(0.5) in (11(12) mm) across with 8–10 scales; seeds relatively few, 6–8 per scale, with tubercles. **CZ9**

AA *Ultimate branchlets not flattened in one plane, but diverging at all angles. Cones 0.4–1.6 in (1–4 cm) wide or long.*

C. macrocarpa **Monterey Cypress.** California. Tree to about 82 ft (25 m), at first pyramidal, finally with a broad crown. Leaves 0.04–0.1 in (1–2.5 mm), densely packed, apices adpressed, rather blunt; bruised foliage with citronella-like smell.

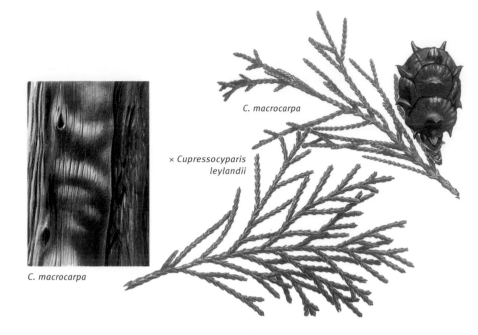

C. macrocarpa

× *Cupressocyparis leylandii*

C. macrocarpa

Mature cones subglobose, 1–1.5 × 0.6–1 in (2.5–4 × 1.75–2.5 cm), with 8–12(14) scales, each with a short, stout, and blunt umbo; seeds minutely tuberculate. Distinguished by its large cones from all other commonly cultivated species except *C. sempervirens,* which has smaller leaves and smooth seeds. Useful as a windbreak on exposed coasts. **CZ8**

C. sempervirens **Italian Cypress, Mediterranean Cypress, Funeral Cypress.** The "classical" cypress of the ancients. Mediterranean area including Crete, Cyprus, and Sicily; Switzerland, and the mountains of N Iran. Tree usually 66–100 ft (20–30 m), but up to 165 ft (50 m) in the Mediterranean area. Branches either spreading (var *horizontalis*) or fastigiate (var *sempervirens*). Leaves dark green, 0.04 in (1 mm), diamond-shaped but apices bluntish; bruised foliage with little or no smell. Mature cones subglobose to broadly elliptical, 1–1.25 × 0.8 in (2.5–3 × 2 cm) with 8–14 scales, the central umbo inconspicuous; seeds smooth. The type is var *sempervirens* and is very striking with its erect, fastigiate branches, the whole tree being lanceolate to narrowly pyramidal in outline. This variety is also known as 'Stricta.' **CZ8**

C. goveniana **Gowen Cypress.** California. Shrub or small tree to 66 ft (20 m). Leaves 0.04–0.08 in (1–2 mm), sometimes with a "pit," gray to blackish-green; bruised foliage with distinct, pleasant, resinous smell; shoots purplish-brown. Mature cones globose, 0.4–0.6 in (1–1.5 cm) across with 6–10 scales, each with a low blunt umbo; seeds smooth. **CZ8**

C. lusitanica **Mexican Cypress, Cedar of Goa.** Mexico, extending to the mountains of Guatemala. Tree to 100 ft (30 m) but variable. Branches commonly spreading and pendulous at the ends; ultimate branchlets not flattened in one plane but diverging at all angles (compare with *C. lusitanica* var *benthamii* above). Leaves acute, glaucous to gray-green, the tips spreading, 0.06–0.08 in (1.5–2 mm); bruised foliage with little or no smell; shoots pinkish-brown. Mature cones subglobose, 0.5–0.6 in (12–16 mm) across with 6–8 scales, the umbo pointed and often hooked; seeds smooth, the wing sometimes little developed. **CZ9**

C. sempervirens

Cupressus always has minute scalelike leaves which are flattened to the branchlet. The cones of *C. macrocarpa* have ridgelike projections in the center of their scales. Scales on the cones of *C. sempervirens* usually rise to a point in the center but can also be flat.

× *Cupressocyparis*

Hybrid Cypresses

The genus × *Cupressocyparis* is a natural bigeneric hybrid—
× *Cupressocyparis leylandii*—between *Cupressus macrocarpa*
(Monterey Cypress) from California and *Chamaecyparis
nootkatensis* (Nootka Cypress or Yellow Cypress) from the
Pacific Northwest coast of the United States.

× *Cupressocyparis* is thought to have arisen in cultivation
in England at Leighton Hall, Shropshire, in 1888 where
seedlings of the Nootka Cypress were being raised and a
Monterey Cypress was growing in the same garden. Further
seedlings were raised here in 1911, this time with seed from
Cupressus macrocarpa. From these original seedlings the
following clones have been established, with differences in
growth habit, color, and texture: 'Green Spire,' 'Haggerston
Gray' (probably the commonest), 'Leighton Green,' 'Naylor's
Blue,' and 'Stapehill.'

Two other *Cupressocyparis* hybrids have also emerged:
× *C. notabilis* (*Chamaecyparis nootkatensis* × *Cupressus glabra*)
—the Arizona Cypress—and × *C. ovensii* (*Chamaecyparis
nootkatensis* × *Cupressus lusitanica*)—the Mexican Cypress.

Hybrid cypress began to attract widespread attention in
the 1950s for fast-growing shelter belts and hedges; by the
1960s, demand began to outstrip limited supplies. Today
× *Cupressocyparis leylandii* is widely planted as a very fast-
growing, hardy, and adaptable conifer. From a distance it
resembles the Nootka rather than the Monterey Cypress in
general appearance but is usually far more columnar and
erect in habit. However, the leaves and branches are less
flattened than Nootka and resemble more the filiform shape
of Monterey. Cones are produced on more mature trees and
they are somewhere between the cone structures of the
parents, with tubercles on the cone-scales.

The hybrid cypress withstands clipping and can be made
into a dense hedge from 6.6 ft (2 m) in height, but it is not
suitable for dwarf hedging.

The timber of the Leyland Cypress is of good quality and
the tree can be readily grown under plantation conditions.

Chamaecyparis

False Cypresses

Chamaecyparis is a northern hemisphere genus, mainly found
on the western and southeastern coasts of North America, and
in Japan and Taiwan. They are hardy, evergreen, mostly
pyramidal trees with similar habit to that of the true cypresses
(*Cupressus*) except that the young shoot systems or sprays
(phyllomorphs) are flattened and in one plane, a characteristic
shared with species of *Thuja* (arbor-vitae). The leaves are scale-
like, opposite, and decussate, but juvenile leaves are sometimes
awl-shaped. Both sexes occur on the same tree, on separate
branches. The female cones are globose and very small—up to

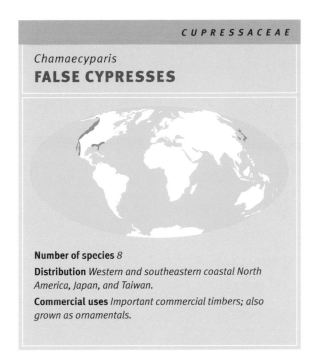

| CUPRESSACEAE |

Chamaecyparis
FALSE CYPRESSES

Number of species *8*
Distribution *Western and southeastern coastal North
America, Japan, and Taiwan.*
Commercial uses *Important commercial timbers; also
grown as ornamentals.*

0.4 in (1 cm) across. They mature in a year apart from
Chamaecyparis nootkatensis (Nootka Cypress), which
requires about eighteen months. The seeds are somewhat
compressed, each with a thin broad wing. They thrive on moist
(but not waterlogged) soils if they are not too calcareous.

The timber of most *Chamaecyparis* species is of high
quality, generally light, durable, easily worked, and resistant
to pests and diseases. The wood of most species has its own
pleasant distinctive odor and color. One of the most valued
species in Taiwan is *C. formosensis*, which has no distinctive
odor. Specimens can reach 165 ft (50 m) high and some may
be over 3,000 years old. The wood of *C. lawsoniana* is as
useful and is used for general building, for floors, furniture,
fence posts, railway sleepers, and boatbuilding. That of
C. nootkatensis is also of excellent quality and similarly used.
It is confusingly known in the trade as "yellow cypress," a
popular name also applied to the Swamp Cypress (*Taxodium
distichum*). The wood of *C. obtusa* is much prized in its
native Japan and is probably unsurpassed for the highest-
quality work in all manner of construction. It is very straight,
evenly grained, and often beautifully marked. Another
Japanese species, *C. pisifera*, is perhaps the least exploited of
the false cypresses but nevertheless extensively used for less
ornamental kinds of carpentry.

Outside their native habitats, species of *Chamaecyparis* and
their cultivars are popular ornamentals for parks and large
gardens, including *C. pisifera*, *C. obtusa*, and *C. nootkatensis*.
The best-known cultivated species is *C. lawsoniana* from
southwest Oregon and northwest California. There are in
excess of 200 cultivars, ranging from dwarf shrubs suitable
for rock gardens to tall, columnar trees exhibiting many
different color forms. *Chamaecyparis* also makes an excellent
hedging or screening subject and will grow in a wide range of
conditions, including shaded or exposed sites. **CZ3–9**

× *Cupressocyparis leylandii*

Chamaecyparis cultivars are
favored for rockeries and
smaller gardens. *Chamaecyparis
lawsoniana* 'Aurea Densa' is a
popular dwarf shrub.

The Main Species of *Chamaecyparis*

Group I: Underside of phyllomorphs partially whitish or at least glaucous, especially on leaf margins (lens). Lateral leaves significantly larger (twice as long) than facial ones and all closely adpressed—except *C. pisifera* where leaves are about the same size (and length), with acute more or less spreading tips.

C. formosensis **Formosa Cypress.** Taiwan. Tree reaching 210 ft (65 m) with a girth of 78 ft (24 m) in its native habitat. Lateral and facial leaves of equal length, about 0.02 in (1.5 mm), keeled or with glandular pit, dull green, bronze-tinged, often whitish beneath, smelling of rotten seaweed when crushed. Mature cones 0.3–0.35 in (8–9 mm) across but ellipsoidal, with 10–11 scales, the outer surfaces more or less wrinkled; seeds 2 per scale, oval with narrow wings and conspicuous resin tubercles. The species is close to *C. pisifera* but differing in color, shape, and the odor of the crushed leaves. It forms pure forests in Taiwan on Mt. Morrison at 7,545–10,800 ft (2,300–3,300 m) in association with *C. obtusa*. It is a valuable timber tree in its native land, being resistant to insect attack and decay, but in danger of extinction through over-felling. **CZ8**

C. lawsoniana **Lawson Cypress.** Extreme W U.S. Tree 82–165 ft (25–50 m), spire-like with spreading branches, pendulous at the tips. Lateral leaves of ultimate branchlets 0.1–0.12 in (2.5–3 mm); facial leaves about half as long, all acute and with glandular dots appearing conspicuously translucent when examined under a lens against light. Male cones

characteristically crimson. Mature cones about 0.3 in (8 mm) across with usually 8 scales, each with 2–4 seeds. Much planted and with 200 or more named cultivars. **CZ8–9**

C. obtusa **Hinoki Cypress.** Japan, with var *formosana* in Taiwan. Tree to 130 ft (40 m), pyramidal. Leaves distinctly obtuse, without glands, the white markings beneath somewhat Y-shaped; lateral leaves about twice as long as the facial ones. Mature cones 0.3–0.4 in (8–10 mm) across with 8(–10) scales, each with up to 5 seeds. Numerous cultivars. Intolerant of lime and a dry climate. **CZ3**

C. pisifera **Sawara Cypress.** Japan. Tree to 165 ft (50 m). Leaves with spreading acute tips, the facial and lateral leaves about the same size and obscurely glandular. Mature cones 0.2(0.3) in (6(8) mm) across with 10(12) scales, each scale with 1–2 seeds. Numerous cultivars. **CZ3**

Group II: Underside of phyllomorphs the same color as the upper side or slightly paler, without whitish or glaucous marking. Lateral leaves about the same size as the facial leaves or only a little longer.

C. thyoides **White Cedar (sometimes also known as White Cypress).** E N. America. Tree to 82 ft (25 m). Branchlets distinctly compressed and phyllomorphs less uniformly disposed in the horizontal plane. Leaves bluish-green on both sides, conspicuously glandular. Mature cones 0.25(0.28) in (6(7) mm) across. **CZ3**

C. nootkatensis **Nootka or Yellow Cypress.** W N. America. Tree 100–130 ft (30–40 m), more or less conical with spreading branches, pendulous at the tips. Phyllomorphs horizontal and characteristically drooping at the sides, giving the appearance of a short circle segment; branchlets not obviously compressed; leaves green above, paler beneath, virtually without glands. Mature cones 0.4–0.5 in (10–12 mm) across with 4–6 scales and 2–4 seeds on each scale. **CZ8**

LEFT The typical columnar habit of *Chamaecyparis lawsonia* 'Pottenii' forms an effective screen. The cultivar is much planted as a garden boundary.

LEFT *Chamaecyparis lawsoniana* has reddish brown furrowed bark, foliage which has scale leaves that are closely pressed to the twigs. Cones are about 0.3 in (0.8 cm) with 8 scales and turn brown when ripe. *Chamaecyparis nootkatensis* is distinguished by the leaves, which are very pungent when crushed and do not have white on the underside, cone scales have a prominent point and the bark is thin and never deeply furrowed.

C. nootkatensis

C. lawsoniana

C. lawsoniana

Thuja

Arbor-vitae

The species (some with numerous varieties) in the genus *Thuja* are generally known as arbor-vitae. They are evergreen trees and shrubs from North America and East Asia, the trees usually of pyramidal habit and the young shoots (phyllomorphs) characteristically flattened in one plane with scale-like decussate leaves. Male and female cones occur on the same plant: the tiny male ones are borne terminally on the smallest shoots; the female cones are erect, solitary with imbricate cone-scales. Only the middle two or three pairs of scales are fertile—each bears two seeds on the lower surface.

Arbor-vitae are often grown as ornamentals, and thrive on well-drained loams, on light moist sandy soils, and in peat. Large cultivars, for example those of the White Cedar (*Thuja occidentalis*) and the Western Red Cedar (*T. plicata*), make excellent specimen trees for large gardens, and may serve as hedging, particularly the latter, which withstands clipping well, though *T. occidentalis* does better in cold climates. The numerous slow-growing, dwarf cultivars are particularly suitable for some gardens and rock gardens.

The wood, which is light, easy to work, and without resin canals, is used for general building, furniture, telegraph poles, etc. The inner, more fibrous, bark serves as a stuffing for upholstery. In the United States, timber of *T. plicata* is used for roofing tiles. This same species has also proved a successful timber tree in Scotland, but in the warmer, southern parts of England it is unsatisfactory, mainly because of extensive shrinkage during the seasoning process, which causes significant gaps to form between the annual rings. Its trunks were frequently used by the North-American indigenous people as totem-poles. **CZ6–8**

CUPRESSACEAE

Thuja
ARBOR-VITAE

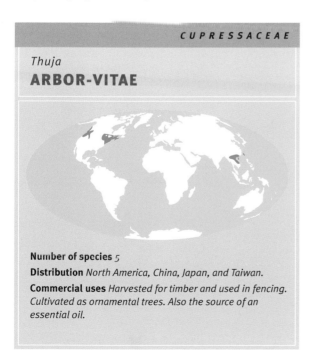

Number of species *5*
Distribution *North America, China, Japan, and Taiwan.*
Commercial uses *Harvested for timber and used in fencing. Cultivated as ornamental trees. Also the source of an essential oil.*

The Species of *Thuja*

T. occidentalis **American or White Cedar.** E N. America. Tree to 66 ft (20 m). Underside leaves of phyllomorphs without white streaks or markings, usually yellowish or bluish-green, each leaf of main axis with conspicuous glandular dot on the back (lens). Cones 0.4–0.5 in (8–12 mm) with 8–10 scales, only half of them fertile. Numerous named varieties. **CZ7–8**

T. plicata **Western Red Cedar.** W N. America. Tree 100–200 ft (30–60 m). Underside leaves with more or less X-shaped white streaks and any glands inconspicuous; bruised foliage strongly aromatic. Mature cones about 0.5 in (12 mm) with 10–12 scales, each with a small spine; about half the scales fertile. Numerous named varieties. **CZ7**

T. standishii **Japanese Arbor-vitae.** Japan. Tree to 60 ft (18 m). Phyllomorphs not obviously flattened; leaves without glands, those on the underside with more or less triangular white markings; bruised foliage not aromatic. Mature cones with 8–10 scales, only the middle 4 fertile. **CZ7**

T. koraiensis **Korean Arbor-vitae.** Korea. Usually a somewhat sprawling shrub, but sometimes a slender conical tree to 30 ft (9 m). Phyllomorphs much flattened; leaves with conspicuous glands, dark green on the upper surface of the phyllomorphs, contrasting with the almost white lower surface; bruised foliage not aromatic. Mature cones 0.4–0.5 in (8–12 mm) with 4 pairs of scales, the middle 2 pairs fertile. **CZ6**

T. sutchuenensis, from NE Szechwan in C China, is little known and is not yet in cultivation. **CZ6**

ABOVE *Thuja plicata* 'Zebrina,' has pleasing two-colored foliage.

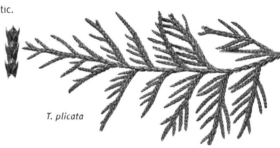

T. plicata

T. occidentalis

T. occidentalis

All *Thuja* have thin shredding bark which makes a useful roofing material. The leaves of *T. plicata* are glossy and dark above, paler with whitish marks below, with a fruity scent. *Thuja occidentalis* leaves are dark green above, yellowish below and smell of apples. Those of *T. standishii* are dull yellowish-green above, and the leaf bases have patches of gray below. Shoots have a lemony smell when crushed.

T. standishii

RIGHT *Calocedrus decurrens* in its native habitat. Although the timber is durable, it is not widely grown in cultivation.

BELOW The distinctly flattened phyllomorphs (young shoots) of *Thujopsis dolabrata* distinguish Hiba from the five species of Arbor-vitae.

Microbiota

Microbiota

This genus, first described in 1923, is allied to the genus *Thuja* and restricted to eastern Siberia. It consists of a single species, *Microbiota decussata*, which is not in general cultivation. **CZ7**

Platycladus

Platycladus

Comprised of one species, *Platycladus orientalis*, now considered distinct from the genus *Thuja*, where it was formerly placed on account of having fleshy female cone-scales and wingless seeds.

    Platycladus orientalis, the Chinese or Oriental Arbor-vitae, from north and west China forms a tree to 16–33 ft (5–10 m), sometimes more or less shrubby. Leaves reveal a small gland on the back and shoots (phyllomorphs), predominantly in vertical planes, are green on both sides. Cone-scales are thick, recurved at the apices and mature cones 0.6–1 in (1.5–2.5 cm), usually with 6 scales. Easily recognized by the subgeneric characters. There are numerous named varieties. **CZ7**

Thujopsis

Hiba

This genus has been separated from *Thuja* to accommodate the single species *Thujopsis dolabrata* (Japan), which differs from *Thuja* in having much more flattened branchlets and each fertile cone-scale maturing three to five seeds, unlike *Thuja*, which matures just two.

    The Hiba Arbor-vitae is a pyramidal tree to 50 ft (15 m), often shrubby in cultivation. The scale leaves are decussate, 0.16–0.25 in (4–6 mm) long, the lateral more or less spreading and acute, the facial obtuse, both virtually white beneath except for a thin green margin. Female cones are broadly ovoid to 0.6 in (15 mm) long, comprising six to eight scales each with a subapical boss or mucro on the outside; the upper pair of scales are sterile and bear winged seeds.

    In cultivation the Hiba is hardy in temperate regions where it thrives on well-drained soils. It is increasingly planted for its handsome and pleasing appearance. It can be distinguished immediately from typical species of *Thuja* by its broader branchlets, its often much denser habit toward the base, the much more rounded cones, and thicker cone-scales. Several cultivars of Hiba have been developed, including the golden-yellow-leaved 'Aurea,' the variegated 'Variegata,' and the dwarf 'Nana.'

    The soft, durable wood is much used locally in Japan for general construction work and the bark is processed for caulking boards. **CZ7**

Libocedrus

Southern Incense Cedars

As now understood, *Libocedrus* comprises five species: two native to New Zealand and three to New Caledonia. They are evergreen trees and shrubs with the branchlets flattened into spray-like phyllomorphs. The juvenile leaves are short and needle-like, the adult ones scale-like, arranged in

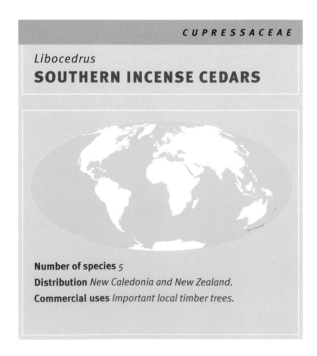

CUPRESSACEAE

Libocedrus
SOUTHERN INCENSE CEDARS

Number of species 5
Distribution *New Caledonia and New Zealand.*
Commercial uses *Important local timber trees.*

decussate pairs and mostly dimorphic. Male and female cones occur on the same tree. Mature cones comprise two pairs of decussate, woody, valvate scales, but only the upper pair is fertile. Each scale is more or less dorsally spined, the fertile scales producing one or two unequally winged seeds.

Only two species are found in cultivation and then only rarely. Pahautea (*L. bidwillii*) is from New Zealand, where it grows at altitudes of up to 6,500 ft (2,000 m) and reaches a height of 82 ft (25 m). Its ultimate branchlets are flattened and the juvenile leaves markedly dimorphic—the facial about 0.04 in (1 mm) long, the lateral about 0.12 in (3 mm). Adult leaves are scale-like, adpressed, triangular, and all about 0.08 in (2 mm) long. Female cones are ovoid, about 0.4 in (10 mm) long, the four scales each with a spine-like horn and the two fertile scales each maturing a single seed. Kawaka (*L. plumosa* = *L. doniana*), also from New Zealand, reaches a height of 110 ft (33 m). Its branchlets are distinctly flattened and the juvenile leaves very dimorphic—the laterals to 0.2 in (5 mm) long, the facial barely 0.04 in (1 mm). The adult scale leaves overlap and are adpressed, subequal, the laterals about 0.12 in (3 mm) long, the facial just over 0.04 in (1 mm). Female cones are ovoid, finally 0.4–0.6 in (10–15 mm) long, each of the four scales with a curved dorsal spine. One seed is produced on each fertile scale. Both these species are only marginally hardy in temperate areas. The wood is of some economic value, fragrant, and durable.

The following species remain in the genus *Libocedrus*, again in the narrowest sense: *L. austro-caledonica*, *L. bidwillii*, *L. chevalieri*, *L. plumosa*, and *L. yateensis*. **CZ9**

Calocedrus
Northern Incense Cedars

Calocedris comprises three species found respectively on the Pacific coast of North America, in China, and in Taiwan. They are evergreen trees with their ultimate branchlets (sprays or phyllomorphs) flattened. The leaves are scale-like, flattened, decussately arranged, with the edges of the lateral ones overlapping and virtually equal in length to the facial ones; both sets are adpressed except at their slightly recurved pointed apices. The cones are unisexual and typically on different branches of the same tree, rarely on separate trees. The male cone is oblong, comprising between six and sixteen decussate pollen sacs. The female cone is elliptic-oblong, comprising three pairs of finally woody, imbricate scales, each scale with a subapical recurved thorn-like process. Only the middle pair of scales is fertile, each bearing two ovules; the inner-most pair is fused together, and the outermost (lowest) pair much shorter and recurved. The cone matures in one year, each seed with two very unequal wings.

The three species were formerly included under *Libocedrus*, in the widest sense, one character separating them out being that the facial and lateral scale leaves are

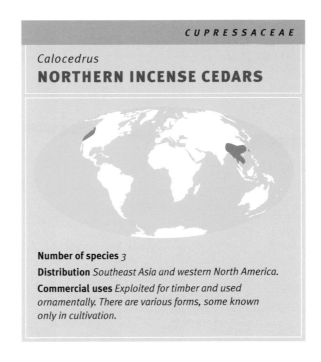

CUPRESSACEAE

Calocedrus
NORTHERN INCENSE CEDARS

Number of species *3*
Distribution *Southeast Asia and western North America.*
Commercial uses *Exploited for timber and used ornamentally. There are various forms, some known only in cultivation.*

nearly equal in length. The Incense Cedar (*C. decurrens*, formerly *Libocedrus decurrens*) grows to 150 ft (45 m) in its native habitat and has an elongated conical canopy in the wild state. Its bark is deeply furrowed and reddish-brown. The leaves are long decurrent, those on the ultimate lateral branches about 0.12 in (3 mm) long, but up to 0.5 in (12 mm) on the main branches with juvenile leaves even longer. Male cones are 0.25 in (6 mm) long, the females ovate, 0.71–0.98 in (18–25 mm) long, pendulous, fleshy at first, finally woody. It is native to Oregon and western Nevada to lower California, growing at altitudes between 3,280 and 9,020 ft (1,000 and 2,750 m).

The Incense Cedar is by far the best known of the species, is fully hardy and is widely planted in temperate regions. There are at least six cultivars, but 'Columnaris,' with its narrow columnar canopy, is most common in cultivation. It is not particular as to soil, but flourishes in a moist, well-drained loam away from atmospheric pollution. Propagation is best from seeds, but cuttings may be taken. The wood is light, resistant to decay, and fragrant. It is used for pencils and general carpentry, boxes, fence posts, etc.

Calocedrus macrolepis is a tree to 115 ft (35 m), which differs from the previous species by its larger leaves on the ultimate lateral branchlets—0.25–0.3 in (6–8 mm) long—and only one seed is usually produced on each fertile scale. It is rare in its native habitat of south China to the Myanmar border and not really hardy in cultivation, but may be grown in warmer parts of temperate regions.

Calocedrus formosana is very close to *C. macrolepis* in form but its leaves are only 0.08 in (2 mm) long, with two stomatal lines on the lateral leaves, whereas there are typically four in *C. macrolepis*. It is native to the broadleaved forests of Taiwan ascending to altitudes of nearly 6,560 ft (2,000 m) and is little known in cultivation. **CZ7–9**

Mature species of *Calocedrus decurrens*, formerly known as *Libocedrus decurrens*, are, in their native habitats, impressive trees and favored as hardy ornaments in temperate regions.

Austrocedrus

Chilean Incense Cedar

Austrocedrus is a genus of one species, the Chilean Incense Cedar (*A. chilensis*), native to Chile and Argentina; it was formerly included under *Libocedrus*. It differs from this genus in having scale leaves that are much more strongly dimorphic—the facial ones being one-quarter (or less) the length of the lateral ones (one-half in *Libocedrus*)—blunter and rhombic to ovate as against triangular, and cones comprising four valvate scales, only two of which are fertile, each with one or two unequally winged seeds.

The Chilean Incense Cedar is an evergreen tree to about 82 ft (25 m) in its native habitat, but little more than 50 ft (15 m) when cultivated in temperate regions. The shoots are compressed, frond-like (phyllomorphs) with the leaves arranged in decussate pairs, the lateral ones 0.08–0.18 in (2–4.5 mm) long, the facial (upper and lower) ones rarely more than a quarter this length. The male cones are about 0.12 in (3 mm) long, and comprise numerous pollen sacs. The female cones are solitary and finally woody, each of the four valvate scales with a minute subterminal dorsal tubercle. Only the upper two scales are fertile, each about 0.3–0.5 in (8–12 mm) long, and therefore much longer than the lower two sterile scales.

The tree is reasonably hardy in temperate regions, where it favors moist but well-drained soils. However, since its attractive qualities are few, it is little planted outside botanical collections. Propagation is usually by cuttings, but seeds can be used. The wood is scented and durable and has been used for general carpentry purposes. **CZ8–9**

ABOVE LEFT *Pilgerodendron uviferum*, an Andean species, yields valuable timber in its native habitat.

LEFT The typical scale-like leaves of the Chilean Incense Cedar (*Austrocedrus chilensis*) which feature a paired arrangement.

Papuacedrus

Papuacedrus

The single species of this genus of evergreen trees from the Moluccan Islands and New Guinea was formerly classified as three doubtfully distinct species, and placed in *Libocedrus* (taken in the widest sense), but it differs from that genus (in the narrowest sense) in leaf form and anatomy and cone structure. Male cones comprise numerous whorled bracts that are not decussately arranged. Female cones have four valvate scales each with a dorsal, short, stumpy spine; only the upper, much larger pair of scales is fertile and these mature into four very equally winged seeds.

Papuacedrus papuaria ssp *arfakensis* grows up to an altitude of 3,300 ft (1,000 m) on the Arfak Mountains of New Guinea. It is a tree up to 115 ft (35 m) with a more or less pyramidal form and red, scaly bark. The juvenile leaves are up to 0.8 in (2 cm) long, almost herbaceous, with a slender spreading point. The facial pair are more or less overlapped by the lateral pair, both pairs tapering downward; the greatest width of about 0.4 in (10 mm) occurs just below the spreading point. The adult leaves are smaller, darker green, widening upward to an erect blunt apex. Female and male cones occur on different branches of the same tree. The two upper (inner) fertile scales are narrowly ovate, each about 0.5 × 0.3 in (12 × 8 mm). The species is not extensively cultivated. **CZ9**

Pilgerodendron

Pilgerodendron

This genus contains a single species formerly placed under *Libocedrus* from which it differs in leaf form and arrangement, and cone structure. Pilgerodendron uviferum is restricted to the Andes of southern Chile and Argentina—including Tierra del Fuego. It is an evergreen tree to 80 ft (25 m), rarely a shrub. The branchlets are quadrangular in outline. Leaves are scale-like, boat-shaped, 0.12–0.3 in (3–8 mm) long, opposite, and decussate. They are all similar in size, overlapping and adpressed to the shoots except at the somewhat spreading bluntish, slightly incurved tips, to which they taper from a broad base.

The cones are 0.3–0.5 in (8–12 mm) long, ovoid, and comprise two pairs of woody, valvate scales, each scale with a subapical curved, dorsal spine. Only the upper pair of scales is fertile, each scale with one, rarely two, ovules; the lower sterile pair is much smaller. The seeds have very unequal wings. *Pilgerodendron uviferum* is sometimes mistaken for *Fitzroya cupressoides*, whose leaves are wider above, narrowing to a decurrent base, and the cones have three pairs of scales.

The species is rare in cultivation, but its timber is extensively used in its native area. **CZ9**

Callitris

Cypress Pines

Callitris is a genus of some fourteen species native to Australia, particularly dry and arid regions. They are evergreen trees or shrubs with sexes on the same plant. Adult leaves are scale like, arranged in alternating whorls of three and adpressed, except at the tips; juvenile leaves are 0.25–0.5 in (6–12 mm) long, arranged in whorls of four. Male cones are solitary or clustered, small and cylindrical to oblong. Female cones are mostly 0.8–1.2 in (2–3 cm) long, globular to narrowly pyramidal, solitary or clustered, and comprising six to eight thick, woody, often pointed, unequal valvate scales that are grossly warted, veined, or smooth on the back. Two to nine seeds are produced per scale, each with one to three wings.

Tetraclinis and *Widdringtonia* are closely related genera (the cones are normally composed of no more than four scales). *Tetraclinis* has its leaves in fours; in *Widdringtonia* they are arranged alternately in opposite pairs.

In north temperate zones, for example Europe, cypress pines require a cool greenhouse, except in the warmest parts. The most frequently cultivated species include the following. The Murray River Pine or White Cypress Pine (*Callitris columellaris* = *C. arenosa*), from New South Wales and the southern coast of Queensland, is a shrub or slow-growing tree to 82 ft (25 m). Its wood is very fragrant, insect resistant, and much used for panels and cabinetmaking. The Black or Red Cypress Pine (*C. endlicheri*), from New South Wales, northeast Victoria, and Queensland, grows to the same height. Its finely figured wood is much used for paneling. The Rottnest Island Pine or Common Cypress Pine (*C. preissii* = *C. robusta*), from southern and western Australia, is a low shrub or tree to 100 ft (30 m). The Oyster Bay Pine or Port Jackson Pine (*C. rhomboidea*), a tree to 33–50 ft (10–15 m), is widely distributed in Australia but only locally frequent; it is also naturalized in New Zealand. The Tasmanian Cypress Pine (*C. oblonga*) from Tasmania is a bush or small tree to 26 ft (8 m).

Cypress pine wood is close-grained, hard, fragrant, and takes a good polish. Often its grain patterns are quite striking. The presence of natural preservatives adds to its resistance to insect and fungal attack. It is used for general carpentry and building, furniture, and turnery. The bark can be slashed for resin and is an economic source of tannins; the cones, leaves, and shoots can be distilled for their fragrant principles. **CZ9**

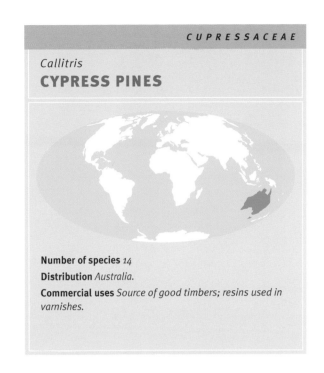

CUPRESSACEAE

Callitris
CYPRESS PINES

Number of species *14*
Distribution *Australia.*
Commercial uses *Source of good timbers; resins used in varnishes.*

Actinostrobus

Actinostrobus

This genus has three species of monoecious trees native to western Australia. The thick leaves, in spirals of three, are closely pressed to the stem. The female cones are globose and woody, and bear winged seeds. The genus is differentiated from *Callitris* on account of the presence of sterile bracts at the base. It is cultivated as an ornamental. **CZ9**

Rottnest Island Pines, (*Callitris preissii*) have greatly divided branches and scalelike adult leaves.

Juniperus

Junipers

There are about fifty species of evergreen trees and shrubs in the genus *Juniperus*, commonly known as junipers. They are widely distributed throughout the northern hemisphere, from the mountains of the Tropics as far south as the Equator and ranging as far north as the Arctic. The Common Juniper (*J. communis*) is extremely widespread in temperate regions, forming dominant scrub on chalk, limestone, and slate.

Junipers have leaves of two kinds: the normal adult leaves are small, scale-like, and decussate, closely pressed to the shoot, crowded, and overlapping; the juvenile leaves are larger and awl-shaped (acicular), growing in threes or opposite pairs at a node. In a number of species the awl-shaped, juvenile leaves are the only ones present. They do not always connect smoothly with the stem (on which, in some species, they are decurrent) but sometimes there may be some kind of constriction at the junction with the stem, as in *J. communis*, where the leaf base is swollen, the swollen tissue being virtually free of the stem. There is thus a constriction between the swollen leaf-base and the stem, the actual connection between the two being much narrower.

Such leaves are referred to as "jointed."

The scale-like leaf margin (lens) is denticulate in some species but smooth (entire) in others. The cones are unisexual, borne either on different plants or separately on the same plant. Male cones are solitary or in more or less crowded catkins; the female cones consist of three to eight fleshy, pointed scales, which coalesce and finally form a more or less globular body or "berry." This so-called berry is often coated and bloomed, with subtending scaly bracts; it matures in the second or third year. There are between one and twelve seeds, according to species.

Propagation is readily effected from seed but germination may be delayed up to about one year. Cultivars and varieties are increased by cuttings from the current year 5 shoot or by grafting on the appropriate stocks.

Juniperus virginiana, known as the Red or Pencil Cedar, is one of the largest conifers cultivated as an ornamental. It prefers a well-drained soil, particularly a chalky one.

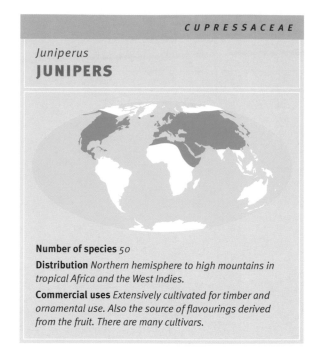

CUPRESSACEAE

Juniperus
JUNIPERS

Number of species 50
Distribution *Northern hemisphere to high mountains in tropical Africa and the West Indies.*
Commercial uses *Extensively cultivated for timber and ornamental use. Also the source of flavourings derived from the fruit. There are many cultivars.*

Juniper wood is generally durable and easy to work; the presence of oils is probably responsible for the juniper's resistance to many insect attacks. The timber is used in general building, for roof shingles, furniture, posts, and fences. In Myanmar, *J. recurva* var *coxii* is the favored wood for coffins. *Juniperus virginiana*, popularly known as the Pencil Cedar, is extensively used in the manufacture of pencils. Cedar wood oil is obtained from a distillation of the sawdust and shavings and, until recently, was the main "immersion oil" used in the highest power light microscopy. *Juniperus oxycedrus* (Prickly Juniper) yields Oil of Cade (*Oleum cadinum*) or juniper tar by distillation of the wood. This oil was once widely used as a treatment for skin diseases—especially psoriasis—but is now largely replaced by coal-tar products, which prove more effective. It is also used in the perfumery industry. Oil of juniper is distilled from the fully grown but unripe berries of *Juniperus communis* and is responsible for the characteristic flavor of gin. It is added to the rectified spirit obtained after fermentation of the mixed grain mash or the spirit is redistilled together with the berries. The word "gin" is a corruption of Geneva, derived from the French word *genévrier,* meaning juniper, and has nothing to do with the eponymous Swiss city. Oil of Savin, from *J. sabina*, is obtained by distilling fresh leaves and shoots. It is a powerful diuretic and has been used as an abortifacient.

Junipers are slow-growing and hardy, and a number of species are frequently grown as ornamentals in parks, large gardens, and graveyards. The most popular species are the Chinese Juniper (*J. chinensis*) and the Pencil Cedar. Dwarf and prostrate forms suitable for ground cover and in rock gardens include the Creeping Juniper (*J. horizontalis*), the Procumbent Juniper (*J. procumbens*), and dwarf cultivars of the Common Juniper, 'Compressa' and 'Stricta.' **CZ2–9**

The Main Species of *Juniperus*

Group I: Caryocedrus Leaves always awl-shaped (acicular) and spreading, in threes, jointed at base, and decurrent on the shoot; white-banded (from stomata) on upper surface. Cones axillary, sexes on separate plants; seeds usually 3.

J. drupacea **Syrian Juniper.** Greece, Asia Minor, Syria. Tree 33–40 ft (10–12 m), usually narrowly pyramidal. Leaves decurrent on stem, narrowly lanceolate, 0.06–1 × 0.01–0.02 in (15–25 × 3–4 mm), 2 white bands on upper side, separated by green midrib, except sometimes at apex. Berries globose to broadly ovoid, 0.6–1 in (1.5–2.5 cm). **CZ8**

Group II: Oxycedrus Leaves always awl-shaped (acicular), in threes and jointed at base but not decurrent on the shoot, white-banded (from stomata) on upper surface.

J. communis **Common Juniper.** Cosmopolitan. Shrub or tree to about 40 ft (12 m). Leaves more or less awl-shaped hard-pointed and skin-piercing, 0.4–0.6 × 0.04–0.08 in (10–15 × 1–2 mm), the upper surface with a single white band, broader than the green margins but divided at the extreme base by the midrib. Berries globose to broadly ovoid, 0.02–0.024 in (5–6 mm), bluish-black. **CZ2–6**

'Hibernica' ('Stricta'). The Irish Juniper, has very dense foliage and short branches bending outward so that the upper surface, in the mass, presents a deep blue-green appearance; *J. communis* ssp *nana* (= *J. sibirica*), the Mountain Juniper, is a prostrate shrub about 1 ft (30 cm) high, the leaves scarcely prickly; it is characteristic of windswept areas—roughly arctic alpine Europe.

A number of other very closely related species have been described but are now regarded as geographical variations, eg var *depressa* from E N. America and var *hemispherica* from S. Europe.

J. rigida **Needle Juniper.** Japan, Korea, Manchuria. Tree to 42 ft (13 m), sometimes a shrub, with pendulous branches. Leaves narrowly awl-shaped, 0.5–1 × 0.04 in (13–25 × 1 mm), sharply pointed, deeply grooved on upper surface with the single white band narrower than the green margins; keeled below. Berries globose, about 0.2–0.3 in (6–8 mm) across, brownish-black. **CZ6**

J. oxycedrus **Prickly Juniper.** Spain, N. Africa, through Syria to the Caucasus. Shrub or small tree to 33 ft (10 m). Leaves linear-lanceolate, 0.5–0.7 × 0.04–0.6 in (12–18 × 1–1.5 mm), apex piercing sharp, the upper surfaces with 2 white bands separated by a narrow green midrib and surrounded by a narrow green marginal band. Berries globose, 0.25–0.5 in (6–12 mm) diameter, distinctly reddish-brown. **CZ9**

The Utah Juniper, *Juniperus osteosperma*, is a short tree that may live as long as 650 years. Under severe conditions of aridity these junipers persist in very stunted forms.

J. communis

J. oxycedrus

J. communis

J. chinensis
male flowers

J. virginiana

J. chinensis fruit

TOP RIGHT The aptly named Prickly Juniper, *Juniperus oxycedrus*, has the characteristic spinelike leaves that minimize transpiration in the plant's native dry habitats.

Group III: Sabina Leaves predominantly scale-like, at least on adult plants, but sometimes wholly awl-shaped (acicular); awl-shaped leaves, when present, always decurrent on the shoot and in opposite pairs or threes. Cones terminal.

J. recurva Drooping Juniper. Myanmar, SW China, E Himalaya. Shrub or small tree to 33 ft (10 m), with spreading, pendulous branches. Leaves only awl-shaped and in threes at a node, crowded, and overlapping, 0.1–0.25 × 0.04 in (3–6 × 1 mm), sharp-pointed, white-banded above without a green midrib; not jointed at base. Berries ovoid, 0.3–0.4 in (8–10 mm), dark purplish-brown to black. **CZ8**

var *coxii* (Coffin Juniper) is a large tree with larger, less crowded leaves, about 0.4 in (1 cm) long, the upper surface of each leaf with 2 whitish bands on upper surface. It is sometimes considered a distinct species but, when typical, is probably only an extreme form of a variable species; there are intermediates.

J. phoenicia Phoenician Juniper. Mediterranean region including Algeria, Canary Islands. Shrub or tree to 20 ft (6 m). Leaves predominantly scale-like, imbricate, and closely adpressed, in threes or opposite pairs, 0.04 in (1 mm) long, blunt-tipped, the margin denticulate; awl-shaped leaves (rarely present) about 0.25 in (6mm) long, 3 at a node. Berries more or less globose, about 0.3 in (8mm) across, brown or reddish-brown. Specimens on the Canary Islands reach an exceptional size and may be 1,000 years old. They have been described as a separate species (*J. canariensis*), but this is not generally accepted. **CZ8–9**

J. thurifera Spanish Juniper. SW Europe, N. Africa, Asia Minor, and the Caucasus. Tree to 40 ft (12 m). Scale leaves more or less diamond-shaped, opposite and decussate, imbricate

and closely adpressed, sometimes in threes on leading shoots; awl-shaped leaves in opposite pairs, 0.2 in (5–6 mm) with 2 whitish bands on each upper surface; margin denticulate. Berries globose, about 0.3 in (8 mm) in diameter, blue or bluish; seeds about 4. **CZ9**

J. chinensis Chinese Juniper. The Himalaya, China, Mongolia, Japan. Tree to 66 ft (20 m), sometimes a low shrub. Leaves either wholly scale-like, diamond-shaped, crowded, imbricate, and closely adpressed, 0.06 in (1.5mm) with blunt tip, or with a few awl-shaped leaves 0.03–0.05 in (8–12 mm), 3 at a node (less often in opposite pairs), with 2 white bands on upper surface, separated by a green midrib; margin entire; apex spiny and skin-piercing. Berries more or less globose, 0.2–0.3 in (6–8 mm) across, brown. A variable species with numerous cultivars. **CZ3–9**

J. sabina Savin. C Europe. Shrub to 16 ft (5 m), the bruised foliage having an unpleasant smell and a bitter taste. Leaves predominantly scale-like, diamond-shaped, imbricate, and closely adpressed, about 0.04 in (1 mm) with a dorsal gland; awl-shaped leaves 0.2 in (5 mm), sharply pointed, each with a glaucous upper surface and prominent green midrib; margin entire. Berries globose to ovoid, 0.25 in (5–6 mm) across, brownish or bluish-black, pendulous. Numerous cultivars. **CZ2–3**

J. virginiana Red or Pencil Cedar. E and C U.S. Tree to 100 ft (30 m), with ascending or spreading branches, ultimate branchlets no more than 0.04 in (1 mm) thick. Leaves predominantly scale-like, imbricate, and closely adpressed, 0.06 in (1.5mm), apex pointed, diverging, and with a small dorsal gland; awl-shaped leaves spiny-pointed, opposite or 3 at a node, 0.2–0.25(0.3) in (5–6(8) mm), and glaucous above; margin entire. Berries ovoid or subglobose, about 0.25 in (6 mm), bluish-glaucous. Numerous cultivars. **CZ9**

Fitzroya

Patagonian Cypress

Fitzroya comprises a single evergreen species (*F. cupressoides*) from Chile and Argentina where it may live to 3,000 years. It grows to 165 ft (50 m) in the wild, and the trunk has a diameter of 30 ft (9 m), with characteristic reddish, furrowed bark. The leaves are spreading and typically arranged in whorls of three (rarely opposite). They are ternate, dark green, obovate, about 0.12 in (3 mm) long, and narrowing into flat decurrent bases, the free end more or less spreading, but with an incurved tip. Male and female cones occur separately on the same trees or on different trees, although some cones may be bisexual. The solitary male cones have up to twenty-four pollen sacs. The female cones comprise three alternating whorls, each whorl of three valvate scales, the lower smallest whorl sterile, the uppermost always fertile and the middle whorl sometimes fertile. They are finally woody, globose, 0.25–0.3 in (6–8 mm) in diameter, the fertile scales bearing two to six seeds each with two or three wings. The mature cone bears a terminal gland, which secretes a fragrant resin.

The Patagonian Cypress is reasonably hardy when cultivated in temperate zones, but then it is often shrubby. Propagation is usually from cuttings taken toward the end of summer, since many cultivated trees are only female, thus setting no seed. The wood yields a valuable timber not unlike that of the redwoods and is used for general construction work locally. **CZ8**

Widdringtonia

African Cypresses

Widdringtonia comprises three species from tropical and southern Africa. They are mostly evergreen trees, rather like *Callitris,* but the adult leaves are smaller and decussate (three-ranked in *Callitris*) and the slender, adpressed base of each scale leaf suddenly expands into an obtuse, incurved,

broad, mucronate apex. The leaves of juvenile plants are needle-like and spirally arranged. Male and female cones occur on separate trees. Mature cones are woody, more or less globose, mostly comprising four similar cone-scales, each with five or more ovules. The seeds are two-winged.

Cypress pines are not generally hardy in temperate regions, although the following two species are marginally hardy in warmer parts of this region. The Berg Cypress (*Widdringtonia cupressoides*), from Table Mountain to Drakensburg in South Africa, is a shrub to 10–13 ft (3–4 m). Its main branches are 4–8 in (10–20 cm) in thickness, the juvenile leaves 0.5 × 0.04 in (12 × 1 mm), and the adult leaves scalelike. The cones comprise virtually smooth scales that are 0.5–0.7 in (12–18 mm) long; 20–30 seeds are produced by each cone.

The Clanwilliam Cedar, Cape Cedar, or Cedarboom (*W. cedarbergensis,* syn *W. juniperoides)* from South Africa's Cedarberg Mountains to an altitude of 4,300 ft (1,300 m), is a tree to nearly 66 ft (20 m), though it is smaller and more bushy in cultivation. The juvenile leaves are 0.6–0.7 × 0.04 in (15–18 × 1 mm) and the adult leaves are scale-like. Mature cones are solitary, borne on short laterals, globose, 0.3–0.7(1) in (8–18(25) mm) across, comprising four, exceptionally six, rough and spine-tipped scales. The timber of this species has some commercial value for furniture and cabinetmaking, while its good resistance to insect attack makes it suitable for fencing posts. **CZ6**

Neocallitropsis

Neocallitropsis

The single member of this genus, *Neocallitropsis pancheri* (syn *N. araucanoides)* from New Caledonia, is related to *Callitris* but has the habit of *Araucaria.* It is a tree to 33 ft (10 m), its branchlets clothed with eight vertical rows of stiff, incurved leaves so that each branchlet has a cylindrical shape. Each leaf is about 0.25 × 0.2 in (6 × 5 mm), keeled below with a pointed apex and serrulate margin. The male cones are ovoid, 0.5 × 0.25 in (12 × 6 mm) comprising about eight rows of bracts bearing sessile pollen sacs. The female cones are terminal and borne on short laterals, each cone consisting of two alternating whorls of four narrowly pointed bracts, each bract maturing a single seed. (In *Callitris* there is only one whorl of six or eight alternating long and short scales.)

This species is very rare in cultivation. **CZ9**

ABOVE *Widdringtonia nodiflora* syn *cupressoldes* Is a common shrub of the Drakensburg flora of South Africa.

LEFT *Fitzroya cupressoides,* the single representative of the *Fitzroya* genus.

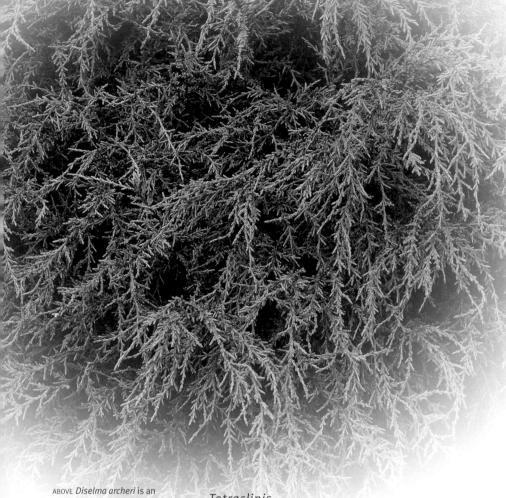

ABOVE *Diselma archeri* is an untidy-looking tree with straggling foliage.

Diselma

Diselma

Diselma

This genus comprises a single species (*Diselma archeri*), which was formerly placed in the genus *Fitzroya*. It is endemic to western Tasmania and Lake St. Clair, where it grows at altitudes of a little over 3,300 ft (1,000 m). It grows to about 26 ft (8 m) and is characterized by minute, decussate or whorled, closely adpressed scale-like leaves, which are blunt, about 0.04 in (1 mm) long, and pear-shaped. Male and female cones are borne on separate plants. The female cones are subglobose, about 0.08 in (2 mm) across, comprising four scales, only the upper (inner) pair of which is fertile. Each fertile scale gives rise to two three-winged seeds. *Diselma* is of no known economic value and is very rare in cultivation. **CZ9**

Fokienia

Fokienia

Fokienia probably contains a single species (*F. hodginsii*), which is native to China, extending westward into Indochina. *Fokienia maclurei* is considered to be a synonym, while *F. kawaii* is doubtfully distinct. *Fokienia hodginsii* is an evergreen tree to 43 ft (13 m), with flattened branchlets arranged in one plane (phyllomorphs). Leaves are scale-like, 0.12–0.3 in (3–8 mm) long, and dimorphic—the shorter ones on older trees. Their apices are pointed or blunt and they are arranged in four ranks, each set of four leaves of equal length, but with the facial pair narrower than the lateral pair. The female cones are globose, about 1 in (2.5 cm) in diameter, comprising twelve to sixteen peltate scales, the outside of each scale with a small papilla in a central depression. They ripen during the second year with two seeds per fertile scale. This unusual species is very rare in cultivation. **CZ9**

Tetraclinis

Tetraclinis

Tetraclinis articulata is the only member of this genus and is native to southern Spain, North Africa, and Malta. It is related to *Callitris* and *Widdringtonia*, but differs at a glance from these genera by having the branchlets (phyllomorphs) distinctly flattened and by its scale leaves, which are arranged in decussate pairs. It is an evergreen tree growing up to 150 ft (50 m) and has erect, articulated branches. The lateral scale leaves somewhat exceed the length of the facial ones, but both have long decurrent bases, the upper free parts more or less boat-shaped with pointed tips. Female cones are solitary, terminal, globose, and 0.3–0.5 in (8–12 mm) in diameter. They are composed of two pairs of nonpeltate woody scales, which are triangular in outline, with a blunt or pointed apex; all the scales are finally grooved or furrowed on the outer surface after separating and bear a very small subapical spine. Only the upper (inner) pair of scales is fertile, each producing two to nine broadly winged seeds.

Its ability to withstand high temperatures and extended periods of drought has led to the replanting of this species in its native areas. In cultivation it is only hardy in the warmest parts of the North Temperate Zone.

The wood has long been greatly esteemed, probably from Roman times; it is hard, sweet-smelling, often with attractive markings, and has been much used for cabinetmaking and high-class furniture. The trunk also yields a resin (commercially known as Sandarac) that is extensively used for the manufacture of varnish. **CZ9**

RIGHT Leaves of *Fokienia hodginsii* are in fours but flattened and amalgamated with only the points free. Each quartet of leaves becomes shorter with age until on flowering shoots they are quite blunt.

PODOCARPACEAE

Podocarpus
Podocarps and Yellow Woods

Podocarpus is a large genus of evergreen trees and shrubs commonly called podocarps or yellow woods on account of the distinctive color of their timber. Some species were formerly placed in the genus *Taxus* (yews) on account of their similar fleshy, edible, aril-covered seed. Sectioning of the genus is not easy and interpretation of the structure of some species is often difficult.

About 115 species have been described of which 94 are generally accepted as "good." They are natives of the Tropics, subtropics, and warm temperate regions of the Old and New Worlds, mainly the southern hemisphere.

Their leaves are mostly alternate, very variable in form, from small and scale-like up to 14 in (35 cm) long and 2 in (5 cm) wide with an equally variable anatomy, which is used in sectioning the genus. The sexes are typically on separate plants, rarely on the same. Male cones are either solitary or clustered. Female "cones" are often reduced to a short, stout stalk with two to four "bracts" of which only one is fertile, and bearing one, sometimes two, inverted ovules fused to these scale-like bracts. The latter either remain small or become more or less expanded above into an aril-like structure—the epimatium. In many species, the sterile "bracts" fuse with the upper part of the stout stalk to give an often brightly colored fleshy receptacle on which the seed matures. In some species this fleshy receptacle is edible. The seed is commonly ovoid or globose and resembles a drupe or nut with an outer layer that may be skin-like or more or less fleshy, surrounding a hard inner shell or "kernel." The homologies of this "cone" structure are not clear: the "bract" is thought to be a bract-scale and the epimatium an ovuliferous-scale.

The podocarps are important timber trees in their native areas. Fine timber is obtained from the South African species *P. falcatus* and *P. latifolius,* from two Australian ones, *P. elatus* and *P. amarus,* and, in New Zealand, from *P. totara*—the tree locally known as "Totara"—which is deeply rooted in the traditions of the Maoris.

Most species are not hardy in temperate regions, though there are some clear exceptions to this rule. The closely related Plum-fruited Yew (*Prumnopitys andinus*), for instance, forms a bushy tree that can be grown to form an excellent hedge, which often provides a welcome alternative to the Common Yew (*Taxus baccata*). It grows well on good soils overlying chalk. Other hardy species include *Podocarpus salignus, P. totara, P. alpinus,* and *P. nivalis*—the latter being the alpine Totara that is normally seen as a low-growing shrub forming a mound of prostrate stems. **CZ7–9**

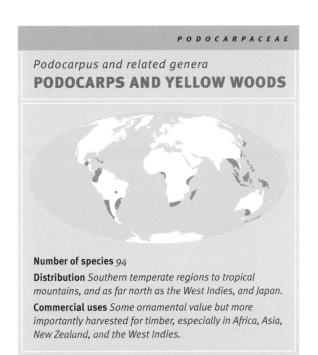

PODOCARPACEAE

Podocarpus and related genera
PODOCARPS AND YELLOW WOODS

Number of species 94

Distribution *Southern temperate regions to tropical mountains, and as far north as the West Indies, and Japan.*

Commercial uses *Some ornamental value but more importantly harvested for timber, especially in Africa, Asia, New Zealand, and the West Indies.*

The Outeniqua Yellow Wood, *Podocarpus falcatus,* is a forest tree from East and southern Africa and the source of quality timber. In their native habitats, mature specimens (this one is in South Africa's Tsitsikama National Park) can reach impressive heights of up to 150 ft (45 m).

The Main Species of *Podocarpus*

Leaves with hypoderm, hypodermal fibers, or well-developed transfusion tissue. Receptacle well developed, fleshy to leathery.

A *Leaves linear to narrow lanceolate, rarely reaching 1 × 0.5 in (25 × 12 mm), typically yew-like.*
B *Typically shrubs. Leaves rounded to slightly mucronate, not tapering; not in spikes.*

P. alpinus Mountains of Victoria, NSW (Australia), and New Zealand. Dense shrub, rarely a low tree to 13–16 ft (4–5 m). Leaves 0.25–0.5 in (6–12 mm) with essentially blunt apex; arranged in 2 ranks. Seed ovoid, 0.2–0.25 in (5–6 mm), single or paired, red, on fleshy receptacle. **CZ9**

    P. nivalis Alpine Totara. Mountains of New Zealand. Dense shrub to 6 ft (2 m). Leaves irregularly arranged, 0.25–0.75 in (6–18 mm), mucronate. Seed a small nutlet on red, fleshy base. **CZ7**

    BB *Trees with stiff, tapering, and acutely pointed leaves.*

    P. totara Totara. New Zealand. Massive tree to over 100 ft (30 m). Leaves irregularly arranged or two-ranked, 0.4–0.8 in (10–20 mm) long, up to 0.2 in (4 mm) wide on adult trees, almost sessile. Seeds mostly solitary, more or less globose, about 0.5 in (12 mm) across, on a red swollen receptacle. **CZ9** var *hallii* (sometimes seen as a distinct species) is similar but smaller, the leaves longer, seed acute not rounded.

AA *Leaves lanceolate to oval, over 1 in (25 mm), not yew-like.*

P. macrophyllus China, Japan. Small shrub or tree to 66 ft (20 m). Leaves densely and irregularly arranged 4(6) × 0.25 in (10(15) × 0.5 cm), with prominent midrib above. Male cones in clusters, female "cones" solitary; seeds elliptic-ovoid, about 0.4 in (1 cm) on purple, fleshy receptacle. Several varieties. **CZ9**
P. salignus Chile. Tree to about 66 ft (20 m). Leaves 2–4(5) × 0.2–0.3 in (5–10(12) × 0.4–0.6 cm), with prominent midrib above, often slightly falcate. Male cones solitary or few but not in spikes; female "cones" solitary; seeds more or less oblong about 0.3 × 0.12 in (8 × 3 mm), red, on slender-stalked fleshy receptacle. A valuable timber tree. **CZ9**
    P. nubigenus Chile, S Argentina. Tree to about 82 ft (25 m), or in cultivation sometimes a bush, and densely branched. Leaves irregularly arranged but sometimes in two ranks, 1–1.6 × 0.2–0.16 in (2.5–3.5 × 0.3–0.4 cm), with apical spine, straight to somewhat falcate and glaucous beneath. Male cones in clusters; seeds ovoid-oblong, about 0.3 in (8 mm) long on a swollen, fleshy receptacle. **CZ9**

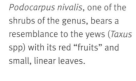

Podocarpus nivalis, one of the shrubs of the genus, bears a resemblance to the yews (*Taxus* spp) with its red "fruits" and small, linear leaves.

Other Genera of Podocarpaceae

Afrocarpus

Three species native to tropical and South Africa, once placed within the genus *Podocarpus* in section *Afrocarpus* but now considered distinct. Leaves alternate, more or less spirally arranged: stomata on both leaf surfaces.
A. dawei Uganda. Tree to 110 ft (33 m). Leaves leathery, 0.45–1.8 × 0.13–0.15 in (1.2–4.75 × 0.34–0.4 cm). Seeds brown to purple, bloomed, subglobose, about 0.8 in (2 cm) long. An important timber tree. **CZ9**

Dacrycarpus

A genus of nine species formerly placed within *Podocarpus* in their own section, now considered distinct. Their distribution is from Southeast Asia to New Zealand. Leaves awl-shaped, flattened, or both. Bract fused with outer seed coat and as long as seed: receptacle fleshy.
D. dacrydioides White Pine. New Zealand. Tree to over 165 ft (50 m). Leaves of young trees soft, flat, 0.3 in (8 mm), in a single row on either side of shoot (and on mature trees scale-like and spirally arranged—or may show both types). Seeds a black nut, 0.25 in (6 mm), on red fleshy stalk. Important timber tree. **CZ9**

Falcatifolium

A recently proposed genus, reported to contain five distinct species, from Malaysia to New Caledonia. **CZ9**

Halocarpus

A genus of three species native to New Zealand. Exhibits linear juvenile foilage becoming scale-like with age and densely clustered. Seeds with a white aril, or fine covering. One species, *Halocarpus biformis*, from the mountains of New Zealand, grows to 33 ft (10 m) tall, and is an important timber tree. **CZ9**

Lagarostrobus

One species, *Lagarostrobus franklinii* (Huon Pine), formerly described in the genus *Dacrydium* and native to Tasmania and New Zealand, forms this genus. The scale-like leaves have scattered white stomata on the upper surface, and the tiny cones are borne at the end of the drooping branch tips. An attractive tree with pendulous branchlets. The red timber is fragrant and used for building, furniture, and cabinetwork. **CZ9**

Lepidothamnus

A genus of three species allied to and formerly placed in *Dacrydium*, native to New Zealand and southern Chile. More shrub than tree-like, especially *Lepidothamnus laxifolius*, which tends to be procumbent, hence its use to reduce soil erosion. Leaves thin, spreading along filamentous branches, shortening and becoming thicker with age. Seeds covered in a distinctive red aril. **CZ9**

Nageia

A recently created genus for five species now considered distinct from the genus *Podocarpus* where they were formerly placed in their own section. Trees to 130 ft (40 m). Leaves more or less oppositely arranged, many-nerved, to 2 × 1 in (5 × 2.5 cm), half as broad as long; opposite or almost so. Native to Southeast Asia, some cultivated as ornamentals, especially *Nageia wallichiana*, the only conifer known to be native to India.

N. nagi China, Japan, Taiwan. Tree to about 82 ft (25 m), but mostly a bush in cultivation. Leaves leathery, ovate, 2 × 1 in (5 × 2.5 cm). Seeds plum-like about 0.5 in (1.25 cm) across on slightly thickened stalk. **CZ9**

Parasitaxus

A genus of a single species, *Parasitaxus ustus*, native to New Caledonia, and until recently included within *Podocarpus*. It is unique in being the only known coniferous parasitic species in the entire gymnosperms, parasitizing *Prumnopitys taxifolia*, also in the family Podocarpaceae. Leaves coppery-red, scale-like, and overlapping, to 3 ft (1 m) tall. **CZ9**

Prumnopitys

Eight species formerly placed in section *Stachycarpus* in the genus *Podocarpus*, native to Central and South America, New Zealand, and New Caledonia, now considered a distinct genus. Leaves lacking a hypoderm, not exceeding 0.2–1.4 in (0.5–3.5 cm), typically appearing to be arranged in 2 ranks; transfusion tissue absent. Receptacle little developed, typically not fleshy.

P. andinus Plum-fruited Yew. Andes region of S. Chile. Tree to about 55 ft (17 m) but mostly a much-branched shrub in cultivation. Leaves linear, 0.8–1.2 × 0.2–0.3 in (2–3 × 0.5–0.7 cm), often distinctly two-ranked with 2 glaucous bands beneath. Female "cones" arising from upper leaf axils on a scaly stalk; seeds with yellowish-green, white-speckled outer fleshy coating, subglobose, about 0.8 in (2 cm) across. **CZ9**

P. spicatus New Zealand. Tree 66–82 ft (20–25 m) with dense, finally erect shoots. Leaves somewhat scale-like, 0.2–0.5 in (6–12 mm), glaucous on each side of midrib below. Male cones sessile, each about 0.16 in (4 mm), about 20 grouped together on short (1 in/2.5 cm) stiff shoot; seeds globose, about 0.3 in (8 mm) across, black with glaucous bloom and without fleshy base. Wood deal-like and in general use. **CZ9**

P. ferrugineus New Zealand (mainly South Island). Tree to 55–100 ft (17–30 m). Leaves similar to those of the Common Yew (*Taxus baccata*), 0.7–1.2 × 0.08 in (18–30 × 2 mm) (but half this size on old trees), the margins more or less revolute. Male cones 0.2–0.6 in (6–18 mm), borne singly; female "cones" subsessile, also borne singly, about 0.6 in (18 mm), with short point, bright red with waxy bloom. Wood strong, hard, but requires treating with preservative for outdoor use. **CZ9**

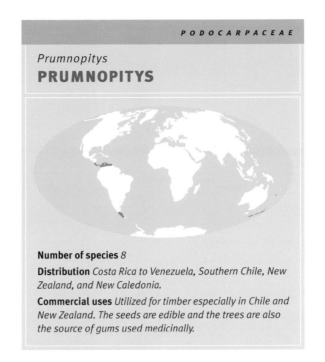

PODOCARPACEAE

Prumnopitys
PRUMNOPITYS

Number of species *8*

Distribution *Costa Rica to Venezuela, Southern Chile, New Zealand, and New Caledonia.*

Commercial uses *Utilized for timber especially in Chile and New Zealand. The seeds are edible and the trees are also the source of gums used medicinally.*

Retrophyllum

A genus of five species (generally composed of what was known as *Podocarpus* section *Polypodiopsis*). Leaves opposite and decussate, but mostly in one plane of two ranks; stomata on both leaf surfaces. The genus contains species from widely different areas: South America, the South Pacific Islands, New Caledonia, and Fiji. Little economic value, little cultivated. **CZ9**

Sundacarpus

Composed of a single species, *Sundacapus amara*. Leaves lacking a hypoderm and at least 2 × 0.25 in (5 × 0.6 cm), more or less spirally arranged around the branchlets; transfusion tissue present. Receptacle little developed and typically not fleshy. Native to northeast Australia, New Ireland, Philippines, and Indonesia. No ornamental value but limited timber use. **CZ9**

P. andinus

P. andinus

P. andinus

Dacrydium

Red Pines

Dacrydium is a genus of evergreen trees and a few shrubs represented by twenty to twenty-five species. These conifers are natives of New Zealand, Tasmania, Australia, New Caledonia, New Guinea, Malaya, the Philippines, Fiji, and Chile. The trees bear two types of foliage—juvenile, which is soft and awl-shaped (acicular), and adult, which is of small, densely arranged, overlapping, leathery scale-like leaves. Both types of foliage often occur on the same tree simultaneously. The two sexes occur on different plants. The male cones are produced in catkins in the axils of upper leaves, and female "cones" occur at or near the tips of branchlets. The seeds have an aril.

The genus, which includes many stately trees of ornamental importance, for example *D. cupressinum*, also comprises smaller species, among them *D. bidwillii*, the Mountain Pine of New Zealand, an erect or prostrate shrub of 2–10 ft (0.6–3 m) and with very widely spreading branches, and *D. laxifolium*, another prostrate shrub of New Zealand, which attains only a few inches in height.

Several species produce timber of economic value, among them the Red Pine (*D. cupressinum*), a native of New Zealand; this tree has a pyramidal shape reaching 60–100 ft (18–34 m) high with *Cupressus*-like branchlets. It produces a wood used for building, railway sleepers, furniture, and cabinetwork. The timber of the Westland Pine (*D. colensoi*) of New Zealand is also of economic value. **CZ9**.

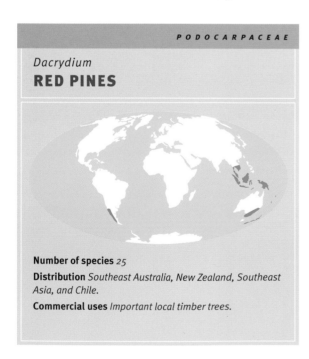

PODOCARPACEAE

Dacrydium
RED PINES

Number of species 25
Distribution *Southeast Australia, New Zealand, Southeast Asia, and Chile.*
Commercial uses *Important local timber trees.*

The drooping branchlets of *Dacrydium cupressinum* are typical of this genus.

Saxegothaea

Prince Albert Yew

Saxegothaea comprises a single species, the Prince Albert Yew (*S. conspicua*), from Chile. It is a remarkable evergreen, a more or less conical and bushy tree to 45 ft (13 m) with foliage resembling that of the true yew (*Taxus baccata*). The shoots are drooping and either opposite or in whorls of three or four. The leaves are more or less two-ranked, spirally inserted, linear, and 0.5–1 in (12–25 mm) long, each with a sharp, distinct horny point. Male and female cones are found on the same tree. The male cones are about 0.04 in (1 mm) long and borne near the shoot apex. The female "cones" are solitary, terminal, and comprise overlapping spine-tipped fleshy scales. The mature structure is cone-like but fleshy, subglobose, 0.5–0.8 in (12–20 mm) in diameter, the bluish-gray scales more or less connate, the upper ones each with two inverted ovules that ripen into broadly ovoid seeds that are about 0.16 in (4 mm) long with a small arillate edge.

The Prince Albert Yew is hardy in the warmer parts of the north temperate region, but shelter is advisable elsewhere. Propagation can be effected by cuttings, but it is a slow grower. The timber is durable and easy to work so that it is used locally for general carpentry. **CZ8**

Microstrobos

Microstrobos

Microstrobus comprises two species of evergreen shrubs characteristic of wettish habitats in Tasmania and southeast Australia. Their leaves are scale-like, overlapping, and spirally arranged in four or five rows. Female cones are very small, comprising four to eight glume-like bracts.

Both species are rare in cultivation, with *M. fitzgeraldi* (New South Wales) the most hardy in temperate zones, hence the most frequently seen. It is a bushy shrub up to 6.6 ft (2.2 m) tall with numerous long slender shoots. The leaves are 0.08–0.12 in (2–3 mm) long, diverge from the stem and are keeled, with an incurved tip. The female "cone" is 0.08–0.12 in (2–3 mm) long, the seed about equal in length to its subtending bract.

The second species, *M. niphophilus,* from the mountains of Tasmania, is a shrub to 6.6 ft (2 m) and is distinguished by its compact, bushy habit and even smaller leaves, which are more densely clustered. **CZ9**

Acmopyle

Acmopyle

Acmopyle comprises three species of evergreen trees with yew-like foliage that are native to New Caledonia and Fiji. They are not hardy in temperate zones, although *A. pancheri* (New Caledonia) is sometimes grown as a glasshouse subject. It is a tree up to 52 ft (16 m) tall with erect branches. The leaves are linear lanceolate, 0.3–0.8 × 0.08–0.12 in (8–20 × 2–3 mm) with obtuse apices and borne in two ranks. The upper leaf surface has broken white stomatic lines and the undersurface is more or less silvery. The male cones are 1.2–1.6 in (3–4 cm) long, borne terminally in clusters of one to three. The female cones are also terminal, each comprising up to nine sterile bracts and a single fertile apical bract, which are all fused together to form a fleshy, more or less warty, receptacle. The fertile bract bears a single globose seed that is longer than the receptacle. This genus is related to *Dacrydium* and *Podocarpus*, differing mainly in fruiting cone character, although some authorities place it in the yew family, Taxaceae. **CZ9**

Microcachrys

Microcachrys

This genus comprises a single species, *Microcachrys tetragona,* from the mountains of Tasmania. It is a straggling bush with a prostrate habit and slender four-angled branchlets. The leaves are scale-like with hairy margins, overlapping, 0.04–0.08 in (1–2 mm) long, and arranged in four ranks. Individual trees may be unisexual or bisexual. Male cones are ovoid, borne terminally, and about 0.12 in (3 mm) long; female "cones" are 0.25–0.3 in (6–8 mm), comprising numerous bracts. The mature cones are fleshy and a translucent red color—each bract with an inverted seed with a fleshy scarlet aril (or epimatium).

This species is marginally hardy in temperate zones although not common in cultivation, when it is sometimes staked for upright habit. It is particularly unusual in its attractive fruits, which yield fertile seeds. **CZ9**

LEFT *Saxegothaea conspicua* has dense evergreen foliage and a typically conical bushy form. It was first identified by Europeans during the mid nineteenth century, and was named in honor of Prince Albert, Queen Victoria's husband.

ABOVE The foliage and cones of *Microcachrys tetragona.*

PHYLLOCLADACEAE

Phyllocladus

Celery-topped Pines

Phyllocladus comprises some five species of evergreen trees and shrubs native to the Philippines, Borneo, the Moluccan Islands, and Australasia. Their striking feature is the flattened and expanded short shoots, which resemble and function as leaves (phylloclades, as in Butcher's Broom, *Ruscus* spp). The true leaves are scale-like and borne on the long shoots.

The following species are more or less hardy in the warmest parts of temperate regions but only marginally so at the limit of cultivation—often stunted with great reduction in size of the phylloclades. The Alpine Celery-topped Pine (*P. trichomanoides* var *alpinus*) from the North and South Island mountains of New Zealand is a bush or tree to 33 ft (10 m). The phylloclades are crenate to somewhat lobed, roughly diamond-shaped, 0.25–1.5 × 0.12–0.7 in (6–38 × 3–18 mm). The female "cones," each with three or four ovules, mature to a globose red fruit. The Celery-topped Pine, Tanekaha (*P. trichomanoides*) occurs throughout New Zealand up to 2,600 ft (800 m). It grows to 66 ft (20 m) with a trunk up to 10 ft (3 m) in diameter. The branches are in whorls, with the phylloclades often reddish-brown when young, up to 1 in (2.5 cm) long, ovate to oblong in outline, more or less lobed. The sexes are borne on the same plant, the female "cones" in groups of about seven mostly near the apex of terminal phylloclades. The fruit comprises a nut-like seed with a swollen, basal fleshy cup formed of fused scales. The wood of this species is of good quality and durability and the bark is rich in tannin from which a red dye is obtained. **CZ9**

CEPHALOTAXACEAE

Cephalotaxus

Cow's Tail Pines

Cephalotaxus comprises six species of evergreen trees and shrubs, native to China, Japan, and India (the Khasi Hills and Assam). The genus resembles *Torreya*, but the leaves are not spiny. The branches are opposite or whorled, with the young branchlets grooved and minutely white-pitted by stomata. The leaves are yew-like, spirally inserted, but, at least on lateral shoots, mostly appearing in two ranks, the upper leaf surface with a prominent midrib, the lower with two wide stomatic bands. The sexes are typically on separate plants, sometimes on the same, with male cones in globose heads in leaf axils and female "cones" at the base of branchlets, each comprising a few pairs of scales, and each scale bearing two ovules. Usually only one fertilized ovule in the whole "cone" matures in the second season to form a

stalked, protruding, green to purple, ellipsoid, drupe-like seed up to 1 in (2.5 cm) long, the outer layer finally fleshy and enclosing an inner woody "kernel."

The Chinese Plum Yew (*Cephalotaxus fortunii*) from central China is a small tree to 43 ft (13 m) in the wild but often an untidy shrub in cultivation. It has evergreen foliage and reddish-brown flaking bark, which peels away in flakes. The leaves are 2–3 in (5–8 cm) long, tapering gradually to a point in two horizontal ranks. The Japanese Plum Yew (*C. harringtonia*) is a similar tree and likewise mostly shrubby in cultivation. Its abruptly pointed leaves, 0.8–2 in (2–5 cm) long, are arranged in a V-shape on the shoot. It is the most widely cultivated species, and its two varieties, var *drupacea* and var *harringtonia*, are known only in cultivation. The cultivar 'Prostrata' provides useful ground cover.

Cephalotaxus species are hardy in temperate regions and require much the same conditions as yews (*Taxus* spp) although are somewhat less tolerant of chalk. Propagation is by seed or cuttings. They stand pruning well and are useful as hedging. The wood has some value, but the yield is low. **CZ6–9**

Amentotaxus

Amentotaxus

Amentotaxus comprises one to four species formerly placed in the Taxaceae. They are evergreen shrubs to small trees, native to India (Assam) and China, including Hong Kong. The shoots are opposite, the leaves decussate, needle-like, conspicuously keeled beneath, with a single whitish stomatal band on either side of the keel. Male and female cones are borne on separate plants, the male in sessile pendent groups of two to four (rarely one or five), the female stalked, solitary, in the axil of a bract, maturing to a drupe-like structure (the seed), which is surrounded by a more or less orange aril, open above with persistent scales at the base.

The type species is *A. argotaenia*, a shrub to 13 ft (4 m), with leaves 1.6–2.8 × 0.25 in (4–7 cm × 6 mm). It has probably not been cultivated. Other recorded species are *A. cathayensis*, and *A. yunnanensis* (China), *A. formosana* (Taiwan and China) **CZ6**.

Taxus

Yews

Yew is the popular name for the seven species (regarded by some as varieties of one species) of *Taxus*, a genus of evergreen trees, shrubs, and subshrubs (used for ground cover). Yews are widely distributed throughout the North Temperate Zone of the Old and New Worlds, with one species, the Chinese Yew (*T. mairei*), virtually on the Equator on the Indonesian island of Sulawesi. Though placed by many authorities in the order Coniferales, yews and other genera of the family Taxaceae lack the typical seed-bearing cone structure and do not have resin canals in the wood and leaves. For these and other reasons, fossil evidence included, the family is sometimes omitted from the Coniferales and transferred to a separate order Taxales.

The leaves of yews are linear and more or less spirally arranged on erect shoots but appear mostly two-ranked on horizontal shoots. Male and female cones are normally borne on different plants and are small and solitary. When ripe, the seed is nut-like and surrounded by a fleshy cup (aril), which is conspicuous by its usually scarlet color and is commonly referred to as a "berry" (strictly only angiosperms have berries). In the absence of its seeds, *Taxus* is often confused with *Abies* and *Tsuga*. It is at once distinguished by the underside of the leaves being uniformly yellow-green without conspicuous white stomatal lines, always evident in the other two genera. All parts of the plant, except the scarlet aril, are

ABOVE All yew species are poisonous, though historically they made popular subjects for topiary and often grace the grounds and parklands of large country houses in western Europe—as well as cemeteries. *Taxus baccata* 'Aurea' is a cultivar with leaves edged or lined with gold.

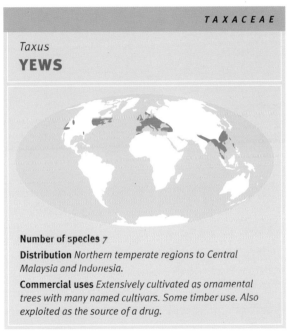

TAXACEAE

Taxus
YEWS

Number of species 7
Distribution *Northern temperate regions to Central Malaysia and Indonesia.*
Commercial uses *Extensively cultivated as ornamental trees with many named cultivars. Some timber use. Also exploited as the source of a drug.*

highly poisonous. The enclosed seed or "stone" of the aril also contains poison, so that children in particular should be discouraged from eating the tempting red fruit in case they swallow the stone. The poison is a mixture of alkaloids collectively referred to as taxine. Yew poisoning, resulting in gastroenteritis and heart and respiratory failure, is extremely serious, and fatal results in both humans and animals are well documented. In many temperate countries, veterinary surgeons consider the yews to be the most dangerous of all native trees and shrubs.

A grim feature of yew poisoning is that the main symptom is sudden death—within five minutes following some sort of convulsion. Thus, countermeasures are difficult and, in cattle, dangerous: opening the rumen, removing the contents, and replacing them with normal foodstuffs. The best approach, as always, is prevention. The poison is also found in dried parts of the plant, so these should be cleared away and burnt.

LEFT The Irish Yew, *Taxus baccata* 'Fastigiata,' is distinctly compact with erect branches.

Yews succeed well on almost any soil from peaty to calcareous, provided it is not liable to waterlogging, which may be fatal to the plant. Propagation is by seed, and for the cultivars by cuttings, grafting (on stocks of *Taxus baccata*), or by layering.

Yew wood is close-grained, durable, and hard but elastic. In Britain it was the traditional material for making bows and is still used for archery sports, being combined with hickory (*Carya*), the latter for the side facing the "string," the former on the side away from it. Despite its high quality, the wood is less popular now than formerly; it is used mainly for floor blocks, panels, posts, mallet heads, etc, and as a veneer in cabinetmaking.

About five species are known in cultivation, the most common being the Common Yew (*Taxus baccata*). In Britain this species has been associated with cemeteries and graveyards and many of these trees are of great age, typically around 1,000 years old. Whatever other reasons may be suggested for this association—religious, bow-making, etc.—there is the highly practical one that these places are least likely to be frequented by cattle and unaccompanied children who might otherwise be victims of its poisonous properties.

The Yew is also planted for ornament throughout western Europe and some of its cultivars make excellent hedges. It is a favorite subject for topiary work. **CZ2–9**

The Main Species of *Taxus*

Group I: Leaves gradually tapering, not abruptly pointed (but see *T. mairei*). Winter bud scales not keeled.

T. baccata **Common or English Yew.**
Europe, N. Africa, W Asia. Tree 40–66 ft (12–20 m), rounded head, sometimes with a few erect stems from the base as well as a main stem. Leaves 0.4–1 in (1–2.5 cm), usually in one plane on either side of stem, suddenly contracted into very short petiole. Seeds with a conspicuous scarlet fleshy edible cup (aril) surrounding an olive-brown poisonous seed 0.25 in (6 mm) long. Very many garden forms and cultivars.

T. cuspidata

T. baccata (topside)

T. baccata (underside)

'Fastigiata' Irish Yew. is a distinctly compact and columnar cultivar with upwardly directed branches. **CZ6**

Group II: Leaves abruptly pointed (but see *T. celebica*). Winter bud-scales keeled.

T. cuspidata **Japanese Yew.** Japan. Tree 52–66 ft (16–20 m). Leaves 0.6–1 × 0.08–0.12 in (1.5–2.5 cm × 2–3 mm), not obviously in one plane, but ascending on either side of the stem in a V-shape. Seeds much as in *T. baccata*. Several cultivars. **CZ4**

T. canadensis **Canada Yew.** Canada and NE U.S. Low, somewhat straggling shrub about 3.2 ft (1 m) tall. Leaves 0.5–0.8 × 0.04–0.08 in (1.3–2 cm × 1–2 mm), arranged horizontally in 2 ranks. Seeds as in *T. baccata*. **CZ2**

T. brevifolia **Western or American Yew.** W N. America (British Columbia, Washington, Oregon, California). Tree 16–50(82) ft (5–15(25) m), rarely shrubby. Leaves 0.4–1 × 0.08 in (1–2.5 cm × 2mm), arranged horizontally in 2 ranks. Seeds as in *T. baccata*. **CZ4**

T. mairei (*T. chinensis*) **Chinese Yew.** Widely distributed in China but extending to Taiwan, the Philippines, and Sulawesi, though there is doubt whether the extra China distributions represent the same species. Shrub or tree to about 40 ft (12 m). Leaves 0.6–1.6 × 1 in (1.5–4 × 2.4 cm), straight or slightly curved, tapering at the apex or more or less abruptly pointed, the lower surface densely covered with minute papillae. Seeds much as in *T. baccata*. This species is sometimes labeled *T. chinensis*. **CZ6**

T. baccata

LEFT The bright red arils of *Taxus baccata* are attractive to birds which ingest and disperse the seeds. The arils are the only part of the yew plant that are not poisonous.

Note: Two hybrids are also in cultivation: T. × hunnewelliana (T. cuspidata × T. canadensis) and T. × media (T. cuspidata × T. baccata).

Detail of the Japanese Nutmeg, *Torreya nucifera*, showing the linear, spiny leaves and lines of male cones that characterize the genus.

Torreya
Nutmeg Trees

Torreya comprises six or eight species of evergreen trees from East Asia and the United States. They are closely related to the yews (*Taxus* spp), but the branches and branchlets are opposite or almost so, the leaves pungent with a sharply pointed apex, and the lower side, which has a single resin canal, shows two narrow but distinct white to off-white stomatal bands. The sexes are mostly but not always on separate plants. The seed is drupe-like, being wholly surrounded by a thin fleshy layer, and requires two years to mature. In *Taxus*, the seed has a basal aril, the lower sides of the needles are uniformly pale yellowish-green, and there is no resin canal. Nutmeg trees are scarcely hardy except in the warmest parts of temperate regions.

The California Nutmeg (*T. californica*) is a tree to 66 ft (20 m) in its native habitat of coastal California, ascending to nearly 6,600 ft (2,000 m) in the Sierra Nevada. The second-year shoots are reddish-brown, the crushed leaves strongly aromatic, 1.2–2.4 × 0.12 in (3–6 cm × 3 mm). The seed is ovoid to 1.4 in (3.5 cm) long and purple-streaked.

The other main American species is the Florida Torreya or Stinking Cedar (*T. taxifolia*), a tree to 43 ft (13 m), rarely 60 ft (18 m), from southwest Florida with yellowish-green second-year shoots. The leaves are 1–1.2 × 0.12 in (2.5–3 cm × 3 mm), pungent (not unpleasant) when crushed; the stomatal bands not obviously in grooves. The obovoid seeds are 1–1.2 in (2.5–3 cm) long, with the same smell. It is the least hardy species.

The Chinese Torreya (*T. grandis* = *T. nucifera* var *grandis*) is a tree to 82 ft (25 m) from eastern and central China, but more usually a shrub in cultivation. Its second-year shoots

are yellowish-green. The leaves are virtually without smell when crushed and the stomatal bands are in grooves. The seeds are ellipsoidal.

The hardiest species is the Japanese Nutmeg or Torreya (*T. nucifera*), which is a tree growing to 82 ft (25 m) but, like the previous species, generally shrubby in cultivation. The second-year shoots are reddish-brown. The leaves are very aromatic when crushed and the stomatal bands are in grooves. The seeds are more or less ovoid, green tinged purplish-red, and are edible. However, they are not the source of the spice, which comes from the genus *Myristica*. **CZ7–9**

Austrotaxus
Austrotaxus

Austrotaxus comprises a single evergreen species from New Caledonia with the foliage of *Podocarpus*, but a seed like that of yews (*Taxus* spp). Its male cones are in spikes like some species of *Podocarpus*, but unlike *Taxus*, where they are in small stalked heads of some six to fourteen pollen sacs.

Austrotaxus spicata is a tree to 82 ft (25 m) with a bushy crown. It grows in moist woods on slopes at 1,300–3,300 ft (400–1,000 m). Leaves are linear, spirally arranged, 0.3–0.5 × 0.16 in (8–12 × 4 mm), with revolute margins, keeled below, grooved above, and the apex pointed. Male cones are axillary in dense spikes up to 0.6 in (15 mm) long; the females are solitary, giving rise to a single stone-like elliptical seed 0.5–0.6 in (12–16 mm) long, with a fleshy, yellowish, aril-like sheath. It has probably not been cultivated. **CZ9**

Pseudotaxus
Pseudotaxus

This genus comprises a single species from China, differing from *Taxus* in leaf epidermal structure, there being no papillae surrounding the stomatal openings, and in the presence of sterile scales in the male cone and a white, not red, aril surrounding the seed. *Pseudotaxus chienii* is an evergreen shrub that grows to 6.5–13 ft (2–4 m), with the sexes borne on separate plants. In the female cone there is a short stalk with about fifteen decussately arranged scale-like bracts, the uppermost and longest one 0.1–0.2 in (4–5 mm) long, concealing the young ovule. **CZ6**

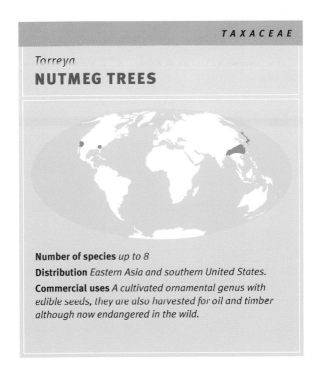

TAXACEAE

Torreya
NUTMEG TREES

Number of species *up to 8*
Distribution *Eastern Asia and southern United States.*
Commercial uses *A cultivated ornamental genus with edible seeds, they are also harvested for oil and timber although now endangered in the wild.*

Temperate Broadleaves

The term "broadleaved tree" is a convenient and popular one used to distinguish trees belonging to the class Angiospermae (flowering plants) from those belonging to the class Pinopsida (conifers). Within the flowering plants, broadleaves are normally considered to be only those trees belonging to the dicotyledons (subclass Dicotyledoneae)— those that have two seed leaves within each seed. Apart from the broadleaves, tree-like forms also occur in the other subclass (Monocotyledoneae) of flowering plants. Monocotyledons (seeds with one seed leaf) differ from "true" broadleaved trees, having typically fanlike leaves and "wood" produced by a quite different process. The main living tree representatives are the palms, considered in "Trees of the Tropics" (*see* pages 246–76).

Most broadleaved trees have leaves that are flattened, and their reproductive structures are borne in flowers, whereas the leaves of conifers are typically needle-like and the reproductive structures are borne in cones. Another vital difference (albeit microscopic) is that the female egg-containing body—the ovule—is enclosed in an ovary, as in all flowering plants, whereas in all gymnosperms, conifers included, it is not enclosed in an ovary but lies naked on the cone-scales. The structure of the wood differs too (*see* page 12).

Flowering plants are the dominant and most successful plants of the modern flora. In the course of evolution, angiosperms and gymnosperms diverged from a common stock, but the angiosperms are far more recent than the gymnosperms. However, the fossil record is scanty and incomplete. The earliest evidence of angiosperms is from the mid Jurassic period (136 to 190 million years ago), and their greatest development took place within the Tropics, primarily as trees. Tropical forests are the richest in flowering plant species and contain the greatest diversity of broadleaved trees in the world. From this evolutionary epicenter many species have migrated to temperate regions where there are seasonal changes of weather, including reduced and intermittent rainfall with alternating warm and cold periods of different intensity limits. Many broadleaved trees have adapted to such changes in the environment by evolving the deciduous habit, so that they pass the winter period in a state of dormancy, to grow again with the return of the warmth in spring.

Environmental and esthetic considerations apart, broadleaves are vital to the economies of most countries as sources of food, fuel, construction materials, paper, pulp, and related products, drugs, tannins, latex, and coloring and flavoring matters—and are horticulturally valued as ornamentals. For centuries, the exploitation of such products has been of crucial significance in the rise of civilizations, and ongoing rates of destruction (logging, burning, and the extension of grazing areas) of native forests, particularly in the Tropics, are of grave concern. In hand with global conservation measures and planting programs must go the curbing of the rich nations' ever-increasing demands for the products of broadleaves (which by their nature are slower to mature than the softwood conifers) and greater commitment to developing alternative materials in order to sustain—not destroy—the remaining natural forests.

Broadleaf Taxonomy

The botanical classification of broadleaved trees is more complex than that of conifers. There are some three to four hundred families of flowering plants but only a relatively small number (about eighty) are purely arborescent. Many angiosperm families contain herbs as well as trees, whereas all conifer families are made up of trees or tree-like shrubs. In evolutionary terms trees evolved before herbs, hence the most primitive family, Magnoliaceae, contains only trees and shrubs. Other so-called primitive traits can be recognized, including (with advanced conditions shown in parentheses): large regular flowers with numerous free parts (small irregular flowers with fewer and fused parts); superior ovaries of free carpels (inferior ovaries of fused carpels); dehiscent fruits (indehiscent fruits). One major branch of evolution has been the development of the wind-pollinated trees, in which petals and sepals are either absent or reduced and the flowers are typically arranged in pendulous catkins. These "anemophilous" trees produce copious amounts of pollen rather like the conifers, which are also wind-pollinated. Some authorities once viewed such wind-pollinated species as primitive, but they are now considered to have evolved from an angiosperm stock that had typical insect-pollinated flowers.

This section details those broadleaved genera whose members are either mainly native or cultivated in temperate and warm temperate regions, such as the Mediterranean and California. Each genus is placed within its family, with the families arranged in order of increasing evolutionary sophistication. The system of arrangement adopted here is based upon that of G.L. Stebbins in his *Flowering Plants—Evolution Above the Species Level*, with amendments for this edition based on D.J. Mabberley's *Plant-Book*.

FACING PAGE Elms (*Ulmus* spp), show a natural preference for riverine sites, but their range has been extended by planting.

Magnolia

Magnolias

The genus *Magnolia* has about a hundred species distributed in Southeast Asia and the Americas and provides some of the most popular ornamental trees and shrubs. The name commemorates Pierre Magnol (1638–1715), an early director of the botanic garden at Montpellier, France, and Professor of Botany and Medicine. The geographical range of the genus exhibits the same discontinuous type as that of *Liriodendron* (Tulip Tree) in the same family. In Asia *Magnolia* species occur in a triangular area extending from the Himalaya in the west, to Japan in the east, and south through the Malay Archipelago to Java. In North America they occur in the eastern United States and extreme southeast Ontario, and range southward into the West Indies, Mexico, and Central America to northern South America. Over fifty species are Asian, most montane, though a few are found at low altitudes, and over half the species are tropical. Only the temperate species can be cultivated outdoors in northern latitudes.

Magnolias have large simple alternate leaves and the flower buds are enclosed in a single scale. The large showy flowers are solitary and borne terminally on the shoots. The entire perianth is petaloid and comprises six or nine segments (exceptionally more) arranged in whorls. These segments, being neither distinctly sepals nor petals, are often referred to as "tepals," though in some cases the outer whorl may be reduced and sepal-like. The fruit is conical.

Magnolias have been cultivated outdoors in Europe for centuries. The first to arrive was the American *M. virginiana* in 1688. Four more American magnolias were brought to Europe by 1786, among them *M. grandiflora*, an evergreen species now widely planted in tropical countries as well as in temperate regions. The first Asian species to be introduced into Europe was *M. coco* (1786) from Java, a nonhardy evergreen shrub to about 3 ft (1 m) with night-scented flowers commonly grown in Southeast Asia. This was soon

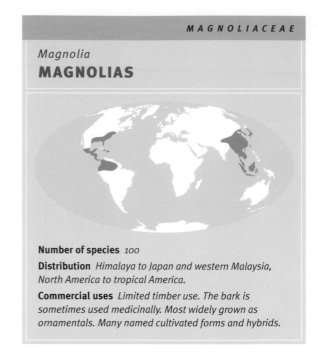

Magnolia
MAGNOLIAS

Number of species *100*

Distribution *Himalaya to Japan and western Malaysia, North America to tropical America.*

Commercial uses *Limited timber use. The bark is sometimes used medicinally. Most widely grown as ornamentals. Many named cultivated forms and hybrids.*

followed by the precocious (early)-flowered *M. heptapeta* (the Yulan of the Chinese) and the semi-precocious *M. liliflora*, two species already long cultivated in China and Japan. By the end of the nineteenth century seven other species had been introduced from North America and Japan, as well as the magnificent Himalayan *M. campbellii*; but it took until the twentieth century, largely as the result of the botanical exploration of west and central China, to complete the fine array of species now available for cultivation in temperate gardens. Currently there are about twenty-eight *Magnolia* species in outdoor cultivation in Europe and North America, three of which are evergreen.

The ever-rising popularity of magnolias as ornamental specimens owes mainly to the striking beauty of such deciduous, precocious-flowered species as *M. campbellii*, *M. sargentiana*, *M. dawsoniana*, *M. sprengeri*, *M. denudata*, *M. salicifolia*, *M. kobus*, and *M. stellata*. There are now also hybrids in increasing numbers, some of which have arisen spontaneously by accident, others the result of deliberate cross-fertilization. The most frequently grown hybrid is *M.* × *soulangiana* (*M. heptapeta* × *liliflora*), which was first grown in Europe during the 1820s and is now represented by many cultivars.

Magnolias favor a well-drained soil with ample humus. Some of them are lime tolerant, others not. Several species produce useful commercial timber, among them the Southern Magnolia (*M. grandiflora*) from the eastern United States, the Japanese Cucumber Tree (*M. hypoleuca*)—often wrongly known as *M. obovata*, an illegitimate name—from Japan, and Campbell's Magnolia (*M. campbellii*) from the eastern Himalaya. The leaves of many species readily yield "skeletons" and these have been used to "set off" bouquets; the bark has been used as a tonic and general stimulant. **CZ4–9**

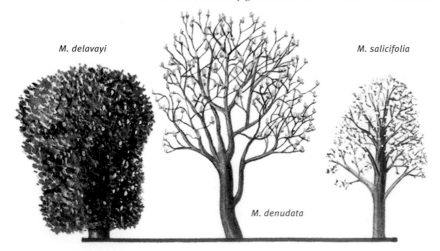

M. delavayi

M. salicifolia

M. denudata

The Main Species of *Magnolia*

Subgenus *Magnolia*

Eight sections of temperate and tropical flowering trees with anthers that shed pollen introrsely (turned inwards). Flowers appear after the leaves; the tepals are in similar whorls. Leaves are evergreen or deciduous and the fruits variously shaped.

Section *Gwillimia*

Eighteen evergreen species with stipules adjoining the leaf stalks and short, nonflattened beaks on the carpels.

M. delavayi Yunnan, China. Large bushy tree up to 40 ft (12 m). Leaves ovate to oblong and very leathery, up to 12 in (30 cm) long and 6 in (15 cm) wide. Flowers with 6 greeny-white tepals; anthers straw-colored. **CZ9**

M. coco SE China. Erect shrub 6.5–13 ft (2–4 m) high. Leaves oblong 3.5–6 in (9–15 cm) long, leathery, shining above. Nodding flowers with 3 green outer tepals and 6 white, fleshy inner tepals. **CZ9**

M. henryi Yunnan, N Thailand. Tree 20–26 ft (6–8 m) tall. Leaves wedge-shaped, 8–25 in (20–65 cm) long, 2.8–9 in (7–22 cm) wide, leathery. Flowers white with 8 or 9 tepals. **CZ9**

M. championi Hong Kong. Shrub or small tree, up to 13 ft (4 m) high. Leaves elliptic. 2.8–6 in (7–15 cm) long and 1–2 in (2.5–5 cm) wide, leathery. Flowers globe-shaped, cream-colored, and very fragrant, with 10 tepals. **CZ9**

Section *Lirianthe*

M. pterocarpa India, Myanmar. Tree similar to *M. henryi* but distinguished by remarkable long flattened beaks on the carpels. **CZ9**

Section *Rytidiospermum*

Nine deciduous species with a whorl-like arrangement of leaves at the end of the branches.

M. macrophylla SE U.S. Tree or large shrub to 33–49 ft (10–15 m). Leaves oblong-ovate, extremely large, 12–39 in (30–100 cm) with auriculate-subcordate bases. Flowers up to 14 in (35 cm) across, 6 tepals white with a purple blotch at the base. **CZ6**

M. tripetala Umbrella Tree. E U.S. Small branching tree to 40 ft (12 m). Leaves obovate, 12–24 in (30–60 cm) long and 7–12 in (18–30 cm) wide. Flowers large, white, and unpleasantly scented. Fruit slightly rose-colored. Closely related species include *M. macrophylla* ssp *ashei* (U.S.), *M. fraseri* (S U.S.), and *M. dealbata* (S Mexico). **CZ5**

M. hypoleuca Japan. Large tree, up to 100 ft (30 m). Leaves obovate, up to 18 in (45 cm) long and 8 in (20 cm) wide. Flowers with 2 distinct whorls of tepals—outer ones red-brown, tinged with green, inner ones large, fragrant, pale creamy-yellow. **CZ6**

M. officinalis E China. Large tree to 72 ft (22 m). Leaves elliptic-obovate, up to 14 in (35 cm) long and 7 in (18 cm) wide. Flowers large, fragrant with creamy-white, fleshy tepals. **CZ8**

M. rostrata China, Tibet, Myanmar. Tree up to 78 ft (24 m). Leaves obovate-oblong, up to 20 in (50 cm) long and 8 in (20 cm) wide. Flowers with green fleshy tepals in the outer whorl and white tepals within. **CZ9**

Section *Magnoliastrum*

M. virginiana Sweet Bay, White Laurel. E U.S. Semievergreen tree up to 66 ft (20 m). Leaves oblong-ovate, 2–4 in (5–10 cm) long, shining green above, bluish-white below. Flowers globular, creamy-white, very fragrant, with bright red fruiting cone. **CZ5**

Section *Oyama*

M. sieboldii Japan, Korea, China. Slender deciduous tree up to 23 ft (7 m). Leaves obovate or oblong-obovate 3.5–6 in (9–15 cm) long. Flowers on a long stalk, cup-shaped, pure white, with a rich, crimson rosette of stamens. **CZ7**

M. sinensis W China. A large spreading shrub, usually 13–20 ft (4–6 m) tall. Leaves sparse, elliptic-oblong, 3–5 in (8–12 cm) long, 1.2–2 in (3–5 cm) wide. Flowers cup-shaped, fragrant, white, with 12 tepals; anthers with red filaments and red carpels. **CZ7**

M. wilsonii China. A spreading shrub or small tree to 26 ft (8 m), with leaves and flowers like those of *M. sinensis*. **CZ7**

M. globosa Sikkim, Yunnan. A small tree up to 26 ft (8 m) tall. Leaves membranous, 4–10 in (10–25 cm) long, oval, with acute or mucronate apex and cordate base. Flowers white with 9 tepals and a purple bract. **CZ9**

Section *Theorhodon*

Fifteen tropical evergreen trees mostly confined to the Caribbean. Flowers have sessile carpels.

M. cubensis Cuba. Tree up to 66 ft (20 m). Leaves narrowly ovate, 23 in (6–8 cm) long and 1–1.6 in (2.5–4 cm) wide, leathery. Flowers small, with white tepals. **CZ7**

M. domingensis Haiti. Tree 11–13 ft (3.3–4 m), with spreading branches. Leaves obovate, thick, leathery, 2.8–4 in (7–11 cm) long and 1.6–2.8 in (4–7 cm) wide. Flowers unknown. **CZ6**

M. grandiflora Laurel Magnolia, Bull Bay. SE U.S. A tall pyramidal tree up to 100 ft (30 m). Leaves oval to oblong, 5–10 in (12–25 cm) long and 2.5–8 in (6–20 cm) wide. Flowers very large, up to 12 in (30 cm) diameter, with thick, creamy-white tepals, purple stamens, and rusty-brown fruits. Many varieties are cultivated. Related species include *M. emarginata* (Haiti), *M. ekmannii* (Haiti), *M. pallescens* (Dominican Republic), *M. hamori* (Dominican Republic). *M. portoricensis* (W Puerto Rico), *M. splendens* (E Puerto Rico). **CZ6**

M. sieboldii

M. virginiana

M. hypoleuca

M. delavayi

M. salicifolia

M. denudata

M. stellata

M. liliflora

M. grandiflora

Section *Gynopodium*

M. nitida NW Yunnan, SE Tibet, NE Myanmar. Shrub or tree up to 20–50 ft (6–15 m) tall. Leaves ovate-oblong, up to 4 in (10 cm) long and 1–2 in (2.5–5 cm) wide, evergreen, very glossy. Flowers creamy-white or yellow, fruit short-stalked, and seeds bright golden-red **CZ9**.

M. kachirachirai Taiwan. The only other member of this section and very similar to *M. nitida*. **CZ7**

Section *Maingola*

Ten tropical Asiatic species, with short, stalked leaves and free stipules.

M. griffithii Assam, Myanmar. Large tree (size unrecorded). Leaves elliptic-oblong and pointed, 7–12 in (18–30 cm) long and 3–5 in (8–12 cm) wide. Flowers white-yellow, small, and leaf-opposed. **CZ8**

M. pealiana Assam. Similar to the previous species but with smaller, hairless leaves. **CZ8**

Subgenus *Pleurochasma*

Three sections of temperate trees with anthers that shed their pollen from lateral or sublateral openings. The flowers are either precocious, appearing before the leaves, or with a reduced calyx-like outer whorl of tepals and appearing with the leaves. The leaves are deciduous, the fruits cylindrical or oblong and usually more or less distorted.

Section *Yulania*

Five species with 9 subequal tepals appearing before the leaves.

M. denudata Yulan, C China. A tree growing up to 60 ft (18 m), with wide-spreading branches and the trunk up to 8 ft (2.5 m) in circumference. Leaves obovate-oblong, 3–7 in (8–18 cm) long and 3–5 in (8–12 cm) wide. Prized for its flowers, which are large, pure white, and bell-shaped with 9 fleshy tepals. The earliest cultivated garden magnolia, known from the Tang dynasty in China. Closely related Chinese species include *M. sprengeri*, *M. dawsoniana*, and *M. sargentiana*. **CZ6**

Section *Buergeria*

Five temperate species with a reduced outer whorl of tepals. Flowers appear before the leaves.

M. kobus N Japan. Large, somewhat round-headed, deciduous tree up to 66–115 ft (20–35 m). The slender branches and young leaves are scented when crushed. Leaves obovate, 3–5 in (8–12 cm) long. Flowers white, with 6 tepals. **CZ5**

M. salicifolia Mount Hakkoda region, Japan. Slender, pyramidal tree up to 16–23 ft (5–7 m). Leaves narrowly oval to lanceolate, up to 4 in (10 cm) long. Flowers like *M. kobus*. **CZ6**

M. stellata Star Magnolia. Japan. Much-branched shrub up to 16 ft (5 m) tall and equally broad. Bark aromatic when young. Leaves narrow oblong, up to 3.5 in (9 cm) long. Flowers pure white with 12–18 tepals. Lesser-known related species include *M. biondii* (E China) and *M. cylindrica* (N and C China). **CZ4**

Section *Tulipastrum*

M. acuminata Cucumber Tree. E U.S. A large pyramid-shaped tree up to 66–100 ft (20–30 m). Leaves oblong, bright green, 5–10 in (12–25 cm) long, hairy below. Flowers greenish-yellow, cup-shaped, erect, and slightly fragrant. Cucumber-like fruit. **CZ4**.

M. cordata E U.S. Shrub or tree up to 33 ft (10 m). Leaves broadly ovate, 3–6 in (8–15 cm) long. Flowers cup-shaped, yellow, the inner tepals marked with reddish lines. **CZ4**

M. liliflora China. A large sturdy bush, 6.6–13 ft (2–4 m) tall. Leaves oblong-ovate, 3.5–8 in (9–20 cm) long, tapering to a point, dark glossy green above, downy below. Flowers with vinous purple and white tepals. **CZ6**

The Species of *Liriodendron*

L. tulipifera **Tulip Tree, Yellow Poplar, Whitewood.** Native to North America, from Nova Scotia south to Florida and into the Midwest, reaching its finest development in the South Alleghany region. A hardy, stately, ornamental deciduous tree of lofty pyramidal habit up to almost 200 ft (60 m). Leaves are alternate, 3–8 in (7.5–20 cm) in length, with long mobile leaf stalks and truncated apex. Flowers greenish-white with orange-stained base to the petals, somewhat resembling a tulip flower. The carpels mature to winged, 1- or 2-seeded nutlets densely packed on a spindle-shaped column. **CZ4**

L. chinense **Chinese Tulip Tree.** Limited regions of C China; first noticed in 1875 in the Lushan Mountains. A more densely growing, smaller tree than *L. tulipifera*, reaching up to 66 ft (20 m). Leaf shape is somewhat similar but the undersides of the leaves are covered with minute hairs, which are visible with a hand lens. The flowers are smaller and more greenish. **CZ8**

Liriodendron
Tulip Trees

Liriodendron is a genus with just two species of deciduous trees, *L. tulipifera* (Tulip Tree) from North America and *L. chinense* (Chinese Tulip Tree) from central China. Both species are hardy in temperate climates, though the latter, first introduced to Europe at the beginning of the twentieth century, is rarely found in cultivation. *Liriodendron tulipifera* is a fast-growing, stately tree, reaching heights of 165–200 ft (50–60 m) in its native habitats. It was one of the first introductions to Europe from the United States in the seventeenth century and some fine specimens may be seen as ornamental trees in large gardens. *Liriodendron tulipifera* 'Fastigiatum' is a more erect cultivar.

The leaves of *Liriodendron* are alternate and very characteristically truncate at the apex. Tulip-like flowers are borne singly at the ends of short branchlets, each one greenish-yellow with orange blotches, with three deflected sepals and six petals. The stamens are numerous and surround a densely packed tapering column of carpels. Flowers are usually produced from May through July on trees of some maturity (twenty to thirty years).

The trees flourish best on a rich, deep soil. They should be given a permanent site at an early stage and do not like being transplanted. They make splendid specimen trees in parkland and amenity areas. The leaves are a bright fresh green throughout the summer, turning gold and lemon in the fall.

The Tulip Tree, or Yellow Poplar or Whitewood, has important timber value, producing a soft, fine-grained, light yellow wood much used for carpentry, furniture, and boat-building. It does not split easily and is readily worked. The inner bark is said to have medicinal properties.

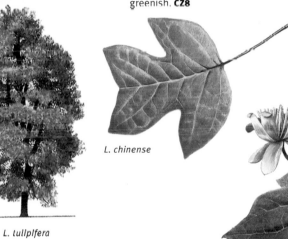

L. chinense

L. tulipifera

L. tulipifera

MAGNOLIACEAE

Liriodendron
TULIP TREE

Number of species 2

Distribution *Eastern North America and China.*

Commercial uses Liriodendron tulipifera *is an important timber tree in North America, and both species of the genus are widely grown as ornamentals.*

TOP LEFT For most of the summer, the Tulip Tree, *Liriodendron tulipifera*, bears flowers which resemble a tulip. The tree can reach 150–200 ft (45–60 m) in the wild and has a magnificent column or trunk. The leaves of *L. chinense* and *L. tulipifera* are of the same shape but the former has a more pronounced waist, the sinus between the lobes is deeper, and the midrib more prolonged.

Laurus
True Laurels

The true laurels belong to the genus *Laurus*, which contains just two species—the Sweet Bay, Bay Laurel, or simply Bay (*Laurus nobilis*) and the Canary Island Laurel (*L. azorica* = *L. canariensis*). Both are evergreen shrubs or trees with hairless branchlets. The leaves are also hairless, entire, and highly aromatic when bruised. The flowers are unisexual and borne on separate plants in small axillary clusters. They have a whorl of four sepals, the male flowers with usually twelve (eight to fourteen) stamens with the anthers opening by valves, the females with four staminodes. The fruit is a berry surrounded by a persistent perianth.

Laurus nobilis is the classical laurel, sacred to Apollo, the symbol of victory and honor in the form of crowns and garlands. In the Middle Ages distinguished men were crowned with a wreath of this berried laurel, whence the title Poet Laureate. University undergraduates were known as Bachelors from the Latin *baccalaureus,* meaning laurel berry. They were forbidden to marry, since this would distract them from their studies. By extension of this, all unmarried men are now referred to as bachelors.

The Sweet Bay is much cultivated outside its native Mediterranean, the aromatic leaves being used as a culinary flavoring. It is generally hardy in most temperate regions and not particular as to soil, but this should be well drained and open to the sun. Many plants are grown in tubs and clipped; they are particularly suitable for growing near coasts. The leaves were once used medicinally and contain about 2 percent of the essential oil cineole—a terpene with a smell like camphor. This oil is widely distributed, being found also, for example, in the oil of *Eucalyptus globulus, Melaleuca quinquenervia* (cajuput oil), both in the family Myrtaceae, and in various worm-seed oils, for example *Artemisia* species (Compositae).

The Canary Island Laurel forms trees to nearly 66 ft (20 m) in the wild. It differs from the previous species in its larger leaves, 2.4–5 in (6–12 cm) long, and its downy branchlets. A native of the Canary Islands and the Azores, it is less hardy than *L. nobilis* and is rarely seen in cultivation.

The term "laurel" is, perhaps, more commonly associated with the Cherry Laurel (*Prunus laurocerasus*) and Portugal Laurel (*P. lusitanica*), both in the rose family (Rosaceae), as well as the Spotted or Japanese Laurel (*Aucuba japonica*) in the family Cornaceae. The first two species have the same dark green, leathery, elliptical entire leaves. This is also true of healthy *A. japonica*, the spotted form of the leaves being due to localized destruction of chlorophyll pigments by virus infection, which does not affect the associated yellow carotenoid pigments. The True Laurel is readily distinguished from all the above species if a leaf is held against the light, when its translucent margin is plainly visible. **CZ8–9**

Umbellularia
Californian Laurel

The evergreen Californian Laurel (*Umbellularia californica*), also known as the Californian Bay, Californian Sassafras, Oregon Myrtle, and Headache Tree, is the only species of its genus, and is native to the Pacific Coast region of California and Oregon. It is a strongly aromatic tree 66–132 ft (20–40 m) tall, though sometimes only a shrub in cultivation.

The leaves are alternate, glossy, more or less ovate-oblong, 2.4–5 in (6–12 cm) long, tapering toward the apex. Small yellowish-green, bisexual flowers are arranged in many-flowered stalked axillary umbels 0.6–0.7 in (15–18 mm) across (racemose in the closely related *Sassafras*) and open in late winter and early spring. Each has a calyx of six lobes, petals are absent, and stamens are arranged in four whorls, the innermost whorl sterile (staminodes). The anthers have four locules (*Laurus* has two). The ovary is single and the resulting fruit is a plum-like ovoid drupe 0.8–1 in (2–2.5 cm) long.

The leaves are particularly pungent when crushed, painfully irritating to nose and throat, and reputed to give headaches—even to people merely sitting under the tree—hence one of its popular names. The foliage may also cause skin irritation and running of the eyes in some people. For this reason perhaps, the tree is rarely grown as an ornamental. It is hardy only in the less extreme parts of temperate regions and tolerant of shade in its early years. It is not particular as to soil provided it is reasonably fertile and free from chalk. The timber is hard and heavy, and used for making ornaments.

ABOVE *Umbellularia californica* can reach heights of 130 ft (40 m) in California's Siskiyou National Forest but, owing to its sometime shrubby habit and irritatingly pungent aroma it is rarely grown in collections and gardens.

LEFT *Prunus laurocerasus*, the Cherry Laurel, showing its leathery, glossy green leaves and spikes of tiny green flower buds which open in early spring. It gets its name from its laurel-like leaves, but is not related to the true laurels (*Laurus* spp).

FAR LEFT The Bay, *Laurus nobilis*, is very popular as a decorative tree for gardens and patios; clipped and grown as a standard, it is often seen in containers placed at the entrance to houses, hotels, and restaurants.

PLANTS WITH THE COMMON NAME "LAUREL"

Common Name	Species	Family
Alexandrian Laurel	*Calophyllum inophyllum*	GUTTIFERAE
Bay Laurel	*Laurus nobilis*	LAURACEAE
Bog Laurel	*Kalmia polifolia*	ERICACEAE
Californian Laurel	*Umbellularia californica*	LAURACEAE
Camphor Laurel	*Cinnamomum camphora*	LAURACEAE
Canary Island Laurel	*Laurus azorica*	LAURACEAE
Cherry Laurel	*Prunus laurocerasus*	ROSACEAE
Chilean Laurel	*Laurelia semperivens*	MONISPERMACEAE
Ecuador Laurel	*Cordia alliodora*	BORAGINACEAE
Great Laurel	*Rhododendron maximum*	ERICACEAE
Indian Laurel	*Terminalia alata*	COMBRETACEAE
Japanese Laurel	*Aucuba japonica*	AUCUBACEAE
Mountain Laurel	*Kalmia latifolia*	ERICACEAE
Portugal Laurel	*Prunus lusitanica*	ROSACEAE
Sheep Laurel	*Kalmia angustifolia*	ERICACEAE
Spotted Laurel	*Aucuba japonica*	AUCUBACEAE
Spurge Laurel	*Daphne laureola*	THYMELAEACEAE
Swamp Laurel	*Magnolia virginiana*	MAGNOLIACEAE
Tasmanian Laurel	*Anopterus spp*	GROSSULARIACEAE

The leaves of *Sassafras albidum* are of variable shapes, although they generally always have a conspicuous lobe on one or both sides with a rounded indentation between. They are 3–7 in (8–18 cm) long and a glossy dark green above and slightly glaucous beneath. The crushed leaf has the strong, sweet aroma of citrus fruit and vanilla.

Sassafras

Sassafras

Sassafras is the common and genus name of three species of deciduous tree, with one species found in each of North America, China, and Taiwan. Best known is the American Sassafras (*S. albidum* = *S. officinale*), which can grow to 100–125 ft (30–35 m) in its native eastern United States.

All three species have leaves that are entire or one- to three-lobed at the apex, depending on age. Yellowish-green flowers are borne in short racemes before the leaves emerge. They are unisexual (the sexes on different plants), sometimes bisexual. Petals are absent but there are six sepal lobes. Males have nine stamens, the four-celled anthers opening by flaps; females have a single ovary and style and occasionally functional stamens are present. The fruit is an ovoid blue-black drupe.

The American Sassafras has gray bark vertically fissured with many horizontal breaks at fairly regular intervals. The leaves are three-nerved from near the base and variable in shape from more or less entire wedge-shaped (young) to three-lobed at the apex (adult). They smell strongly of oranges, lemons, and vanilla when crushed. Mature trees have only a few lobed leaves. The fruit is 0.4 in (1 cm) long, bluish-black and is carried on a bright red stalk. This species is hardy in temperate regions and is widely planted as an ornamental for its fall foliage, which is yellowish-pink, finally turning orange to scarlet. The tree succeeds on rich, moisture-retaining soil.

The fragrant principle is in all parts of the plant and has been used for flavoring tobacco and root beer. Sassafras oil, extracted from the dried inner bark of the root, contains about 80 percent of the phenolic compound safrole and has

been used to destroy lice, and to treat insect stings and bites. The older name *S. officinale* recalls its use in medicine (*Oleum sassafras*)—it has been prescribed as both carminative (curing flatulence) and stimulant, presumably where these two requirements are not in conflict! Its use is now restricted to perfume and cosmetics: the British Government recommended its prohibition as a flavoring agent in 1965, after a report that 0.5–1.0 percent of the oil in the diet of rats could result in cancer of the liver.

The timber is durable enough to be used for fence posts as well as fuel. American indigenous people use the hollowed-out trunks to make canoes of excellent durability. **CZ5–8**

WINTERACEAE

Drimys

Winter's Bark

Drimys is a genus of about eleven species of evergreen shrubs and small trees, the bark and other parts of which are aromatic and/or acrid—hence the generic name, which is derived from the Greek *drimus* = acrid. They are natives of Australia (including Tasmania), New Caledonia, Malaysia, Central and South America. Their leaves are entire, hairless, and the stipules are either absent or minute. The flowers are produced in axillary clusters, rarely solitary, and usually less than 2 in (5 cm) across.

In cultivation *Drimys* species are hardy only in the warmer parts of temperate regions, and cannot survive prolonged freezing conditions in winter. Outside such areas they require a cool conservatory. Winter's Bark (*D. winteri*) is the best-known species in cultivation. It has considerable potential for arboreta and parks in warmer regions of temperate zones.

WINTERACEAE

Drimys
WINTER'S BARK

Number of species *11*
Distribution *Central and South America to central Malaysia, Australia, and Tahiti.*
Commercial uses *The dried fruits are edible and used as pepper; the trees are often planted as hedging.*

It is most often seen as a tree, 26–52 ft (8–16 m) in height, though sometimes it reaches only the stature of a large shrub. The leaves are more or less elliptic to oblanceolate, reaching up to 8 in (20 cm) in length. The flowers are white, fragrant, each up to 1.5 in (4 cm) across with between five and twenty narrow petals. The fruits are fleshy berries. *Drimys winteri* var *andina* (Andean—its range is from Tierra del Fuego to Mexico) was named after one Captain Winter who sailed with Sir Francis Drake. He collected the highly aromatic bark from a tree in the vicinity of the Magellan Straits and used it to treat the crew against scurvy. It is of dwarf habit, reaching about 3 ft (1 m) in height, and very floriferous at an early stage.

The Mountain Pepper (*D. lanceolata* = *D. aromatica*) is also sometimes found in cultivation. It is a shrub or small tree up to 16 ft (5 m) and is native to Tasmania and eastern Australia. Its branchlets are a fine red color and the leaves elliptic to oblanceolate, 0.6–2.8 in (1.5–7 cm) long, with short red petioles. The white flowers are borne in fascicles, each flower about 0.5 in (13 mm) across. The sexes are on separate plants, the male flowers with twenty to twenty-five pinkish-buff stamens, the female with a single carpel. The fruit is a pungent black berry, which, when dried, has been used as a seasoning. **CZ4–8**

CERCIDIPHYLLACEAE

Cercidiphyllum

Katsura Tree

An ornamental of increasing popularity, the Katsura Tree (*Cercidiphyllum japonicum*) is a graceful deciduous tree native to China and Japan. One of only two members of its genus, it was originally described from Japan, where it is the largest native deciduous tree, reaching up to 100 ft (30 m). However, it is represented in China by the variety *sinense*, which may reach 130 ft (40 m) and has a single main trunk. In cultivation it is smaller and it usually produces more than one main stem.

The leaves are heart-shaped like those of the Judas Tree (*Cercis siliquastrum*), typically in opposite pairs, appearing as if arranged in layers. They can turn to magnificent shades of scarlet-crimson, orange, and finally yellow in the fall, but are variable. The flowers are solitary, insignificant, lack petals, and the sexes are on separate trees. The males have a minute calyx and fifteen to twenty stamens, while the females have four slightly larger, fringed, green sepals and four to six (rarely three) carpels with long purplish-red styles. The fruit is a many-seeded dehiscent green to yellowish pod and the seeds winged.

Hardy in temperate regions (but may be nipped by a spring frost), the Katsura Tree is one of the most attractive of shade ornamentals, though it will still grow in semi-shade or full sun. It prefers moist, fertile soil and is ideal for woodland

settings. The timber is fine-grained and used for making furniture and interior fittings for houses and other buildings.

The taxonomic position of the genus is not certain, which is due largely to the interpretation of the female flower: whether it is considered to be a single flower or a condensed inflorescence, in which case the number of individual flowers corresponds to the number of carpels. The genus is currently placed in its own family in the subclass Hamamelidae. **CZ5**

ABOVE *Drimys winteri* flowers in early summer in 4–5 in (10–12 cm) loosely globular inflorescences. The individual flowers are borne on pedicels up to 1 in (2.5 cm) long, and have white petals with a yellow center.

BELOW *Cercidiphyllum japonicum* is extremely variable in color. Generally, young trees are scarlet and crimson at the beginning of fall; older trees are pale yellow and pink, but as the season progresses they can turn gold, pink, purple, red, and orange. However, in dry years trees can fail to color at all.

PLATANACEAE

Platanus

Planes and Buttonball Trees

Planes, also known as sycamores or buttonball trees in the United States, are tall deciduous trees with often very characteristically scaling bark, as in the London Plane. The genus comprises some nine species, all natives of America except *Platanus orientalis* (southeast Europe to the Himalaya) and *P. kerrii* (confined to Indochina). Not all species are hardy in temperate regions (some of which are noted in the species table, on the facing page).

The London Plane *Platanus × hispanica* 'Acerifolia' is incredibly vigorous even in difficult conditions, and due to its roots' ability to cope in compacted and restricted soil, it is often chosen for streets and avenues.

All parts of the plants are covered with stellate (star-shaped) hairs. The leaves are alternate, simple, palmately three- to nine-lobed (except in *P. kerrii*, where the leaves are elliptic-oblong with pinnate veins). The long petiole is swollen at the base and forms a hood over the axillary bud; the stipules are large and embrace the shoot but soon fall away. The flowers are unisexual, but borne on the same plant in one to several globose heads on separate long stalks. There are three to eight small sepals, which are free and hairy. The male flowers have three to eight stamens and as many spoon-shaped petals, and the females have the same number of separate ovaries, each one with a basal tuft of long hairs. The plane fruit comprises a dense hanging cluster of one-seeded nutlets, each of which is shed along with its basal tuft of hairs.

The planes are grown predominantly for their ornamental value. They are at their best planted in a deep loam. Most of the cultivated specimens are probably of hybrid origin. They form magnificent mature trees and, for example, in the Balkan Peninsula, *P. orientalis* has historically been frequently planted in public squares for the shade it gives— "and plane trees large enough to afford shade to quaffers" (Virgil: *Georgics*, translated by H. Gilbert-Carter). The Buttonwood, Buttonball Tree, American Plane, or American Sycamore (*P. occidentalis*) is one of the two major ornamental species. It is a fast-growing, beautiful, and massive tree, reaching 130–165 ft (40–50 m). It is commonly grown in North America, particularly the southeastern United States, both for ornament and timber, but does not grow well in Europe.

The London Plane (*P. × hispanica* 'Acerifolia,' *P. hybrida* of some authors) is famous for its tolerance of grime and its ability to grow in the paved streets of cities, and is also equally at home at water edges. It is a common sight in many European town squares and lining avenues. In England, as its common name suggests, it has been the most popular tree planted in the capital city since the eighteenth century, shortly after its appearance in the Oxford Botanic Gardens, probably as a result of a cross between *P. orientalis* and *P. occidentalis*. Like the Buttonwood, the London Plane has a tall trunk with attractively scaling bark and a beautiful winter silhouette characterized by arching branch tracery and the hanging fruiting balls. Against this, as with other *Platanus* species, there is a long-held and widespread belief that the stellate pubescence and especially the pappus-like hairs on the seed can cause not insignificant irritations of the upper respiratory tract, resulting in "catarrhal" conditions, hayfever symptoms, and may even affect the lungs. The wood is hard and fine-textured and has been used for fancy goods, as a veneer, and for decorative purposes generally. It also burns very well in open grates.

The species of *Platanus* are very similar, so much so that in the past they have been considered as a single, albeit highly variable, species. **CZ5–9**

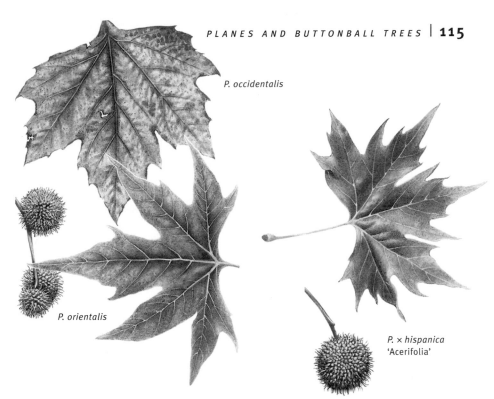

P. occidentalis

P. orientalis

P. × hispanica 'Acerifolia'

Platanus
PLANES AND BUTTONBALL TREES

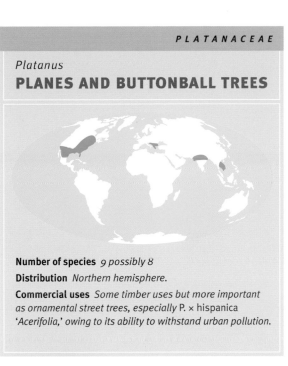

Number of species *9 possibly 8*
Distribution *Northern hemisphere.*
Commercial uses *Some timber uses but more important as ornamental street trees, especially P. × hispanica 'Acerifolia,' owing to its ability to withstand urban pollution.*

P. × hispanica 'Acerifolia'

P. acerifolia frequently grows to over 100 ft (30 m) high and has a smooth, straight trunk. The bark is brown or dark grey and flakes off to reveal large white or yellow patches. This creates an attractive feature even after leaves have fallen.

The Main Species of *Platanus*

Group I: Fruiting heads 3–7, rarely 2, on each stalk. Leaves mostly deeply lobed.

P. orientalis Oriental Plane. Europe (Balkan Peninsula), Crete, Asia, and the Himalaya. Tree to about 100 ft (30 m). Bark scaling, pallid, tinged gray or green. Leaves 8 in (20 cm) wide, 5–7 lobed, the cleft reaching at least to half-way, usually coarsely toothed, glabrous on lower surface. Between 2 and 6 fruiting heads, each up to 1 in (2.5 cm). Of the few named varieties, some are probably of hybrid origin. Variety *insularis* (Cyprian Plane) is sometimes incorrectly attributed to this species, but is now considered a variety of *P. orientalis*. **CZ7**

P. racemosa (P. californica) Californian Plane. California. Tree to 131 ft (40 m). Leaves 6–12 in (15–30 cm) across, 5 lobed, rarely 3, tomentose, at least beneath, the lobes virtually entire or with a few teeth. Between 2 and 7 fruiting heads, each 1 in (2.5 cm) across. A rare and much less vigorous species outside SW America. **CZ8**

P. wrightii Mexico and adjoining S U.S. Tree to 82 ft (25 m). Leaves deeply divided into 3–5 lanceolate, entire or almost entire lobes, at first tomentose on both sides, the underside becoming hairless. Between 2 and 5 fruiting heads, mostly stalked and smooth, the achenes truncate or rounded with an often deciduous style. Very closely related to *P. racemosa*, of which it is sometimes regarded as a variety, but the leaves are more deeply divided with an often cordate base and the fruiting heads do not exceed 4. **CZ8**

Group II: Fruiting heads 1 or 2, rarely more, on each stalk. Leaves mostly with shallow lobes.

P. occidentalis Buttonwood, Buttonball Tree, American Plane, American Sycamore. E and SE U.S. Fine tree to 131–170 ft (40–50 m). Bark creamy-white, scaling, much darker at base especially in older trees. Leaves 4–9 in (10–22 cm) wide, about the same or less in length, typically 3 lobed, rarely 5; clefts shallow. Fruiting head about 1.2 in (3 cm) across, usually single, rarely 2. **CZ5**

P. × hispanica 'Acerifolia' (P. hybrida) London Plane. Extensively planted in Europe and N. America. Tree to 115 ft (35 m) with characteristic scaling bark. Leaves 5–10 in (12–25 cm) across, 3–5 lobed, the cleft extending about one-third leaf length, middle lobe about as long as broad; petiole 1.2–4 in (3–10 cm) long. Fruiting heads typically 2, rarely more. Fertile seed is set, but the germination rate is low. Seedlings said to be variable, as would be expected from a hybrid. Origin unknown, but was once thought to be a variety of *P. orientalis* stabilized by cultivation, though the prevailing view is that it is a hybrid between *P. orientalis* and *P. occidentalis*. Some still consider it as a possible variety of *P. orientalis*. Earlier names, still in use for the London Plane, are *P. hybrida* and *P. hispanica*, but no authentic specimens exist to clinch the identity. The binomial *P. hispanica* was, however, applied by one Augustus Henry to a plant received from a Belgian nursery in 1878. It differs markedly from *P. × hispanica 'Acerifolia'* both in habit and foliage, the latter being on average larger and of a lighter, almost sea-green color, the lobe margins more toothed and the whole leaf tending to turn downward at the edges. It is now distinguished under the name *Platanus* 'Augustus Henry.' It may be another hybrid variant from the same parentage as *P. × hispanica 'Acerifolia' (P. orientalis × P. occidentalis)*. **CZ7**

HAMAMELIDACEAE

Hamamelis

Witch Hazels

The genus *Hamamelis* comprises four or five (perhaps six) species of deciduous shrubs or small trees native to eastern Asia and eastern North America. They are deservedly popular with gardeners, for most of the species—and their hybrids and cultivars—produce spider-like yellow or rusty-red flowers from December to March (with the exception of *H. virginiana*), which stand up to the severest weather. Petals, sepals, and stamens are typically in fours, but sometimes in fives. The leaves resemble those of the Common Hazel (*Corylus avellana*) and usually turn an attractive yellow or red in the fall. This resemblance to hazel led early settlers in North America to use the twigs for water divining, and the popular name arose because of the pliant properties of the branches. (Witch Hazel is a name used also for the Witch Elm (*Ulmus glabra*) and for the Hornbeam (*Carpinus betulus*), the term "witch" or "wych" being an old English word used to denote any tree with particularly pliant branches.)

The Common Witch Hazel (*Hamamelis virginiana*) of the eastern United States and Canada is a large spreading shrub or tree to 23–33 ft (7–10 m) whose leaves turn yellow in the fall. The small yellow flowers are produced in the fall and are particularly resistant to cold weather. The bark, leaves, and twigs yield the pharmaceutical preparation witch hazel, which is widely used as an astringent and coolant, and can be applied to cuts and bruises. The extract contains substances that tend to constrict the blood vessels, which can prevent bleeding.

The Japanese Witch Hazel (*H. japonica*), from Japan, is a shrub or small tree to 33 ft (10 m) and has slightly scented wavy-petaled flowers in roundish heads; the leaves turn yellow in the fall. This species is somewhat variable in form—'Arborea' is taller growing, var *flavopurpurescens* has reddish petals, 'Sulphurea' has much crumpled pale yellow petals, and 'Zuccariniana' has pale lemon flowers produced in March.

The Chinese Witch Hazel (*H. mollis*), from western and western central China, is the most handsome of the genus. It is a shrub or small tree to 33 ft (10 m) producing very fragrant flowers, the petals of which are not wavy. The best cultivar is 'Pallida,' with large sulfur-yellow flowers produced in January and February.

Hamamelis × intermedia is a hybrid between the above two species, with many good named cultivars. It was first produced at the Arnold Arboretum in the United States. The Ozark Witch Hazel (*H. vernalis*) is a shrub to 6.5 ft (2 m) and produces small scented flowers, which vary in color from pale yellow to red, in January to February. **CZ5–6**

Liquidambar

Sweet Gums

Liquidambar is a small genus of resinous trees of scattered distribution in both hemispheres. Their leaves are palmate, long-stalked, with three to seven lobes, much as in maples (*Acer* spp) but distinguished from that genus by being alternate and not opposite. The greenish-yellowish inconspicuous flowers are unisexual but on the same tree, the males in short clusters, each with stamens only, the females in globose heads, each flower with more or less closely adpressed ovaries. The fruits are capsules containing winged seeds.

Sweet gums are grown mostly as ornamentals for their splendid fall colors, though only *L. styraciflua* is seen at all extensively. It grows best in good, deep, not too moist soil and is propagated by seed, though germination may not occur until the second year. The fall coloring can be magnificent, from scarlet through dark red, but its quality and quantity can vary immensely.

The timber, known commercially as satin walnut, is valued for furniture, cabinetmaking, and veneer. Fragrant resinous gums known as American storax and liquid storax are obtained from the bark of *L. styraciflua* and *L. orientalis* respectively. They are used to scent soap, as an expectorant in cough pastilles, and as a fumigant in the treatment of skin diseases such as scabies. The old-fashioned Friar's balsam contains liquid storax and is used as an inhalant in bronchial upsets. The word "storax" is also the popular name derived from a quite different group of resinous flowering plants of the genus *Styrax*, family Styracaceae.

Liquidambar formosana is rare in cultivation but in its native regions the wood is used for making tea chests and the leaves to feed silk worms. **CZ5–8**

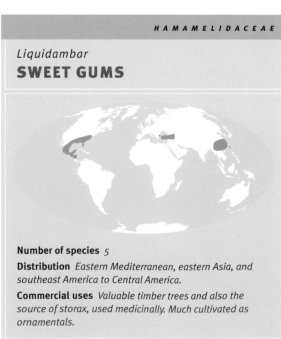

HAMAMELIDACEAE

Liquidambar
SWEET GUMS

Number of species 5
Distribution *Eastern Mediterranean, eastern Asia, and southeast America to Central America.*
Commercial uses *Valuable timber trees and also the source of storax, used medicinally. Much cultivated as ornamentals.*

ABOVE The Chinese witchhazel *Hammamelis mollis* has narrow, scented yellow petals throughout the winter months, which, together with its stout, spreading branches, make it highly distinctive.

ABOVE The Sweet Gum *Liquidamber styraciflua* is often mistaken for a Maple but can be distinguished by its alternate leaves. During the fall, the foliage turns to striking shades of red, purple, and orange.

L. orientalis

L. formosana

♀

♂

L. styraciflua

L. styraciflua

L. styraciflua

The Main Species of *Liquidambar*

L. styraciflua Sweet Gum. E U S , Mexico, Guatemala.
Deciduous tree to 150 ft (45 m) in the wild state but nearer
33–50 ft (10–15 m) in cultivation. Leaves 4–7 in (10–18 cm)
wide, 5–7 lobed, turning a fine red color in the fall. Fruiting
head with small, blunt scales. **CZ5**
'**Levis**' Branches without corky bark. Leaves brilliantly
colored in the fall.
'**Variegata**' Leaves marked with yellow.
'**Rotundiloba**' Leaves with 3–5 short rounded lobes.
'**Pendula**' Branches deflexed, pendulous, forming a
narrow crown.

L. orientalis Asia Minor. Deciduous tree to about 100 ft (30 m)
in the wild, but under 33 ft (10 m) in cultivation, where it is
less common than the previous species. Leaves (1.6)2–2.8
(3.5) in ((4)5–7(9) cm) wide usually with 5 inconspicuously
toothed smallish lobes.**CZ8**

L. formosana Taiwan, S and C China, Indochina. Deciduous tree
to about 130 ft (40 m) in the wild. Leaves 3 (rarely 5) lobed,
(3)4–6 in ((8)10–15 cm) wide. Fruiting head with slender awl-
shaped bristles.
var *monticola* Leaves hairless, usually truncate at the base,
cordate only in young seedlings, plum purple when
unfolding, later bronzy-crimson, then finally dull green,
crimson again in the fall. **CZ5**

L. styraciflua

RIGHT The Persian Ironwood is
a compact tree or shrub. Its
flowers (inset) have numerous
stamens which are a bright red,
surrounded by rich brown
bracts, and open before the
leaves, giving excellent early
spring color.

Parrotia

Persian Ironwood

The Persian Ironwood (*Parrotia persica*) is the only
member of its genus. It is a small deciduous tree that is too
infrequently found cultivated in parks and large gardens
in temperate regions. In its native northern Iran and the
Caucasus it forms dense thickets with interlacing main
stems and branches that may fuse together. Such natural
grafting is also seen in cultivated specimens. It reaches
50–65 ft (15–20 m) in the wild but only 16–26 ft (5–8 m)
in cultivation, and then it is sometimes shrubby.

All parts of the tree are covered with star-shaped (stellate)
hairs. The bark is flaking, rather similar to that of the
London Plane (*Platanus × hispanica*), and the leaves are
alternate, sinuous, and toothed. The flowers are small,
bisexual, and borne during early spring in dense clusters
surrounded by large bracts. Petals are absent, but there is a
five- to seven-lobed calyx. The five to seven stamens are
conspicuous for their size and red color. The fruits comprise
three to five nut-like capsules, which open at the top. The
seeds are 0.3–0.4 in (8–10 mm) long and shining brown.

The Persian Ironwood is fully hardy in temperate regions
and its value as a year-round ornamental is underestimated.
It is particularly attractive for its early spring flowers, which
open before the leaves, and the splendid golden to crimson
foliage in the fall. The leaves often have a reddish tinge in
spring and the bark stands out well in the winter. In summer
the flower buds are deep brown and characteristically down-
curved at the tip. It grows well in a sunny or partly shaded
position on fertile, well-drained soil. Cultivar 'Pendula' has
a weeping habit and exceptional fall colors. **CZ5**

FAGACEAE

Quercus

Oaks

Quercus is a large and economically important genus including many trees prized for their noble aspect and fall colors. Specimens have been recorded up to 700 years old.

In the wider sense, as accepted here, the genus includes over 400 species, predominantly of the northern hemisphere, the majority in North America, but twenty in Europe, the Mediterranean, and western and eastern Asia. In South America, oaks occur only in the Andes of Colombia. The relatively small tropical distribution is virtually confined to high mountains. The altitudinal range of oaks is from sea level to 13,000 ft (4,000 m) in the Himalaya. They like a reasonably rich soil, not too sandy or too dry. They grow best in well-drained soils and produce a better crown if grown in an open site in full sun.

Oaks are predominantly trees, but some are shrubs. They may be evergreen, half-evergreen (the leaves survive winter, but fall by springtime), or deciduous. The leaves are rarely entire, and the margins are usually cut or lobed in various ways. Male and female flowers are borne on the same tree, the males in pendulous catkins, the females solitary or in spikes of two or more flowers. The fruit is a large, solitary, characteristic nut (acorn) more or less enclosed from the base upward by a cup (cupule) composed of variously shaped scales more or less imbricate, less often connate, to form concentric rings.

Oaks are wind-pollinated, and interspecific hybridization (between species) is extensive, which greatly complicates identification.

The Importance of Oak

Oaks provide the finest hardwoods, and this wood is in the forefront of all timbers because of its great strength and durability. It is not easy to distinguish the various commercial oak timbers, but a distinction is made between the white oaks and the red oaks, the former being somewhat harder and more durable. Both kinds are used for the same purposes: furniture, and bridge, ship, and many other types of construction. The wood will take a high polish and, cut radially, is a favorite for paneling because of the fine "silver grain" formed by the wood rays. Important white oak species are *Q. alba*, *Q. macrocarpa*, *Q. robur*, and

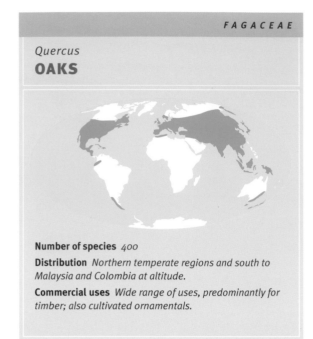

Quercus
OAKS

FAGACEAE

Number of species *400*

Distribution *Northern temperate regions and south to Malaysia and Colombia at altitude.*

Commercial uses *Wide range of uses, predominantly for timber; also cultivated ornamentals.*

The Durmast oak *Quercus petraea* differs from the Common Oak, *Q. robur*, in its habit—it has much straighter branches and the trunk extends further into the crown, and the leaves which are not as markedly obovate. Its other common name, Sessile Oak, refers to the fruit which is borne on the twig rather than on long slender stalks, as in *Q. robur*.

Q. sessiliflora; among the red oaks are *Q. rubra (borealis)*, *Q. velutina*, and *Q. palustris*. Live Oak is the popular name for *Q. virginiana*, considered to be the most durable of all oak timbers. It is used for trucks, ships, and toolmaking, but unfortunately is now in short supply.

The timber of some oaks is used for inlay work, for example "brown oak," which is oak timber stained by the mycelium of the bracket fungus *Fistulina hepatica*. Similarly, oak timber may be stained a deep emerald green by the mycelium of the cup fungus *Chlorosplenium aeruginascens*. The green coloring substance has attracted considerable attention and it has been isolated and characterized as a rare type of green pigment named xylindein.

Oak and Winemaking

The association of wine and oak goes back to classical times. The Romans knew that oak's qualities made it ideal for constructing barrels and vats, not least its impermeability to water—or wine—for storage or transport. While other timbers may be used to make the characteristic oval or egg-shaped barrels used for fermenting and maturing wine, new oak is much favored for another characteristic of the wood: its ability to impart an added flavor dimension to the wine.

The main species used for barrelmaking are *Q. alba* from eastern North America and *Q. robur* and *sessilis* from Europe, and there are nuances in flavor between the type of oak and its source. Growth rates are influenced by the climate and the soil, the density of the tree stands, and the age of the trees. The slower the growth rate, the tighter the grain, the better the flavor in the wine, because more of the desirable phenols are extracted from slower-growing oak.

Cork is obtained from the outer bark of the Cork Oak (*Q. suber*). Trees are first stripped at about twenty years and subsequently at nine-year intervals. The freshly stripped bark is dried, then boiled in water to remove impurities and soften it. It is finally cut either parallel to the lenticels, giving corks that are permeable, or at right angles to them so that the resulting corks are airtight. Cork oaks survive this "surgery" for anything from 100 through 500 years.

Other Uses

It is paradoxical that a timber as near indestructible as oak comes from a tree that, when growing, attracts a host of invaders, especially fungi and insects. Rarely serious but numerous are the gall-forming insects, over 800 of which have been recorded in oak. Some galls are, in fact, of economic importance. Thus, the oak apple or oak marble gall, caused by the gall wasp *Andricus kollari*, contains tannin. Various oak species, among them *Q. lusitanica* and the closely related *Q. pubescens*, are major sources of tannins, which are extracted from the bark and from galls by chopping the material into fragments, which are then cooked and extracted by steam. In addition to leather tanning, tannins are used to make the

"blue black" type of ink used in fountain pens. A fine, scarlet, cochineal-like dye has been extracted since medieval times from a scale insect, *Coccus ilicis*, which lives on the Kermes Oak or Grain Tree (*Q. coccifera*) ("kermes" is the Arabic name for the insect, "grain" is from *granatinctorum*, the Latin equivalent.)

Acorns are of little economic value, but they are eaten by game birds and have been used to fatten hogs and poultry.

Oaks have a long history in mythology, being associated with Zeus, the god of thunder. It is often held that oak trees are particularly susceptible to being struck by lightning, and Shakespeare refers to "oak-cleaving thunderbolts" in *King Lear*. Plants with supposed magical properties are regarded as being especially superior if found growing on oak. Thus, Mistletoe (*Viscum album*), with an extensive mythology of its own, is much prized when found on oak, which is a rare host for this semi-parasite.

Outside their native ranges many oaks are grown as ornamentals. Most are hardy, long-lived trees often producing attractive fall colors. They grow best in well-drained soils and produce a better crown if grown in an open position in full sunlight. Some of the better-known cultivated species are Red Oak (*Q. rubra*) for its crimson to red-brown fall foliage, the Turkey Oak (*Q. cerris*) for its rapid growth, the Scarlet Oak (*Q. coccinea*) for its scarlet fall foliage, and the Holm Oak (*Q. ilex*) for its evergreen foliage. The Holm Oak is also used for screens, windbreaks, and for hedging, particularly in coastal areas. **CZ3–9**

The Oregon Oak, *Q. garryana*, can reach 80 ft (25 m) high and has a broad crown of tortuous branches. Native to western North America, it tolerates cool humid sites near the coast and is equally at home on hot dry hillsides inland.

Q. rubra Summer

Q. rubra Fall

The Main Species of *Quercus*

Group I: Leaves evergreen, persisting more than 1 year, hairless beneath when mature.

Q. coccifera **Kermes Oak, Grain Tree.** Mediterranean. Usually a shrub to 6.5 ft (2 m), rarely a small tree. Leaves dentate, broad elliptic to 2 in (5 cm), the teeth spine-tipped. Cupular scales spreading. **CZ6**

Q. myrsinaefolia China, Japan. Tree to 60 ft (18 m). Smaller in cultivation. Leaves lanceolate, 2–5 in (5–12 cm), serrate. Cupular scales in concentric rings. **CZ7**

Group II: Leaves evergreen (half-evergreen in *Q.* × *hispanica*) persisting more than 1 year, white or grayish-downy beneath when mature.

Q. suber **Cork Oak.** S Europe, N Africa. Tree to 66 ft (20 m), bark corky. Leaves more or less ovate-oblong, 1.2–2.8 in (3–7 cm) with mucronate teeth and 5–7 pairs of veins. **CZ9**

Q. × *pseudosuber* (*Q* × *hispanica*) **Spanish Oak.** Occurs naturally in S Europe. Tree to 100 ft (30 m) with thick but only slightly corky bark. Leaves persisting through fall to spring, ovate to oblong, 1.6–4 in (4–10 cm) long with 4–7 pairs of shallow, mucronate, triangular lobes. **CZ7**
Cultivar 'Lucombeana' or Lucombe Oak belongs to this hybrid group, one striking form of which is recognized by the main branches being much swollen where they join the main trunk and the terminal buds are surrounded by subulate bristles, which are absent from the lateral buds (a useful distinction from *Q. cerris* in which all buds have subulate bristles).

Q. ilex **Holm Oak, Evergreen Oak.** Mediterranean, N Spain, W France. Tree to 66 ft (20 m). Leaves ovate-lanceolate, apex acute, 1.2–2.8 in (3–7 cm), entire or more or less serrate with 7–10 pairs of veins. Acorns bitter and unpalatable. **CZ7**

Q. rotundifolia SW Europe. Very similar to *Q. ilex*, which it replaces in SW Spain, but lateral veins of leaf make wider angle with midrib. Acorns sweet and edible.

Q. virginiana **Live Oak.** S U.S., Mexico. Tree to 66 ft (20 m). Leaves oblong, apex rounded, 1.6–5 in (4–13 cm), typically entire and margin revolute. The finest evergreen oak. Wood much prized. **CZ7**

Group III: Leaves deciduous or half-evergreen, not persisting more than one year; entire.

Q. phellos **Willow Oak.** N. America. Tree to 100 ft (30 m). Leaves lanceolate, 2–4 in (5–10 cm), pale green fading to yellow. **CZ6**

Group IV: Leaves deciduous as above, but lobed, the lobes bristle-tipped.

Q. marilandica **Blackjack Oak.** SE U.S. Tree to about 33 ft (10 m). Leaves markedly obovate, 3–5 lobed, 4–8 in (10–20 cm), rusty pubescent below. **CZ5**

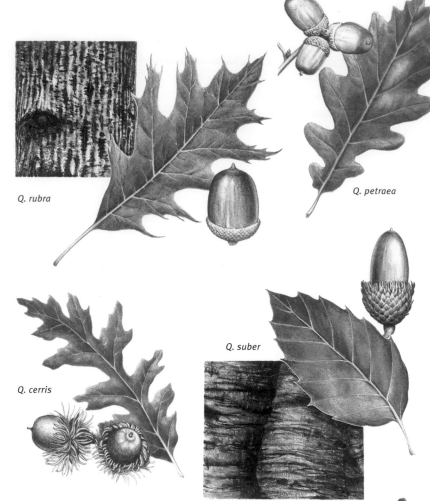

Q. rubra

Q. petraea

Q. suber

Q. cerris

Q. velutina (*Q. tinctoria*) **Black Oak.** N. America. Tree 100–165 ft (30–50 m). Leaves ovate to oblong, 4–10 in (10–25 cm), with 7–9 lobes, which are toothed and more or less wavy, hairy beneath. Its bark and acorns yield a yellow dye "quercitron." **CZ6**

Q. rubra (*Q. borealis*) **Red Oak.** E U.S. Tree to 82 ft (25 m). Branchlets dark red. Leaves oblong, 5–8 in (12–20 cm) with 7–11 lobes, the lobes cut less than half-way to midrib, hairless below except for axillary tufts of hair. **CZ3**

Q. palustris **Pin Oak.** N. America. Tree to 100 ft (30 m). Leaves elliptic-oblong, 4–6 in (10–15 cm), 5–7 lobed to more than half-way to midrib, hairless below, but with conspicuous axillary tufts of hair. Fall leaves a duller red than following species. **CZ6**

Q. coccinea **Scarlet Oak.** N. America. Tree to 82 ft (25 m). Branchlets scarlet red. Leaves elliptic-oblong, 3–6 in (8–15 cm), 7–9 lobed almost to midrib, hairless below except for inconspicuous axillary tufts of hair. Much admired for its brilliant scarlet fall leaf colors. **CZ4**

Group V: Leaves deciduous as before but with bristle-tipped serrations, not lobes.

Q. libani **Lebanon Oak.** Syria, Asia Minor. Tree to 33 ft (10 m). Leaves oblong-lanceolate, 2–4 in (5–10 cm); veins 9–12 pairs. **CZ6**

Q. robur

Q. ilex

Q. robur

The Cork Oak, *Quercus suber*, native to the west Mediterranean region, is easily distinguished from other evergreen oaks by its thick and corky bark. Once stripped, the trunks are a rich red color. They are low, domed spreading trees with low, heavy twisting branches.

Q. acutissima China, Japan, Korea, Himalaya. Tree about 50 ft (15 m). Leaves oblong-obovate, 3–7 in (8–18 cm); veins 12–16 pairs. **CZ5**

Group VI: Leaves deciduous as before, but without bristle-tips to teeth or lobes—but these may be mucronate.

Q. cerris Turkey Oak. S Europe, W Asia. Tree to about 125 ft (38 m). Leaves elliptic-oblong, toothed; blade without basal auricles, 2–4 in (5–10 cm), with 4–10 pairs of narrow lobes. Cupular scales conspicuously long, filiform, and spreading. **CZ7**

Q. robur English Oak, 'Pedunculate Oak.' Europe, N Africa, Asia Minor. Tree to 150 ft (45 m). Leaves obovate-oblong, lobed, with basal auricles, 2–5 in (5–12 cm), the 3–7 rounded lobes cut less than half-way to midrib. Fruiting stalk 0.8–2.8 in (2–7 cm) long. **CZ6**

Q. petraea Durmast Oak, 'Sessile Oak.' Europe, Asia Minor. Tree up to 130 ft (40 m). Leaves obovate-oblong, 3–5.2 in (8–13 cm), the 5–9 rounded lobes cut less than half-way to midrib; basal auricles absent. Fruits virtually sessile. **CZ4**

Q. alba White Oak. E U.S. Tree 150–67 ft (45–50 m). Leaves obovate-oblong with 5–9 rounded lobes, some lobes cut more than half-way to midrib. **CZ4**

Q. bicolor Swamp White Oak. E N. America. Tree to about 100 ft (30 m). Branchlets hairless. Leaves oblong-obovate, 4–6.5 in (10–16 cm), sinuate-dentate, hairy beneath, 6–8 lobed. Cupule much shorter than acorn. **CZ4**

Q. macrocarpa Burr Oak. N. America. Tree usually to 82 ft (25 m), sometimes reaching 180 ft (55 m). Branchlets hairy (at first). Leaves more or less obovate, lyrate-pinnatified, 4–10 in (10–25 cm), hairy beneath, terminal lobe large, more or less crenate to twice-lobed. Rim of cupule with filiform fringe of scales. **CZ3**

Fagus

Beeches

Beeches are a closely knit group of between eight and ten species of deciduous trees belonging to the genus *Fagus*. They grow to 100–150 ft (30–45 m) and occur throughout the northern hemisphere, in all three continents, where they are frequently dominant or codominant in temperate forests. Tertiary fossils said to be beeches have been reported as far north as Iceland. Pre-Roman peats in Great Britain have yielded pollen of the Common Beech (*F. sylvatica*), in spite of Julius Caesar's statement that it did not occur. It is likely that he was referring to the Sweet Chestnut (*Castanea sativa*).

The southern beeches belong to the closely related genus *Nothofagus* and are native to the southern hemisphere.

Beeches have rounded, spreading canopies and smooth, gray bark. The leaves are alternate, more or less ovate, acute, with coarsely dentate to wavy margins, and are usually thin and shining green; the slender, elongated winter buds are a very distinctive feature. The flowers are unisexual and appear on the same tree after the leaves have opened. Numerous male flowers crowd into slender-stalked globose heads, each flower with a four to seven-lobed perianth (calyx) surrounding eight to sixteen stamens. The female inflorescence has two flowers, each flower with three styles and a perianth of four or five lobes. The fruit is an ovoid-triangular nut, and one or two nuts are wholly or partly enclosed in the involucre of fused bracteoles, which becomes woody and four-valved and is then referred to as the cupule. It is borne on a peduncle, which may be stout and short (up to 1 in/2.5 cm) or slender and longer (up to 3 in/8 cm). The cupule is covered with prickly, bristly, bract-like or short, deltoid appendages.

The species are quite hardy, lime-tolerant, and flourish on light to medium soil. The Common Beech is the typical woodland species of many calcareous soils. Such woods often lack ground flora as the dense mosaic of leaves effectively reduces the light. In the fall, however, beechwoods are some of the best locations for finding many fine species of gill fungi (Agaricales), some of which are edible: *Pleurotus ostreatus*, the Oyster Mushroom, for one, is an excellent edible fungus that is commercially cultivated in some countries.

The Uses of Beech

Beech timber, for example that of Common Beech, is valuable as it is strong, tough, hard, and of high compressive strength. Its uses are many where these qualities are important, such as ships' wedges, plane blocks, furniture, and flooring, but it deteriorates when exposed to the weather. Beech is often used for the wrest plank in pianos, which has to withstand the

The fresh green foliage of Common Beech, *Fagus sylvatica*, turns golden bronze in the fall, making beech woods a magnificent sight.

strain of 225 or more strings, each one under a tension of over 150 lb (68 kg). In the main, the wood is fairly plain in figure and texture, though spalted beech (where the wood has been infected by a fungus) is often prized by furniture-makers for the effect it has—random jet black lines across the cut surface—which can be most striking.

The nut or "mast" of some *Fagus* species is sufficiently rich in oil to provide valuable food for browsing animals, including hogs.

Several beeches are widely cultivated for their handsome shape and foliage. For the species, propagation is from seeds, but cultivars have to be grafted. The Common Beech is particularly rich in varieties and cultivars. The Fern-leaved Beech (*F. sylvatica* 'Asplenifolia') has leaves varying between narrowly strap-shaped to shallowly to deeply pinnately lobed, sometimes down to the midrib. Dawyck's Beech (*F. sylvatica* 'Dawyck') is a fastigiate form that arose in Scotland in 1860 and is planted by roadsides and in avenues. The Cut-leaved Beech (*F. sylvatica* var *heterophylla*) exists in two forms: *forma laciniata* has ovate-lanceolate leaves tapering at both ends, the margin with seven to nine deep serrations on each side, extending about one-third of the way to the midrib; *forma latifolia* has larger leaves than the type—in young trees up to 3 x 5.5 in (8 x 14 cm), rather less in older trees. "Weeping" beeches ('Pendula') come in various forms some with horizontal main branches draped with pendulous branchlets and others with the main branches also pendulous. The Purple or Copper Beeches (*forma purpurea*) are forms in which the chlorophyll of the leaves is masked by an anthocyanin pigment, which colors them varying shades of purplish, purplish-black, or dark red. They are commonly planted and admired by many, reviled by some. *Fagus sylvatica* 'Zlatia' has golden-yellow young leaves, which later turn green. **CZ4-7**

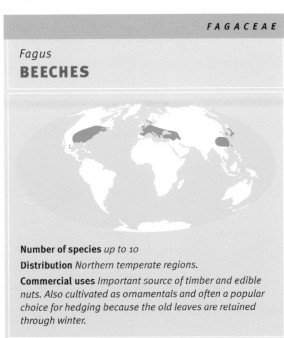

FAGACEAE

Fagus
BEECHES

Number of species *up to 10*

Distribution *Northern temperate regions.*

Commercial uses *Important source of timber and edible nuts. Also cultivated as ornamentals and often a popular choice for hedging because the old leaves are retained through winter.*

F. sylvatica

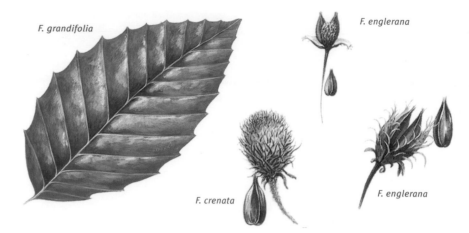

F. grandifolia

F. englerana

F. crenata

F. englerana

F. sylvatica

The Main Species of *Fagus*

Group I: Nut a third to half its length longer than the cupule; peduncle 2–3 times longer than cupule. Leaves glabrous beneath.

F. japonica Japanese Beech. Japan. Tree 70–82 ft (21–25 m). Leaves elliptic to ovate, acuminate, 2–3 in (5–8 cm), more or less glabrous beneath, margin almost entire to sinuate-crenate; veins (9)10–14(15) pairs. Cupule processes short deltoid. **CZ5**

Group II: Nut not exceeding its cupule; peduncle stout, shortly hairy, 0.2–1 in (5–25 mm) long. Leaves green beneath.

F. grandifolia American Beech. E N. America. Tree 70–82 ft (21–25 m), suckering. Leaves ovate to oblong, 2.2–5 in (6–12 cm), with coarse serrations; veins (9)11–14(15) pairs. Cupule appendages awl-shaped. **CZ4**

F. sylvatica Common or European Beech. C and S Europe, including British Isles, extending to Crimea. Tree 100(150) ft (30(45) m). Leaves ovate to elliptic, 2–4 in (5–10 cm), margin remotely denticulate, mostly more or less wavy; veins 5–9 pairs. Cupule appendages prickly, awl-shaped. **CZ5**

F. sylvatica ssp *orientalis* Oriental Beech. Asia Minor, the Caucasus, N Iran. Tree to 100 ft (30 m). Leaves widest above middle, ovate to obovate-oblong, 2.3–4.3(5) in (6–11(12) cm), margin entire, slightly wavy; veins 7–12(14) pairs. Cupule appendages bract-like linear to spathulate (spoon-shaped) below, more bristle-like above, peduncle 0.8–3 in (2–7.5 cm). **CZ5**

F. longipetiolata

F. × *moesiaca* and *F. taurica* are binomials for two beech populations intermediate in (mainly) fruit and leaf characters between *F. sylvatica* and *F. sylvatica* ssp *orientalis* and generally occurring where they overlap. **CZ5**

F. crenata (*F. sieboldii*) Siebold's Beech. Japan. Tree to 100 ft (30 m). Leaves widest below middle, more or less ovate, 2–4 in (5–10 cm), margin somewhat crenate; veins 7–10(11) pairs. Cupule appendages linear and bristle-like above, more spathulate below, peduncle 0.2–0.6 in (5–15 mm). **CZ4**

F. lucida Hupeh Province (E China). Tree 20–33 ft (6–10 m). Leaves elliptic to ovate, 2–4 in (5–8 cm), shiny-glossy on both sides, margin weakly sinuate; veins (8)10–12(14) pairs, exserted as small prickle in leaf-margin sinus. Cupule woolly, the appendages scale-like, deltoid, adpressed. **CZ6**

Group III: Nut not exceeding its cupule but peduncle slender, glabrous, rarely slightly pubescent, 1–3 in (2.5–7 cm). Leaves more or less glaucous or glossy beneath.

F. engleriana Chinese Beech. China. Tree 20–50(75) ft (6–15 (23) m). Leaves elliptic to ovate (1.6)2–3(4.3) in ((4)5–8(11) cm), margin sinuate, the nerves of lower surface with silky hairs, otherwise glabrous; petiole to 0.4 in (10 mm); veins 10–14 pairs. Cupule appendages bract-like, more or less linear. **CZ6**

F. longipetiolata C and W China. Tree to 82 ft (25 m). Leaves ovate to somewhat oblong, 2.8–5 in (7–12 cm), margin with a few teeth, the lower surface finely but conspicuously pubescent; petiole 0.4–0.8 in (1–2 cm); veins 9–12(13) pairs, extending to leaf margin teeth. Cupule with slender, curled, bristle-like appendages. **CZ6**

The Common Beech, *Fagus sylvatica*, has a wide spreading form in isolated positions. When growing in close association with others, it develops a tall, smooth column-like trunk.

Summer   *F. sylvatica*   Winter

Nothofagus
Southern Beeches

Nothofagus is an important southern hemisphere genus of shrubs and trees with a discontinuous distribution between the Old World and the New. It includes temperate species ranging in South America from about 33° south latitude to Cape Horn and from New Zealand northward through Tasmania to Eastern Australia, and species in the more tropical islands of New Guinea and New Caledonia. Many species are dominants or codominants in the cool temperate and tropical montane forests south of the Equator, though some grow in subtropical lowland conditions.

There has been much speculation on the causes of the discontinuous distribution of *Nothofagus*, since its Old and New World ranges are separated by the broad wastes of the Southern Oceans and Antarctica. The fruits have poor powers of dispersal, ruling out long-distance transport by birds, wind, or ocean currents, which have been shown to be responsible for similar discontinuities in other plants. However, fossil *Nothofagus* of Cretaceous age (about 100 million years ago) have been found in Antarctica, showing that the southern beeches were present at a time when Australasia, South America, and Antarctica were joined together in the supercontinent Gondwanaland. Its subsequent fragmentation by plate tectonics into the modern southern continents explains the distribution of *Nothofagus* and, perhaps, other ancient groups.

The southern beeches are deciduous or evergreen shrubs or, more usually, trees up to 165 ft (50 m), having nonpersistent stipules and separate male and female flowers on the same plant. The male flowers are solitary, in pairs or in groups of three (rarely five), with numerous nonpersistent bracts, a campanulate perianth, and five to ninety stamens. The female flowers, which have a minute dentate perianth,

N. obliqua

N. procera

N. solandri

The evergreen *Nothofagus solandri* has oval, not toothed, leaves, which are glabrous and glossy above and covered with a close down beneath. However, young trees or those in shade are glabrous on both sides.

FAGACEAE

Nothofagus
SOUTHERN BEECHES

Number of species 35
Distribution *New Caledonia, New Guinea, Australia, New Zealand, and temperate South America.*
Commercial uses *Important timber trees in the southern hemisphere and also cultivated as ornamental trees with several named cultivars.*

are solitary or in groups of three (rarely seven) surrounded by a two- or four-partite cupule, derived from a lobed extension of the flower-stalk (pedicel), which hardens in fruit. The fruit is a one-seeded nut.

The genus, which is most closely related to the northern hemisphere beeches (*Fagus* spp), is divided into two sections: section *Calucechinus* is deciduous and, apart from one Tasmanian species, is entirely South American; section *Calusparassus* is evergreen, with all but three species in the Old World, mostly in New Guinea and New Caledonia.

The temperate species of *Nothofagus* are parasitized by "mistletoes"—by members of the genus *Elytranthe* (Loranthaceae) in New Zealand, while *Misodendendrun*, the only genus in its family, is restricted to the South American beeches.

Several of the temperate species of *Nothofagus*, particularly those from South America, produce a hardwood timber, which, though somewhat softer than *Fagus*, finds a wide range of uses in furniture manufacture, building construction, fencing, and so on. *Nothofagus nervosa* ('Rauli'), *N. obliqua* ('Roble'), *N. glauca*, and *N. alessandri* (the last two used for boat-building in Chile) have the best timber quality, while that of *N. dombeyi* and *N. pumilio* is slightly poorer. Some temperate species, principally *N. antarctica* ('Ñire'), *N. obliqua*, and *N. nervosa*, have been grown as garden ornamentals for their form and splendid fall coloring. However, since the earliest forest plots were set out in Britain in the 1930s, there has been increasing interest in planting *Nothofagus* for timber production. *Nothofagus obliqua* and *N. nervosa* have demonstrated their ability to outyield all the native hardwoods on a wide range of soils and rainfall regimes, and there is currently much work being carried out on testing species from a variety of natural habitats to extend the *Nothofagus* plantations in Britain.

The Main Species of *Nothofagus*

Section *Calucechinus*

Deciduous trees. Leaves plicate (folded like a fan) in bud.

Subsection *Antarctica*

Cupule 4-partite (in 4 parts). Female flowers in threes
(or rarely sevens).

N. alessandri **'Ruil'** C Chile. Tree to 130 ft (40 m). Leaves 2–5 x
3–3.5 in (55–135 x 80–90 mm), ovate-oblong, finely dentate,
glabrous. Male flowers in threes, with 10–20 stamens. Nuts
0.25–0.3 in (6.5–7.5 mm), having 3 acute angles and
3 concave surfaces (triquetrous), winged and glabrous. **CZ9**

N. antarctica **'Ñire' or 'Guindo'** S Chile, S Argentina. Tree to 60 ft
(18 m) or small shrub. Leaves 0.45–1.8 x 0.2–0.9 in (13–45 x
5–22 mm), oblong to ovate-suborbicular, somewhat lobed,
crenate, usually glabrous but slightly pubescent (puberulent)
on veins beneath. Male flowers solitary, in twos or threes,
with 8–13 stamens. Nuts about 0.25 in (6 mm), triquetrous,
and glabrous. **CZ7**

N. glauca **'Roble de Maule'** or **'Hualo'** C Chile. Tree to 130 ft
(40 m). Leaves 1.8–3 x 1.2–2 in (45–80 x 30–50 mm), ovate-
oblong, doubly serrate, glabrous but fine-haired (ciliate)
on veins beneath. Male flowers solitary, with 40–90
stamens. Lateral nuts 0.6–0.65 in (15–16 mm),
triquetrous, not winged. **CZ7**

N. obliqua **'Roble Pellin,' 'Coyan,'** or **'Hualle'** C and S Chile,
C and S Argentina. Tree to 115 ft (35 m). Leaves 0.8–3 x
0.4–1.4 in (20–75 x 12–35 mm), elliptic-oblong, doubly
serrate, subglabrous. Male flowers solitary, with
20–40 stamens. Nuts 0.2–0.25(0.4) in (5–6(10) mm),
distinctly winged. **CZ8**

N. nervosa **'Rauli'** C and S Chile, C and S Argentina. Tree to
100 ft (30 m). Leaves 1.6–5 x 0.8–1.6 in (40–120 x 20–40 mm),
oblong to narrowly ovate, finely denticulate; male flowers
solitary, with 20–30 stamens. Nuts about 0.25 in (6 mm),
pubescent or glabrous, the lateral 3-winged, the central
2-winged. **CZ7**

N. gunnii **Tanglefoot Beech.** Tasmania. Tree or shrub 5–8 ft
(1.5–2.5 m). Leaves 0.4–0.5 x 0.4–0.5 in (10–15 x 10–15 mm),
orbicular-ovate, crenate, with long adpressed hairs on veins
beneath. Male flowers solitary in twos or threes, with 6–12
stamens. Nuts about 0.3 in (8 mm), the lateral broadly
3-winged, the central flat and 2-winged. **CZ8**

Subsection *Pumiliae*

Cupule 2-partite. Female flower solitary.

N. pumilio **'Lenga'** or **'Roble Blanco'** S Chile, S Argentina. Tree
to 82 ft (25 m) or small shrub at higher elevations. Leaves
0.8–1.4 x 0.4–1 in (20–35 x 10–25 mm), broadly ovate to
broadly elliptical, obtusely doubly dentate, subglabrous.
Male flowers solitary, with 20–30 stamens. Nuts about 0.3 in
(7 mm), triquetrous, and puberulent. **CZ7**

Section *Calusparassus*

Evergreen trees. Leaves not plicate in bud.

N. antarctica

N. moorei

N. procera

N. obliqua

N. procera

N. pumilio

N. menziesii

Subsection *Quadripartitae*

Cupule 4-partite. Female flowers in threes, lateral flowers with parts in threes, central with parts in twos. Leaves subentire to lobed or deeply divided.

N. betuloides **'Coigüe de Magallanes'** S Chile, S Argentina. Tree to 100 ft (30 m). Leaves 0.5–1 × 0.2–0.8 (12–25 x 6–19 mm), ovate-elliptical, serrate, glabrous. Male flowers solitary, with 10–16 stamens. Nuts 0.25 in (6 mm), triquetrous, and glabrous. **CZ7**

N. dombeyi **'Coigüe'** C and S Chile, C and S Argentina. Tree to 165 ft (50 m). Leaves 0.8–1.2 × 0.3–0.6 in (20–30 × 7.5–15 mm), ovate-oblong to lanceolate, unevenly denticulate, and glabrous. Male flowers in threes, with 8–15 stamens. Nuts about 0.25–0.28 in (6–7 mm), sparsely pubescent, the lateral 3-winged, the central 2-winged. **CZ8**

N. nitida **'Roble de Chiloe'** C Chile, C Argentina. Tree to 100 ft (30 m). Leaves 0.85–1.4 × 0.45–0.8 in (22–35 × 12–20 mm), ovate-oblong to triangular, coarsely dentate and glabrous. Male flowers in threes, with 5–8 stamens. Nuts about 0.25 in (6 mm), triquetrous, winged, and sparsely pubescent. **CZ7**

N. cunninghamii **Myrtle Beech.** SE Australia. Tree to 165 ft (50 m). Leaves 0.2–0.8 × 0.2–0.8 in (6–20 × 6–20 mm), suborbicular, distantly crenate and glabrous. Male flowers solitary, rarely in threes, with 8–12 stamens. Nuts about 0.25 in (6 mm), glabrous, the lateral 3-winged, the central 2-winged. **CZ9**

N. moorei **Australian Beech.** E Australia. Tree to 165 ft (50 m). Leaves 0.6–4.5 × 0.3–2.4 in (15–115 × 8–60 mm), ovate-oblong, serrate, glabrous but with hairs on mid-vein above. Male flowers solitary, with 15–20 stamens. Nuts about 0.25 in (6 mm), lateral triquetrous and 3-winged, central flat and 2-winged. **CZ9**

N. menziesii **Silver Beech.** New Zealand. Tree to 100 ft (30 m). Leaves 0.2–0.6 × 0.19–0.6 in (6–15× 5–15 mm), broadly ovate to suborbicular, doubly crenate, glabrous except on veins beneath. Male flowers solitary, with 30–36 stamens. Nuts about 0.2 in (5 mm), puberulent, the lateral triquetrous and 3-winged, the central flat and 2-winged. **CZ9**

N. fusca **Red Beech.** New Zealand. Tree to 100 ft (30 m). Leaves 1–1.4 × 0.5–1 in (25–35 × 12–25 mm), broadly ovate to ovate-oblong, rather deeply serrate, glabrous except on veins beneath. Male flowers solitary, in twos and threes, rarely in groups of 5, with 8–11 stamens. Nuts 0.3 in (8 mm), glabrous, triquetrous or flat and winged. **CZ9**

N. truncata **Hard Beech.** New Zealand. Tree to 100 ft (30 m). Leaves 1–1.4 × 0.8 in (25–35 × 20 mm), broadly ovate to elliptic-oblong or suborbicular, shallowly, coarsely, and obtusely serrate, glabrous or subglabrous. Male flowers solitary, in twos or threes, with 10–13 stamens. Nuts about 0.3 in (8 mm), puberulent. **CZ8**

Nothofagus species form the tree line in the southern Andes. They are vigorous growers, reaching 50 ft (15 m) in height, but can become straggly on exposed mountain sites.

N. codonandra

N. grandis

Subsection *Tripartitae*

Cupule 3-partite. Female flowers in threes, lateral flowers with parts in threes, central flower with parts in twos. Leaves entire.

N. solanderi var *cliffortioides* Mountain Beech. New Zealand. Tree to 50 ft (15 m) or a shrub. Leaves 0.4–0.6 × 0.28–0.4 in (10–15 × 7–10 mm), ovate to ovate-oblong, glabrous above, densely grayish, white- or brownish-tomentose beneath. Male flowers solitary, in twos or threes, with 8–14 stamens. Nuts 0.25–0.3 in (6–8 mm), glabrous or puberulent, wings with acute tips. **CZ8**

N. solanderi Black Beech. New Zealand. Tree to 82 ft (25 m). Leaves 0.4–0.6 × 0.2–0.4 in (10–15 × 5–10 mm), narrowly to elliptic-oblong, glabrous or subglabrous above, densely grayish white-tomentose beneath. Male flowers solitary or in pairs, with 8–17 stamens. Nuts up to 0.3 in (8 mm), with broadly based wings. **CZ8**

Subsection *Bipartitae*

Cupule 2-valved. Female flowers solitary or in threes, all with parts in twos.

Series *Triflorae*

Cupule with 3 nuts.

N. perryi New Guinea. Tree 46–130 ft (14–40 m). Leaves 1.2–3 × 0.4–1.4 in (30–80 × 12–35 mm), ovate-oblong, crenate in upper part, glabrous. Male flowers in threes, with 13–15 stamens. Nuts 0.2–0.3 in (5–8 mm), ovoid, more or less winged near apex. **CZ8**

N. nuda New Guinea. Tree about 66 ft (20 m). Leaves 3–4 × 1.2–1.6 in (80–100 × 30–40 mm), elliptical, shallowly crenate toward apex, glabrous. **CZ8**

N. balansae New Caledonia. Tree. Leaves 1.8–3 × 0.8–1.2 in (47–80 × 20–30 mm), obovate-elliptical, glabrous. Male flowers in threes, with 12–30 stamens. Nuts 0.5 in (13–15 mm), orbicular, narrowly winged. **CZ7**

N. discoidea New Caledonia. Tree to 130 ft (40 m). Leaves about 3 × 1–1.6 in (80 × 25–40 mm), lanceolate, glabrous. Male flowers in threes, with 12–30 stamens. Nuts 0.6 in (16–19 mm), more or less orbicular, narrowly winged. **CZ7**

N. starkenborghi New Guinea. Tree 52–150 ft (16–45 m). Leaves 1.2–3 × 0.5–1.3 in (30–80 × 12–35 mm), elliptical, rarely obovate, glabrous. Male flowers in threes, with about 12–14 stamens. Nuts about 0.25 in (6 mm) ovoid, more or less winged. **CZ9**

N. aequilateralis New Caledonia. Tree to 100 ft (30 m). Leaves 3.2–4 × 1.2–1.6 in (85–100 × 30–40 mm), elliptical, glabrous. Male flowers in threes, with 12–30 stamens. Nuts orbicular, narrowly winged. **CZ9**

N. brassii New Guinea. Tree 66–150 ft (25–45 m). Leaves 1–3.5 × 0.6–1.6 in (25–90 × 15–40 mm), elliptic- to ovate-oblong, glabrous. Male flowers in threes, with about 15 stamens. Nuts 0.25–0.4 in (6–10 mm), ovoid to subglobose, winged toward apex. **CZ7**

N. baumanniae New Caledonia. Tree. Leaves 2.5–5 × 1–2.3 in (6–12 × 2.5–5.5 cm), more or less oblong, glabrous. Male flowers in threes, with 12–30 stamens. Nuts 0.7–1.2 in (20–30 mm), more or less orbicular, narrowly winged. **CZ9**

N. codonandra New Caledonia. Tree to 100 ft (30 m). Leaves 3.5–5 × 1.2–2.2 in (9–12 × 2.8–5.5 cm), oblong, glabrous. Male flowers in threes, with 12–30 stamens. Nuts 0.6–0.7 in (17–20 mm), more or less orbicular, narrowly winged. **CZ9**

Series *Uniflorae*

Cupule with 1 nut.

N. pullei New Guinea. Shrub 6.5– 13 ft (2–4 m) or tree to 66– 165 ft (20–50 m). Leaves 0.4–1.8 × 0.28–1.1 in (10–45 × 7–28 mm), broadly elliptical to elliptic-oblong, glabrous above, sparsely hairy on mid-vein beneath. Male flowers solitary, with 10–15 stamens. Nut 0.2–0.25 in (5–6 mm), orbicular to elliptical. **CZ8**

N. crenata New Guinea. Tree to 130 ft (40 m). Leaves 1–2 × 0.5–0.8 in (25–50 × 12–20 mm), ovate-oblong, crenate toward apex, glabrous. Male flowers solitary. Nut about 0.2 in (5 mm), more or less orbicular, narrowly winged. **CZ7**

N. resinosa New Guinea. Tree 50–165 ft (15–50 m). Leaves 1.6–4 × 1–2 in (40–100 × 25–50 mm), elliptical, minutely dentate near apex, glabrous. Male flowers solitary, with 13–15 stamens. Nut 0.4 in (9–10 mm), broadly ellipsoid, winged, puberulent. **CZ7**

N. pseudoresinosa New Guinea. Tree 100–150 ft (30–45 m). Leaves 1–2.1 × 0.5–1 in (25–55 × 12–25 mm), elliptic-oblong, and glabrous. Male flowers solitary. Nut 0.3 in (7–8 mm), ovoid. **CZ7**

N. carrii New Guinea. Tree 66–150 ft (20–45 m). Leaves 0.9–2.4 × 0.4–1.2 in (20–60 × 10–30 mm), obovate, rarely elliptical, glabrous. Male flowers in threes, with about 10 stamens. Nut 0.2–0.4 in (7–11 mm), ellipsoid to ovoid-oblong. **CZ8**

N. flaviramea New Guinea. Tree 50–150 ft (15–45 m). Leaves 2–5 × 1–2 in (50–120 × 25–50 mm), ovate-oblong, glabrous. Male flowers in threes; nut 0.4 in (8–10 mm), obovate. **CZ8**

N. grandis New Guinea. Tree (40)82–156 ft ((12)25–48 m). Leaves 1.8–4 × 0.9–2 in (45–100 × 20–50 mm), broadly elliptical to elliptic-oblong, glabrous. Male flowers in threes, with 10–17 stamens. Nut 0.28–0.4 in (7–10 mm), rhomboid, narrowly winged. **CZ8**

N. rubra New Guinea. Tree 56–150 ft (17–45 m). Leaves 1–4 × 0.6–1.8 in (25–100 × 15–45 mm), ovate-oblong to elliptical, glabrous. Male flowers in threes. Nut 0.2–0.25 in (4–6 mm), orbicular to broadly ovoid. **CZ8**

N. womersleyi New Guinea. Tree about 66 ft (20 m). Leaves 2–3.8 × 1–1.6 in (50–90 × 25–40 mm), ovate-oblong, glabrous. Nut 0.28–0.4 in (7–10 mm), ovate-oblong, flat, winged toward apex. **CZ8**

Castanea

Chestnuts

Castanea is a genus of about ten species from the northern hemisphere. The Sweet Chestnut (*C. sativa*) is a native of the eastern Mediterranean countries but is now naturalized further north and has been in Britain since Roman times.

The chestnuts are fast-growing, long-lived deciduous trees, often growing to a great size, branching low down and spreading horizontally. The trunk has a characteristic spirally ridged bark. The leaves are elliptical, serrate, with a polished surface that makes the tree readily identifiable from a distance even in dense mixed woodland. The flowers are small and are borne in catkins in the axils of the leaves, the upper part of the catkin with groups of male flowers, the female flowers below in groups of three, yielding three nuts (strictly they are seeds) enclosed in a prickly capsule, which splits open when they are ripe. Improved cultivated varieties contain a single large nut.

The trees and fruits of chestnut are susceptible to disease, the most serious of which is Chestnut Blight caused by the sac fungus (Ascomycotina) *Endothia parasitica* (Sphaeriales), which was responsible for the decimation of the forests of *Castanea dentata* of the eastern United States. It was first noticed in 1904 and thought to be a local parasite. It is now understood that the fungus was introduced from China and Japan, where it occurs on other locally indigenous species of chestnut, doing little harm. The parasite appeared in Europe in 1938, with serious consequences in Italy and in Turkey. Invasion takes place only through wounds, killing bark and sap wood. The tree usually dies in a matter of a few years. The fruits themselves may also become infected and this probably contributes to the spread of the disease. Control of

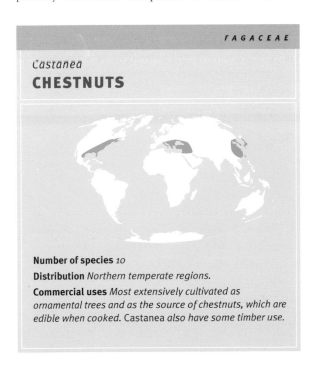

FAGACEAE

Castanea
CHESTNUTS

Number of species *10*

Distribution *Northern temperate regions.*

Commercial uses *Most extensively cultivated as ornamental trees and as the source of chestnuts, which are edible when cooked. Castanea also have some timber use.*

spread is almost impossible, because the spores are carried by birds, insects, rain, and winds. Attempts have been made to produce disease-resistant hybrids by crossing the American species with resistant oriental species.

Chestnuts are edible when cooked and were very popular in the days of the Roman empire. They are energy-rich and highly nutritious and still constitute a basic food in many countries in southern Europe, including Sardinia, Corsica, parts of northern Italy, and upland regions of southern, central, and western France, where they are typically ground into a flour. They can be variously prepared to produce such diverse delicacies as *marrons glacés* (cooked whole and preserved in a vanilla-flavored syrup) and chestnut purée, used as a stuffing for turkey or as the basis for many sweet desserts. Fresh chestnuts, available in the winter months, are also often roasted in their shells, then peeled and eaten as they are.

The timber of young trees is used for hop-poles and hoops for barrels, but older wood is too weak for exploitation. The wood does not burn satisfactorily and for this reason it was often deployed in wine-producing countries in Europe to stake vines, because the stakes were less likely to be stolen from the vineyards for use as fuel. Chestnut continues to have limited application in barrelmaking in some European countries. The bark is used in the tanning industry.

Other species of *Castanea* also supply timber, which is often used for railway sleepers; many of these species also produce edible nuts. Best known are the American Chestnut (*C. dentata*) from eastern North America, the Japanese Chestnut (*C. crenata*), and two species from China, *C. henryi* and *C. mollissima*.

Some of these species are also among the most popular ornamental trees of the genus. They are all hardy, but like warm situations, and are tolerant of drought conditions. Although of basically a similar structure to *C. sativa*, they can be distinguished mainly on leaf characters. *Castanea henryi* and *C. pumila* have a possibly more fundamental difference: the nuts are solitary rather than the usual three or more (rarely two) in the other species. **CZ4–8**

BELOW The fruit of *Castanea sativa* ripen in one season into edible, red-brown nuts. These are usually in twos, one globose and one smaller, and they narrow to a tip bearing the remains of the styles. They are enclosed in a globose prickly bur.

ABOVE The smooth-leaved American Chestnut, *Castanea dentata*, is a popular ornamental tree with edible fruits.

The Main Species of *Castanea*

Group I: Leaves hairless or with only a few hairs on the veins beneath.

C. dentata American Chestnut. E N. America. Tree to 100 ft (30 m). Leaves hairless beneath. Catkins 4–8 in (15–20 cm). **CZ4**

C. henryi China. Tree 66–82 ft (20–25 m). Leaves with a few hairs on the veins beneath. Catkins about 4 in (10 cm). Fruit with solitary nut. **CZ6**

Group II: Leaves hairy on the lower surface. Fruits usually with solitary nuts.

C. pumila Chinquapin. E U.S. Shrub or tree to 66 ft (20 m). Hairs on leaves whitish. **CZ7**

C. alnifolia SE U.S. Shrub less than 3 ft (1 m) tall. Hairs on leaves brownish. **CZ8**

Group III: Leaves hairy on the lower surface. Fruits with 2–3 nuts.

C. molissima Chinese Chestnut. China. Tree to 66 ft (20 m). Young twigs remaining hairy. Leaves lacking scaly glands beneath, the margins with triangular teeth. **CZ6**

C. sativa Sweet or Spanish Chestnut. S Europe, N Africa, and Asia Minor. Tree about 100–130 ft (30–40 m). Young twigs soon losing their downiness. Leaves with scaly glands beneath, margins with pointed, coarse teeth. **CZ5**

C. crenata Japanese Chestnut. Japan. Tree to 33 ft (10 m). Young twigs soon losing their downiness. Leaves with scaly glands and hair beneath, the margins with pointed but small teeth. **CZ4**

C. seguinii China. Shrub or tree to 33 ft (10 m). Leaves with scaly glands beneath, hairs only on veins, margin coarsely toothed. **CZ6**

C. alnifolia

C. pumila

C. dentata

C. henryi

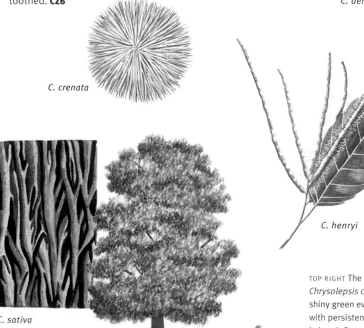

C. crenata

C. sativa

C. sativa

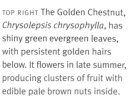

C. pumila

TOP RIGHT The Golden Chestnut, *Chrysolepis chrysophylla*, has shiny green evergreen leaves, with persistent golden hairs below. It flowers in late summer, producing clusters of fruit with edible pale brown nuts inside.

Chrysolepis/Castanopsis

Golden Chestnut, Chinquapins

The taxonomy of this group of evergreen trees continues to be a matter of considerable debate. *Chrysolepis*, *Castanopsis*, and also *Lithocarpus* are considered living links between the oaks (*Quercus* spp) and chestnuts (*Castanea* spp). The system followed here is as follows. *Chrysolepis* is a genus of two species from the west coast of the United States, which were originally placed in the genus *Castanea*, transferred to *Castanopsis*, then moved again to *Chrysolepis*. *Castanopsis* is now a genus of some 110 species exclusively native to the subtropics and Tropics of Asia. Chief differences between the genera are: *Castanea* is deciduous and its fruit matures in one year; *Chrysolepis* and *Castanopsis* are evergreen and in the former the fruit takes two years to mature; *Castanopsis* has unisexual inflorescence spikes, while in the other genera the sexes are mixed in a single spike. To add to the confusion, the popular name Chinquapin is also given to *Castanea pumila*.

The Giant Chinquapin or Golden Chestnut (*Chrysolepis chrysophylla*, formerly *Castanopsis chrysophylla*) has shiny green leaves that are covered with persistent golden yellow scales below. It may be found in cultivation for its attractive foliage but, as with the other members of the genus, it is not hardy in cold climates, though at its northern limits it will form a shrub. It grows to almost 115 ft (35 m) in the wild, but only 33 ft (10 m) in cultivation and then it is sometimes shrubby. It is intolerant of lime-rich soils. The Bush Chinquapin (*Chrysolepis sempervirens*, formerly *Castanopsis sempervirens*) is a shrubby plant to about 13 ft (4 m) but spreading to about 20 ft (6 m) in cultivation.

The best-known Asian species is the Japanese Chinquapin (*C. cuspidata*), which has a grayish down on the undersides of the leaves. In Japan it is valued for its timber and edible nuts, and hence much planted in gardens and parks. Logs of this species are also used in Japan to cultivate edible fungi. In north temperate regions it is hardy but makes poor growth. Other *Castanopsis* species are widespread in tropical forests and are valued for their timber and as sources of food—the Greater Malayan Chestnut (*C. megacarpa*) yields top-quality wood much used for cabinetmaking in the Orient. **CZ7–8**

BETULACEAE

Betula
Birches

The genus *Betula* comprises thirty to forty species of trees and shrubs native to the north temperate and Arctic regions that are outstanding for their beauty and usefulness. Most species are extremely hardy, *B. nana* reaching the tree limit in the northern hemisphere.

The birches are deciduous, wind-pollinated trees or shrubs. The bark is often extremely handsome, particularly in the White Birch (*B. pubescens*), the Silver Birch (*B. pendula*), and the Paper Birch (*B. papyrifera*) in which it peels off in papery layers. Some species are characterized by trunks of yellow, orange, reddish-brown, or almost black shades. The lenticels are horizontal and the leaves alternate and serrate. The flowers, which appear at the same time as leaves, are borne in unisexual "catkins" on the same plant. Each catkin-bract has three flowers. The male flower has a perianth of four minute calyx lobes and two stamens, the catkins being produced in the fall and overwintering; the female flower has a single ovary with two styles and a three-lobed bract. The fruit is a two-winged nutlet with a membranous wing on each side for wind dispersal. The genus is distinguished from *Alnus* by the fact that the fruiting catkins disintegrate when ripe.

In cultivation, *Betula* species succeed in good well-drained loam, though *B. pendula* likes a poor sandy soil. *Betula pubescens* flourishes on acid heathland among heather, spreading rapidly over clearings and wastelands by means of vast numbers of wind-dispersed seeds. *Betula nana* and *B. nigra* occur normally on wet ground.

Useful timber is obtained from the Black Birch (*B. lenta*), the Himalayan Birch (*B. utilis*), the Silver, Common or White Birch (*B. pendula*), and the White or Downy Birch (*B. pubescens*). This timber is too soft for use in the building construction trade, but the handsome grain makes it valuable for furniture. It turns and works easily and is employed in chairs, coopering, clog- and spoon-making. It provides much firewood, particularly in parts of Russia, and considerable quantities of charcoal. When wet, the wood is exceptionally durable, so can be used for supports in certain places, but it decays quickly if exposed to alternate wetness and dryness. The flexible branches, cut in winter, are made into besoms, still much used by gardeners. The bark is impermeable to water and can therefore be used for roofing, household utensils, and to make a variety of containers. The bark of the Canoe or Paper Birch (*B. papyrifera*) is used by North American indigenous people in the construction of canoes; these are made from sheets of bark tied together with root-fibers of the White Fir and smeared with resin from the Balsam Fir. Birch twigs and bark also yield an oil, which is used as a preservative and gives the fragrance to Russian leather. **CZ1–9**

BETULACEAE

Betula
BIRCHES

Number of species *up to 40*
Distribution *Northern hemisphere.*
Commercial uses *Highly valued for good-quality timber and also for horticultural use; various oils are also extracted from the bark for a wide range of uses.*

B. papyrifera

B. pendula

B. pubescens

ABOVE *Betula pendula* is the popular ornamental choice with its graceful, pendulous branching habit compared to *B. papyrifera*, which has a thin open head of branches. *B. pubescens* is the least attractive.

LEFT Birch trees are among the first species to colonize bare ground, being able to make rapid early growth in full light and on poor soils.

The Main Species of *Betula*

Section *Betula*

Fruiting inflorescences subglobose or ovoid or shortly cylindrical and solitary. Wings of the nutlets entirely or almost hidden by the fruiting bracts.

B. lutea

Subsection *Nanae*

Shrubs to 6.6 ft (2 m), though often prostrate. Leaves small, 0.2–1.8 in (0.5–4.5 cm), distinctly reticulate with 2–6 veins. Male inflorescences on shortened leafless branchlets; fruiting female inflorescences small and erect.

B. nana Dwarf Birch. North temperate regions in moist places on mountains. Bush 20–39 in (50–100 cm), with erect downy branches, not warty. Leaves orbicular, 0.2–0.6 in (0.5–1.5 cm) diameter, with round teeth, dark green above, glabrous at maturity; veins in 2–4 pairs. Fruiting catkins 0.2–0.4 in (5–10 mm), scales with lobes of equal length. **CZ2**

Subsection *Costatae*

Trees or largish shrubs. Leaves large, 1–4 in (25–100 mm), 7 to many pairs of veins, not or only indistinctly reticulate. Male inflorescences terminal on elongated branchlets, more rarely on laterals as well; fruiting female inflorescence erect or pendulous, bracts often elongated.

B. nigra River Birch. C and E U.S. A graceful pyramidal tree, 50–100 ft (15–30 m), with striking blackish curling shaggy bark. Shoots warty and downy. Leaves rhomboid-ovate, cuneate at base, 1.6–3.5 x 0.8–2.4 in (4–9 × 2–6 cm), double-toothed, glaucous beneath; veins underneath hairy in 6–9 pairs. Female catkins 1–1.6 in (2.5–4 cm), scales downy, middle lobe smallest. **CZ4**

B. utilis Himalayan Birch. The Himalaya and China. Tree to 66 ft (20 m) with peeling creamy-white bark. Twigs very downy becoming reddish-brown. Leaves ovate, 2–3 in (5–7.5 cm), irregularly toothed; veins in 9–12 pairs. Fruiting catkins cylindrical, 1.4 × 0.4 in (3.5 × 1 cm); scales ciliate, middle lobe longer and rounded. **CZ7**

B. lenta Black, Cherry, or Sweet Birch. E N. America. Tree to 66–82 ft (20–25 m), bark very dark, not peeling. Young branches softly hairy, soon becoming glabrous. Leaves 2.8–6 × 1.2–3.5 in (7–15 × 3–9 cm), ovate to oblong, cordate at base, toothed; veins in 10–12 pairs, bearing silky hairs underneath. Petiole 0.4–1 in (1–2.5 cm). Female catkins about 1 × 0.4 in (2.5 × 1 cm); scales glabrous. The young bark has a sweet aromatic smell when bruised. Attractive in the fall when the leaves turn yellow. **CZ3**

B. alleghaniensis Yellow Birch. E N. America. Tree to 100 ft (30 m), bark smooth, shining, yellowish-brown, peeling. Leaves rich yellow in the fall. Young shoots hairy with bitter aromatic bark. Leaves 2.4–5 × 1.2–2.4 in (6–12 × 3–6 cm), apex pointed, base cordate, margin doubly toothed, ciliate: veins in 9–12 pairs, hairy beneath. Fruiting catkins 1–1.6 × 0.8 in (2.5–4 × 2 cm), erect; scales downy on outside and margin. **CZ3**

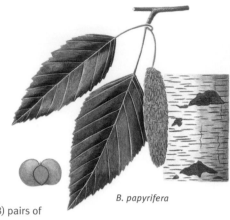

B. papyrifera

Subsection *Albae*

Leaves large, 1–4 in (2.5–10 cm), usually with 5–7(8) pairs of veins, not or only indistinctly reticulate. Male inflorescences usually situated terminally on elongated branchlets; female fruiting inflorescences usually cylindrical, bracts short.

B. pendula Silver, White, or Common Birch. Europe, N Asia, and N Africa. Tree to 82 ft (25 m) with silvery-white peeling bark and more or less pendulous branches. Twigs glabrous with pale warts. Leaves 0.8–2.4 × 0.8–1.6 in (2–6 × 2–4 cm), ovate-deltoid, acuminate, cuneate at base, sharply doubly serrate. Fruiting catkins 0.6–1.4 × 0.4 in (1.5–3.5 × 1 cm); scales glabrous, central lobe smallest. A number of forms and cultivars: 'Purpurea' has purple leaves. **CZ1**

B. pubescens Downy Birch. Europe and N Asia. Tree to 66 ft (20 m) with peeling white bark, becoming dark and rugged at the base. Twigs covered in down and wartless. Leaves ovate, 1.4–2 in (3.5–5 cm), rounded at base, downy; veins in 5–7 pairs. Fruiting catkins 1 in (2.5 cm); scales ciliate, center one larger and pointed, lateral rounded. Hybrids between this species and *B. pendula* occur but are rare. There are a number of cultivars. **CZ1**

B. papyrifera Paper or Canoe Birch. N. America. Tree 50–100 ft (15–30 m) of thin graceful habit. The bark is one of the whitest among all the birches, peeling off in papery layers. Young shoots warty and hairy when young. Leaves 1.6–3.5 × 1–2.8 in (4–9 × 2.5–7 cm), ovate, cordate at base, margins doubly toothed, upper and lower surfaces hairy; 6–10 pairs of veins and small black glands present on lower surface. Fruiting catkins drooping, 1.6 × 0.4 in (4 × 1 cm); scales glabrous, lateral lobes broader than middle. The most widespread of all the American birches, used for fuel, roofing, and canoe-making. A number of varieties are recognized and cultivated. **CZ2**

B. pubescens

B. nana

B. pendula

Section *Betulaster*

Female fruiting inflorescences cylindrical in conspicuously elongated racemose heads or solitary through abortion. Wings of the nutlets markedly wider than the fruiting bracts.

B. maximowicziana Japan. Tree to 100 ft (30 m) in its native habitat. Bark orange-brown becoming grayish. Leaves heart-shaped, pointed, 3–6 in (7.5–15 cm) (the largest in the genus) turning a lovely clear butter-yellow in the fall. **CZ6**

B. nigra

Alnus

Alders

The genus *Alnus* comprises some twenty-five species, predominantly natives of north temperate regions, with one or two species extending down the Andes of South America to Chile, Peru, and Argentina. The species are mainly characteristic of cool climates as well as being moisture-loving. Their tolerance of wet soils gives rise to a particular type of alder scrub or woodland. This is an association of plants on predominantly alkaline (or very slightly acid), more or less permanently wet peat commonly known as fen. Above the winter water level and thus free from standing water, plants—notably alders—become established. Such woods are known in parts of England as carrs, associated with the Icelandic word *kjarr*, meaning a bog- or fenwood.

Alders are deciduous trees and shrubs, with alternate, usually serrate or dentate simple leaves. The flowers are unisexual and occur in catkins, with both sexes appearing on the same plant. The pendulous male catkins are borne at the tips of the previous year's shoots and overwinter unprotected by bud-scales; the female catkins are erect or pendulous, with a four-lobed perianth of one whorl (calyx). After fertilization, the female catkin forms a characteristic woody fruit, which somewhat resembles a small pine cone. These "cones" persist after the seed is shed and can normally be seen throughout the following winter.

Most of the alders in cultivation are hardy, and include Italian Alder (*Alnus cordata*), Common or Black Alder (*A. glutinosa*), Gray Alder (*A. incana*), and Red Alder (*A. rubra*). They flourish in wet soil conditions, making them popular for planting by rivers, streams, and ponds.

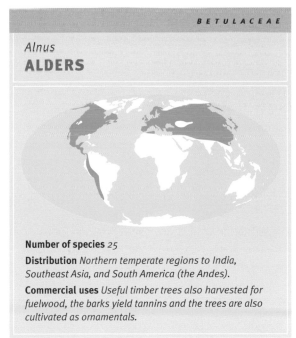

BETULACEAE

Alnus
ALDERS

Number of species 25
Distribution *Northern temperate regions to India, Southeast Asia, and South America (the Andes).*
Commercial uses *Useful timber trees also harvested for fuelwood, the barks yield tannins and the trees are also cultivated as ornamentals.*

An important feature is the presence of large nodules on the roots housing a symbiotic bacterium *Frankia alni*, which is capable of vigorous nitrogen fixation, from which the alders benefit.

The wood is used for decorative purposes, clog- and toy-making. Alder bark, obtained from various *Alnus* species such as *A. glutinosa* and *A. incana*, has long been used for its tannin content. The tannins have the property of coagulating proteins, and this is the basis for their use in converting raw hides into leather. Alder tannin is similar to oak tannin, obtained from the so-called oak-apple galls. Alder tannin has also been used for dyeing linen, using a suitable mordant. **CZ2–9**

ABOVE The Mountain Alder, *Alnus tenvifolia*, thrives in wet, nutrient-rich areas—here on the Rogue River in Oregon, U.S.A. They grow up to 33 ft (10 m).

BELOW Male catkins of *Alnus glutinosa* can make the tree appear purple in winter. They turn a dark yellow when they open in spring.

The Main Species of *Alnus*

Subgenus *Alnaster*

Winter buds sessile. Female catkins terminal, appearing with the leaves in spring, on short, few-leaved branches. Fruit winged.

A. pendula Japan. Small tree 26–42 ft (8–13 m). Leaves unlobed, oblong-lanceolate, acuminate, 2–5 in (5–12 cm), base cuneate to rounded, margin sharply serrate: veins in 12–18 pairs. "Cones" 2–5, pendulous, 0.3–0.6 in (8–15 mm), peduncle 1.2–2.5 in (3–6 cm). **CZ4**

A. viridis European Green Alder. Europe, especially montane. Shrub 3–10 ft (1–3 m) with sticky branchlets. Leaves unlobed, roundish-ovate, 1–2.4 in (2.5–6 cm), apex acute, base cuneate, margin finely serrate; veins in 5–10 pairs. "Cones" 0.4 in (1 cm), in racemes. Very hardy, thriving in cold and heavy soils. **CZ3**

A. crispa American Green Alder. Mountains of E N. America (Labrador to N Carolina). Eastern. American counterpart of *A. viridis*. Shrub to 10 ft (3 m). Young leaves sticky, pleasantly aromatic. Leaves 1.2–3 in (3–8 cm), not lobed, more or less roundish-ovate, the base more rounded than *A. viridis* to subcordate, margin finery serrate; veins in 5–10 pairs; 3–6 "cones" in racemes, each 0.4–0.6 in (1–1.5 cm) long. **CZ2**

A. sinuata W U.S. (Alaska to N California). Western counterpart of *A. viridis*. Shrub or small tree to 42 ft (13 m). Leaves with 5–10 pairs of veins but more or less lobed; 3–6 "cones," each about 0.4 in (1 cm) long, peduncle to 0.8 in (2 cm). **CZ2**

(Some view *A. crispa* and *A. sinuata* as subspecies of *A. viridis*.)

Subgenus *Cremastogyne*

Winter buds stalked. Male and female catkins solitary in the axils of leaves, the peduncles 2–3 times longer than the catkins. Female flowers naked. Spring-flowering.

A. cremastogyne China. Tree 85–100 ft (26–30 m). Leaves off-whitish, pubescent beneath in vein axils, soon glabrous, oblong-obovate, 2.8–5.6 in (7–14 cm), apex acute, base round to slightly cuneate, margin toothed; veins in 8–9 pairs. "Cones" 0.6–0.8 in (1.5–2 cm), pendulous, peduncles 0.8–2.4 in (2–6 cm). Fruit with broad wings. Rare in cultivation. **CZ8**

A. lanata Akin to above; leaves reddish-woolly beneath. **CZ8**

Subgenus *Clethropsis*

Winter buds sessile. Female catkins single or racemose in leaf axils, "cone" mostly longer than peduncle. Male catkins long and slender, the flower perianth lobes free to the base or, if connate at base, then with fewer than 4 lobes. Fall-flowering.

A. nitida W Himalaya. Tree to 100 ft (30 m) in its native habitat. Leaves more or less oblong-ovate, 3–5.8 in (8–14 cm); veins in 9–10 pairs, anastomosing at the weakly serrulate margin. Male catkins to 6 in (15 cm). "Cones" 0.8–1.2 in (2–3 cm), single in a leaf axil. Seed with thick leathery wing. **CZ8**

A. nepalensis Himalaya, Nepal to W China. Silver-barked tree 50– 66 ft (15–20 m). Leaves ovate-lanceolate, 3–5(6.5) in (8–12 (17) cm), serrate; veins in 12–14(16) pairs. Seed with thin, membranous wing. **CZ9**

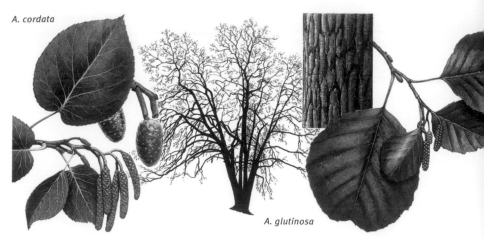

A. cordata

A. glutinosa

Subgenus *Alnus* (*Gymnothyrsus*)

Winter buds sessile. Leaves conspicuously serrate. "Cone" typically longer than its peduncle, single or racemose in the axils of leaves. Male flowers with 4-partite perianth connate at base and, like the female catkins, formed on previous year's wood, over-wintering to flower in spring.

A. glutinosa Black Alder or Common Alder. Europe, extreme N. Africa, Asia Minor, Caucasus to Siberia, naturalized locally in E N. America. Tree 82–115 ft (25–35 m). Leaves plicate in bud, green beneath, more or less oval to broadly obovate, 1.6–3.5(4) in (4–9(10) cm), coarsely and doubly serrate, the rounded apex notched, lateral veins in 5–7(8) pairs. Catkins 3–5, the "cone" 0.6–0.8 in (1.5–2 cm). Many named varieties, those with variously cut or divided leaves—var *laciniata*, var *incise*—being particularly striking. **CZ5**

A. glutinosa

A. rubra (*A. oregona*) W N. America. Tree 66–82 ft (20–25 m). Shoots soon bright red. Leaves plicate in bud, more or less oblong-ovate, 2.8–5 in (7–12 cm), apex acute, almost truncate at base, somewhat lobed, glaucous beneath; veins in 12–15 pairs. "Cones" 0.6–1 in (1.5–2.5 cm), peduncle present, orange-colored. **CZ6**

A. incana Speckled or Gray Alder. Europe (not British Isles), Caucasus, and N. America. Tree to 66 ft (20 m), occasionally shrubby, with grayish bark. Leaves plicate in bud, more or less glaucous beneath, broad elliptic to obovate, 1.6–4(5) in (4–10(12) cm), apex acute; veins in 9–12 pairs; 4–8 "cones," each about 0.6 in (1.5 cm), sessile or almost so. European specimens are sometimes known as var *vulgaris*. Numerous named varieties: var *acuminata* has leaves lobed to about half-way. **CZ2**

A. incana

A. cordata Italian Alder. Corsica and S Italy. A handsome pyramidal tree to 50 ft (15 m). Shoots and leaves glabrous. Leaves not plicate in bud, orbicular to broadly ovate, 2–4 in (5–10 cm), apex more or less acuminate, cordate at base; veins in 6–10 pairs. "Cones" 0.6–1 in (1.5–2.5 cm). **CZ6**

Note: There are a number of hybrids, e.g. *A. glutinosa × incana* = *A. hybrida*; *A. cordata × glutinosa* = *A. × elliptica*.

A. viridis

Carpinus
Hornbeams

Carpinus is a distinctive group of species distributed throughout temperate regions of the northern hemisphere. They are deciduous, wind-pollinated trees of moderate size with conspicuously ribbed alternate leaves and branches ascending at an angle of 20–30°. The flowers are pendulous, unisexual, and borne in catkins, with both sexes found on the same tree: male catkins arise on the old wood; the slender female catkins are in loosely constructed cones terminating the young shoots. At the base of each flower is a small, three-lobed, hairy bracteole. After fertilization the small ovary becomes woody to form a ribbed nut, and the large collar-like bracteole serves as a wing for dispersal.

Hornbeams are extremely hardy and handsome, especially when in flower and fruit. For this reason, about half of the species have been brought into cultivation, including several of the more widespread American and Asiatic species. Twenty-six are recognized as "good."

The spring-flowering Common Hornbeam (*C. betulus*) is often cultivated. Ranging from 5 ft (1.5 m) to 82 ft (25 m) tall in its mature state, it resembles the beech, for which it is easily mistaken. However, its stalked leaves are much more pointed than those of the beech, with double-toothed margins and prominent parallel veins emerging from the midrib. Its winter buds are very much shorter and more squat, and the flattened, ridged, and fluted trunk appears much duller. It is a native of Europe and southwest Asia. The timber is very tough, with almost a horned texture, and is difficult to work. However, its hard texture is valued for the manufacture of piano-key movements, for wooden axles and spokes. It burns well and makes excellent charcoal for burning and for the manufacture of gunpowder. During the Middle Ages, hornbeams were coppiced and pollarded for firewood and charcoal. Hornbeam coppices well, retaining its leaves after clipping, and because it branches profusely, it makes an excellent hedge. Seven well-known cultivars are grown in Europe, varying in color, leaf shape, tree morphology (form), and branching habit.

BETULACEAE	
Carpinus **HORNBEAMS**	

Number of species *26*

Distribution *Northern temperate regions to Central America and East Asia.*

Commercial uses *Widely planted as specimen trees and also sometimes used as hedging. The source of a good timber used for tools and musical instruments.*

C. betulus

C. caroliniana

The American Hornbeam or American Muscle Tree (*C. caroliniana*), native to the eastern United States, is similar to the Common Hornbeam, but is usually smaller, differing in its whitish, downy leaves, which turn orange-yellow or scarlet in the fall. The Japanese Hornbeam (*C. japonica*) is a widely cultivated, sturdy, pyramidal tree, which grows to 12–15 m (40–50 ft). It is valued for its large, handsome leaves and the large bracteoles on its pendulous female catkins. Less cultivated but beautiful species include the Oriental Hornbeam (*C. orientalis*), the hardy, vigorous Chinese Henry's Hornbeam (*C. henryana*), and the Cordate Hornbeam (*C. cordata*). **CZ5–8**

BELOW *Carpinus betulus*, the Common Hornbeam, is cultivated in North America as a park, street, or hedging tree. They are particularly attractive in the summer, laden with hanging clusters of fruit.

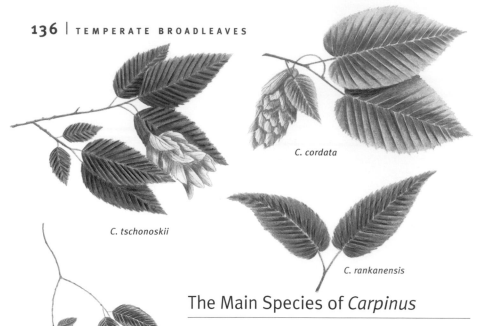

C. cordata

C. tschonoskii

C. rankanensis

C. orientalis

C. macrocarpa

C. betulus

The Main Species of *Carpinus*

Subgenus *Carpinus*

Scales of male flowers ovate and scarcely stalked. Bracts of fruiting catkins loosely packed and thus little infolded, leaving the nut exposed. Veins of leaves in 10–17 equal or subequal pairs. Fifty-four species.

C. betulus Common Hornbeam. Eurasia. Tree to 50–82 ft (15–25 m). Leaves oval, 1.6–3.5 × 1–2 in (4–9 × 2.5–5 cm), their bases rounded or heart-shaped, one side longer than the other, shortly pointed at the apex, unequally and doubly toothed, dark green and initially downy above, underside more downy, especially on the midrib, but both sides glabrous by the fall; veins in 10–13 pairs, petiole 0.2–0.4 in (0.5–1 cm). Fruiting catkins 1.2–3 in (3–8 cm), with large, conspicuous, 3-lobed bracts, the central lobe 0.8–1.6 in (2–4 cm) and often toothed, produced in facing pairs, each with an ovate, ribbed nut at the base. **CZ5**

C. caroliniana American Hornbeam, American Muscle Tree. E N. America. Somewhat similar to the above but grows more slowly and never attains such a size. Its leaves turn a deeper color in the fall. In winter, the best distinctions come from bud characters. In *C. betulus* they are slender and spindle-shaped and about 2.8 in (7 cm) long; in *C. caroliniana* the buds are egg-shaped and only 0.2 in (0.5 cm) long. **CZ5** Closely related species (all from China) include: *C. tientaiensis*, *C. lanceolate*, *C. londoniana*, *C. acrostachya*, *C. davidii*, *C. kempukwan*, *C. viminea*, *C. kweichowensis*, *C. poitanei*, and *C. tropicalis*.

C. macrocarpa Iran. Tree to 66 ft (20 m), rounded when mature. Leaves narrow, oblong-acute to rounded acuminate, 2.4–4.5 × 1.2–2 in (6–11 × 3–5 cm), densely hairy on the veins and with woolly axils; veins in 10–15 pairs, petioles 0.4–0.6 in (1–1.6 cm). Fruiting catkins about 3 × 1.8 in (8 × 4.5 cm) when mature, peduncles up to 2.4 in (6 cm); bracts semi-ovate, 1.2–1.4 × 0.8 in (3–3.5 × 2 cm), unevenly serrate toward the apex, bases unlobed, margin conduplicate.
Ripe nut ovoid and hairy with a hairy coronate apex. **CZ7** Morphologically similar species include *C. schuschaensis* (SW Asia), *C. geokczaica* (Russia), *C. grosseserrata* (Iran), and *C. hybrida* (Caucasus).

C. orientalis Oriental Hornbeam. SE Europe. Usually a small tree or large shrub but sometimes a shrubby bush. Leaves ovate, 1–2 × 0.4–1 in (2.5–5 × 1–2.5 cm), round to somewhat wedge-shaped at the base, pointed at the apex, with sharply and regularly double-toothed margin, dark, glossy green above and silky down on both surfaces of the midrib; veins in 12–15 pairs, petiole 0.2–0.3 in (5–7 mm). Fruiting catkins 1.2–2.4 in (3–6 cm) when mature, with short stalks, bracts more or less ovate, slightly longer on one side, coarsely and irregularly toothed but not lobed, each enclosing a tiny nut up to 0.2 in (0.5 cm) long. Its small leaves and unlobed bracts distinguish it from *C. betulus* and *C. caroliniana*. **CZ5** Morphologically related species include *C. turczaninowii*, *C. paxii*, *C. cowii* (all China), and *C. coreana* (Korea).

C. tschonoskii Japan and NE Asia. A small, deciduous tree to 33 ft (10 m). Leaves ovate, 1.6–3.2 × 0.8–1.6 in (4–8 × 2–4 cm), with tapered apex, unequally and doubly toothed margins, rounded base, dark green upper surface and flattened hairs on midrib; veins in 9–15 pairs, petiole slender, downy, 0.28 in (7 mm). Ripe fruiting catkins develop to 2–2.4 in (5–6 cm) on long silky stalks with narrowly ovate bracts 0.4–0.8 in (1–2 cm), toothed on one side, and silky-hairy especially on the veins and at the base, where they become slightly boat-shaped to accommodate the ovoid nut in the hollow. **CZ7** Allied species include *C. tsiangiana*, *C. chuniana*, *C. polyneura*, *C. henryana*, *C. seemeniana*, *C. fangiana*, *C. rupestris*, *C. kweitingensis*, *C. austrosinensis*, *C. bandelii*, *C. tungtzeensis*, *C. tschonoskii* (*C. yedoensis*), *C. fargesiana*, *C. sungpanensis*, *C. huana*, *C. putoensis*, *C. pubescens*, and *C. monbeigiana* (all from China), *C. fauriei* and *C. tanakeana* (Japan), *C. eximea* and *C. coreana* (Korea, *C. multiserrata*, *C. kawakamii*, *C. hogoensis*, *C. sekii*, and *C. hebestroma* (Taiwan).

Subgenus *Distegocarpus*

Scales of male flowers narrow-oblong with distinctive stalks. Bracts of fruiting catkins closely packed together, thus overlapping and infolded at the base to enclose the nut. Veins of leaves in 15–25 prominent equal pairs. Five species.

C. japonica Japanese Hornbeam. Japan. Tree to 60 ft (18 m). Leaves ovate or oblong, 2–4 × 0.8–2 in (5–10 × 2–5 cm), mostly heart-shaped at the base, but sometimes rounded or wedge-shaped, sharply double-toothed and often with an alternating large and small tooth. **CZ8**

C. cordata and ***C. mollis*** China. Distinguished from *C. japonica* by their large, deeply cordate leaves and enormous winter buds. They are very similar, however, in the curious manner in which the nut is protected by basal portions of the bract infolding over it. **CZ5**

C. rankanensis and ***C. matsudai*** Taiwan. Both are deciduous trees to 66 ft (20 m). Leaves ovate-oblong, 3–4 × 1.2–1.6 in (8–10 × 3–4 cm), membranous, papery, with caudate bases and the margins irregularly serrate becoming serrulate toward the acuminate apex; veins in 20–24 distinct pairs. **CZ7**

Corylus

Hazels

Corylus is a genus comprising some fifteen species of trees or shrubs from the temperate northern hemisphere including Europe, Asia, and North America. Hazels do well in a loam soil and are especially good in chalky areas. They are deciduous, wind-pollinated shrubs, less often trees. The leaves are soft, alternate, and singly or doubly toothed. The flowers, which appear before the leaves in late winter or early spring, are unisexual, with both sexes on the same plant, and the perianth is absent. The male flowers are borne in the familiar clusters of two to five pendulous catkins (commonly referred to as "lambs' tails"), each bract (scale) subtending a single flower with four to eight stamens, branched almost to the base, and two bracteoles. The female cluster is budlike, the upper bracts each with two flowers and associated bracteoles, and each flower has a single ovary surmounted by two styles. Their stigmas are strikingly red at pollination. The fruit is an edible nut enclosed in a leafy green involucre or husk, which originates from the enlarged bract and associated bracteoles.

The hazels are a very hardy group, with economic and decorative value. They are commercially grown for their nuts, which can be eaten fresh (sold in their green husks) but are usually dried and eaten roasted or salted. They are much used in patisserie and confectionery. The nuts have a high fat content (about 60 percent) and contain several important trace elements. A flavorsome oil is also extracted from the nut, which is used for cooking and as a salad dressing.

In North America, the principal native cultivated species are the American Hazel (*C. americana*) and the Beaked Hazel (*C. cornuta*); the European Hazel or Cobnut (*C. avellana*) has also been introduced from Europe. This last is a vigorous shrub or sometimes a small tree up to 7 m (23 ft), which forms dense thickets of erect, much-branched stems. At one time it was an important economic species, grown in coppices to supply wood for fuel, the regular straight stems for making hurdles and walking sticks, and also its nuts (variously known as hazelnuts, cobnuts, filberts) for fall cropping. *Corylus avellana* is still grown commercially, but the true Filbert is *C. maxima* from southeastern Europe and Asia Minor, which is widely cultivated for its nuts, both in its native areas and elsewhere, for example in southeast England, where the chief commercial variety is known as "Kentish Cob." Annual world production is over 800,000 tons.

Species that are cultivated for their nuts and ornamental value are the Chinese Hazel (*C. chinensis*), Turkish Hazel (*C. colurna*), and Tibetan Hazel (*C. tibetica*). Ornamental cultivars are *C. avellana* 'Aurea' with soft, yellow leaves, *C. avellana* 'Contorta' (the Corkscrew Hazel) with twisted branches, and *C. maxima* 'Purpurea' with purple leaves. **CZ4–8**

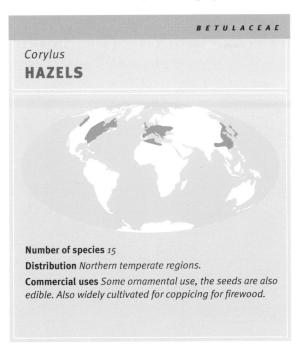

BETULACEAE

Corylus
HAZELS

Number of species 15

Distribution *Northern temperate regions.*

Commercial uses *Some ornamental use, the seeds are also edible. Also widely cultivated for coppicing for firewood.*

TOP *Corylus avellana* in fruit; the edible nuts ripen in October. These are set in a green husk or involucre the same length as the nut and cut into shallow, toothed lobes. It is the husk that best distinguishes the various hazel species.

ABOVE In the wild, hazel forms bushy thickets of 14–20 ft (4–6 m) when coppiced and sometimes develops into small trees. They make ideal hedging plants. Its branches are very supple and they are often grown for coppicing and the cut branches used for woven fencing and plant supports.

The Main Species of *Corylus*

Group I: Involucral lobes free or partly united at the base, not forming a distinct tube, but rather a deeply lobed, wide-spreading campanulate husk. The first 3 species are closely related and could be regarded as the local representatives of one "macro" species.

C. avellana **Common** or **European Hazel, Cobnut.** Europe, W Asia, N Africa. Typically a much suckering, bushy shrub to 20 ft (6 m). Leaves more or less broadly ovate, cuspidate, hairy, 2–4 in (5–10 cm). Male catkins yellow, 1.2–2 in (3–5 cm), very conspicuous in early spring. Female flowers minute, crimson-scarlet. Fruit in clusters of 1–4, 0.7 in (18 mm) long, nut barely enclosed in its campanulate involucre, divided to about half-way by more or less lanceolate toothed lobes. **CZ4**
'Contorta' (Corkscrew Hazel) A unique slow-growing variety with twisted stems. 'Aurea' is a cultivated form.

C. americana **American Hazel.** Canada, E U.S. Similar to above. Shrub 6.6–10 ft (2–3 m). Leaves 2–5 in (5–13 cm). Nut about 0.6 in (1.5 cm), concealed by an irregularly lobed involucre, connate at the base, about 1.2 in (3 cm) long. **CZ4**

C. heterophylla China, Japan. Shrub or small tree to about 23 ft (7 m). Leaves variable in shape, mostly widest above the middle, 2–4 in (5–10 cm) long. Involucre campanulate, 0.7–1 in (18–25 mm) long, somewhat longer than the nut, deeply divided into 6–9 triangular teeth with essentially smooth margins, about 0.2–0.25 in (4–6 mm) deep. **CZ6**

Group II: Like Group I but involucre resembling a small round-bottomed flask (more conical in *C. maxima*), the "bulb" enclosing the nut, the "neck" somewhat grooved, as long as, mostly 2–3 times longer than, the bulb, more or less toothed above.

C. cornuta (*C. rostrata*) **Beaked Hazel.** E and C U.S. Shrub to about 10 ft (3 m). Leaves more or less ovate to obovate, 1.6–4.5 in (4–11 cm), irregularly toothed to slightly lobed, petiole less than 0.4 in (1 cm). Involucre with distinct "bulb," conspicuously bristly. The nuts are said to be inedible. Var *californica*, from the western states of North America, has the involucral "neck" only about as long as the "bulb." **CZ4**

C. maxima **Filbert.** S Europe (not British Isles). Bushy shrub or tree to 23 ft (7 m). Leaves broadly ovate, widest above the middle, 2–5 in (5–13 cm) long. Involucre downy, without bristles, more conical without evident "bulb," the free end more deeply toothed. Extensively cultivated for its nuts, and parent of the cultivated English Filbert, of which there are a number of varieties. **CZ5**

C. sieboldiana **Japanese Hazel.** Japan. Shrub to 16 ft (5 m). Leaves elliptic to obovate, 2–4 in (5–10 cm), petiole 0.6–1 in (1.5–2.5 cm). Involucre bristly and with distinct "bulb," its "neck" only 1½ times longer. Var *mandshurica* (the Manchurian Hazel) has leaves to 6 in (15 cm) and the involucre with more spreading bristles, its "neck" about twice as long as the "bulb." **CZ6**

Group III: Species with unusual features either of bark or fruits, but the latter quite unlike fruits of Group II.

C. colurna **Turkish Hazel.** E Europe, Asia Minor. Pyramidal tree to 82 ft (25 m). Bark strikingly furrowed on shoots more than 2 years old, soon becoming corky. Leaves broadly ovate, (2.8)3–5(6) in ((7)8–12(15) cm), margin more or less lobed, petioles 1–1.8 in (2.5–4.5 cm), at first downy and with glands. Involucre of fruit with numerous linear, pointed, somewhat curved, hairy lobes with gland-tipped bristles. **CZ5**

C. chinensis **Chinese Hazel.** China. Similar to *C. colurna*, of which it was once made a variety. Tree approaching 100 ft (30 m) in the wild, about half that in cultivation. Leaves (4)6–7 in ((10)15–18 cm), uniformly serrulate, not lobed. Involucre strikingly constricted above the enclosed nut into a tube with slender, sometimes forked lobes. **CZ6**

C. tibetica **Tibetan Hazel.** Tibet. Tree, sometimes shrub-like, to about 23 ft (7 m). Leaves more or less ovate, 2–5 in (5–13 cm), petiole 1 in (2.5 cm) in length. Fruit a group of 3–6 nuts, the involucres quite unique with their slender, branched, glabrous spines, the whole looking like a burr, commonly recalling the fruit of Sweet Chestnut (*Castanea sativa*). **CZ7**

C. colurna

C. avellana 'Contorta'

C. cornuta

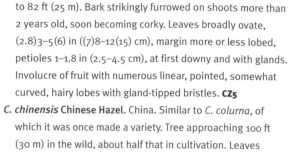

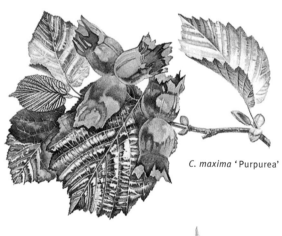

C. maxima 'Purpurea'

C. avellana

B. tibetica

Ostrya

Hop Hornbeams

The genus *Ostrya* comprises five species of medium-sized deciduous trees with wide-spreading horizontal branches. They are found throughout the temperate regions of the northern hemisphere, extending in Central America south to Guatemala and Costa Rica.

The leaves of hop hornbeams are alternate, more or less oval, with parallel veins and a toothed margin. The flowers appear with the leaves in spring. The male flowers, which occur in pendulous catkins, exposed throughout the winter, have three to fourteen stamens and no perianth. The female flowers are borne in erect bracteate catkins, with two flowers per bract. The calyx is adherent to the ovary, which is enclosed in an open involucre (husk); this closes after fertilization and then expands to form a bladder-like casing around a nutlet, the whole fruiting catkin not unlike a Hop (*Humulus lupulus*) "cone." The species resemble the true hornbeams (*Carpinus* spp), but here the involucre that surrounds the nutlet stays open and the male catkins are not exposed during winter.

Three species are occasionally cultivated as ornamentals and are quite hardy in temperate regions. The most common are the European Hop Hornbeam (*Ostrya carpinifolia*), a native of southern Europe and Asia Minor, and the American Hop Hornbeam (*O. virginiana*), which occurs in the eastern United States. Neither is particular as to soil. The European Hop Hornbeam is a tree growing to 66 ft (20 m), with gray bark. The leaves are acuminate, 1.6–5 in (4–12 cm) long, with 11–15 pairs of veins; the ovoid nutlet is 0.16–0.2 in (4–5 mm) long. The American Hop Hornbeam, also known as Ironwood, is likewise a tree to 66 ft (20 m), with dark brown bark and leaves akin to O. *carpinifolia*. The nutlet is

spindle-shaped and 0.25–0.3 in (6–8 mm) long. The wood is extremely hard—hence its popular name—and widely used for tool handles and fence posts. It is very similar to the Japanese Hop Hornbeam (*O. japonica*), native to Southeast Asia, which is valued for flooring and furniture. **CZ4–5**

BETULACEAE

Ostrya
HOP HORNBEAMS

Number of species *5*
Distribution *Northern temperate regions to Central America.*
Commercial uses *Important timber trees.*

BELOW European Hop Hornbeam, *Ostrya carpinifolia*, has attractive long male catkins.

BOTTOM Fruiting catkins of *Ostrya japonica*, Japanese Hop Hornbeam.

ABOVE *Juglans regia* has leaves which usually have 5–7 leaflets. They are thick and leathery with entire margins, the only species to grow like this. It is also the only species to have a nut that splits into two halves. The short male catkins are dark yellow and appear in early summer.

RIGHT In France walnut trees are much planted as ornamentals as well as for their crop of nuts.

JUGLANDACEAE

Juglans
Walnuts

Juglans is a genus of some twenty-one species distributed from the Mediterranean to eastern Asia, and in Indo-China, North and Central America, and the Andes. They are deciduous trees (rarely shrubs) with pinnate leaves, which are aromatic when crushed. Male flowers are in unbranched catkins with the few female flowers on the same tree. The fruit is a drupe with a fleshy outer layer and an inner "nut" containing the single seed, which contains abundant oil. The closely related *Carya* (hickories) differs in having three-branched catkins.

The Common, Persian, or English Walnut (*J. regia*), from southeast Europe to China, is perhaps the most distinct species, as it is the only one where the nut splits into two halves. The other species are distinguished on vegetative characters and sometimes on details of the fruit; they all further differ from *J. regia* in having serrate, not entire, margins to the leaflets.

Juglans is prized for the beautifully marked, often hard and durable wood and is used to make furniture, gunstocks, veneers, and turning; best known are *J. neotropica* (Ecuador), *J. mollis* (Mexico), *J. nigra* (North America), *J. ailanthifolia* (China and Japan), and the Common Walnut. This last is also widely exploited for food and the oil used for soaps and paints. It is cultivated commercially in the United States (especially California), France, Italy, China, and India. The Black Walnut and the Butternut (*J. cinerea*) from North America are also exploited for their nuts. The latter, and *J. mollis*, provides a dye from the fruit pericarp. Several species, particularly the Common Walnut, make magnificent ornamentals. **CZ4–10**

JUGLANDACEAE

Juglans
WALNUTS

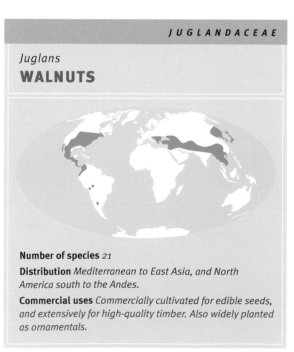

Number of species *21*
Distribution *Mediterranean to East Asia, and North America south to the Andes.*
Commercial uses *Commercially cultivated for edible seeds, and extensively for high-quality timber. Also widely planted as ornamentals.*

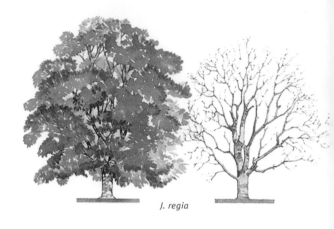

J. regia

The Main Species of *Juglans*

Group I: Leaflets more or less entire. Nuts with a thin partition, splitting when mature.

J. regia **Common, English, or Persian Walnut.** SE Europe to the Himalaya and China. Tree 66–100 ft (20–30 m). Leaflets usually 7–9, hairless. Fruits smooth, about 1.5–2 in (3.7–5 cm) long. Nuts variously sculpted. **CZ5**

Group II: Leaf-scars without a row of hairs on upper edge. Leaflets 9–25, serrate. Fruits hairless or finely hairy. Nuts with a thick partition, not splitting, 4-celled at base.

J. californica S California. Large shrub or small tree. Leaflets 11–15, hairless; nuts deeply grooved. Fruits globose, 0.4–0.8 in (1–2 cm) across. **CZ8**

J. hindsii California. Tree 40–66 ft (12–20 m). Leaflets 15–19, downy on the veins beneath. Nuts shallowly grooved. Fruits nearly globose, 1–1.4 in (2.5–3.5 cm) across. Commonly planted in Californian streets. **CZ8**

J. microcarpa (*J. rupestris*) **Texas Walnut.** SW U.S. to Mexico. Small tree to 33 ft (10 m). (The related *J. major* grows to 50 ft (15 m).) Leaflets hairless except on the veins beneath. Fruits globose, 0.6–1 in (1.5–2.5 cm) across. Nuts deeply grooved. **CZ6**

J. nigra **Black Walnut.** E and C U.S. Tree 66–115 ft (25–35 m). Leaflets downy beneath. Fruits compressed-globose, 1–1.4 in (2.5–3.5 cm) wide. Nuts irregularly ridged. **CZ4**

Group III: Leaf-scars with a row of hairs on the upper edge. Leaflets 7–19, toothed. Fruits with sticky hairs. Nuts with a thick partition, not splitting, 2-celled at base.

J. ailanthifolia (J. sieboldiana) **Japanese Walnut.** Japan. Tree to 66 ft (20 m). Leaflets downy on both surfaces. Fruits in long pendulous racemes, ovoid, about 2 in (5 cm) long, sticky from down. Nuts not ridged or angled. **CZ4**

J. cinerea **Butternut.** E N. America. Tree 50–66 ft (15–20 m) or more. Leaflets downy, with spreading teeth. Mature bracts red or purplish. Fruits 3–5 in pendulous racemes, each more or less ovoid, 1.6–2.6 in (4–6.5 cm), sticky. Nuts strongly ridged. **CZ4**

J. cathayensis China. Tree to 66 ft (20 m). Leaflets remaining downy, with serrate margins. Mature bracts gray or yellow-brown. Fruits ovoid in pendulous racemes, each 1.2–1.8 in (3–4.5 cm) long. Nuts with 6–8 spiny toothed angles. **CZ5**

J. mandshurica N China. Tree 50–66 ft (15–20 m). Leaflets becoming hairless above, with serrate margins. Mature bracts gray or yellow-brown. Fruits in a short raceme. Nut grooved, deeply pitted. **CZ5**

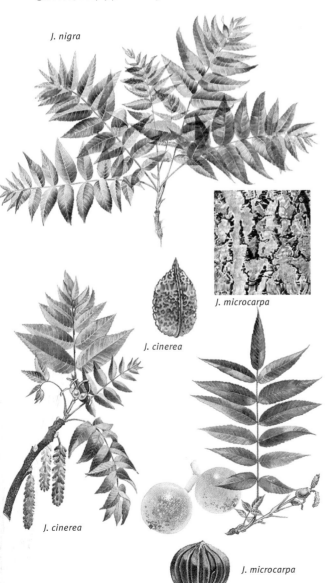

J. nigra

J. microcarpa

J. cinerea

J. cinerea

J. microcarpa

Pterocarya

Wing Nuts

Pterocarya are deciduous trees growing to 82–100 ft (25–30 m) with laminated pith and large alternate, pinnate leaves. Walnuts (*Juglans* spp) have laminated pith but are distinguished by the large, tough-fleshed drupe with its wrinkled, unwinged stone. In *Carya* (hickories) the pith is continuous and the calyx absent or nearly so. Flowers are unisexual, borne in catkins on the same plant, with one to four sepals and the petals absent: male flowers have six to eighteen stamens; the female a one-celled ovary with a short style and a two-lobed bright pink stigma. The fruit is a small one-seeded nut with two leafy wings, borne on 8–20 in (20–50 cm) catkins. Several species are grown in temperate regions as ornamentals. These moisture-loving trees, best planted in a deep loam beside lakes and rivers.

The most commonly cultivated species, the Caucasian Wing Nut (*Pterocarya fraxinifolia*) from northern Iran, is a tree with several superposed naked buds. It is liable to sucker in moist habitats and produce a thicket. The leaves, which have eleven to twenty-five leaflets and a leaf rachis (central stalk), turn bright yellow in the fall. The fruit is distinctly winged.

The Chinese Wing Nut (*P. stenoptera*) has naked buds, five to nine leaflets, and fruiting catkins 8–12 in (20–30 cm) long. *P. × rehderana* (*P. fraxinifolia × P. stenoptera*) is hardier and more vigorous than its parents and produces root suckers. The leaves have some twenty-one leaflets and the rachis is flanged or grooved. The fruiting catkins grow to 18 in (45 cm). The Japanese Wing Nut (*P. rhoifolia*) has buds at first with two or three dark brown scales and eleven to twenty-one leaflets. Winged fruits hang in catkins 8–12 in (20–30 cm) long. **CZ6–8**

ABOVE The leaves of the Chinese Wing Nut, *Pterocarya stenoptera*, are shorter than *P. fraxinifolia* at 12 in (30 cm) with 11–21 leaflets. These are oblong, taped at both ends and regularly finely toothed.

BELOW The fruiting catkins of *P. fraxinifolia* are longer than the male ones, lengthening to 10–20 in (25–50 cm). Each fruit has two wings.

JUGLANDACEAE

Pterocarya
WING NUTS

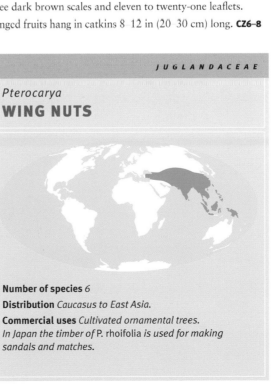

Number of species *6*
Distribution *Caucasus to East Asia.*
Commercial uses *Cultivated ornamental trees. In Japan the timber of* P. rhoifolia *is used for making sandals and matches.*

Carya

Hickories

C. ovata

Carya are large, stately, fast-growing, deciduous trees, chiefly confined to North America, with two species in Tonkin and China. They grow to over 100 ft (30 m) and may be elegantly conical, as in *C. cordiformis*, or broadly conical (*C. glabra* and *C. ovata*). The bark is gray and smooth but in the latter it becomes rugged and shaggy, hence its common name Shagbark Hickory. The pith of the shoots is solid. The leaves are opposite, large and compound, yellowish-green, often oily, thick, and sweet-smelling, with three to seventeen leaflets per leaf. Leaflet size, shape, and number vary with the species. The flowers are unisexual, borne on the same tree, the males in terminal three-pronged catkins, the females in terminal spikes, with two stigmas. The corolla is absent and the calyx absent or nearly so. The fruit is a round to pear-shaped nut surrounded by a husk.

Hickories are cultivated for their tough, elastic wood, ornamental value, and edible fruits, of which the most important is the Pecan nut from *C. illinoinensis* (*C. pecan*) This species is a native of the southeastern United States, Mexico, and other parts of Central America. The wild trees produce edible fatty nuts (dry drupes). Though individual trees may live as long as 1,000 years, the life of a commercial orchard is considered to be 100 years.

Over 300 varieties of Pecan are grown. Their food value is high: the nuts contain more fat than any other vegetable product—over 70 percent. Most of the harvest is used for confectionery, ice cream, and the fresh and salted nut trade; and the oil is extracted for cooking and cosmetic production. Thin-shelled varieties are now grown, so-called "paper-shelled pecans," which can be broken with the fingers. **CZ4–8**

JUGLANDACEAE

Carya
HICKORIES

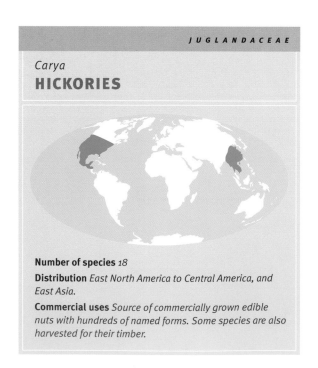

Number of species *18*
Distribution *East North America to Central America, and East Asia.*
Commercial uses *Source of commercially grown edible nuts with hundreds of named forms. Some species are also harvested for their timber.*

C. tomentosa

C. cordiformis

C. cordiformis

Carya are large, stately trees which generally have conical crowns until old when they broaden.

The Main Species of *Carya*

Group I: Leaflets 5–17. Scales of overwintering buds paired, scales valvate, 4–6, broad.

C. illinoiensis (*C. pecan*) **Pecan.** Mississippi Basin. Fast-growing tree to 150 ft (45 m). Trunk buttressed; bark thick-furrowed. Leaflets 9–17. Scales of overwintering buds with bright yellow hairs. Kernel sweet. **CZ5**

C. aquatica **Water Hickory, Bitter Pecan.** Generally in swamps and rice fields of N. America. Tree to 50 ft (15 m). Leaflets 7–13, narrow to broadly lanceolate. Scales without yellow hairs but with red-brown buds and yellow glands. Kernel bitter. **CZ6**

C. cordiformis (*C. amara*) **Swamp Hickory, Pignut, Bitternut.** Woodland and mountains of N. America. Tree to 88 ft (27 m). Leaflets 5–9. Scales of overwintering buds without yellow scales but with permanent yellow scurf and curving shape. **CZ4**

Group II: Leaflets 3–9. Scales of overwintering buds imbricate, 6–12, very narrow.

C. ovata (*C. alba*) **Shagbark Hickory.** N. America. Tree to 118 ft (36 m). Bark exfoliating in narrow strips; young branches scurfy, red-brown, becoming gray. Leaflets 5–7, serrate, strongly ciliate, with tufts of hairs at apex of teeth of leaves. Nuts white; kernel sweet. **CZ6**

> *C. laciniosa* **Kingnut, Big Shellbark.** N. America. Similar to *C. ovata* but stouter and buds less pointed. Young branches orange, scurfy. Leaflets ciliate when young but without tufts. Nuts yellow-brown. **CZ6**

> *C. tomentosa* (*C. alba*) **Mockernut Hickory.** N. America. Tree to 60 ft (18 m). Bark dark and deeply furrowed; petioles, branches, etc. permanently tomentose with curly dense hairs. Velvet gray terminal bud twice as thick as stem behind it. Leaflets usually 7, very large, rarely 5–9, drooping and sweet-smelling, on yellow-pink rachis; largest leaflet in terminal position. Fruits with very thick hard shell and almost empty inside. **CZ4**

C. glabra (*C. porcina*) **Pignut, Smoothbark Hickory.** Borders of swamps in N. America. Tree to 78 ft (24 m). Bark gray-purple, smooth but becoming wrinkled with rust and black folds. Buds, leaves, etc. unusually small. Nuts smooth, pale brown. **CZ4**

C. ovalis **Sweet Pignut, False Shagbark.** N. America. Similar to *C. glabra* but old bark becoming more shaggy. Branches, leaves, etc. scurfy. Kernel sweet. **CZ6**

C. pallida **Pale Hickory.** N. America. Bark very pale gray and furrowed. **CZ6**

C. texana **Black Hickory.** N. America. Nuts coarsely ridged and reticulate veined. **CZ6**

C. cathayensis **Chinese Hickory.** E China. Tree to 82 ft (25 m). Leaflets 5–7, green above, rusty-brown below. Fruits with 4-ridged nuts. **CZ6**

CASUARINACEAE

Casuarina
She Oaks

This genus of highly distinctive semi-evergreen to more or less deciduous trees and shrubs is the only member of the family Casuarinaceae, and comprises some seventeen species native to northeast Australia and Southeast Asia. They are mostly tall trees with a characteristic weeping habit and slender and wiry shoots that recall the horsetails (*Equisetum* spp). The leaves are reduced to form whorls of many-toothed sheaths surrounding the articulations of the jointed stems. The flowers are also highly reduced and usually unisexual, with the sexes on the same or different plants. The male flowers are borne in simple or branched terminal spikes, each flower with a single conspicuous stamen and one or two perianth lobes, and the females in dense, spherical or oval heads, each a single one-celled ovary without perianth. The fruits occur in globular clusters, and each fruit is a winged nutlet enclosed in two hard bracts, which later open to reveal the fruits, so that the whole fruiting structure resembles a pine cone. The whole appearance is more that of a conifer rather than a flowering plant.

She Oaks are well adapted to very dry habitats, and though not able to survive sustained frost, a number of species are grown as ornamentals outside their native regions. They will grow in a sandy loam, in alkaline and brackish soils. Species such as *Casuarina campestris*, *C. cunninghamiana*, and *C. littoralis* are grown in parks and as street trees in frost-free regions of southern Europe and the United States. The Horsetail Tree (*C. equisetifolia*), also known as the South Sea Ironwood or Mile Tree, is a pioneer colonizer of seashores in its native Pacific regions, and this tolerance has been exploited in its use for hedges and windbreaks in seaside resorts. It is widely cultivated in tropical America and naturalized in parts of Florida and East Africa.

The larger species of *Casuarina* yield a hard and conspicuously grained wood, used for constructional work and ornamental furnishings. The popular name Beefwood refers to the reddish color of the wood. **CZ8**

CASUARINACEAE

Casuarina
SHE OAKS

Number of species *17*
Distribution *Southeast Asia to the western Pacific.*
Commercial uses *Source of a dense hard wood widely used for timber and firewood, also sometimes planted as windbreaks.*

Casuarinas are cultivated for their foliage, which is modified into tiny scales that are in a ring around each node. She Oaks make fine specimen trees, windbreaks, or screening plants, as they are tolerant of strong wind and maritime conditions.

BUXACEAE

Buxus

Boxes

Best known as shrubs used for hedges and in topiary, the genus *Buxus* contains about fifty species of evergreen shrubs and small trees native to western Europe, the Mediterranean region, temperate and eastern Asia, the West Indies, Central America, and Africa. The leaves are entire, opposite, oval, mostly leathery, dark green, shining above, often with inrolled edges and an apical notch. The flowers are unisexual and lack petals; they occur in clusters with a single terminal female flower surrounded by several male flowers below. The male flowers have four sepals and four protruding stamens, the females four to six sepals and a three-celled ovary with three styles. The fruit is a capsule, which splits into three horned valves each containing two shining black seeds.

About six species are commonly cultivated and hardy (except *B. harlandii*) in temperate regions. They do well on any average soil and are lime and shade tolerant. The most widely cultivated species is the Common Box (*B. sempervirens*), which is extensively used for hedges, especially in towns. Its great tolerance of pruning and shearing makes it a favorite for topiary work. It is a densely bushy shrub or tree growing to 20 ft (6 m), rarely 30 ft (9 m). The young shoots are four-angled, slightly winged, and minutely hairy with the leaves sub-sessile, ovate to oblong, widest at or below the middle, 0.6–1.2(1.6) in (1.5–3(4) cm) long, with somewhat inrolled margins. The horns on the fruit are about half the length of the capsule. Common Box is native to Europe (and probably the British Isles), North Africa, and western Asia. There are numerous cultivars including: 'Argentea' (*aureo-variegata*), a very bushy form

The Common Box, *Buxus sempervirens*, is a spreading bush or small tree which is usually wider than it is tall. It is used often in gardens as an extremely useful hardy evergreen. Boxes provide shelter or screens and are often planted in formal designs. They are adaptable to pruning and can be clipped for topiary or box hedging.

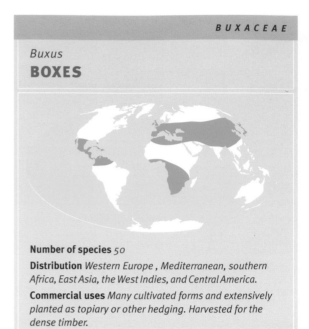

Buxus
BOXES

Number of species 50
Distribution *Western Europe , Mediterranean, southern Africa, East Asia, the West Indies, and Central America.*
Commercial uses *Many cultivated forms and extensively planted as topiary or other hedging. Harvested for the dense timber.*

with leaves more or less bordered white; 'Longifolia' with leaves to 1.5 in (3.8 cm); and 'Suffruticosa' (the Edging Box) a long-established edging plant, which will grow to about 5 ft (1.5 m) but is normally kept to a height of 4–5 in (10–12 cm) by regular clipping. In 'Suffruticosa' the leaves are oval to obovate, 0.4–0.8 in (1–2 cm) long. 'Arborescens' is an excellent cultivar for screening purposes, 'Gold Tip' has its upper leaves of the terminal shoots tipped with yellow, and 'Pendula' has pendulous shoots.

Buxus microphylla from China, Korea, and Japan is a small cultivated shrub growing to about 3 ft (1 m) with square, glabrous shoots and leaves that are somewhat papery, oblong to obovate, 0.5–0.8 × 0.16–0.3 in (12–20 × 4–8 mm), sometimes notched at the apex and generally wider above the middle. It is a variable species with regional varieties: var *japonica* (Japanese Box), for instance, has more rounded leaves; *koreana* (Korean Box) has obovate to elliptic-oblong leaves 0.25–0.6 in (6–15 mm) long; while *sinica* from China is a shrub growing to 18 ft (5.5 m) with downy shoots and ovate to obovate leaves 0.3–1.4 in (8–35 mm) long. Var *koreana* is very hardy and much prized in the United States. The Balearic Box (*B. balearica*) from the Balearic Islands, Sardinia, and southwest Spain has larger and duller leaves than *B. sempervirens*, which it replaces as a cultivated plant in southern Europe. It forms a shrub or tree growing to 30 ft (9 m) with square shoots that are downy at first. Its leaves are more or less elliptic to oblong, 1–1.6 in (2.5–4 cm) long and hardly glossy, and the fruits have recurved styles that are about as long as the capsule.

The wood of boxes is hard and often described as of "bony" texture. It was once used for engravings and is still in demand for decorative work, sculpture, and for making musical instruments, rulers, and furniture. **CZ5–8**

SALICACEAE

Salix

Willows, Sallows, Osiers

Salix is a large, well-known genus of species popularly known as willows, sallows, and osiers. The great majority of species occur in cool temperate or colder situations in the northern hemisphere; they are rare in most parts of the Tropics and the southern hemisphere, and are totally absent from Australasia.

Willows vary from creeping shrubs a few inches high to tall trees up to 60 ft (18 m) or more, but very few are forest trees. Most occur in rather open places, the larger species usually in swampy areas or along streams and rivers, the smaller species more often in boggy places on heaths and moors or in damp, stony ground on mountains and in the Arctic. Some species send masses of rootlets into the water that they grow beside. In the White Willow (*S. alba*) they are whitish and in the Crack Willow (*S. fragilis*) red. The small seeds, each with a tuft of hairs, are easily scattered by the wind, and many species of *Salix* are strong colonizers of wasteland or newly exposed, neglected, or reclaimed ground, in some cases quickly forming dense thickets.

The flowers are borne in rather stiff catkins, the male and female on different trees. Each flower is held in the axil of a scale, and consists of a single ovary with two stigmas in the case of the female and a small group of two to about twelve stamens in the case of the male, together with one or two small, club-shaped glands, which secrete nectar and are considered by some to represent the vestiges of a perianth.

These characters, among others, are used to divide the genus into three major groups or subgenera, all of which are well represented in most north temperate regions. Subgenus *Salix* (*Amerina*) consists of trees or tall shrubs with narrow and pointed leaves (true willows), subgenus *Caprisalix* of tall or short shrubs with narrow and pointed or broad and rounded or blunt leaves (osiers and sallows respectively), and subgenus *Chamaetia* of dwarf, creeping mountain or Arctic shrubs with small, broad, and rounded or blunt leaves (dwarf willows).

Hybridization between different species of *Salix* is a very widespread phenomenon and many artificial hybrids have been made, to add to the considerable number of natural ones. At least 180 hybrids have been listed, about forty of these being triple or quadruple ones. Since most of these hybrids are fully fertile, and can cross with their parental species or with other species or hybrids, the boundaries between many species have become somewhat blurred and the identification of specimens of *Salix* can be very difficult. Any one species is able to cross successfully with many others, but, in general, species of subgenus *Salix* (true willows) do not hybridize with species of the other two subgenera, though the latter do interbreed. A notable exception is the Almond-leaved Willow (*S. triandra*), which, though a true willow, hybridizes with certain species of osier and sallow. In the past, much *Salix* hybridization has been carried out by taxonomists and geneticists in Sweden, and one plant has been obtained with thirteen different species in its parentage.

Propagation of willows is effected by leafless cuttings and by seeds, but because of the ease with which hybridization takes place, seeds should be used only if the parentage is beyond doubt. "Weeping" forms can be grafted on tall stems. Any average soil, provided there is an ample water supply, is suitable—for example a deep heavy loam by a waterside.

SALICACEAE

Salix
WILLOWS, SALLOWS, OSIERS

· **Number of species** *400*
Distribution *Circumpolar and northern temperate regions.*
Commercial uses *Some timber use and widely coppiced for firewood and basketry. Extensively planted as horticultural trees with many hybrids and named forms in existence. The bark was once used as the source of aspirin.*

LEFT The Golden Weeping Willow, *Salix × chrysocroma*, is a hybrid whose crown is broadly domed with large, sinuous, curving branches and long, slender shoots which hang straight down. Leaves are narrow, with silky hairs on both sides, pale yellow in spring and becoming richer and brighter in the summer.

BELOW The crown of *Salix* spp can vary greatly. *Salix caprea* is bushy and low on a sinuous bole. *Saxlix fragilis* has a broadly conic crown with upswept branches that are long and slender. *Salix babylonica* has a rugged trunk that supports a wide spreading head of branches.

S. caprea

S. fragilis

S. babylonica

The stems of willows, whether saplings or ancient trunks, show remarkable powers of regeneration, particularly in winter and early spring before the leaves appear. *Salix* sticks pushed into the ground quickly take root, and this characteristic, together with a very rapid growth rate, is much exploited.

Willow timber is light, fairly soft, but tough and elastic and not given to splintering when subjected to strain. It is thus useful for making boxes, polo balls, steamer paddles, tool handles and, because it is relatively nonflammable, for the brake blocks of railroad stock. Cricket bats are made from the Cricket-bat Willow (*S. alba* var *caerulea*), which can be harvested about twelve years after planting. Baskets and other wickerwork (including lobster pots) are made from the young (mostly one-year-old) sucker shoots of the Common Osier (*S. viminalis*) and other osiers and true willows. These species can be encouraged to put out long, straight, flexible suckers by severe pruning (pollarding) of old trunks, from which the suckers can be harvested annually.

Willow thickets are commonly associated with mammals that eat bark, branches, and leaves, while the buds and catkins may provide food for a number of bird species. The glucoside salicin, which has mild analgesic properties, is widely distributed in the genus and is extracted from the bark of, for example, *S. purpurea* and its hybrid with *S. viminalis* (*S.* × *rubra*). The use of salicin has now been virtually abandoned in favor of acetylsalicylic acid (well known as aspirin) and other synthetic analgesics.

Willows generally may be cultivated for their rapid growth (*S. alba* has been measured to grow 65 ft (20 m) in fifteen years) and as attractive waterside and ornamental trees. The "weeping" forms are particularly popular, but quickly outgrow small gardens. Most of them are hybrids that obtain their weeping habit from *S. babylonica*, variously considered to be a native of the Middle East or China.

Hybrids of *S. babylonica* with *S. alba* and *S. fragilis* are grown extensively. The commonest weeping willow in Europe is *S. alba* var *vitellina* × *S. babylonica*, which has pale to bright yellow twigs and a beautiful weeping habit. It has received a wide range of names, such as *S. alba* 'Tristis,' and *S. alba* 'Vitellina Pendula,' but botanically it is correctly known as *S.* × *sepulcralis*. Most of the forms of weeping willow in cultivation are derivatives of the two above hybrids, but the American Weeping Willow is *S. purpurea* 'Pendula.' *Salix babylonica* itself is a brown-twigged tree of poor growth in Europe. It is traditionally associated with Psalm 137 of the Old Testament ("*We hanged our harps upon the willows …*"), but the tree in question is now believed to have been *Populus euphratica*. Other ornamental willows include the Violet Willow (*S. daphnoides*) with purple twigs overlaid by a white bloom, the Coral Bark Willow (*S. alba* 'Chermesina') with twigs at first dark red, finally bright orange-red, the Golden Willow (*S. alba* var *vitellina*) with yellowish twigs, and the Japanese Willow (*S. melanostachys*) with black and scarlet catkins. Dwarf rock

S. fragilis

S. caprea

garden plants include the Woolly Willow (*S. lanata*) with long, silky pubescence and large golden catkins, and the Dwarf Willow (*S. herbacea*), which forms little more than a carpet over the ground. A striking cultivar of a distinctly rare species is the Contorted Willow (*S. matsundana* 'Tortuosa') with unmistakable twisted and contorted 2–3 in (5–8 cm) long narrow-lanceolate leaves. **CZ1–8**

The Main Species of *Salix*

Subgenus *Salix* (*Amerina*)

The true willows. Male flowers with 2 to about 12 stamens and 2 nectaries. Catkins long and narrow, arising from lateral buds of the previous year, appearing with or after the leaves.

S. alba White Willow. Lowland regions from W Europe to C Asia. Tree to 82 ft (25 m) with upward-growing main branches, forming a rather narrow shape, and often with pendulous twigs. Leaves long and narrow, with white silky hairs on both surfaces. Male flowers with 2 stamens.

var *caerulea* Cricket-bat Willow. Differs in its more erect growth- habit and bluish-gray leaves, which lose their silky hairs during the summer. Most cricket-bat willows are female and may belong to a single clone.

var *vitellina* Golden Willow. Bright yellow or orange first-year shoots, and leaves that lose their hairs in summer. Hard pruned to produce thickets of colored suckers. **CZ2**
A commonly grown form known as 'Chermesina' (Coral-bark Willow) has bright red shoots. The pendulous form of this variety is held to be one of the parents of the most commonly cultivated weeping willow, known as *S.* × *chrysocoma*. The other putative parent is *S. babylonica*.

S. babylonica Probably native to Iran. One of the so-called "weeping willows," uncommon and not particularly hardy in Europe. Tree to 50 ft (15 m) with widely spreading main branches and long, pendulous ("weeping") twigs. Leaves long and narrow, smooth. Male flowers with 2 stamens. **CZ5**

S. fragilis Crack Willow. Europe, W Asia. Tree to 88 ft (27 m) with spreading main branches, forming a broad crown, and twigs that are very fragile at their joints. Leaves long and narrow, deeper green than *S. alba* and losing their hairs when still very young. Male flowers with 2 stamens, but most trees are females. Hybrids between this and *S. alba* are common. **CZ5**

S. babylonica

S. arctica

S. reticulata

S. pentandra Bay-leaved Willow. Europe, W Asia. Tree to 60 ft (18 m). Leaves long and pointed but broader than in other species of this group (up to 2 in/5 cm wide). Male flowers with usually 5(12) stamens. A very handsome species, which commonly hybridizes with *S. alba* and *S. fragilis*. **CZ5**

S. triandra Almond-leaved Willow. Europe, Asia. Tall shrub or small tree to 30 ft (9 m). Leaves long and pointed, smaller than in other species of this group, dark green and smooth. Male flowers with 3 stamens. An attractive shrub, commonly grown also as an osier, which forms hybrids with species not only of this group but also with *S. viminalis* and others in subgenus *Caprisalix*. **CZ5**

S. nigra Black Willow. N. America. Tree to 100 ft (30 m). Leaves long and narrow, with sparse hairs especially near the main vein. Male flowers with 3–7 stamens. Quite commonly cultivated in Europe, where it usually reaches only 30–40 ft (9–12 m) and resembles a small, densely branched *S. alba*. There are related species in S. America and S. Africa, where the genus as a whole is rare. **CZ4**

Subgenus *Caprisalix*

The osiers and sallows. Male flowers with 2 stamens and 1 nectary. Catkins short arising from lateral buds of the previous year, appearing with or before the leaves.

S. viminalis Common Osier. Europe, Asia. Tall shrub or small tree to 20 ft (6 m) with very long, gray to yellowish, straight twigs, which are very hairy when young. Leaves very long and narrow, smooth above but with dense silky hairs beneath. Stamens separate. This species hybridizes with many others, particularly *S. triandra*, *S. purpurea*, and various sallows. Several hybrids involving 3 species occur. **CZ4**

S. elaeagnos Hoary Willow. C and S Europe, W Asia. Shrub to 16 ft (5 m), resembling a slender *S. viminalis* but with less hairy twigs and partially fused stamens. A characteristic species of mountain rivers in C Europe. **CZ4**

S. purpurea Purple Willow. Europe, Asia. Shrub to 16 ft (5 m) with slender, smooth, yellowish-reddish twigs. Leaves narrow, smooth, very pale beneath, distinctive among the genus in that at least some of them are borne oppositely not alternately. Stamens fused, appearing as if 1 but with 2 anthers. Hybrids with various sallows and with *S. viminalis*. In the latter, the stamens are intermediate between those of the parents, fused in the bottom half and separate above. **CZ5**

S. daphnoides Violet Willow. Europe (but not Britain) to C Asia, and the Himalaya. Tall shrub or tree to 30 ft (9 m) with long, straight, purple twigs covered with a whitish, waxy bloom. Leaves long and rather narrow, soon smooth. Stamens separate. Commonly cultivated for its attractive twigs, for which it is pruned hard. **CZ5**

S. caprea Sallow, Goat Willow, Pussy Willow. Europe and W Asia. Shrub or small tree to 30 ft (9 m) with strong twigs at first hairy but soon smooth. Leaves broad, blunt at the apex, densely and softly hairy beneath. Stamens separate. A very familiar plant in NW Europe, the twigs with male catkins being collected for decoration in the spring, especially on Palm Sunday. There are two common and very closely related species, which often hybridize with each other and with *S. caprea*: *S. cinerea* (Gray Sallow), differing in its narrower leaves with sparser hairs, more persistently hairy twigs, and raised striations under the bark of 2-year-old branchlets, and *S. aurita* (Eared Sallow), a smaller plant, differing from the former in its wrinkled leaves and widely spreading twigs. **CZ5**

S. nigricans Dark-leaved Willow. N and C Europe, Asia. Shrub to 13 ft (4 m) with hairy, dull twigs. Leaves broad, blunt at the apex, more or less hairy beneath, becoming blackish when dried. A characteristic upland species, only on mountains in the south of its range. **CZ5**

S. phylicifolia Tea-leaved Willow. N and C Europe. Shrub to 13 ft (4 m) with smooth twigs. Leaves oval, pointed, hairless when mature. A plant that grows in similar habitats to, and often with, *S. nigricans*, with which it frequently hybridizes and forms a range of intermediates. **CZ5**

S. repens Creeping Willow. Europe, Asia. Small shrub to about 4 ft (1.2 m), with creeping (often underground) main stems and usually ascending, somewhat hairy twigs. Leaves small, very variable in shape and hairiness, usually oval and at least slightly hairy. This variable species occupies a wide range of habitats. The more distinctive forms are considered by some to be separate species, e.g. *S. rosmarinifolia* from C Europe, with very narrow leaves and short catkins, and *S. arenaria* (*S. argentea*) from damp sand-dunes on the Atlantic coasts of Europe, with very hairy twigs and dense silvery hairs on the leaves. The last two are favored by gardeners. **CZ5**

S. lanata Woolly Willow. Arctic and subarctic Europe and Asia. Small shrub to 4 ft (1.2 m) with stout, densely hairy twigs. Leaves oval, pointed, with dense white hairs on both surfaces. Catkins cylindrical, with golden-yellow hairs so that even the female plants are very attractive in flower. A very popular garden shrub. **CZ2**

S. viminalis

S. pentandra

S. daphnoides

LEFT *S. x sepulcralis*, the Weeping Willow most commonly cultivated in Europe, is a rapid grower though its need for ample water means it can deprive other plants.

Subgenus *Chamaetia*

The dwarf willows. Male flowers with 2 stamens and 1 or 2 nectaries. Catkins short, arising from terminal buds of the previous year, appearing with or after the leaves.

S. herbacea **Dwarf Willow.** Arctic lowlands and temperate mountains of Europe and N. America. A truly dwarf shrub rarely over 2 in (5 cm) high. Leaves about 0.5 in (13 mm) long, often almost circular, smooth, and shining with rather prominent veins. Catkins very short, few-flowered. A characteristic plant of mountaintops in temperate Europe, often forming large patches by its creeping underground stems. Commonly described as the smallest shrub, though in reality there are many other equally dwarf shrubs in *Salix* and other groups. It hybridizes with many other dwarf willows. **CZ2**

S. arctica **Arctic Willow.** Arctic regions. Dwarf shrub a few inches high with small, broad, pointed, more or less smooth leaves with slightly prominent veins. Catkins cylindrical. Representative of a large group of dwarf arctic willows, differing from *S. herbacea* in that the stems creep on the surface of the ground, but also often forming large patches. **CZ1**

S. retusa Mountains of C Europe. Similar to *S. arctica* but the leaves are often rounded or notched at the apex and the catkins shorter. This and some related species more or less replace the *S. arctica* group on the mountains of the temperate zone. **CZ2**

S. reticulata **Reticulate Willow.** Arctic lowlands and temperate mountains of Europe, Asia, and N. America. Dwarf shrub a few inches high with broad, rounded, slightly hairy leaves with prominent veins beneath but with impressed veins above. Catkins narrow, on long stalks. Another patch-forming dwarf willow with surface-creeping stems, this is very distinctive and prized by rock-gardeners. **CZ1**

The Weeping Willow is comonly cultivated in parks and gardens, or planted in avenues for a graceful and striking effect. Although usually found by water, these trees will thrive on ordinary dry land providing the soil is deep.

Populus

Poplars, Aspens, Cottonwoods

The *Populus* species are found from Alaska to Mexico, from North Africa through Europe, Asia Minor, the Himalaya, China, and Japan. They are nearly all fast-growing trees that can grow to a large size. All poplars have resinous buds and alternate leaves with long stalks, and in many the stalks are flattened laterally. The flowers are on pendulous catkins, which open before the leaves and have a cup-shaped disc at the base. The two sexes are on separate trees, except in some (not all) specimens of the Chinese Necklace Poplar (*P. lasiocarpa*), which was introduced by the distinguished plant hunter E.H. Wilson. Some of these bear catkins that have male flowers below, bisexual and female flowers above.

Poplars are wind-pollinated and the fruits are capsules containing numerous seeds, which are surrounded at the base by long silky hairs, hence the American vernacular name Cottonwood. These form a carpet of cottonwool around a fruiting tree in midsummer when the seeds are shed, and so male trees are preferred in public places.

Poplars are classified into four distinct sections: *Populus* (*Leuce*), white poplars and aspens; *Leucoides*, a small group that includes *P. lasiocarpa*; *Tacamahaca*, the balsam poplars; and *Aegiros*, the black poplars. Poplars hybridize readily within their own section, but there are important hybrids between species of balsam and black poplars. Many of the hybrids exhibit even greater vigor than the parent species, and are the fastest-growing trees in regions too cool for eucalypts to grow at their best. For timber production, these hybrids are planted in most places to the exclusion of the parent species. The sections to which these hybrids belong comprise species most easily raised from cuttings.

Members of the aspen group are propagated by seed or from their abundant root-suckers and are hard to grow from cuttings. The Aspen itself (*P. tremula*) is a dainty small tree, common throughout Europe. Its leaves are gray-green during summer, turning yellow in the fall. The leaf stalks are long and flattened so that the leaves "tremble" in the slightest breeze, as in the American Quaking or Trembling Aspen (*P. tremuloides*). The White Poplar (*P. alba*) makes a medium-sized domed tree, rarely straight, and is conspicuous in the summer because the underside of the leaf is densely matted with brilliant white hairs, as are the shoots. It grows dense thickets of suckers, which can help stabilize blowing sands, and the trees withstand severe exposure to sea winds. The Gray Poplar, *P. × canescens* (*P. alba × tremula*) is the giant of this section, often attaining 100–115 ft (30–35 m) rapidly. It is a hybrid or intermediate between the two species and differs from the White Poplar mainly in its stature; the leaves also differ slightly, being grayer beneath than the dense bright white of *P. alba*.

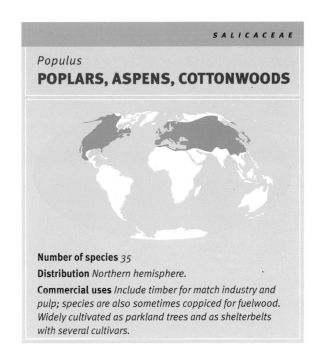

SALICACEAE

Populus
POPLARS, ASPENS, COTTONWOODS

Number of species *35*
Distribution *Northern hemisphere.*
Commercial uses *Include timber for match industry and pulp; species are also sometimes coppiced for fuelwood. Widely cultivated as parkland trees and as shelterbelts with several cultivars.*

The Chinese Necklace Poplar (*P. lasiocarpa*) is a rather sparsely branched small tree with shaggy dark gray bark, noted for its very large fresh green leaves with red midribs, veins and (usually) petioles; it is rare.

Balsam poplars are native to North America, Siberia, and eastern Asia and have large, sticky buds and usually large leaves, hairless but whitened beneath. Many species give out a delicious aroma as the buds burst, especially following rain. The Western Balsam or Black Cottonwood (*P. trichocarpa*) can be almost 200 ft (60 m) tall in its native range on the Pacific coast of North America and can grow 8 ft (2.5 m) in a year in Britain, where it is commonly planted. The firm, thick leaves are long-triangular to 10 in (25 cm) long and turn yellow in the fall. The recently introduced decorative poplar, *P. × jackii* 'Aurora,' is a balsam and the only variegated poplar seen, the dark green of its leaves being often replaced by white, cream, or pink over much of their surface.

The Quaking Aspen, *Populus tremuloides*, can reach heights of 100 ft (30 m) in the wild but usually only half that in cultivation. The trunk is slender and paler and yellower than *P. tremula* when young. Bark also has horizontal dark marks when young. Leaves emerging in spring have flattened petioles or stalks which make them quake in the wind.

The true European Black Poplar (*P. nigra*) is native to Britain in the form ssp *betulifolia* (Downy Black Poplar). It is now rare in the wild, but is much planted in industrial areas. The Lombardy Poplar (*P. nigra* 'Italica') is the narrow columnar tree widespread in northern Europe and North America. By 1750, the Eastern Cottonwood (*P. deltoides*), a familiar tree throughout the eastern United States, which has luxuriant large deltoid leaves, was growing in France and had hybridized with the Black Poplar, giving rise to the group known as *P. × canadensis* (*P. × euramericana*). The oldest and commonest of these is the Black Italian Poplar 'Serotina,' a male form of great vigor, making a huge tree with an open crown and leaves that unfold very late, orange-brown at first turning grayish-green. A similar—but more shapely—recently introduced hybrid is 'Robusta,' a conical tree with larger leaves that open weeks earlier and show orange-red for a few days. Its bright red male catkins are profuse in early April. The Berlin Poplar, *P. × berolinensis* (*P. laurifolia* × *P. nigra* 'Italica') is often seen in Germany, and has an upswept, dense crown of leaves that taper to their bases and are whitish beneath.

Propagation of poplars by seed is not recommended; hybrids are likely to arise since male and female plants of the same species rarely grow in close proximity. The polygamous *P. lasiocarpa* will come true from seed; otherwise propagation is mainly by cuttings of leafless wood stuck in open ground. To produce new hybrids, cuttings from the two parent species can be grown in water and brought to flower under glass. With simultaneous flowering, cross-pollination can be effected and seed obtained in a few weeks. It should be sown without delay.

Like willows, poplars are prey to many diseases, control of which is predominantly one of prevention: the planting of resistant cultivars, the rapid removal of infected trees—in other words, good management.

Poplars are unusually rapid growers, but this is best achieved in sheltered conditions when there is a warm summer and on a reasonably good soil with ample water supply but no danger of waterlogging. The Lombardy Poplar is commonly used for shelter purposes and as a screening to hide unwanted sights such as factories, and balsam hybrids, for example *P. tacamahaca × trichocarpa*, are also used for the same purpose. Poplars are not favored for planting in confined areas, such as towns. Furthermore, in clay soils the extensive root system and high transpiration rate can result in soil shrinkage with damage to road and building foundations. Other disadvantages are the poplars' relatively short lifespan, the untidiness of the shed female catkins and seeds, and the extensive suckering of many species. For growing on a large scale, planting should be at intervals of about 26 ft (8 m), as poplars are notoriously intolerant of competition. In spite of this limitation, there is increasing interest in poplar cultivation and much effort has gone into producing ever better cultivars for particular purposes.

Poplar wood is soft, pale in color, does not readily splinter, and is virtually without smell, the last two properties making it especially useful for containers of various sorts, including food. Being relatively nonflammable, the timber is much used for domestic flooring and for brake blocks of railway stock. It is extensively used for matches, its relative nonflammability being countered by dipping in paraffin wax. For outside work, poplar wood must be treated with preservative. **CZ1–7**

Populus nigra 'Italica,' the Lombardy Poplar, can reach 100 ft (30 m) and is often grown for ornamental effect, shelter, and on roadsides, chosen for its distinctive slender, tapering shape.

The Main Species of *Populus*

Subgenus *Populus* (*Leuce*)

White and gray poplars and aspens. Young trunks and branches of older trees smooth and gray, pitted with dark, diamond-shaped lenticels. Leaves toothed or lobed, petioles rounded, quadrangular, or laterally flattened.

A *White and gray poplars. Petioles rounded or quadrangular, not or scarcely flattened. Leaves on long shoots densely tomentose (woolly) beneath; other leaves less so, becoming glabrous and of different shape.*

P. alba **White Poplar.** *Europe (excluding British Isles). Medium-sized tree rarely to 60 ft (18 m), usually with leaning bole. White patches on bark of old trees, pitted black. Shoot, leaf stalk and underside densely felted bright white. Leaves on strong shoots with angular lobes; on old shoots nearly round, shallowly toothed. Frequently cultivated in Europe; less common in N U.S. as an introduction. **CZ3**

P. alba f *pyramidalis* Large tree with erect branches and resembling the Lombardy Poplar, but broader. 'Richardii' A less vigorous tree with golden-yellow leaves that are white beneath.

P. × canescens **Gray Poplar.** *Europe (excluding British Isles). Vigorous, very large tree to 125 ft (38 m) with many-domed crown somewhat pendulous with age. Leaves as in *P. alba* but grayish-white beneath and less often lobed. Commonly cultivated and naturalized across U.S. especially in Gulf states, fewer in NE and to Montreal. Naturalized in England and Ireland, forming big trees in chalk and limestone valleys. **CZ4**

AA *Aspens. Petioles much laterally flattened. Leaves glabrous beneath or almost so, without translucent margin, uniform in size and shape, and characteristically rounded.*

P. alba

P. grandidentata **Big-toothed Aspen.** *NE U.S., SE Canada. Slender tree to 56 ft (17 m) with smooth pale gray-green bark. Leaves solid to touch, orbicular, 10 curved teeth each side, fresh green, 4 × 3 in (10 × 8 cm) on pale yellow 3.5 in (9 cm) petiole. Very rarely cultivated in Europe. **CZ3**

P. tremula **Aspen.** *Europe. Conical, lightly branched, often leaning tree to 66 ft (20 m) with pale gray-green, smooth but pitted bark. Suckers widely. Leaves round, slightly pointed with incurved teeth, gray-green above, paler beneath. **CZ2**

P. tremuloides **Quaking Aspen.** *Mexico to Alaska and Newfoundland. Narrow small tree usually in dense stands with pale gray-green to clear white bark. Leaves abruptly pointed with fine blunt teeth, fresh green above, whitish beneath, bright yellow in the fall. **CZ1**

Subgenus *Leucoides*

Small section of 4 species. Bark roughened and scaly. Petioles rounded or quadrangular.

P. lasiocarpa **Chinese Necklace Poplar.** *C and W China. Gaunt, broad-conical tree to 72 ft (22 m). Few level branches and peeling, flaking gray-green bark. Leaves 8–13.5 in (20–35 cm), cordate base, broadly ovate, finely toothed, finely hairy beneath, red midrib and veins, on pink flattened 8 in (20 cm) petiole. The only poplar with male and female flowers on the same tree, often on the same catkin, 5 or 6 females at the base of a male catkin. **CZ5**

P. tremula

P. × canescens

P. trichocarpa   *P. nigra* 'italica'   *P. canescens*   *P. alba*

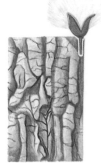

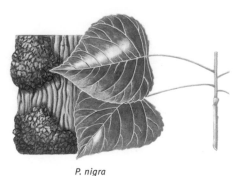

P. deltoides

P. nigra

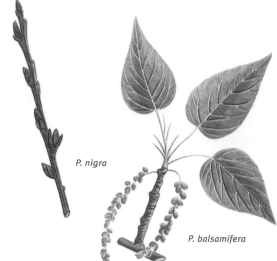

P. nigra

P. balsamifera

P. trichocarpa

P. trichocarpa

Subgenus *Taacmahaca*

Balsam poplars. Trunk with furrowed bark. Unfolding leaves gummy, pale or whitish beneath without pubescence, appearing early, margin translucent, cordate to subcordate at base; petioles rounded or quadrangular, often grooved above. Winter buds very viscid, perfuming the air on bursting.

P. balsamifera (*P. tacamahaca*) **Balsam Poplar.** *Alaska, Canada, N U.S. Upright narrow tree to 100 ft (30 m). Long brown resinous buds fragrant in spring. Leaves to 6 in (15 cm), thickly whitened beneath but smaller, less whitened in the wild. Suckers freely. **CZ2**

P. × jackii **Balm of Gilead.** Hybrid balsam of unknown origin growing wild in NE U.S. and SE Canada. **CZ2**

'Aurora' **Variegated Poplar.** A relatively recent cultivar with dark green leaves 4 × 3 in (10 × 8 cm) and more, variably splashed with or very largely cream, white, and pink on red or white petiole.

P. trichocarpa **Western Balsam Poplar, Black Cottonwood.** *W N. America. Very vigorous, untidy, rather erect tree to 120 ft (37 m) (196 ft/60 m in U.S.) often with a few suckers at the base of some trees. Leaves highly variable in size, 4–12 in (10–30 cm), thick to touch, whitened like paint beneath. Males bear thick green and dull crimson catkins; females bright green, soon setting, fruit covered in white wool. The cultivar 'TT 32' is a hybrid between this and *P. balsamifera* and has a narrowly erect crown and exhibits great vigor. **CZ5**

Subgenus *Aegiros*

Black poplars, cottonwoods. Trunk with furrowed bark (smooth in *P. nigra* 'Italica'). Leaves more or less triangular (rhomboid to cordate), green on both sides, margins translucent, more or less coarsely crenate; petioles laterally flattened.

P. deltoides **Eastern Cottonwood.** *E U.S. Big leafy tree to 150 ft (45 m) with gray bark and heavy branches. Leaves to 8 × 8 in (20 × 20 cm), rich, shiny green; incurved teeth to near abrupt tip. Many minor variants in the wild.

P. nigra **Black Poplar.** *Europe, SW Asia. Broad-domed tree to 115 ft (35 m) with burry bole and heavy branches. Foliage in dense upswept tufts. Leaves 3 × 3 in (8 × 8 cm). **CZ2**

'Italica' **Lombardy Poplar.** *N Italy; other forms farther east. Fastigiate, columnar-conical tree to 130 ft (40 m) in W U.S. Male only.

P. × canadensis (*P. × euramericana*). A series of garden hybrids between *P. deltoides* and *P. nigra* arising in S Europe since 1750.

'Robusta' Tree to 130 ft (40 m) with conic, regular crown. Exceptionally vigorous. Leaves similar to *P. deltoides*, orange at first. Male only.

'Serotina' **Black Italian Poplar.** Tree to 153 ft (46 m). Wide cup-shaped crown on clean bole and pale gray, vertically fissured bark. Very late in leaf, brownish-orange at first. Male only.

'Serotina Aurea' **Golden Poplar.** Tree to 107 ft (32 m) with dense, many-domed crown; less vigorous. Foliage a good yellow. Good in towns.

'Marilandica' Tree to 118 ft (36 m) with rounded dome, dense when young, more open and heavily branched when mature. Leaves small, very triangular, coarsely toothed. Female only.

'Regenerata' Vase-shaped tree with arching branches and slender hanging shoots. Leaves opening early, pale brown soon green. Female only.

'Eugenei' Very vigorous and neat tree to 115 ft (35 m), conical until old when broad-columnar, hanging shoots. Male only.

*Many species of Populus are cultivated and naturalized well beyond their natural range. The geographical distribution given at the beginning of each entry refers to the natural distribution.

The true Black Poplar, *Populus nigra*, is not often seen as it has been supplanted by hybrids that have sprung up between it and *P. deltoides*. It is, however, more leafy than the hybrids with a shapely crown and a fine branching habit, as can be seen in this female tree in springtime.

TILIACEAE

Tilia

Limes, Lindens, Basswoods

The genus *Tilia* is singularly uniform, all forty-five limes or lindens being trees of moderate to large size with long-petioled, ovate-acuminate leaves, toothed and with an abrupt point, and small cymes of fragrant flowers from a pedicel that is fused to about half-way along a pale green bract. The flowers are small, white or yellow, with five petals alternating with five sepals and five bundles of stamens and often five petaloid scales or staminodes. The fruit is indehiscent and nut-like. The genus is widespread in the north temperate zone but absent from western America, central Asia, and the Himalaya.

There are two species native to limestone cliffs and damp woods in the west of Britain. One is the Small-leafed Lime (*T. cordata*), which, like most limes, is long lived, and can grow to a height of 115 ft (35 m). It bears elegant, small, cordate leaves, slightly silvered beneath, and numerous small flowers spreading or erect from their bracts. In North America it is abundant as a tree of city streets from St. Louis and Atlanta north and east to Montreal. The other British native is the Large-leafed Lime (*T. platyphyllos*), which makes a good clean tree with a hemispheric crown until very old, when it can be up to 110 ft (33 m) tall. The cymes bear only three to five large flowers, which open early. This lime species is used as an understock for grafts of some rarer species and for cultivars.

The Common Lime (*T. × europaea* = *T. vulgaris*) is a natural hybrid between the two previous species and grows to be the tallest broadleaved tree in Britain at 150 ft (45 m).

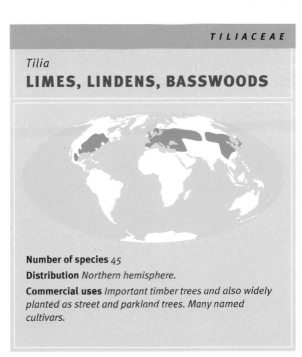

TILIACEAE

Tilia
LIMES, LINDENS, BASSWOODS

Number of species 45
Distribution *Northern hemisphere.*
Commercial uses *Important timber trees and also widely planted as street and parkland trees. Many named cultivars.*

Though often planted in town streets it has the two disadvantages of sprouting continually around the base and weeping honeydew from the aphids that infest it throughout the summer months. It is because of these defects that the Caucasian Linden (*T. × euchlora*) is often planted instead of the Common Lime. It has insect-free, handsome glossy leaves but tends to make a crown like a mushroom.

The American Lime or American Basswood (*T. americana*) makes a splendid conical tree in most American cities, with deep, rich green, large leaves with white veins, but it seldom flourishes in Europe, unlike its hybrid with the Silver Pendent Lime, which arose in Berlin, *T. ×* 'Moltkei.' This has very large leaves with fine white down beneath and on the petiole. The Silver Pendent Lime (*T. petiolaris*) grows to be a fine tall tree with leaves silvered beneath and outer branchlets pendulous. The Silver Lime (*T. tomentosa*) is more sturdy and domed with harder leaves, darker above, which thrives in cities. The Mongolian Lime (*T. mongolica*), which is rare but in demand, has red-stemmed dark leaves cut into acute lobes. The choicest Lime is the Oliver's Lime (*T. oliveri*) from China, with large pale leaves with sharp whitish teeth and a silvered underside, held out level from a drooping petiole.

Lime trees thrive on any moderately damp soil that is neither too acid or peaty, and many species are tolerant of considerable exposure. Propagation can be by seeds, but these are sometimes difficult to obtain and often infertile, so that layering is commonly resorted to, with grafting for rare species and cultivars.

The timber from *Tilia* species is light, soft, and pale-colored. It is prized for furniture, carving, paneling, for making matches and boxes, and especially for the manufacture of piano keys. The main timber-yielding trees are the American Basswood, the Small-leafed Lime, and the Japanese Linden (*T. japonica*). The inner bark fibers of these three species and the Tuan Linden (*T. tuan*) are used for making mats, cordage, and, when plaited, for shoes. Lime timber is also used to produce charcoal for drawing and burning. The fragrant flowers of the Linden—also known as vervaine—make one of the best-known and widely enjoyed herbal teas, which is said to have calming and restorative properties. **CZ3–7**

ABOVE *Tilia × europaea* is a naturally occurring hybrid between *T. cordata* and *T. platyphyllos*. It is often planted for shade and ornament in streets, parks, and gardens.

BELOW Branches of mature *Tilia* spp are ascending then branching, with the center of the crown often filled with masses of young growth.

T. × europaea

T. × europaea

T. mongolica

The Main Species of *Tilia*

Group I: Leaf green beneath, glabrous but for veins and vein axillary tufts, pubescent in *T. platyphyllos* but hairs simple.

T. cordata Small-leafed Lime. *Europe, Caucasus Mountains. Domed, broad, densely crowned tree to 115 ft (35 m). Leaves 2 in (5 cm), cordate-ovate or narrow triangular, pale beneath, slightly glaucous; orange tufts of hair in vein-axils. Flowers erect or at any angle, whitish, 5–10 from each pale green bract. Common in American city streets from Virginia to Colorado and Washington and in S Canada. **CZ3**
'Green Spire,' a neatly conic form with orange shoots, is now grown in N U.S.

T. americana American Basswood or Linden. *NE U.S. and SE Canada. Conic until mature, when broadly domed. Peculiarly luxuriant rich green foliage, with large leaves, 5 × 4 in (12 × 10 cm), but some sprout-leaves to 8 × 7 in (20 × 18 cm). Underside same color but veins white. Flowers 10–12 from big pale green bract. Widely planted in streets and squares beyond its natural range in Midwest states, Colorado, South Dakota, Manitoba, and, in the west, Montana to Washington and British Columbia. **CZ3**
'Fastigiata' is a narrowly conic-columnar occasional in the streets in America.

T. × euchlora Caucasian Linden. *Caucasus Mountains. Related to *T. cordata*. Domed and pendulous crown when maturing. Leaves bigger than *T. cordata*, 4(6) in (10(15) cm), glossy deep green above. Shoots yellow-green. Flowers 3–7, rich yellow from greenish-white bract. Patches of bright yellow leaves in the fall. Infrequent in streets and parks in Europe; rare in collections in America. **CZ6**

T. × europaea (T. × vulgaris) Common Lime or Linden. *Europe. Natural hybrid *T. cordata* × *T. platyphyllos*. Very tall tree to 153 ft (46 m), with narrow domed crown opening toward the top and numerous sprouts from base and bole, rarely clean. Leaves dull green above, a little paler beneath with small tufts of white hair in all vein-axils. Flowers 4–10, pale yellow, hanging from yellow-green bract. Abundant in streets, parks, and gardens in Europe; in N. America, a few in New York, New England, and British Columbia. **CZ4**

T. americana

T. oliveri

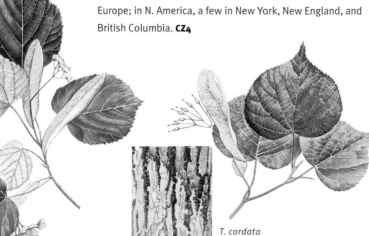

T. cordata

T. mongolica Mongolian Lime. *N China, Mongolia. Medium-sized domed tree. Leaves on red petiole, small, hard, dark shiny green, unique in genus for deeply and jaggedly toothed lobes. Very hardy but scarce. Planted where available in Europe and in NW U.S. in cities. **CZ3**

T. platyphyllos Large-leafed Lime. *Europe. Tree with hemispherical crown to 110 ft (33 m). Leaves softly hairy above and below (hairs simple), as are shoot and petiole. Flowers 3(4–6), large and early, yellowish-white from whitish bract. Common in Europe, frequent in N. U.S. cities (Baltimore to St. Louis); occasional in Virginia, Washington, and British Columbia. **CZ5**

'Laciniata' Cut-leaf Lime. Tree to 50 ft (15 m) leaves small, acuminate, toothed and lobed deeply, nearly to midrib.

'Rubra' Red-twigged Lime. Tree to 82 ft (25 m). Shoots dark red in winter, green in summer. Foliage denser and paler than type and flower-bract cream-white.

Group II: Leaves silvery-white beneath with typically fascicled or stellate hairs.

T. × 'Moltkei' Hybrid *T. americana* × *T. petiolaris*. Vigorous tree to 82 ft (25 m) with somewhat pendulous crown. Leaves big, 8–10 in (20–25 cm), coarsely toothed like *T. americana* but with dense, soft gray-white pubescence beneath. Arose in Berlin, before 1880.

T. heterophylla White Basswood. *E U.S. Probably a form of *T. americana* with intermediates but striking in some roadside woods in Ohio as wind shows silver underside of leaves. Leaves only to 5 in (12 cm) more finely toothed, densely white-haired beneath. **CZ5**

T. oliveri Oliver's Lime. *China. Tall, narrowly domed tree to 80 ft (23 m). Shoot and bud apple-green and pink, leaves big, 5–8 in (13–20 cm), pale green above with whitish sharp teeth, silvered beneath, flowers 2–4 from big pale green bract. Very handsome. **CZ6**

T. petiolaris Silver Pendent Lime. Perhaps from the Caucasus. Tall, narrow-domed pendulous tree to 110 ft (33 m), usually grafted at 6.6 ft (2 m) onto *T. platyphyllos*. Shoot, petiole, and underside of leaves closely matted with white simple hairs. Leaves very oblique at base, 5 × 5 in (12 × 12 cm), dark green, sharply toothed, on slender petiole 2.4–5 in (6–12 cm). Flowers 7–10, cup-shaped, broad-petaled, fragrant, and late. **CZ6**

T. tomentosa Silver Lime. *SW Asia. Broadly domed tree to 100 ft (30 m) with stout branches when old, regular hemispheric crown when young. Leaves broad, dark, hard, crinkled, very oblique, 5 × 4 in (12 × 10 cm) on 2 in (5 cm) petiole. Flowers cup-shaped, yellow, fragrant. Scarce in cities and big gardens in N U.S., mostly in New York, and New England; frequent in European cities. **CZ6**

Many species of Tilia are cultivated well beyond their natural range. The geographical distribution given at the beginning of each entry refers to the natural distribution.

ULMACEAE

Ulmus

Elms

The genus *Ulmus*, to which the various elms are allocated, comprises some thirty species of deciduous trees. It has a good continuous fossil record from the Upper Cretaceous onward, and its salient characters have shown little variation during its long geologic history. It has always been a north temperate genus, with three species in the Tropics. It now occurs throughout Europe, north to Scotland and Finland. It is absent from most of Siberia but present in Turkey, Israel, Iran, Afghanistan, parts of central Asia, and the Himalaya. In the Far East it is widespread in China (possibly its center of origin), Japan, the far east of Russia, and Korea, and extends south through Malaya to Sarawak and Sulawesi. In Africa, it is restricted to northern Algeria. In North America, it is confined to the eastern states, and extends south to Mexico.

Though the species are difficult to distinguish, the genus is usually identifiable by two salient leaf characters: bilateral asymmetry and bidentate leaf margins. The flowers may be stalked as in the American White Elm (*U. americana*) or sessile as in the European Field Elm (*U. minor*). In most species, the flower buds develop in spring after the leaves, in whose axils they were produced, have been shed—the vernal flowering habit.

In some subtropical species, for example the Chinese Elm (*U. parvifolia*), flowers develop from the buds while the leaves that subtend them are still attached—the fall flowering habit. The fruit is the main character used in specific discrimination, in particular the distribution of hairs upon it. Hybridization between most of the elm species can be accomplished artificially and it also occurs frequently in nature.

U L M A C E A E

Ulmus
ELMS

Number of species *30*
Distribution *North temperate regions to Mexico.*
Commercial uses *Formerly important timber and ornamental trees but susceptible to disease. Many cultivated forms and clones exist as a result of previous widespread cultivation.*

U. procera

A solitary *Ulmus glabra*, the Wych Elm, displays its noble form. In the open, it forms a stout, short trunk and a crown of branches which are often pendulous at the ends.

Throughout their natural range, elms show a preference for riverine sites. It is, however, difficult to ascertain the exact natural distribution of several species, as their areas have been much extended by human planting over the past 2,000 years, particularly in Europe, central Asia, and China.

The elms, in particular the English Elm (*U. procera*), American Elm (*U. americana*), Slippery Elm (*U. rubra*), and Rock Elm (*U. thomasii*), are of manifold utility. The foliage has been a preferred cattle feed over wide areas. This use is frequently mentioned in Roman agricultural writings and persisted in parts of Europe until the beginning of the twentieth century. It is still important in the Himalayan species *U. wallichiana*. Extensive lopping for cattle by prehistoric man is a possible explanation for the widespread "elm decline" that occurred in northwest Europe about the time when neolithic agriculture was spreading.

Elm timber has a number of special characteristics. In particular it is cross-grained and resists splitting. Consequently it has been the timber of choice for wheelwrights for the hubs of spoked wheels, a use that goes back to Mycenean Greece. The polished wood of elm shows a beautiful zigzag pattern, the so-called partridge-breast grain so skillfully exploited in the wooden sculptures of Arp, Moore, and Hepworth. Another characteristic of the timber is its resistance to decay under continuously waterlogged conditions. This accounts for its choice for underwater piles, the wooden water mains in former urban use, and the floats of water wheels.

A local use of elm, more widely known from its frequent mention by the Roman poets, is as a support for the vine. This practise was important in central Italy only.

The principal medicinal product of the elms is the mucilaginous bark of the Slippery Elm (*U. rubra*), which is used to treat inflamed conditions of the alimentary canal.

The elms have associated with them a large flora and fauna of species found nowhere else. The flora mainly comprises fungi, most of which cause little harm. Exceptional, however, in its destructive effect is the so-called Dutch Elm Disease caused by the fungus *Ceratocystis ulmi*. Dutch Elm Disease was first recognized as such in 1918. The fungus kills by inducing blockage of the vessels. It is distributed by bark-boring beetles, mainly *Scolytus* spp. It caused widespread death of elms in much of Europe between the world wars, whence it was introduced into North America. In Europe, the disease attenuated after this outbreak, but another flare-up began after 1965, perhaps through reintroduction of virulent strains from North America. In 1975 several counties in England recorded the extent of the catastrophe of Dutch Elm Disease, noting the loss of 98 percent of all their smooth-leaved elms, culminating in a major change to the English landscape. A few disease-resistant forms are now grown.

Elms have been widely cultivated as ornamentals, particularly in avenues and formal plantings. **CZ3–9**

U. americana

U. mexicana

The Main Species of *Ulmus*

Group I: Flowers in fall, stalked. Fruit hairy, wing narrow.

U. crassifolia Cedar Elm. SE U.S. Tree to 82 ft (25 m) with broad round-topped head, branches often with 2 corky flanges. Leaves ovate, rough above, 1–2 in (2.5–5 cm). Fruit oval, about 0.4 in (1 cm). **CZ7**

U. serotina SE U.S. Spreading tree to 66 ft (20 m). Leaves oblong, smooth above, 2–3 in (5–8 cm). Fruit oval, 0.4–0.6 in (1–1.5 cm). **CZ6**

U. monterreyensis An imperfectly known species from Nuevo Leon, Mexico. Tree to 50 ft (15 m). Leaves elliptic, shiny, but rough above, 0.8–1.6 in (2–4 cm). Mature fruits not observed. **CZ6**

U. parvifolia

Group II: Flowers typically in the fall, sessile. Fruit glabrous, wing conspicuous.

U. parvifolia Chinese Elm. China, Korea, Japan, SE Asia. Tree to 66 ft (20 m) with rounded head. Leaves lanceolate, smooth above, 0.8–1.6 in (2–4 cm), 30–50 secondary teeth, sub-evergreen in the south. Fruit oval, about 0.4 in (1 cm). **CZ5**

U. lanceifolia E Himalaya, SW China, Myanmar, SE Asia, Sumatra, Sulawesi. Spreading tree to 150 ft (45 m). Leaves lanceolate, smooth above, 1.6–2.4 in (4–6 cm), 50–70 secondary teeth. Fruit orbicular, sometimes markedly asymmetrical, about 1 in (2.5 cm). **CZ9**

Group III: Flowers vernal, stalked. Fruit densely hairy, no wing.

U. mexicana Mexican Elm. Mexico. Tree to 66 ft (20 m). Leaves elliptic, smooth above, 3–4 in (8–10 cm), with fewer than 100 secondary teeth. Fruit elongate oval, about 0.4 in (1 cm). **CZ6**

U. villosa W Himalaya. Tree to 82 ft (25 m). Mature leaves usually on long shoots, elliptic, smooth above, 2.8–3.5 in (7–9 cm), more than 100 secondary teeth. Fruit elongate oval, 0.5–0.6 in (1.2–1.5 cm). **CZ5**

U. americana

The American Elm has a crown of arching branches with shoots that are gracefully pendulous at the ends. It can reach heights of 120 ft (37 m), with a trunk of 6 ft (2 m) in diameter.

U. minor 'Sarniensis'

Group IV: Flowers vernal, stalked. Fruit densely hairy throughout, wing narrow.

U. alata **Wahoo, Winged Elm.** SE U.S. Round-headed tree to 50 ft (15 m). Branches usually with 2 corky flanges. Leaves oblong, smooth above, 1.2–2 in (3–5 cm). Fruit elongate oval, about 0.4 in (1 cm). **CZ4**

U. thomasii **Rock Elm.** E Canada, NE U.S. Tree to 100 ft (30 m) with rounded head. Leaves elliptic, smooth above, 2–3 in (5–8 cm). Fruit oval, 0.6–0.8 in (1.5–2 cm). **CZ3**

Group V: Flowers vernal, stalked. Fruit hairy along the edge only.

U. laevis **European White Elm.** E Europe, as far north as S Finland and as far west as NE France. Tree to 100 ft (30 m) of irregular habit. Trunk often bossy with buttressed roots. Leaves elliptic, tapering abruptly, often highly asymmetrical at the base, smooth above, 2.4–5 in (6–12 cm). Fruit oval, 0.4–0.6 in (1–1.5 cm). **CZ5**

U. americana **American White Elm.** SE Canada, E U.S. Regular, wide-spreading tree to 130 ft (40 m). Leaves elliptic, tapering abruptly, smooth or rough above, 3–5 in (7–12 cm). Fruit oval, about 0.4 in (1 cm). The only species known to be tetraploid (56 somatic chromosomes). **CZ3**

U. divaricata Known only from Nuevo Leon, Mexico. Spreading tree to 33 ft (10 m). Leaves elliptic, rough above and below, subsessile, 1.6–3 in (3.5–8 cm). Fruit oval, 0.2–0.3 in (0.5–0.8 cm); styles persistent.

U. procera

U. americana

U. wallichiana

U. alata

Group VI: Flowers vernal, sessile or subsessile. Fruit broadly winged, seed central in fruit. Leaves large.

U. rubra **Slippery Elm.** SE Canada, E U.S. Tree to 66 ft (20 m) with spreading, open canopy. Leaves oblong, tapering gradually, rough above, 4–5 in (10–12 cm). Fruit orbicular, hairy over the seed only, 0.4–0.8 in (1–2 cm). **CZ3**

U. macrocarpa N China, far east Russia, Korea. Bushy tree to 33 ft (10 m). Leaves elliptic, tapering abruptly, very rough above, 1.5–3 in (4–8 cm). Fruit orbicular, hairy over the entire surface, 0.8–1 in (2–2.5 cm). **CZ5**

U. wallichiana W Himalaya. Tree to 100 ft (30 m) with spreading crown. Leaves elliptic, tapering abruptly, rough above, 3.5–5 in (9–12 cm). Fruit orbicular, hairy throughout or only over seed, 0.4–0.45 in (1–1.3 cm). **CZ6**

U. uyematsui Taiwan and facing Chinese hinterland. Tree to 82 ft (25 m). Leaves elliptic, tapering abruptly, subsessile, rough above, about 4 in (10 cm). Fruit oval, glabrous, about 0.4 in (1 cm); fruit stalks about 0.25 in (0.6 cm).

U. bergmanniana C China. Tree to 82 ft (25 m). Leaves elliptic, tapering abruptly, subsessile, rough above, 3–4.5 in (8–11 cm). Fruit orbicular, glabrous, about 0.4 in (1.5 cm); fruit stalk 0.06–0.12 in (0.2–0.4 cm). **CZ6**

U. glabra **Wych Elm.** N Europe, N China, Korea, far east Russia, N Japan, Sakhalin, mountains farther south. Spreading tree to 130 ft (40 m). Leaves elliptic, tapering abruptly, subsessile, rough above, 3.5–5 in (9–12 cm). Fruit orbicular, usually glabrous, sessile, about 0.8 in (2 cm). **CZ5**

'Horizontalis' Weeping Wych Elm. Originated at Perth, Scotland, in the early nineteenth century. Frequently planted in cemeteries in the British Isles. Main branches spread horizontally in a low flat crown; lesser branches pendulous.

'Camperdownii' Camperdown Elm. Originated at Camperdown House, Scotland, around 1850 and used as the previous elm. Another weeping elm, but main branches grow upward and form a round head; lesser branches pendulous.

'Exoniensis' Exeter Elm. Originated in a nursery at Exeter, SW England, about 1826, now widespread in parks in N Europe. Branches grow upward to constitute a narrow columnar head. Leaves coarsely toothed, wrinkled, and twisted.

var elliptica Caucasus and SE Russia. Differs from typical *U. glabra* in having hairs over the seed on the fruit.

Group VII: Flowers vernal, sessile. Fruit broadly winged, seed central in fruit. Leaves usually small.

U. pumila **Siberian Elm.** C Asia, Mongolia, far east Russia, N China, Korea, Tibet. Tree to 82 ft (25 m). Mature leaves often on long shoots, elliptic, smooth above, 0.8–2 in (2–5 cm). Fruit orbicular, 0.4–0.5 in (1–1.5 cm). **CZ3**

U. glaucescens Mongolia and N China. Tree to 82 ft (25 m). Leaves ovate, smooth above, 1.2–1.6 in (3–4 cm). Fruit oval, 0.8–1 in (2–2.5 cm).

U. chumlia W Himalaya. Tree to 82 ft (25 m) with spreading branches. Leaves elliptic, smooth above, 2.4–3 in (6–8 cm). Fruit orbicular, 0.4–0.5 in (1–1.2 cm).

Elm species are widespread throughout all but the north and west of North America. The elms' natural preference is for the damp conditions afforded by riverine sites. The timber of *Ulmus* resists decay under waterlogged conditions, a property which has ensured its utillity for hundreds of years.

Group VIII: Flowers vernal, sessile. Fruit broadly winged, seed displaced to apex of fruit. **CZ9**

U. davidiana China, Korea, far east Rusia, Japan, Sakhalin. Tree to 100 ft (30 m). Leaves elliptic, rough above, 2–4 in (5–10 cm); petioles densely hairy. Fruit oval, glabrous or hairy over the seed, about 0.8 in (2 cm). **CZ6**

U. wilsoniana SW China. Tree to 82 ft (25 m). Leaves elliptic, smooth or rough above, 2–3 in (5–8 cm). Fruit oval, glabrous, about 0.6 in (1.5 cm). **CZ6**

U. castaneifolia C China. Tree to 66 ft (20 m). Leaves narrow, lanceolate, rough above, 5–5.5 in (12–14 cm). Fruit oval, glabrous, about 0.8 in (2 cm).

U. minor (U. carpinifolia) **European Field Elm.** C and S Europe, E England, Algeria, Near East. Tree to 100 ft (30 m) of variable habit; canopy open. Leaves elliptic, often highly asymmetrical at the base, usually smooth above, 2–3 in (5–8 cm); petioles glabrous or hairy. Fruit oval to orbicular, glabrous, 0.4–0.8 in (1–2 cm). **CZ5**

'Modiolina' **Orme Tortillard, Cross-grained Elm.** France. Small tree with gnarled and twisted branches. Variable leaves. Timber extremely cross-grained. Formerly much used for wheel hubs.

'Umbraculifera' Widely distributed in C Asia and N Iran. Habit highly characteristic, the head formed of a dense network of branches with an almost spherical perimeter. Leaves elliptic, 1.2–2.4 in (3–6 cm). One of the most distinctive landscape elements of C Asia, trees often marking shrines and wells.

'Viminalis' Originated in Kent, SE England, in 1817. Branches ascending; crown narrow. Leaves lanceolate, 0.8–2 in (2–5 cm).

var *cornubiensis* **Cornish Elm.** The principal elm in Cornwall and W Devon, England. Tall tree with straight bole and narrow crown. Leaves elliptic, about 2 in (5 cm).

'Sarniensis' **Guernsey Elm.** The predominant elm species of Guernsey, Channel Islands, and once extensively planted as a roadside tree in England. Medium-sized tree of stiff pyramidal habit. Leaves ovate, 1.6–2.4 in (4–6 cm).

var *lockii (U. plotii)* **Lock's Elm.** N Midlands of England. Trunk crooked; crown narrow; the leading branch characteristically droops to one side resembling an ostrich feather in profile. Mature leaves often on long shoots, oblong, about 1.2 in (3 cm).

U. procera **English Elm.** S and C England, NW Spain. Tree to 130 ft (40 m) with stout, straight bole and figure-of-eight or violin-shaped silhouette; canopy dense. Leaves orbicular, highly asymmetrical at base, usually rough above, 2–2.4 in (5–6 cm); petioles hairy. Fruit orbicular, glabrous, 0.4–0.8 in (1–2 cm). **CZ6**

Group IX: Hybrids between members of Groups VI and VIII.

U. × hollandica (U. glabra × U. minor) Numerous hybrids of this parentage occur in Europe, and in many regions, such as the Netherlands and parts of E England, they outnumber either parent. Vigorous trees to 130 ft (40 m); habit variable. Leaves large, usually petiolate, typically more than 3 in (8 cm). Fruit variable, tending to be intermediate between that of the parental species. **CZ5**

'Major' **Dutch Elm** (of England). Introduced from France to the Netherlands by nurserymen, then taken from the Netherlands to England in the time of William III. No longer common in the Netherlands. Planted extensively in exposed places in the British Isles such as Land's End and the Scilly Isles; also frequently planted in Ireland. Irregularly branched and of open, scraggy habit. Leaves ovate, usually rough above, with characteristic black blotchy discoloration toward the fall, 3–4.5 in (8–11 cm).

'Belgica' **Dutch Elm** (of the Netherlands). Of Belgian origin, apparently first recorded at Bruges in the eighteenth century. Mainly planted in the Netherlands, where it is the most frequent elm, and in Belgium. Tidy habit and broad, rounded head. Leaves narrow elliptic, 3–5 in (8–12 cm).

'Vegeta' **Huntingdon Elm.** Originated in Hinchingbrooke Park, near Huntingdon, England, about 1750. Mainly planted in S England. Trunk usually divides into a radiating fan of principal branches. Leaves elliptic, smooth above, 3.5–4.5 in (9–11 cm).

'Høersholmiensis' **Hørsholm Elm.** Originated at the Hørsholm nursery, Denmark, around 1885 and planted as a street tree in Denmark and S Sweden. Leaves narrow lanceolate, 4–5 in (10–12 cm).

Note: Leaf descriptions normally apply to well-developed leaves on dwarf shoots.

Zelkova

Caucasian Elms

Zelkova is a small genus composed of just four species from the eastern Mediterranean, the Caucasus, Iran, and western and eastern Asia. They are deciduous trees or shrubs with smooth peeling bark and alternate leaves with conspicuously toothed margins and a short petiole. The flowers are bisexual, unisexual (and then borne on the same plant), or polygamous (unisexual and bisexual flowers on the same plant), with a four- to five-lobed calyx but no petals. The male flowers are borne in groups of two to five in the axils of the lowermost leaves and have four to five stamens. The female or bisexual flowers are solitary or few in the axils of the uppermost leaves and have a single ovary and excentric style. The fruit is unwinged, nut-like (or like a dry drupe) with a wrinkled surface subtended by the persistent calyx and crowned by the remains of the style, forming two minute beaks. Zelkovas are hardy in temperate regions and succeed on any well-drained, deep, good soil. Flowering occurs in spring when the leaves appear. Propagation is by seed or by grafting onto elm stocks.

Hemiptelea davidii, the only species of its genus, is sometimes included in *Zelkova* but this species has hairy shoots with long, stout spines and a broadly ovoid, stalked, winged fruit. It is a native of China, Mongolia, and Korea and is hardy in temperate regions.

The timber from all species of *Zelkova* is used in cabinetmaking and inlay work. *Zelkova serrata*, a native of China and Japan, which forms lowland forest with maple, beech, and oak, produces a hard, fine-grained wood similar to that of English Elm (*Ulmus procera*) and is highly valued in Japan for special building purposes such as temples. The Asiatic name for the wood is "Keaki." It resists moisture well because of its high oil content, but this imparts flavor to the wood and makes it unsuitable for food containers or vessels. In Korea it is highly prized for making the rims of wagon wheels. The species was introduced into Britain in 1862 and is grown for ornamental purposes. The Caucasian Elm (*Z. carpinifolia*) was introduced in 1760 and has been used as a replacement tree for elms lost through Dutch Elm Disease. Unfortunately, it is now evident that some zelkovas are also subject to the disease.

The foliage of zelkovas is cut in summer, dried and used as winter feed for livestock. The Caucasian word *zelkoua* translates as "stonewood," a reference to the hardness of the timber. **CZ5–8**

Leaves of *Zelkova carpinifolia* have 6–12 pairs of veins, as opposed to *Z. serrata* which has 8–12. The leaves are dark green and have hairs on the main vein beneath and are roughly hairy above. The fruit are borne singularly at each leaf base; they are bright green, round, and distinctly ridged.

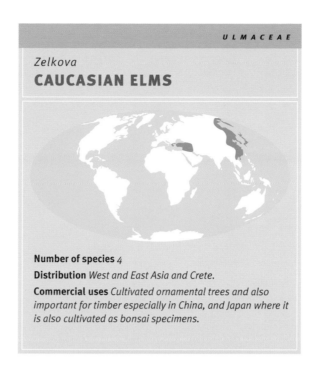

ULMACEAE

Zelkova
CAUCASIAN ELMS

Number of species 4
Distribution *West and East Asia and Crete.*
Commercial uses *Cultivated ornamental trees and also important for timber especially in China, and Japan where it is also cultivated as bonsai specimens.*

Z. serrata

The Species of *Zelkova*

Group I: Bark pinkish to orange or with close-set horizontal pink stripes. Shoots glabrous or more or less pubescent but not hispid (ie without rough bristly hairs).

Z. serrata (*Z. acuminata*) **Keaki.** Japan. Tree to 130 ft (40 m) in the wild, much less in cultivation. Bark gray, horizontally striped with pink. Shoots pubescent, soon glabrous. Leaves more or less ovate, 1.2–4(5) in (3–10(12) cm), with about 10 mucronate teeth on each side, veins 8–12(14) pairs. Fruit roundish, 0.1–0.2 in (3–5 mm) across. **CZ5**

Z. sinica **Chinese Zelkova.** C and E China. Tree to 50(55) ft (15(17) m). Bark orange or pink not striped. Shoots gray-woolly. Leaves ovate to oval, 0.8–2.8 in (2–7 cm), margin entire toward cuneate base, but shallowly crenate-toothed toward apex, veins 6–8 pairs. Fruit 0.2–0.25 in (5–6 mm) across. **CZ6**

Group II: Not the characters of Group I. Crown unique in its ovoid-oblong shape formed by very numerous branches vertically ascending from apex of 3–10 ft (1–3 m) trunk.

Z. carpinifolia (*Z. crenata*) **Siberian or Caucasian Elm.** Caucasus. Tree to 82 ft (25 m). Shoots pubescent. Leaves more or less elliptic, 0.8–2(3.5) in (2–5(9) cm), margin broadly crenate, ciliate, veins 6–12 pairs, petiole 0.04–0.08(0.12) in (1–2(3) mm). Fruit 0.16–0.25 in (4–6 mm) across. **CZ5**

Group III: Not the characters of Groups I or II. Branches spreading to give a more or less dome-shaped crown.

Z. abelicea (*Z. cretica*) **Cretan Zelkova.** Mountains in Crete, possibly endemic. Recorded from Cyprus in 1840 by a competent botanist (Kotschy) but not since re-collected; now possibly extinct. Shrub to 16 ft (5 m) or tree to 50 ft (15 m). Shoots slender, at first with short bristles, which soon fall off. Leaves subsessile, ovate to oblong, 0.4–1(1.6) in (1–2.5(4) cm), rough above, pubescent or glabrescent beneath, the margin with 7–10 broad rounded crenations. Flowers white, sweet-scented. Fruit pubescent. **CZ8**

Z. carpinifolia 'Verschaffeltii' **Cut-leaf Zelkova.** Possibly Caucasus. Shrubby bush or small tree. Leaves subsessile, oval to lanceolate, rough above, 1.2–2.4(3) in (3–6(8) cm), the margin with 5–8(9) coarsely triangular teeth on each side and as many paired veins. Fruit globose, green, 0.16–0.2 in (4–5 mm) across, grooved. Very close to *Z. carpinifolia* possibly a form of that species, differing mainly in habit. **CZ5**

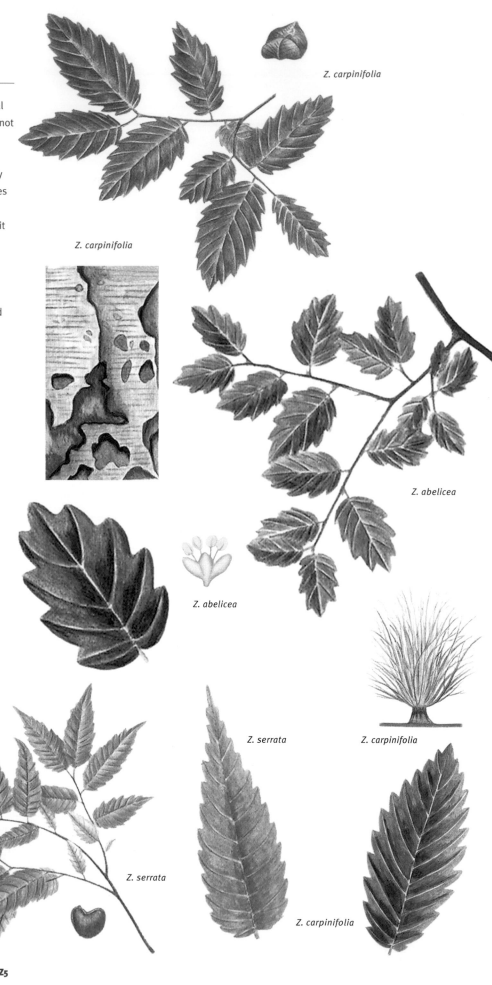

Z. carpinifolia

Z. carpinifolia

Z. abelicea

Z. abelicea

Z. serrata

Z. carpinifolia

Z. serrata

Z. carpinifolia

Celtis

Hackberries

The genus *Celtis* comprises some hundred species from North and South America, Africa southeastern Europe, and the Near and Far East (China, Korea, Japan). They are related to the elms from which they differ in having leaves with three main veins instead of one and globose fleshy fruits (dry and winged in elms).

Hackberries are mainly deciduous, hardy trees with decorative leaves, though the tropical and subtropical species are often evergreen. The flowers are green, with a perianth of one whorl (calyx) usually produced in the spring with the young leaves, and are either bisexual or male, both occurring on the same tree. The male flowers are found in clusters (below the bisexual), with four or five calyx segments and stamens; the bisexual flowers (above the males) are typically solitary (sometimes up to three), and borne in the young leaf axils. The cherry-like fruit is a globose drupe with a central stone covered by a thin pulp, which may be edible, and a thick skin usually colored red or purple.

A few more or less hardy species, for example the Common Hackberry (*C. occidentalis*), are grown in temperate regions but are not outstanding, apart from the bright yellow fall leaves of some species. They prefer a well-drained, loamy soil.

The fruit of *C. australis* is said to have been the "Lotus" of the Homeric Lotus-eaters, consumption rendering them unmindful of home and family. Pliny used the name *Celtis* for an African species of *Lotus*, perhaps because of the sweet berries. The timber is used for manufacturing utensils, walking sticks, whip handles, and fishing rods.

Other species of *Celtis* yielding usable timber of medium to low quality, which is utilized locally, are *C. brasiliensis* from Brazil, the Stinkwood (*C. kraussiana*) of Africa, from the Cape to Ethiopia, *C. mildbraedii* from west and central tropical Africa, and *C. philippinensis* from the Philippines to New Guinea. The Granjeno (*C. iguanaea*) from tropical Central America also has edible fruits, and *C. cinnamomea* from the Indian subcontinent and Indonesia has strongly scented wood, which, when powdered, is known as "kajoo lahi." This is used medicinally as a blood purifier and tonic. **CZ2–9**

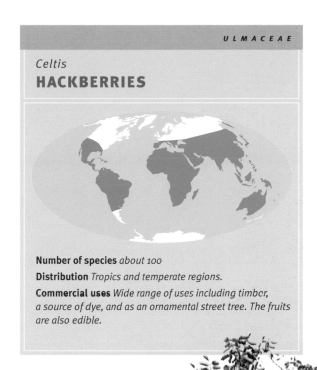

ULMACEAE

Celtis
HACKBERRIES

Number of species *about 100*

Distribution *Tropics and temperate regions.*

Commercial uses *Wide range of uses including timber, a source of dye, and as an ornamental street tree. The fruits are also edible.*

Celtis australis is a spreading deciduous tree producing a mellow fall color and edible fruit. It has a broad rounded canopy and makes a good shade tree.

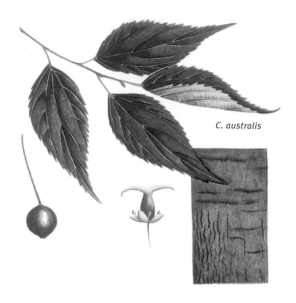

C. australis

C. occidentalis   *C. australis*

The Main Species of *Celtis*

Group I: Leaf margins toothed or serrate at least in upper half.

A *Lower surface of leaves plainly pubescent. Fruit with pitted stone.*

C. australis **European Hackberry.** Mediterranean region: S Europe, N Africa, SW Asia. Tree to 82 ft (25 m), girth to 10 ft (3 m). Bark gray, like a beech (*Fagus*). Shoots hairy. Leaves ovate-lanceolate, bases wedge-shaped, upper surface with short, stiff hairs at first, falling later. Fruit globose, 0.3–0.5 in (9–12 mm) across, finally (purplish) black. Reputed to reach 1,000 years. Timber valuable, tough. **CZ6**

C. caucasica **Caucasian Nettle Tree.** Caucasus, Afghanistan, India. Tree to 66 ft (20 m). Closely related to *C. australis*, but leaves shorter and wider and fruit yellow. Also hardier than *C. australis*. **CZ6**

AA *Lower surface of leaves glabrous, at least between the veins, rarely with sparse down. Fruit with pitted or smooth stone.*

C. occidentalis **Sugarberry, Common Hackberry.** S U.S. Tree to 130 ft (40 m). Bark gray, rough, corky. Leaves ovate with cordate base. 2–4 in (5–10 cm), petiole 0.4 in (1 cm) or more. Fruit globose, 0.3–0.35 in (8–9 mm) across, at first more or less orange, finally dark purple: stone pitted. **CZ2**
var *crassifolia* has larger and thicker leaves, (3.5)4.5–6 in ((9)11–15 cm). **CZ2**
var *pumila* resembles a small *C. occidentalis* and is a shrub or small tree to 13(16) ft (4(5) m). Leaves more or less ovate, 1.2–3 in (3–8 cm), apex acute, larger leaf margins sometimes with a few wider spaced teeth in upper half of leaf. Fruit 0.25–0.3 in (6–8 mm) across, orange to purplish.

C. sinensis **Chinese Hackberry.** E China, Korea, Japan. Tree 66 ft (20 m) in the wild, about 36 ft (11 m) in cultivation. Leaves broadly oval, shiny, dark green, deeply toothed toward apex, petiole under 0.4 in (1 cm). Fruit rich orange; stone pitted. **CZ9**

C. bungeana Mountains of N China. Tree 33–50 ft (10–15 m). Leaves ovate to lanceolate, 2–3.5 in (5–9 cm), toothed only toward apex, petiole less than 0.4 in (1 cm). Fruit ovoid, 0.25–0.28 in (6–7 mm) across, black; stone smooth. **CZ5**

C. occidentalis

C. glabrata Caucasus, Asia Minor. Shrub or small tree to 13 ft (4 m). Shoots at first downy, quickly glabrous. Leaves ovate, 0.1–0.25(0.28) × 0.6–1.4 in (2.5–6(7) × 15–34 mm), margins of upper half with coarse, deep, incurved teeth; entirely hairy and rough to the touch. Fruit globose, 0.16–0.2 in (4–5 mm) across, rusty brown; stone very slightly pitted. **CZ6**

C. tournefortii Balkans, Asia Minor, Crimea, Sicily. Shrub or small tree, 20–24 ft (6–7 m). Leaves ovate, 1.2–2.8 in (3–7 cm), wide, blunt teeth on margins of upper half. Fruit orange; stone smooth. This and the previous species are closely related to *C. bungeana*. **CZ7**

Group II: Leaf margins more or less entire or slightly wavy. Fruit with pitted stone.

C. laevigata (*C. mississippiensis*) **Mississippi Sugarberry** or **Hackberry.** S U.S. Tree 66–82 ft (20–25 m). Bark warty. Leaves more or less ovate, 2–4 in (5–10 cm), the apex long, drawn out, and tapering (long acuminate). Fruit (0.2)0.25–0.28 in ((5)6–7 mm) across, orange, finally dark purplish, its stalk 0.4–0.8 ln (1–2 cm) long, longer than the 0.25–0.4(0.5) in (6–10(12) mm) leaf stalk. **CZ5**
var *smallii* has sharply serrate leaves.

C. reticulata SW U.S. Tree 33–40(50) ft (10–12(15) m), sometimes shrubby. Leaves mainly ovate, 1.2–3(4) in (3–8(10) cm), apex typically acute. Fruit 0.3–0.35 in (8–9 mm) across, orange-red; stalk 0.4 in (1 cm) long, about equal to length of leafstalk. **CZ6**

FACING PAGE *Ficus religiosa*, a giant of a tree, is a symbol of Buddhism throughout Asia. In its native India, where it is known as the Bo-tree or Peepul, a tincture made from its leaves is used to treat a variety of medical conditions.

MORACEAE

Ficus

Figs

Ficus is a large pantropical genus of approximately 750
species, mostly from the Old World but some from the New
World, for example *F. paraensis*. Members vary from small
shrubs to large trees up to 150 ft (45 m) tall, and are
important constituents of many upland tropical forests. They
are frequently evergreen in tropical zones, but tend to become
deciduous in temperate zones. Some species are glabrous
(for instance *F. elastica*), others hairy, or with stinging hairs
(*F. minahassae*), or with silica bodies in the leaves (*F. hispida*).
Leaf arrangement is usually alternate, occasionally opposite
(*F. hispida*). The leaves vary from 1.5 in (4 cm) (*F. pumila*)
to 20 in (50 cm) (*F. gigantifolia*) long, can be undivided or
lobed, the venation palmate or pinnate, and in shape may be
asymmetrical about the midrib (*F. tinctoria*) or dimorphic; in
F. pumila, for example, the young leaves are cordate and
sessile, while the older ones are large, elliptic, and petiolate.
Caducous stipules are universally present, usually in pairs.
Also universal is the presence of latex vessels throughout the
plant: the India-rubber Fig (*F. elastica*) was used extensively
in rubber manufacture up to the mid-nineteenth century.

Figs have a characteristic inflorescence termed a syconium,
a flask-shaped fleshy container with many minute flowers
densely arranged on the inner walls. Fig flowers may be one
of three types: male flowers with one or two short stamens
(rarely three or six), and female flowers, which may be long
or short-styled, each type with an ovary containing one ovule.
The long styled flower is capable of being fertilized to produce
seed. The short-styled flower is infertile and known as a

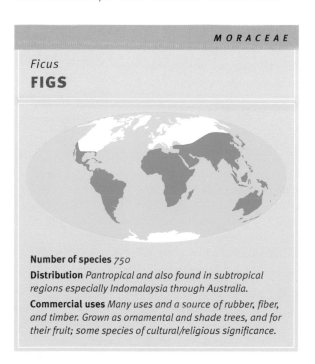

MORACEAE

Ficus
FIGS

Number of species *750*

Distribution *Pantropical and also found in subtropical
regions especially Indomalaysia through Australia.*

Commercial uses *Many uses and a source of rubber, fiber,
and timber. Grown as ornamental and shade trees, and for
their fruit; some species of cultural/religious significance.*

"gall flower," because the female fig insect lays her eggs in it and the young insect develops to maturity inside the ovary of the flower. The difference in style length is adapted to the egg-laying habits of the insect, whose ovipositor is too short to reach the ovary of the long-styled flower. However, in her attempts, the insect effectively pollinates the stigma with pollen picked up from the male flowers she has already crawled over. The common fig insect is the gall-wasp *Blastophaga psenes* (Hymenoptera), but it is thought that each *Ficus* species may support its own species of *Blastophaga*.

Fig Types

Several species of fig are classed as "stranglers." This strange habit is common to many tropical species, among them *F. pertusa* and *F. cordifolia*. The strangler fig begins as a seed dropped in the fork of a twig by a fig-eating mammal or bird. As the seed germinates it begins to grow downward, the roots wrapping round the host. The effect is to crush the bark, thus ringing the tree and destroying its food-bearing vessels. Eventually the fig survives as a freestanding tree.

The Edible Fig (*F. carica*) has a long history of cultivation, beginning in Syria probably before 4000 B.C.E. Since then it has held an important place in folklore and literature. The art of fig culture was first documented by the Greek poet Archilochus, around 700 B.C.E., and there are many biblical references to the fig. It grows successfully in many tropical and some temperate

F. sycomorus

F. aurea

F. carica

F. macrophylla

F. benghalensis

Ficus capensis is a tropical fig, known as the famine food in parts of Africa. Fruits, leaves and aerial roots may be eaten.

habitats, usually on dry, higher ground. The main cultivation areas are California, Turkey, Greece, and Italy. The Cultivated Fig is a small tree, under 33 ft (10 m) tall, with large palmately lobed leaves 4–8 in (10–20 cm) in length. There are two fruiting types: Adriatic and Smyrna. The more common Adriatic Fig does not have male flowers and the fig fruits develop from the female flowers without need for pollination and fertilization. Its seeds are undeveloped and infertile. Likewise the Smyrna Fig has no male flowers, but its female flowers do require pollination. To achieve this, branches of wild figs with male flowers are attached to Smyrna Fig trees at the time fig wasps are expected to emerge, thus allowing cross-pollination. The Wild Fig with male flowers is known as the Caprifig.

There are other fig species with edible fruits, for example *F. racemosa*, a common tree of eastern Asia, though its fruits are hardly palatable by Western standards, being full of insects or hard seeds. *Ficus religiosa* (Peepul Tree) and *F. pertusa* are Indian species that are often planted as shade trees because of their dense spreading crowns. Several species act as host trees for the lac insect, including *F. semicordata* and *F. rumphii*. This insect secretes a resinous substance (lac), which, in its purified form (shellac), is used for industrial purposes, particularly varnish manufacture, and for electrical insulation. In temperate zones some species are grown as houseplants. The commonest is the Rubber Plant, a sapling of *F. elastica* 'Decora.' The Climbing Fig (*F. pumila*) and the Weeping Fig or Java Willow (*F. benjamina*) are also grown. A number of species can be grown outside in warm temperate areas, for example the Moreton Bay Fig (*F. macrophylla*).

Banyans

Several species of the genus are called banyans, best known of which is *F. benghalensis*. This species is a large tree, which, though indigenous to the Himalayan foothills, is now widespread throughout India, as for centuries it has been planted in many villages for the excellent shade it provides. The Hindus regard it as sacred, for it is said that Buddha once meditated beneath a banyan tree.

Perhaps its most interesting botanical features are its pillar-like aerial roots. They grow downward from the branches and thicken once established in the ground below, so that the tree assumes the unusual appearance of being supported by pillars. By this manner of growth the tree is able to spread outward almost indefinitely, and many examples are of immense size and great antiquity. Some probably cover the largest area of all the living plants; one giant tree growing in the Andhra Valley in India is quoted as having a crown measuring 2,000 ft (600 m) in circumference and being supported by 320 aerial pillar-roots. There was at one time a very old specimen growing in the Calcutta Botanic Garden that had over 460 such roots around its main trunk, and another in Sri Lanka with over 300 pillars, whose umbrella-like crown provided enough shade to cover an entire village. **CZ7–10**

The Main Species of *Ficus*

Section *Urostigma*

Monoecious. Figs with small bracts around the apical pore and at the base. Flower tube 3-, rarely 4- or 2-lobed; 1 stamen. Fruits usually in axillary pairs. A large group from Asia, Australia, Africa, and America, many of which are climbers and/or epiphytic ("stranglers.")

F. elastica **India-rubber Fig, Caoutchouc Tree.** India, SE Asia. Seedlings epiphytic, becoming large trees to 196 ft (60 m) with thick, buttressed, multiple trunks and spreading surface roots. Leaves thick, 5–12 × 2.4–6 in (12–30 × 6–15 cm), elliptic, apex and base more or less rounded, surface smooth and glossy. Terminal bud sheathed by only 1 stipule (2 being more usual). Figs sessile, spherical, about 0.4 in (1 cm) diameter, surface smooth, pale green with darker flecks. **CZ10**

F. religiosa **Bo-tree, Peepul Tree.** India. Seedlings epiphytic, becoming large trees with many trunks and dense leaf canopies. Leaves thin, to 6.5 × 5 in (17 × 12 cm), more or less triangular, the apex drawn out into a slender tip to 2.4 in (6 cm). Figs sessile, cylindrical, surface smooth, green to purple with bright red flecks. **CZ10**

F. benjamina **Weeping Fig, Benjamin Banyan, Java Willow.** India, SE Asia. Several distinct varieties:

var *benjamina* Tree to 100 ft (30 m) with aerial roots, trunks never buttressed, branches drooping. Leaves thin, leathery, to 4.5 × 2 in (11 × 5 cm), elliptic, broader toward the base, the apex drawn out to a long curving tip. Figs on short stalks, spherical to cylindrical, about 0.4 in (1 cm) long, surface smooth, green, bright red and/or black flecked with white. Cultivated for its ornamental value.

var *comosa* Tufted Fig. As above but leaves in dense clusters at the tips of shoots. Figs on short stalks, more or less spherical, 0.8 in (2 cm) diameter, surface yellow to orange.

var *nuda* As above but leaves narrow. Figs pale green to reddish-brown, the bracts at the base of the fig falling before the fruit is mature. **CZ10**

F. benghalensis **Banyan Fig.** India. Large trees with multiple, buttressed trunks supporting dense leaf canopies. Spreading surface roots. Leaves leathery, 6–10 × 5–6.5 in (15–25 × 12–17 cm), ovate, the apex rounded or tipped by a short point, base more or less rounded, surface with soft velvet-like covering of short hairs. Figs sessile, spherical to cylindrical, about 0.8 in (2 cm) long, surface hairy, bright red flecked with white. Prominent yellow bracts at base of fig. **CZ10**

F. thonningii C and W Africa. Seedlings epiphytic, becoming large trees with multiple buttressed trunks and dense leaf canopies. Leaves leathery, smooth, about 5.5 × 2 in (14 × 5 cm), elliptic, apex and base broadly rounded, upper surface dark green, lower surface light green. Figs sessile, sometimes solitary, more or less cylindrical, about 0.6 in (1.5 cm) long, surface sparsely hairy, green flecked with white. **CZ10**

F. gigantifolia

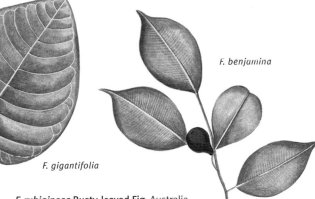

F. benjamina

F. salicifolia

F. rubiginosa **Rusty-leaved Fig.** Australia. Seedlings epiphytic, becoming large trees with multiple trunks, buttressed, if not conspicuously so. Leaves leathery, to 6.5 × 2.4 in (17 × 6 cm), elliptic, apex and base rounded, rough in texture, red-brown when young, becoming smooth when mature. Figs spherical on short stalks, about 0.6 in (1.5 cm) across, surface smooth to very rough, green, yellow, or rust-colored; green or white flecked. **CZ10**

F. pretoriae **Wonderboom.** S Africa. Tree to 75 ft (23 m) with a broad, spreading crown, supported by many trunks. Leaves stiff, papery, elliptic, 3–8 in (7.5–20 cm) long, up to 2.8 in (7 cm) wide, apex more or less acute, base rounded to shallowly cordate, surface dull above without hydathodes (water-secreting glands) or hairs. Figs singly or in pairs in leaf axils or clustered in the axils of leaf scars, very short-stalked, spherical to broadly pear-shaped, approximately 0.3 in (0.7 cm) across, surface green to reddish-brown, hairy, flecked with greenish-white. Basal bracts green, becoming red with age. **CZ10**

Section *Pharmacosycea*

Monoecious. Figs usually solitary and lacking basal bracts. Flower tube 4-lobed; stamens 1–3, usually 2. Trees, never climbers or stranglers. Mainly tropical America, but a few species in Asia and one in Madagascar.

F. maxima C America, W Indies, Amazon Basin. Fairly common. Tree to 100 ft (30 m). Leaves thin, papery, 2.4–8 × 0.8–3.5 in (6–20 × 2–9 cm), variable in shape, usually elliptic, apex blunt or pointed, base continuing into short petiole. Figs short-stalked, spherical, 0.4–0.8 in (1–2 cm) across, surface smooth, sometimes sparsely hairy, green or yellowish-green, apical pore 0.04–0.08 in (1–2 mm) diameter. **CZ10**

F. insipida C America, from Mexico to S Brazil. Tree to 130 ft (40 m), trunk buttressed. Leaves thick, leathery, 2–10 × 0.4–4.5 in (5–25 × 1–11 cm), narrowly to broadly elliptic, apex blunt or pointed, base narrowing into petiole. Figs sessile or short-stalked, spherical, 0.4–1.2 in (1.5–3 cm) across, green or yellow, apical pore 0.08–0.16 in (2–4 mm) diameter. **CZ10**

F. gigantoscyce Colombia. Tree to 66 ft (20 m). Leaves 5.5–11 × 2–6 in (13–28 × 5–15 cm), elliptic, apex acute, sometimes with a distinct tip, base deeply cordate forming 2 deep lobes. Figs very large, spherical, 1.2–3 in (3–8 cm) across, yellow or reddish. **CZ10**

F. elastica

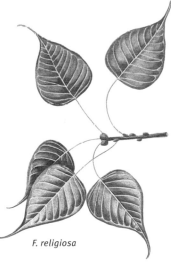

F. religiosa

F. paraensis

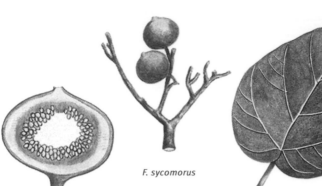

F. sycomorus

F. pumila (young leaves)

F. pumila (older leaves)

F. carica

Section *Sycomorus*

Monoecious. Figs pear- or top-shaped, in clusters on leafless stems, branches and on the main trunk. Stamens 1 or 2, rarely 3. Africa, SW Asia, and Australia.

F. sycomorus Mulberry Fig, Pharaoh's Fig. N to E Africa, SW Asia. Small tree to 50 ft (15 m). Leaves rough, leathery, to 6 × 5 in (15 × 13 cm), broadly ovate, margins undulate, the apex bluntly rounded, the base cordate, upper surface glabrous, dark green, lower surface paler, slightly hairy. Figs on slender stalks, pear-shaped, to 1.2 in (3 cm) long, surface green with dense velvet-like covering of white hairs. **CZ10**

F. racemosa Cluster Fig. India, SE Asia, Australia. Tree to 82 ft (25 m) with spreading crown. Leaves thin, leathery, margins undulate, elliptic or ovate, to 8 × 3 in (20 × 8 cm), apex pointed, base cordate, surface smooth and glossy with a silvery appearance. Figs in large clusters borne directly on the trunk and leafless parts of branches, shortly pear-shaped, to 1.2 in (3 cm) long, green becoming bright red flecked with white at maturity. **CZ10**

Section *Ficus*

Dioecious. Figs in clusters or pairs on leafless branches or behind leaves. Female flowers with styles much longer than those of gall-flowers, 2 stamens (4 in *F. carica*). Trees and climbers. Many species, in Africa, Asia, and Australasia.

F. carica Edible or Cultivated Fig. Native of SW Asia. Small spreading tree to about 13 ft (4 m), deciduous in temperate climates. Leaves broadly lobed, large, 4–8 × 4–8 in (10–20 × 10–20 cm), base truncate or rounded, lower surface sometimes sparsely covered with rough hairs. Male flowers with 4 stamens. Figs usually in pairs or singly on leafless branches or behind leaves, pear-shaped; surface usually green, sometimes tinged with purple or brown. Extensively cultivated; many varieties. The Wild Fig, var *caprificus*, is very variable. **CZ7**

F. pumila Climbing Fig. Asia, common in China and Japan. Vine-like, attaching itself to rocks and buildings by short sticky roots that develop at the nodes. Leaves dimorphic, young leaves sessile, small, heart-shaped; older leaves petiolate, larger, to 5.5 × 1.6 in (11 × 4 cm), elliptic, surface smooth, glabrous, or lower surface sparsely hairy. Figs on short, thick stalks, mostly solitary, more or less cylindrical with apex prominent, large, to 2.4 × 1.4 in (6 × 3.5 cm), surface pale green or gray flecked with white, densely hairy. Cultivated. Young specimens popular as house plants. **CZ9**

F. hispida Opposite-leaved Fig. India, SE Asia, and N Australia. Shrub or small tree with hairy twigs. Leaves opposite on some branches, alternate on others, large, ovate, to 12.5 × 5.5 in (31 × 11 cm), apex blunt or sharply pointed, base rounded, both surfaces very rough, the upper surface having a dense covering of rigid hairs, hydathodes present, margins toothed. Figs on short stalks, in axillary pairs, more or less spherical, very hairy, green or yellow flecked with white; 3 bracts prominent at the base of each fig. Fruits reputed to be poisonous. **CZ10**

F. auriculata Roxburgh Fig. India, SE Asia into China. Shrub. Leaves with long petioles, ovate, very large, up to (sometimes exceeding) 18 × 13.5 in (46 × 35 cm), base deeply cordate, the 2 lobes sometimes overlapping or becoming united, apex acute, upper surface with scattered hydathodes, lower surface hairy. Figs in clusters on the main branches and trunk, on thick stalks, pear-shaped, very large, up to 2.6 × 2 in (6.5 × 5 cm) long, surface greenish-white to brown with red flecks, hairy; 3 large bracts at the base of each fig. **CZ10**

F. tinctoria Dye Fig, Humped Fig (named for the asymmetry of the leaves). SE China, Philippines, Indonesia, N Australia. Leaves thin, approximately ovate, the blade unequal in shape about the midrib, to 7 × 2.8 in (18 × 7 cm), apex acute, base rounded or narrowing into petiole, margins angular, as in holly (*Ilex*), surface hairless with scattered hydathodes. Figs axillary, singly or in pairs, more or less sessile, spherical, about 0.4 in (1 cm) diameter, surface sometimes rough and hairy, yellowish-green flecked with paler green. The juice from the fruits is used as a base for a green dye. The bark fibers are used to make poor-quality cordage and those of young shoots to make fishing nets. **CZ10**

F. minahassae Philippines, Sulawesi. Tree. Young twigs with sharp stinging hairs. Leaves ovate, to 8 × 5.2 in (20 × 12.5 cm), apex rounded to acute, base deeply cordate, the lobes meeting or overlapping, margins finely toothed and fringed with hairs, both upper and lower surfaces with rigid hairs and many scattered hydathodes. Fruits in clusters on long rope-like spurs arising from the main trunk and up to 10 ft (3 m) long. Figs very small, less than 0.2 in (0.5 cm) across, red. **CZ10**

F. pseudopalma Palm-like Fig. Philippines. Small tree to 25 ft (7.5 m). Leaves papery, obovate, to 39 × 6 in (100 × 15 cm), margin coarsely toothed near the apex, entire at the base, upper surface glossy with scattered hydathodes. Figs short-stalked up to 1.2 × 0.8 in (4 × 2 cm), surface ribbed lengthwise, dark brown to green/purple, with raised white flecks. Basal bracts prominent. **CZ10**

Morus
Mulberries

The genus *Morus* is best known for its fruit, the mulberry. All its members are deciduous and most are tropical. There are probably about twelve distinct species of *Morus*, though over 100 have been described, on the basis of the large variation found in the fruits. The cultivated forms are of Asiatic and American origin.

In common with the rest of the Moraceae, the milky sap from cut *Morus* stems contains latex. The leaves are cordate, simple or lobed, with three to five veins originating at the junction of the leaf blade with the petiole. Leaf shapes may vary from tree to tree, or even on the same branch. The flowers are unisexual, small, and individually inconspicuous with male and female on the same tree. They are clustered into green, pendulous, male or female catkins. The mulberry fruits form around a central core in blackberry-like clusters, in which the colored juicy parts have developed from the perianth segments of the individual flowers. The seeds are small, hard, and embedded in the flesh. Cultivated mulberries may be about 0.8 in (2 cm) long, but those from the wild are usually less than 1 cm (0.4 in) long.

The White Mulberry (*M. alba*) was probably the parent of the original American "Downing" Mulberry, selected for its fruit yield. It forms a wide-spreading tree up to 50 ft (15 m) tall, with gray bark and small leaves, 2–6 in (5–15 cm) long, which are shiny above and may be hairy beneath, with coarsely toothed margins. The fruits are red. It is thought to have escaped from its native China to North America. In China its primary functions were to provide silkworm fodder from the soft tender leaves and also to provide timber. It was not selected for its fruit until it became established in America. With the Chinese Catalpa (*Catalpa ovata*), the White Mulberry used to be considered one of the two most important timber trees of China, and most Chinese homesteads had one or two of each planted nearby. The expression "Sang Tzu" means literally "Land of the mulberry and catalpa," and is still a common phrase in Chinese usage meaning "home" or "homeland."

The Russian Mulberry (*M. alba* var *tatarica*) is a very hardy variety grown not for its fruit but as an ornamental low-growing shrub in cold northerly climates.

The Red or American Mulberry (*M. rubra*) is a native of North America and a common tree of American woodland. It may reach 40–65 ft (12–20 m) in height and has larger, more bluntly toothed leaves than *M. alba*. The fruits are red to purple, and drop from the branches when ripe. The fallen fruit is juicy and very sweet, and is collected to make pies and jellies. From American literature it is known that the mulberry was an important food source of North American indigenous people and early explorers and settlers. The tree also provides useful timber.

MORACEAE

Morus
MULBERRIES

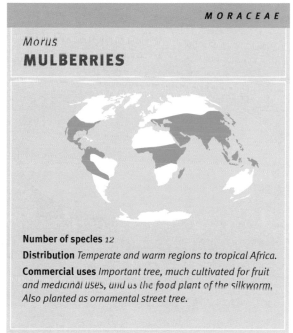

Number of species *12*
Distribution *Temperate and warm regions to tropical Africa.*
Commercial uses *Important tree, much cultivated for fruit and medicinal uses, and as the food plant of the silkworm, Also planted as ornamental street tree.*

The Black, Persian, or English Mulberry (*M. nigra*) is the most commonly cultivated species in Europe. It grows up to 33 ft (10 m), the bark is brown and the leaves have a rough upper surface and blunt-toothed margins. The fruits are purple to black. It was introduced into Europe in the early sixteenth century from its native Persia (Iran), some time before *M. alba*. *Morus nigra* is reputedly slow-growing and long-lived, with specimens recorded to be three hundred years old.

In Africa, large tree species are more common than shrubs. *Morus mesozygia* is a central African species, up to 100 ft (30 m) tall. It is utilized as a shade tree; the top branches are removed and the lateral branches are weighted to produce an umbrella-shaped crown. It yields edible mulberries, but they are small and not usually harvested.

M. nigra

M. alba

TOP The fruit of *Morus rubra* appear in clusters and are long and cylindrical. They are red, later turning dark purple, and are larger than other species.

ABOVE The White and Black Mulberry can be distinguished by their crowns, *Morus alba* being tall and narrow and *M. nigra* making a low, broad dome. Old trees are often crooked or leaning.

The Main Species of *Morus*

M. alba White Mulberry. A native of China;
escapees have become naturalized in
N. America and Europe. Tree to 50 ft (15 m)
with spreading, umbrella-shaped crown,
branches gray to yellow-gray, bark smooth,
young twigs slender. Leaves thin, small,
2–6 in (5–15 cm), broadly ovate, sometimes
almost orbicular, or triangular, apex
pointed; surface pale green, smooth and
rather glossy above, hairy beneath,
particularly on veins and in vein-axils;
margins irregularly lobed, coarsely toothed. Fruit on short
stalks as long as fruits, white to pinkish-purple, usually red
when ripe, globose, 0.8 in (2 cm) diameter, often smaller
in wild specimens; sweet. Widely cultivated, the leaves
are used as food for silkworms. There are numerous
varieties and cultivated forms, some useful as
ornamental shrubs and trees. **CZ4**

var *heterophylla* Variously lobed leaves on same plant.
'Laciniata' Leaf margins jaggedly toothed.
'Macrophylla' Large leaves to 12 in (30 cm).
'Pendula' Pendulous habit.
var **tatarica** Hardy, shrubby form.
var **venosa** Leaves broadly diamond-shaped with
conspicuous pale yellow or white veins.

The following five species are closely related to *M. alba*:

M. serrata NW Himalaya. Similar to *M. alba*, but young
shoots and leaves with velvet-like covering of short hairs.
Styles longer, hairy, united below (styles freein *M. alba*).
Fruit not juicy.

M. laevigata (***M. macroura***) E India, Java, Sumatra. Fruit more or
less cylindrical in shape, to 2 in (5 cm) long. **CZ8**

M. australis Component of secondary forests in C Africa. Young
shoots hairy. Leaves small, 1.2–5 × 1.1 in (3–12 × 2.8 cm),
surface dark green, rough. **CZ6**

M. microphylla C. America from Mexico to Peru. Bears edible
fruit. **CZ6**

M. rubra Red or American Mulberry. Common in N. American
woods. Tree to 66 ft (20 m) with wide, spreading crown.
Leaves larger than those of **M. alba**, 3–8 in (8–20 cm), ovate
to oblong, surface dull green, rough above, hairy beneath,
margins bluntly toothed. Fruits globose, 1.2–1.6 in (3–4 cm)
diameter, reddish-purple, very sweet. A popular source of
edible fruit. **CZ5**

'Nana' A slow-growing, dwarf form with a compact habit.

M. nigra Black, English, or Persian Mulberry. Native of Iran,
cultivated and perhaps also naturalized in parts of Europe.
Small spreading tree to 33 ft (10 m). Young twigs thick, dark
brown with a velvet-like hairy covering. Leaves thick, 2–8 in
(5–20 cm) long, ovate with deeply cordate base and abruptly
acute apex; surface dull, dark green, rough above, hairy
beneath; margins sometimes lobed, coarsely and sharply

M. tartarica

M. alba

M. rubra

M. nigra

toothed. Fruits more or less sessile, dark purple, about
0.8 in (2 cm) diameter, acid, becoming sweet only when
completely ripe; of good quality, though considered
inferior to that of *M. rubra*. In the past the leaves were
used for silkworm fodder. **CZ5**

M. mesozygia Fairly common in C Africa, planted to provide
shade. Large tree to 100 ft (30 m) with spreading umbrella-
shaped crown. Young shoots hairless, reddish-brown. Leaves
rather thin, 2.8–4.5 × 1.2–2.8 in (7–11 × 3–7 cm), elliptic, base
shallowly cordate, surface hairless above, sparsely hairy on
veins and in axils beneath. Fruits on long stalks, about 0.4 in
(1 cm) diameter, sweet, rather dry in texture. **CZ6**

Mulberries, the fruit of *Morus
nigra*, grow to as much as 1 in
(2.5 cm) long. They have an
unusual flavor and can be
eaten raw but are more often
used in jelly- and winemaking.

Maclura
Osage Orange

The Osage Orange (*Maclura pomifera*) was once the only member of this genus; *Maclura* is now considered to include *Cudrania* and *Pecospermum*, raising the number of species to about twelve. *Maclura pomifera* is a fast-growing spiny, deciduous tree, up to 60 ft (18 m) tall. It is native to the fertile lands of Arkansas and Texas, and naturalized elsewhere in the United States. The name Osage derives from the Osage River, the largest tributary of the Missouri, and is also the name of a tribe of North American indigenous people. The tree is distinguished by its orange, fissured bark and the sharp spines on the young shoots and leaf stalks (var *inermis* has no spines on the shoots). The leaves are alternate, ovate, with pointed tips, and glossy green above with whitish veins below. The leaves turn bright yellow in the fall. Crushed leaves and shoots yield a sticky milky latex that can be a mild skin irritant. The flowers are unisexual, with male and female occurring on separate trees in inconspicuous globose clusters. The fertilized female flowers fuse together to form a globose, yellow-green, orange-like false fruit up to 5 in (13 cm) across, which contains many hard true fruits (drupelets) and is full of milky latex. It is inedible. Outside its native range the fruits are less frequently seen, since trees of opposite sexes are rarely close enough for the female flowers to be fertilized.

The Osage Orange was once very widely used as a thorny hedging plant throughout America, and though still used as such, its decline was in part due to the introduction of more efficient, barbed-wire fences. It grows well in a wide range of soils, including those that are poor, its spreading roots making it resistant to drought. The timber is hard, strong, and flexible, and is used for fence posts. When first cut, the wood is bright orange, later discoloring to brown. It was once used by the North American indigenous people for making bows and fighting clubs (hence its other popular name—Bow Wood) and is still valued as such by present day archers.

THEACEAE

Stewartia
Stewartias

The eight to ten members of the genus *Stewartia* are native to eastern Asia and eastern North America. They are small deciduous trees or shrubs, with characteristic, attractive, smooth, flaking bark. The leaves are alternate, simple, ovate to obovate, toothed dark green and shiny, turning shades of red, orange, and yellow in the fall. The showy, cup-shaped, bisexual white flowers are borne singly over a long period of the summer.

A number of *Stewartia* species are planted as ornamentals, preferring humus-rich, well-drained, neutral or slightly acid soil. Best known in cultivation are the Japanese Stewartia or Deciduous Camellia (*S. pseudocamellia*) from Japan, and *S. koreana* from Korea, both trees to 60 ft (18 m), and the Chinese Stewartia (*S. sinensis*) from central China, a shrub or small tree to 33 ft (10 m). American species are represented in cultivation by the Silky Camellia (*S. malacodendron*) and the Mountain Camellia (*S. ovata*), both shrubs growing to 16–20 ft (5–6 m).

CZ5–8

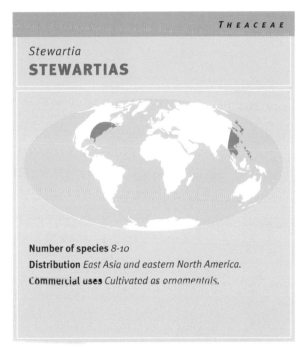

THEACEAE

Stewartia
STEWARTIAS

Number of species 8-10
Distribution *East Asia and eastern North America.*
Commercial uses *Cultivated as ornamentals.*

ABOVE *Maclura pomifera* only sets fruit when male and female trees grow close to each other. The fruit are round and finely wrinkled with a bright pale green color, and contain an inedible stringy white pulp.

LEFT *Stewartia pseudocamellia*, the Deciduous Camellia, has white cupshaped flowers about 2 in (5 cm) across. Petals have a broad wavy edge and they open to show clusters of bright yellow anthers.

EBENACEAE

Diospyros

Persimmons

Diospyros is an economically important genus of 400–500 tropical, subtropical and some temperate species including the persimmons, which yield edible fruits, and the ebonies, which yield valuable timber. They are deciduous or evergreen trees and shrubs with shoots without terminal buds. The sexes are normally on separate plants and the flowers inconspicuous, whitish, with calyx and corolla usually four-lobed (sometimes three- to seven-); there are one to four times as many stamens as there are corolla lobes. The fruit is a large, juicy berry with an enlarged calyx. *D. armata*, *D. lotus* (commonly called the Date Plum), and *D. virginiana* (the Common or American Persimmon) are hardy in temperate regions, but *D. kaki* (the Kaki, Chinese, or Japanese Date Plum, or Oriental Persimmon) only in the warmer parts.

Ebony is the heavy, hard, dark heartwood derived from several species of *Diospyros*, the dark color being caused by deposition of resins; the sapwood is usually uncolored. Although the word is synonymous with black, ebony wood can be other colors: coromandel and calamander ebonies, for instance, have brown or gray mottling. Clearly, ebony has been valued since earliest times, for two inlaid ebony stools were found in the tomb of Tutankhamun. It has always been carved into images and, being reputed to be antagonistic to poison, in India it was used for royal drinking cups. Some tribes in Africa use a bark extract as a fish poison. The wood takes a high polish and in more recent times has been used principally for small objects such as piano keys, knife handles, chess pieces, hairbrushes, and walking sticks. Most trade names refer to country or port of origin.

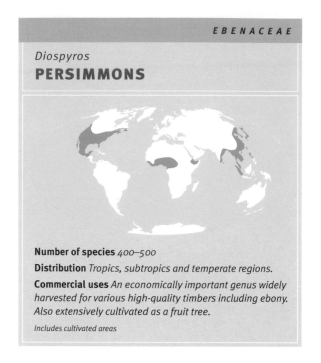

EBENACEAE

Diospyros
PERSIMMONS

Number of species *400–500*
Distribution *Tropics, subtropics and temperate regions.*
Commercial uses *An economically important genus widely harvested for various high-quality timbers including ebony. Also extensively cultivated as a fruit tree.*

Includes cultivated areas

D. virginiana

D. lotus

ABOVE *Diospyros virginiana* is much taller and straighter than *D. lotus* at 40–66 ft (12–20 m). The latter species reaches 40 ft (12 m) and has a domed crown which often forks low down on the trunk.

Though several species of *Diospyros*, including *D. reticulata* (Mauritius) and *D. ebenum* (Sri Lanka), are described as the producers of the best ebony, *D. virginiana* is the only species of commercial value. It grows wild in forests from New Jersey to Texas. The strong, hard timber (known as North American Ebony) is used to make the heads of golfclubs. The sapwood, white when fresh, deteriorates to reddish or bluish. In the United States, *D. virginiana* is often used as a rootstock to produce dwarf trees, which are convenient to handle but often last as little as ten years; in China and Japan, local seedlings are used as rootstocks for large trees, which are very long lived.

The persimmon is the round, edible fruit of certain species of *Diospyros*. The warm temperate *D. kaki*, first cultivated in China, is now grown in the subtropics throughout the world. In Japan it is the national fruit, with a total crop approaching that of the citrus fruits. The Kaki Persimmon was brought to Europe in 1796, but outside China and Japan it was of little commercial significance until its introduction into the United States (where it is now mostly concentrated in California) after Commodore Perry's expeditions to Japan (1852–54).

The scaly-barked trees grow to 46 ft (14 m) on well-drained lighter soils. They have dark green ovate leaves and produce yellowish-white flowers two or three years after being grafted. The flowers may be male, female, or bisexual. Male pollinator varieties are usually needed to obtain fruit production on female types, but some female varieties produce fruit without fertilization, hence need no pollination to form fruit.

Persimmons need very little winter chilling to induce satisfactory flower and fruit development. The orange-yellow fruit is 1.2–2.8 in (3–7 cm) across and, when fully ripe, jelly-like and sweet. Before it softens, the fruit tastes very astringent owing to the presence of tannin, which disappears as the persimmon ripens. **CZ4–8**

LEFT Ripening Persimmons. *Diospyros* are underused, for they are good for landscaping purposes as well as for the edible fruit of some species.

D. lotus

D. virginiana

The Main Species of *Diospyros*

Group I: Native to the U.S.

D. virginiana **American Persimmon.** E and C U.S. in fields and
woodland. Stately evergreen tree to about 50 ft (15 m), in
primeval forest sometimes to 100 ft (30 m). Bark dark gray-
black cracked into small rectangular plates. Leaves on long
petioles, very variable even on individual shoots, from 0.4 in
(1 cm) oval to 8 in (20 cm) oval-ovate, with sizes mixed along
shoot; fine fall colors. Anthers slender. Edible fruits 0.8–1.6 in
(2–4 cm) diameter, green, yellow, or red; seeds flat, thin-
skinned, much longer than wide. **CZ4**

var *pubescens* has branches villous, leaves pubescent below.

D. mosieri E and C U.S.: pinelands. Shrub, similar to above
species but smaller overall. Anthers stout. Seeds turgid, only
slightly longer than wide.

Group II: Native to Africa.

D. abyssinica E Africa. Forest tree to 100 ft (30 m). Bark black
with oblong plates, wood beneath bark orange. Leaves 4 ×
1 in (10 × 2.5 cm), veins prominent. Fruit glabrous, yellow
becoming red or black, small and 1-seeded on saucer-shaped
3-lobed calyx; calyx much shorter than fruit, lobes with flat
margins.

D. barteri W Africa. Forest scrambler. Stems rusty hirsute.
Leaves brown, hairy below.

D. mannii W Africa, Congo, Angola. Forest tree to 66 ft (20 m).
Red-brown bark. Distinctive densely bristly hairy twigs,
flowers (lobes with flat margins), and fruit. Fruit orange with
dense red bristles on calyx of long starfish-like lobes.

D. mespiliformis **W African Ebony, Swamp, Calabar, or Lagos
Ebony.** Widespread throughout tropical Africa in lowland
rainforest. Tree to 100 ft (30 m). Bark with rectangular
plates, black outside, pink inside. Leaves elliptic, 6 × 2 in

(15 × 5 cm). Male flowers in stalked clusters, female
flowers single. Fruit round, yellow, surrounded at base by
small cup-shaped calyx of 4 or 5 distinctive lobes with
wavy margins.

D. monbuttensis **Yoruba Ebony, Walking-stick Ebony.**
Forest tree with red, papery, peeling bark; spines on
trunk. Fruit glabrous, round on much shorter cup-
shaped calyx with flat margins.

D. soubreana W Africa. A shrub of drier rainforests.

D. tricolor W Africa. Thick-stemmed shrub with
zigzag rusty silky branches; forms a dense thicket
immediately behind beaches.

Group III: Native to Asia.

D. ebenum **Ceylon or East Indian Ebony.** India and Sri
Lanka. Large evergreen forest tree. Leaves thin and
leathery, with minutely netted raised venation on
both surfaces. Male corolla hairless; female flowers
usually solitary, calyx much enlarged and reflexed
in fruit. Heartwood jet black, not streaked. **CZ4**

D. kaki **Kaki, Chinese or Japanese Date Plum, Oriental
Persimmon.** China, Japan, Myanmar, and India.
Similar to *D. lotus* but branchlets and leaves softly
hairy; leaves with depressed midrib. Male and female
flowers similar, female flowers usually solitary; calyx
deeply 4-lobed with silky hairs, corolla downy at
apex. Fruit yellow or red, hanging on the tree long
after the leaves have fallen. **CZ8**

var **sylvestris** is smaller, distinguished by smaller
female flower, densely hairy ovary and smaller fruit.

D. kurzii **Andaman Marble, Zebra Wood.**
Andaman, Nicobar, and Coco Islands, Sri
Lanka, India. Large evergreen tree with smooth
gray bark. Only female flowers known, in short-
stalked cymes, with 2–10 flowers; calyx almost
hairless, corolla velvety outside.

D. lotus **Date Plum.** China, Japan to W Asia. Tree to 82–100 ft
(25–30 m), deciduous, with dome-shaped crown, often
forked lower down. Foliage very glossy, dark green, glaucous
and hairy on veins beneath, petiole pubescent (with fine
hairs); male and female flowers on separate plants, the
female usually solitary; calyx lobed to half-way
down, slightly pubescent; corolla hairless
outside. Fruit finally yellowish or purplish. **CZ5**

D. melanoxylon **Coromandel Ebony.** India. Tree to
50 ft (15 m). Dark gray bark with rectangular
scales. Leaves thickly leathery. Male calyx
cup-shaped, woolly, corolla woolly; female
flowers usually solitary, calyx with broad
edges recurved. Fruit yellow. Heartwood
streaked jet black.

D. tomentosa Very similar to *D. melanoxylon* and
often included with it, but smaller leaves.

D. kaki

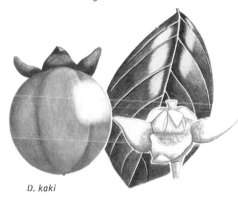

D. ebenum

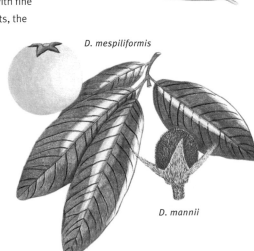

D. mespiliformis

D. mannii

AQUIFOLIACEAE

Ilex
Hollies

There are about four hundred species of hollies worldwide; the only temperate or tropical regions in which they do not feature are western North America and southern Australasia. They are sometimes deciduous, more often evergreen trees or shrubs, with shoots often angled, leaves alternate, and the white unisexual flowers axillary and usually borne on separate male and female plants. The red or black "berries" are technically drupes containing two to eight seeds. The evergreens are exceptionally hardy attractive plants for temperate climates— the European and Asiatic species will adapt to most soils and sites, while the North American species generally prefer a neutral or acid soil. The name *Ilex* derives from the Latin for the Holm Oak (*Quercus ilex*)—also an evergreen. Holly wood is prized for veneer, inlay, and musical instruments.

Holly has a diverse and international folklore. It was held by Celtic druids to symbolize the sun, and sprays of holly were taken into dwellings during winter months. It is still used as a decoration during the Christmas season, as it was by the Romans during their Saturnalia. Holly was used in divination in Europe, and as a martial emblem by North American indigenous people, their Black Drink ceremony being based on the emetic leaves of the Yaupon or Carolina Tea Holly (*Ilex vomitoria*). Birdlime is partly made from holly bark, and *I. paraguariensis* leaves are the source of maté, a kind of tea.

The European Holly (*I. aquifolium*) from Europe, North Africa, and western Asia is a dense pyramidal tree to about 82 ft (25 m) tall. Its dark green, glossy, spiny foliage and red winter berries have made it one of the best known and most popular of ornamental plants. About 120 different cultivated varieties have been selected over several hundred years, some being variegated, others with spineless, crisped, or puckered leaves of diverse shape. The American Holly (*I. opaca*) is the best-known evergreen American species, growing to about 50 ft (15 m) and containing some 115 cultivars, some providing commercial crops at Christmas. The Black Alder or Winterberry (*I. verticillata*) is a large deciduous eastern North American shrub with copious bright red fruit in winter; its purple leaves turn yellow in the fall. There are two cultivars.

Among Asian evergreen hollies are the Horned Holly (*I. cornuta*), with three- to five-spined leaves, the Japanese Holly (*I. crenata*), a shrub with often tiny obovate leaves and black berries, which are sometimes clipped or used as a dwarf hedge, and *I. pernyi,* with stalkless three-spined leaves; all attractive natives of China. The large serrate leaves, to more than 6 in (15 cm) long, and orange-red fruits distinguish the Tarajo Holly (*I. latifolia*), a species from Japan. *Ilex insignis* (*I. kingiana*) from the eastern Himalaya is another large-leaved species grown in gardens. **CZ3–6**

I. crenata

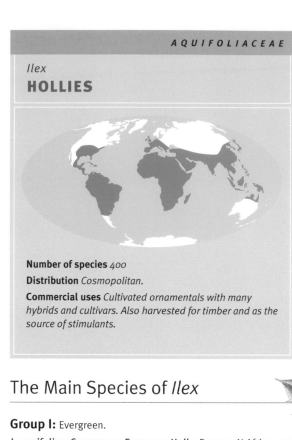

	AQUIFOLIACEAE
Ilex **HOLLIES**	

Number of species *400*
Distribution *Cosmopolitan.*
Commercial uses *Cultivated ornamentals with many hybrids and cultivars. Also harvested for timber and as the source of stimulants.*

The Main Species of *Ilex*

Group I: Evergreen.

I. aquifolium **Common** or **European Holly.** Europe, N Africa, and W Asia. Bushy tree to 82 ft (25 m), of a much-branched habit, forming a dense pyramidal mass. Leaves glossy dark green, 1–3 in (2.5–7.5 cm) long, with wavy margins and large triangular spine-tipped teeth; size, outline, and toothing of leaves variable within the species and with position on the tree (lower branches tend to carry more spined leaves, possibly a protection against browsing animals). Flowers small, dull white, and axillary; plants male, female, or bisexual. Fruits round, red, and persistent in the winter, containing 2–4 nutlets. About 120 cultivated varieties, many noted for brilliant gold and silver variegation (often on leaf margins) and variety in shape and size of leaves and habit. **CZ6**

I. cornuta **Horned Holly.** China. Dense shrub 6.6–10 ft (2–3 m) tall. Leaves bat-shaped, rectangular with few (3–5) spines. Fruits red. **CZ6**

I. crenata **Japanese Holly.** China and Japan. Dense shrub, usually 5–10 ft (1.5–3 m) high, with small, often tiny, obovate, shallowly toothed leaves. Fruits tiny, black. Long cultivated; several varieties. **CZ6**

I. dipyrena **Himalayan Holly.** E Himalaya. Tree to 50 ft (15 m). **CZ7**

I. glabra **Inkberry.** E U.S. Small to medium-sized shrub 3–6 ft (1–2 m) high. Leaves small, dark shining green. Fruits black. **CZ3**

I. insignis E Himalaya. Remarkable large-leaved species. **CZ8**

I. opaca

I. aquifolium

I. latifolia **Tarajo Holly.** Japan. Magnificent large-leaved species. Dark, glossy green serrate leaves up to 32 in (80 cm) long, similar to *Magnolia grandiflora*. Fruits orange-red. **CZ7**

I. opaca **American Holly.** E and C U.S. Best-known. American species. Large shrub or small tree to 50 ft (15 m). Spiny leaves, pale olive-green. Red, stalked fruits. About 115 cultivars. **CZ5**

I. paraguariensis **Yerba Maté.** S. America. Small tree with oval leaves to 5 in (12 cm). Cultivated and wild. **CZ9**

I. perado **Azorean or Madeira Holly.** Madeira. Small tree with flattish leaves with few spines. **CZ7**

I. pernyi C and W China. Densely branched tree to 30 ft (9 m), with distinctive diamond-shaped triangular-spined leaves. Fruits red. **CZ5**

I. perado ssp *platyphylla* **Canary Island Holly.** Canary Islands. Similar to *I. perado* and regarded by some as a variety of that species. **CZ7**

I. vomitoria **Carolina Tea, Cassena, Yaupon, Emetic Holly.** SE U.S. To 26 ft (8 m). Fruits red. **CZ7**

Group II: Deciduous.

I. decidua **Possumhaw Holly.** SE U.S. Medium-sized shrub 6.6– 10 ft (2–3 m) high, occasionally a small tree up to 33 ft (10 m). Stems slender, leaves obovate, crenately toothed. Fruits bright orange or red, lasting well into winter. **CZ6**

I. macrocarpa C China. Small to medium tree. Large fruits resembling black cherries. **CZ7**

I. serrata Japan. Shrub to 16 ft (5 m), with spreading branches, downy ovate leaves, and many tiny red fruits. **CZ5**

I. verticillata **Black Alder.** Winterberry. E U.S. Shrub. 6.6–10 ft (2–3 m). Purple-tinged leaves, especially in spring, turning yellow in the fall. Fruits bright red and persistent. **CZ3**

'Xmas Cheer' A selected American clone which bears masses of bright red fruits, normally persistent throughout the winter. **CZ3**

STYRACEAE

Styrax

Snowbell Trees

Styrax is a large genus of tropical and subtropical deciduous or evergreen trees or shrubs with alternate, entire or slightly serrated leaves, somewhat mealy, with stellate pubescence. The bell flowers are typically bisexual, white, and borne in pendulous simple or branched racemes. The calyx is shortly five-toothed, the corolla five-lobed (perhaps eight), and there are eight to ten (sometimes sixteen) stamens inserted on the corolla base. The ovary is superior or nearly so. The fruit is a dry or fleshy drupe with a pericarp that may be dehiscent.

Some species are hardy enough to be cultivated in temperate regions. They like a good but lime-free soil in a sheltered frost-free site. Commonly cultivated are *S. hemsleyaus* from central and western China, an attractive tree to 20 ft (6 m) with racemes of white flowers in early summer, and *S. japonica* from China and Japan, a shrub or tree to 33 ft (10 m) with masses of elegant snowdrop-like flowers appearing even earlier than those of *S. hemsleyaus*. Also hardy is the Big Leaf Storax (*S. obassia*) from Japan, a shrub or tree to 33 ft (10 m), with broad elliptic-obovate leaves, 2.8–8 in (7–20 cm) long, partly obscuring the long racemes of white fragrant flowers. *Styrax americana* from the southeastern United States is a shrub with one to four flowers in a pendulous cluster. It is not very hardy in temperate regions. *Styrax benzoin*, from Bolivia, Sumatra, and Thailand, yields a resin, gum benzoin, which is used medicinally. The species is not hardy in temperate regions. Storax (*S. officinalis*) from southeast Europe and Asia Minor is a shrub or small tree growing to 20 ft (6 m). It is hardy in the milder areas of temperate regions. **CZ5–10**

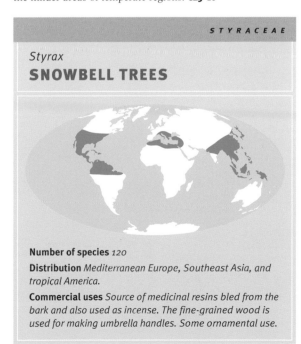

STYRACEAE

Styrax
SNOWBELL TREES

Number of species *120*

Distribution *Mediterranean Europe, Southeast Asia, and tropical America.*

Commercial uses *Source of medicinal resins bled from the bark and also used as incense. The fine-grained wood is used for making umbrella handles. Some ornamental use.*

LEFT *Ilex aquifolium* is a leafy branching tree which naturally forms a dense pyramidal mass. Holly makes a cheerful sight in the winter months, laden with its bright red fruit.

ABOVE *Styrax japonica* is often grown as an ornamental in gardens for its abundant flowers. The underside of each branch is densely packed with clusters of 3–4 flowers. These open in June and July and are white with pale orange stamens.

Halesia

Snowdrop Trees

Halesia (pronounced Hails-ía after Stephen Hales, 1677–1761, an outstanding English experimental biologist) is a genus of five species native to the eastern states of North America, and China. They are deciduous trees with simple, serrate leaves. The flowers are bisexual, occurring in axillary fascicles, white or, less often, pale pinkish. The calyx and corolla each consist of four segments, the latter more or less lobed; there are eight to sixteen stamens and the ovary is inferior. The fruit is a ribbed drupe with two to four wings. The genus formerly included other species from China and Japan, now transferred to *Pterostyrax*, which, among other differences, have perianth members in fives and the flowers arranged in panicles.

The plants are grown for their attractive snowdrop-like flowers, produced abundantly in the spring. The best-known species are the Snowdrop Tree or Silver Bell (*Halesia tetraptera = H. carolina*) from the southeastern United States, a beautiful small, spreading tree, which grows well in cultivation in sheltered, lime-free sites, and the much taller pyramidal Mountain Snowdrop Tree or Silver Bell Tree (*H. monticola*) from the mountains of the southeastern United States. This species has some value as a timber tree.

The Species of *Halesia*

Group I: Corolla lobed to less than half-way, except in *H. carolina* forma *dialypetala*. Fruit with 4 prominent wings.

H. tetraptera (*H. carolina*) Silver Bell, Snowdrop Tree. SE U.S. Dense, rounded, twiggy shrub in cultivation, 23–26 ft (7–8 m) high, but a tree to 50 ft (15 m) in the wild. Leaves oval-obovate, 2–4 in (5–10 cm) long, covered beneath with gray stellate hairs. Flowers abundant in spring, pendulous, bell-shaped, white like snowdrops (*Galanthus nivalis, G. elwesii*) 0.4–0.6 in (1–1.5 cm) long. Fruit club-shaped, 1–1.5 (1.6) in (2.5–3.5 (4) cm) long. Very fine; the best known in cultivation. **CZ5**

forma *dialypetala* Corolla divided well beyond the middle of petals.

H. monticola Mountain Snowdrop Tree or Silver Bell Tree. Mountains of SE U.S., ascending to about 3,300 ft (1,000 m). Tree to 100 ft (30 m) with trunk up to 3 ft (1 m) across, carrying a high canopy of branches; bark separates from trunk in large, loose, plate-like scales. Leaves more or less glabrous, otherwise, like the flowers, much as in *H. carolina*, but corolla larger, 0.6–1 in (1.5–2.5 cm). Fruits 1.4–2 in (3.5–5 cm) long. **CZ5**

var *vestita* Leaves distinctly tomentose, at least to begin with, especially dense on the veins; forma *rosea* has pale pink flowers.

Group II: Corolla lobed well below middle. Fruit with 2 prominent wings.

H. diptera SE U.S. Usually a small shrub in cultivation to 8–16 ft (2.5–5 m), but sometimes a small tree to 33 ft (10 m) in the wild. Leaves elliptic to obovate. Flowers with corolla (0.6)0.8–1 in ((18)20–25 mm) long. Fruit usually club-shaped, 1.4–2 in (3.5–5 cm) long, with 2 prominent wings. Less attractive than *H. carolina*; less free-flowering. **CZ6**

LEFT The Silver Bell, *Halesia tetraptera*, has beautiful white flowers developing from a pale pink bud during May. They hang on slender stalks in clusters of 3–5 from the joints of the naked previous year's wood.

BELOW *Halesia* have wide spreading lower branches and a broadly conic crown arising from a curved bole.

H. monticola var *vestita*

H. diptera

H. monticol

H. monticol

H. carolina

H. carolina

H. carolina

H. carolina

ERICACEAE

Arbutus

Strawberry Trees

Arbutus species are native to North and Central America, and western Europe to the Mediterranean. They are evergreen trees or shrubs, the bark of some species exfoliating to reveal a smooth underbark of a splendid reddish-brown or reddish-cinnamon color. The leaves are alternate and leathery. The flowers, resembling those of Lily of the Valley (*Convallaria majalis*), are borne in terminal clusters. They are pale pinkish or greenish, urn-shaped with a five-lobed calyx, white corolla, and ten stamens. The fruit (edible in *Arbutus unedo*) is a strawberry-like subglobose berry with mealy flesh and a warted surface. It tastes, however, not at all of strawberry.

Strawberry trees are much cultivated as ornamentals. They do well on peaty or loamy soils, but some of the best, unlike many ericaceous plants, are equally happy on calcareous soil. The American species *A. menziesii* yields a useful wood. **CZ6–8**

The Main Species of *Arbutus*

Group I: Young leaves tomentose beneath and flowers (spring or early summer), white to pinkish, in more or less erect panicles. Leaf margin entire or serrate, the petiole more than 0.6 in (1.5 cm) long. Species from SW U.S.

A. xalapensis SW U.S., Mexico, Guatemala. Shrub or small tree to 50 ft (15 m). Underbark reddish-brown. Leaves more or less oval-oblong, (1.4)1.6–4(4.5) × 0.6–1.8 in ((3.5)4–10(11) × 1.2–4.5 cm), the lower surface brown-tomentose when young. Flowers in an erect to nodding cluster, each flower with an inflated basal ring. Fruit dark red. **CZ8**

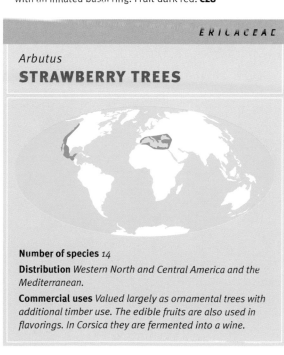

A. arizonica Mts of Arizona south into Mexico. Tree to 50 ft (15 m). First-year twigs hairy and reddish-brown; older wood grayish or whitish bark. Leaves narrowly oval, 1.6–3.2 × 0.6–1.2 in (4–8 × 1.5–3 cm). Possibly a variety of previous species. **CZ6**

Group II: Leaves at no time tomentose beneath (may be a few hairs on veins or petioles); adult leaves of mature plants normally serrate, tapering below into a petiole less than 0.4 in (1 cm) long (but see *A. × andrachnoides*). Flowers white or greenish tinged in pendulous or nodding panicles. Young plants 3–6 ft (1–2 m) may have some entire leaves , e.g. *A. undedo* forma *integerrima*.

A. unedo Strawberry Tree. SW Ireland, SW France, Spain and Mediterranean region, including Balkans, Asia Minor. Tree (16)33(42) ft ((5)10(13) m). Bark soon grayish-brown, fibrous. Leaves elliptic to obovate, blackish-green above, paler green below, 2–4 × 0.8–1.2 in (5–10 × 2–3 cm). Flowers in hairy not glandular clusters, corolla white-pinkish or greenish-white, 0.3 in (8 mm) across, appearing midfall as previous season's fruits ripen. Fruit subglobose, about 0.6 × 0.4 in (18 × 15 mm), warty. A fine fall and winter sight. Lime tolerant. **CZ7**
forma *integerrima* Leaf margins entire. Occurs as a wild plant.

A. × andrachnoides (*A. unedo* × *A. andrachne*) Greece. Up to 33 ft (10 m). Underbark smooth and reddish-brown. Flowers spring or late fall. Distinguished from *A. unedo* by leaves sometimes with virtually smooth margin, base always rounder and less tapered, underside paler, fruit less warty, 0.04 in (10 mm) across, and from *A. andrachne* by leaves most always toothed, flower clusters nodding. **CZ8**

A. canariensis Canary Islands. Shrub or small tree 29–50 ft (9–15 m). Leaves 2–5 × 0.2–1.8 in (5–12 × 0.5–4.5 cm). Rather like *A. unedo*, but has drooping to suberect glandular-hairy, somewhat leafy clusters of greenish-tinged flowers, each flower corolla a little longer, 0.3–0.35 in (8–9 mm) against 0.2–0.25 in (6–7 mm) in *A. unedo*. Fruit 0.8–1.2 in (2–3 cm) across, yellow-orange, warty. Half-hardy only. **CZ8**

Group III: As Group II but adult leaves normally entire (some serrate in *A. andrachne*), the base broadly or narrowly rounded and not tapering into the (0.5)0.6–1.2 in ((1.3)1.5–3 cm) long petiole. Flowers white or pinkish or white with pale greenish tinge, in erect panicles. Bark reddish-brown.

A. andrachne SE Europe (E Mediterranean). Tree in the wild to 29–40 ft (9–12 m), in cultivation mostly shrub to about 20 ft (6 m). Leaves oval, 2–4 × 1–2 in (5–10 × 2.5–5 cm), dark, shining green above, paler below. Flowers (spring) on glandular hairy stalks, in hairy pyramidal clusters 2.8 × 2 in (7 × 5 cm), corolla pale yellowish-green. Fruit globose, 0.5 in (13 mm) across. Tolerant of lime, but rarely cultivated. **CZ8**

A. menziesii Madrona. British Columbia to California. Tree to over 100 ft (30 m) in the wild, 33–50 ft (10–15 m) in cultivation. Terracotta underbark, shiny leaves oval, 2–5 in (5–13 cm) long, dark green above, pale glaucous to near white below. White flowers in glabrous pyramidal clusters, 6 × 5 in (15 × 12 cm), corolla pure white. Fruit orange-red, ovoid, 0.4–0.5 in (10–13 mm). **CZ7**

A. andrachne

A. unedo

A. unedo

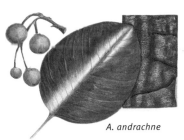

A. andrachne

A. × andrachnoides

BELOW *Oxydendrum arboreum* is a fine ornamental with its leaves turning scarlet and eventually deep red in fall while the clusters of white flowers are still open.

BOTTOM *Eucryphia glutinosa* is the finest of the *Eucryphia* species, blossoming in late summer with large pure white petals and an attractive tuft of slender stamens with pink anthers.

Oxydendrum
Sorrel Tree, Sourwood

The Sorrel Tree (*Oxydendrum arboreum*) is the only member of its genus and is native to the southern United States. Its best-known features are the yellow, red, and purple colors of the fall foliage, and the leaves are apparently pleasantly acid-tasting—for those who wish to try them! It is a small deciduous tree or shrub, growing to 82 ft (25 m) in the wild but to about 23–26 ft (7–8 m) in cultivation. The leaves are alternate, elliptic-oblong, finely serrated, and glossy green, the flowers bisexual, in terminal one-sided panicles that develop from midsummer on the end of branches to form fragrant hanging clusters up to 8 in (20 cm) long. There are five sepals and the petals are urn-shaped, white, with five short lobes, not unlike Lily of the Valley (*Convallaria majalis*). The fruit is a five-valved capsule containing numerous reticulate seeds.

The Sorrel Tree is a fairly popular park and garden tree in temperate regions, growing most vigorously in a sheltered, semi-shaded position on acid, humus-rich soil, though the best flowers and fall colors occur in a sunny position. The leaves have some medicinal properties, having been used to treat heart complaints and by some people to allay thirst.

Eucryphia
Eucryphias

Eucryphia, the only genus of its family, comprises six species from the temperate zone of the southern hemisphere—two from Chile and four from Australasia. There are also various hybrids. Eucryphias are evergreen or semievergreen trees, sometimes shrubby, with leaves that are opposite and simple or pinnate; the stipules are connate. The flowers are white, very abundant, bisexual, axillary, with the sepals and petals in fours; the stamens are numerous. The fruit is a tough dehiscent capsule that ripens after one year.

In cool temperate regions only *E. glutinosa* is generally hardy; the others, including the hybrids, are suitable only for the warmer temperate regions. In general they prefer a moist soil on the acid side of neutrality with no free lime. Two exceptions are the hybrid *E. × nymansensis* and *E. cordifolia*, though the latter is distinctly tender and few calcareous areas have a sufficiently mild climate for it to survive a cold winter. Woodland protection is helpful.

In its native Chile, *E. cordifolia* makes a fine tree to some 78 ft (24 m), and the timber has been used to make canoes, railroad sleepers, telegraph poles, oars, and cattle yokes. Indoor uses include furniture and flooring. The bark is a source of tannin. The timber of the Tasmanian species *E. lucida* is pinkish and utilized for general building as well as for cabinetmaking. *Eucryphia moorei* from New South Wales (Australia) has similar applications.

Outside their native areas, those species hardy enough to be cultivated are planted for their attractive evergreen leaves, which enhance the beauty of the white flowers. **CZ7–9**

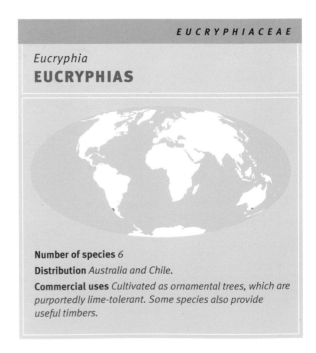

EUCRYPHIACEAE

Eucryphia
EUCRYPHIAS

Number of species *6*

Distribution *Australia and Chile.*

Commercial uses *Cultivated as ornamental trees, which are purportedly lime-tolerant. Some species also provide useful timbers.*

The Species of *Eucryphia*

Group I: All the leaves simple, i.e. not made of paired leaflets.

E. cordifolia Evergreen native of rainforests of Chile. Shrub or tree to about 78 ft (24 m) with pubescent branchlets. Leaves oblong with wavy margins, 1.4–3 in (3.8–7.6 cm) long, base cordate, densely pubescent beneath (the leaves of young specimens are longer, more pointed at the apex, and with the margin distinctly toothed). Flowers white, 2 in (5 cm) across, each with 4 petals arising in terminal leaf axils; stamens numerous, the anthers reddish-brown. **CZ9**

E. lucida (*E. bilardieri*) Leatherwood. Tasmania. Evergreen tree commonly 23–55 ft (7–17 m), occasionally over 100 ft (30 m) with a 10 ft (3 m) girth. Branchlets pubescent. Leaves opposite, resinous (as are young shoots), oblong, 1.5–3 × 0.4–0.6 in (3.8–7.5 × 1–1.5 cm), margin entire; petiole 0.1 in (3 mm). Flowers white, 1–2 in (2.5–5 cm) across, scented, pendulous on a 0.5 in (1.25 cm) pedicel and arising singly in leaf axils; stamens numerous, the anthers yellow. **CZ8**

E. milliganii Tasmania. Very similar to *E. lucida* of which it has been regarded as a mountain variety, differing by being a shrub to 13 ft (4 m) high, having smaller flowers and leaves only 0.3–0.7 in (8–19 mm) long. In its native habitat found at higher altitudes than the previous species. **CZ8**

E. (*lucida* × *cordifolia*) A hybrid that arose in southwest England, with the leaves larger than *lucida*, the margin wavy and somewhat toothed toward the apex. **CZ9**

E. × *hybrida* (*lucida* × *milliganii*) A hybrid from Australia, sometimes with pink forms.

Group II: All the leaves compound, i.e. with mostly 2–3 pairs of leaflets and an odd terminal one (imparipinnate) or trifoliolate (one pair of leaflets and an odd terminal one).

E. glutinosa (*E. pinnatifolia*) Chile. Evergreen or half-evergreen (occasionally deciduous) tree, 10–16 ft (3–5 m) high with upright branches; branchlets pubescent. Leaves clustered toward ends of shoots with 3–5 leaflets each more or less oval, 1.4–3 in (3.8–7.6 cm) long with marginal teeth; petiole pubescent. Flowers in ones or twos toward ends of shoots, about 2.2 in (6 cm) across, each with 4 white petals and numerous stamens having, normally, yellow anthers. Generally considered to be the finest in the genus, it is now rare in its native habitat. **CZ8**

E. × *hillieri* (*E. lucida* × *moorei*) More or less intermediate between the parents. Leaflets 2–3 pairs, rarely trifoliolate, wider and more rounded at apex than in *E. moorei*, margin entire. 'Winton' and 'Penrith' are 2 named cultivars. **CZ8**

E. moorei Plumwood. New South Wales (Australia). Evergreen tree to about 60 ft (18 m) in cultivation, the branchlets with short, brown hairs. Leaves of 5–13 leaflets, somewhat hairy above at first, subsessile, with oblique base, narrowly oblong, 0.6–3 in × 0.1–0.6 in (1.7–7.6 × 0.3–1.5 cm), with entire downy margins, the midrib protruding beyond the lamina as a short spine, veins of underside shortly hairy. Flowers pure white, 1 in (2.5 cm) across, with 4 petals and arising singly in leaf axils; pedicel hairy, 0.6 in (1.8 cm) long; stamens numerous, white. **CZ9**

Group III: Hybrids bearing simple, pinnate, and trifoliolate leaves.

E. × *intermedia* (*glutinosa* × *lucida*) Evergreen tree, the branchlets faintly grooved. Leaves simple, subdentate, up to 2.6 in (6.5 cm) long, with small apical mucro; trifoliolate leaves with terminal leaflet to 2.6 in (6.5 cm), the lateral ones sessile and to 1 in (2.5 cm). Flowers pure white, 1–1.2 in (2.5–3 cm) across, with 4 petals, arising singly at the ends of branches. A vigorous hybrid that arose spontaneously in NE Ireland. **CZ8**

E. × *nymansensis* (*glutinosa* × *cordifolia*) Erect shrub or small tree to 52 ft (16 m), the branchlets grooved. Intermediate between the parents, having both simple and compound leaves, but mostly trifoliolate, the odd terminal leaflet the largest, 1.5–3.5 × 1–1.5 in (3.8–9 × 2.5–3.8 cm), all with rather pointed marginal teeth; flowers pure white, 2.5 in (6.4 cm) across, mostly with 4 petals, a few with 5; stamens numerous, pinkish-purple when ripe. This much-admired fertile hybrid arose at Nymans Gardens in Sussex, England, and is frequently seen though not as hardy as *E. glutinosa*. **CZ7**

A deciduous and partially evergreen tree, *Eucryphia glutinosa* is small at 25 ft (7 m) with erect branches.

E. glutinosa

E. cordifolia

E. milliganii

E. moorei

E. x nymansensis

PITTOSPORACEAE

Pittosporum

Pittosporums

The species included in *Pittosporum* are natives predominantly of Australia and New Zealand but with representatives in Macaronesia (Canary Islands), West and East Africa, Hawaii, Polynesia, the Himalaya, China, and Japan. These evergreen shrubs and trees have alternate, leathery, entire leaves. The flowers are a very dark purple, with the sepals, petals, and stamens each of five parts, the respective whorls alternating, the petals mostly united below. The ovary ripens to a capsular fruit of two to five leathery to woody valves, containing numerous seeds covered with a viscid resinous layer, to which the generic name refers (*pittos* = pitch). An unusual feature of *P. tenuifolium* and *P. crassifolium* is that the seedlings have three or four cotyledons, not the normal two.

Within their native areas, the wood has some value, but outside that the species are grown mainly for ornament. Few are hardy in the climate of most of Europe, except in the south and especially the southwest, including areas such as the Isles of Scilly off the Cornish coast of England, where they are "at home." The hardiest, generally, is *P. tenuifolium* from New Zealand, which may grow to a tree of 33 ft (10 m).

The evergreen, elliptical leaves have a pronounced but shallowly wavy margin and are an attractive pale grass-green, making them a popular foil for cut flowers. The flowers, which are produced abundantly in the spring, are very sweet-smelling at dusk. It is said that the flowers of the genus as a whole are inconspicuous. This may be true at a distance of some feet, but at close hand, once the flowers are recognized, the effect is very pleasing.

Pittosporum tenuifolium 'Golden King' is popular in gardens as well as with florists, who commonly use its deeply waved and crinkled evergreen foliage in floral displays. The bright, pale green leaves contrast well with the young black shoots.

Pittosporum crassifolium, also from New Zealand, is grown for ornament but is less hardy than *P. tenuifolium*. It has the same very dark purple, but larger, flowers, and the ripe dehisced capsules produce smooth, sticky, and shiny black seeds that are equally attractive. It has a special interest in coastal areas because it is resistant to salt spray and used as a most successful windbreak for enclosing small plots of land where bulbs are cultivated. Locally, these windbreaks are called "fences." It was one of the introductions of a remarkable man, Augustus Smith, who became the first Lord Proprietor of the English Isles of Scilly in 1834, and who laid out the famous gardens at Tresco.

Pittosporum 'Garnettii' is of interest in that the variegated leaf margins become tinged pinkish toward winter. Its exact status is not clear, and though usually regarded as a cultivar of *P. tenuifolium* it may prove to be a hybrid between that species and *P. ralphii*. Another unusual species is *P. bullata*, which has puckered leaves that resemble an eiderdown quilt. One with perhaps more conspicuous flowers is *P. tobira*, a bushy shrub to 16–20 ft (5–6 m). It has obovate leaves and the flowers are white and fragrant, about 1 in (2.5 cm) across. It is a native of the Far East (China, Taiwan, and Japan). Again, it is not really hardy, but is commonly grown in southern Europe. **CZ9**

PITTOSPORACEAE

Pittosporum
PITTOSPORUMS

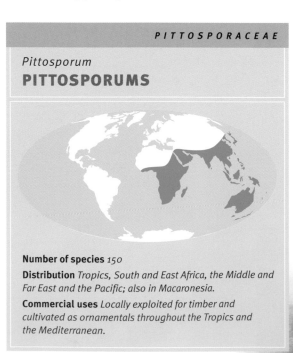

Number of species *150*

Distribution *Tropics, South and East Africa, the Middle and Far East and the Pacific; also in Macaronesia.*

Commercial uses *Locally exploited for timber and cultivated as ornamentals throughout the Tropics and the Mediterranean.*

ABOVE In sheltered conditions the Common Hawthorn, *Crataegus monogyna,* forms a slender trunk, which supports a rounded head of dense branches that are pendulous at the ends.

BELOW The Common Hawthorn, *Crataegus monogyna,* has the ability to thrive on the harshest mountainside or windswept clifftop where, though stunted and blown by the elements, it maintains a dense head of foliage.

ROSACEAE

Crataegus

Thorns

Crataegus is predominantly a genus of eastern and central North America. It is a genus of about 200 "good" species commonly known as thorns, hawthorns, or mays and some 1,000 binomials have been published, but it is now clear that most of these are either synonyms, hybrids, or variants of one sort or another. Of the "good" species about 100–150 occur in North America, 20 in Europe, 20–30 in central Asia and Russia, and 5–10 in the Himalaya, China, and Japan.

The species are deciduous, rarely semievergreen shrubs or trees, usually thorny, with leaves that are alternate, simple or variously lobed. The flowers are small, rarely more than 0.6 in (1.5 cm) across, mostly white, rarely more or less reddish and sometimes fragrant, with five sepals and petals arising from a disk at the margin of the receptacle (hypanthium); there are 5–25 stamens, the anthers variously colored, and a single ovary adnate to the receptacle with between one and five chambers, each with one ovule. The fruit (haw) is a red, yellow, or blackish pome falling with the receptacle and maturing between one and five hard nutlets. The number of styles and nutlets is typically the same.

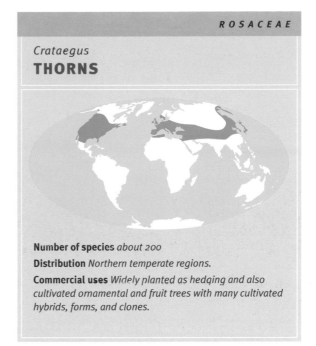

ROSACEAE

Crataegus
THORNS

Number of species *about 200*
Distribution *Northern temperate regions.*
Commercial uses *Widely planted as hedging and also cultivated ornamental and fruit trees with many cultivated hybrids, forms, and clones.*

The genus is one of great taxonomic difficulty, partly because of extensive hybridization and partly because the species do not fall into easily differentiated sections. Good material comprising foliage, flowers, and fruit is essential. Leaf venation, stamen number, anther color, and nutlet characteristics are important features to have available.

Diseases of *Crataegus* are few and none is particularly serious. Species are widely used for hedges and as specimen ornamentals; many are prized and planted for their abundance of flowers—often fragrant—and the red and scarlet fruits, which are an important food for birds. The best known is the Pink May, a variety of *C. laevigata* (European Midland Thorn). A few species have pleasing fall colors.

The fruits of several species are made into jellies or preserves and those of *C. cuneata* are used in China for the treatment of stomach complaints; *C. laevigata* provides a leaf-infusion tea, which is said to reduce blood pressure, dizziness, and palpitations; a coffee substitute from the seeds, and a tobacco substitute from the leaves.

The wood of *Crataegus* is very hard and has been used for engraving. The Cockspur Thorn (*C. crus-galli*) from the eastern and southeastern United States produces a heavy wood used for tool handles, and that of *C. laevigata* is used for a variety of articles, from wheels to walking sticks. **CZ2–8**

The Main Species of *Crataegus*

Group I: Leaves large, at least on long shoots, with veins extending to base of sinuses as well as lips of lobes. Included here are species with small fruits, 0.2–0.25 in (4–6 mm) across.

A *Nutlets variously pitted on ventral side.*
B *Styles and nutlets 1–2(3). Fruit yellow or red, 0.25–0.35 in (6–9 mm) across. (Section* Oxycanthae.*)*

C. laevigata (*C. oxycantha*, *C. oxycanthoides*) **May, Midland Hawthorn.** Europe, N. Africa. Shrub or tree to 16 (20 ft) 5(6) m; thorns to 1 in (2.5 cm). Leaves obovate with 3–5 lobes, base wedge-shaped, soon glabrous. Inflorescence glabrous, 5–12 flowered; stamens typically 20, anthers red; styles 2–3. Fruit red, broadly oval with 2 nutlets. Extensively cultivated. **CZ5**

C. monogyna **Common Hawthorn.** Europe, W Africa, W Asia. Shrub or tree to 33 ft (10 m), similar to previous species but leaves larger, more deeply lobed with 3–7 lobes, thorns more numerous, style 1(2), fruit subglobose with 1 nutlet. Extensively cultivated. **CZ5**
'Biflora' Glastonbury Thorn. Will flower a second time in mild winter months.

BB *Styles and nutlets 4–5. Fruit black or purplish-black. (Section* Nigrae = Pentagynae.*)*

C. pentagyna SE Europe, Caucasus, Iran. Shrub or small tree to 20 ft (6 m). Leaves 3–7 lobed, hairy beneath but finally glabrous. Flowers in pubescent clusters, anthers pink. Fruit oval not shiny. **CZ6**

C. nigra **Hungarian Thorn.** SE Europe (Hungary). Tree to 20–23 ft (6–7 m). Leaves with 7–11 lobes, hairy on both sides. Flowers in densely hairy clusters, anthers yellow. Fruit subglobose, shiny. **CZ6**

AA *Nutlets smooth on ventral side.*
C *Fruits small, 0.2–0.3 in (4–6 mm) across. Sepals more or less deciduous. Styles and nutlets 3–5. Leaves glabrous or quickly so.*

C. phaenopyrum **Washington Thorn.** SE U.S. Tree to 33 ft (10 m); thorns to 2.8 in (7 cm). Leaves broadly triangular, 3–5 lobed. Fruit oblate, red, persisting through winter. Pleasing scarlet and orange fall colors. (Section *Cordatae*.) **CZ5**

C. spathulata S and SE U.S. Shrub or small tree to 26 ft (8 m). Leaves of flowering shoots obovate, sometimes broadly 3(5) lobed at apex, base tapering. Fruit subglobose, red with reflexed sepals, ripening late and persisting through fall. (Section *Microcarpae*.) **CZ7**

CC *Fruits more than 0.4 in (1 cm) across with persistent sepals.*
D *Shoots and/or inflorescence at least virtually glabrous. Leaves more than (2)2.4 in ((5)6 cm) long, more or less deeply lobed, the lowest lobe pair divided almost to midrib; petioles more than 0.4 in (1 cm). Fruit ovate, 0.8–1.2 × 0.4–0.9 in (2–3 × 1–2.3 cm), red with whitish dots. (Section* Pinnatifidae.*)*

C. pinnatifida N China. Tree to 20 ft (6 m); thorns short or absent. Leaves more or less triangular, 2–4 in (5–10 cm) long, with 5–9 lobes, the lowest pair cut almost to midrib, dark shiny green above; petioles 0.8–2.5 in (2–6 cm). Flowers with 3–4 styles. Fruit red, 0.6 in (1.5 cm) across. **CZ6**
var *major*, with larger leaves and fruits to 0.9 in (2.3 cm) across, and glabrous inflorescence, is the better ornamental.

DD *Shoots, leaves, and inflorescence more or less densely hairy. Leaves 1.2–2.8 in (3–7 cm) long; petioles less than 0.4 in (1 cm). Fruits almost round or smaller than previous Section, yellow to orange-red without dots. (Section* Azaroli, *formerly* Orientales.*)*

C. orientalis (*C. laciniata*) SE Europe and Spain. Tree to 20(23) ft (6(7) m), almost without thorns. Leaves with 5–9 pinnatifid lobes, more or less hairy on both sides, can be tapering or flat at base. Flowers with 3–5 styles. Fruit oblate to 0.8 in (2 cm) across; nutlets 4–5. Much planted for attractiveness in flower and fruit. **CZ6**

C. tanacetifolia **Tansy-leaved Thorn.** Asia Minor. Tree to 33 ft (10 m), sometimes a shrub. Young shoots woolly tomentose, mostly without thorns. Leaves rhomboid-ovate to obovate, 0.8–2 in (2–5 cm) long with 5–7(8) deepish lobes, the margins glandular-serrate. Flowers 0.8–1 in (2–2.5 cm) across, 5–8 in a densely woolly corymb; stamens 20, anthers red, styles 5; calyx woolly, glandular-serrate. Fruit globose, 0.8–1 in (2–2.5 cm) across, yellow to red with characteristic laciniate bracts below; nutlets 5. **CZ6**

Group II: Large leaves at least of long shoots, with veins extending to lobes or teeth and not to base of sinuses. Leaves not or only shallowly lobed, except Section *Sanguineae*.

E *Nutlets variously pitted on ventral surface.*
F *Fruit black or purplish-black. Stamens 10. Nutlets (3)4–5.*

C. douglasii N. America. Tree to about 40 ft (12 m), often without thorns; young shoots glabrous reddish-brown. Leaves 1.2–3 in (3–8 cm), more or less ovate, sometimes slightly lobed, base tapering. Flowers with 2–5 styles. Fruit shining black. (Section *Douglasianae*.) **CZ5**

C. chlorosarca comes here with its black fruit but is referred to Section *Sanguineae*, having distinctly lobed leaves (see **GG** on page 181).

C. monogyna

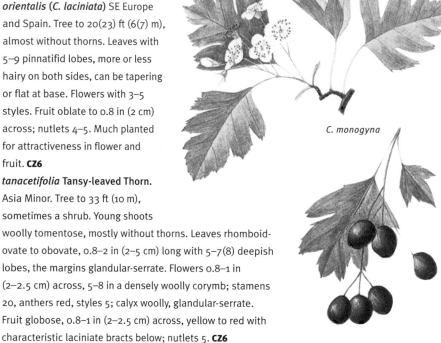

C. monogyna

C. flava

C. tanacetifolia

FF *Fruit yellowish, orange or (bright) red. Stamens (8)10–20.*
  G *Leaves entire or slightly lobed. Sepals finely serrate often with glands, or incised, longer than receptacle (hypanthium). (Section* Macrantha.*)*
  C. succulenta E N. America. Tree to 20 ft (6 m), thorns 1.2–2 in (3–5 cm). Leaves 2–3 in (5–8 cm), more or less obovate, doubly serrate, base tapering. Flower clusters densely hairy, sepals glandular serrate, stamens 15–20, anthers pink, styles 2–3. Fruit globose, 0.6 in (1.5 cm) across, red. **CZ4**

  GG *Leaves obviously lobed, sharply serrate. Sepals typically entire, shorter, than receptacle. (Section* Sanguineae.*)*

  C. wattiana C Asia (Altai Mountains to Baluchistan). Small tree with shining mahogany-colored shoots, often without thorns. Leaves broadly oval, 2–3.5 in (5–9 cm) long, base rounded-flat to somewhat tapering, lobes 3–5 pairs divided almost to half-way. Flowers with 15–20 stamens, anthers whitish to pale yellowish. Fruit globose, orange to reddish, 0.3–0.5 in (8–12 mm) across. **CZ5**

  C. altaica is very close to above with leaves lobed beyond halfway, the lowest pair almost to midrib and resembling *C. pinnatifida.* **CZ5**

  C. chlorosarca E Asia. Small tree with warted shoots. Leaves broadly ovate, 2–3.5 in (5–9 cm) long with 3–5 pairs of short, broad lobes, base broad. Flowers with serrulate calyx lobes, styles 5. Fruit oblate, 0.4 in (1 cm) across, black (atypical for its section). **CZ3**

  C. sanguinea Siberia, SE Russia. Shrub or tree to 23 ft (7 m), usually without thorns; shoots soon brownish-purple, shiny. Leaves broad ovate with tapering base and 2–3 pairs of shallow distinct lobes. Flowers with 20 stamens, anthers pinkish to purple. Fruit globose, 0.4 in (1 cm) across, bright red. Widespread in its native habitat where it is much used for hedgerows. A variable species; determination difficult because of hybridization with closely allied species. **CZ4**

EE *Nutlets smooth on ventral surface.*
  H *Flowers typically solitary, rarely 2–5. Leaves to 0.6 in (1.5 cm) long, tapering at base, not or only slightly lobed, margin more or less toothed above middle. Calyx lobes foliaceous laciniate or deeply glandular-serrate. (Section* Parvifoliae.*)*

  C. uniflora SE U.S. Shrub or low tree to 8 ft (2.5 m), with numerous thorns. Leaves obovate to 1.4 in (3.5 cm), with coarse, blunt teeth. Flower clusters with woolly pedicels and calyces. Stamens 20 or more with whitish to pale yellow anthers. Fruit subglobose, yellow or with greenish tinge, 0.4–0.5 in (10–13 mm) across; nutlets 3–5. **CZ5**

  HH *Flowers in simple or slightly branched clusters of 4 or more. Lobes of calyx not foliaceous, either entire or glandular-serrate.*
  I *Leaf blades at least, end flowers somewhat, conspicuously glandular. Flowers in clusters of 4–7(8).*
  J *Leaves with 1–3 pairs of shallow lobes in upper part and variable in shape on flowering shoots of same plant, mostly*

less than 0.8 in (2 cm) wide, base tapering into a less than 0.8 in (2 cm) long, densely glandular petiole. (Section Flavae.)

  C. aprica SE U.S. Shrub or tree to 20 ft (6 m), with zigzag shoots; thorns to 1.4 in (3.5 cm). Leaves oval to obovate, toothed, and sometimes slightly lobed in upper part. Flowers with 10 stamens, anthers yellow. Fruit globose, 0.5 in (12 mm) across, orange to red. **CZ6**

  C. flava is very similar but flowers have 20 stamens and purple anthers. **CZ6**

  JJ *Leaves mostly with 4–5 pairs of pointed lobes, rarely unlobed, more or less uniform in shape on flowering shoots of same plant, mostly more than 0.8 in (2 cm) wide, base tapering or more abruptly narrowing; petiole virtually without glands and/or more than 0.8 in (2 cm) long.*

  C. intricata N. America. Shrub to 13 ft (4 m) with curved thorns to 1.6 in (4 cm). Leaves elliptic to ovate, 0.8–2.8 in (2–7 cm) long, margin doubly serrate, lobes 3–4 pairs. Flowers with 10 stamens, anthers yellow, the bracts densely glandular. Fruit broadly oval, 0.3–0.5 in (9–13 mm) across, bronze-green or brownish; nutlets 3–5. (Section *Intricatae.*) **CZ5**

  C. coccinioides N America. Tree to about 20(23) ft (6(7) m); thorns 1.2–2 in (3–5 cm). Leaves 2–3 in (5–8 cm) long with 4–5 pairs of pointed lobes. Flowers (4)5–7 in a cluster, stamens 20, anthers pink. Fruit subglobose, 0.6–0.7 in (15–18 mm) across, red; nutlets 4–5. Pleasing orange to red fall colors. (Section *Dilatatae.*) **CZ5**

II *Leaf blades and flowers, except sometimes the sepals, virtually without glandular hairs. Petioles sometimes more or less glandular. Flowers few or many in a cluster.*
  K *Flowers 2–6(7) in a cluster. Leaves unlobed, rarely slightly so, typically tapering at base.*
  L *Young shoots, at least rough-warty. Thorns less than 0.4 in (1 cm) long.*

  C. cuneata Japan and C China. Bushy shrub to 5 ft (1.5 m). Leaves obovate, 0.8–2.4 in (2–6 cm) long. Flowers hairy, styles 5, stamens 20, anthers red. Fruit more or less subglobose, 0.5–0.6 in (12–15 mm) across, red with 5 nutlets. (Section *Cuneatae.*) **CZ6**

  LL *Young shoots smooth. Thorns longer than 0.4 in (1 cm).*

  C. aestivalis SE U.S. Tree to 33 ft (10 m); thorns 0.8–1.4 in (2–3.5 cm). Leaves oblong to obovate, to 1.2 in (3 cm) long; petiole 0.3–0.8 in (6–20 mm) long, sometimes 3 lobed. Flowers in glabrous clusters appearing before or with the leaves. Fruit red, 0.3 in (8 mm) across, with 3 nutlets. (Section *Aestivales.*)

C. pruinosa

C. mollis

C. crus-galli

ABOVE The striking deep red fruit of *Crataegus monogyna* brighten up the countryside in fall and provide food for birdlife.

BELOW *Crataegus prunifolia*, the Broadleaved Cockspur Thorn, is a particularly beautiful thorn with its leaves turning a rich glowing crimson in fall. Fruit are a deep red and ripen in September.

C. triflora Shrub or tree to 23 ft (7 m). Leaves 0.8–2.8 in (2–7 cm) long with a few shallow lobes. Flowers 2–5 in a cluster, 1–1.2 in (2.5–3 cm) across, sepals glandular serrate, stamens 20, anthers yellow. Fruit globose, 0.5–0.6 in (12–15 mm) across, red; nutlets 3–5. (Section *Triflorae.*) **CZ7**

KK *Flowers numerous in a cluster (more than 7). Leaves tapering at base, lobed or not.*
M *Petiole up to 0.4 in (1 cm) long, rarely to 0.6 in (1.5 cm). Leaves unlobed or only slightly lobed, tapering at base.*
N *Fruit large, 0.8–1.2 × 0.6–0.8 in (2–3 × 1.5–2 cm). Leaves ovate-lanceolate, unlobed, tapering at base, and hairy on both sides.*

C. pubescens forma *stipulacea* (*C. stipulacea*) Mexico. Tree to 20 ft (6 m); thorns mostly absent. Leaves 1.6–4 in (4–10 cm) long, sometimes with a few glandular serrations in upper part. Flowers with hairy pedicels and calyx, stamens 15–20, anthers pink, styles 2–3. Fruit yellowish or orange, speckled, with 2–3 nutlets. (Section *Mexicanae.*)

NN *Fruit smaller. Flowers appearing with or after the leaves. Leaves oblong to obovate.*
O *Leaves typically unlobed on flowering shoots, leathery, dark green, and shining above, veins inconspicuous or slightly impressed above, fruit hard, inedible; nutlets 1–3, rarely 5. (Section* Crus-galli.*)*

C. crus-galli Cockspur Thorn. E and C N. America. Shrub or tree to about 40 ft (12 m), less in cultivation; thorns 1.6–3 in (4–8 cm). Leaves obovate, 0.8–2(4) in (2–5(10) cm) long. Styles 2, stamens 10, anthers pink. Fruit subglobose, red, 0.4 in (10 mm) across, persisting through winter. **CZ5**

C. × lavallei (?*C. crus-galli* × *C. pubescens* f. *stipulacea*) Tree to over 23 ft (7 m); thorns few, stout, 1–1.6(2) in (2.5–4(5) cm). Leaves 2–4 in (5–10 cm) long, and mostly oblong to obovate. Flowers 0.8–1 in (2–2.5 cm) across, styles 1–3, stamens 15–20, anthers yellow-orange to reddish-brown. Fruit ellipsoidal, 0.5–0.6 in (13–15 mm) long, orange-red with brown dots, persisting throughout winter; nutlets 2–3. **CZ5**

OO *Leaves sometimes slightly lobed above middle, more or less papery, not shining above; veins typically and obviously impressed above. Fruit fleshy, edible; nutlets 3–5, rarely 2. (Section* Punctatae.*)*

C. punctata E N. America. Tree to 33(40) ft (10(12) m); thorns 2–3 in (5–7.5 cm), sometimes absent. Leaves more or less ovate, 2–4 in (5–10 cm) long. Flowers with 5 styles and 20 stamens. Fruit subglobose, about 0.8 in (2 cm) across. **CZ4**

MM *Petiole, at least of some leaves on long shoots, 0.6–1.2 in (1.5–3 cm) long. Leaves tapering or broad at base.*

P *Inflorescence, flowers, and both surfaces of leaves more or less densely hairy. Leaves more or less lobed and truncate to subcordate at base. (Section* Molles.*)*

C. mollis C U.S. Tree 33–40 ft (10–12 m); thorns 1–2 in (2.5–5 cm). Leaves leathery, broadly ovate, 2.4–4.3 in (6–11 cm) long, with 4–6 pairs of shallow lobes. Flowers about 1 in (2.5 cm) across, styles 4–5; stamens 20, anthers pale yellow. Fruit subglobose, hairy, red, 0.5–0.6 in (12–15 mm) across. **CZ5**
C. submollis NE U.S., SE Canada. Similar to previous species, but leaves more papery and stamens 10. **CZ5**

PP *Both inflorescence and flowers glabrous, or almost so. Leaves sparsely hairy only when young, soon become virtually glabrous.*

Q *Leaves not or only slightly lobed and with tapering base. (Section* Virides.*)*

C. viridis E and S N. America. Tree to 40 ft (12 m); thorns to 1.5 in (3.8 cm). Leaves ovate to oval, 1.6–3.5 in (4–9 cm) long, usually 3 lobed above. Flowers with 2–5 styles, 20 stamens, anthers pale yellow. Fruit globose, 0.2–0.3(0.35) in (6–8 (9) mm) across, red. **CZ5**

QQ *Leaves obviously lobed, base broad, not gradually tapering.*

C. pruinosa U.S. Tree to 20 ft (6 m) or large shrub; thorns stout, 1–1.5 in (2.5–3.8 cm). Leaves more or less ovate, 1.2–2 in (3–5 cm) long, with broad cuneate base with 3–4 pairs of triangular lobes and unfolding reddish. Flowers 0.4–1 in (2–2.5 cm) across; stamens 20, anthers pink. Fruit roundish, 0.04–0.06 in (1–1.5 mm) across, long remaining green, finally purplish with sweet yellow flesh; nutlets 5. (Section *Pruinosae.*)

Mespilus
Medlar

Medlar is the common name for *Mespilus germanica*, a small spreading deciduous tree growing to about 23 ft (7 m), found in southeastern Europe extending eastward to central Asia. It is the better known of the two species (the second being *M. canescens*) that comprise the genus, and is related to the hawthorns (*Crataegus* spp) though differing in its solitary flowers, and fruits with five carpels. So closely related are *Mespilus* and *Crataegus* that both graft and sexual hybrids have been synthesized between the two. The branches are often armed with hard spines to 1 in (2.5 cm) long, and the leaves are hairy, subsessile, oval to ovate, 2–4(5) in (5–10(12) cm) long. The flowers are white, about 1.2 in (3 cm) across, and appear in late spring. Medlars often persist in cultivation as old, gnarled, but attractive specimens.

The brownish apple-shaped fruits are traditionally eaten with wine after frosting or "bletting" (rotting) has softened the hard fruit tissues. Jellies and preserves can also be made from the fruits, though the taste is rather an acquired one.

The leaves color well in the fall after the showy flowers—the medlar is cultivated as much as an ornamental as for its fruit. It prefers an open sunny site on well-drained soil. Cultivar 'Nottingham' has an erect habit and produces small, richly flavored fruits; 'Dutch' has a spreading habit with larger fruits. It is very hardy and grows in any reasonable soil.

Cydonia
Common Quince

The Common Quince (*Cydonia oblonga*) was formerly the only species of its genus but *Cydonia* now also includes *Pseudocydonia, and C. sinensis* is the other species. Other species, formerly placed in this genus, and conveniently distinguished as flowering quinces, are now transferred to the closely related genus *Chaenomeles*. This has involved a number of sometimes confusing nomenclatural changes, of which the more important ones are dealt with under *Chaenomeles*. *Cydonia* differs by its entire (not toothed) leaf margin, the free styles (not united below) and the almost invariably solitary flowers (compared to solitary or clustered in *Chaenomeles*).

The Common Quince is a densely branched, thornless, deciduous tree, which grows to 16–20 ft (5–6 m). The leaves are alternate, elliptical to ovate, 2.4–4 in (6–10 cm) long, with an entire margin, more or less woolly beneath and with glandular hairy stipules. The flowers are either white or pink, 0.8–1.2(2) in (2–3(5) cm) across, with numerous stamens. The yellow fruit is usually shaped like a rounded pear, 2.4–4 in (6–10 cm) long, very fragrant, with numerous seeds in each of its five chambers (unlike apples and pears, which

have only two seeds per chamber). When ripe it is covered with a fine down.

The origin of the Common Quince is uncertain; it appears to be wild (or naturalized) in parts of the Near East and central Asia and may have originated in northern Iran and Turkistan, where it is known as the Pear of Cydonia. It has been cultivated in Europe for millennia. The Greeks apparently ate the fruit hollowed out, filled with honey and cooked in a pastry case, and the Romans extracted an essential oil used in perfume. For centuries it has been used in France, in cooking, in perfumery, and medicine. (The seeds contain a bassorin-type gum, which is used as a lubricant in toilet preparations. An infusion of the seeds is listed in some pharmacopoeias.)

The fruit has a strong scent and the flesh, though quite unpalatable raw, is rich in tannin and pectin. It must always be cooked and is used to make fragrant dishes, sweet and savory. In many European countries it is used to make confectionery, liqueurs, and jellies. The word marmalade derives from the Portuguese *marmelo*, meaning quince. It is an excellent flavoring for pies and tarts; in the East it is enjoyed salted, stuffed, or in stews.

The Common Quince grows best in a deep moist loam in warm sheltered sites, either as a freestanding tree or trained on walls and also serves as a stock for grafting pears. It may live to a great age. Cultivars include 'Lusitanica' (Portuguese Quince), which is very vigorous and floriferous but less hardy, and 'Maliformis', where the fruits are apple-shaped. **CZ4**

TOP AND ABOVE The Common Quince, *Cydonia oblonga*, bursts into flower in early spring with its dense branches seemingly dripping with flowers. They are pink or white and cup-shaped, and have conspicuous stamens.

Chaenomeles

Flowering Quinces

Chaenomeles comprises three or four species from China and Japan, and is very similar to *Cydonia,* in which genus they were formerly placed. They are deciduous or half-evergreen shrubs or trees, often suckering, with alternate, more or less toothed leaves (entire in *Cydonia*). The flowers are solitary or clustered with the parts in fives, except the stamens, which may number twenty or more, and the styles are united below (whereas they are free in *Cydonia*). The fruit is a pome (false fruit), each of the five chambers containing numerous brown seeds.

All species are hardy and do well on any average well-drained loamy soil, preferably in a sunny position.

Perhaps the most widely cultivated species is *Chaenomeles speciosa* (formerly *C. lagenaria*), commonly known in the United States as the Japanese (Flowering) Quince and in Britain as "Japonica." This has been, and in some quarters remains, the center of nomenclatural confusion. *Pyrus japonica* was described by Thunberg from the Hakone Mountains in Japan in 1784. Long before its introduction into Europe, a different species from China had been introduced and was taken to be identical with Thunberg's species. This became known as Japonica. In 1818 the Chinese species was shown to be distinct from Thunberg's Japanese species and renamed *Pyrus speciosa*. The specific part of the name (*speciosa*) has been retained, in spite of the transfer first to genus *Cydonia* and then to *Chaenomeles. Chaenomeles speciosa* is a profusely branching, suckering shrub growing to 6 ft (2 m), bearing single or double scarlet flowers, 1.4–2 in (3.5–5 cm) across, in early spring. The aromatic fruits are more or less ovoid, 1.2–2.8 in (3–7 cm) long, yellowish-green with white speckles, and can be used in the same way as those of the Common Quince.

Maul's Flowering Quince (*C. japonica*) is a deciduous, thorny, wide-spreading shrub over 3 ft (1 m) tall with orange-red to scarlet flowers and a red-blotched yellow fruit like an apple, 1.6 in (4 cm) across. The Chinese Quince (*C. sinensis*) is a deciduous tree growing to over 40 ft (12 m) with pinkish flowers, a deep yellow, woody, egg-shaped fruit, 4–6 in (10–15 cm) long, and leaves that turn red in the fall. All species are adaptable as wall shrubs, in borders or hedges.

Cultivated hybrids include *C. × superba* (*C. japonica × C. speciosa*) and *C. × superba* 'Vermilon' (*C. cathayensis × C. speciosa*), both of which exist as a number of cultivars. **CZ5**

Clusters of scarlet and blood red flowers are produced on the old wood of *Chaenomeles speciosa*. The dense, tangled habit of this species makes for a dramatic display.

Sorbus

Whitebeams, Mountain Ash

Sorbus is a genus of almost two hundred species of deciduous trees and shrubs of the northern hemisphere. They are found as far south as Mexico and the Himalaya. The genus includes the rowans or mountain ashes, the whitebeams, and the service trees. Many of the species are grown as ornamentals and can tolerate shade and atmospheric pollution.

The branches bear alternately arranged leaves; in whitebeams these are simple but in the rowans they are pinnately compound with ovate leaflets. However, every kind of intermediate shape, from simple through lobed through compound, is found in representatives of the genus as a result of interspecific hybridization. The inflorescence consists of tight flattened clusters (compound cymes) of flowers with five white, or occasionally pink, petals. The fifteen to twenty stamens surround a semi-inferior ovary, which ripens into a pome (a false fruit, commonly called a "berry"), which is white, yellow, orange, pink, or red, according to species. The seeds are small and scattered in the pulp of the fruit.

One of the most attractive trees is the Rowan, European Mountain Ash, or Quickbeam (*Sorbus aucuparia = Pyrus aucuparia*), which grows wild at altitudes of up to 2,000 ft (600 m) in its native Scottish Highlands. It is often planted elsewhere as an ornamental in parks and gardens, where it attains a height of about 40 ft (12 m). At one time rowan wood was used as firewood and for making furniture and tools in the more barren and relatively treeless districts of northern Scotland. The leaves are pinnate with seven pairs of leaflets, each with a serrated margin. It produces large clusters of bright orange-red fruits, which in var *edulis* are edible and used for making jams and jellies. The berries, in common with of other species, are particularly attractive to birds that digest the pulp and excrete the seeds, which may subsequently germinate in a variety of habitats, including clefts on cliff faces and even in the hollow trunks of old trees.

Sargent's Rowan (*S. sargentiana*), native to western China, is a thick-shooted bushy tree, which grows to about 16 ft (5 m) tall. It is very common in parks and gardens, most often as a graft on the stem of *S. aucuparia*. It is recognizable by its very long pinnate leaf—up to 16 in (40 cm)—with 9–11 leaflets, its large, sticky, red winter buds and very small bright red fruits. Other Asian rowans are much less commonly grown, including the Kashmir Rowan (*S. cashmiriana*), the Japanese Rowan (*S. commixta*), and Vilmorin's Rowan (*S. vilmorinii*).

The Common Whitebeam or Chess Apple (*S. aria*) is a native of Europe, found on chalky or sandy soils, growing to a height of 15 m (50 ft). It bears ovate toothed leaves, covered on the lower side with white downy hairs, and has large white flowers and fruits that are ovoid and scarlet. The Swedish Whitebeam (*S. intermedia = S. suecica*) usually grows to 15 ft (4.5 m) tall and is commonly used for planting

S. aria

S. aucuparia

ABOVE The Rowan and Whitebeam differ in habit, with *Sorbus aria* having an irregularly domed crown of erect main branches. The crown of *S. aucuparia* is irregularly ovoid, becoming more spreading and graceful with age.

RIGHT The Mountain Ash, *Sorbus aucuparia,* is beautiful in leaf and flower but most of all when its branches are laden with clusters of ripe red fruit.

in town streets and parks. The leaves are deeply lobed and covered on the underside with grayish hairs. Large clusters of white flowers are followed in August and September by conspicuous scarlet fruits.

The Wild Service Tree (*S. torminalis*) is native to southern England. It rarely exceeds 40 ft (12 m) in height and is recognizable by its five-lobed leaves, which are very similar to those of the maples though they are not borne in opposite pairs. The flowers are white, the fruits globose and brown with dull reddish speckles. Although the fruits are rather acid they are edible and were once sold in Kent in southeast England as "chequers berries." The true Service Tree (*S. domestica*) is found all over Europe, growing to a height of about 60 ft (18 m). The flowers are creamy-white and the fruits are large, pear-shaped, brownish-red, and edible. In some areas the fruits are fermented with grain to produce an alcoholic beverage and the bark is used for tanning leather.

Species of *Sorbus* hybridize readily and a number are grown as ornamentals, among them the Bastard Service Tree (*S. × thuringiaca*)—the result of a cross between *S. aucuparia* and *S. aria*—and the Service Tree of Fontainebleau (*S. latifolia*), which is possibly derived from *S. torminalis* and *S. aria*. **CZ2-7**

ROSACEAE

Sorbus
WHITEBEAMS, MOUNTAIN ASH

Number of species *193*
Distribution *Northern hemisphere.*
Commercial uses *Cultivated ornamental trees with many named forms. The timber is used in joinery and tannins are extracted from the bark. The fruits are also edible.*

The Main Species of *Sorbus*

Group I: Leaves pinnate with at least 4 pairs of leaflets.

S. americana (*Pyrus americana*) **American Mountain Ash, Dogberry, Missey-moosey, Roundwood.** E N. America. Shrub or tree to 33 ft (10 m). Leaflets 11–17, narrowly oblong-lanceolate, 2–5 in (5–12 cm) long, acuminate (narrowing to a point), sharply toothed (serrated) on margins, bright green and glabrous above, paler below. Fruits shining red, globose, 0.2–0.25 in (4–6 mm). **CZ2**

S. aucuparia (*Pyrus aucuparia*) **Rowan** or **European Mountain Ash, Quickbeam.** Europe and W Asia. Shrub or tree to 60 ft (18 m). Leaflets 11–15, oblong-lanceolate, 1.2–2.4 in (3–6 cm) long, more or less rounded, serrated on margins, dark green above, grayish below. Fruits orange-red (but yellow in 'Xanthocarpa'), subglobose, 0.25–0.35 in (6–9 mm). **CZ2**

S. domestica **Service Tree.** S Europe, N. Africa, and Asia Minor. Leaflets 11–21, narrow, oblong-lanceolate, 6.2 in (16 cm) long, acute, the margins sharply serrated from near the base. Fruits brownish, tipped with red, pear-shaped, about 1.2 in (3 cm) long. **CZ2**

S. scopulina Rocky Mountains, U.S. Shrub to 13 ft (4 m). Leaflets 11–13, glossy, lanceolate or oblong-lanceolate, 1.2–2.4 in (3–6 cm) long, cuneate (wedge-shaped) at the base and shortly acute or acuminate at the apex. Fruits bright red, subglobose, 0.3–0.4 in (8–10 mm). **CZ5**

S. sargentiana **Sargent's Rowan.** China. Shrub to 16 ft (5 m). Leaflets 7–11, oblong-acute, 1.6–2.4 in (4–6 cm) long, mid-green turning to red in the fall. Fruits orange-red, globose, 0.2–0.3 in (6–8 mm). **CZ6**

S. vilmorinii **Vilmorin's Rowan.** W China. Shrub to 13 ft (4 m). Leaflets 19–25, narrow ovate with serrated margins. Fruits rose-red, ripening to whitish-pink, 0.2–0.3 in (6–8 mm). **CZ6**

S. decora E U.S. and Canada. Shrub or small tree to 33 ft (10 m). Leaflets 11–17, oblong, sharply acute, 1.6–3 in (4–8 cm) long but the lowermost pair usually smaller, margins coarsely serrated from the tip to the middle below. Fruits glossy red, subglobose, 0.2–0.4 in (6–10 mm). **CZ2**

S. californica California. Small shrub 3.3–6.6 ft (1–2 m). Leaflets 7–9, oblong-oval, simply or doubly serrate from the tip to below the middle, 0.8–1.6 in (2–4 cm) long, glabrous on both sides, glossy above. Fruits scarlet, globose, 0.28–0.4 in (7–10 mm). **CZ7**

S. cascadensis British Columbia to N California. Shrub 6.6–16 ft (2–5 m). Leaflets 9–11, oval but sharply acute at the apex, somewhat rounded at the base, sharply serrate from the apex to below the middle. Fruits scarlet, globose, 0.3–0.4 in (8–10 mm). **CZ6**

Group II: Leaves simple, serrate, lobed, sometimes basally pinnate.

S. pseudofennica (*S. fennica*) Scotland. Small tree to 23 ft (7 m). Leaves oblong or ovate, 2–3 in (5–8 cm) long with 1–2 pairs of free leaflets at the base, sharp serrated margins, dark

S. aria

S. aucuparia

S. intermedia

yellowish-green above, grayish and felty below. Fruits scarlet, subglobose, 0.28–0.4 in (7–10 mm). **CZ5**

S. hybrida Scandinavia. Small tree up to 33 ft (10 m). Leaves lobed ovate, 2.4–6 in (6–15 cm) long with 2–3 pairs of oblong, serrate, mid-green (grayish and felty below) leaflets at the base; fruits red, subglobose, 0.2–0.3 in (6–8 mm). **CZ5**

S. × thuringiaca (*S. aria* × *S. aucuparia*) Europe. Tree to 42 ft (13 m). Leaves oblong, 2.8–4.3 in (7–11 cm) long, with 1–3 pairs of free leaflets at the base (sometimes they are not free and the leaf is merely lobed at the base, with no free leaflets), serrated margins, dull green and glabrous above, grayish and felty below. Fruits red, subglobose, 0.3–0.4 in (8–10 mm). **CZ6**

Group III: Leaves entire, without true leaflets.

S. aria **Common Whitebeam, Chess Apple.** Europe. Tree to 40 ft (12 m). Leaves ovate-elliptic to elliptic-oblong, toothed or shallowly lobed, 2–5.5 in (5–14 cm) long, acute rounded or cuneate at the base, often more than twice as long as broad, whitish when young, turning to dark green (or yellow in 'Aurea') and finally red in the fall. Fruits scarlet, subglobose, 0.3–0.6 in (8–15 mm). **CZ5**

S. torminalis

S. hybrida

S. torminalis Wild Service Tree. Europe, N. Africa, Asia Minor. Tree to 66 ft (20 m). Leaves broad ovate, 2–6 in (5–15 cm) long, cordate to broad cuneate at the base, deeply lobed with 3–5 angular, serrated lobes, the lowest pair much deeper than the rest. Fruits brown, ellipsoid. 0.5–0.6 in (12–16 mm). **CZ6**

S. intermedia Swedish Whitebeam. N Europe. Small tree to 29 ft (9 m). Leaves deeply lobed, serrate, 2.8–5 in (7–12 cm) long, elliptic, 1.5–2 times as long as broad, rounded or broad cuneate at the base, mid-green, but gray and hairy on the underside. Fruits bright red, oval or oblong, 0.5–0.6 in (12–15 mm). **CZ5**

S. leptophylla Endemic to Wales. Small shrub to 10 ft (3 m). Leaves obovate, 2.4–4.8 in (6–12 cm) long, 1.5–2.5 times as long as broad, acute, cuneate at the base, doubly serrate, dark green above, greenish-white below. Fruits scarlet, subglobose, 0.8 in (2 cm). **CZ5**

S. rupicola British Isles and Scandinavia. Small shrub to 6 ft (2 m). Leaves obovate or oblanceolate, 3–5.5 in (8–14 cm) long, 1.4–2.4 times as long as broad, unequally toothed, dark green above but white and felty below. Fruits green-red, subglobose, 0.5–0.6 in (12–15 mm). **CZ7**

S. vexans Endemic to SW England. Small tree to 26 ft (8 m). Leaves obovate, 2.8–4.5 in (7–11 cm) long, up to twice as long as broad, cuneate at the base, coarsely serrate, yellowish-green above but white and felty below. Fruits scarlet, subglobose, 0.5–0.6 in (12–15 mm). **CZ7**

S. subcuneata Endemic to SW England. Small tree to 30 ft (9 m). Leaves elliptic, acute, cuneate or rather rounded at the base, 2.8–4 in (7–10 cm) long, lobed in the upper parts (the lobes being rather triangular) and sharply toothed, bright green above but grayish and felty below. Fruits brownish-orange, subglobose, 0.4–0.5 in (10–13 mm). **CZ7**

Amelanchier
Serviceberry, Shadbush

Amelanchier is a genus of over thirty species often cultivated for their abundant white flowers in spring and brilliant red fall foliage. About twenty species are found in North America, extending as far south as Mexico, the remainder distributed throughout central and southern Europe and parts of Asia, including China, Japan, and Korea. Popular names for the genus are numerous and are often applied indiscriminately to various species. The most common are: Shadbush, Shadblow, Serviceberry, Juneberry, and Snowy Mespilus.

These are deciduous shrubs or trees, sometimes stoloniferous or suckering. The leaves are alternate, simple, and the stipules soon fall away. The flowers are bisexual, white, and borne in terminal racemes of six to twenty, rarely only one to three, before or with the leaves. The calyx-tube (hypanthium) is bell-shaped with five small lobes, and there are five petals and some ten to twenty stamens. The ovary is solitary with two to five chambers and two to five styles. The small fruit is a purplish to black, often juicy and sweet, pome containing five to ten seeds.

The species are generally hardy in temperate regions and are not particular as to soil as long as it is not waterlogged. Grafting on hawthorn (*Crataegus* spp) stock has been practised but is not recommended. They are cultivated chiefly for their abundant white flowers produced in the spring. Some species, for example *A. laevis* and *A. lamarckii*, have an attractive bronze or purplish tinge to their leaves, especially the young ones; *A. asiatica* and *A. lamarckii*, among others, give pleasing reddish leaves in the fall. The sweet and juicy fruits of some species are greatly attractive to birds, while those of *A. canadensis* and *A. stolonifera*, especially the 'Success' strain of the latter, are edible by humans and are made into jellies.

The genus is taxonomically difficult both in terms of nomenclature and species identification. There are perplexing intermediates, many, no doubt, the result of natural hybridization. This is especially true for the binomial *A. canadensis*, which covers four different species: *A. arborea*, *A. canadensis (sensu stricto)*, *A. laevis*, and *A. lamarckii*, all with ovary tops glabrous and not hairy-woolly. This is an important character to note for identification purposes. Others are: examination of just opened leaves for any indumentum or bronze or purplish tints, and the number of styles and whether they are free to the base or more or less joined from the base upward. **CZ2–5**

LEFT The lower slopes of Mount Rainier in Washington state on America's Pacific Northwest are home to wild Mountain Ash (*Sorbus* spp), the seeds of which are dispersed by birds feeding on the berries.

BELOW The graceful form of the Serviceberry (*Amelanchier* spp) is an abundance of starlike pure white flowers, that appear among the unfolding leaves.

Malus

Apples

Malus is a genus of over fifty species of deciduous, fruit-bearing trees and shrubs, the fruits of some being known as crabs or crab apples. The genus includes the many varieties of the long-cultivated Edible Apple, *M. pumila* (see the table for synonyms and crosses), which are probably the result of crosses between several species. They are characterized by simple, more or less lobed leaves and clusters of bisexual flowers, ranging from white through pink to purplish, with five petals, five sepals, fifteen to fifty stamens, the anthers typically yellow, and two to five styles united toward the base.

The Cultivated or Edible Apple is an upright or spreading tree with dark, gray-brown, irregularly fissured, scaly bark, and gray to reddish-brown twigs. The leaves are simple, ovate or oval, broad cuneate or rounded at the base, crenate-serrate, and generally hairy on the undersurface. The flowers are white, suffused with varying degrees of pink, and are formed in clusters of four to seven. They arise sometimes on year-old wood (axillary fruit buds), on apical buds of most year-old shoots (cultivars known as "tip-bearers") but more generally on tips of short, about 2.8 in (7 cm), vegetative growths ("dards" and "brindilles") and from simple or compound spurs on wood more than two years old. Most cultivars are partially selfsterile and are pollinated by insects such as bees

M. baccata

ABOVE *Malus baccata*, the Siberian Crab Apple, forms a round, wide, spreading head of branches, with the lower branches arching or pendulous.

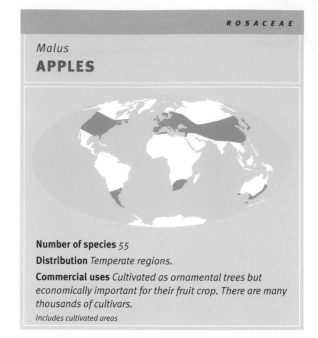

Malus
APPLES

Number of species 55
Distribution *Temperate regions.*
Commercial uses *Cultivated as ornamental trees but economically important for their fruit crop. There are many thousands of cultivars.*
Includes cultivated areas

ROSACEAE

BELOW The cultivar 'Discovery' is a delicious early dessert apple, lasting long on the tree as well as the shelf. It is crisp and crunchy, and has a yellow skin with bright red stripes.

and flies. The fruit is a pome (a false fruit), green or yellow to red, having five leathery chambers (loculi), each normally containing two seeds or pips.

As with many cultivated plants the origin of the Cultivated Apple—and other species of *Malus* that have contributed to its hybrid constitution—remains uncertain. The available evidence indicates that it originated in the upland regions between the Black Sea, Turkistan, and India. Some of the better forms spread westward to be established elsewhere as varieties still capable of future variation.

Apple cultivars have arisen as chance seedlings, by deliberate selection from seedlings of unknown parentage or from naturally occurring bud-sports (atypical shoots that can throw a flower of different colour to the parent plant). Scientific breeding began only when Thomas Andrew Knight (1750–1835) showed that desirable characters in different parents could be combined by their controlled cross-pollination, an approach now pursued with vigor on a worldwide basis. Irradiation techniques are also used to induce desirable mutations. Interestingly, though, 'Cox's Orange Pippin,' 'Bramley's Seedling,' 'Golden Delicious,' 'Granny Smith,' 'Ribston Pippin,' and 'Discovery' all originated as chance seedlings.

The global interest in, and importance of, this crop is demonstrated by the existence of over 2,000 named cultivars.

Apple Types

Economically, apples can be classified into four main groups: dessert, cooking, cider, and ornamental. Worldwide emphasis has been on the development of **Dessert types**. These are normally cultivars producing average-sized fruits, about 2.4–2.75 in (6–7 cm) diameter. They are mainly red and/or yellow (rarely green), with a high sugar content, the particular flavor largely imparted by the amount of aromatics present.

Cooking types are normally large-fruited cultivars, on average 4 in (10 cm) in diameter, mainly green, with a high acid content. In England, it has been suggested that the large, ribbed, green, early cultivars, such as the 'Costard' (first recorded in 1292, which gave rise to the term "costermonger") and "codlins," and the smaller, more rounded, sweeter "pippins" (imported in 1609 by Henry VIII's gardener, Richard Harris) were, respectively, the forerunners of present-day cooking and dessert types.

Cider varieties are grown mainly in the British Isles, northern France, and other northern European countries. They are subdivided into sweets, sharps, bitter-sweets, and bitter-sharps, depending on the proportions of sugars, acids, and tannins in their expressed juices, all of which, along with certain organic and aromatic substances, have a profound effect on the "vintage" quality of the cider produced. Most commercial ciders are made by mixing juices from the different cultivars to produce the desired blend of sweetness, acidity, or astringency.

Present-day demands cannot be met by the juice from true cider varieties so they are normally supplemented from quantities of downgraded dessert types.

Other apple products are unfermented apple juice, wine, liqueurs, vinegar, fillings for tarts, pies, and sauces, and pectin from dried apple pulp after juice extraction. More than 75 million tons of apples are grown annually throughout the world.

A number of *Malus* species, particularly the crab apples, are grown exclusively as **Ornamentals**. Their decorative attributes include the profusion of spring blossom, attractive leaves, shoots, and bark, and pleasing form. Of especial note are the two hybrids *Malus* 'Eleyi' and *M.* × *purpurea*—the latter with many fine forms. Many produce copious quantities of small fruits which are of little culinary use other than for making jelly but they add distinctive splashes of color in parks and gardens in the fall. Their potential as pollinators in commercial orchards and for providing useful characters for apple breeding has also aroused some considerable interest.

Apples can be cultivated only in regions where winter temperatures are sufficiently low to provide the chilling required to break bud dormancy. Without it, budbreak in spring fails or is erratic, so making the crop an uneconomic proposition. Cultivation, therefore, is confined to the northern and southern temperate zones and the higher altitudes of warmer regions. Soils with adequate depth, drainage, texture, structure, and fertility are also required.

Conversely, however, excessive winter cold, which is most likely to occur in regions centered on large land masses, such as Russia and North America, can cause injury or death of buds, bark-splitting, root damage, and withering of the stigmas, thus preventing pollination. It is possible to reduce such losses by using rootstocks and cultivars selected for resistance to low temperatures. **CZ2–9**

The Main Species of *Malus*

Section *Malus (Calycomeles)*
Calyx usually persistent.

Subsection *Malus*
No stone cells in fruit; leaves entire.

M. pumila (**M. domestica, M. communis, M. sylvestris** ssp **domestica, M. pumila** ssp **domestica**) **The Cultivated or Edible Apple.** *Malus pumila* is used here to cover only those varieties cultivated for their fruit and does not include the main wild ancestors. The principal species contributing to the Cultivated Apple have been *M. sylvestris*, *M. orientalis*, and *M. sieversii* with significant contributions from *M. baccata*, *M. prunifolia*, and *M.* × *robusta* and lesser contributions from other species, including *M. floribunda*, *M.* × *atrosanguinea*, *M.* × *zumi*, and *M.* × *micromalus*. Through controlled breeding, some of the last species are now making significant contributions to resistance to diseases and pests. The Cultivated Apple has been distributed throughout the temperate zones of the northern and the southern hemispheres. Chromosome numbers range from diploids ($2n = 34$) via triploids ($2n = 51$) to tetraploids ($2n = 68$). **CZ3**

M. sylvestris ssp **sylvestris** Wild Crab. C, N, and E Europe. Small tree. Leaves much less hairy than those of *M. sylvestris* ssp *paradisiaca*. It is used as a rootstock. The fruits, 0.8–1.6 in (2–4 cm) diameter, are usually acid and used in the production of jelly. Chromosome number is $2n = 34$ and 51. The name "Crab Apple," as distinct from Wild Crab, is sometimes used to distinguish crosses between various cultivated apples and so-called Siberian crabs such as *M.* × *robusta*. *Malus* × *astracanica*, the Astrakhan Apple, and *M. prunifolia* have also been involved in such crosses.

M. sylvestris ssp **paradisiaca** (**M. praecox, M. paradisiaca, M. dasycarpa**) Types include 'Paradise' and 'Doucin.' Leaves much more hairy than those of ssp *sylvestris*, fruits usually far sweeter and less acid. Chromosome number is $2n = 34$ and 68. Has been widely used throughout Europe as a dwarfing rootstock for many hundreds of years but is rarely found growing wild. Some authorities consider it to be a hybrid between ssp *sylvestris* and *M. orientalis* and/or *M. sieversii*.

M. orientalis The Caucasus, occurring especially in sparse oak forest areas. Closely related to *M. pumila*. The tall trees produce late-ripening sweet fruit, which transports well. The species is involved in the origin of some Caucasian, Crimean, and Italian cultivars, though elsewhere it is not very winter-hardy.

M. sieversii Closely related to *M. pumila*.
ssp **kirghisorum** Valleys of the Pskem, Ugam, and Kok-Su rivers. Found in the underbush of the Wild Walnut (*Juglans regia*) in W T'ien Shan (W China). Introgressed into cultivars.

M. pumila   'Herefordshire Pearman'

M. floribunda

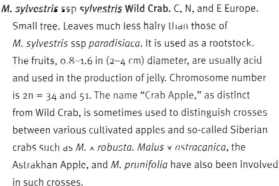

M. sylvestris sylvestris

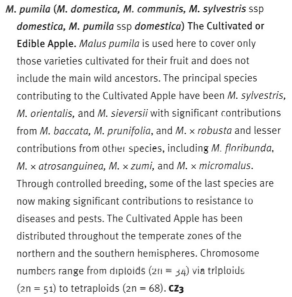

M. × purpurea

M. coronaria

M. coronaria

M. × purpurea

Malus × purpurea has an untidy, spreading crown with long, sparse branches. It is, however, more open and erect than M. floribunda.

spp *turkmenorum* Kopet-Dag Mountains, Turkmenistan. Large early maturing fruit. The cultivar 'Babaarabka' is characterized by the death of the main trunk at around twenty years of age, followed by rejuvenation from soboles (creeping underground stems).

forma *niedzwetzkyana* Sometimes regarded as a distinct species or a variety of *M. pumila*. SW Siberia, Turkistan, T'ien Shan Mts (W China). Small tree with red leaves, dense purple-red flower clusters giving rise to large conical dark red fruits. A parent of many very attractive ornamentals. Chromosome number is 2n = 34.

The hybrid species *M. × purpurea* (*M. atrosanguinea* × *sieversii* forma *niedzwetzkyana*) has produced attractive types, such as 'Eleyi,' 'Aldenhamensis' (a useful pollinator for cultivars), and 'Lemoinei.' The cross 'Lemoinei' × *M. sieboldii* gave rise to the fine ornamental 'Profusion' with wine-red scented flowers borne in large clusters, copper-crimson young leaves, and small ox-blood-red fruits.

M. prunifolia Chinese Crab Apple, Plum-leaf Crab. N China, E Siberia. Small tree bearing white-pink flowers (rose-crimson in the bud), 1.2 in (3 cm) diameter; fruits yellow-red, globose, and about 0.8 in (2 cm) across. Very resistant to frost and drought. It has been used in the breeding of numerous cultivars, including 'Bellefleur-Kitaika' and 'Saffran Pippin.' The chromosome number of the species includes diploids (2n = 34), triploids (2n = 51) and tetraploids (2n = 68). It has been suggested that *M. prunifolia* has arisen as a result of hybridization between *M. baccata* and some other species.

var *rinki* (*M. asiatica, M. ringo*) Ringo Crab. China, Korea, Japan. Cultivated for its abundant bright red or yellow fruit. Dwarf almond-pink double-flowered selections are prized as ornamentals. The trees prefer sunny dry limestone outcrops, mountain slopes or hillsides, and are not well adapted to moist bottom lands. Chromosome number is 2n = 34. Segregation pattern of seedlings suggests hybrid origin. **CZ3**

M. spectabilis Hai-Tang Crab Apple, Chinese Crab, Chinese Flowering Apple. China, Japan. Cultivated in China as an ornamental and for its fruit, which is used to make the confection called "Tang-Hu-Lu." Flowers semidouble to single, rose-red to blush-pink, 1.6–2 in (4–5 cm) diameter. There is a diversity of fruit types, including deep red, pink, or purple forms that are angular, long, or flat. In China the selections are usually propagated on *M. baccata* rootstocks. The species is not found growing wild. Chromosome number is 2n = 34 or 51. The *M. × micromalus* (*M. spectabilis* × *baccata*) hybrid forms a small tree of upright habit with pink flowers, 1.6 in (4 cm) diameter and roundish red fruit, 0.6 in (1.5 cm) diameter, with a calyx that is either deciduous or persistent. **CZ4**

Subsection *Chloromeles*

No stone cells in fruit; leaves dissected; fruits green. Native to N. America.

M. ioensis Prairie Crab. Central U.S. One of the few diploids (2n = 34) in this subsection, the remainder being mostly triploids or tetraploids. Leaves coarsely serrated or shallowly lobed. Flowers 1.6 in (4 cm) diameter. Fruits 1.2 in (3 cm) diameter, waxy and green. *Malus ioensis* 'Plena' (Bechtels' Crab) is an attractive ornamental tree with violet-scented double flowers. The hybrid *M. × soulardii* (*M. pumila* × *ioensis*)—Soulard Crab—is another very attractive ornamental with large almond-pink flowers and yellow (red-flushed) fruit, 2 in (5 cm) diameter. Another hybrid is 'Red Tip Crab' (*M. ioensis* × *sieversii* forma *niedzwetzkyana,* characterized by red young leaves and reddish-purple flowers. **CZ2**

M. glaucescens E U.S. Tree or shrub forming a wide dense head. Leaves with short triangular lobes (most deeply lobed on the vegetative shoots). When mature the leaves are glabrous and turn an attractive yellow to dark purple in the fall. Flowers 1.6 in (4 cm) diameter, with styles that are shorter than the stamens. Fruits waxy, yellow-green, fragrantly scented, 1.6 in (4 cm) diameter. Chromosome number is 2n = 68. The species is related to *M. glabrata* (2n = 68), which differs in having styles that are longer than the stamens. **CZ5**

M. angustifolia Southern Crab. E U.S. (Virginia to Florida and Mississippi). Slender tree or shrub remaining semi-evergreen in favorable locations. Leaves sharply lobed on vigorous shoots but narrow and toothed on mature shoots. Flowers salmon-pink, violet-scented, 1 in (2.5 cm) diameter. Fruits yellowish-green, roundish, 1 in (2.5 cm) diameter. Chromosome number is 2n = 34 or 68. *Malus angustifolia* ssp *pendula* has slender weeping branches. **CZ6**

M. × platycarpa SE U.S. (N Carolina to Georgia). Low spreading tree, characterized by leaves with several pairs of triangular lobes. Flowers large and pink. Fruits pale yellow-green, 2 in (5 cm) diameter. The fruit is sometimes used to make preserves. Chromosome number is 2n = 51 or 68. **CZ6**

M. coronaria Garland Crab. E and C U.S. Strong-growing tree. Leaves slightly lobed and short and broad on vigorously growing shoots. Flowers scented, 1.4 in (3.5 cm) diameter. Fruits green, 1.2 in (3 cm) diameter and slightly ribbed at the apex. Chromosome number is 2n = 51 or 68. *M. coronaria* 'Charlottae' has large lobed leaves, which become richly colored in the fall. It also has interesting large, shell-pink, semidouble violet-scented flowers, which open in late May/early June. *M. bracteata* (2n = 51) is a closely related species, which usually has less lobed leaves.

M. lancifolia U.S. Medium-sized spreading, often spiny, tree. Leaves rather thin, lanceolate (especially on flowering shoots), slightly lobed on vigorous shoots and glabrous at maturity. Flowers shell-pink, 1.4 in (3.5 cm) diameter. Fruits waxy, green, round, 1 in (2.5 cm) diameter. Chromosome number is 2n = 51 or 68. **CZ5**

M. tschonoskii

The narrowly erect crown of *Malus tschonoskii* has a pyramidal habit with long upright branches.

M. tschonoskii

M. tschonoskii

M. baccata

M. 'Yellow Siberian'

Subsection *Eriomeles*

Stone cells in fruit; leaves not, or slightly, lobed.

M. prattii C and W China. Tree growing to 33 ft (10 m). Leaves 2.4–6 in (6–15 cm) long, red-veined, nonlobed, attractively colored in the fall. Flowers white, 1 in (2.5 cm) diameter, occurring in many-flowered clusters. Fruits red or yellow, roundish, 0.6 in (1.5 cm) diameter. *M. ombrophila* is a related species with fewer styles per flower and slightly larger fruit. **CZ6**

M. yunnanensis W China. Tree similar in size to *M. prattii* but having pointed leaves with 3–5 pairs of short, broad lobes. Flowers white, 0.6 in (1.5 cm) diameter, up to 12 per cluster, with 5 or more styles. Fruits deep red, round, 0.4–0.6 in (1–1.5 cm) diameter, with a reflexed calyx. The crimson and orange fall leaf coloring makes it an attractive ornamental. **CZ6**

Subsection *Eriolobus*

Stone cells in fruit; leaves lobed; very late flowering.

M. trilobata W Asia, E Mediterranean, NE Greece. Tree or shrub. Leaves maple-leaf-like, deeply 3 lobed and sublobed, toothed. Flowers 1.4 in (3.5 cm) diameter, opening very late and often failing to set fruit. Fruits (if present) yellow or red. **CZ6**

Subsection *Docyniopsis*

Stone cells in fruit; leaves not, or slightly, lobed.

M. tschonoskii Japan. Large tree. Leaves slightly lobed, 2.8–5 in (7–12 cm) long, turning yellow, orange, purple, and scarlet in the fall. Flowers white, pink-tinged, 1.2 in (3 cm) diameter. Fruits yellow-green, purple-tinged, round, 1.2 in (3 cm) diameter. This species, which rarely sets fruit, is an attractive ornamental often planted in public parks for its attractive foliage. **CZ6**

M. doumeri (*M. formosana*) Taiwan. Tree growing to 50 ft (15 m). Leaves pointed, finely serrated, glabrous, 3.5–6 × 1.6–2.5 in (9–15 × 4–6.5 cm), without lobes. Flowers 1–1.2 in (2.5–3 cm) diameter. Fruits about 2.2 in (5.5 cm) diameter, with a relatively large core. In its native Taiwan it is found at 3,300–6,600 ft (1,000–2,000 m) above sea level. The species is tolerant of warm, moist climatic conditions. *M. laoensis* (*M. laosensis*), from Laos and neighboring areas, is probably related to *M. doumeri*. **CZ8**

M. melliana China. Tree growing to 33 ft (10 m). Leaves pointed, finely serrated, hairy, 2–4 × 1–1.6 in (5–10 × 2.5–4 cm), without lobes. Flowers about 0.8 in (2 cm) diameter. Fruits about 1 in (2.5 cm) diameter, consisting almost exclusively of core. In its native China the species is found at 2,300–8,000 ft (700–2,400 m) above sea level.

Section *Gymnomeles*

Calyx usually deciduous.

Subsection *Baccatae*

Leaves entire; fruit soft-fleshed.

M. baccata Siberian Crab. N and E Asia, N China, E Siberia. Tree growing to 50 ft (15 m); very frost resistant. Leaves 1.2–3 in (3–8 cm) long, with finely serrated leaf margins. Flowers white, about 1.4 in (3.5 cm) across, with styles normally longer than the stamens. Fruits red or yellow, berry-like, roundish, about or just under 0.4 in (1 cm) diameter. Chromosome number is 2n = 34, 51 or 68. It is found up to 5,000 ft (1,500 m) above sea level, and it is used as a rootstock for fruiting apples and flowering crab apples and as an ornamental for its showy flowers and handsome foliage. *M. × robusta* is a hybrid between *M. baccata* and *M. prunifolia*. *Malus × robusta* 5 is a Canadian selection from this hybrid and is used as a very cold hardy rootstock for commercial apple cultivars. The ornamental hybrid *M. × hartwigii* (*M. halliand × baccata*) forms a small tree with semidouble pink-white flowers, 2 in (5 cm) diameter. **CZ2**

ssp *mandshurica* Manchurian Crab. C China, Korea, Japan, E Siberia. Tree similar to *M. baccata* but with styles scarcely as long as the stamens and fruit to about 0.5 in (1.2 cm) diameter. It grows at 300–800 ft (100–2,100 m) above sea level. It is cultivated for its fragrantly scented flowers and also serves as a hardy rootstock. **CZ2**

ssp *sachalinensis* Sakhalin Apple. **CZ2**

ssp *gracilis* Small pendent-branched tree. Leaves small, 0.6–1.2 in (1.5–3 cm) long, on long stalks. Fruits to 1.2 in (3 cm) diameter **CZ2**

ssp *nickovsky* In some cases growing to only 3.3 ft (1 m) in height in 100 years. **CZ2**

M. rocki (*M. himalaica*?) Himalayan Apple. W China, Himalaya. Closely related to *M. baccata*. Leaves 5 in (12 cm), pubescent on the lower surface. Fruits more or less round, about 0.4 in (1 cm) across, calyx very slow to dehisce. Chromosome number includes types with 2n = 68. The species grows at 8,000–12,500 ft (2,400–3,800 m) above sea level. **CZ5**

M. sikkimensis Sikkim Apple. The Himalaya. Closely related to *M. baccata*. Small tree with stout branching spurs at base of the branches. Flowers white or at most slightly pink. Fruits often slightly pear-shaped, dotted and about 0.6 in (1.5 cm) long. Reported to be a triploid with 51 chromosomes. **CZ6**

M. hupehensis (*M. theifera*) Hupei Apple. China, Japan, Assam (NE India). Medium-sized tree with stiff branches. Flowers fragrant, pink then white, 1.6 in (4 cm) diameter. Fruits yellow-green (red-tinted), about 0.4 in (1 cm) diameter. Chromosome number is 2n = 51 or 68. The species grows at 150–9,500 ft (50–2,900 m) above sea level. **CZ4**

M. halliand Hall's Apple. China, Japan. Small tree. Leaves dark, glossy, glabrous (except for midrib), sometimes slightly purple. Flowers red in the bud but paler when open, 1.2 in (3 cm) diameter. Fruits purple, 0.3 in (8 mm) diameter. Chromosome number is 2n = 34 or 51. 'Parkmanii' is an attractive ornamental selection with pendulous semidouble, rose-red to shell-pink flowers on crimson pedicels. **CZ5**

M. sargentii

M. sargentii

Malus × purpurea 'Eleyi' has exceptionally red fruit borne in clusters, each on a slender stalk. Their color and shape is such that they resemble the Morello Cherry.

Subsection *Sorbomalus*

Leaves dissected; clusters of red or yellow fruit.

Series *Sieboldianae*

Styles with long weak loose hairs at base; calyx and pedicels glabrous or slightly pubescent.

M. sieboldii (*M. toringo*) **Toringo Crab.** Korea. Shrub 6.5–33 ft (2–10 m) high, with profusely branching, spreading (or semi-weeping) habit. Leaves 3–5 lobed. Flowers pink or red in the bud, fading to white when open, 0.8 in (2 cm) diameter; often self-fertile. Fruits red (or sometimes yellow-brown) and about 0.2–0.3 in (6–8 mm) diameter. Chromosome number is 2n = 34, 68 or 85. The species is tolerant of salt. The dwarf types are cultivated in Japan as ornamentals; they are also of some value as a dwarfing rootstock. *M. × sublobata* (*M. prunifolia × sieboldii*) is a small pyramidal tree with slightly lobed leaves, pink flowers, and yellow fruit. *M. × zumi* (*M. baccata* var *mandshurica × sieboldii*) —the Zumi Crab—is similar to *M. sieboldii* but has larger flowers (1.2 in/3 cm) and bright red fruit (0.4 in/1.2 cm). *M. × zumi* var *calocarpa* is a variant with a more spreading habit, attractive small leaves and flowers, and fruit that stays on the tree through the winter. *M. × atrosanguinea* (*M. halliand × sieboldii*)—the Carmine Crab—is an attractive hybrid forming a small tree with green, glossy, nearly glabrous leaves and a profusion of flowers which are crimson in the bud and rose-colored when open. It much resembles *M. floribunda* and produces red-tinted yellow fruit. A selection from both *M. floribunda* and *M. atrosanguinea* has been used in breeding for resistance to Apple Scab (*Venturia inaequalis*) in commercial apples. **CZ5**

M. sargentii **Sargent's Apple.** Japan. Shrub growing to 6 ft (2 m), producing a mass of white flowers and red cherry-like fruit. Chromosome number is 2n = 34, 51 or 68. **CZ4**

M. floribunda **Japanese or Showy Crab.** Japan. A highly attractive tree flowering abundantly. Flowers deep carmine-red in the bud, fading to pale blush and eventually to white when open, 1.2 in (3 cm) diameter. Fruits red (or sometimes yellow), round, 0.3 in (8 mm) diameter. Chromosome number is 2n = 34. The hybrid *M. × arnoldiana* (*M. baccata × floribunda*) is a small floriferous tree produced in the Arnold Arboretum in Boston in 1883. It has red buds, white flowers, and red-tinted yellow fruit 0.4 in (1 cm) diameter). Another hybrid, *M. × schiedeckeri* (*M. floribunda × prunifolia*) is a slow-growing tree producing a profusion of semidouble fragrant pale pink flowers, 1.4 in (3.5 cm) diameter, and yellow fruit, 0.6 in (1.5 cm) diameter. The trees do not perform well on thin alkaline soils. The species *M. brevipes* (2n = 34) is related to *M. floribunda* but has a more compact habit. **CZ4**

Series *Florentinae*

Styles with long, weak, loose hairs at the base; calyx and pedicels hairy; leaves distinctly lobed.

M. florentina (*M. crataegifolia*) Italy. Small tree with hawthorn-like foliage; undersurface of the leaves hairy; flowers white, 1.2 in (3 cm) diameter; fruits 0.5 in (1.2 cm) long. In the fall the orange and scarlet leaves make a fine ornamental display. **CZ6**

Series *Kansuenses*

Styles glabrous.

M. toringoides China. Very attractive small tree with flowing wide-spreading branches. Flowers creamy-white, 1 in (2.5 cm) diameter, occurring in subsessile umbels. Fruits red and yellow, round or pear-shaped, 0.6 in (1.2 cm) long. Chromosome number is 2n = 51 or 68. *M. transitoria* (NW China) is related to *M. toringoides* but is more elegant in general appearance and with much more deeply lobed leaves and smaller, rounder yellow fruit. Both species have attractive fall leaf coloration. **CZ5**

M. kansuensis NW China. Small tree. Leaves with hairs on the veins of the lower surface. Flowers creamy-white, 0.6 in (1.5 cm) diameter, each having a hairy calyx. Fruits red or yellow, 0.4 in (1 cm) long. The related species, *M. honanensis* (NE China), has dotted roundish fruits, 0.3 in (8 mm) diameter. **CZ5**

M. komarovii China. Small tree growing to 10 ft (3 m). Leaves lobed as in *M. kansuensis* and 1.6–3.2 × 1.2–2.8 in (4–8 × 3–7 cm). Flowers 1.4 in (3.5 cm) diameter. Fruits 0.3–0.4 in (8–10 mm) diameter. In its native China the species is found at altitudes of 3,600–4,300 ft (1,100–1,300 m).

M. fusca (*M. diversifolia, M. rivularis*) **Oregon Crab.** U.S. (mainly Washington and Oregon but also California to Alaska). Large shrub or small tree with vigorous dense growth, often producing an almost impenetrable thicket. Flowers white or pink, 0.8–2 in (2–5 cm) diameter. Fruits red or yellow, 0.6 in (1.5 cm) long. **CZ6**

Pyrus
Pears

Pears are the popular edible fruits produced by the twenty-five species of the genus *Pyrus*. They are deciduous shrubs or trees, sometimes with spines, and the leaves are simple and alternate. The flowers are bisexual, occurring in simple umbel-like corymbs. They have five sepals and petals, twenty to thirty stamens with typically red to purplish anthers, and two to five styles, free to the base; the ovary is inferior, consisting of two to five cells united together and with the receptacular calyx-tube (hypanthium). The "fruit" is in fact a pome (false fruit), mostly pyriform (pear-shaped), the enlarged receptacular tissue forming the edible flesh with its numerous grit or stone cells and surrounding the papery to cartilaginous ovary wall, which, with its seeds, comprises the true fruit—the core.

Pears have evolved over a period of more than 2,000 years from a primary center in central Asia with secondary centers arising in both China and the Caucasus. In China and Japan *P. pyrifolia* (*P. serotina*), a species with hard, crisp fruit, formed the population from which that region's cultivated varieties were selected, these being known by the various names of Oriental, Chinese, Sand, or Japanese pears. They are distinctly gritty (from stone cells), lack flavor, and are mostly used for culinary purposes. Oriental pears have not spread beyond China and Japan to any significant extent except as rootstocks or as parents in breeding programs.

The European or Common Pear (*P. communis*) is an aggregate species with a center of origin in Asia Minor and complex history of hybrid origin, believed to involve ancestral wild species such as *P. pyraster*, *P. syriaca*, *P. salvifolia*, *P. nivalis*, *P. austriaca*, *P. cordata*, and possibly others. From this "mixture" the cultivated or orchard pears are derived. Over a thousand different kinds of cultivated pears are known. These have frequently escaped back to wild conditions and

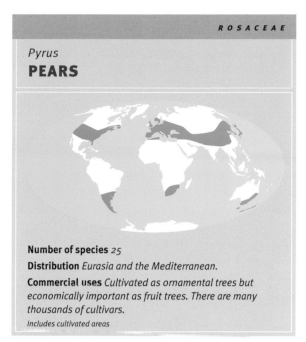

ROSACEAE

Pyrus
PEARS

Number of species 25
Distribution *Eurasia and the Mediterranean.*
Commercial uses *Cultivated as ornamental trees but economically important as fruit trees. There are many thousands of cultivars.*
Includes cultivated areas

P. bretschneideri

P. betulaefolia

P. communis

The 'Bartlett' or 'Williams' Bon Chrétien' Pear is cultivated widely on a commercial basis .

"back-crossed" with one or other of the supposed ancestors. It is thus impossible to distinguish with certainty how "wild" the present descendants of the supposed ancestors are. These are sometimes treated as subspecies of *P. communis*, but recent treatments maintain their specific rank. Thus *P. communis* may be taken as a species that has "bred itself back" into natural habitats. *Pyrus pyraster* is little more than a form with a greater frequency of spines, smaller flowers and fruits which lack a sweet taste. Some authorities regard *P. pyraster* as the correct name for the nearest thing to a wild pear. Unlike some of the ancestral species, the leaves of the Common and Wild Pear are most always shallowly crenate.

Pears have been cultivated since ancient times. Homer spoke of their cultivation in 1000 B.C.E. and Theophrastus described grafting of selected varieties in 300 B.C.E. Following the fall of the Roman Empire, little or no progress was made in the cultivation of pears until interest revived in France in the early seventeenth century. Pear breeding was initiated in 1730 by the Abbé Nicolas Hardenpont in Belgium. He is credited with being the first person to select varieties with the soft melting flesh that is a feature of most modern commercially produced pears. Jean-Baptiste Van Mons (1765–1842), who continued Hardenpont's breeding work, at one time had 80,000 seedlings under test in his nursery and released several dozen new varieties during his lifetime.

In Europe, pears were grown mostly in gardens and propagated by grafting, but when they were first taken to North America most propagation was undertaken by seed. Only during the nineteenth century, when the need to produce uniform commercial (rather than garden) products developed, did it become the general practise in North America to select varieties for propagation by grafting. The selections chosen were often of European origin. Historically, European pear breeders have been given credit for adding quality to the fruit, while North American breeders have added cold hardiness and resistance to disease.

The Oriental Pear (*P. pyrifolia*) crossed with the European or Common Pear (*P. communis*) gave rise to important commercial varieties, such as 'Le Conte,' 'Kieffer,' and 'Garber.' These are more resistant to fireblight (caused by the bacteria *Erwinia amylovora*) than the standard European pears but the fruit is of poorer quality, which makes them more suitable for canning than for fresh consumption. Resistance to fireblight has also been obtained from Chinese varieties such as 'Ba Li Hsiang' (*P. ussuriensis*).

In North America, pears have usually been grafted on pear seedlings obtained from commercial varieties such as 'Winter Nelis,' 'Bartlett' (known in Europe as 'Williams' Bon Chrétien'), and 'Beurre Rose.' On such rootstocks large trees are produced, which, though relatively slow to come into fruit production, are able to withstand cold winter conditions. By contrast, in Europe the Quince (*Cydonia oblonga*), including vegetatively propagated selections such as 'Quince A,' are used as rootstocks because of their ability to dwarf and induce trees to fruit early in their life. When the quince/pear graft union is incompatible, as is the case with such varieties as 'Williams' Bon Chrétien,' it is necessary to insert a piece of a compatible pear variety such as 'Beurre Hardy' or 'Old Home' between the quince rootstock and the incompatible scion variety.

The current world production of pears is over 17 million tons per year. Major producers are Italy, China, Germany, the United States, France and Japan.

A few pear species are grown as ornamentals, the most notable being three closely related species, all characterized by abundant pure white flowers, whitish leaves with entire margins and a tapering leaf base: *P. salicifolia* 'Pendula' which, with its elegant weeping branches and silvery-gray foliage, is probably the best form, *P. nivalis* and *P. elaeagrifolia*. **CZ4–9**

The Main Species of *Pyrus*

Section *Pyrus*

Fruit typically with persistent calyx (but finally deciduous in *P. cordata*). Species native to Europe, N. Africa through to C Asia, Manchuria, and Japan.

P. communis **Common or European Pear.** Europe. W Asia; doubtfully native in Britain. Tree to 50(66) ft (15(20) m). Shoots with variable number of spines. Leaves more or less ovate, 0.8–3 × 0.4–0.8 in (2–8 × 1–2 cm), margin finely crenate, rarely smooth. Flowers 1.2 in (3 cm) across. Fruits roundish to pyriform (pear-shaped), 2.4–6.2 in (6–16 cm) long, finally soft-fleshed, and sweet-tasting. An important contributor to cultivated pears, these being sometimes referred to as var *culta*. **CZ4**

P. pyraster **Wild Pear.** W Asia, C Europe. Very similar to previous species, but more constantly thorny with smaller flowers.

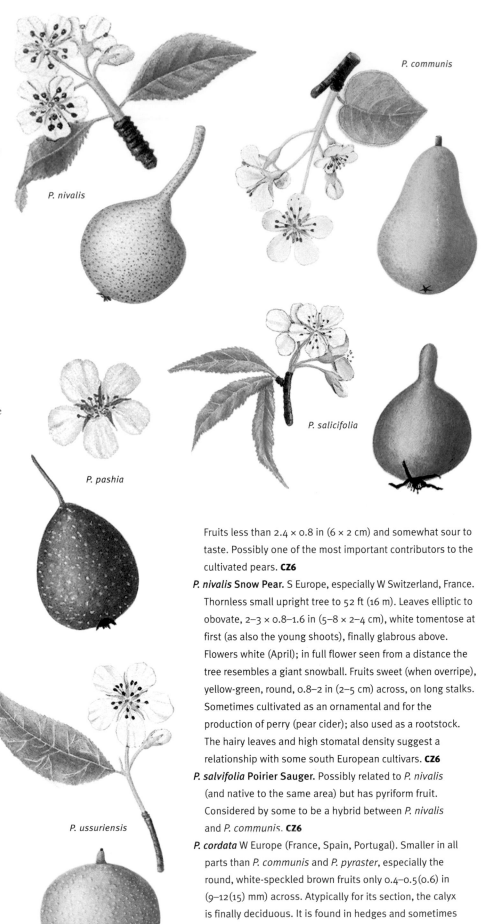

P. communis

P. nivalis

P. salicifolia

P. pashia

P. ussuriensis

Fruits less than 2.4 × 0.8 in (6 × 2 cm) and somewhat sour to taste. Possibly one of the most important contributors to the cultivated pears. **CZ6**

P. nivalis **Snow Pear.** S Europe, especially W Switzerland, France. Thornless small upright tree to 52 ft (16 m). Leaves elliptic to obovate, 2–3 × 0.8–1.6 in (5–8 × 2–4 cm), white tomentose at first (as also the young shoots), finally glabrous above. Flowers white (April); in full flower seen from a distance the tree resembles a giant snowball. Fruits sweet (when overripe), yellow-green, round, 0.8–2 in (2–5 cm) across, on long stalks. Sometimes cultivated as an ornamental and for the production of perry (pear cider); also used as a rootstock. The hairy leaves and high stomatal density suggest a relationship with some south European cultivars. **CZ6**

P. salvifolia **Poirier Sauger.** Possibly related to *P. nivalis* (and native to the same area) but has pyriform fruit. Considered by some to be a hybrid between *P. nivalis* and *P. communis*. **CZ6**

P. cordata W Europe (France, Spain, Portugal). Smaller in all parts than *P. communis* and *P. pyraster*, especially the round, white-speckled brown fruits only 0.4–0.5(0.6) in (9–12(15) mm) across. Atypically for its section, the calyx is finally deciduous. It is found in hedges and sometimes cultivated for its wood.

P. longipes Algeria. Shrub or small tree with fine-toothed leaves. It is closely related to *P. communis* but has a partly deciduous calyx. Fruits brown and dotted, round and about

P. betulifolia

P. bretschneideri

0.6 in (1.5 cm) diameter. Probably involved with *P. communis* in the origin of some cultivars. *Pyrus boissieriana* is a closely related Iranian species. **CZ8**

P. syriaca Armenia through W Asia to Cyprus. Forms a small thorny tree with glossy green leaves. The species is closely related to *P. communis* and was probably involved in the origin of some cultivars where *P. communis* is the main contributory species. **CZ7**

P. bulunsae W Asia. Long-stalked turbinate (top-shaped) fruit borne on a long stalk. Related to *P. communis*. **CZ6**

P. caucasica Caucasus (forest zone). Vigorous tree that spreads rapidly in open areas. The lowland type is vigorous, frost-, and drought-resistant; the highland type is less vigorous and susceptible to frosts and drought. The species was involved in the origin of some E European cultivars.

P. turcomanica Related to *P. communis* and *P. caucasica*. Well characterized by the snow-white pubescence of all young parts and sepal lobes adpressed to the fruit.

P. korshinskyi W T'ien Shan (W China), the Pamir region of Tadjikistan. Fruits roundish, 0.8 in (2 cm) diameter, with a characteristic stout stalk. Another species that is related to *P. communis*. **CZ6**

P. armeniacaefolia China. This species was first reported in 1963 and is similar to *P. communis* in some respects but with apricot-like leaves.

P. salicifolia **Willow-leafed Pear.** W Asia, SE Europe. Young leaves covered with silvery hairs but becoming glabrous and grayish-green on the upper surface later. Fruits pyriform, 1 in (2.5 cm) long, with a short stalk. The species is involved in the origin of some cultivars. It makes an attractive ornamental and is a graft-compatible drought-resistant rootstock. **CZ4**

'Pendula' is a graceful tree to 26 ft (8 m) with slender pendulous branches; leaves narrow-lanceolate, 1.2–3.5 × 0.28–0.8 in (3–9 × 0.7–2 cm), appearing whitish when young from a dense matting of silvery hairs, finally shining green above.

P. × canescens (*P. nivalis* × *salicifolia*) is a fine small, silver-leafed hybrid.

P. glabra is a related subglobose-fruited species from Iran.

P. amygdaliformis W Asia, S Europe. Shrub or small tree, sometimes thorny. Leaves narrow, silvery, hairy when young but becoming sage-green and less hairy. Fruits yellow-brown, globose, 1.2 in (3 cm) diameter, borne on stout 1.2 in (3 cm) long stalks. The hairs and high stomatal density of the leaves suggest an involvement in the origin of some S European cultivars. The *P. × michauxii* (*P. amygdaliformis* × *nivalis*) hybrid forms a small tree with gray to glossy green leaves. **CZ6**

P. elaeagnifolia Asia Minor. Small, usually thorny tree with attractive grayish-white hairy leaves. Fruits are green, short-stalked, rounded or turbinate (top-shaped), about 1 in (2.5 cm) in diameter. Very closely related to *P. nivalis*. **CZ5**

P. regelii Bukhara region of Uzbekistan and Pamir region of Tadjikistan, W T'ien Shan (W China). Shrub or small tree, extremely resistant to drought. Leaves very variable, more or less unlobed and coarsely serrate or with 3–7 narrow lobes almost to the midrib. Fruits nearly pyriform, 1 in (2.5 cm) long. **CZ6**

P. takhtadzhiani W Asia. Tree with same growth habit as Common Pear cultivars but now found only in the wild, though formerly cultivated.

P. ussuriensis **Ussurian Pear.** Manchuria, especially the valley of the Ussuri River. Small to medium-sized tree that is very winter-hardy and well adapted to cold dry areas. Leaves glabrous, turning crimson-bronze in the fall. Flowers 1.4 in (3.5 cm) diameter, appearing very early in the spring. Fruits green-yellow, short-stalked, roundish, 1.6 in (4 cm) diameter. This species was possibly involved with *P. communis* in the origin of some ancient cultivars. It often lacks resistance to Pear Scab (*Venturia piri*) but includes types resistant to Fireblight (*Erwinia amylovora*). It is used as a rootstock (though inducing susceptibility to pear decline disease), as an ornamental, and widely as a parent in scion variety breeding programs.

Pyrus ussuriensis var *ovoidea* (N China, Korea) has ovoid-round fruits. The long-stalked species, *P. lindleyi*, is closely related to *P. ussuriensis*. **CZ4**

P. hopeiensis Hopeh Province (NE China). The species was first reported in 1963 and is probably related to *P. ussuriensis* but has fewer seeds, smaller fruit, very short stamens, and long styles.

P. pseudopashia China. First reported in 1963 and possibly related to *P. xerophila*.

P. xerophila China. First reported in 1963. Leaves small, pointed, with only a few small serrations; fruits round, 0.6 in (1.5 cm) diameter, with a very large core; stamens extending well beyond the ends of the styles. It is adapted to a hot dry climate.

BELOW Ripening pears hang from the bough of the productive 'Beurre Hardy' cultivar which fruits in late fall.

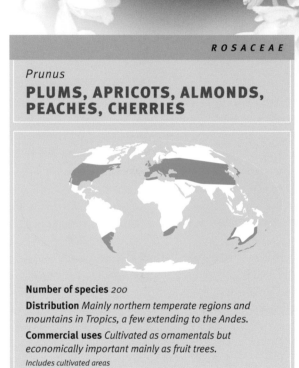

Section *Pashia*

The calyx is typically deciduous (but see *P. cordata* in section *Pyrus*). The species are native to China and the Himalaya.

P. pyrifolia (*P. serotina*) **Chinese, Japanese, Oriental, or Sand Pear.** Widely cultivated in China and Japan and named "Sand" for the stone cells, that give the fruit a firm crisp texture. The collective name for the numerous cultivated pears is var *culta*. The roundish brown fruit travels and stores well. It has been hybridized with the Common Pear to improve the storage and resistance to Fireblight (*Erwinia amylovora*) of Western cultivars. Among the hybrids of *Pyrus* × *lecontei* (*P. communis* × *pyrifolia*) are 'Kieffer' and 'Le Conte.' The Japanese selection 'Twentieth Century' is one of the best cultivars. As a rootstock, however, *P. pyrifolia* induces susceptibility to pear decline disease. *Pyrus bretschneideri* (*P. betulaefolia* × *pyrifolia*), from N China, is slightly less hardy than the extremely winter-hardy *P. ussuriensis*, but it bears medium-sized fruit of better flavor and texture than other oriental pears. **CZ6**

P. betulifolia N and C China. Small, slender, and graceful tree. Fruits 0.4 in (1 cm) diameter, borne in long-stalked cherry-like clusters. Some selections are resistant to Pear Scab (*Venturia piri*). The species is used as a rootstock for which it has the advantage of inducing resistance to pear decline disease. **CZ5**

P. phaeocarpa N China. The brown pyriform fruit rapidly becomes soft after harvest. **CZ5**

P. calleryana China, Japan, Korea. Medium-sized tree. Leaves glabrous, glossy green. Flowers with as many as 20 stamens but normally only 2 styles. Fruits brown, dotted, about 0.4 in (1 cm) diameter. The species is used as a rootstock, which induces resistance to pear decline disease. 'Bradford' is a nonthorny selection producing dense blooms in early spring and attractive colored leaves in the fall. **CZ5**

P. pashia W China, the Himalaya. Can grow to be a fairly large spiny tree, though some selections are small. Leaves hairy when young but becoming nearly glabrous when older; vigorous shoots sometimes have 3 lobed leaves. Flowers with up to 30 stamens (with red anthers) and 3–5 styles. Fruits brown, round, about 1 in (2.5 cm) diameter. The species is used as a rootstock and is sometimes cultivated for its fruit. **CZ5**

P. serrulata China. Fruits brown (with pale dots), rounded, with a calyx that is sometimes more or less persistent. **CZ6**

P. sinkiangensis Sinkiang region (W China). The species was first reported in 1963 and is possibly closely related to *P. serrulata*.

ROSACEAE

Prunus

PLUMS, APRICOTS, ALMONDS, PEACHES, CHERRIES

Number of species *200*

Distribution *Mainly northern temperate regions and mountains in Tropics, a few extending to the Andes.*

Commercial uses *Cultivated as ornamentals but economically important mainly as fruit trees.*

Includes cultivated areas

Prunus

Plums, Apricots, Almonds, Peaches, Cherries

The commercially important stone fruit crops, together with the almond, ornamental cherries, and cherry laurel, all belong to the genus *Prunus*. They are mostly deciduous shrubs or trees with alternate leaves that are typically serrate, with stipules. The flowers are bisexual, solitary, fascicled or in racemes with five sepals and petals, the latter mostly white, sometimes pink to red. There are usually more than fifteen stamens situated on the edge of a calyx-tube (hypanthium), which surrounds the single two-ovuled ovary with a single style. The fruit is a drupe that typically matures one seed.

There are almost countless cultivars, varieties, and hybrids, some selected for their ornamental value of spring blossoms, fall colors, edible fruits, and sometimes the edible seed (kernel).

The flowers of *Prunus subhirtella* 'Pendula Rubra,' a cultivar from Japan, are a deep pink and borne in clusters. The petals are notched at the end.

Prunus yedoensis

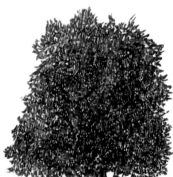

Prunus laurocerasus

Prunus cerasifera

Prunus *Orchard Fruits*

The genus is divided into five subgenera (which some treat as separate genera), which fall into two broad groups. The first, in which the fruit typically has a longitudinal furrow (sulcate) and the skin has a bloom, comprises the subgenera *Prunus* = *Prunophora* (plums), *Armeniaca* (apricots), *Persica* (peaches), and *Amygdalus* (almonds). The second group, in which the fruit is sometimes furrowed but to less than half-way, and the skin has no bloom, comprises subgenera *Cerasus* (cherries), *Padus* (bird cherries), and *Laurocerasus* (cherry laurels).

Plums are remarkable among orchard fruits for their very great diversity of tree vigor, habit, and fruit shape. There is good evidence, genetic included, that plums, bullaces, damsons, and greengages should be referred to the binomial *Prunus domestica* agg as subspecies, and that this taxon has resulted from a cross between *P. spinosa* (Sloe, Blackthorn) and *P. cerasifera* (Cherry Plum, Myrobalan). The latter, known only in cultivation, has arisen from the very closely related *P. divaricata*, a genuinely wild species from western Asia that forms natural but sterile hybrids with *P. spinosa*. Plums have been cultivated in the Old World for at least two thousand years.

Prunus × domestica, and cultivars, is the true plum, which can be eaten fresh, cooked, or preserved. Many cultivars are dried and sold as prunes, often consumed for their mild purgative action. In cooler areas cultivars tend to bear smaller fruits more suited to canning and preserves. In Croatia plum brandy (slivovitz) is produced by distilling fermented juices of such plums. World production of plums is about 9 million metric tons a year, mainly from Europe and North America.

The **Bullace** and **Damson** (ssp *insititia*) are found wild in many parts of Europe, naturalized in Britain, and Asia (the name derives from Damascus). The purplish astringent fruits are more or less globose in the Bullace, oval in the Damson. A group of clones of this subspecies known as St. Julien is used extensively as rootstocks for the European plums.

The **Greengage** (spp *italica*) originated from the cultivar 'Reine Claude,' a cross between ssp *domestica* and *insititia*. It is widely cultivated for the delicate and sweet flavor of its yellowish-green fruits.

The **Sloe** or **Blackthorn** (*P. spinosa*) is a dense suckering shrub with spiny branches and small white flowers, usually single or in pairs, appearing in early spring before the leaves. The blue-black, globose fruits, 0.4 in (1 cm) across, are very astringent but are used for flavoring, for example to make the liqueur sloe gin. The plant is native and widespread throughout Europe, extending to parts of northern Asia.

The **Japanese Plum** (*P. salicina*) is grown in frostfree areas, (parts of the United States, Italy, and South Africa). Extensively cultivated in Japan, it probably originated in China. Cultivars of this species flower very early—before European types. Most cultivars have large (2.8 in/7 cm) highly colored fruits, but of an inferior quality. Their lower perishability, however, permits export of fresh fruit over long distances.

The **Cherry Plum** or **Myrobalan** (*P. cerasifera*) is known only in cultivation, but is undoubtedly derived from the very closely related *P. divaricata*, which is genuinely wild from the Balkans to central Asia. Only occasionally grown for its cherry-like fruits, it is perhaps more appreciated for its very early spring flowering. The types known as the Myrobalans are often used as rootstocks for plums where trees of high vigor and tolerance to heavy soils are required. Cultivar 'Pissardii' ('Atropurpurea') is commonly planted for its reddish-purple leaves which appear before the pinkish flowers in early spring.

Other ornamentals include *P. × blireana* (*P. cerasifera* 'Pissardi' × *P. mume*), with double rose-pink flowers, and *P. × cistena*, another hybrid involving *P. cerasifera* 'Pissardi' × *P. pumila* or, possibly, *P. besseyi*: it has crimson to bronzy-red leaves and white flowers appearing in spring before the leaves.

The **Apricot** (*P. armeniaca*) is believed to have originated in western China and to have been brought to Italy about 100 B.C.E., reaching England in the thirteenth century and America by 1720. The fruit is smaller than a peach, orange-yellow when ripe, and has drier flesh. Its food value ranks higher than most common fruits, particularly as a source of vitamin A, as well as proteins and carbohydrates. Iran is the biggest producer, others being the United States, Hungary, Turkey, Spain, and France. The annual world production is about 2.7 million tons. About half the commercial crop is dried, with smaller quantities canned or sold fresh. A well-drained soil is required and freedom from spring frost. Too-warm winters encourage flower bud fall, and a more or less semi-arid locality is important in the ripening season as maturing fruits tend to split during heavy rain.

The main all-purpose cultivar is 'Royal.' Propagation is by budding onto apricot and peach seedling stocks. Nearly all cultivars are self-fertile. Fruits are produced on year-old shoots and short lived spurs. Trees usually fruit after the third year and may be productive for up to twenty years.

Sweet Almonds (*P. dulcis* = *P. amygdalus* var *dulcis*) include those grown for their flowers as well as those cultivated for their sweet almonds, which are the most widely consumed of all edible nuts. Almonds are grown in Italy (the main exporter), Spain, north and South Africa, and California. Annual world production is about 1.8 million tons. **Bitter Almonds** (var *amara*) contain potentially dangerous amounts of prussic acid if consumed in quantity. Medicinal *Oleum amygdalae* (almond oil) is expressed from both types of almond, but more especially the latter. It is also used for toilet preparations and as a food flavoring.

The **Peach** (*P. persica*), closely related to the almond, is prized for its delicious fleshy (furry) fruit. It originated in China under conditions that gave selective advantage to self-pollination. Consequently, peaches can normally be planted without pollinators. There are many varieties, including so-called "flowering" ones. Var *nectarina* is the **Nectarine**, which has a smooth skin. Annual total world production of peaches and nectarines is over 13 million tons.

P. avium

The fleshy, velvety fruit of the peach cultivar 'August Lady' ripening on the tree. Their red-infused color develops on the side exposed to the sun.

In the nineteenth century increased interest in high-quality fruit for commercial distribution switched attention from seed to vegetative propagation to ensure a uniform fruit. The best seedlings were selected and grafted following procedures long used for peaches grown in walled English gardens. Today most rootstocks are grown from seed—either wild types or selected commercial varieties. Other *Prunus* species may also be used, such as *P. tomentosa* (dwarfing). In France peach × almond (*P. dulcis*) hybrids have done well as rootstocks for peaches on soils subject to lime-induced iron deficiency. Varieties underwent dramatic changes, owing much to the efforts of nineteenth-century American fruit breeders and to new genetic material from China. The Chinese Cling, brought to America from China via England in 1850, was the parent of well-known varieties such as 'Elberta' and 'J.H. Hale' and involved in the ancestry of many modern varieties. Peaches are of two main types—"freestones" (mostly consumed fresh) and "clingstones" (mainly for canning). Since peaches can be stored for only a few weeks, a very high proportion is processed, either canned or as preserves.

Extending the area of fruit production is constrained by lack of winter hardiness (in colder regions) and chilling limitations; varieties need 500–1,000 hours and winter temperatures below 45°F (7°C) to promote normal flowering and fruit setting.

Cherries belong to the subgenus *Cerasus*. The **Sweet Cherry, Gean,** or **Mazzard** (*P. avium*) is an ancestor of the commercial fruiting cherries, especially the black ones. Its center of origin is now believed to be northwest and central Europe. Var *duracina* is the firm-fleshed Bigarrean Cherry; var *Juliana*, the Heart Cherry, has soft flesh. **Sour Cherries** are derived from *P. cerasus*, which is not known as a genuinely wild plant but is naturalized in Europe, including Britain. Cultivars of the Morello Cherry, var *austera*, are used in cooking and preserves.

Sweet cherries, excepting var 'Stella,' are self-incompatible, therefore two compatible varieties must be grown together to produce fruit crops. Most sour cherries, however, are self-compatible and fruit well without special pollinators. Annual world production of both types is about 1.7 million tons.

Ornamentals

The deciduous **Dwarf** or **Ground Cherry** (*P. fruticosa*) is a low spreading shrub about 3 ft (1 m) tall. Native to Europe, it extends north to eastern Siberia and has been cultivated in England for over 300 years. Its fruits are cherry flavored, but are too astringent to be palatable. Hybrids between it and *P. cerasus*, known as *P.* × *eminens* (or *P. reflexa*) occur naturally and may be found in gardens. Hybrids between *P. avium* and *P. cerasus*, known as *P.* × *gondouinii*, are cultivated in Europe as "Duke" cherries.

The so-called **Flowering Cherries** are the most outstanding and widely cultivated of all *Prunus* ornamentals. There are hundreds of cultivars and selections in cultivation, ranging from *P.* 'Plena,' the finest of the geans (*P. avium*), to the

Japanese flowering cherries such as *P.* 'Kanzan' with huge clusters of double purple-pink flowers. Japanese cherries derive mostly from the white-flowered Oshima Cherry (*P. speciosa* or *P. lannesiana* forma *albida* held by some to be the same and has priority) or from the very closely related *P. serrulata*. Whatever the species, no confusion arises if the generic name is followed immediately by the cultivar name in single inverted commas, for example, *Prunus* 'Kanzan.' (In English texts they are commonly treated under the binomial *P. serrulata*, principally to maintain a long-standing practise.)

Bird Cherries and **Cherry Laurels** belong to subgenera *Padus* and *Laurocerasus* respectively. Both have flowers in racemes of ten or more flowers, each up to 0.4–0.6 in (1–1.5 cm) across. They are sometimes treated as one subgenus (*Laurocerasus*), but bird cherries are typically deciduous and cherry laurels always evergreen. The Cherry Laurel (*Prunus laurocerasus*) is a vigorous shrub with leathery obovate-lanceolate leaves 6 in (15 cm) long, white flowers, and small black fruits. It is widely planted for hedging and screening and tolerant of shade.

The Main Species of *Prunus*

Subgenus *Prunus* (*Prunophora*)

Fruit with longitudinal groove (sulcate), typically hairless and with bloom. Often spring-flowering before the leaves. No terminal bud, axillary buds solitary.

Section *Prunus*

Typically 1–2-stalked flowers per cluster. Leaves in bud convolute. Ovary and fruit glabrous.

P. spinosa Blackthorn, Sloe. W Asia, Europe, N. Africa. Very thorny shrub or small tree to about 13 ft (4 m). Flowers solitary before the leaves. Fruit blue-black with distinctive bloom, globose, 0.4–0.6 in (1–1.5 cm), very astringent. Generally accepted as involved with *P. cerasifera* in the ancestry of *P. domestica*. **CZ4**

P. × domestica agg (*P. spinosa* × *P. cerasifera*) Plums, Bullaces, Damsons, Greengages. Natural hybrids of this parentage occur in the Caucasus. The cultivated plants grown for their fruits and widely naturalized. **CZ5**
  ssp **domestica** European or Garden Plum. W Asia, Europe. Tree 33–40 ft (10–12 m), spineless. Flowers in pairs, greenish-white, 0.8 in (2 cm) across. Fruit 1.6–3 in (4–7.5 cm) long, blue-black, purple, red. Widely cultivated in temperate zones. **CZ5**
  ssp **insititia** Bullace, Damson, St. Julien. W Asia, Europe. Shrub or tree to 20 ft (6 m), often with thorns. Flowers white, about 1 in (2.5 cm) across. Fruit 1 in (2–5 cm) long, blue-black; round and sweet in Bullace, oval and astringent in Damson. **CZ5**
  ssp **italica** (ssp **domestica** × ssp **insititia**) Greengage ('Reine Claude'). ?Armenia. Introduced into England by the Gage family between 1494 and 1547. Fruit more or less globose, greenish, sweet taste very characteristic. **CZ5**

P. × *domestica*
ssp *domestica*

P. × *domestica*
ssp *domestica*

P. × *domestica*
ssp *insititia*

P. spinosa

P. spinosa

P. cerasifera

P. cerasifera

P. armeniaca

P. amygdalus

P. amygdalus

P. persica

P. cerasifera Myrobalan, Cherry Plum. W Asia. Shrub or tree 26–33 ft (8–10 m), often spiny. Flowers solitary, about 1 in (2.5 cm) across, appearing with or a little before the leaves, mostly white. Fruit globose, cherry-like, 0.8–1.2 in (2–3 cm) across, red. Only known in cultivation, more as an ornamental, only to limited extent for its fruit, but important as rootstock for other plum species. **CZ4**

'Pissardii' has reddish, purple-tinged leaves with pinkish flowers, and is much more common as an ornamental. **CZ4**

P. cerasifera var *divaricata* Caucasus east to Asia. The wild form of the species differing virtually only by smaller fruits, which are yellow. **CZ4**

P. × *syriaca* (*P. cerasifera* × *P. domestica*) Mirabelle Plum This species, with its subglobose yellow fruits, is known in a semi-wild state in Europe. **CZ5**

P. salicina Salicine, Japanese Plum. China. Tree to about 40 ft (12 m). Flowers white, about 0.8 in (2 cm) across, typically in clusters of 3, appearing well before the leaves. Fruit sweet, more or less globose, 2–2.8 in (5–7 cm) long, depressed at stalk end, varying (greenish) yellow, orange, red. Long cultivated in Japan and elsewhere in nineteenth century, especially U.S., but fruit inferior in quality to most other cultivated plums. Probably only seen in Europe as an ornamental. **CZ6**

Section *Prunocerasus*

2–5 flowers per cluster. Leaves mostly conduplicate in bud, rarely convolute. Ovary and fruit glabrous. Stone mostly smooth.

P. americana American Red Plum. N. America. Tree to 33 ft (10 m). Flowers white, about 1.2 in (3 cm) across. Fruit virtually round, about 1 in (2.5 cm) across, usually finally red, rarely yellowish. Hybrids with *P. salicina* have been made in America to produce new varieties. **CZ3**

Section *Armeniaca*

Shrubs or trees, thornless. Flowers appearing before leaves, usually sessile or subsessile. Leaves convolute in bud. Ovary and fruit pubescent.

P. mandshurica Manchurian Apricot. Korea and Manchuria. Tree to 16 ft (5 m) with pendulous, somewhat spreading branches. Flowers pink, solitary, about 1.2 in (3 cm) across. Fruit nearly round, 1 in (2.5 cm), yellow. Selections widely cultivated as ornamentals. **CZ6**

Subgenus *Amygdalus*

Fruit with external groove, more or less pubescent. Terminal bud present; axillary buds 3; leaves conduplicate in bud. Flowers typically sessile, rarely stalked, in clusters of 1–2, appearing before leaves.

Section *Amygdalus*

Calyx-tube cup shaped and about as long as its sepal lobes.

P. dulcis Almond. W Asia. Tree to 25 ft (8 m). Flowers subsessile, pale pink, 1.2–2 in (3–5 cm) across, usually solitary. Fruit velvety, compressed roundish to 2.5 in (6 cm) long; stone smooth but with pits. Widely cultivated in California and S Europe, and as an ornamental for its early spring flowering. **CZ4**

var *dulcis* Sweet Almond of commerce. In Britain planted only as an ornamental.

var *amara* Bitter Almond. Very bitter to taste with potentially lethal amounts of prussic acid.

Section *Chamaeamygdalus*

Calyx-tube (hypanthium) much longer than its sepal lobes.

P. tenella Dwarf Russian Almond. SE Europe to W Asia and E Siberia. Bushy shrub to about 6 ft (2 m). Flowers in clusters of 1–3, a fine rose-red, 0.4–0.8 in (1–2 cm) across. Fruit like a small almond, velvety, 1 in (2.5 cm) long, ovoid. Used in breeding and several ornamental types have been selected. **CZ2**

Subgenus *Armeniaca*

P. armeniaca Apricot. W Asia. Tree to 33 ft (10 m). Bark reddish. Flowers white or pink, mostly solitary, 1 in (2.5 cm) across. Fruit round, 1.6–3.2 in (4–8 cm), short, velvety, yellow with red blush, stone smooth but furrowed along one margin. Widely cultivated in warmer parts of temperate zones of both hemispheres. **CZ5**

P. brigantina Briançon Apricot. SE France. Shrub or tree to 20 ft (6 m). Flowers white in clusters of 2–5. Fruit clear yellow, almost round, about 1 in (2.5 cm), quite smooth and glabrous. An inflammable, perfumed oil, "huile de Marmotte," is expressed from the seeds. **CZ6**

Subgenus *Persica*

P. persica Peach. China. Tree 2.4–2.8 in (6–7 m). Flowers solitary, pink, to 1.4 in (3.5 cm) across. Fruit globose, velvety, 2–2.8 in (5–7 cm), yellowish tinged reddish on exposed side; stone furrowed, deeply pitted. Widely and long cultivated in temperate zones. **CZ5**

var *nectarina* Nectarine. Fruits quite glabrous like a plum skin.

P. subhirtella

P. laurocerasus

P. × yedoensis

P. serrulata

Subgenus *Cerasus*

Fruit virtually without groove or bloom. Flowers 1–10(12), sometimes in short (to 2 in/5 cm) racemes of fewer than 10 flowers. Terminal bud present; leaves conduplicate. Stone either smooth or furrowed and pitted.

Section *Microcerasus*

Flowers solitary or in short few-flowered (fewer than (12) racemes. Leaf axils with 3 buds.

P. tomentosa Downy Cherry. China, Japan, and the Himalaya. Sprawling shrub to about 10 ft (3 m), rarely tree-like. Flowers white or pink-tinged, 0.6–0.8 in (1.5–2 cm) across. Fruit almost round, 0.4 in (1 cm) across, bright red, edible, may be slightly hairy. Ornamental value short-lived. Himalayan collections possibly from cultivated plants. **CZ2**

P. glandulosa Dwarf Flowering Almond. China, Japan. Bushy shrub to about 5 ft (1.5 m). Flowers white or pinkish. Fruit round, red, 0.4–0.6 in (10–12 mm) across. Double-flowered plants 'Alba Plena' (white), 'Rosea Plena' (pink) are of much greater ornamental value. **CZ4**

P. pumila Dwarf American Cherry, Sand Cherry. N. America. Shrub 3.3–8.2 ft (1–2.5 m). Flowers (almost) white in clusters of 2–4. Fruit subglobose, purplish-black, 0.3–0.5 in (8–12 mm) long, too bitter to be really palatable. The species has been hybridized with plum species such as *P. cerasifera*. **CZ2**

P. besseyi Rocky Mountain Cherry, Western Sand Cherry. N. America. Similar to previous species but with slightly larger flowers and edible sweet fruits of commercial promise. Both species have potential in rootstock breeding. **CZ3**

Section *Pseudocerasus*

As section *Microcerasus* but sepals upright or spreading and buds solitary. Flowers in bunches of few-flowered short racemes. A high proportion of the ornamental flowering cherries are derived from Chinese and Japanese species of this section or from their hybrids.

P. subhirtella Wild Spring or Higan Cherry. Japan. Tree to 30 ft (9 m). Flowers in clusters of 2–5, each about 0.8 in (2 cm) across, pale pinkish, tending to fade with age. Includes many attractive ornamentals, especially cultivar 'Autumnalis,' flowering late fall to early spring. **CZ5**

var *ascendens* The wild, mountainous form of the species in W China, Japan, and Korea. Leaves larger and tree to 66 ft (20 m). Of interest essentially for its involvement in cultivated varieties.

P. canescens Gray Leaf Cherry. China. Bushy shrub to 6(10) ft (2(3)m). Of little ornamental value except as parent, with *P. avium*, of the hybrid *P. × schmittii* with pale pink flowers and polished bark. **CZ6**

P. incisa Fuji Cherry. Japan. Bushy shrub to 16 ft (5 m), sometimes a tree to 33 ft (10 m). The female parent with *P. campanulata* of the very fine floriferous, hardy hybrid 'Okame.' **CZ6**

P. nipponica Japanese Alpine Cherry. Japan. Bush or bushy-headed tree to 20 ft (6 m). Another fine early flowering cherry. **CZ5**

P. 'Kursar' is raised from seed of *P. nipponica* var *kurilensis*.

P. campanulata Bell-flowered Cherry. Taiwan and S Japan. Tree to 30 ft (9 m), less hardy than other species within this section. The pollen parent of 'Okame'—see *P. incisa* above. **CZ7**

P. rufa A Himalayan pink-flowered type, closely related to *P. tricantha* from Sikkim. **CZ8**

P. serrula W China, Tibet. Tree 33–50 ft (10–15 m) prized for its fine, flaky, bright brown bark. Flowers white in clusters of 1–3. **CZ5**

P. concinna China. Produces a profusion of white flowers before the leaves appear. **CZ6**

P. conradinae China. Includes some semidouble-flowered selections. **CZ8**

P. × yedoensis Yoshino Cherry. Japan. A source of several attractive ornamental selections. Origin uncertain; not known wild. Possibly a hybrid *P. speciosa × P. subhirtella*. See *P. speciosa*. **CZ5**

P. sargentii Sargent Cherry. N Japan, Sakhalin. Tree to 80 ft (25 m). Flowers rose-pink, 1.2–1.6 in (3–4 cm) across, 2–6 held in an umbel. Fruit almost black, subglobose, 0.3–0.4 in (8–10 mm) across. Very attractive both in flower and its orange to red fall foliage. **CZ4**

P. serrulata Now regarded as a garden form, with scentless double white or pink flowers, of the Hill Cherry, a native of China and Japan, distinguished as *P. serrulata* var *spontanea,* which is the national tree of Japan, and grows up to 66 ft (20 m). Some 60 Japanese flowering cherries ("Sato Zakura" in Japanese, meaning "domestic cherries") are commonly listed under it and some are thought to have their origin from *P. serrulata,* but the majority probably derive from *P. speciosa* (*P. lannesiana* forma *albida*), the Oshima Cherry. **CZ5**

P. speciosa Oshima Cherry. Japan. Very closely related to *P. serrulata* and included by some authorities under that species but not synonymous with it. Flowers single, white, and fragrant. **CZ6**

P. sieboldii Japan. Generally regarded as a hybrid (*P. speciosa ×* ?). Tree reaching 26 ft (8 m) with 2–4 large, often double flowers on each short peduncle. **CZ6**

Section *Lobopetalum*

As section *Pseudocerasus* but with reflexed sepals. Petals notched at apex or 2-lobed. Chinese species.

P. cantabrigiensis Cambridge Cherry. Tree with 3–6 pink flowers in each short stalked umbel. Fruit like a bright red cherry, 0.4 in (1 cm) across. Often confused with the following species.

P. pseudocerasus Similar to previous species but the 2–6 flowers are in a raceme and there are gland-toothed bracts at the base of each pedicel. **CZ6**

A selection intermediate between this and *P. cantabrigiensis* was hybridized with *P. avium* to produce the new rootstocks 'Colt' (for sweet and sour cherries) and 'Cornflower' (for ornamental cherries).

Section *Eucerasus*

As section *Lobopetalum* but petals not notched or lobed. Flowers usually in sessile umbels with persistent bud-scales at the base.

P. avium Mazzard, Gean, Wild (Sweet) Cherry. Europe, SW Russia, N. Africa (mountains). Tree to 65–80 ft (20–24 m). Flowers pure white, 1 in (2.5 cm) across, the calyx-tube (hypanthium) constricted above. Fruit globose, 0.35–0.5(0.7) in (9–12(18) mm) across, typically blackish-red, can be sweet or bitter-tasting but not sour (acid). The ancestor of most of the sweet cherries. **CZ3**

P. cerasus Sour Cherry. Not known as a wild plant. Widely cultivated and often naturalized in parts of Europe and W Asia. Similar to preceding species but often shrubby and not exceeding 33 ft (10 m); commonly suckering. Calyx-tube (hypanthium) not constricted above. Fruit bright red, sour (acid), but not bitter. The ancestor of Morello cherries. **CZ3**

P. fruticosa Ground Cherry. Europe to parts of Siberia. Dwarf, spreading shrub to 3.3 ft (1 m). Flowers white, 0.6 in (1.5 cm) across. Fruit dark red, round, nearly 0.4 in (1 cm) across, of cherry-like taste but scarcely palatable. Long cultivated in Europe. **CZ4**

Section *Mahaleb*

As section *Eucerasus*, but basal scales at base of flower clusters dropping before flowers open. Flowers mostly in racemes of 12 or fewer, less often in umbels. Bracts deciduous and leaf teeth rounded.

P. mahaleb St. Lucie Cherry, Mahaleb Cherry. C and S Europe. Tree to 33(40) ft (10(12) m). Flowers white, 0.5–0.7 in (12–18 mm) across, fragrant, in 6–10(12)-flowered racemes up to 1.2–1.6 in (3–4 cm) long. Fruit black, ovoid, 0.3–0.4 in (8–10 mm) long. Sometimes used as rootstock for grafting cherries, though the resulting trees tend to have a relatively short life. **CZ5**

P. pennsylvanica Pin or Wild Red Cherry. N. America. Shrub or tree to 40 ft (12 m) with very slender red, shiny, often pendulous branches. Flowers white, 0.5 in (12 mm) across in 2–5(10) umbels or short racemes. Fruit round, 0.2 in (6 mm) across, red, abundantly produced. **CZ2**

Section *Phyllocerasus*

As section *Mahaleb*, but bracts persistent, leaf teeth pointed, and 1–4 flowered umbels.

P. pilosiuscula C and W China. Shrub or tree to 40 ft (12 m). Flowers white, 0.7–0.8 in (18–20 mm) across. Fruit ellipsoidal, 0.3–0.35 in (8–9 mm) long, red. **CZ5**

P. laurocerasus

Section *Phyllomahaleb*

As section *Mahaleb*, but flowers in (4)5–10 flowered racemes.

P. maximowiczii Japan, Korea, Manchuria. Attractive tree to 52 ft (16 m). Flowers dull yellowish-white, 0.6 in (1.5 cm) across, with 6–10 in the raceme. Fruit round, 0.2 in (5 mm) across, red finally black. Foliage often strikingly red in the fall. **CZ4**

Subgenus *Padus*

As subgenus *Cerasus* but flowers in long (2.4 in/6 cm or more) racemes of (10)12 or more flowers. Leaves deciduous.

P. padus European Bird Cherry. Europe to Japan. Tree 33–50 ft (10–15 m) (or more). Flowers white, 0.3–0.5 in (8–12 mm) across, petals 0.2–0.35 in (6–9 mm) long, fragrant, in pendulous racemes with leafy peduncle. Fruit round, black, 0.2–0.3 in (6–8 mm) across, calyx deciduous; taste astringent. **CZ3**

P. serotina Rum Cherry. N. America. Tree to 100 ft (30 m), usually about 50 ft (15 m) in cultivation. Flowers white, 0.3–0.4 in (8–10 mm) across, petals 0.08-0.16 in (2–4 mm) long; peduncle of raceme leafy; fruit round 0.3–0.4 in (8 10 mm) across, finally black, with persisting calyx. **CZ3**

Subgenus *Laurocerasus*

As subgenus *Padus* but leaves evergreen. Peduncles of racemes always leafless.

P. lusitanica Portugal Laurel. Portugal, Spain. Shrub or tree to 20(50) ft (6(15) m). Shoots and petioles red. Leaves shining, elliptical, 2.8–5.2 in (7–13 cm) long. Flowers white, 0.3–0.5 in (8–13 mm) across. Fruits dark purple, rounded cone-shaped to 0.3 in (8 mm) long, but very unpalatable. **CZ7**

P. laurocerasus Cherry Laurel. Asia Minor, SE Europe. Shrub or tree to 20 ft (6 m). Shoots and petioles pale green. Leaves more or less obovate to oblong, (2)4–6 in ((5)10–15 cm) long, margin more or less serrate. Flowers white, 0.3–0.35 in (8–9 mm) across. Fruit purplish-black, rounded cone-shaped, about 0.3 (8 mm) long, palatable when cooked (makes an acceptable jelly). **CZ7**

P. avium

P. avium

P. cerasus

P. padus

LEGUMINOSAE

Acacia

Acacias

Acacia is a very large genus of species native to the Tropics and subtropics, about three-quarters of them in Australia. Many are highly attractive plants, with feathery silvery-gray foliage and yellow flowers in large conspicuous clusters; some have economic importance. Acacias are mostly evergreen trees and shrubs (rarely herbs); a few are twiners and hook climbers. Most are xerophytic (able to withstand prolonged drought). The leaves are typically bipinnate, often silvery, without terminal leaflets, and sometimes remarkable in being reduced to a more or less expanded petiole that functions as a leaf (phyllode). The stipules can be thorn-like. The minute flowers are unisexual or bisexual, predominantly yellow, rarely whitish, and borne in dense globose or cylindrical heads of twenty to thirty, each flower with five (rarely four) blunt tooth-like sepals, five (rarely four) petals about 0.06 in (1.5 mm) long, and numerous protruding yellow stamens making each head attractively conspicuous; the sepals and petals are sometimes absent. The ovary is sessile or stalked and the fruit is a roundish to elongated pod (legume). The phyllode-bearing species (section *Phyllodineae*) are mostly native to Australia.

The species are not particularly hardy, but about two dozen, of which the Silver Wattle or "Mimosa" (*Acacia dealbata*) is the most popular, can be grown in milder parts of temperate regions, but may succumb in a hard winter. Any reasonably good soil is adequate, but most species, except *A. longifolia* and *A. retinodes*, will not tolerate free lime.

Acacias are a major component of the widespread scrub found in Australia where they are called wattles, named for their use by early settlers for building huts of wattlework plastered with mud. Other species form a conspicuous part of

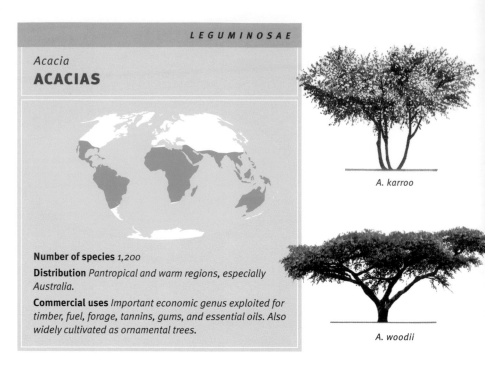

Number of species *1,200*
Distribution *Pantropical and warm regions, especially Australia.*
Commercial uses *Important economic genus exploited for timber, fuel, forage, tannins, gums, and essential oils. Also widely cultivated as ornamental trees.*

LEGUMINOSAE

Acacia
ACACIAS

A. karroo

A. woodii

A. baileyana

A. dealbata

the landscape in desert areas and dry savannas of Africa and dry plains of India, where they are frequently the only trees. They are called thorns or thorn-trees in Africa and tropical America, in reference to the large thorns found in many species which protect the tree against grazing animals. These thorns are mostly modified stipules and may be swollen at the base.

The Bull-horn Acacia (*A. cornigera*) from Mexico and Central America (and widely naturalized in the Antilles) has developed an excellent example of symbiosis with the ant *Pseudomyrmex ferruginea*. The ants are attracted to the trees by nectaries at the base of the petioles, which provide them with sugars, and by curious sausage-shaped food organs called Beltian bodies at the tips of the leaflets, which provide them with a diet of oils and proteins. At the base of each leaf the acacia has a pair of massive swollen thorns 0.8–1.2 in (2–3 cm) long. They are inhabited by colonies of the ants, which bore into them and hollow them out.

This remarkable association, first described by Thomas Belt in his book *The Naturalist in Nicaragua* (1874), has subsequently been found in a number of other acacia species, such as *A. drepanolobium*. There has been considerable debate as to what benefit the acacia obtains from the presence of the ants, but it has been shown that the plant obtains protection from herbivores through the action of the worker ants, which swarm over it if disturbed, stinging and biting any predators in a bid to protect their own territory. In addition, the ants cut away any branches of other plants that touch their host acacias, thereby ensuring a tunnel through the foliage to the light above, allowing the acacia to grow rapidly and compete effectively with other vegetation.

The best ("genuine" or "true") gum arabic is obtained from *A. senegal*, a native of tropical Africa from Senegal through Nigeria. Certain other species, such as *A. nilotica*

LEFT A Camel Thorn Acacia (*Acacia erioloba*) on the dry, barren expanses of Namibia. It is an extremely important species for the survival of people and their domestic animals in Africa.

and the Whistling Thorn (*A. seyal*), yield an inferior product. The gum exudes largely from the branches, and is used in pharmacy, confectionery, and as an adhesive. Black catechu or cutch, a dark extract rich in tannin, is obtained from *A. catechu* by steeping the wood in hot water. The original khaki cloth is said to have been dyed and shrunk in this tanning agent. Other tannin-producing species include the Australian Black Wattle (*A. mearnsii*), the Golden Wattle (*A. pycnantha*), and Silver Wattle (*A. dealbata*), which are planted in Spain, Portugal, and Italy for this purpose. The last species is also widely cultivated for timber, ornament, and soil stabilization in southern Europe and is the "Mimosa" of florists, which is used as a winter cut-flower. Silver Wattle is conspicuous on the Côte d'Azur in the south of France, where whole hillsides are covered by it, though occasionally it is devastated by a combination of drought, frost, and fire. Several species, Australian Blackwood (*A. melanoxylon*) is one, yield valuable timber used for a wide range of purposes from furniture to boomerangs, boats, and spears, and are now grown in southern Europe. Others are planted as shade trees, or for stabilizing coastal dunes.

Ornamental plants (all Australian) for the milder parts of temperate regions include *A. dealbata*, which has particularly attractive silvery, feathery foliage and conspicuous, globose clusters of fragrant flowers. *Acacia podalyriifolia* is a splendid shrub growing to 3 m (10 ft), with more or less ovate, mucronate phyllodes, 1–1.2 in (2.5–3 cm) long, and abundant racemes of stalked, globose heads of fragrant flowers. The Sydney Golden Wattle (*A. longifolia*) is noted for its cylindrical heads of strongly perfumed flowers, and the Wirilda (*A. retinodes*), with fragrant flowers in globose heads, can flower at all times of the year. The Kangaroo Thorn (*A. armata*), is unusual in its ribbed young shoots, spiny at the apex. It has deep yellow flowers and is popular as a glasshouse plant, as hedging, or as a sand binder. *Acacia cyanophylla* (the Orange Wattle or Blue-leaf Wattle), a western Australian plant, with more or less lanceolate to oblanceolate, blue-green phyllodes which may reach 12 in (30 cm), and globose flower heads, is also planted for soil stabilization, as well as for ornament, in southern Europe. The Karroo Thorn (*A. karroo*) from South Africa is grown in southwest Europe (sometimes becoming naturalized) and has striking whitish, piercing spines 2–4 in (5–10 cm) long.

The Opopanax (or Opoponax) (*A. farnesiana*), known also as Huisache, Sweet Acacia, Popinac, and West Indian Black Thorn, is naturalized in all tropical countries and much cultivated in the subtropics, but is believed to be a native of tropical and subtropical America. It is prized for its fragrant violet-scented flowers—Cassie flowers—which are extracted by the perfume industry. Opopanax is also a valid generic name for two or three herbaceous species of the family Umbelliferae (Apiaceae), natives of southern Europe including Greece, gum opopanax being obtained from *Opopanax chironium*. **CZ8–9**

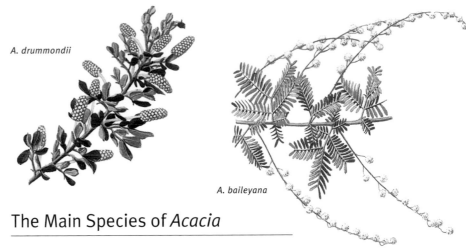

A. drummondii

A. baileyana

A. dealbata

The Main Species of *Acacia*

Group I: Leaves bipinnate.

A *Nutlets smooth on ventral side.*

A. baileyana Golden Mimosa, Bailey's Mimosa, or Cootamundra Wattle. Australia. Small graceful tree. Leaves gray-glaucous with 2–4 pairs of pinnae. Flowers in globose heads in racemes. Pods glaucous. **CZ8**

A. dealbata Silver Wattle. Australia. Tree to 100 ft (30 m) with silvery-gray bark. Leaves downy with (8)15–20(25) pairs of pinnae. Flowers strongly scented in globose heads borne in long panicles. Cultivated in S France for perfumery and as florists' "Mimosa." Produces a gum-arabic substitute. **CZ8**

A. drummondii W Australia. Shrub or small tree to 10 ft (3 m). Shoots furrowed. Flowers lemon-yellow in dense, solitary, cylindrical, drooping spikes. **CZ9**

A. mearnsii (*A. mollissima*) Black Wattle. Tasmania. Tree with softly hairy shoots and leaves. Flowers in heads borne in leaf-axils. Pods strongly constricted between the seeds. A source of tannin. Similar to previous species, but pinnules (leaflets on pinnae) much smaller (to 0.08 in/2 mm) and young shoots and leaves yellowish. **CZ9**

A *Plants spiny.*
B *Flowers in spikes or spike-like racemes.*

A. catechu Black Catechu, Cutch, Black Cutch, or Khair. W Pakistan to Myanmar. Small to medium-sized deciduous tree with short hooked spines. Flowers in solitary spikes or 2–3 together. Pods flat. The heartwood is a source of tannin and dyeing extract. **CZ9**

A. albida Tropical and subtropical Africa, Syria, and Palestine. Wide-spreading tree to 100 ft (30 m) with straight spines in pairs. Leaves blue-green. Flowers cream-colored in long spikes. Pods bright orange, indehiscent, curved or curled into a circular coil. **CZ9**

A. cornigera Bull-horn Acacia. Mexico to Costa Rica. Shrub or small tree with large, swollen, twisted spines, the latter partly hollow. **CZ9**

A. gummifera Morocco or Barbary Gum. Morocco. Tree to 33 ft (10 m). Pods white-tomentose, constricted between the seeds. **CZ9**

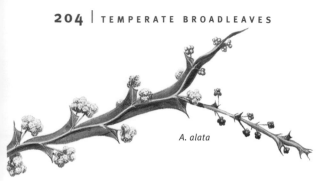

A. alata

A. longifolia

A. melanoxylon

A. karroo

A. horrida **Cape Gum Tree.** India, tropical E Africa, Somalia, and Sudan. Low tree or shrub, usually flat-topped. Spines 1–4 in (2.5–10 cm) long. Flowers creamy-yellow. Material in cultivation under this name is usually misidentified and is probably *A. karroo*. **CZ8**

A. senegal **Gum Arabic Tree.** Tropical Africa. Shrub or tree to 40 ft (12 m) with spiny prickles in threes, the middle one recurved, or solitary. Flowers white or creamy-yellow, in axillary spikes. Pods flat. The source of "true" gum arabic of commerce. **CZ9**

BB *Flowers in globose heads (capitate).*

A. farnesiana **Opopanax (Opoponax), Popinac, Huisache, Sweet Acacia, West Indian Blackthorn, or Cassie.** Tropical and subtropical America and Australia but widely introduced in other tropical areas and cultivated. Deciduous shrub or small tree to 20 ft (6 m), much branched. Flowers very fragrant, bright golden-yellow. Widely grown as an ornamental and for the essential oil from its flowers used in perfumery. **CZ8**

A. erioloba **Camel Thorn.** South Africa, Zimbabwe. Tree to 42 ft (13 m) with straight stout paired spines. Flowerheads in clusters. Pods curved, velvety-gray, indehiscent. **CZ9**

A. karroo **Karroo Thorn.** South Africa. Deciduous shrub or small tree with pungent ivory-white spines, 2–4 in (5–10 cm) long on older parts of plant. Flowers fragrant, the heads in clusters of 4–6 in leaf-axils. Pods flattened. Used as a hedging plant or sand-binder. **CZ8**

A. nilotica (*A. arabica*) **Gum Arabic Tree, Babul,** or **Egyptian Thorn.** Tropical and subtropical Africa and Asia extending to India. Variable tree to 82 ft (25 m) with long straight spines. Flowers bright yellow on axillary pedunculate heads. Source of gum arabic substitute, tannin, and a hard timber. **CZ9**

A. seyal **Gum Arabic Tree or Tahl Gum.** Tropical and subtropical Africa, Sudan to Zimbabwe. Tree to 40 ft (12 m) with straight spines (with or without ant galls). Flowers bright yellow on axillary pedunculate heads. Pods curved, constricted between seeds. Source of good-quality gum arabic. **CZ9**

A. woodii (*A. sieberana* var *woodii*) **Paperbark Thorn.** S Africa. Large tree. Young shoots golden-tomentose. Spines very short. Flowers cream, in solitary or paired heads. **CZ9**

Group II: Adult leaves apparently simple, modified to phyllodes, occasionally with a few pinnate leaves.

C *Flowers in globose heads (capitate), which may be solitary, clustered, or in racemes.*

A. acinacea **Gold Dust.** Australia. A branching shrub to 8 ft (2.5 m) with oblong phyllodes. Flowers yellow in solitary, golden heads or 2 together. **CZ9**

A. alata W Australia. Shrub up to 8 ft (2.5 m). Phyllodes narrowly triangular or ovate-lanceolate, 1-veined, with decurrent linear-oblong wing, tipped with a slender spine. Flowers creamy-yellow in axillary, solitary or paired heads. **CZ8**

A. paradoxa **Kangaroo Thorn.** Australia. Shrub to 10 ft (3 m); young shoots ribbed, spiny at the apex. Stipules spine-like. Phyllodes semi-ovate. 0.5–1 × 0.12–0.25 in (12–25 × 3–6 mm), curved at the tip, each node with its 2 stipules modified as forked spines to 0.5–0.52 in (12–13 mm) long. Flowers bright yellow in heads that are simple or paired in axillary stalks. **CZ8**

A. melanoxylon **Blackwood Acacia.** S Australia, Tasmania. Large tree 66–130 ft (20–40 m). Stipules not spine-like. Phyllodes 3–5 veined, oblong-lanceolate, curved; some bipinnate leaves produced. Flowers cream-colored; heads in axillary racemes. Important timber tree, now grown in southern Europe. **CZ8**

A. pycnantha **Golden Wattle.** Australia. Shrub or medium-sized tree to 23 ft (7 m). Stipules not spine-like; phyllodes 1-veined, lanceolate-curved. Flowers fragrant, bright yellow; heads in racemes. Widely used for tanning. **CZ8**

A. pycnantha

A. retinodes **Wirilda.** Tasmania, Australia. Shrub or small tree to 33 ft (10 m). Stipules not spine-like. Phyllodes linear-lanceolate-curved. Flowers pale yellow; heads in branched racemes. Widely cultivated. **CZ8**

CC *Flowers in cylindrical spikes.*

A. acuminata **Raspberry Jam Tree.** Australia. Tree to 33 ft (10 m) or shrub. Phyllodes linear, 4–10 × 0.16–0.3 in (10–25 cm × 4–8 mm). Flowers in axillary spikes. Wood scented like raspberry jam, hence its popular name. **CZ9**

A. longifolia (inc. *A. floribunda*) **Sydney Golden Wattle.** Australia, Tasmania. Shrub or tree up to 33 ft (10 m). Phyllodes oblong-lanceolate, 3–6 × 0.4–0.07 in (7.5–15 cm × 9–18 mm). Flowers bright yellow in lax, axillary spikes. Often cultivated for ornament. **CZ8**

A. retinodes

C. siliquastrum

C. siliquastrum

Cercis

Judas Trees, Redbuds

Cercis is a genus of about six species from North America and southern Europe to eastern Asia (China). They are deciduous shrubs or trees, some species with characteristic dark red buds. The leaves are more or less round with a cordate base, alternate and entire with five or seven prominent veins arranged fan-wise. The flowers are rose-purplish borne in clusters, sometimes directly on the trunk (cauliflorous), and appear before or with the leaves. The calyx is bell-shaped, shortly and bluntly toothed, and the corolla has five petals, the upper three smaller; there are ten stamens. The fruit is a flat pod, green to pinkish, finally brown, with several flat seeds.

Cercis are mostly hardy species grown for their floral beauty and their characteristic and pleasing leaf shape. Best known is the Judas Tree (*C. siliquastrum*), which is one of two trees (the other is an elder, *Sambucus* sp) on which Judas is said to have hanged himself—the cauliflorous flowers being no doubt symbolic of blood. The legend explains the frequent occurrence of the species beside churches and in graveyards. It is a tree of low and irregular spreading habit, about 15–20 ft (5–6 m) tall, and with a spread of similar dimensions. Old trees often become one-sided with branches bending to the ground. The bark, which is purplish and ridged when young, becomes grayish-red and fissured on mature trees.

Cercis racemosa, from China, is unique among the species in that its flowers are arranged in a raceme, that is the flowers in the unbranched cluster are stalked.

The name Redbud is more properly applied to *C. canadensis*, a popular ornamental choice in North America, though this species is much less popular in Europe than the Judas Tree.

Judas trees like a good average loamy soil. Adult specimens do not transplant easily and so should be given their permanent position at an early stage. Propagation is best by seed; the usual stocks for grafting are *C. canadensis* or *C. siliquastrum*. **CZ4–8**

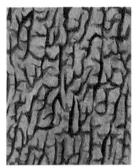

C. siliquastrum

C. siliquastrum

The pale rose flowers of the Redbud, *Cercis canadensis*, are produced in clusters in early summer, before the leaves appear. They are smaller than the popular *C. siliquastrum*.

C. canadensis

The Main Species of *Cercis*

Group I: Leaves rounded or notched at apex, 2.4–4 in (6–10 cm) wide.

C. siliquastrum Judas Tree. S Europe and Asia. Tree to 40 ft (12 m) but generally less, with spreading, irregular habit. Leaves almost round, not quite so long as wide, sinuate at base, apex usually rounded, very rarely pointed, brightish green above, glaucous below. Flowers bright purplish-rose, 0.4–0.8 in (1–2 cm) long, in clusters of 3–6 produced in great quantities. Pods up to 6 in (15 cm) long. **CZ6**
var *alba* White-flowered.

C. reniformis Texas, New Mexico. Tree to 40 ft (12 m). Leaves broadly ovate to reniform, leathery, sometimes downy beneath. Flowers rose-pink, 0.4 in (1 cm) long. Pod about 2.4 in (6 cm) long. **CZ8**

Group II: Leaves shortly pointed at apex

C. canadensis Redbud. C and E N. America. Usually shrubby but occasionally tree to 40 ft (12 m). Leaves broadly ovate to cordate, 3–5 in (8–12 cm) wide, heart-shaped, dull beneath and downy at vein-axils, thinner and brighter green than *C. siliquastrum*. Flowers in clusters of 4–8, pale rose-pink, smaller and paler than *C. siliquastrum*. **CZ4**
var *alba* White-flowered.
var *pubescens* Leaves downy beneath.

C. chinensis (C. japonica) China. Tree to 40–50 ft (12–15 m) but shrubby in cultivation. Leaves rounded, 3–5 in (8–12 cm) long, glossy green on both surfaces. Flowers in clusters of 4–10, purple-pink, larger than those of *C. canadensis*. Pods 3.5–5 in (9–12 cm) long. **CZ6**

C. racemosa China. Shrub or small tree to 40 ft (12 m). Leaves 2.4–5 in (6–12 cm) long, broadly ovate, bright green above, downy below. Flowers rosy-pink, borne in very distinctive racemes 4 in (10 cm) long. Pod 3.5–5 in (9–12 cm) long. **CZ7**

Gleditsia

Honey Locusts

Gleditsia (incorrectly, *Gleditschia*) is a genus of over a dozen species of deciduous trees from eastern North America, China, Japan, and Iran. The trunk and branches are armed with simple or branched spines, which are stem structures arising from the leaf-axils and can be very aggressive. The leaves are bipinnate or pinnate and the flowers inconspicuous small, green, in racemes 2–6 in (5–15 cm) long. Unlike those of most legumes, the petals are uniform. Nearly all species have numerous seeds embedded in pulp in pods 12–20 in (30–50 cm) long. Seeds are dispersed in the pod, which is often spirally twisted to aid wind dispersal.

Many species are cultivated for their fern-like foliage, for example the Honey Locust (*G. triacanthos*). Its cultivar 'Sunburst' has golden-yellow foliage in the spring and the fall; 'Moraine' (a clone of forma *inermis*) lacks the spines and is sterile. Also cultivated is the spineless hybrid *G. × texana*, which·arose naturally where populations of *G. aquatica* and *G. triacanthos* grew together in Texas. The pods of *G. × texana* are many-seeded but without pulp, thus intermediate between *G. aquatica*, which has one-seeded pods with little pulp, and *G. triacanthos*, which has many-seeded pods with pulp. They succeed in all types of well-drained soil and are finding favor as town trees since they tolerate atmospheric pollution.

Some species have domestic applications. The pulp from *G. triacanthos* is sweet (hence the common name) and pods may be fermented to make "beer" or fed to stock. Pods of the Caspian Locust (*G. caspica*), *G. japonica* (Japan), and *G. macracantha* (China) are used in soap. Pods of the last are also used in tanning. The wood of many species is hard and durable. **CZ3–8**

LEGUMINOSAE

Gleditsia
HONEY LOCUSTS

Number of species *14*
Distribution *India and Japan through New Guinea, the Caspian region, South America, and eastern North America.*
Commercial uses *Widely cultivated for hedging, timber, and as shade and ornamental trees.*

The Main Species of *Gleditsia*

Group I: Pods many-seeded, flat, usually twisted, not dotted. Spines compressed at least at the base.

G. triacanthos **Honey Locust.** N. America. Tree to 150 ft (45 m). Trunk and branches usually armed with simple or branched spines 2.4–4 in (6–10 cm) long. Leaves 5.5–8 in (14–20 cm) long, dark and glossy, pinnate with more than 20 oblong-lanceolate pinnae 0.8–1.4 in (2–3.5 cm) long or bipinnate with 8–14 pinnae. Pods 12–16 in (30–40 cm) long; seeds embedded in pulp. Several varieties and cultivars. **CZ3**
'*Butjoti*' Slender pendulous branches.
'*Nana*' Compact and shrub-like.
forma **inermis** Slender habit, no spines (includes 'Moraine').
'**Elegantissima**' Bushy habit, no spines.
'**Sunburst**' Golden yellow leaves in the spring, no spines.

G. japonica Japan. Tree 66–82 ft (20–25 m). Trunk armed with branched spines 2–4 in (5–10 cm) long; young branches purplish. Leaves 10–12 in (25–30 cm) long, pinnate with 16–20 oblong pinnae 0.8–1.6(2.4) in (2–4(6) cm) long, or bipinnate with 2–12 pinnae. Pods twisted, 10–12 in (25–30 cm) long. **CZ6**

G. ferox Tree closely related to **G. japonica.** Trunk armed with very stout compressed spines. Leaves often bipinnate with 16–30 ovate pinnae. Of doubtful status; cultivated specimens may be *G. caspica*. **CZ6**

G. caspica **Caspian Locust.** N Iran. Tree to 40 ft (12 m). Trunk armed with many spines 6 in (15 cm) or more long; young branches bright green and glabrous. Leaves shiny, 6–9.5 in (15–24 cm) long, pinnate with 12–20 ovate-elliptic pinnae or bipinnate with 6–8 pinnae. Pods about 8 in (20 cm) long. **CZ6**

G. delavayi SW China. Tree to about 33 ft (10 m). Trunk armed with spines up to 10 in (25 cm) long; young branches downy. Leaves pinnate with 8–16 ovate pinnae 1.2–2.5 in (3–6 cm) long, the lower pinnae smaller (young plants often have bipinnate leaves). Pods 6–13.5(20) in (15–35(50) cm) long; walls leathery. **CZ8**

G. triacanthos

G. triacanthos

TOP LEFT One of the most striking of the golden-leaved honey locusts, *Gleditsia triacanthos* 'Sunburst', has rich golden yellow leaves in the spring, which turn to yellowish-green in the summer.

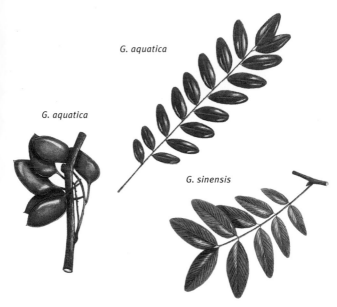

G. aquatica

G. aquatica

G. sinensis

Group II: Pods many-seeded, not twisted, but with minute dots. Spines terete.

G. macracantha C China. Tree to 50 ft (15 m). Trunk armed with long, very stiff branched spines and the branches are ribbed and warted. Leaves 2–2.8 in (5–7 cm) long, glabrous, pinnate with 6–12 ovate-oblong pinnae 2–2.8 in (5–7 cm) long, the lower pinnae smaller. Pods 6–12 in (15–30 cm) long.

G. sinensis C China. Tree to 50 ft (15 m). Trunk armed with stout conical spines, which are often branched. Leaves pinnate, 5–7 in (12–18 cm) long, rather dull yellowish green, with 8–14(18) ovate pinnae 1.2–3 in (3–8 cm) long. Pods 5–10 in (12–25 cm) long, dark purplish-brown. **CZ5**

Group III: Pods many-seeded and straight. Trunk usually without spines.

G. × texana Texas. Natural hybrid tree, arising from the cross *G. triacanthos × G. aquatica*. It grows to 130 ft (40 m) and has smooth, pale bark and glabrous young shoots. Leaves 2–8 in (5–20 cm) long, dark green and glossy, pinnate or bipinnate with 12–14 pinnae. Male flowers in dark orange-yellow racemes 3–4 in (8–10 cm) long. Pods, without pulp, 4–5 in (10–12 cm) long, dark chestnut brown. **CZ6**

Group IV: Pods 2–3-seeded. Leaflets entire and pubescent beneath.

G. heterophylla NE China. Shrub or small tree. Spines slender, simple, or trifid and up to almost 14 in (35 cm) long. Leaves pinnate with 10–18 oblong pinnae 0.4–1.2 in (1–3 cm) long, gray-green. Pods 1.4–2.2 in (3.5–5.5 cm) long, thin, and glabrous. **CZ6**

Group V: Pods 1–2-seeded. Leaflets crenulate, and glabrous beneath.

G. aquatica Water Locust. SE U.S. Tree to 66 ft (20 m); in Europe only reaching shrub size. Trunk bears branched spines 4 in (10 cm) long. Leaves 8 in (20 cm) long, glabrous, pinnate with 12–18 ovate-oblong pinnae 0.8–1.2 in (2–3 cm) long or bipinnate with 6–8 pinnae. Pod, thin, 1–2 in (2.5–5 cm) long, usually with only 1 seed. **CZ6**

Laburnum

Laburnums

Laburnum is a genus of small trees and shrubs with attractive foliage and pendulous racemes of bright yellow flowers, but poisonous leaves and seeds. As now conceived, there are two species—and their hybrid—native to southern Europe.

The leaves are alternate and trifoliolate, with petioles but no stipules. The flowers are bisexual, yellow, and pea-like on slender pedicels and borne in terminal pendulous racemes. The calyx is bell-shaped and two-lipped, the lips not longer than the corolla tube, which is yellow, with the petals all free. The filaments of the ten stamens are united into a tube. The style is slender, with a small, upcurved terminal stigma, and the ovary is short-stalked. The narrow oblong pod is constricted between each of the one to eight seeds, the upper suture thickened or more or less winged. The seeds are kidney-shaped.

Both species (*L. anagyroides* and *L. alpinum*) are much planted as ornamentals. They are not particular as to soil, provided it is not waterlogged. Pods are freely formed, which, if removed early, will prolong the life of what are relatively short-lived plants. They are reasonably free from disease.

Laburnum seeds (and those of their hybrid *L. × watereri*) are freely formed and can be fatally poisonous to humans and domestic animals. Horses are more susceptible than cattle and goats, though sheep and rodents have eaten leaves and bark without harm. While the hybrid has equally poisonous seeds, it forms far fewer seed-pods (between one and three per raceme) and is therefore the most widely planted *Laburnum*. Where poisoning is suspected, hospital aid should be sought immediately. The poisonous principles are the alkaloids cytisine and laburnine.

Laburnum	*LEGUMINOSAE*

LABURNUMS

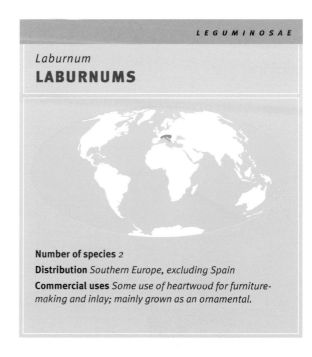

Number of species 2

Distribution *Southern Europe, excluding Spain*

Commercial uses *Some use of heartwood for furniture-making and inlay; mainly grown as an ornamental.*

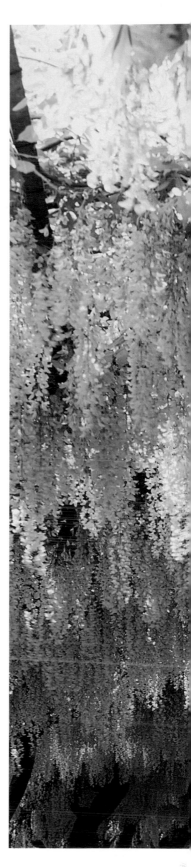

ABOVE Laburnums are laden with streaming racemes of bright yellow color through the early summer months and are often trained in formal gardens as arches and walkways.

A third species, first described as *Podocytisus caramanicus*, from the southern Balkans and Asia Minor, is on occasion transferred to *Laburnum*, but some authorities retain it in its original genus. It is a shrub to about 3 ft (1 m), with terminal racemes of golden-yellow laburnum-like flowers, but the inflorescence is erect, not pendulous.

Laburnum anagyroides forms an interesting graft-hybrid with *Cytisus purpureus*. It is designated (*Cytisus* + *Laburnum*) and referred to as + *Laburnocytisus adami*. It is not, though, a normal intergeneric hybrid, as the tissues of the "parents" remain separate, those of *Cytisus* forming the outer layers, which surround inner tissues derived solely from *Laburnum*. At points *Laburnum* tissues break through the *Cytisus* covering, while some of the branches are pure *Cytisus*. Seeds are occasionally formed, and, being derived from inner layers, will produce only *Laburnum* plants. This type of hybrid is also called chimaera. It can be propagated vegetatively. The habit resembles the normal laburnums, but the leaflets are smaller and almost glabrous; the racemes are nodding rather than pendulous and smaller, and the flowers a rather dirty purplish colour. *Laburnum* heartwood is used in cabinetwork and inlay. Very interesting botanically but otherwise its ornamental value is that of a botanical curiosity of little visual appeal. **CZ5–6**

The Species of *Laburnum*

L. anagyroides (*L. vulgare*) **Common Laburnum, Golden Chain, Golden Rain.** Mountain woods of C Europe, the Alps, Italy, and the Balkans. Large shrub or small tree, 23–30(33) ft (7–9(10) m). Leaflets more or less elliptic, 1.2–3 in (3–8 cm) long, gray-green above, silky-glaucous beneath from the adpressed pubescence. Flowers in pubescent racemes 6–10 in (15–25 cm) long, appearing late spring and early summer, the bright yellow flowers about 0.8 in (2 cm) long on usually shorter pedicels. Fruiting pods rounded in cross-section, the upper suture thickened and keeled, but not obviously winged, averaging 2 in (5 cm), long, dark brown; seeds black. Numerous cultivars. **CZ5**

L. alpinum **Scotch** or **Alpine Laburnum.** Mountainous woods of Austria, Switzerland, the Czech and Slovak republics, Italy, the Balkans. Shrub or tree to 40 ft (12 m). Leaflets mostly elliptic-oblong, 1.6–2.8 in (4–7 cm) long, ciliate on edge but glabrous or virtually so on lower side. Flowers in slightly pubescent racemes 10–15 in (25–40 cm) long, appearing 2–3 weeks later than in *L. anagyroides*, averaging less than 0.8 in (2 cm) long on pedicels of about same length. Fruiting pods almost flat in cross-section, glabrous, the upper suture clearly winged; seeds about 5, brown. There are a number of cultivars and this species is a better ornamental choice than the previous one. **CZ5**

L. anagyroides × *alpinum* = **L. × watereri** (*L.* × *vossii* of horticulturalists). This hybrid has the long racemes of *L. alpinum* and the more striking flowers of *L. anagyroides*. Lower surface of leaves and pods also intermediate in pubescence, that is sparingly adpressed pubescent; fruiting pod about 1.6 in (4 cm) long, less winged than *L. alpinum* and on average fewer seeds. Pods are rarely developed and for this reason the hybrid is the most commonly planted to reduce chance consumption of the seeds, which are just as poisonous. There are a number of cultivars, of which 'Vossii' is the finest.

L. × *watereri*

LEFT During the spring the three species flower in sequence, with *L. anagyroides* flowering first, followed by *L. alpinum* and finally *L.* × *watereri*, which is a hybrid of the two.

L. alpinum

L. anagyroides

L. alpinum   *L. anagyroides*

R. pseudacacia

Robinia
False Acacias, Locust Trees

Robinia is a genus of about seven species all native to North America. They are deciduous shrubs or trees with alternate pinnate leaves that have an odd terminal leaflet (imparipinnate); the stipules are often spinose. The leaflets are opposite, entire, and stipelate (with small stipules = stipels). The flowers are typically pea-like, borne mostly in axillary pendulous racemes and flowering in late spring or early summer. The calyx is bell-like, weakly two-lipped, while the corolla has short-clawed petals with a large round standard and the keel petals united below. There are ten stamens, the upper one free or almost so from the remaining nine, which are united into a tube. The pod is linear to oblong, flat, two-valved, containing three to ten seeds.

False acacias or locusts are hardy in temperate regions and commonly planted for their showy and often scented white or pink to purplish flowers. The wood is somewhat brittle and branches are liable to be broken by strong winds. Accordingly, they are more useful for planting in poorish soils, which reduces lush growth. Propagation is by seed or by grafting with *Robinia pseudacacia* (False Acacia, Black Locust) as a stock.

Probably the most widely planted is the False Acacia, a highly ornamental tree that may reach 85 ft (26 m) and bears pendulous racemes of fragrant white, sometimes pinkish, flowers. Other very attractive species are *R. kelseyi* with deep rose-colored flowers and glandular hispid (with rough bristly hairs) pods, and *R. hispida* with rose to pale purplish flowers, also with glandular hispid pods, which are, however, rarely formed. There are a few hybrids with *R. pseudacacia* as one parent. **CZ3–5**

R. pseudacacia

The Species of *Robinia*

Group I: Shoots glabrous or at most downy, but not glandular-hispid.

R. pseudacacia False Acacia, Locust Black Locust. N. America, naturalized in many parts of Europe. Tree to 85 ft (26 m), with coarsely fissured bark. Shoots glabrous, stipules usually thorny (spinose). Leaflets 11–23. Flowers in dense, 4–8 in (10–20 cm) long, racemes, fragrant and white (pink in var *decaisneana*). Pod smooth linear-oblong, 2–4 in (5–10 cm) long with 3–10 seeds. Much planted as an ornamental. Stipules are not thorny in varieties umbraculifera and bessoniana. **CZ3**

R. boyntonii SE U.S. Shrub to 10 ft (3 m), without thorny stipules. Leaflets 7–13. Flowers in long (2.4–4 in/6–10 cm), loose racemes, pink to rosy-purplish. Pod glandular-hispid (with rough bristly hairs). **CZ5**

R. kelseyi SE U.S. Shrub or small tree to 10 ft (3 m). Shoots with thorny stipules. Flowers deep rosy-pink, 5–8 in each raceme. Pod 1.4–2 in (3.5–5 cm) long, densely purple, and glandular-hairy. **CZ5**

R. elliottii SE U.S. Shrub to 5 ft (1.5 m). Shoots hairy to tomentose at first, stipular spines small. Flowers pinkish-purple or purple and white. Pod hispid. **CZ5**

Group II: Shoots and peduncles glandular-hispid. Pod hispid.

R. hispida Rose Acacia, Bristly Locust. SE U.S. Shrub to 6 ft (2 m). Shoots and peduncles glandular-bristly. Leaflets 7–13. Flowers pink or pinkish-purple in 3–5 flowered hispid racemes. Pod rarely developed, 2–3 in (5–8 cm) long, glandular-hispid. Often grown as a graft on *R. pseudacacia*. **CZ5**

R. luxurians SW U.S. Shrub or tree to 33(40) ft (10(12) m). Shoots and peduncles glandular-hairy or downy, not hispid. Stipules thorny; leaflets 13–25; rachis of leaf pubescent, virtually glandless. Flowers pale pink or almost white. Pod (2.4)2.8–4 in ((6)7–10 cm) long with gland-tipped bristles. **CZ5**

R. viscosa Clammy Locust. SE U.S. Tree 33–40 ft (10–12 m). Shoots and peduncles glandular-hairy. Stipular spines small or absent; leaflets 13–25; rachis of leaf glandular or clammy. Flowers pink with yellow patch on standard. Pod 2–3 in (5–8 cm) long, with gland-tipped bristles. **CZ3**

R. kelseyi

R. hispida

LEGUMINOSAE

Robinia
FALSE ACACIAS, LOCUST TREES

Number of species 7
Distribution *North America.*
Commercial uses *Exploited for timber used in construction and for fuel. Species are also cultivated as garden and parkland trees and many different forms exist.*

Gymnocladus

Kentucky Coffee Tree

Gymnocladus is a genus of five species native to central and eastern North America and eastern China. This widespread distribution, which is apparent in other genera, is thought to indicate the remains of a vast Tertiary forest flora, which, 65–50 million years ago, occupied the northern hemisphere up to the present Arctic regions.

These are deciduous trees with large bipinnate leaves. The flowers are inconspicuous, regular (therefore not pea-like), and the sexes may be on the same or different plants. Each flower has a tubular calyx comprising five sepals, with five petals and ten stamens. The fruit is a large, thick pod, which contains large, flat seeds.

The Kentucky Coffee Tree, Chicot, or Knicker Tree (*G. dioica* = *G. canadensis*) from the east central United States grows to about 100 ft (30 m) high. Its bipinnate leaves may reach 45 in (115 cm) long and 24 in (60 cm) wide, the lowest two leaflets are simple, and there are three to seven pinnae, each with six to fourteen leaflets (rarely four) and one terminal leaflet. The greenish-white flowers are borne on long stalks on separate trees, the females in panicles 4–8 in (10–20 cm) or more long, the males about one-third as long. The pod is oblong, 6 in (15 cm) long and 1.6–2 in (4–5 cm) across. It is hardy in temperate regions, where it is grown for its foliage, but it is often reluctant to flower. As winter approaches, the leaflets drop off leaving behind the yellow leaf and leaflet stalks, with the result that the whole tree assumes a rather severe if distinctive appearance. Early settlers used to grind the seeds to make a drink bearing some resemblance to coffee—hence its popular name. The tree also yields useful timber.

Gymnocladus chinensis from China is a tree which reaches heights of 42 ft (13 m), and has leaves about as long as the previous species but with twenty to twenty-four oblong leaflets and lilac-purple blooms. Bisexual and unisexual flowers occur on the same tree. The pods are 2.8–4 in (7–10 cm) long and 1.6 in (4 cm) across. This species is not hardy in temperate regions.

The bark and pods of the two main species yield saponins, which have lather-producing properties.

LEGUMINOSAE

Gymnocladus
KENTUCKY COFFEE TREE

Number of species *5*
Distribution *Eastern North America and Southeast Asia.*
Commercial uses *Cultivated as ornamental trees and for timber and the seeds, which are roasted and used as a coffee substitute.*

Sophora

Pagoda Tree

Sophora is a genus of forty-five species of evergreen or deciduous trees or shrubs, and sometimes spiny, rarely stout, herbaceous perennials. They are native to warm and temperate regions of North and South America, Asia, and Australasia. *Sophora tetraptera* has a disjunct distribution between New Zealand, Tristan da Cunha, and southern Chile and, since its pods float on seawater and retain viable seed for up to three years, it was probably dispersed by the ocean currents. One species, *S. toromiro*, from Easter Island, was considered extinct. No specimens remain in its native habitat, the population having been destroyed by sheep introduced to this island in the eighteenth century. However, a number of seedlings were successfully raised at Göteborg Botanic Garden, Sweden, from seeds collected by the ethnologist Thor Heyerdahl during his *Kon-Tiki* expedition in 1947.

The leaves of sophoras are alternate, odd pinnate, with either numerous (between seven and eighty) small or few large opposite leaflets; the stipules are membranous and deciduous. The flowers, which are up to about 1 in (2.5 cm) long, are white, yellow, or rarely bluish-violet and are borne in terminal panicles or leafy racemes up to 20 in (50 cm) long.

ABOVE The contorted trunk and branches of the Pagoda Tree, *Sophora japonica*, make an open crown for the leaves, which are pale yellow when they emerge.

LEFT The open crown of a mature Kentucky Coffee Tree (*Gymnocladus canadensis*), displaying its flaking and scaling gray-brown bark and beautiful foliage, a fresh green above, a pale whitish green below.

Sophora
PAGODA TREE

Number of species 45
Distribution *Northern temperate regions to the Tropics.*
Commercial uses *Some species are the source of dyes and the timber is used in construction and for carving. Also grown as ornamental trees.*

The calyx comprises five short teeth and the corolla is either typically pea-like or more or less tube like, the petals pointing forward. The pod is cylindrical or slightly flattened, sometimes winged, up to 10 in (25 cm) in length, and is constricted between the seeds to appear rather like a bead necklace; in some cases it is indehiscent.

A few species are more or less hardy in temperate regions and are grown as ornamentals, the clusters of flowers being particularly attractive. They are distinctly sun-loving plants and some, for example the Kowhai, New Zealand Laburnum, or Fourwing Sophora (*S. tetraptera*), are happiest against a wall. Best known in cultivation is the Japanese Pagoda Tree or Scholar's Tree (*S. japonica*), which is native to China and Korea but not Japan. Other species cultivated in temperate regions include *S. macrocarpa* (Chile), *S. affinis* (southwest United States), and *S. davidii* (China). The timber is very hard: that of *S. tetraptera* is used for cabinetmaking, as shafts, and for turnery work. The fruits of *S. japonica* have purgative properties, and in China its leaf and fruit extracts are used to adulterate opium. The fruits of the Mescal Bean or Frijolito (*S. secundifolia*) are used as intoxicants by various American Indian tribes, and the red seeds for making necklaces. **CZ5–10**

Cladrastis

Yellow Woods

Cladrastis is a genus of six species of medium-sized, round-headed, deciduous trees from North America, China, and Japan. They somewhat resemble the locusts (*Robinia* spp) but have longer clusters of larger flowers. Their leaves are usually large, up to 13 in (33 cm) long, alternate and pinnate with seven to fifteen entire-margined leaflets, the odd one terminal. The flowers are pea-like, white or pinkish, and borne in panicles.

Each flower has ten near free stamens. The fruit is a dehiscent flattened pod containing three to six seeds. The yellow woods' most characteristic feature is the petiole which has a hollow, swollen base that encloses the following year's three buds, which later appear by the horseshoe-shaped leaf-scar.

Yellow woods are hardy in temperate regions and are often planted as ornamentals, preferring a reasonable loam soil and sunny position.

The Yellow Wood (*C. lutea*), from the southern United States, is the most frequently grown ornamental species, notably for its young bright green foliage, which turns a brilliant yellow in the fall. It can reach 66 ft (20 m) but usually grows to only 40 ft (12 m) in cultivation. The leaves are 8–12 in (20–30 cm) long and bear (5)7–9(11) leaflets, which lack stipels. The flowers are white, fragrant, and borne in pendulous panicles up to 14 in (36 cm) long. The pod is 3–4 in (7–10 cm) long and wingless. The heartwood of *C. lutea* yields a yellow dye, and the wood is used for making gunstocks. *Cladrastis sinensis* from China is often planted, possibly grafted onto *C. lutea*, on account of its relatively late summer flowering. It reaches 82 ft (25 m) in the wild, but otherwise about 50 ft (15 m). Each leaf bears (9)11–13(17) leaflets, which lack stipels. The flowers are white or suffused pinkish and borne in erect panicles 5–12 in (12–30 cm) long; the pod is 2–3 in (5–7.5 cm) long and wingless. Another Chinese species, *C. wilsoni*, is closely related to *C. sinensis* but does not flower in cultivation, hence it is infrequently seen. The Japanese Yellow Wood (*C. platycarpa*), from Japan, resembles species of *Sophora*, in which genus it was once placed. It is distinguished from the other *Cladrastis* species by its winged pod and the presence of stipels to the leaflets. **CZ3–6**

The Yellow Wood, *Cladrastis lutea*, has a very distinct and handsome foliage, vivid green in the summer, large and pendulous, turning a bright yellow before falling.

Cladrastis
YELLOW WOODS

Number of species 6
Distribution *East Asia and North America.*
Commercial uses *A source of decorative yellow wood and a yellow dye.*

The leaves of *Elaeagnus angustifolia* are distinct for the silver scales on the underside. They are narrow and lanceolate and a dull green and scaly above. The twigs are also white and combined with the leaves make a striking tree. Foliage becomes whiter in the sun.

ELAEAGNACEAE

Elaeagnus

Oleaster

The species in the *Elaeagnus* genus are all native to North America, southern Europe, and Asia. They are evergreen or deciduous trees or shrubs with alternate leaves, the undersurfaces of which are often covered with fringed, silvery scales. The flowers are mostly fragrant, bisexual (sometimes unisexual) with a perianth comprising one whorl (calyx) with four petaloid lobes that are more or less at right angles to the inverted, bell-like tube. The fruit is a one-seeded drupe.

They are mostly quite hardy species, often cultivated for their attractive foliage and fragrant flowers. They grow best on a light, sandy loam, a poor soil positively enhancing the silvery appearance of the leaves.

The fruits of some species are consumed as preserves or as jellies, for example those of *E. multiflora* (Japan), which are tart, but have a good flavor, and *E. philippinensis* (Philippines). The fruit of *E. angustifolia* (southern Europe, western and central Asia, the Himalaya) is made into a sherbet-like drink. **CZ2–9**

The Main Species of *Elaeagnus*

Group I: Spring flowering; leaves deciduous.

E. angustifolia Oleaster, Russian Olive. W Europe, naturalized in S Europe. Shrub or small tree mostly 16–23 ft (5–7 m), sometimes to 40 ft (12 m), shoots and leaves (both sides) with only silvery scales (none brown). Leaves more or less lanceolate, 1.6–2.8 in (4–8 cm) long. Flowers with perianth yellow inside, silvery scaly outside. Fruit oval, up to 0.55 in (13 mm), silvery scaly, yellow, edible. Much prized for its white shoots and silvery undersides of leaves. **CZ2**

E. commutata Silver Berry. The only species native to N. America. Shrub to 13 ft (4 m), shoots and often leaves (lower side) with brownish scales in addition to silvery ones. Leaves more or less lanceolate, (1.4)1.6–3.5 in ((3.5)4–9 cm) long. Flowers pendulous, freely produced, very fragrant, yellow within, the calyx-tube much longer than its lobes. Fruit ovoid, silvery, 0.3–0.35 in (8–9 mm) long. One of the most attractive shrubs with its silvery foliage and yellow, and very fragrant flowers. **CZ2**

E. multiflora Japan. Shrub 2–3 m. Shoots and lower side of leaves with brownish scales as well as more numerous silvery scales. Leaves elliptic to obovate, 1.4–2.5 in (3.5–6 cm) long. Flowers fragrant, yellowish-white within, silver and brown scales on outside. Fruit oblong, 0.5–0.55 in (12–13 mm) long, a fine orange color. Grown for its abundant, orange-colored fruits. Differs from *E. commutata* and *E. umbellata* by its longer fruit-stalk (0.6–1 in/18–25 mm) and the calyx-tube and its lobes about the same length. **CZ6**

Elaeagnus
OLEASTER

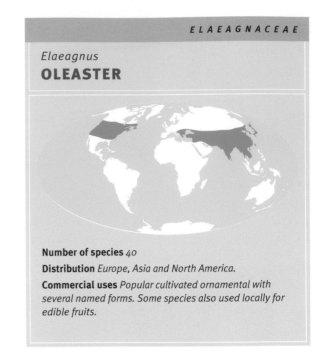

Number of species *40*
Distribution *Europe, Asia and North America.*
Commercial uses *Popular cultivated ornamental with several named forms. Some species also used locally for edible fruits.*

E. umbellata The Himalaya, China, Japan. Wide-spreading shrub often wider than its 13–20 ft (4–6 m) height, shoots and leaves with brown and silvery scales. Leaves lanceolate to oval, 2–4 in (5–10 cm) long. Flowers on stalks, 0.2–0.3 in (6–8 mm), pale primrose within, silvery scaly outside, the calyx-tube much longer than its lobes. Fruit round, 0.2–0.3 in (6–8 mm) across, silvery, finally red. Grown for its flowers and fruits. **CZ3**

Group II: Fall flowering; leaves evergreen.

E. pungens Japan. Shrub to 16 ft (5 m), shoots mostly spiny and with the leaves (underside) brown scaly. Leaves toughish, more or less oval, (1.6)2–4 in ((4)5–10 cm) long. Flowers fragrant, pendulous, silvery-white, the calyx-tube longer than its lobes and contracted above ovary. Fruit 0.5–0.8 in (12–20 mm) long, at first brown, finally red. Popular for its fragrant flowers. There are a number of cultivars with more or less variegated leaves, of which, perhaps, 'Maculata' is outstanding. **CZ7**

E. macrophylla Korea, Japan, possibly China. Spreading shrub 10–13 ft (3–4 m), brown scales absent, the shoots silvery-white, usually spiny. Leaves more or less oval, 2–4.5 in (5–11 cm) long, the upper surface silvery scaly at first, less so when adult, lower surface strikingly and persistently silvery scaly. Flowers very fragrant, more or less pendulous. Fruit oval, 0.6–0.65 in (15–16 mm) long, scaly, with persistent calyx, red. **CZ8**

E. glabra China, Japan. A rambling or climbing shrub to about 20 ft (6 m), often confused with and sold as *E. pungens*, but the shoots are without spines and the lower surfaces of the leaves are dull brownish from the yellow and brown scales, whereas in the latter the color is whitish. Not uncommonly grown, possibly in mistake for *E. pungens*. **CZ8**

MYRTACEAE

Eucalyptus

Eucalypts

The eucalypts are a large genus of evergreen trees and shrubs, found chiefly in Australia, with a few extending to New Guinea, eastern Indonesia, and one of the Philippine islands, Mindanao. None is native in New Zealand. They range in height from less than 3 ft (1 m) to over 330 ft (100 m) in specimens of *Eucalyptus regnans*. This species, known in the state of Victoria (Australia) as Mountain Ash, is the tallest of flowering plants, though surpassed by the coniferous *Sequoia sempervirens*, California's Coast Redwood.

Large or small, in forests, scrubs, or heaths, eucalypts are in the dominant stratum, virtually never the undergrowth. By far the majority of natural forest and woodland in nonarid Australia, from the Tropics to cool-temperate southern Tasmania, is dominated by *Eucalyptus* species, usually without any other genus in the upper story. Such dominance of a single genus has no parallel in other continents.

Fire-adaptation is a vital determinant in the distribution of eucalypt dominated communities. Some species regenerate from seed only after destructive fire, but most survive it by growth of epicormic shoots from dormant buds in the bark. Many smaller species are mallees (shrubby, with several trunks arising from a massive lignotuber beneath or partly above the soil). Small lignotubers also mark young stages of single-stemmed species, which can regenerate from epicormic shoots.

Eucalyptus is traditionally distinguished by the presence in the flower-buds of a floral operculum; the flowers open by shedding these lidlike coverings to expose the style and the numerous stamens. The latter are the conspicuous organs of the flower, attracting various insects (often honeybees) and birds in search of the usually copious nectar. The opercular structures vary considerably in morphological equivalence in the nine subgenera recognized here (on these and other grounds), and must have arisen independently in several parallel evolutionary lines.

In *Angophora* (sometimes treated as a separate genus but bound by a complex of morphological and chemical characters to two eucalypt subgenera), the flowers have separate sepals and petals. In certain of the other subgenera the sepals are free but the petals are united into an operculum; in others the two whorls form an outer and an inner operculum, while in subgenus *Monocalyptus* the single operculum is apparently derived from sepals alone.

Each subgenus or, as in the case of *Symphyomyrtus* (the largest, with about 300 species), each section into which they may be divided has a characteristic range of habitats. Subgenus *Monocalyptus*, for instance, is almost entirely restricted to acid soils particularly poor in phosphates and other nutrients in regions of favorable rainfall—especially winter rainfall.

The Bluegum Tree (*Eucalyptus globulus*) in the Blue Mountains National Park, New South Wales, Australia, named for the fine mist of oil which is given off by the leaves and appears as a blue haze.

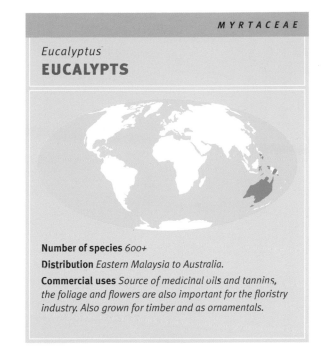

MYRTACEAE

Eucalyptus
EUCALYPTS

Number of species *600+*
Distribution *Eastern Malaysia to Australia.*
Commercial uses *Source of medicinal oils and tannins, the foliage and flowers are also important for the floristry industry. Also grown for timber and as ornamentals.*

Eucalypt Bark and Timber

Popular classification of eucalypts is based on the more obvious features of bark and timber. Such names as Stringy-bark, Ironbark, Peppermint, Box, Blood-wood, Blackbutt, Red Gum, and Blue Gum are widely and often inconsistently applied—similar names being used in different regions of Australia for quite unrelated species. Nevertheless there is some degree of correspondence with the natural affinities expressed in the botanical classification. The characteristic bark of the so-called **Gums**, for example, is smooth and deciduous (peeling); **Boxes** are rough and fibrous-barked, while **Peppermints** are finely fibrous; **Stringy-barks** are long and fibrous, and **Ironbarks** are hard, rough, and fissured.

Identification is rendered difficult for the nonspecialist by the nature of some of the fundamental criteria (for example opercular structure, anther shapes, leaf venation patterns) and by the sheer number of species in some areas: over a hundred are found within a radius of under 95 miles (150 km) from Sydney. Further complication is caused by variation within species, especially geographic and altitudinal clines (gradients in the absolute or statistical expression of characters). Moreover, there are many species that, though distinct over much of their areas, in certain contact zones produce hybrids or hybrid swarms intergrading to the parent species. This phenomenon was certainly widespread in Australia before European settlement but has increased as habitat distinctions have become blurred by clearing, drainage, altered fire regimes, and other human activity, over the past one hundred to two hundred years.

Apart from differences in flowering period, there seem to be few intrinsic barriers to effective interbreeding between species within any one section (and few if any absolute barriers within any one subgenus). In direct contrast, no natural or manipulated hybrids are known between species of different subgenera. Thus many species remain distinct only through geographic isolation or by survival of their progeny in ecologically different habitats within the same region, which likewise act as a barrier to interbreeding. Consequently, in any one site associated species usually belong to different breeding groups, that is, subgenera or sections. In areas of complex physiography or fine mosaics of soil types, this phenomenon is often evident only by careful inspection of the distribution patterns of the species and the environmental determinants.

Eucalypts constitute the major hardwood timber resource of Australia: among the particularly valuable species for sawlog and pole production are the Jarrah (*E. marginata*), Blackbutt (*E. pilularis* and Messmate (*E. obliqua*). Recently, emphasis has swung to pulp for paper and similar products and especially to chipwood for hardboard production. Massive clearance of timbered land for woodchip production and the subsequent export of the product have met with opposition from environmentalists. Forestry authorities claim

ABOVE Flowers of *Eucalyptus globulus* are usually borne singly in the leaf axils. Buds are glaucous and ridged and wrinkled. The most conspicuous feature is the numerous stamens, which are pale yellow/white.

FACING PAGE The tall smooth trunk of *Eucalyptus grandis* is characteristic of the mountain forests of Australia.

E. parvifolia

E. glaucescens

that by rotation of such exploitation the eucalypts can be managed as a renewable resource. Nevertheless, general considerations point to widespread adverse affects on wildlife and the esthetic values of the countryside. Many eucalypt species are important food plants for the indigenous Koala (*Phascolarctos cinereus*), whose metabolism and anatomy have become especially adapted to digest this plant material.

Among the minor products derived from the genus, the best known are eucalyptus oils, essential oils that have been used medicinally and in flavoring. A frequent constituent is cineole (or eucalyptol). Several species yield kinos, which are astringent tannin-containing exudates used in medicine and tanning. The bark of *Eucalyptus sideroxylon* ('Mugga') was formerly much exploited for use in tanning processes.

Eucalypts are widely planted (in Brazil, North Africa, the Middle East, southern and tropical Africa, California, India, and on the Black Sea coast of Ukraine and Russia) for timber, pulpwood, firewood, shelter (shade trees and windbreaks), erosion control, essential-oils production, and ornament. In suitable climates, many species make much better growth in exotic situations than in their native habitat, thanks to higher nutrient status of soils and the absence of destructive insects. The most important species grown outside Australia number only thirty or forty and are often different from those of greatest importance for timber in Australia.

Cultivation outside the eucalypts' native regions is beset with difficulties. Economic and reliable methods of vegetative propagation have not been developed, so that seed is the only means available. This brings many difficulties, not least that seed from sources outside Australia is likely to be unreliably identified. Even seed samples from wild-growing trees may be wrongly named, be mixtures of more than one species, or often include hybrid seed from outcrossings. It is equally important to have appropriate instructions as to germination procedure, potting-off, and final transplanting to the permanent position.

Many eucalypts are fast-growing; seedlings can grow to 5 ft (1.5 m) in a year and to 33 ft (10 m) or more in ten years in some tropical and subtropical species. Some species were planted extensively during the nineteenth century in swampy areas in Italy and also in similar areas in North Africa. It was claimed that their high rates of transpiration helped to dry out the land, with consequent antimalarial benefits. One swamp-tolerant species is the Swamp Mahogany (*E. robusta*), a medium-sized tree with rough, brownish bark. Many other species are cultivated outside Australia: the most widely planted species in California and the Mediterranean region is probably the Tasmanian Blue Gum (*E. globulus*), a tree reaching 115–150 ft (35–45 m) with grayish inner bark annually exposed by stripping away of the outer bark. California has the richest introduced eucalypt flora in the United States.

In cooler regions, eucalypts are mostly grown for ornament or curiosity. Among these is the Cider Gum (*E. gunnii*), a tree reaching 100 ft (30 m) with strips of pinkish bark peeling to expose a more or less smooth gray underbark. Another hardy species is the Alpine Snow Gum (*E. pauciflora* ssp *niphophila*), a small tree in the subgenus *Monocalyptus* that grows to about 20 ft (6 m), with smooth gray or white-streaked bark, peeling every second or third year. Also hardy, except for the coldest areas of temperate regions, is the Tasmanian Snow Gum (*E. coccifera*), a small tree often pruned to keep it shrubby, with strikingly spiraled bark. A vigorous and hardy species less often seen in cultivation is the Urn-fruited Gum (*E. urnigera*), a tree reaching 100–115 ft (30–35 m), the fruit of which is constricted like an urn. **CZ8–10**

SOME OF THE EUCALYPTS GROWN OUTSIDE AUSTRALIA IN WARM TEMPERATE REGIONS

Common Name	Species
Marri, Red Gum	E. calophylla
Murray Red Gum	E. camaldulensis
Lemon-scented Gum	E. citriodora
Mountain Gum	E. dalrympleana
	E. glaucescens
Rose Gum =	E. gomphocephala
	E. grandis
Coarse-leaved Mallee	E. grossa
Kruse's Mallee	E. kruseana
Mottlecah	E. macrocarpa
Flooded Box	E. microtheca
Flat-topped Yate	E. occidentalis
Swamp Gum	E. ovata
Small-leaved Gum	E. parvifolia
Round-leaved Snow Gum	E. perriniana
	E. pileata
Sydney Blue Gum =	E. saligna
	E. sideroxylon
Forest Red Gum =	E. tereticornis
White-leaved Marlock	E. tetragona

Noticeably absent are members of the subgenus Monocalyptus, *mentioned above as important in Australia. This group appears to be particularly dependent on mycorrhizal associations.*

The Main Species of *Eucalyptus*

Subgenus *Blakella*
Section *Lemuria*, series *Clavigerae*

E. papuana Ghost Gum. N Australia, New Guinea. Tree 33–60 ft (10–18 m). Bark shed to ground level, leaving strikingly white surface. Leaves concolorous. Inflorescences lateral with aggregated, mostly 7-flowered umbels. Fruit 0.4 × 0.28 in (10 × 7 mm), papery in texture, valves deeply enclosed. **CZ10**

Subgenus *Corymbia*
Section *Rufaria*, series *Gummiferae*

Bloodwoods. Bark short-fibered, persistent in thick scales. Leaves typically discolorous with fine close lateral veins at a wide angle to the midrib. Inflorescences terminal or lateral, with numerous 7-flowered umbels. Fruit woody, ovoid-urceolate; valves deeply enclosed.

E. ficifolia Red-flowering Gum. SW Australia. Bushy tree to 33 ft (10 m). Flowers large, stamens red. Fruit about 1.2 × 0.5 in (30 × 12 mm). **CZ9**

E. gummifera Red Bloodwood. E Australia. Tree to 115 ft (35 m). Fruit about 0.6 × 0.5 in (15 × 12 mm).* **CZ10**

Section *Ochraria*, series *Maculatae*

Spotted gums. Smooth, pinkish, often mottled bark. Leaves with fine, close lateral veins. Umbels 3 flowered. Fruits urceolate; valves deeply enclosed.

E. citriodora Lemon-scented Gum. NE Australia. Slender tree to 130 ft (40 m). Leaves contain citronellal. Fruit about 0.5 × 0.35 in (12 × 9 mm).** **CZ10**

E. maculata Spotted Gum. E Australia. Usually fairly robust tree 115–130 ft (35–40 m). Leaves slightly discolorous without citronellal. Fruit about 0.6 × 0.5 (15 × 12 mm).** **CZ10**

Subgenus *Eudesmia*
Section *Quadraria* series *Tetrodontae*

E. tetrodonta Darwin Stringybark. N Australia. Tree usually 50–78 ft (15–24 m). Bark fibrous, persistent. Leaves concolorous, grayish, pendulous. Umbels 3-flowered. Fruit somewhat campanulate, about 0.6 × 0.35 in (15 × 9 mm), with 4 prominent external teeth (not to be confused with the small valves about rim level).** **CZ10**

Subgenus *Symphyomyrtus*
Section *Transversaria*

Mainly large trees. Bark persistent or gum type. Leaves mainly discolorous, lateral veins fine, usually at large angles (50–75°) to midrib. Fruit with valves slightly or strongly exserted.

Series *Diversicolores*

E. diversicolor Karri. W Australia. Tree 150–215(245) ft (45–65 (75) m). Gum bark. Umbels 7 flowered. Fruit pyriform-globose, 0.5 × 0.5 in (12 × 12 mm); valves deeply enclosed.*** **CZ10**

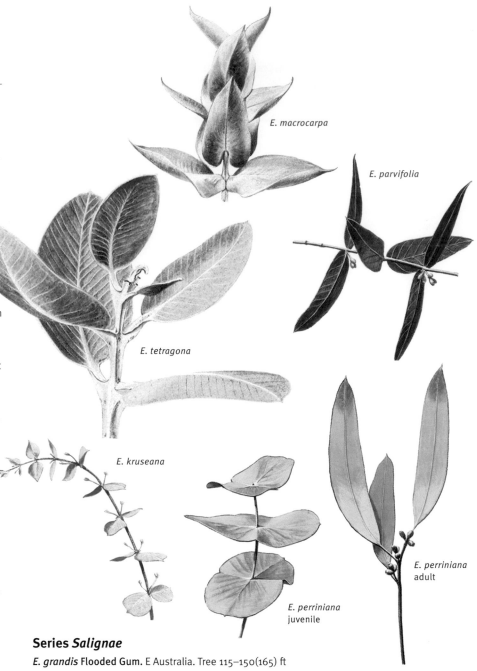

E. macrocarpa

E. parvifolia

E. tetragona

E. kruseana

E. perriniana juvenile

E. perriniana adult

Series *Salignae*

E. grandis Flooded Gum. E Australia. Tree 115–150(165) ft (35–45(50) m). Gum bark. Umbels 7 flowered. Fruit pyriform, about 0.3 × 0.2 in (8 × 6 mm), often sessile; valves thin, slightly exserted, incurved. **CZ10**

E. saligna Sydney Blue Gum. E Australia. Tree 115–150(165) ft (35–45(50) m). Gum bark, but often with basal stocking. Umbels 7–11 flowered. Fruit like that of *E. grandis* but usually smaller and valves straight or spreading outward.** **CZ10**

E. propinqua Small-fruited Gray Gum. E Australia. Tree 100–115 ft (30–35 m). Gum bark. Umbels typically 7 flowered. Fruit hemispherical or obconic, about 0.2 × 0.2 in (5 × 5 mm); valves prominent.* **CZ10**

Section *Bisectaria*, series *Salmonophloiae*

E. salmonophloia Salmon Gum. W Australia. Tree 50–80(100) ft (15–25(30) m). Gum bark salmon pink in color. Leaves concolorous. Umbels 7 flowered. Fruit globular, about 0.2 × 0.2 in (5 × 5 mm); valves very long.* **CZ10**

E. pileata

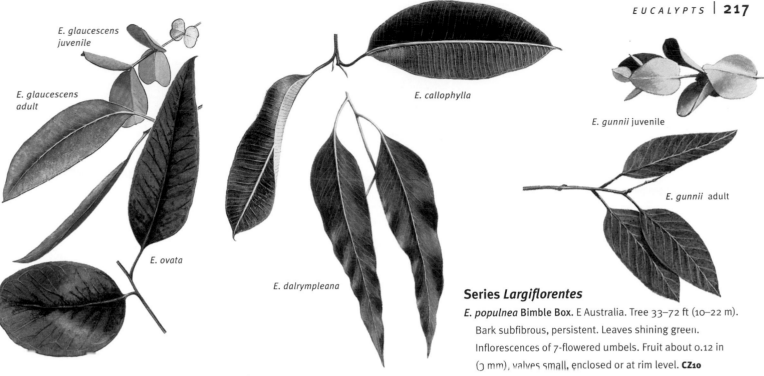

E. glaucescens juvenile

E. glaucescens adult

E. ovata

E. callophylla

E. dalrympleana

E. gunnii juvenile

E. gunnii adult

E. dalrympleana

E. pauciflora ssp niphophila

Section *Exsertaria*

Includes Red Gums. Mainly gum-barked. Leaves concolorous. Umbels often 7–20+-flowered. Fruit typically globular to hemispherical, with strongly exserted valves. Ratio of operculum length to diameter often important in identification.

Series *Tereticornes*

E. tereticornis Forest Red Gum. E Australia, New Guinea. Tree 100–130(165) ft (30–40(50) m). Umbels 7-flowered. Operculum 2.5–4 times longer than wide. Fruit about 0.2 × 0.2 in (6 × 6 mm).** **CZ10**

E. camaldulensis River Red Gum. Most of Australia. Robust tree 82–100(115) ft (25–30(35) m). Operculum typically rostrate but bluntly conic in northern forms. Fruit 0.16 × 0.2 in (4 × 6 mm).** **CZ9**

Section *Maidenaria*, series *Viminales*

E. globulus Tasmanian Blue Gum. SE Australia. Tree 115–150(165) ft (35–45(50) m). Gum bark. Leaves concolorous. Flowers solitary in typical form, buds warty. Fruit top-shaped, about 0.6 × 1 in (15 × 25 mm), sessile.* **CZ9**

E. viminalis Manna Gum. S and SE Australia. Tree 66–115(165) ft (20–35(50) m). Gum bark. Leaves concolorous. Umbels usually 3-flowered. Fruit subglobular, about 0.28 × 0.2 in (7 × 5 mm) (2 lateral ones sessile): valves prominent, exserted.* **CZ8**

Section *Adnataria*, series *Oliganthae*

E. microtheca Coolabah. Inland and N Australia. Tree 40–66 ft (12–20 m). Bark subfibrous, usually persistent on stem and large branches. Leaves bluish-green. Moderately large inflorescences of 7-flowered umbels. Fruit hemispherical, 0.12 × 0.16 (3 × 4 mm), with large, exserted valves. **CZ10**

Series *Largiflorentes*

E. populnea Bimble Box. E Australia. Tree 33–72 ft (10–22 m). Bark subfibrous, persistent. Leaves shining green. Inflorescences of 7-flowered umbels. Fruit about 0.12 in (3 mm), valves small, enclosed or at rim level. **CZ10**

Series *Paniculatae*

E. paniculata Gray Ironbark. SE Australia. Tree 80–100(130) ft (25–30(40) m). Bark ironbark, persistent. Leaves moderately discolorous. Panicles with mostly 7-flowered umbels. Fruit pyriform to ovoid, about 0.35 × 0.28 in (9 × 7 mm); valves small, usually enclosed.** **CZ10**

Series *Melliodorae*

E. melliodora Yellow Box. SE Australia. Tree 50–100 ft (15–30 m). Bark subfibrous, variably persistent. Leaves concolorous. Umbels 7-flowered. Fruit subpyriform, about 0.28 × 0.2 in (7 × 5 mm); valves enclosed. **CZ10**

Section *Sebaria*, series *Microcorythes*

E. microcorys Tallowwood. E Australia. Tree 100–150(165) ft (30–45(50) m). Bark subfibrous, soft, persistent. Leaves discolorous. Umbels 7-flowered, mostly in small terminal inflorescences. Fruit elongated obconical, about 0.3 × 0.2 in (8 × 5 mm); valves very small, slightly protruding. **CZ10**

Subgenus *Telocalyptus*
Section *Equatoria*, series *Degluptae*

E. deglupta Kamerere. Philippines, Sulawesi, New Guinea, and New Britain. Tree 115–200(250) ft (35–60(75) m). Gum bark. Leaves discolorous. Terminal and axillary inflorescences of 3–7-flowered umbels. Fruit hemispherical, about 0.12 × 0.2 in (3 × 5 mm); large, exserted valves.** **CZ10**

Subgenus *Monocalyptus*
Section *Renantheria*, series *Marginatae*

E. marginata Jarrah. SW Australia. Tree 80–115 ft (25–35 m). Bark fibrous persistent. Leaves discolorous. Umbels 7-flowered. Fruit spherical-ovoid, woody, about 0.7 × 0.6 in (18 × 15 mm); valves enclosed.*** **CZ10**

Series *Capitellatae*

Stringybarks. Bark fibrous, persistent. Leaves usually concolorous. Umbels 7–20+ flowered. Fruit hemispherical to globular, typically with exserted valves.

E. baxteri **Brown Stringybark.** SE Australia. Tree 80–115 ft (25–35 m). Umbels 7-flowered. Fruit about 0.4 × 0.35 in (11 × 9 mm), almost sessile.* **CZ10**

E. eugenioides **Thin-leaved Stringybark.** E Australia. Tree 66–80 ft (20–25 m). Umbels 7–11 flowered. Fruit about 0.25 × 0.28 in (6 × 7 mm), with very short pedicels.* **CZ10**

Series *Pilulares*

E. pilularis **Blackbutt.** E Australia. Tree 35–60 m. Bark finely fibrous, persistent on lower half of trunk. Leaves discolorous. Umbels 7–11 flowered. Fruit pilular, about 0.45 × 0.5 in (11 × 12 mm); valves small, enclosed, or to rim level.*** **CZ10**

Series *Obliquae*

Height varies from world's tallest hardwood (*E. regnans*) to mallee. Bark fibrous, persistent, or gum. Leaves typically concolorous, often with oblique base and lateral veins at small angle (15–25°) to midrib. Fruit ovoid to pyriform, mainly with sunken valves.

E. obliqua **Messmate.** SE Australia. Tree 33–200 ft (10–60 m). Bark persistent. Leaves green. The first eucalypt named as such, though some species had been described under other genera. Fruit about 0.35 × 0.3 in (9 × 8 mm).*** **CZ9**

E. delegatensis **Alpine Ash.** SE Australia. Tree 115–165(230) ft (35–50(70) m). Bark persistent on lower trunk. Leaves bluish. Umbels 7–15 flowered. Fruit 0.6 × 0.5 in (15 × 12 mm).*** **CZ9**

E. regnans **Mountain Ash.** SE Australia. Tree 165–250(330) ft (50–75(100) m). Bark persistent on lower part of trunk. Leaves green, small. Umbels 7–11 flowered, often in pairs. Fruit about 0.3 × 0.2 in (8 × 6 mm).*** **CZ9**

E. pauciflora **Snow Gum.** SE Australia. Tree, sometimes crooked, 50–60 ft (15–18 m). Gum bark. Leaf venation conspicuous, major lateral veins almost parallel to midrib. Umbels 7–15 flowered. Fruit about 0.35 × 0.3 in (9 × 8 mm).

Series *Piperitae*

(Peppermints and scribbly gums). Small to moderate trees. Bark fibrous or smooth. Leaves concolorous, often with lateral veins at small angle to midrib. Fruit typically small, with inconspicuous valves often about rim level.

E. radiata **Narrow-leaved Peppermint.** SE Australia. Tree 40–78 ft (12–24 m). Bark subfibrous, persistent. Fruit subglobular to subpyriform, about 0.2 × 0.2 in (4 × 4 mm).* **CZ9**

Commercial importance

*** significant contributor to commercial pulpwood and timber production

** important, but sometimes restricted to a limited geographical area

* limited importance, due to log form, gum pockets (e.g. *E. gummifera*), etc.

E. eugenioides

FACING PAGE *Nyssa aquatica* is a valuable tree in its native habitat for its fruit and its timber.

BELOW The Dove Tree or Handkerchief Tree, *Davidia involucrata*, flowers in late spring, but the small, round heads are hidden by the remarkable creamy white bracts which surround them. These large bracts are of unequal size. Flowers are copious on trees over twenty years old.

Davidia

Dove Trees

Davidia is a genus of only one species, *D. involucrata* (the Dove Tree, Ghost Tree, or Handkerchief Tree) from central and western China, where it reaches 66 ft (20 m) in height. It is a deciduous tree, somewhat resembling a lime tree (*Tilia* spp), bearing alternate, broadly ovate leaves with a heart-shaped base and long-pointed tip. The outstanding feature of this species is the conspicuous enormous white or creamy-white bracts, two of which surround each of the small globose flower heads. The flowers lack petals, each head comprising a mass of male flowers with purple anthers and a single bisexual flower. In early summer the sight of a mature tree clothed in the white bracts is quite spectacular. However, trees under twenty years of age flower sparsely. Later in the season the deep green ovoid fruits, 1.2 × 1 in (3 × 2.5 cm), form a distinctive feature, dangling on long stalks below the leaves and later the leafless shoots.

Dove trees grow well only on fertile soil. The type most frequently seen in cultivation is var *vilmoriniana*, which lacks the white hairs on the undersurface of the leaves that occur on the type variety. **CZ6**

Nyssa

Tupelos

The tupelos, outstanding for their fall colors, comprise a genus of about eight North and Central American and Asian deciduous trees and shrubs.

Tupelos have simple, alternate leaves, without stipules, and minute unisexual flowers, with the sexes on the same or different plants or polygamous. Each flower has five minute sepals and five greenish petals; the females are either solitary or occur in small clusters while the males are clustered in globular heads. The males have 5–10(12) stamens and the females a single style plus a one- or two-chambered ovary. The fruit is a plum-like drupe, often red or purple, containing a single seed (stone).

Best known of the species is the Black Gum, Pepperidge, or Tupelo (*Nyssa sylvatica*), which is renowned both in its native eastern United States and in cultivation throughout temperate regions for its striking scarlet and gold colors produced early in the fall. In cultivation the Black Gum is particularly valuable for wet or acid soils but it can survive in drier areas, particularly coastal regions when protected from winds. Propagation is from seeds or by layering, but seedlings should be planted out as soon as they are manageable, since older saplings do not transplant well.

The Water Tupelo, Cotton Gum, or Large Tupelo (*N. aquatica*) is another notable species. It grows in the swamps of the eastern and southern coasts of the United States, and is often in standing water for much of the year. The Water Tupelo and Sour Tupelo (*N. ogeche*) are both valued as bee plants, and the latter's fruits (ogeche limes) are eaten locally. The soft yet tough wood of tupelos is valued in commerce for making furniture, boxes, and shoes. **CZ3–7**

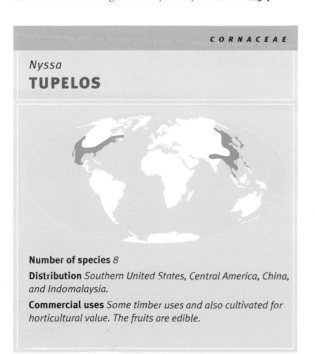

CORNACEAE

Nyssa
TUPELOS

Number of species *8*

Distribution *Southern United States, Central America, China, and Indomalaysia.*

Commercial uses *Some timber uses and also cultivated for horticultural value. The fruits are edible.*

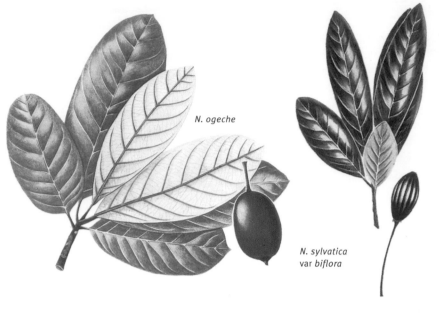

N. ogeche

N. sylvatica var biflora

N. sylvatica

N. sinensis

The Main Species of *Nyssa*

Group I: Native to the United States

A *Female flowers borne 2 or more together. Fruit small and black; stone smooth or bluntly ridged.*

N. sylvatica (N. villosa) Tupelo, Black Gum, Pepperidge.
Hillsides or swampy sites. Calcifuge. Oak-like tree to 100 ft (30 m), crown broadly conic, branches level but curved up at the tip. Bark angular with checkered pattern. Leaves ovate to obovate, 2–5 in (5–12 cm) long, entire, glossy dark or yellow-green above, whitish-green below. Female flowers usually 2, sometimes 3, on a single peduncle. Stone almost ribless. **CZ3**
var *biflora* Tupelo, Water Gum, Twin Flowered Nyssa. Peaty and swampy habitats. Tree to 50 ft (15 m). Bark with long ridges. Distinguished by its spathulate, elliptic leaves. Stone ribbed. **CZ3**

N. ursina A much-branched shrub. Leaves smaller than previous species. Flowers conspicuous in clusters. Drupe (fruit) globular.

AA *Female flowers borne singly. Fruit large, purple-red; stone ridged and winged.*

N. acuminata Pine swamps. Shrub to 16 ft (5 m) with underground stems. Branches with narrow leaves. Female flower short-stalked. Drupe (fruit) red; stone winged.

N. ogeche (N. candicans, N. capitata) Sour Tupelo, Ogeche Lime, Ogeche Plum. Riverbanks. Spreading tree to 30 ft (9 m). Stem often crooked. Leaves broad. Drupe (fruit) oblong, longer than stalk, red-purple; stone winged.

N. aquatica (N. uniflora) Cotton Gum, Water Tupelo. Tree to 100 ft (30 m). Leaves ovate, 4–6 in (10–15 cm) long, downy underneath. Female flower long-stalked, the drupe (fruit) purple-blue, shorter than stalk; stone sharply ridged.

Group II: Native to Eastern Asia.

N. sinensis Shrub or tree to 60 ft (18 m). Bark gray, finely fissured. Leaves oblong-ovate up to 6 in (15 cm) long, deep shiny green above, pale green below, pubescent on veins and midrib; petiole flattened. Flowers axillary, aggregated; stalk slender with silky brown hairs. Young growth red-brown pubescent. **CZ7**

N. javanica Tree to 50 ft (15 m). Branches gray-brown with dense silky pubescence, spotted with prominent lenticels. Leaves as long but broader than *N. sinensis*, green above but silky brown below; peduncle short. **CZ7**

N. sylvatica

TOP LEFT *Nyssa sylvatica* is native to eastern North America, growing in swamps and badly draining wet ground. With a tapering trunk, it reaches 100 ft (30 m). It is one of the first trees in the U.S. to display fall foliage.

Cornus

Cornels, Dogwoods

Cornus is a genus of over sixty species of mostly deciduous trees or shrubs with a scattered distribution over temperate regions of the northern hemisphere, especially the United States and Asia. The leaves are mostly opposite and the flowers normally small, white, less often greenish or yellowish, their parts in fours. They are clustered in terminal heads or cymes, sometimes surrounded by more or less conspicuous involucral bracts. The fruit is a drupe and the seed a two-celled stone.

These are primarily ornamental plants cultivated for the beauty of their flowers, particularly the bracts, and stem color (often red), and some for the fall color of their leaves. The Cornelian Cherry (*C. mas*), the Flowering Dogwood (*C. florida*), the Pacific Dogwood (*C. nuttallii*), and *C. kousa* have especially attractive flowers. All these tree-like species grow best in sheltered, semi-woodland, or particularly shaded sites, preferring moist, lime-free organic soils. The colored-stem dogwoods are shrubby, thicket-forming species,

The Flowering Dogwood, *Cornus florida*, has insignificant flowers in four parts—green, tipped with yellow. The beauty is in the four bracts, white and heart-shaped, which surround them. These enclose the flowerhead in winter, and open in early spring.

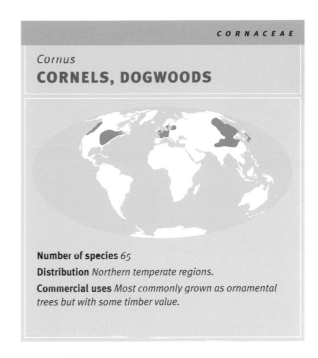

CORNACEAE

Cornus
CORNELS, DOGWOODS

Number of species 65
Distribution *Northern temperate regions.*
Commercial uses *Most commonly grown as ornamental trees but with some timber value.*

often with vivid winter color showing on the current season's growth. "Stooling," or removal of older wood in the spring, is undertaken to maintain stems of the young wood for the full effect. This group grows well in moist waterside habitats and includes the Red Osier Dogwood (*C. stolonifera*), 'Flaviramea' with golden-green stems, and *C. alba* 'Sibirica' with vivid dark red stems. In the European species Common Dogwood (*C. sanguinea*), the specific name refers to the fall red color of the leaves rather than the stems, which may be a patchy red on one side.

A few species have some value other than esthetic. Fruits of the Common Dogwood yield an oil, which can be used for illumination as well as for making soap; the twigs are flexible enough for basketmaking. The wood of the Cornelian Cherry is very durable and suitable for small articles such as skewers, handles, and similar; its fruit can be made into a preserve.

The genus is commonly divided into four sections, which some authorities would raise to generic rank. In the following species selection, the wider concept of the genus is maintained, the four sections being referred to as four Groups, each Group being given a name, which would be the generic name used by those authorities who favor segregation. Relevant for present purposes is the common exclusion of two species from *Cornus*, essentially because they are herbaceous. These are the Dwarf Cornel (*C. suecica*), a beautiful arctic-alpine herb growing to 8 in (20 cm), the flower clusters surrounded by four spreading white involucral bracts—each individual flower purplish-black and fruits red; and the Bunch-berry (*C. canadensis*), which grows to about 10 in (25 cm) and is slightly woody at the base and has a creeping rootstock; individual flowers are greenish and the flower clusters are surrounded by four to six white involucral bracts; the fruit is scarlet. The genus created for them, *Chamaepericlimenum*, is most likely an unnecessary creation. **CZ2–8**

The Main Species of *Cornus*

Group I: (*Swida = Thelycrania*). Flowers white in clusters without involucral bracts or bracteoles.

A *Leaves opposite. Fruit purplish-black or green.*

C. sanguinea **Common Dogwood.** Europe including S England. Shrub to 11(13) ft (3.5(4) m). Leaves ovate, 1.6–3 in (4–8 cm) long, with 3–5 pairs of veins; petiole 0.16–0.5 in (4–13 mm) long. Fruit globose, 0.2–0.3 in (6–7 mm) across, purplish-black. Leaves red in the fall, stems patchy red. 'Viridissima' has green young stems and also fruit. **CZ5**

AA *Leaves opposite. Fruit white or blue.*

C. alba **Tatarian Dogwood.** China, Siberia. Shrub producing a dense thicket, to 10 ft (3 m), young shoots turning a fine red in the fall. Leaves more or less ovate, 2–4.5 in (5–11 cm) long, dark green above, whitish to glaucous beneath, both sides with minute (lens) adpressed hairs, veins 5–6 pairs; petiole 0.3–1 in (8–25 mm) long. A number of variegated cultivars; also 'Sibirica' with brilliant crimson-red winter shoots ('Westonbirt,' 'Westonbirt Dogwood,' and 'Atrosanguinea' are considered to be identical with 'Sibirica'). **CZ3**

C. amomum **Silky Dogwood.** Mainly E U.S. Shrub to 10 ft (3 m), winter stems reddish-purple. Leaves more or less elliptic, 2–4 in (5–10 cm), brownish woolly-hairy beneath, at least on veins; petiole 0.3–0.6 in (8–15 mm) long. Fruit blue or partly white, 0.25 in (6 mm) across. **CZ5**

C. baileyi E N. America. Shrub to 10 ft (3 m), not stoloniferous, branches reddish-brown. Leaves ovate to lanceolate, 2–5 in (5–12 cm), woolly beneath when young; petiole 0.5–0.7 in (12–18 mm) long. Fruit white, 0.2–0.35 in (6–9 mm) across. (See. *C. stolonifera*.) **CZ2**

C. stolonifera **Red Osier Dogwood.** N. America. Vigorous suckering shrub to 8 ft (2.5 m); young shoots red-purple. Leaves ovate to lanceolate, 2–4 in (5–10 cm) long, dark green above, glaucous beneath, both surfaces with adpressed hairs; petiole 0.5–1 in (12–25 mm) long. Fruit white, 0.2–0.25 in (5–6 mm) across. Not dissimilar to *C. alba* and *C. baileyi*, but is stoloniferous. **CZ2**

'Flaviramea' is unusual in its greenish-yellow winter stems.

AAA *Leaves alternate. Fruit black or bluish-black.*

C. alternifolia E N. America. Shrub or small tree to 20 ft (6 m). Leaves oval to ovate, 2–5 in (5–12 cm) long, lower surface adpressed pubescent base tapering into 1–2 in (2.5–5 cm) long petiole. Flower clusters 1.6–2.5 in (4–6 cm) across. Fruit 0.2–0.28 in (6–7 mm) across. **CZ3**

C. mas 'Sibirica'

C. mas

C. florida

Coppicing *Cornus sanguinea* 'Midwinter Fire' produces vibrant fresh new growth, bringing striking winter color to the garden. It is effective planted in clumps or for informal hedging.

The deciduous dogwoods are much valued as ornamentals, especially those with large fruit and striking red stems which add color and interest to gardens during the winter months.

C. controversa Table Dogwood. Japan, China, the Himalaya. Tree 33–52 ft (10–16 m), branches horizontally tiered. Leaves ovate to oval, 3–6 in (8–15 cm) long, lower surface with adpressed hairs centrally attached; veins 6–8(9) pairs; petiole 1–2 in (2.5–5 cm); fall colors sometimes purplish. Flower clusters 2.5–5(6.5) in (6–12(17) cm) across. Fruit 0.25–0.28 in (6–7 mm) diameter. **CZ5**

Group II: (*Cornus*). Clusters of flowers with a yellowish involucre (bracts) that is not longer than the flowers and falls off as these open.

C. mas Cornelian Cherry. C and S Europe, W Asia. Shrub or small tree to 26 ft (8 m). Leaves ovate, 1.6–4 in (4–10 cm) long, both sides with adpressed, centrally attached hairs; veins 3–5 pairs; petiole 0.25 in (6 mm) long. Flowers yellow, open before the leaves in early spring, in umbels 0.7–0.8 in (18–20 mm) across, enclosed in 4 short involucral bracts that drop off as the umbel expands. Fruit scarlet, ellipsoidal, (0.5)0.6 in ((12)15 mm) long. A splendid sight in flower and fruit. Too seldom seen. **CZ5**

Group III: (*Benthamidia*). Clusters of flowers with the involucral bracts white or pink and conspicuously longer than the flowers and persisting after they open. Fruits clustered but distinct from each other.

C. florida Flowering Dogwood. E U.S. Shrub or tree 10–20(23) ft (3–6(7) m). Leaves oval to ovate, 2.8–5.5 in (7–14 cm) long. Flowers inconspicuous in a small cluster 0.5 in (12 mm) across, but surrounded by 4 obovate white very conspicuous involucral bracts, notched at the apex and 1.6–2 in (4–5 cm) long. Fruit 0.4 in (1 cm) long. Flowers liable to succumb to frost in temperate regions. **CZ5**
rubra has pinkish-red bracts.

C. nuttallii Nuttall's Dogwood, Pacific Dogwood. W N. America. Tree mostly up to 52 ft (16 m), but may reach to 100 ft (30 m) in the wild. Leaves oval to obovate, 3–5 in (7.5–12 cm) long. Flowers small in a cluster, 0.7–0.8 in (18–20 mm) across, but surrounded by (4)6(8) large, 1.6–3 in (4–8 cm) long more or less broadly oval involucral bracts, pointed or somewhat blunt but not notched at the apex. A magnificent plant, but not succeeding in the north temperate regions except in the warmer parts. The leaves and "flower" (flower cluster plus bracts) sometimes much exceed above measurements. **CZ7**

Group IV: (*Dendrobenthamia*). Involucral bracts as in Group III, but fruits united into a compound structure or syncarp. (The following species flower spring, summer.)

C. capitata Bentham's Cornel. The Himalaya, China. Half-evergreen tree to 45 ft (14 m) in cultivation. Leaves more or less obovate, (0.8)1.2–2.5 in ((2)3–6 cm) long, densely pubescent on both sides, light green above, glaucous beneath. Flowers with 4–6 yellowish obovate bracts, 1.6–2 in (4–5 cm) long. Fruit strawberry-like, 0.6–1 in (1.5–2.5 cm) across. Not really hardy in temperate regions. **CZ8**

C. kousa C China, Japan, Korea. Shrub or tree to 20 ft (6 m). Leaves ovate, 1.8–3(3.5) in (4.5–8(9) cm) long, margin wavy, veins with tufts of brown hair in their axils; petiole 0.16–0.2 in (4–6 mm). Flowers in a small dense cluster surrounded by 4 lanceolate, ivory-colored, involucral bracts, 1–2 in (2.5–5 cm) long. Fruit strawberry-like, 0.6–1 in (1.5–2.5 cm) across. Hardy in temperate regions and a fine ornamental plant. **CZ5**

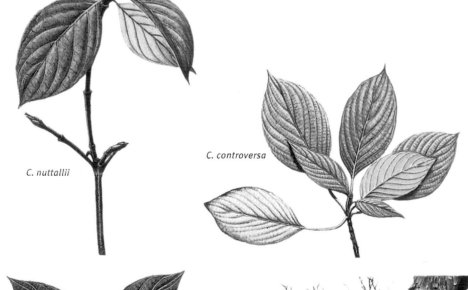

C. nuttallii

C. controversa

C. kousa

C. mas

CELASTRACEAE

Euonymus

Spindle Tree

Euonymus is a genus of at least 175 species from Europe, Asia, North and Central America, tropical Africa, and Australia but centered on the Himalaya and eastern Asia. The plants are deciduous or evergreen trees and shrubs, rarely creeping or climbing by rootlets, with the young shoots often four-angled. The leaves are typically opposite and sometimes toothed. The flowers, which appear in the spring, are small, white, greenish or yellowish (rarely purple), bisexual, and are borne in three- to seven- (sometimes fifteen-) flowered cymose inflorescences. The calyx, corolla, and sub-sessile stamens are in fours or fives and the disk is flat, four, or five lobed, adherent to the three- to five-chambered ovary. The style is short or absent. The fruit is a fleshy capsule, which splits into three to five valves, each containing one to four white, red, or black seeds partially enclosed by a brilliant orange or red aril. The seeds (believed to be poisonous in all species) are dispersed by birds, which are attracted by the colorful fruits.

The species of _Euonymus_ are mainly cultivated for the colors of the fruits and leaves in the fall. They are hardy and require a well-drained loamy soil. Propagation of the deciduous species is by seed, cuttings, or by layering; for the evergreen species, cuttings can be taken at almost any time if bottom heat is available. The Common Spindle Tree (_E. europaeus_) favors calcareous soils and grows to 30 ft (9 m) in cultivation. _Euonymus japonicus_, an evergreen species with golden and variegated leaf cultivars, is a popular hedging plant often seen in towns and on coasts. _Euonymus alatus_ is one of the most valuable fall coloring shrubs and, in common with some of the other species, has curious growths of cork on its branches. Several species have particularly

CELASTRACEAE

Euonymus
SPINDLE TREE

Number of species _up to 177_
Distribution _Northern temperate regions, and Australia._
Commercial uses _Widely planted as ornamental trees with many cultivars and used as hedging. Euonymus were also previously much valued for timber._

unusual fruits for which they are cultivated. Another evergreen species, _E. wilsonii_, has conspicuous awl-shaped spines on its four-lobed fruits, and _E. americanus_ has red spiny warty fruits resembling those of the Strawberry Tree (_Arbutus unedo_). _Euonymus nanus_, a dwarf species from the northern Caucasus, is grown in rockeries.

The wood of some species was formerly used to make spindles—hence the common name—and small items including clothes pegs and skewers; it also makes excellent artists' charcoal. The fruit of _E. europaeus_ is sufficiently poisonous to kill sheep and goats. In powdered form it has been used to delouse children's hair.

This species is also one of the plants on which the Black Bean Aphid (_Aphis fabae_) lays its eggs, and suggestions for its eradication in commercial fava-bean growing areas have been made. **CZ2–9**

BELOW The Common Spindle Tree, _Eunonymus europaeus_, is valued, not for its flowers, but for its colorful fall leaves and branches laden with red fruit. These are four-lobed and contain fleshy orange-covered seeds.

Aesculus

Horse Chestnuts, Buckeyes

Aesculus is a genus of some 13 north temperate species native mainly to North America, the others from southern Europe and East Asia. They are imposing, deciduous trees (one or two more or less shrubby) with a large spreading habit. The familiar sticky brown buds open into large leaves that are opposite and palmate, each one with five to seven (rarely three or nine) leaflets radiating from the end of a long stalk. The flowers, which may be white, pink, or red, are polygamous, irregular, borne in terminal panicles, with four or five sepals, sometimes forming a tube, and four or five petals. There are five to nine stamens on an annular disk, with the filaments free, and the ovary is three-celled with two ovules per cell and a single style. The fruit is a smooth or spiny, firm capsule commonly maturing a single, large shining seed popularly called the "conker" or "buckeye."

LEFT *Koelreuteria bipinnata* can be distinguished from *K. paniculata* by its doubly and sometimes trebly pinnate leaves. The papery brown fruits have rounder and broader valves.

BELOW The Horse Chestnut (*Aesculus hippocastanum*) has flowers with 4–5 petals borne in large panicles. They are white with a patch of yellow then turning red on the base of the petals. They are one of the most beautiful of flowering trees.

HIPPOCASTANACEAE

Aesculus
HORSE CHESTNUTS, BUCKEYES

Number of species *13*
Distribution *North America, southeast Europe, India, and East Asia.*
Commercial uses *Widely planted as ornamentals. Some species also the source of a valued timber. Harvested for edible seeds as a cattle feed.*

Koelreuteria

Golden Rain Tree

Koelreuteria is one of the very few genera of the tropical family Sapindaceae which are cultivated in temperate regions. All three species are native to China and Taiwan. Best known is the Golden Rain Tree or Pride of India (*K. paniculata*), a wide-spreading, medium-sized tree reaching 45 ft (14 m) and a native of central China but long cultivated in Japan. It bears alternate, odd-pinnate leaves, 6–16 in (15–40 cm) long, with 11–13(15) leaflets, which are coarsely and irregularly toothed. Small bright yellow flowers are produced in late summer in large erect terminal panicles up to 16 in (40 cm) high. The flowers are followed by yellow-brown papery fruits containing small black seeds.

The Golden Rain Tree is a sun-loving species that thrives on well-drained soil. It is normally propagated from seeds or by taking root cuttings. An erect columnar cultivar, 'Fastigata,' is sometimes found in cultivation as well as a late-flowering form, 'September.' The other two members of the genus, *K. bipinnata* (southwest China) and *K. elegans* (Taiwan and Fiji), are found cultivated in warmer regions; the former is exceptional in its bipinnate leaves; it grows to 20 ft (6 m) but is not hardy in temperate regions.

Seeds of the Golden Rain Tree are used to make necklaces and in China the flowers are reputed to have medicinal properties. **CZ7**

There are a number of hybrids. Species with four petals and a smooth capsule are transferred by some to a distinct genus *Pavia,* but intermediates do not justify this separation.

Almost all the species and many varieties of them have become well-known ornamentals in parks in temperate regions, in particular the Eurasian Horse Chestnut (*Aesculus hippocastanum*), a native of mountainous regions of Greece and eastward to Iran and northern India, which was introduced into Britain in the middle of the sixteenth century. It is the largest of the chestnuts, growing to over 130 ft (40 m) tall. The flowers are white with a pattern of crimson and yellow spots toward the center. Another fine ornamental is the Red Buckeye (*A. pavia*), a small tree from the southern United States with crimson flowers and smooth spineless fruits. There is a popular hybrid between these two species, *A.* × *carnea*, which has pink flowers and smoothish fruits. A number of cultivars and varieties are found in cultivation.

Floral forms of the Horse Chestnut include 'Alba' with pure white flowers, 'Baumannii' with double white flowers, 'Rosea' with pink flowers, and 'Rubricunda' with red flowers. 'Pumila' is a dwarf form with deeply cut leaves and 'Pyramidalis' has a broad pyramidal habit.

Most species are hardy in temperate regions except in the more extreme areas and require only a good, deep, well-drained soil. Propagation is best from seed for the species, otherwise budding must be resorted to. Stock for the larger species is commonly *A. hippocastanum*; for the smaller ones, *A. flava* or *A. glabra*.

There are various possible explanations for the derivation of the common name. The bitter fruits may have been used in the treatment of respiratory diseases and other ailments of horses. Another explanation is that it refers to the leaf-scar resembling a horseshoe. It is much more likely, however, that in popular English botany "horse" simply means "coarse" or "unpleasant," thus distinguishing the Horse Chestnut (inedible by humans) from the Sweet Chestnut (much esteemed).

Experiments have shown that mashed horse chestnuts could be a useful and palatable cattle feed. The timber is soft and not durable, but is sometimes used for interior work such as flooring, cabinetmaking, boxes, as well as charcoal. Esculoside, a coumarin glycoside, present in the bark, leaves, and seeds of *A. hippocastanum,* is used as a sunscreen agent in skin protection creams and is also prescribed in the treatment of hemorrhoids and other conditions associated with capillary blood vessel fragility. The bark and fruit of some species are used locally to stupefy fish.

The springtime sticky shiny buds are a favorite in some countries for use in floral decoration, while in the fall the beautiful red-brown, polished chestnuts are widely appreciated by children of all ages in the game of conkers. **CZ3–6**

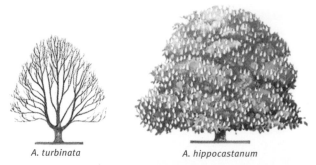

A. turbinata   *A. hippocastanum*

The Sweet Yellow Buckeye *Aesculus flava* is a handsome, roundheaded tree between 50 and 100 ft (15–30 m) high. Leaves have 5–7 leaflets, which give good fall colors of bright orange. The leaf veins however remain white and pale green at first, finally turning orange-brown all over.

The Main Species of *Aesculus*

Group I: Corolla with 4 petals, their claws usually longer than the sepals. Winter buds usually not resinous. Fruits smooth or at least not spiny.

A. splendens SE U.S. Shrub 10–13 ft (3–4 m). Corolla scarlet, leaves downy beneath; fruits smoothish. **CZ5**

A. pavia Red Buckeye. S U.S. Shrub 10–13 ft (3–4 m). Leaves slightly downy beneath, especially near the veins. Corolla red but not opening; petals with glands along the margins. Fruits smooth. **CZ5**

A. flava (*A. octandra*) Sweet or Yellow Buckeye. U.S. Tree to 100 ft (30 m). Leaves often reddish downy beneath. Corolla yellow; margins of petals with nonglandular hairs. Fruits smooth. **CZ5**

A. chinensis Chinese Horse Chestnut. N China. Tree up to 100 ft (30 m). Corolla white. Fruits rough. Winter buds resinous. **CZ6**

A. indica Indian Horse Chestnut. NW Himalaya. Tree to 100 ft (30 m) or more. Corolla white with yellow or red blotches at the base of the petals. Fruits rough. Winter buds resinous. **CZ7**

A. californica California. Tree to 40 ft (12 m). Corolla white or pink. Fruits rough. Winter buds resinous. **CZ7**

A. glabra Ohio Buckeye. SE and C U.S. Smallish tree to 26 ft (8 m), rarely more. Leaflets, usually 2, 1.2–1.6 in (3–4 cm) wide.

Corolla yellow-green. Fruits rough. *Aesculus arguta* from E Texas, which is similar but has 7–9 leaflets, 0.8–1.2 in (2–3 cm) wide, is closely related. **CZ5**

A. parviflora SE U.S. Shrub 6–13 ft (2–4 m). Corolla white, occasionally with 5 petals. Fruits smooth. **CZ5**

Group II: Corolla with 5 petals, their claws shorter than the sepals. Winter buds resinous. Fruits spiny.

A. hippocastanum Horse Chestnut or Conker Tree. N Greece, Albania. Tree to 115 ft (35 m). Corolla whitish with red spots. There are a number of cultivars. For example 'Baumannii' has double flowers and does not form fruits. **CZ3**

A. × carnea Red Horse Chestnut. A polyploid hybrid probably with *A. pavia* and *A. hippocastanum* as parents. Tree 33–80 ft (10–25 m). Corolla red. **CZ4**

A. turbinata Japanese Horse Chestnut. Japan. Tree to 100 ft (30 m). Leaflets 5–7, sessile, obovate, 8–12(16) in (20–30(40) cm) long. Flowers 0.6 in (1.5 cm) across, creamy colored with red spot, in panicles 10 × 2.5 in (25 × 6 cm). Fruit pyriform, warty 2 in (5 cm) maximum across; seed brown. **CZ6**

A. × hybrida (*A. flava* × *A. pavia*) A hybrid often mistaken for *A. pavia*. Flowers mixed pink or red, the margins of the petals with glands as well as hairs.

A. hippocastanum

A. pavia

A. pavia

A. turbinata

A. × carnea

A. californica

A. indica

A. flava

A. hippocastanum

Acer
Maples

Acer is a sizeable genus of species commonly called maples, ranging over almost all the northern temperate region and extending into the Tropics in Southeast Asia. The great majority are Asian, and many are extremely rare.

Maples are predominantly deciduous trees, infrequently evergreen or shrubby, with scaly or smooth bark, which in the small "Snakebark" group is beautifully striped vertically, bright white on a smooth green or gray background. The inflorescence is variable, being in the form of long, pendent, catkin-like racemes, as in the Sycamore (*A. pseudoplatanus*) and Oregon Maple (*A. macrophyllum*), tight bunches against the shoot, as in Red (*A. rubrum*) and Silver (*A. saccharinum*) Maples, small spreading panicles, as in the Norway Maple (*A. platanoides*), or open, erect panicles, as in Van Volxem's Maple (*A. velutinum* var *vanvolxemii*) and Trautvetter's Maple (*A. trautvetteri*). There are five petals (when present), usually yellow, but bright yellow in the Norway Maple and pale in the Italian Maple (*A. opalus*), green in the Hornbeam Maple (*A. carpinifolium*), and red in the Japanese (*A. palmatum*) and Red Maples. There are usually eight stamens (sometimes four to ten) on a prominent disc. Each inflorescence usually bears flowers of both sexes, the females toward the base, but a few maples, for instance Père David's (*A. davidii*), have each inflorescence entirely of one sex, while a few more, among them *A. argutum*, *A. negundo*, and *A. tetramerum*, have sexes on separate plants. Leaves vary in size from the 1.2 in (3 cm), entire, elliptic evergreen type on *A. sempervirens* through those 10 × 14 in (25 × 35 cm) and deeply lobed on *A. macrophyllum*, and through an eastern Asian group of five with trifoliolate leaves to the American *A. negundo* with compound leaves of five and seven leaflets.

Stature in maples varies from the often shrubby species like *A. tschonoskii* and *A. tataricum*, seldom above 20 ft (6 m) tall, to large trees, the Sycamore growing as high as 120 ft (37 m) and *A. macrophyllum* and *A. platanoides* growing to 100 ft (30 m).

There is a maple for every soil and situation, for winter color, spring flowers, summer foliage, and above all for fall color. The Sycamore is among the most resistant of all trees to polluted air and severe maritime exposure, though its native range scarcely includes any seaboard. *Acer* ssp *ginnala* is able to tolerate city pollution and severe cold and is planted in tubs in the streets of Montreal. *Acer rubrum*, *A. saccharum*, and *A. saccharinum* thrive in city squares in their native eastern United States, alongside the European *A. platanoides*. The Japanese *A. palmatum* decorates town parks and gardens everywhere with a plethora of fancy-leaved and colored form.

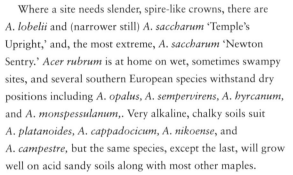

Number of species *100+*
Distribution *Northern temperate regions and tropical mountains.*
Commercial uses *Important source of a hard pale wood but predominantly grown as garden or street trees with many hundreds of cultivars. Also the source of edible syrups.*

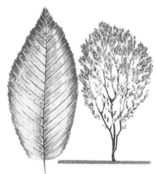

A. carpinifolium

Where a site needs slender, spire-like crowns, there are *A. lobelii* and (narrower still) *A. saccharum* 'Temple's Upright,' and, the most extreme, *A. saccharum* 'Newton Sentry.' *Acer rubrum* is at home on wet, sometimes swampy sites, and several southern European species withstand dry positions including *A. opalus*, *A. sempervirens*, *A. hyrcanum*, and *A. monspessulanum,*. Very alkaline, chalky soils suit *A. platanoides*, *A. cappadocicum*, *A. nikoense*, and *A. campestre,* but the same species, except the last, will grow well on acid sandy soils along with most other maples.

A. rubrum

Winter color is nowhere better displayed than by the brilliant coral and scarlet shoots of *A. palmatum* 'Seiun-kaku' and the deeper red of *A. pennsylvanicum* 'Erythrocladum,' while the shoots of *A. giraldii* display a violet bloom and the trunks of the several snakebark maples and of *A. griseum* add much to the winter prospect. In March, before the trees are in leaf, the bright red flowers clustering along the shoots of *A. rubrum* are decorative though far less spectacular than the acid-yellow larger bunches of flowers on big crowns of *A. platanoides* and the pale but larger still flowers hanging from *A. opalus*. As the leaves unfold in late April, the purplish-red flowers of *A. diabolicum* 'Purpurascens' hang beneath the leaves as on a parachute.

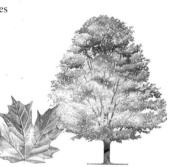

A. saccharum

For summer foliage, the best are: *A. buergeranum*, the snakebarks *A. capillipes*, *A. forrestii*, and *A. maximowiczii* for attractive small leaves, *A. acuminatum*, *A. argutum*, and *A. pectinatum* for decorative lobing, and, for their handsome substantial foliage, *A. macrophyllum* and *A. velutinum vanvolxemii*. For fall color almost any maple earns a place. In New England, *A. saccharum* is supreme for the intensity of its orange-scarlet and *A. rubrum* runs the gamut from lemon-yellow to deep

A. palmatum

purple, but in Europe the species which offer the best colors are *A. palmatum* 'Osakazuki,' *A. capillipes, A. grosseri* var *hersii*, and *A. japonicum* 'Vititolium.'

Propagation for the species is best from seed. For the numerous varieties graftings will be necessary and should be made on stocks of the same species.

Maples are subject to a number of fungal attacks but, in general, few are serious. Pest attacks are more damaging, some maple species being badly defoliated in spring and summer by leaf-eating insects and weevils.

The timber of a number of maples is used commercially. The light-colored, close-grained, and soft wood of *A. campestre, A. macrophyllum*, and *A. negundo* is much used for tool handles, turnery, and cheap furniture. The harder, heavier, tougher, and closer-grained wood of *A. platanoides, A. pseudoplatanus*, and *A. saccharum* is more extensively used for furniture, flooring, and interior finishing of buildings. The Sugar Maple (*A. saccharum*) has orange sap, which is collected in spring and yields a rich aromatic syrup. Maple syrup is used as a sweetener for foods, in the manufacture of sugar, a cider-like drink (in Louisiana especially), and is an essential accompaniment to waffles. Kitchenware and countertops are also made from Sycamore as it scrubs clean easily and does not taint food. **CZ2–9**

BELOW The leaves of *Acer rufinerve* 'Albolimbatum' turn a rich crimson before they fall. They also have a broad margin that is completely covered in white spots.

The Main Species of *Acer*

Group I: Leaves simple.

A *Unlobed leaves only.*

A. carpinifolium **Hornbeam Maple.** Japan. Bushy tree to 33 ft (10 m). Shoots brown. Leaves slender, lanceolate, to 6.5 in (17 cm), sharply toothed with 20 or more parallel pairs of veins, turning a good gold in the fall. **CZ5**

A. distylum **Lime-leafed Maple.** Japan. Tree to 40 ft (12 m) with ascending arched branches. Leaves thick, ovate, cordate, 5 in (12 cm). Flowers on upper half of 2 in (5 cm) erect spike. Fruit pink-brown. **CZ7**

A. davidii **Père David's Maple.** China. Two forms of this variable species, one a small domed tree to 33 ft (10 m) with small, 2.5 in (6 cm) lanceolate leaves, the other a spreading tree to 46 ft (14 m) with large 6 in (15 cm) oblong-lanceolate leaves turning orange in the fall. **CZ6**

AA *Unlobed mixed with 3-lobed leaves.*

A. davidii **'George Forrest'** Most frequent form of the previous species. Snakebarked tree to 52 ft (16 m). Leaves broad, dark leathery, oblong-ovate to 6 in (15 cm), unevenly toothed, petiole scarlet. Flowers prolific on arched stalks.

A. grosseri var *hersii* **Hers's Maple.** China. Snakebarked tree to 52 ft (16 m) with long, arching, spreading branches, few minor shoots. Leaves rich green, leathery, broad, petiole yellow; crimson and orange in the fall. Fruit big-winged, 2.5 in (6 cm) across on arching, hanging 5 in (12 cm) stalk. **CZ6**

A. sempervirens (A. creticum, A. orientale) **Cretan Maple.** E Mediterranean. Low domed tree or bush. Leaves dark, 1.2–2 in (3–5 cm), entire, wavy-edged with variable lobules or lobes. Fruit small in bunches, finally red. **CZ7**

AAA *Leaves predominantly 3 lobed.*

A. buergeranum (incorrectly *A. buergerianum*) **Trident Maple.** China, Japan. Tree to 50 ft (15 m) with brown flaking bark. Leaves in dense masses, narrowed base, with 3 veins, nearly entire, bluish beneath, crimson in the fall. Occasional unlobed leaf. Flowers yellow in domed heads. **CZ6**

A. capillipes Japan. Snakebarked tree to 52 ft (16 m). Leaves glossy green turning orange and red, with 10 parallel veins and small lobe each side. Fruit prolific, small, finally pink. **CZ5**

A. crataegifolium **Hawthorn-leafed Maple.** Japan. Slender tree to 33 ft (10 m) with level branches. Leaves and fruit small, red-winged. **CZ6**

A. forrestii **Forrest's Maple.** China. Snakebarked tree to 36 ft (11 m). Leaves finely toothed, deep green but pale around veins; petiole scarlet. **CZ6**

A. tataricum ssp *ginnala* **Amur Maple.** NE Asia. Bush or small graybarked tree to 33 ft (10 m). Leaves deeply toothed, tapered to 2.8 in (7 cm), turning deep red early in the fall. Flowers white, small, in erect domed heads. **CZ4**

A. maximowiczii W China. Slender snakebarked tree to 42 ft (13 m). Leaves deeply lobed with white tufts in vein-axils beneath, margin incised and twice serrate. **CZ5**

A. monspessulanum Montpellier Maple. S Europe, N. Africa. Densely domed tree to 50 ft (15 m). Leaves at first fresh green but soon dark as if evergreen, 1.6 × 2.8 in (4 × 7 cm), lobes widely spread, margins entire. **CZ5**

A. pectinatum E Himalaya. Rare handsome snakebarked tree to 50 ft (15 m). Leaves large, the central and side lobes drawn out into long, sharply toothed tails. **CZ6**

A. pennsylvanicum Moosewood, Snake-bark Maple. NE U.S. Small tree with bright green or gray snakebark. Leaves large, to 8 × 8 in (20 × 20 cm), turning bright gold in early fall. **CZ3**

A. rubrum Red Maple. E N. America in all low-lying woods. Slender-twigged, rather shapeless tree to 75 ft (23 m). Flowers bright red along shoots before leaves out. Leaves silvered beneath, petiole red. In the wild, fall colors every shade from bright yellow through reds and crimson to deep purple, side by side. **CZ3**

A. rufinerve Gray-budded Snake-bark Maple. Japan. Spreading tree opening out to 42 ft (13 m). Leaves often broader than long; rusty hairs or stain on basal veins beneath; rich reds in early fall. **CZ6**
'Albolimbatum' Grayish-green leaves variably speckled and narrowly margined white.

AAAA *Leaves predominantly 5 lobed.*

A. argutum Japan. Small tree, usually many-stemmed. Leaves deep green with deeply sunk veins and slender serrated tails to lobes. **CZ5**

A. campestre Field Maple, Common Maple. Europe, Africa, W Asia. Domed tree to 80 ft (25 m), shoots often ridged with cork. Leaves small, dark, deeply lobed, with few large, round-tipped teeth, turning a good yellow, sometimes purple in the fall. Fruit 2.5 in (6 cm) across, wings horizontal, stained pink. **CZ4**

A. cappadocicum Cappadocian Maple. Caucasus to China. Domed crown on smooth gray bole among a mass of suckers. Leaves bright green with wire-tipped entire lobes, butter-yellow in the fall. **CZ6**
'Aureum' New leaves (spring and midsummer) bright gold. An elegant and attractive tree.

A. heldreichii Heldreich's Maple. Balkan Mts. Tall domed tree with open crown to 66 ft (20 m). Leaves lobed almost to base, with few triangular teeth; petiole pink, 6 in (15 cm) long. Flowers in erect panicle, yellow. **CZ6**

A. lobelii Lobel's Maple. Italy. Vigorous erect tree with few branches all nearly vertical. Leaves with almost entire lobes twisted at tips. **CZ8**

A. macrophyllum Oregon Maple. Alaska to California. Tree with high dome to 100 ft (30 m); bark fissured, orange-brown. Leaves to 10 × 12 in (25 × 30 cm), deeply lobed; petiole to 12 in (30 cm). Flowers in catkins to 10 in (25 cm). Fruit with white bristles. **CZ6**

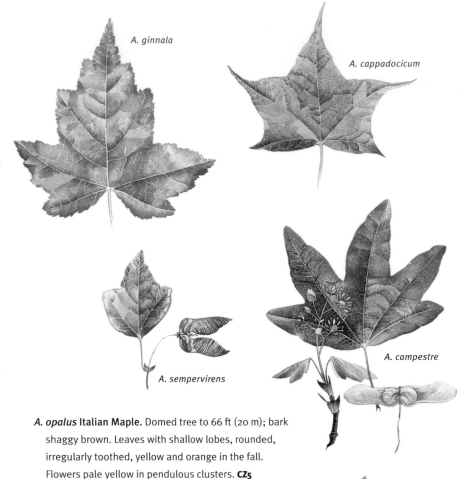

A. ginnala

A. cappadocicum

A. sempervirens

A. campestre

A. opalus Italian Maple. Domed tree to 66 ft (20 m); bark shaggy brown. Leaves with shallow lobes, rounded, irregularly toothed, yellow and orange in the fall. Flowers pale yellow in pendulous clusters. **CZ5**

A. platanoides Norway Maple. Europe and Caucasus. Tree with densely leafed crown to almost 100 ft (30 m) on pale gray finely ridged bole. Leaves with lobes and the few big teeth wire-tipped, bright gold then orange in the fall. Flowers bright yellow in bunches open before leaves. **CZ3**
'Cucullatum' Erect crowned tree to 78 ft (24 m). Leaves semicircular, hooded, and crinkled.
'Drummondii' Dense domed crown of generously white-splashed and margined small leaves.
'Faassen's Black' Big, deep muddy purple leaves.
'Goldsworth Purple' Dark purple-leaved form seen in gardens in the U.S. from coast to coast south to Denver and Atlanta, and in NW Europe.
'Schwedleri' Flowers open 2 weeks later than in the species type, with dark red calyx and stalk amid red-brown unfolding leaves. Leaf purple-tinged until the fall, when orange and crimson.

A. heldreichii

A. pseudoplatanus Sycamore, Great Maple. S and C Europe to Caucasus. Tree with dense, domed crown to over 80 ft (25 m). Leaves dark green, petiole red or yellow. Flowers on 8 in (20 cm) catkin, appearing with the leaves, petals inconspicuous. **CZ5**
'Brilliantissimum' Dense low crown. Leaves bright pink, then orange to yellow for 2 weeks, then white until dull green.
'Prinz Handjery' Differs from the previous cultivar in purple underside to leaf. Flowers freely.

A. capillipes

'Purpureum' A group variably stained purple on underside of leaf.

'Variegatum' Dense trees to over 80 ft (25 m). Leaves with bold angular patches and fine speckles of cream or white.

'Leopoldii' Has brightest leaves with some patches stained pinkish or purple.

'Worley' Leaves bright yellow with red petiole.

A. saccharinum Silver Maple. E N. America. Tree with open crown to 100 ft (30 m) and ascending arched branches. Leaves deeply lobed and sharply toothed, whitish beneath. Flowers greenish-red to red before leaves, petals absent. **CZ3**

A. saccharum Sugar Maple. E N. America. Tree to over 80 ft (25 m). Leaves pale green at first, brilliant orange-scarlet in the fall. Flowers bunched, small on very slender stalks, petals absent. **CZ3**

'Newton Sentry' Vertical stem clothed in leaves; few short branches. Bizarre form in some American parks and streets.

'Temple's Upright' Erect but broader than 'Newton Sentry;' branches erect. Frequent in cities of N U.S.

A. trautvetteri Trautvetter's Maple. Caucasus Mountains. Tree to 66 ft (20 m). Like *A. pseudoplatanus* except acute brown buds, erect heads of flowers, deeply lobed leaves, and big broad wings on fruit bright pink in summer. **CZ6**

A. griseum

A. japonicum

A. negundo

A. pseudoplatanus

A. saccharum

A. velutinum var vanvolxemii Van Volxem's Maple. Caucasus Mountains. Tree to over 80 ft (25 m). Like *A. pseudoplatanus* with huge pale green leaf to 7 × 6 in (18 × 15 cm), petiole 11 in (27 cm), brown buds acute and domed flowerhead erect. **CZ5**

AAAAA *Leaves with more than 5 lobes.*

A. circinatum Vine Maple. N. America (British Columbia to California). Slender, usually leaning small tree to 40 ft (12 m). Shoot smooth bright green. Leaves circular with 7 neat doubly toothed lobes turning scarlet early in the fall. **CZ5**

A. japonicum Downy Japanese Maple. Bush, but in cultivar 'Vitifolium' a tree to 50 ft (15 m). Leaves to 6 in (15 cm) with 7–11 triangular irregularly toothed lobes, scarlet gold and lilac in the fall. Flowers purple. **CZ5**

A. palmatum Smooth Japanese Maple. Broad tree to 50 ft (15 m) with 7(5) narrow finely toothed tapered lobes, varied red in the fall. **CZ5**

'Seiun-kaku' Coral-bark Maple. Shoots in winter bright pinkish-scarlet. Leaves small, much toothed, yellowish.

Group II: Leaves compound.

B *Leaves trifoliolate.*

A. cissifolium Vine-leafed Maple. Japan. Wide, low, mushroom-like tree to 33 ft (10 m) tall but 66 ft (20 m) across with pale brown and white bark. Leaflets on very slender stalks, ovate, acute, coarsely toothed. Flowers prolific and fruit spreading stiffly on 5 in (12 cm) spikes. **CZ6**

A. griseum Paper-bark Maple. China. Tree to 46 ft (14 m) with open, rather upright crown; dark orange to mahogany red, peeling in papery rolls laterally. Leaflets paired, unstalked, but central leaflet shortly stalked, few teeth, dark green, silvery beneath, crimson and scarlet in the fall; petiole dark pink, hairy. Flowers bell-like, yellow, with leaves, in threes. **CZ5**

A. nikoense Nikko Maple. C China, Japan. Sturdy conical tree to 46 ft (14 m) with smooth dark gray bark. Leaflets broad elliptic, densely white-hairy beneath, scarlet and crimson in the fall; petiole dark pink, densely hairy. Yellow flowers in threes. **CZ5**

A. triflorum Korea, Manchuria. Similar to Nikko Maple but smaller in all parts and with rough, shredding, peeling bark. Bright scarlet and crimson briefly in the fall. **CZ6**

BB *Pinnate leaves; 5–7 leaflets.*

A. negundo Ash-leafed Maple, Box Elder. E Canada to California. Low bushy, sprouty tree to 50 ft (15 m). In the wild, foliage rich, shining, bright green; in cultivation, less bright and the colored cultivars are usually planted instead. Flowers before leaves in dense clusters hanging on slender stalks, male and female on separate trees. **CZ2**

'Variegatum' Leaf mostly white in splashes and broad margins, some wholly white. Female only.

'Auratum' Vividly splendid rich gold foliage, greening a little by late summer.

A. nikoense

ANACARDIACEAE

Rhus

Sumacs

The genus *Rhus*, commonly known as sumacs or sumachs, contains species from the subtropics and temperate regions of the Old and the New World. Some dozen of these are grown as ornamentals in temperate regions for their shape, vivid fall coloring, and attractive dense fruiting heads appearing as dark red pyramids at the branch ends.

Sumacs are predominantly small deciduous or evergreen shrubs, rarely climbers or trees, with a characteristic antler-like branching pattern. The leaves are alternate, odd-pinnate, with entire or serrate-margined leaflets. The flowers are borne in conspicuous panicles with male, female, and bisexual flowers occurring together on the same plant or separated on different plants. There are usually five sepals and petals (sometimes four or six) and the ovary is superior, maturing to a single-seeded dry globose drupe with a resinous mesocarp. They are not difficult to grow and can be readily propagated by cuttings or layers.

The genus is characterized by a resinous juice and in such species as Poison Ivy (*R. radicans*), Oakleaf Poison Ivy (*R. radicans*), and Poison Sumac (*R. vernix*) this juice is a powerful skin irritant and on contact all parts of the body may become inflamed, swollen, ulcerated, and very painful. Though not all people react, some claim to be affected by merely being near a plant but this is more likely the result, in very susceptible people, of contact with the pollen (especially where the eyes are involved) or the smoke of burning wood. The treatment is to wash affected parts as quickly as possible with a 1 percent solution of potassium permanganate. The same juice is, however, outstanding as an ink for marking linen, being virtually ineradicable. The poisonous principle is urushiol, a derivative of the polyhydric phenol, catechol.

The only sumac native to Europe, *Rhus coriaria*, known as the Tanner's or Elm-leaved Sumac, was used by the ancient Greeks as a source of spice, medicine, and tannin. Several species of *Rhus* are commercially important in the leather industry. Tannins from the North American species *R. copallina* (Shining Sumac) and *R. typhina* (*R. hirta*, Stag's-horn Sumac) produce a dark colored leather, while the tannins of Eurasian species such as *R. coriaria* and *R. javanica* (*R. chinensis*, *R. semialata*) yield a paler leather. In the case of the latter, the tannin is extracted from galls ("nut galls" or "gall apples") which have a high tannin concentration, and are caused by a louse of the genus *Schlechtendalia*.

Resin from the bark of the Varnish or Japanese Lacquer Tree (*R. verniciflua*) produces the well-known Japanese lacquer and varnish. The crushed fruits of the Wax Tree (*R. succedanea*) give a wax or tallow which was once the main source of artificial light in Japan. **CZ2–9**

Rhus
SUMACS

ANACARDIACEAE

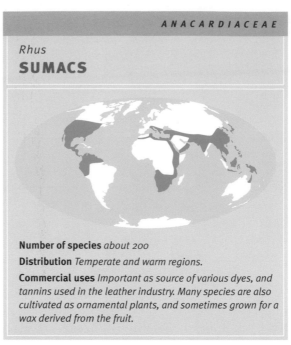

Number of species *about 200*
Distribution *Temperate and warm regions.*
Commercial uses *Important as source of various dyes, and tannins used in the leather industry. Many species are also cultivated as ornamental plants, and sometimes grown for a wax derived from the fruit.*

R. typhina

ABOVE The Stag's Horn sumach, *Rhus typhina,* is a small tree with a gaunt, flat-topped habit. The young bark is densely covered in red hairs.

BELOW The brilliant red-orange foliage of *Rhus typhina* 'Laciniata' makes a stunning fall display in any garden.

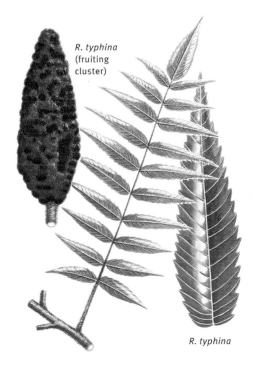

R. typhina
(fruiting
cluster)

R. typhina

R. succedanea

R. tomentosa

R. typhina

R. toxicodendron

R. typhina

The Main Species of *Rhus*

Group I: *Rhus* in strict sense. N. America, Europe, and Asia. Leaves usually pinnate. Flowers short-pediceled, in dense terminal spikes. Fruits reddish. Plants not poisonous.

R. javanica (*R. chinensis*, *R. semialata*) Widespread in Asia from the Himalaya to Vietnam, Korea, China, and Japan. Tree to 20 ft (6 m), with antler-like branching. **CZ8**

R. copallina Shining Sumac. N. America. Deciduous shrub or small tree, unusual in having entire leaflets. A source of tannin. **CZ5**

R. coriaria Tanners or Elm-leaved Sumac. The only native *Rhus* of mainland Europe; widespread from the Canaries to Afghanistan. A small semievergreen shrub characteristic of Mediterranean "maquis." The Arabic name "sumac" belonged originally to this species. Source of tannins (known commercially as "sumac" or "sumach") used in the production of Cordoba and Morocco leathers. **CZ9**

R. glabra N. America. Closely allied to *R. typhina*, differing in its shrubby habit and in having glabrous leaves and branches. The cultivar 'Laciniata' has leaflets deeply cut. **CZ2**

R. typhina (= *R. hirta*) Stag's-horn Sumac. N. America. Small gauntly branched deciduous tree to 26 ft (8 m) or more with thick pithy branches, often grown in European gardens. Male and female flowers on separate trees, the male tree sometimes known as *R. viridiflora*. The cultivar 'Dissecta' has leaflets deeply cut. *R. typhina* forma *laciniata* is a monstrous form, quite common in the wild, with leaves and bracts deeply cut and the inflorescence partly transformed into twisted bracts. **CZ3**

Group II: *Toxicodendron*. N. America, N S. America, C and SE Asia. Leaves ternate (trifoliolate) or pinnate. Flowers long-pediceled, in lax lateral panicles. Fruits whitish or yellowish. Plants with poisonous exudates.

R. diversiloba Poison Oak. W N. America. Shrub with ternate leaves. **CZ5**

R. ambigua (*R. orientalis*) Japan and China. Species closely related to *R. radicans*, differing only in having coarsely hairy rather than smooth or downy fruits. **CZ7**

R. radicans Poison Ivy, Cow-itch. N. America. Deciduous shrub with ternate leaves, found in two forms: the climbing form attaches itself to rocks, tree trunks, and buildings by aerial roots and can grow to a considerable height; the bushy form is a loosely spreading shrub up to 10 ft (3 m). The sap is highly poisonous, causing severe blisters to the skin, and even the pollen is irritating to the eyes. **CZ7**

R. succedanea Wax Tree. India to Japan, Malaysia. Deciduous tree to 40 ft (12 m). Leaves pinnate, the leaflets glossy, glabrous, purplish, entire, with numerous parallel lateral veins almost at right angles to the midrib. Formerly much cultivated in Japan for the fruit, which supplied wax for candles, and for the resin, used as lacquer. **CZ5**

R. verniciflua Varnish or Japanese Lacquer Tree. The Himalaya to China, possibly also native in Malaysia. Deciduous tree to 66 ft (20 m). Leaves pinnate, velvety. Tapped for the resin, which turns black on exposure to air and is used to make Japanese lacquer. The fruit is a source of wax for candles. **CZ9**

R. vernix Poison Sumac. E N. America. Deciduous tree to 20 ft (6 m), often with 2 or 3 main stems. Leaves pinnate, glabrous. Renowned for its outstandingly fine fall coloration and for being perhaps the most poisonous tree in North America. **CZ3**

Group III: Africa and Asia. Leaves 3(5–7) foliolate. Flowers long-pediceled, in lax terminal or lateral panicles. Fruits green, white, red, or brown. Plants not poisonous.

R. chirindensis Red Currant. S. Africa, Zimbabwe. Tree to 82 ft (25 m). Young plants spiny. Leaves not woolly tomentose beneath. Fruit edible.

R. tomentosa S. Africa. Shrub or small tree to 15 ft (4.5 m). Leaves trifoliolate, terminal leaflet the largest, 2–33 × 0.8–1.2(1.6) in (5–8.5 × 2–3(4) cm), sometimes smaller; all leaflets elliptic to obovate, glaucous, gray to dull green, densely whitish to reddish tomentose below, almost glabrescent above, entire or with 1–2(3) teeth beyond middle; midrib and veins prominent beneath; petiole often red, 0.6–1.6 in (1.5–4 cm). Flowers minute in dense, terminal, very pilose panicles. Fruit a subglobose drupe, 0.2–0.25 × 0.12–0.16 in (5–6 × 3–4 mm), and densely tomentose.

Ailanthus

Tree of Heaven

Ailanthus is a genus of five species, all tall deciduous trees from Southeast Asia and northern Australia. The alternate, pinnate leaves resemble those of ashes (*Fraxinus* spp) but have large glandular teeth near the base of the leaflets. They are unusual in that abscission layers form at the base of the leaflets, which often fall before the leaf. The flowers are small, greenish-yellow, and borne in long panicles, with male and female flowers often on separate trees; the ovary is deeply divided. The fruit is a one-seeded samara.

The bark of several species is tapped for resin, which is used for incense and locally to treat dysentery and other abdominal complaints. The hard yellowish wood is light and, despite its coarse grain, takes a fine polish. It is used for furniture, fishing boats, and wooden shoes.

The Tree of Heaven (*Ailanthus altissima = A. glandulosa*) is a suckering tree growing up to 20 m (66 ft) high. It is often grown as a street tree in Europe and is easily propagated by root cuttings, grafts, or suckers. The female tree is preferred as the flowers of the male have an unpleasant odor. The bark is marked with numerous gray fissures and the handsome pinnate leaves grow to 24 in (60 cm) long with 13–30 leaflets. The russet-colored fruits are twisted at each end so that they revolve as they fall, thus traveling farther.

In China the silkworm *Attacus cynthia* feeds on *Ailanthus altissima* and produces a silk that is cheaper and more durable than mulberry silk, though inferior in fineness and gloss. *Ailanthus malabarica* is cultivated in North Vietnam for the leaves, which yield a black dye for silk and satin.

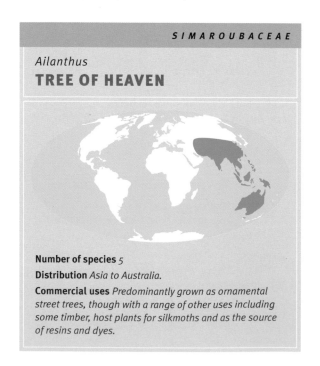

SIMAROUBACEAE

Ailanthus
TREE OF HEAVEN

Number of species 5
Distribution *Asia to Australia.*
Commercial uses *Predominantly grown as ornamental street trees, though with a range of other uses including some timber, host plants for silkmoths and as the source of resins and dyes.*

Citrus

Citrus Fruits

The citrus fruits are a well-known and distinctive group of commercially important tropical and subtropical fruits. The most important genus is *Citrus*, which includes Sweet Oranges, Seville Oranges, Mandarins, Grapefruits, Pomelos (Shaddocks), Lemons, Limes, and Citrons.

Taxonomically, *Citrus* is a difficult genus of perhaps 20 "good" species, but varying from 8 to 145 depending on the species concept of the taxonomist. The center of origin is China where written references go back to 2000 B.C.E. The closely related *Fortunella*, now included in *Citrus*, yields the Kumquat (or Cumquat), and the related but monospecific, distinct genus *Poncirus* is used as a cold-resistant rootstock and for breeding purposes.

Citrus trees, though originating from warm, wet areas of Southeast Asia, grow well over a belt extending from 35° south to 35° north (occasionally as far as 42° north in well-protected Mediterranean areas). Orange-gold types apparently come from cooler climates, the intense color being attained when temperatures drop toward winter, whereas the lemon-yellow types are probably more tropical in origin and growth habits.

For the fresh fruit market the best quality is obtained in a narrower subtropical belt (23° to 35° either side of the Equator) where seasonal alternation of temperatures and precipitation occurs. In uniformly wet and warm tropical climates, vegetation tends to be continuous and fruiting irregularly recurrent. The fruit from these climates is juicy and sweet, but the rind has a yellowish-green tinge and the crop does not transport well, so that the fruit is best suited to processing. Low temperatures are the main obstacle to cultivation outside the subtropics, for citrus fruits are highly sensitive to frost.

The Tree of Heaven, *Ailanthus altissima*, usually produces male and female flowers on separate trees in mid summer. From a distance, they look similar but male flowers are borne in dense green-yellow clusters, and have a most unpleasant smell. The pinnate leaves are 12–20 in (30–50 cm) in adult trees, but in young, vigorous specimens they can reach up to 3 ft (1 m).

The citrus fruits are borne on evergreen trees or shrubs bearing alternate leaves which are dotted with glands that are apparent when held against the light. Leaf-like wings occur on the stalk (petiole). The buds sometimes have a single accompanying spine. The flowers, which occur mostly in clusters (occasionally solitary), are white or purplish-tinged, bisexual, with typically five sepals and petals. The stamens are numerous (fifteen plus), united into bundles, and the ovary has eight to fifteen (eighteen) cells and a solitary style. The fruit is a large, rather unusual kind of berry known as a hesperidium, with the compartments or segments containing up to eight seeds (although sometimes none) embedded in a pulpy flesh. The skin is a thick peel comprising an outer thin, colored and fragrant exocarp (flavedo), a whitish spongy mesocarp or pith (albedo), and an inner endocarp, the latter forming the lining of the segments. From the endocarp multicellular juice vesicles grow centripetally to fill the segments, which may also contain seeds. The relative amounts of peel and pulp, the overall size, juiciness, acidity, and flavor vary widely according to species.

Total world cultivated area is about 5.5 million acres (2.2 million ha), 1.5 million acres (0.6 million ha) being in the Mediterranean area. Total production in 2002 was 104 million tons (over half the crop oranges and mandarins, 10 percent lemons and limes, and 5 percent grapefruit and pomelos). Relative to other tree fruits, a high percentage of the citrus world crop is exported as fresh fruit, because the very good shipping properties of the fruit. Competition on European markets is keen between Mediterranean producing countries, but production from the southern and northern hemispheres is complementary because of opposite seasonal rhythms. **CZ8–10**

ABOVE AND BELOW The Mandarin Orange (*Citrus reticulata*), is generally more densely foliated than other citrus species, with long, pointed leaves. These trees, originally from South Vietnam, are vigorous growers.

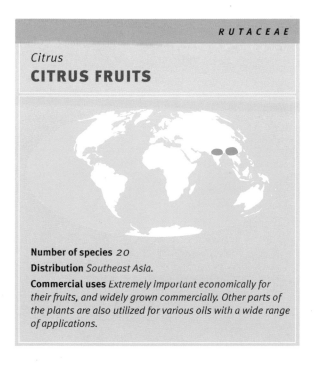

RUTACEAE

Citrus
CITRUS FRUITS

Number of species 20
Distribution *Southeast Asia.*
Commercial uses *Extremely important economically for their fruits, and widely grown commercially. Other parts of the plants are also utilized for various oils with a wide range of applications.*

The Main Species of *Citrus*

Group I: Mature fruits predominantly yellow with or without a greenish tinge. Lemons and Grapefruits.

A *Fruits broadly elliptic oblong (limoniform), less than 4 in (10 cm) across equatorial diameter.*

C. × *aurantifolia* Lime. NE India and Malaysia. Species producing small, very acid, fruits resembling the lemons, except for their greenish-yellow peel and flesh. The juice is high in vitamin C and is much used in drinks, confectionery, and other foods. Oil expressed from the fruit is used in confectionery and perfumery. *C. latifolia* (Persian Lime) is sometimes considered a hybrid of the lime and citron; the fruit is larger than the lime and the tree is less susceptible to frost. **CZ9**

C. limettioides Sweet Lime. South America. The fruits are used fresh and the roots as rootstocks for other *Citrus* species. **CZ10**

C. limetta Sweet Lemon. Tropical Asia. Produces fruits similar to *C.* × *limon*, but with sweeter, more insipid, flavor. **CZ9**

C. × *limon* Lemon. Probably Himalayan region. The most important acid citrus fruit, ranking second only to oranges in overall economic significance. Produces juicy, acid, yellow fruits on evergreen, thorny, bushy trees that are normally grafted onto a rootstock. The juice is widely used in fruit drinks, confectionery, and as a flavoring. It is also a commercial source of citric acid. Oil of lemon, extracted from the peel, is used in perfumery, for flavoring, and as an aid to digestion. Lemon seed oil is used in the manufacture of soap. **CZ9**

C. medica Citron. NE India or S Arabia. Large yellow fruits, with thick fragrant peel and small pulp, produced on small shrubby trees. The peel is used for making candied peel and the fruits used in the Jewish ceremony of the Feast of Tabernacles. **CZ9**

The Sweet Orange (*Citrus sinensis*) a native of Asia, is now a significant commercial crop in several Mediterranean countries (Israel, Spain, Italy) and the U.S. (Florida and California). They are attractive trees with the blossom of the following year's fruit forming while the current crop is still on the branch. The flowers have a heady scent.

AA *Fruits subglobose, 4 in (10 cm) or more across equatorial diameter.*

C. maxima Shaddock, Pomelo, Pummelo, Forbidden Fruit. Malaya. Produces large yellow fruits with yellow or pink flesh. Similar to grapefruit, but lacks bitterness and has thicker peel and firmer flesh. Little commercial value, but is eaten raw in India and has limited use in candying and for making marmalade. **CZ9**

C. paradisi Grapefruit, Forbidden Fruit. Probably originated in West Indies as a chance seedling of the Shaddock. Large yellow fruits with juicy, bitter-flavored pulp produced in clusters on dense, dome-shaped evergreen trees. The third most important citrus fruit, large quantities being consumed raw, canned, or as juice. Grapefruit seed oil is used in soap manufacture. **CZ9**

Group II: Mature fruits predominantly orange color. Oranges.

B *Fruits globose or the polar diameter a little larger than the equatorial diameter. Skin adherent, not easily peeled off.*

C. aurantium Seville, Bitter or Sour Orange, Bigarade. SE Asia. Produces bitter fruits resembling the Sweet Orange. The bulk of the crop is used to make marmalade and the peel is used to relieve digestive complaints, in the distilation of orange liqueurs, and to produce oil of bitter orange, an ingredient of some perfumes. Neroli oil derived from the flowers is also used in perfumery. The rootstocks are used for grafting other *Citrus* species. Also known in culinary terms as the Temple orange. **CZ9**

C. × bergamia (*C. aurantium* ssp *bergamia*) Bergamot. Tropical Asia. Similar to Seville Orange. Bergamot oil extracted from the peel is used in perfumery, especially in the manufacture of eau de Cologne. **CZ9**

C. sinensis Sweet Orange. NE India and adjoining regions of China. The most important citrus fruit. Produces round, orange-colored fruits with sweet-flavored pulp, large quantities being consumed raw, canned, or as juice. Also used for flavoring, in marmalades, and oil of sweet orange extracted from the peel is used in perfumery, and as a flavoring agent. Orange seed oil is used in the manufacture of soap. **CZ9**

BB *Fruits slightly flattened (oblate). The polar diameter less than the equatorial diameter. Skin loose, peels easily.*

C. reticulata Mandarin Orange. S Vietnam. Produces loose-skinned, tender, sweet, orange-colored fruits, which have increased in commercial importance as dessert fruits because of their easy peeling character. Several important varieties are cultivated, including the Satsuma (var *unshiu*) and Tangerine (var *deliciosa*). **CZ9**

C. × mitis Calamodin, Musk Lime. Malaysia. Produces small orange-colored fruits with an acid flavor and musty smell. Has limited use in marmalade, jellies, and drinks. **CZ9**

SOME POPULAR CITRUS HYBRIDS

Numerous hybrids between *Citrus* species occur and have been given popular names. Those with an asterisk (*) are economically and horticulturally important.

Bitter Sweet Orange	*C. aurantium* × *C. sinensis*
Chironja *see* Orangelo	
Citrange	*C. sinensis* × *Poncirus trifoliata**
Limequat	*C. maxima* × *C.* sp. poss. *C. margarita* (= *F. marginata*)
Orangelo	*C. paradisi* × *C. sinensis*
Satsumelo	*C. paradisi* × *C. reticulata* var *unshiu*
Siamelo	*C. paradisi* × *C. reticulata*
Siamor	*C. sinensis* × Tangelo
Sopomaldin	*C. paradisi* × *C. × mitis*
Tangelo	*C. paradisi* × *C. reticulata* var *deliciosa**
Tangelo	*C. paradisi* × Tangelo
Tangor Temple Orange	*C. sinensis* × *C. reticulata**
Ugli *see* Tangelo	

Tetradium

Euodias

The genus *Tetradium* comprises about six species native to Southeast Asia and Japan. They are medium-sized trees, deciduous or evergreen, often aromatic, with naked exposed buds (hidden in the leafstalk base in the closely related genus *Phellodendron*). The leaves are opposite and pinnate, and the flowers, which are often unisexual, are small, in flat-topped clusters; there are four or five sepals, petals, stamens, and carpels. The fruits are capsular and split open when ripe. Some species are hardy in temperate regions, but these attractive and unusual trees are uncommon in temperate cultivation. The leaves of some species are used for poultices and medicinal teas.

The following hardy species are all deciduous and succeed in all types of soil. *Tetradium daniellii* from northern China and Korea is a handsome species in flower and fruit. It grows to 52 ft (16 m) and has odd-pinnate leaves 9–15 in (22–38 cm) long with between five and eleven more or less lanceolate to ovate leaflets 2–5 in (5–12 cm) long. The flowers are small, white, and the fruits purplish.

A Chinese (Szechwan) form of *T. danielli*, formerly known in the genus *Euodia* as *E. hupehensis*, is a useful fall-flowering species growing to about 62 ft (19 m) in cultivation, with smooth, streaked, or speckled bark. The leaves are odd-pinnate, 8–10 in (20–25 cm) long, with five to nine leaflets. The flowers are unisexual on the same tree and similar to those of *Tetradium daniellii*. It is recognized by the shoots, leaves, and fruit being variably downy to hairy. It grows to about 43 ft (13 m) and has leaves 10 in (25 cm) long with seven to eleven leaflets. It flowers abundantly in late summer followed by purplish-brown fruits. **CZ9**

ABOVE *Ptelea trifoliata* produces fruit in dense clusters, each being a thin, flat disk up to 0.8–2 in (2–5 cm) across. An almost circular wing surrounds one central seed. They eventually ripen to a pale straw color.

BELOW *Tetradium daniellii* is often cultivated for ornament in parks and gardens for both its flower and fruit. Flowers open in late summer and are strongly aromatic.

Ptelea

Hop Tree

Ptelea is a genus of about ten species of shrubs and small trees that are native to North America and Mexico. They are well known for their aromatic foliage. Each leaf is usually trifoliolate and dotted with translucent glands that are visible when held against light. The flowers are mostly unisexual and densely clustered, each with four or five minute sepals but larger petals and either four or five stamens (abortive in female flowers) or a single typically two-celled ovary. The latter develops into a two-seeded, somewhat disc-like, circular samara with a distinct surrounding wing.

The best-known species is the Hop Tree, Wafer Ash, or Stinking Ash (*P. trifoliolata*), which grows to a height of 26 ft (8 m) and has bitter bark and fragrant, greenish-white flowers that appear in early summer, each with four sepals and petals and four stamens in the males. The distinctive winged fruit is greenish-yellow when ripe and the wing is reticulated. The Hop Tree is native to southern Canada and the eastern United States and is not uncommonly cultivated elsewhere—indeed, it has become naturalized in several places including central Europe. Its common name recalls the practise of using the fruits for making home-brewed beer, the flavor of the fruits (and bitter-tasting bark) resembling that of hops.

Hop trees grow best in slightly shaded conditions on well-drained soils. Cultivated plants in some areas rarely set fertile seeds but the tree can be propagated by layering in the spring. A number of cultivars exist, such as 'Aurea' with bright yellow leaves. Variety *mollis* has densely hairy inflorescence and underside of the leaflets. The only other species found in cultivation is *P. crenulata*. **CZ5–8**

Phellodendron

Amur Cork Tree

The species of *Phellodendron* are all native to northeast Asia. They are deciduous, aromatic trees with bright yellow inner bark. The young buds are enclosed in the petiole base and the leaves are opposite and pinnate, with odd terminal leaflets. The flowers are inconspicuous, greenish, with the sexes on separate trees. There are five to eight sepals and petals and five to six stamens (sterile in the female flowers). The fruit is a black drupe with five chambers, each with one stone-like seed. Phellodendrons are fairly hardy in temperate regions where they are grown for their attractive yellow leaves in the fall.

The Amur Cork Tree (*P. amurense*), from north China and Manchuria, grows to 50 ft (15 m) with fissured, corky bark when mature and yellowish shoots. The leaves are 10–15 in (25–38 cm) long with five to eleven (rarely thirteen) ciliate leaflets, hairless beneath (midrib slightly hairy), and more or less glaucous. The fruit, 0.4 in (1 cm) across, when bruised, smells of turpentine. The seeds yield an insecticide and extracts of the bark have been used in a preparation for treating various skin diseases.

Phellodendron chinense from Hupeh in central China grows to about 33 ft (10 m) with a thin, reticulately ridged bark and purple-brown branches. The leaves are up to 15 in (38 cm) long with seven to thirteen (rarely fourteen) leaflets that are broadly cuneate at the base and more or less hairy beneath, especially on the midrib. The flowers are borne in loose clusters about as broad as they are deep, and the fruit is globose, 0.4 in (1 cm) across. As with *P. amurense*, the bark is used medicinally, and is known to the Chinese as "huang-peh." *Phellodendron japonicum* from central Japan is a similar species but the leaflets are truncate to subcordate at the base and the flower clusters are deeper than they are broad.

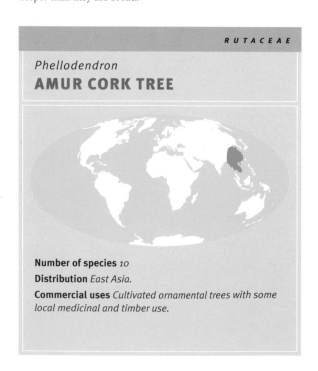

RUTACEAE

Phellodendron
AMUR CORK TREE

Number of species *10*
Distribution *East Asia.*
Commercial uses *Cultivated ornamental trees with some local medicinal and timber use.*

OLEACEAE

Olea

Olives

Olea is a genus of some twenty species native to warm temperate or tropical regions from southern Europe (Mediterranean) to Africa (the main center), southern Asia, eastern Australia, New Caledonia, and New Zealand. They are small to medium-sized trees or shrubs with opposite, simple leaves. The flowers are white, mostly bisexual, borne in axillary panicles or fascicles. The calyx and the tube of the corolla are four-lobed, the corolla lobes valvate or absent, and there are two stamens. The fruit is a more or less ovoid drupe, dark blue to black when ripe.

The silvery-green foliage and gnarled trunks of ancient olive trees form one of the most characteristic aspects of the vegetation of the Mediterranean basin. Indeed, the olive is often regarded as an indicator of the Mediterranean climate and of the limits of Mediterranean vegetation. The best-known species is the Common Olive (*O. europaea*). The Cultivated Olive, subspecies *europaea*, is distinguished from the wild form, subspecies *sylvestris*, by the latter's wider leaves, thorny branches, and smaller fruits.

Phellodendron chinense has opposite pinnate leaves with 7–13 leaflets, which are similar to *P. japonicum* but less downy. When crushed, the leaves give off an aromatic scent and also turn an attractive yellow in the fall, making them popular ornamentals.

Olives have been cultivated since prehistoric times, and constitute a crop of fundamental importance in the daily life, economics, and sociology of the peoples of Mediterranean countries, providing them with their main source of edible oil. The ancients used olive oil for lighting as well as cooking and for anointing the body in religious ceremonies. There are frequent references to the olive in the Bible and in Greek and Roman texts, and the olive branch is still an emblem of peace. The olive provided much of the wealth of many Mediterranean communities and still plays a major role in the economy, though production is in decline today and the acreages under cultivation have been diminishing for some time. Not only is the crop an ancient one but it has changed little over the millennia and its present decline is largely due not only to changed patterns of agriculture and eating habits but to the fact that the methods of cultivation, propagation, and oil production are not properly adapted to modern conditions.

The longevity of the olive has had a major influence on its history and evolution. Trees may survive for fifteen hundred years or more (they regenerate from suckers) and are among the oldest trees known in Europe.

Olives are exacting in their climatic requirements—they cannot survive temperatures of 16°F (–9 °C) or an average temperature of 37°F (3°C) during the coldest winter months, though they require some degree of winter chilling to ensure the induction of flowering. Olives are generally grown in groves or orchards, sometimes interplanted with catch crops, though they produce best when grown alone. They survive on dry soils without artificial irrigation, but heavier and more reliable crops are obtained with irrigation.

There are hundreds of olive cultivars, comprising mixtures of clones, often occupying extensive areas. They are budded onto seedlings or propagated by cuttings, often by layering. Propagation by these means was a slow process until mist propagation techniques were introduced for the rooting of cuttings. Often cuttings are grafted onto the stumps of old trees. Growth is very slow and the olive requires several decades to reach maturity and full productivity.

Different styles of cultivation are employed in the various Mediterranean countries: in Spain, for example, three main stems are allowed to develop, either by planting or by splitting the crown, giving a low-growing tree, while in other countries, such as Greece, the trees are allowed to develop a single tall straight trunk.

The olive is not reliable in its cropping, and a heavy crop one year is liable to exhaust the plant and be followed by a light crop the next year. It is also highly susceptible to wind and heavy rain, which can beat down the young fruits and leaves, and to spring frosts, which can kill the flowers.

Harvesting of the crop is undertaken by hand or by mechanical shakers. The fruits are handpicked when straw-colored for green table olives and left to mature on the tree until black and ripe for table use, cooking, or, more usually, for oil. Olives are inedible when gathered from the trees, and need to undergo various treatments including a period in a potash or salt solution, which gives rise to a lactic acid fermentation; they are then preserved in brine. Black olives may be stored direct in a brine solution, but the best-quality table ones are preserved in a marinade of olive oil, often with various herbs such as thyme or rosemary. Green olives are often sold stoned and stuffed with sweet red bell pepper, anchovy, or almonds.

Apart from its major use as a cooking and salad oil, olive oil is widely used for medicinal purposes, for canning sardines and other preserves, in dressing wool, and in soap manufacture and cosmetics.

Other cultivated species include the Indian Olive (*O. ferruginea* = *O. europaea* ssp *cuspidata*) and the Wild Olive (*O. europaea* ssp *africana*). The wood from several species is decorative and can be finely worked, especially that of the Black Iron Wood (*O. capensis*). **CZ8–9**

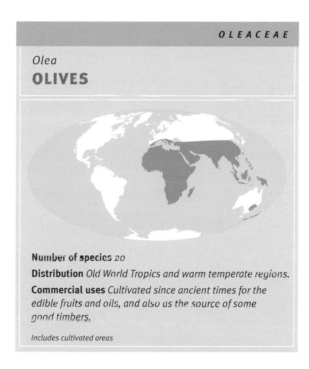

	OLEACEAE

Olea
OLIVES

Number of species 20
Distribution *Old World Tropics and warm temperate regions.*
Commercial uses *Cultivated since ancient times for the edible fruits and oils, and also as the source of some good timbers.*

Includes cultivated areas

Olea europaea, the Common Olive, is usually found in groves, the silver tinge of their leaves lending that tone to much of the Mediterranean landscape. The rugged, heavily branching habit of olives makes them attractive specimens in favorable climes.

Fraxinus

Ashes

Fraxinus as a genus is comprised of some sixty-five species from the northern hemisphere, in particular east Asia, North America, and the Mediterranean region. The ashes are deciduous trees, with opposite and mostly pinnate leaves. Their clusters of small greenish flowers, often without petals, are bisexual or unisexual, the sexes variously distributed, and there are usually two stamens. The fruit is winged (samara).

The best-known species is the European or Common Ash (*F. excelsior*), a tree growing to 130 ft (40 m) with light gray bark and black winter buds. Its handsome "keys" (bunches of winged fruits) hanging from the shoots are a characteristic sight in the fall.

Nordic myths tell that Man was created from ash wood: the Norse word "aska" means man. Medicinally, decoctions of the bark of the European Ash were once used to cure jaundice and other complaints of the liver, and to bring relief from toothache, gout, and stiff joints. A strong extract made from ashes of the wood was used for scabby heads; other extracts were apparently able to counteract snakebites. The Flowering or Manna Ash (*F. ornus*) yields a pale yellow juice when the bark is cut, which acts as a mild laxative and has long been given to children, particularly in Italy and Sicily.

The principal use of ash, however, has been for its timber, that of European Ash in particular. It is hard but elastic, scarcely warps, is not very susceptible to attack by insects and is thus durable. In the past it was used for making spears and staffs, then for carriage- and waggon-building, as well as for such uses as hop-poles and tool handles. Furniture-makers appreciate the close grain and few knots of this pale timber. It burns very well and was the original Yule log.

The genus is also valuable as a source of ornamental street and park trees. Some of these have the calyx remaining when in fruit, the best known being the Arizona Ash (*F. velutina*), the White Ash (*F. americana*, and the Red Ash (*F. pennsylvanica*). Others, in which the calyx is absent or falls early, include the Blue Ash (*F. quadrangulata*), the Black Ash (*F. nigra*), and the European Ash. The Flowering Ash is also frequently seen as a handsome ornamental tree. **CZ3–8**

OLEACEAE

Fraxinus
ASHES

Number of species 65
Distribution *Northern temperate regions to the Tropics.*
Commercial uses *Important timber trees used in a host of ways. Also utilized in forestry and grown widely as ornamentals.*

F. excelsior

RIGHT *Fraxinus angustifolia* 'Raywood,' a form of the Narrow-leaved Ash, is an elegant tree that can be distinguished from the Common Ash by its knobbly, deeply ridged bark, its brown rather than black buds in winter, and its glabrous leaves. These turn a glorious rich plum purple in fall.

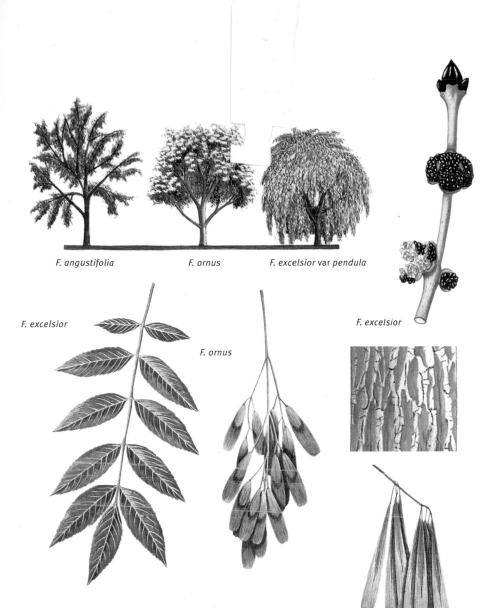

F. angustifolia   F. ornus   F. excelsior var pendula

F. excelsior

F. ornus

F. excelsior

F. pennsylvanica

The Main Species of *Fraxinus*

Section *Ornus*

Flowers appearing with or after leaves in terminal and lateral clusters on leafy branches. Filaments of stamens usually longer than their anthers. "Flowering" or "Manna" Ashes.

A *Corolla present.*

F. ornus Flowering or **Manna Ash.** S Europe, Asia Minor. Tree to 50–66 ft (15–20 m). Leaflets usually 7, hairless except along the midrib beneath. **CZ6**

F. floribunda **Himalayan Manna Ash.** The Himalaya. Tree to 130 ft (40 m). Leaflets usually 7 or 9, hairless above but hairy on the veins beneath. **CZ8**

AA *Corolla absent.*

F. chinensis China. Tree to 50 ft (15 m). Closely related to *F. ornus.* **CZ6**

F. bungeana China. Shrub or small tree to 16 ft (5 m). Closely related to *F. ornus.* **CZ5**

Section *Fraxinaster*

Flowers appearing before leaves from leafless, lateral buds of previous year's growth. Filaments of stamens mostly shorter than their anthers.

B *Flowers with calyx.*

F. dipetala California and adjacent areas. Shrub to 13 ft (4 m). Leaflets usually 5, hairless. Petals 2. **CZ8**

F. americana **White Ash.** N. America. Tree to 130 ft (40 m). Leaflets 7–9, usually hairless, occasionally downy underneath. Calyx small, persistent; corolla absent. Wing of fruit terminal. **CZ3**

F. velutina **Arizona Ash.** SW U.S. Tree 26–40 ft (8–12 m). Leaflets 3–5, usually hairy on both surfaces. Calyx present at fruiting; corolla absent. **CZ7**

F. pennsylvanica **Red Ash.** E N. America. Tree 40–66 ft (12–20 m). Leaflets usually 7–9, downy at least beneath. Calyx persistent; corolla absent. Wing of fruit decurrent. **CZ4**

BB *Flowers lacking calyx and corolla.*

F. excelsior **Common or European Ash.** Europe. Tree to 150 ft (45 m). Leaflets 7–11, hairless except for the midrib beneath. **CZ4**

F. angustifolia **Narrow-leaved Ash.** W Mediterranean, N. Africa. Tree 66–80 ft (20–25 m). Leaflets 7–13, hairless. **CZ6** ssp *oxycarpu* (*F. oxycarpa*) E Mediterranean to Turkestan. Similar but with fewer leaflets, each with a row of hairs near the midrib beneath. **CZ6**

F. nigra **Black Ash.** E N. America. Tree 82–100 ft (25–30 m). Leaflets 7–11, hairless except along the veins beneath. Calyx present, small, deciduous. **CZ7**

F. quadrangulata **Blue Ash.** N. America. Tree to about 66 ft (20 m). Leaflets 5–11, hairless above, downy beneath. Calyx present, minute, soon falling. **CZ4**

F. americana

F. ornus

F. ornus

F. excelsior

Syringa

Lilacs

Syringa is a genus of over twenty species from Asia and southeast Europe, cultivated for their showy flowers in spring and early summer. They are deciduous shrubs or small trees with opposite leaves that are usually entire, rarely lobed or pinnate. The flowers, which are borne in panicles, are bisexual, fragrant, and waxy, ranging in color from white to deep purple. The calyx is four-toothed and the corolla tubular with four valvate lobes. There are two stamens, either included or exserted, and the ovary has two cells. The fruit is a leathery capsule maturing winged seeds, two to each chamber.

The Common Lilac (*S. vulgaris*) from southeast Europe is a very popular species with over 500 named cultivars, many originating in France. It grows to 23 ft (7 m) and is given to suckering and the formation of epicormic shoots. Such suckers and shoots need to be removed. Lilacs flourish in a good moist loam and are distinctly sun-loving. Propagation is best by layers, but seeds and cuttings can be used. In some instances, grafting on Common Lilac stocks is required.

There are a number of excellent species of *Syringa* from China and central Europe, including *S. reflexa, S. villosa,* and *S. josikaea* (Hungarian Lilac), which have been used as parents for a great many hybrids, among them the "Canadian hybrids" raised at Ottawa in the 1920s.

The name Syringa may derive from the Greek word "surinx," meaning tube, and alluding to the use of its stems to make pipes. **CZ4–7**

TOP AND ABOVE The attractive flowers of *Syringa* are strongly scented and borne in panicles which are often pyramidal. They are good for cutting and range in color and shade from white to a deep purple.

SCROPHULARIACEAE

Paulownia

Empress Tree

The genus *Paulownia* contains six species of fast-growing deciduous trees native to China. Best known is the Empress Tree (*P. tomentosa* = *P. imperialis*) also named the Foxglove Tree for its fragrant, pale violet or rich purple foxglove-like flowers, which are borne in tall erect panicles during early spring, before the leaves emerge. The latter are long-stalked opposite, ovate, large—normally 5–12 in (12–30 cm), but up to 3.3 ft (1 m) on suckering shoots—hairy on the upper surface and distinctly downy on the lower. Leaves of young trees may be lobed and bear one to three points. The fruit is a woody, ovoid capsule containing winged seeds.

The Empress Tree is widely grown in temperate zones, but its habit of producing flower buds in late summer and fall, which are then susceptible to winter frosts, means that flowering the following spring can be unpredictable in northern regions. Other species found in cultivation include *P. fortunei* (flowers with a pale yellow blotch) and *P. × taiwaniana* (flowers purple-white with purple lines). Paulownias thrive in a well-drained, deep loam in a sheltered sunny position. They can be propagated from seeds or by root, shoot, and leaf cuttings. The Empress Tree yields top-quality wood much used in cabinetmaking in the Orient. **CZ5–7**

SCROPHULARIACEAE

Paulonia
EMPRESS TREE

Number of species *6*
Distribution *China*
Commercial uses *High quality wood for cabinet making.*

BIGNONIACEAE

Catalpa

Bean Trees

Catalpa is a genus of about eleven species of hardy deciduous, rarely evergreen trees, sometimes shrubs, native to America, the West Indies, and east Asia, some of which are popular ornamentals. Their leaves are opposite or in whorls of threes, borne on long stalks, and large with an entire or broadly lobed margin. The flowers occur in terminal clusters, each flower with a tubular mostly two-lipped calyx and a tubular corolla with five spreading lobes—two above and three below. There are five stamens but typically only two are fertile. The fruit is a narrow, flattish capsule, 12–24 in (30–60 cm) long, which splits into two valves. The seeds are numerous, compressed, and tufted at each end with white hairs.

Catalpas are vigorous and hardy in temperate regions. The persistent long fruits recall Runner Beans (*Phaseolus coccineus*), a feature reflected in their popular name. They are favorite ornamentals, prized for their large leaves, showy clusters of large tubular flowers, and the long and persistent pendent fruits. Any reasonably good, moist soil is suitable and they are seen to best advantage as isolated specimens on lawns or lining an avenue. Propagation can be from seed or by cuttings of mature wood. Named varieties are propagated by grafting on seedlings.

The best-known species is the Indian Bean, Common or Southern Catalpa (*Catalpa bignonioides*) the crushed leaves

of which, however, have an unpleasant odor. Under favorable conditions, it can reach 60–66 ft (18–20 m) and has a round, spreading head. There is a dwarf form: cultivar 'Nana,' which grows to no more than 6 ft (2 m). Cultivar 'Aurea' is attractively conspicuous by its more yellowish leaves. The coarse-grained durable timber of this species and also that of the Western Catalpa, Catawba, or Cigar Tree (*C. speciosa*) is used for fence posts and railway sleepers. The bark of *C. longissima* is used for tanning in the West Indies. **CZ5–9**

BIGNONIACEAE

Catalpa
BEAN TREES

Number of species *11*

Distribution *East Asia, southeast United States and the West Indies.*

Commercial uses *Some timber use but predominantly grown as horticultural specimens with various named cultivars in existence.*

Bean trees (*Catalpa* spp) in mid summer are without doubt among the most beautiful of flowering trees. Flowers are borne in panicles, racemes, or corymbs up to 12 in (30 cm) tall and are generally white with yellow and red spotting.

The Main Species of *Catalpa*

In the following selection, the petal background color is white or pinkish, except *C. ovata* where it is yellowish.

Group I: Leaves pubescent with typically unbranched hairs on the lower surfaces—at least on the veins.

C. ovata (*C. kaempferi*) **Chinese or Yellow Catalpa.** China. Tree 20–33(50) ft (6–10(15) m) with spreading head. Leaves opposite, broadly cordate-ovate, 5–10 in (12–25 cm) long, simple, but with 3–5 pointed lobes. Flowers fragrant, in many-flowered panicles, 4–10 in (10–25 cm) long, the corollas less than 1 in (2.5 cm) long, yellowish-white, with striped orange and violet-purple spotted markings on the inside of the tube. Fruit up to 12 in (30 cm) long. Long cultivated in Japan. **CZ5**

C. bignonioides **Common Catalpa, Indian Bean, Southern Catalpa.** N. America. Rounded tree 20–66 ft (6–20 m). Leaves often in whorls of 3, broadly cordate-ovate, 5–8 in (12–20 cm) long, simple, but sometimes with 2 small lobes, giving a strong unpleasant odor when crushed or bruised. Flowers in many-flowered panicles, 5.3–10 in (13–25 cm) , the corollas 1.6–2 in (4–5 cm), white, with striped yellow and purple spotted markings on the inside of the tube, which is frilled at the mouth. Fruit 6–15 in (15–40 cm). Cultivar 'Aurea' has more or less yellow leaves; 'Nana' is a dwarf form to 6 ft (2 m), possibly covering more than one clone. **CZ5**

C. × *hybrida* (*C. teasii* = *C. ovata* × *C. bignonioides*) **Hybrid Catalpa.** Tree to 100 ft (30 m). Leaves opposite, broadly cordate-ovate, 6–15 in (15–40 cm), similar to those of *C. ovata* but bluish-purple before fully expanded. Flowers in many-flowered panicles, 6–15 in (15–40 cm) and similar to those of *C. bignonioides*, but rather smaller. Fruit to 15 in (40 cm), but does not contain seeds. Cultivar 'J.C. Teas' has purplish unfolding leaves. **CZ5**

C. speciosa **Western Catalpa, Catawba, Cigar Tree.** N. America. Tree to 100 ft (30 m). Leaves cordate-ovate, 6–12 in (15–30 cm) long. Flowers in relatively few-flowered panicles, 6–7 in (15–18 cm) long, the corollas large, 2–2.5 in (5–6 cm) across and 1.6–2 in (4–5 cm) long, white with a few purplish spots on the inside of the tube, the mouth of which is frilled. Fruit 9–18 in (22–45 cm) long. **CZ5**

Group II: Leaves quite glabrous on the lower surface.

C. bungei China. Small tree, 18–33 ft (6–10 m) with pyramidal shape. Leaves opposite, triangular-ovate, 3–6.3 in (8–16 cm) long, sometimes toothed or angled near the base. Flowers in 3–12-flowered racemes 4–8 in (10–20 cm) long, the corollas 1.2–1.6 in (3–4 cm) long, white with purple spots on the inside of the tube. Fruit 10–13.5 in (25–35 cm) long. **CZ6**

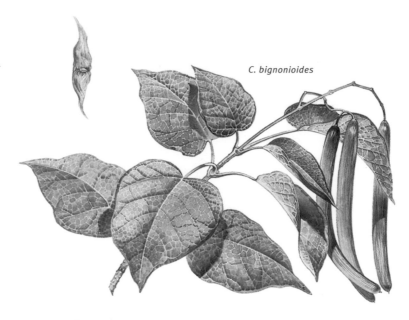

C. bignonioides

C. bignonioides

C. bignonioides

CAPRIFOLIACEAE

Sambucus

Elders

Sambucus comprises about nine species from the temperate and subtropical regions of the Old and the New World. They are mostly deciduous shrubs or small trees (occasionally herbaceous) with opposite, odd-pinnate leaves. The abundant flowers are bisexual, white and small, in flat or more or less pyramidal clusters. There are usually five sepals (minute) and petals (rarely three or four) and five stamens; the ovary is three to five chambered. The fruit is a small berry with three to five one-seeded nutlets.

CAPRIFOLIACEAE

Sambucus
ELDERS

Number of species 9
Distribution *Temperate and subtropical regions.*
Commercial uses *Some species cultivated as ornamentals or for edible fruit (though the fruit of certain species is toxic), and several named forms are grown. The fruits are also sometimes used to make wine.*

S. nigra

S. canadensis

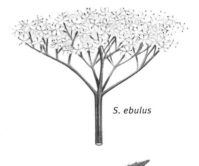

S. ebulus

S. caerulea

S. racemosa

Some half dozen species are either native or hardy in temperate regions, and are grown as ornamentals. They are mostly vigorous, invasive, sun-loving shrubs thriving in many soils and habitats, especially where there is a good moisture supply. Among the species cultivated as ornamentals are *S. canadensis* (the American Elder) and its cultivars 'Maxima' with huge flower heads, 'Aurea' with greenish-yellow foliage, and *S. racemosa*, an attractive bright red-berried elder with masses of flowers in a distinctly pyramidal cluster. The Common Elder (*S. nigra*) exists in several cultivar forms, including 'Aurea' with leaves golden-yellow, and 'Purpurea' with leaves flushed purple.

In Britain, the Common Elder has for long been the basis for excellent country wines made both from the flowers and the berries ("the English-man's grape"). At one time, in Britain, elderberry wine was used to adulterate red wine made from grapes and thus fell somewhat into disrepute. Allowed to mature for at least six months, elderberry wine is a fine alcoholic drink. Infusions of roots of this same species are said to have purgative properties. **CZ4–8**

The Main Species of *Sambucus*

Group I: Flower clusters flat. Pith white. Fruit dark purple or black.

S. caerulea **Blue Elderberry.** W N. America, especially California. Shrub or small tree, 10–50 ft (3–15 m). Leaves 6–10 in (15–25 cm) long, compound with 5–7 leaflets. Flowers yellowish-white in early summer in flat umbels. Berries black but covered with an intensely glaucous (blue) bloom. In California this species is more tree-like, the trunk being up to 16 in (40 cm) diameter. The cooked berries are used as a food. It was also introduced to France and cultivated in Paris during the nineteenth century. **CZ5**

S. canadensis **American Elder.** E N. America. Deciduous shrub to 13 ft (4 m) with soft pithy stems and branches. Leaves pinnate with 5–11 leaflets, 5 in (12 cm) long. Flowers in convex umbels up to 8 in (20 cm) across, white, produced soon after midsummer. Berries purple-black. Closely related to *S. nigra*. **CZ3**

'Maxima' An extremely robust variety with large leaves and enormous flat flower heads 12 in (30 cm) across.

S. nigra **Common Elder.** Europe. A very common and widespread deciduous shrub or small tree, 13–26 ft (4–8 m). Branches and young wood pithy, with rugged fissured bark on older trees. Leaflets 5–7, 4–12 in (10–30 cm) long. Flowers yellowish-cream or dull white with characteristic scent, in flat umbels 5–8 in (12–20 cm) across, beginning early summer. Berries prolific, shining black, ripening in September. The juice of the berries has many pharmaceutical properties. It is also used for domestic winemaking and as a syrup for colds and chills. *Sambucus nigra* 'Aurea' is the Golden Elder; *S. nigra* 'Albo-variegata' is an attractive variegated form. **CZ5**

S. ebulus **Dane's Elder** or **Danewort.** Europe and N. Africa, naturalized in British Isles. An unusual herbaceous species producing stout, grooved stems 3.3–4 ft (1–1.2 m) high each year. Leaves with 9–13 leaflets. Flowers white, tinged pink in flat umbels, 3–5 in (7.5–10 cm) across. Fruit black. Formerly an important medicinal plant, the plant was recommended for the healing of all manner of ailments, from jaundice to gout. **CZ5**

Group II: Flower clusters more or less pyramidal (not flat). Pith mostly brown. Fruit red, yellow, or white (brownish to black in *S. melanocarpa*).

S. racemosa **Red-berried Elder.** Europe, Asia Minor, Siberia, and W Asia. A medium-sized deciduous shrub, 10–16 ft (3–5 m) with coarsely toothed compound leaves. Flowers are produced in April as terminal white pyramidal panicles, followed by the brilliant red fruits in July. Two outstanding cultivars are 'Laciniata,' a decorative cut-leaved variety, and 'Plumosa Aurea,' a fine, golden, cut-leaved shrub. **CZ4**

S. pubens North American species closely related to *S. racemosa*. **CZ5**

S. melanocarpa Shrub to 13 ft (4 m). Leaflets 5–7. Flower clusters about as deep as wide. Fruits black but reddish-brown in some. **CZ6**

S. nigra

S. nigra

Trees of the Tropics

Nowhere else on earth has a richer diversity of trees than the Tropics. Entire families occur pantropically which are totally absent from colder parts of the globe, and of the four hundred species of oak worldwide, over eighty of them are found only in Malaya.

Tropical forests have abundant, almost daily, rainfall, a high and constant temperature throughout the year, and soils enriched by a very considerable animal population —a combination of factors favorable to evergreen plant life. Indeed, the great majority of tropical trees are evergreen (*see* pages 27–29 for a consideration of the different forest types).

In this section, the majority of entries are broadleaves, though monocotyledonous trees (the palms predominantly, but also screwpines, dragon trees, and grass trees, and some species of bamboo which attain tree-like dimensions) have their place. Most monocotyledonous species are appreciated mainly for their esthetic value, though bamboos are vitally important in the economy of the seasonally dry tropical countries where they are most abundant, being traditionally used as a building material, conduits and food vessels, and increasingly as a source of fibers and cellulose for the manufacture of paper.

For centuries, tropical trees have yielded many fine woods and continue to provide most of the world's hardwood timber. In addition, they are the source of many of the world's spices, gums, resins, latexes, fruits, and medicines. Vast areas of the more accessible rainforest have been depleted of their timber, to the extent that plantations are increasingly seen as the future source of the major tropical hardwoods, such as Teak (*Tectona grandis*), African Mahogany (*Khaya* spp), ebonies (*Diospyros* spp), and rosewoods (*Dalbergia* spp).

Coffee (*Coffea arabica* and *C. liberica*) is the most important tropical tree crop of African origin, while tropical America's principal crops are the true Mahogany (*Swietenia macrophylla*), the American cedars (*Cedrela*) and two species of pine, *Pinus caribaea* and *P. oocarpa* (both of which are planted on a huge scale) and fruit trees of global significance, including the Brazil Nut (*Bertholletia excelsa*), the Avocado Pear (*Persea americana*), and Cacao (*Theobroma cacao*)—the source of chocolate. Other South American trees yielding so-called minor products include: *Hevea brasiliensis*, on which a major industry grew up within the Amazon, based on collecting rubber latex from this species; the Kapok Tree (*Ceiba pentandra*), used for its cotton-like seed covering, and *Strychnos* spp, from which curare, a powerful nerve poison is derived. Many species from Asia and Africa have similarly important economic and medicinal properties, such as *Melaleuca* spp from Indomalaysia, the source of the medicinal cajaput oil, and *Derris* spp, from Asia and Australia, which contain various chemicals used as insecticides, among other applications. From *Cinnamomum*, a tree found in tropical Asia and America, the spice cinnamon as well as camphor are derived, and the seeds of *Ricinus*, a tree of Africa and the Middle East, yield oils used in soaps, varnishes, and cosmetics.

Apart from providing some of the world's most economically important timber trees, the Tropics also offer up some of its most ornamentally appealing. From Africa the Flame of the Forest or Flamboyant (*Delonix regia*) must rival Asia's *Amhertsia nobilis* (both members of the Leguminosae) as the world's most glorious flowering tree. *Delonix* originates in Madagascar but is now common throughout the Tropics and subtropics, known for its vivid scarlet flowers and finely feathery foliage. Tropical America is home to a number of superb ornamental flowering trees, among them the thirty-plus species of Jacaranda, prized for their lilac blooms and delicate foliage, the coral trees (*Erythrina* spp) sporting robust red or yellow flowers and, perhaps loveliest of all, the Frangipani (*Plumeria alba* and *P. rubra*)—small, open-crowned trees bearing masses of blossoms exuding an exquisite, heady perfume.

It is a fact that many tropical countries look to the exploitation of their rainforests as a means of attaining a "developed" economy. Such forests contain numerous plant and animal species threatened with extinction which have yet to be described. It is disturbing to reach the conclusion that, at the present rate of destruction, there will be very little, if any natural forest cover left fifty years hence. Conservation of tropical forests requires their proper management on an international basis for the overall good. However, it is understandably difficult to persuade underdeveloped nations of the need to conserve this last resource when the developed world has already destroyed its own natural forests. Therefore, hand in hand with conservation must go the curbing of the ever-increasing demands of rich developed nations for the products of tropical forests.

OPPOSITE The Mahogany, *Swietenia*, is planted all over the Tropics, and is propagated easily from cuttings. They grow to be towering giants of up to 165 ft (50 m), with heavy trunks of hard, rich red-brown, straight-grained timber.

ABOVE *Aloe vaombe,* displaying its rather garish scarlet, yellow, and orange tubular flowers. The viciously spined leaves are borne in spiral rosettes.

BELOW *Adansonia digitata* can develop a trunk up to 30 ft (10 m) in diameter while its branches may only reach 40 ft (13 m). These trees can live for an extraordinarily long time; some in Africa are estimated to be over 5,000 years old.

Adansonia   BOMBACACEAE

Baobab

A genus of eight species of distinctive trees up to 66 ft (20 m) tall, restricted to Africa and Madagascar with a single species in northern Australia. All have the characteristic swollen trunk and relatively short branches. The best-known species is probably *Adansonia digitata* from Africa, popularly called the Monkey Bread Tree, which is thought to live for thousands of years.

All species flower during darkness and are pollinated mainly by bats but also by insects and bushbabies. The nocturnal flowers are pendulous on long stems and the petals overlap clockwise and anticlockwise in equal numbers. The bark of *A. digitata* is used to make cloth and rope and the dried fruit also provides a nutritious drink. *Adansonia gregorii,* the Australian species, provides enormous quantities of water for birds and indigenous people alike.

Albizia   LEGUMINOSAE

Silk Tree

This genus is composed of approximately 120 species of deciduous trees, shrubs, and lianas, and representatives can be found in Asia, Africa, and a few in the Americas. All have showy flowers in umbels or spikes, the flowers themselves being pink, cream, or yellow in color, the conspicuous stamens lending a delicate appearance to the flowers.

Albizias are extensively cultivated as ornamentals, especially *A. julibrissin* (Silk Tree), which produces a dome-shaped tree to 20 ft (6 m) and is surprisingly hardy especially in areas experiencing long summers—in particular the form 'Rosea.' They are generally found as specimen trees in gardens rather than as street trees owing to susceptibility to pests and diseases. Some species are cultivated as shade trees for coffee and tea crops, e.g. *A. chinensis,* or, in a few cases, for timber (*A. grandibracteata*) from Africa.

Aloe   ASPHODELACEAE

Aloe

Aloe is a large genus of over 350 species of succulent trees and prostrate, sessile plants, which range from tropical and South Africa through Madagascar, Arabia, and the Canary Islands.

The succulent leaves are borne in terminal spiral rosettes and are usually spined along their edges and sometimes on the surface. The yellow or red flowers, which are bird-pollinated, are held in axillary or terminal panicles and racemes.

Aloes are widely cultivated as ornamental plants on account of their diversity of form and architectural stature, though many species have additional commercial applications, among them *A. ferox* and *A. vera.* The latter, originally from Asia, is now widely naturalized and cultivated in the southern United States, Mexico, and the Caribbean where it is the major source of commercial aloes used in many shampoos and other cosmetics. A purgative drug, bitter aloes, is extracted from the leaves of several species.

Amhertsia   LEGUMINOSAE

Pride of Burma

A genus of a single species (*Amhertsia nobilis*), native to Myanmar, where it is so rare it has been reported only twice from the wild. It is now, however, cultivated as an ornamental tree in the moist Tropics, largely for its beautiful pink flowers.

The 3 ft (1 m) long pinnate leaves, composed of several léaflets to 12 in (30 cm) long, are spotted red or purple when young, becoming lush green as they mature. The tree can grow to 40 ft (12 m) and bears long pendent racemes of tubular pink-red flowers. Both the young leaves and flowers are edible.

Anacardium   ANACARDIACEAE

Cashew

The eleven species of trees and shrubs in this genus are all native to hot, semiarid areas of the American Tropics. Only one is widely cultivated, *Anacardium occidentale* (the Cashew Nut)—so widely that it is now naturalized throughout the Tropics. It forms a tree to 40 ft (12 m) tall with simple leaves that can be quite variable in size and unremarkable flowers held in short panicles.

Anacardium occidentale is cultivated for its fruit. An outer fleshy covering contains the familiar cashew, though the nut must be roasted to remove toxins in the shell prior to eating to make it edible. The pedicel (flower stalk) also forms an edible fruit (known as the Cashew Apple) as it swells. An oil used in lubricants can be extracted from the nut, and a gum widely used in dyes and inks is obtained from the wood.

Annona ANNONACEAE
Cherimoya, Soursop, Sweetsop, Custard Apple

A large genus of over 130 species of evergreen trees and shrubs widely distributed throughout the American and African Tropics, the tree species not exceeding 33 ft (10 m). The species exhibit a wide variation in leaf and flower arrangement; the fleshy bisexual flowers are solitary in some, clustered in others.

Many species are edible and hence widely cultivated in many tropical countries, such as *Annona cherimola* (the sweet-sour flavored Custard Apple), originally from Peru, and *A. muricata* (the Soursop or Prickly Custard Apple). Others—the Sweetsop (*A. squamosa*) is one—in addition to providing edible fruits, have been found to contain insecticides in their seeds and are used locally medicinally.

Areca PALMAE
Betelnut

Areca is a widely cultivated palm genus comprising some sixty species native throughout Indomalaysia, Australia, and the Solomon Islands. They form trees to 66 ft (20 m) and have characteristic arching feathery leaves to 6 ft (2 m). They form understory plants in tropical rainforests in their natural state, and are now cultivated as ornamental plants in the Tropics and sometimes also in temperate areas under glass.

The most well-known species is *A. catechu* (the Betelnut). In Southeast Asia its seeds are sliced then wrapped in a wad of leaves from the pepper *Piper betle*, and chewed with lime. The chewing action releases an alkaloid, which is mildly narcotic, and which promotes a feeling of wellbeing, while at the same time turning saliva bright red. In other species (for instance *A. vestiaria*) the leaves are shredded and the outermost layer used in the manufacture of textiles.

Arenga PALMAE
Sugar Palm

A genus of twenty usually monocarpic, palm species found throughout Malaysia to Northern Australia. They range in stature from 6–66 ft (2–20 m) and bear the typical feather-like palm foliage, the leaf bases of which persist and can often be seen still clinging to the trunk after the leaves have fallen. The leaf bases are useful in the production of fiber.

The most commonly known and widely cultivated species is *Arenga pinnata* (Sugar Palm) from Malaysia. The male flowers are tapped for their sap, which produces palm sugar. This may be used to make palm wine or "toddy," or distilled into a spirit, *arrack*. Various other species, among them *A. microcarpa* (Sago), are often cultivated as ornamental trees.

Artocarpus MORACEAE
Breadfruit, Jackfruit

A monoecious genus of fifty latex-bearing tree species native to tropical Asia. The leaves are arranged alternately and are often very large and may also be deeply divided (pinnate), and often bear large stipules.

Some species are cultivated for timber (e.g. *Artocarpus chama*), others are used as shade trees for coffee or, most widely, for their fruit. Many species produce large edible fruits: *A. altilis* is the breadfruit famously exported to the West Indies by Captain Bligh in the eighteenth century (before the *Bounty* voyage it had been cultivated in Asia for thousands of years). The fruits are an important source of carbohydrates and vitamins and are commonly used as vegetables. The Jackfruit (*A. heterophyllus*) produces one of the largest fruits in the world, up to 3 ft (1 m) long and weighing up to 90 lb (40 kg).

Avicennia AVICENNIACEAE
White Mangrove

These trees are native to the warm coastal mangroves found in the Tropics. The genus is the single member of the family and is thought to comprise up to seven species. All species produce the characteristic "pneumatophores" (aerial roots) of mangroves, which are erect and grow upward from the main roots, becoming exposed at low tide above the estuarine mud in which the trees grow.

Large areas of mangrove have been cleared for timber as many species produce good hardwood (*Avicennia marina*), and are used to make charcoal. The bark is often useful in the production of dyes. The trees also produce live or "viviparous" young, whereby the active fruits drop from their terminal or axillary position on the parent tree directly into the mud where they stick and begin to grow into a new tree.

ABOVE The Jackfruit, *Artocarpus heterophyllus*, produces one of the largest fruits in the world. They can appear anywhere on the trunk or older branches. A heavy, spiky rind covers a sweet, juicy pulp, which can be eaten raw or cooked.

BELOW *Areca* have a narrow, upright habit and broad, feather-shaped leaves. The seeds (betelnuts) are one of the most popular stimulants in the world.

Banksia   PROTEACEAE
Banksias

Named for the botanist Sir Joseph Banks who collected
the first specimens of this genus on the *Endeavour*
voyage led by Captain James Cook in the late eighteenth
century. There are over seventy species of trees and
shrubs, all except one (endemic to New Guinea) native
to Australia.

These evergreen plants are widely cultivated as
ornamental plants (especially *Banksia aemula*). The
leaves, sometimes with serrated edges, are tough and
leathery and variable in size; the dense attractive terminal
flower spikes are much utilized in the cut flower trade.
The leaves, flowers, and cone-like fruits can all be dried
for decorative purposes.

Some species (*B. ornata*) require fire in order for the
fruits to open and release the seed. Many species also
provide abundant nectar to attract nectiferous birds,
which serve to pollinate the plants. The nectar is also
reported to be eaten by indigenous people.

Bertholettia   LECITHYDIACEAE
Brazil Nut

A genus of a single species of deciduous tree, growing to
a height of 130 ft (40 m), and native to the rainforests of
Amazonia. The statuesque trees produce a long straight
trunk, branch only toward the top, and bear large,
oblong leathery leaves. The erect spikes of flowers held
aloft in the axils of the leaves or terminally at the ends
of the branches produce the large, heavy fruits that
contain the nut.

Most fruit of *Bertholettia excelsa* is collected from wild
trees, which are self-infertile and rely on specific species
of bee to pollinate the often widely scattered individuals.
The fruit itself is produced only on trees of at least ten
years maturity, and then takes up to fourteen months to
mature. The white kernel is highly nutritious and has a
high fat content.

Bixa   BIXACEAE
Annato

Bixa contains one species, *B. orellana*, native to tropical
America and growing up to 23 ft (7 m). It is intensely
branched, has large elliptical leaves with the veins
arranged palmately, and pink flowers held in terminal
spikes of five, each flower being approximately 2 in
(5 cm) in diameter.

Sometimes cultivated as an ornamental garden
specimen in warm climes or, on account of its tolerance of
quite radical pruning, as a hedge, *Bixa* is most valued for
the red seed coat, which contains bixin, a carotenoid
coloring widely used in foodstuffs— and as bodypaint by
Amerindian people.

Blighia   SAPINDACEAE
Akee

Introduced to the West Indies by Captain Bligh of the
Bounty, this genus of four evergreen trees, which grow
to 66 ft (20 m), originates from tropical Africa. The
hairless pinnate leaves alternate along the stems, with
the small fragrant greenish-white flowers held in racemes
growing from the axils of the leaves.

Akee (*Blighia sapida*) is widely cultivated in the West
Indies and Africa as an ornamental tree, and also for the
edible white aril surrounding the black seeds which is
exposed when the bright yellow-red fruit ripens and
splits. However, when unripe, both fruits and seeds are
poisonous, and can cause hypoglycemia.

Bombax   BOMBACACEAE
Silk Cotton, White Kapok

Bombax are large deciduous trees to 130 ft (40 m)
originating in tropical Asia and Africa. As they mature,
the twenty species often form buttresses at the base to
help support the spreading, horizontal branches. The
leaves are large and palmate and the colorful cup-shaped
flowers either solitary or in small clusters at the ends of
the branches, appearing before the leaves.

Bombax ceiba (Silk Cotton Tree), is the source of a
soft timber as well as being a cultivated ornamental.
Kapok is derived from the hairs surrounding the ovary
of the flowers from many species. *Bombax buonopozense*
is likewise the source of a soft commercial timber.

The pear-shaped fruit of the
Akee (*Blighia sapida*) are
sometimes known as "vegetable
brains" on account of their
spongy white to yellow flesh.
The soft edible arils now a major
feature of various Caribbean
cuisines—in Jamaica, salt cod
and akee is the national dish.

Borassus   *PALMAE*
Palmyra Palm

An Old World genus of eleven dioecious long-lived
palms to 100 ft (30 m) tall. All have palmate foliage with
individual leaves sometimes 10 ft (3 m) in diameter. The
flower spikes can be over 3 ft (1 m) in length, the tiny
male flowers densely crowded together, the larger female
flowers solitary.

Cultivated as ornamental trees in the Tropics but also
for myriad other uses. *Borassus flabellifer* (Palmyra Palm)
is used for timber, roof thatch, paper, and the leaf fibers
for weaving. The fruit is also edible—as are the young
seedlings—and the inflorescence is a significant source of
"palm toddy."

Boswellia   *BURSERACEAE*
Frankincense

Of the family that includes the source of Myrrh, this
genus of perhaps twenty deciduous trees is native to dry
forests and hillsides in tropical Africa and Asia. (Other
members of the family occur throughout the Tropics,
including South and Central America.)

Pinnate leaves are clustered in spirals at the ends of
the branches, and the flowers, individually insignificant,
are held in panicles, also usually at the branch tips.
All parts of the plants, the bark especially, contain resin.
This resin is the source of frankincense, derived from
Boswellia sacra, B. carteri, and *B. fereana.* Another
species, *B. serrata,* is commonly found throughout dry,
deciduous forests on hillsides in India, and has some
local economic significance in the production of
timber and charcoal.

Broussonetia   *MORACEAE*
Paper Mulberry

The eight species of deciduous, dioecious trees and shrubs
in this genus, are originally native to tropical Asia with a
single species in Madagascar. The leaves have serrated
edges or may also be deeply lobed, both examples being
sometimes found on the same tree, and are usually green
and rough to the touch above, and soft, velvet-like, and
gray underneath.

Members of *Broussonetia* are generally grown for
ornamental purposes. They form small trees and bear
attractive flowers—the males are pendent catkins,
the females are in globe-like heads—and have
large colorful fruits.

The genus is now widely cultivated and may even
be naturalized in parts of North America, and there
are many named cultivars. The inner bark of
B. papyfiera was formerly used in Japan to make
paper and in the Pacific islands to produce a
paper-like cloth known as tapa.

Brugmansia   *SOLANACEAE*
Angels Trumpet

A small but ornamentally important genus of some
fourteen species of shrubs and trees to 33 ft (10 m) tall
native to South America, especially the Andean region.
The leaves are large, simple, and arranged alternately, and
the spectacular white to yellow, or red flowers, over 8 in
(20 cm) in length, are solitary and pendulous.

Brugmansia aurea, of which there are many cultivars,
is particularly attractive with large fragrant white to
yellow flowers. It is the parent, along with *B. versicolor,*
of the widely cultivated hybrid *B.* × *candida.* Many of
the Brugmansias contain alkaloids that can cause
hallucinations and are widely cultivated by shamans in
indigenous populations.

Caesalpinia   *LEGUMINOSAE*
Pride of Barbados, Peacock Flower

A pantropical genus of up to ten or perhaps over one
hundred species of trees, shrubs, and perennial herbs,
some climbers. A wide variety of forms is exhibited and
the bark may be thorny or not, depending on the species.
The trees can grow to over 33 ft (10 m) and all have the
characteristic foliage of the pea family, each leaf being
composed of many smaller leaflets.

The genus is largely grown as ornamental specimens
on account of the flamboyant terminal racemes of often
colorful tubular flowers with conspicuous stamens, often
a different color to the rest of the flower. *Caesalpinia
pulcherrima* (Pride of Barbados or the Peacock Flower)
makes a particularly attractive specimen: up to 10 ft
(3 m) tall with bright yellow flowers and red stamens.
Other species are cultivated as street trees (*C. ferrea*),
as the source of tannin (*C. coriaria* and
C. paraguariensis), and also grown as a
hedging plant (*C. decapetala*).

Cananga   *ANNONACEAE*
Ylang-Ylang

Cananga comprises two species of aromatic
evergreen trees, which grow up to 100 ft
(30 m) tall. They are native to tropical Asia
and Australia, which bear alternately
arranged, largely simple elliptical leaves,
and drooping axillary clusters of small,
fragrant, colorful flowers.

Widely cultivated for its attractive habit,
foliage, and highly fragrant flowers throughout
Asia and the Mascarenes, *C. odorata* is also
grown for the essential oil ylang-ylang,
distilled from the flowers and extensively used
in the haircare and perfume industries.

The female flowers of
Broussonetia are always
produced on a separate
plant and form a round,
fuzzy head almost 1–2 in
(2–5 cm) in diameter.

LEFT *Carica papaya* can produce fruit for fifteen years, bearing masses of melon-sized pawpaw close to the trunk. They are hollow with delicious flesh.

BELOW *Carnegeia giganteus* thrives on the desert slopes and flats. They are a distinctive sight with their large armlike branches curving upward.

Cassia   LEGUMINOSAE

Indian Laburnum

A pantropical genus of about thirty species of deciduous or semi-evergreen trees growing up to 100 ft (30 m) tall. All species have pinnate leaves, which range from glossy green to dull or soft and downy, and some species have spines. The long-lasting pea-like flowers, which are often fragrant, may be red, orange, pink, or yellow, and are held in drooping or erect racemes.

Cassias are extensively cultivated as ornamental trees on account of these attractive long-lasting blooms, especially *Cassia fistulosa* (Indian Laburnum, Golden Shower Tree). Many have medicinal properties derived from the latex found in the fruit (*C. grandis*), while others are a source of timber (*C. javanica*).

Cedrela   MELIACEAE

West Indian Cedar, Cigar-box Cedar

Formerly including the Old World Chinese Cedars (now referred to the genus *Toona*), this genus now comprises eight tree species that reach heights of 100 ft (30 m), all native to tropical America. These relatively smooth-barked trees all bear pinnate leaves and dense panicles of flowers held either in the axils of the leaves or at the ends of the branches.

Cedrelas are an important timber crop in Central America and the Caribbean, where *Cedrela odorata* (West Indian Cedar) is widely cultivated. The wood is aromatic and also has insect-repellent properties and consequently is used extensively to make closets and cigar boxes, giving rise to its alternative common name. *Cedrela fissilis* is also utilized for its timber.

Ceiba   BOMBACACEAE

Kapok Tree

Ceiba is a genus of perhaps a dozen species of large deciduous trees, native to the rainforests and savanna habitats in South America, with one species, *C. pentandra*, also extending into tropical Africa. *C. pentandra*, reaches 230 ft (70 m), making it the tallest tree in Africa. Ceibas often form sizeable buttresses and may also be covered in spines.

The seeds are embedded in a white fiber, from which is derived commercial kapok, harvested from *C. pentandra*, now extensively cultivated and naturalized in many parts of the Tropics. The fiber may also be gathered locally from other species, and some, including *C. insignis*, are cultivated as ornamentals on account of the colorful flowers, which appear before the palmate leaves.

Carica   CARICACEAE

Pawpaw, Papaya

Carica is a genus of twenty-three trees native to South America. The trees are usually dioecious with deeply lobed palmate foliage, the male tubular flowers in axillary racemes and the female flowers, which are usually less tubular and wider than the males, either solitary or clustered together in the leaf-axils.

Carica papaya, a stout tree growing to 33 ft (10 m), is extensively commercially cultivated today as the source of the Pawpaw or Papaya, borne on a short stalk, almost directly on the trunk. The fruit is rich in vitamins and consumed throughout the world. Species native to higher altitudes which are therefore somewhat more tolerant of cooler temperatures, such as *C. stipularis*, are now also commercially cultivated in New Zealand and Australia. The skin of the unripe fruit is also an important source of the enzyme papain, which has a wide variety of medicinal and industrial uses.

Carnegeia   CACTACEAE

Sahuaro, Saguaro

A giant columnar cactus to 66 ft (20 m) tall with a tree-like habit native to the deserts of the southwest United States and Mexico. The genus is composed of a single species, the aptly named *Carnegeia giganteus*. The plant forms a main stem up to 2 ft (60 cm) thick, which eventually branches to produce a candelabra-like architecture. It is covered in spines up to 2.8 in (7 cm) long, with large white tubular flowers, which are pollinated by birds, insects, and also by bats, appearing near the top of the stem.

The reddish-green fruit of *C. giganteus* is edible and was previously an important source of food and drink for the indigenous population, who still use it ceremonially.

ABOVE The Tree Cactus (*Cereus repandus*) is more like a tree in outline than any other cactus with its cylindrical, branching stems. These contain an acrid, milky juice and are covered in clusters of small spines.

Ceratonia   *LEGUMINOSAE*
Carob

A small genus, comprising just two evergreen species that form shrubs, or trees to 33 ft (10 m). Originally from Arabia and Somalia but cultivated in the Mediterranean basin since ancient times, and now naturalized as far as the warmer parts of the southern United States. The glossy foliage is finely divided into many leaflets, and the tiny greenish-red flowers are clustered together into short racemes.

Occasionally used as a street tree, especially in hot areas as it is drought tolerant, the main species *Ceratonia siliqua* is more extensively used for the fruits (beans), which contain a refreshing, sugar-rich pulp used as a foodstuff or animal fodder, and provide a source of alcohol. In the food industry, carob meal (E410) is used as a jelling agent (for jellies) and as a texturing agent. The wood is also a valuable timber crop.

Cereus   *CACTACEAE*
Tree Cactus

A genus of some thirty-six species of tree-like cacti native to the dry areas of the West Indies and eastern South America. *Cereus* has been subject to extensive revision over the last century and formerly included many other columnar-type forms, including the nocturnal flowering species now placed in the genus *Hylocerus*.

These cacti generally grow up to 33 ft (10 m) tall and with extensive branching. The stems of *Cereus* are often glaucous (blue-green) and the white tubular flowers may be up to 12 in (30 cm) in length. Cultivated for their horticultural and botanical interest, the young stems of some species, such as *C. repandus*, are also edible—once the spines are removed.

Ceroxylon   *PALMAE*
Wax Palm

Native to the Andes from Venezuela to Bolivia, this genus of about fifteen species comprises both the tallest palm, *Ceroxylon quindiuense* from Colombia (where it is the national flower), and also claims the highest recorded altitudinal growth for a palm at 13,000 ft (4,000 m). Wax palms form tall trees with a single, sometimes slightly swollen, stem bearing a typical palm-like crown of pinnate leaves.

The trunks of the trees become coated with a heavy coating of wax, formerly harvested for use in such household items as matches and candles. Many also produce masses of round bright red-, orange-, or purple-colored fruits.

Chamaerops   *PALMAE*
Dwarf Fan Palm

A monotypic genus, *Chamaerops humilis* is a small palm with large fan-like leaves growing no taller than 20 ft (6 m). It is Europe's only mainland palm, found in the western Mediterranean. *Chamaerops* occur naturally in clumps in maquis landscapes, where they often tolerate poor sandy soils, or in open woodland.

Widely cultivated as ornamentals and easy to grow, *Chaemerops* are also able to cope with relatively cold temperatures. Their tough leaf fibers are used as stuffing in upholstery.

Chrysobalanus   *CHRYSOBALANACEAE*
Coco Plum, Icaco Plum

Two species of small shrubs or trees form this genus. Native to the West Indies and Central America, one species, *Chrysobalanus icaco*, extends to western tropical Africa and is now extensively naturalized throughout East Africa, the Seychelles, Vietnam, and Fiji. Both species naturally occur close to the shoreline.

The trees grow to up to 16 ft (5 m) and bear simple leaves, glandular at the base, and small racemes of insignificant flowers. They are cultivated for their edible fruits, which may be eaten raw or used as a preserve. The flesh is white, soft, and sour-tasting. Oil extracted from the seeds is sometimes used for candles.

Chrysophyllum   **SAPOTACEAE**
Star Apple

A pantropical genus of about forty species of evergreen trees or shrubs concentrated in the Americas where they are widely cultivated. The trees can reach 66 ft (20 m) and have alternate or spirally arranged leaves, with flowers occurring in small clusters either in the axils of the leaves or directly on the stem.

Chrysophyllum cainito, the Star Apple, is naturally found in the hot tropical lowlands of Central America and the West Indies. Many species in the genus produce edible fruits, but the Star Apple is the most commonly—and extensively—cultivated tree. They also make beautiful ornamental trees with their purple fruits and pubescent leaves, which are tinged coppery red. Some species are also useful for timber.

Cinnamomum   **LAURACEAE**
Camphor, Cinnamon

An economically important genus of perhaps 350 species of aromatic trees and shrubs from Southeast Asia, through Australia, Fiji, Samoa, and tropical America. The trees may be up to 100 ft (30 m) tall with aromatic leathery leaves, which are usually opposite.

Cinnamomum verum is the source of commercial cinnamon, extracted from the aromatic bark. However, *C. aromaticum* from Myanmar is similarly cropped and widely cultivated in China for this purpose. Camphor was also originally extracted from a member of this genus, *C. camphora*, by distilling the leaves for oils, though this tree is now mainly grown for its timber, which is prized for fine woodwork.

Many other species, including *C. iners* and *C. burmanii*, are harvested for their bark, which may be sold as spice or for its medicinal properties.

Cloroxylon   **RUTACEAE**
Satinwood

A monotypic genus native to southern India and neighboring Sri Lanka. The sole species, *Cloroxylon swietenia*, has alternate, pinnate, glandular foliage and small flowers in axillary or terminal panicles. It is a small, aromatic, deciduous tree to 66 ft (20 m) tall, originally described from Sri Lanka, and now cultivated for its quality wood, which is used in furniture and veneers.

Coccoloba   **POLYGONACEAE**
Sea Grape

Coccoloba is a large genus of some 120 species of mostly evergreen trees, shrubs, and lianas with large variable alternate leaves. The flowers are in dense or loose spikes, and the fruits are grape-like, hence the common name, which refers to *C. uvifera*. This species, which is native

to the Atlantic shores of the tropical Americas and the Caribbean, has edible fruits and is consequently cultivated on a wide scale.

The genus occurs throughout the tropical Americas and the Caribbean. The trees can be up to 66 ft (20 m) tall, and some species (for instance *C. pubescens*) are also occasionally planted as street trees or ornamental specimens in parks.

Cocos   **PALMAE**
Coconut

The *Cocos* genus comprises a single monoecious palm tree, *C. nucifera*, growing to 100 ft (30 m) tall. Now cultivated throughout the Tropics, it is thought to have originated in the western Pacific. It exhibits an often curved stem, swollen at the base, supporting the crown of large pinnate leaves up to 16 ft (5 m) in length.

Cocos nucifera is the picture postcard palm of the Tropics, often cultivated along seashores for ornamental purposes and to prevent erosion. The nuts are water-dispersed and can remain viable even after immersion in seawater for two weeks, a further reason why the tree is so often seen along seashores.

The species is an important economic crop—the nuts are processed to produce coconut milk, cream, oil, and desiccated coconut, all ingredients which are extensively used in Asian cuisine. There are many other uses: the fibrous outer layer of the nut is used as matting, for ropes, and, ground down, as a horticultural growing medium that is now an significant peat alternative. Additionally, the Coconut is very important locally—in fact, all parts of the plant are used: the leaves for shelter and weaving and the stem for timber.

The Coconut Palm, *Cocos nucifera*, has a tall, unbranched trunk topped by a crown of fronds. Older leaves have leaflets on either side of a central stem; on seedlings they are entire.

Coffea · RUBIACEAE
Coffee

A genus of ninety small trees, up to 33 ft (10 m) tall, and shrubs, native to tropical Africa and the Mascarenes but now widely cultivated in the Tropics, especially in South America. *Coffea* was first cultivated by the Arabs who roasted the seeds to produce coffee beans. It was they who subsequently introduced the drink to Europe. The highest concentration of cultivation is in high altitudes in Brazil, Colombia, and the West Indies. Kenya and Ethiopia are other sources of quality coffee. *Coffea arabica* produces the best coffee, though *C. canephora* and *C. liberica* are also used—especially in instant coffee.

Coffea make fine ornamental specimens with evergreen glossy opposite leaves and small whitish, often fragrant flowers, either solitary or in small clusters. The ripe red fruits containing the important seeds are attractive in their own right. *Coffea arabica* is also utilized for timber.

Cola · STERCULIACEAE
Kola

A large genus of up to 125 usually monoecious species, native to tropical Africa. These trees are evergreen or deciduous and up to 66 ft (20 m) tall, the alternately arranged leaves may be entire, lobed, or deeply divided, and the flowers are held in axillary clusters or racemes.

Plants of this genus, especially *Cola acuminata*, are widely grown for their bitter seeds (nuts), which contain caffeine. These are either chewed, used in cookies, or in Cola drinks—though they have largely been replaced by synthetic cola today. Many species, including *C. nitida* and *C. verticillata*, also make attractive ornamentals in subtropical regions and are often planted in gardens.

ABOVE The white starlike flowers of *Coffea arabica* emerge in axillary clusters. They have five petals and a jasmine scent and only last for 2–3 days. Plants do not begin flowering until they are 2–4 years old, and generally flower after rain.

BELOW Indigenous to the desert regions of North Africa, *Commiphora glaucescens* grows only to about 10 ft (3 m) and has tough, knotted branches.

Commiphora · BURSERACEAE
Myrrh

A widely distributed genus of almost two hundred species from tropical and subtropical Africa, Madagascar, Arabia, Sri Lanka, and South America, with two species found in Mexico. Commonly found in hot dry scrub or savanna, but some species inhabit mangroves and tropical forest. Up to 66 ft (20 m) tall with spirally arranged pinnate leaves clustered at branch tips, and panicles of small flowers, also clustered toward the tips of the branches.

All species exude resins from the bark, with Myrrh, used in perfumes and incense, principally sourced from *Commiphora myrrha*, which is cultivated in Arabia and Ethiopia. Many other species also have medicinal properties: *C. merkeri* and *C. wrightii* are a source of oleo-resin widely used locally for various treatments.

Copernicia · PALMAE
Carnauba Wax Palm

This genus includes some twenty-nine species of slow-growing palms, ranging in height from 3 to 100 ft (1–30 m), from South America and the West Indies with a concentration of species in Cuba. They are native to savanna areas but are also found in tropical forests, being tolerant of a wide range of conditions. They bear large palmate leaves, attractive when young, and large inflorescences up to 10 ft (3 m) long with many small flowers. Some (*Copernicia prunifera* and *C. alba*) are important cultivated ornamental plants. *Copernicia prunifera* is a source of carnauba wax which is used in such products as shoe polish.

Corypha
Talipot Palm
PALMAE

Six species of fan palms native to tropical Asia and Australia make up this genus. They grow up to 66 ft (20 m) tall and have palmate leaves up to 16 ft (5 m) wide borne on erect solitary trunks. All are hapaxanthic (having a single flowering period), but may live for up to 50 years in cultivation prior to flowering. They have impressive erect inflorescences—up to 26 ft (8 m) tall—bearing millions of tiny individual flowers, which result in up to 250,000 fruits.

Various species are cultivated including *Corypha utan*, the inflorescence of which is a good source of toddy and palm sugar. *Corypha umbraculifera* is also exploited, its leaves being used for thatch and as writing paper.

Couroupita
Cannonball Tree
LECYTHIDIACEAE

Native to the warm forests of tropical America, the four species of *Couroupita* are all trees, growing to a height of 115 ft (35 m) with spirally arranged simple leaves, sometimes with serrated edges and pendulous panicles of large showy flowers. The inflorescences are cauliferous (growing directly from the trunk, on the oldest wood) and can be over 10 ft (3 m) in length in the case of *C. guianensis*. The fruits, up to 8 in (20 cm) across, are at first fleshy but become encased in a woody capsule—hence the popular name.

They are occasionally grown as street trees, and are also a source of good timber.

Daemonorops
Dragons Blood
PALMAE

Daemonorops is a genus of over a hundred species of dioecious climbing palms from Indomalaysia, some of which (e.g. *D. grandis*) are exploited for their tough stems, which are the source of rattan, a material widely used in wickerwork and furniture manufacture. The stems are usually clad in spines, as are the pinnate leaves, and the interfoliar inflorescence is short and branched.

The species also often exploit a close relationship with ants that live among the stems and protect the plant against browsers or insect infestation. The fruits also produce resins used in varnishes.

Dalbergia
Rosewood, Blackwood, Kingwood
LEGUMINOSAE

Composed of lianas, shrubs, and trees up to 82 ft (25m) tall, this genus of perhaps a hundred species occurs naturally throughout the Tropics, usually in savanna or coastal woodland. Dalbergias all bear the alternately arranged pinnate leaves and axillary or terminal panicles of small pea-like flowers typical of members of the pea family.

Dalbergias are widely cultivated commercially for their beautiful and often dramatically colorful grained wood. *Dalbergia decipularis* is an important timber tree from Brazil, *D. latifolia* is widely cultivated in Asia, and *D. melanoxylon* is much used in Africa for its wood. *Dalbergia nigra*, another species from Brazil, has been so extensively harvested for its fine timber to make musical instruments and furniture that it is now endangered in the wild state.

Dasylirion
Sotol
DRACAENACEAE

A genus of arborescent evergreen perennial herbs, which can become tree-like, though no more than 10 or 13 ft (3 or 4 m) tall. These plants, restricted to the southwest United States and Mexico, are related to the *Yucca*. The linear leaves are usually spiny along their edges and the tiny creamy-white flowers are held in a dense inflorescence, which may be up to 5 ft (1.5 m).

The leaves have a variety of local uses and the sap is the source of a drink (Sotol). *Dasylirion wheeleri* is rumored to be a source of alcohol. Some species are virtually stemless while others take the form of stocky trees. They are occasionally cultivated as ornamentals within flower schemes.

Delonix
Flamboyant, Flame Tree
LEGUMINOSAE

A small genus of fast-growing beautiful trees up to 33 ft (10 m) tall, comprising both deciduous and evergreen species. All are characterized by pinnate leaves with tiny leaflets and racemes of large, long-lasting flowers, which range in color from scarlet through orange, white, and yellow. This combination of fast growth and long-lasting showy flowers borne on a tall umbrella-like tree makes the Flame Tree (*Delonix regia*) a favorite ornamental, popular for urban planting schemes.

Delonix regia is perhaps the widest planted species, grown throughout the subtropics and Tropics as a street tree or in parks. A native of Madagascar, where it is now very rare, the species has become naturalized in southern Florida, where it has proved to be perfectly tolerant of maritime locations.

The flowers of the Cannonball Tree (*Couroupita*) are a rich apricot pink and gold color with an unusual lopsided mass of stamens. They are strongly fragrant, and grow from the old wood of the trunk.

Dendrocalamus GRAMINEAE
Giant Bamboo

Though members of the grass family are not generally considered to be trees, the bamboo *Dendrocalamus giganteus* attains such stature that it is taller than many other plants commonly referred to as trees. The genus is composed of between thirty and thirty-five species of woody, clump-forming bamboos, native to India, China, Malaysia, and the Philippines. Individual stems can grow at incredible rates: up to 12–16 in (30–40 cm) a day, and mature plants can top 130 ft (40 m).

The genus is now cultivated throughout the world in tropical regions. All species are easily recognizable as typical bamboos with thin linear-shaped leaves and cane-like stems. Some species, such as *D. asper* from Malaysia, have edible shoots, while much use is made of the tall strong stems of *D. giganteus* in the construction industry, often as scaffolding.

Derris LEGUMINOSAE
Derrisroot

Derris has forty species of lianas, shrubs, and trees, all of which are native to lowland tropical forests in Southeast Asia and northern Australia, with one climber species,

D. trifoliata, extending as far as East Africa and the Pacific in mangrove swamps. With typical leguminosae pinnate foliage and terminal or axillary racemes of colorful flowers, these are attractive plants.

Derris are most commonly used as a source of rotenones, chemicals found in the swollen roots, especially of another climber, *D. elliptica*, formerly used as a fish poison, and in dried powdered form in the horticultural industry as an insecticide. The plants are also often found in specialized botanical collections.

Dipterocarpus DIPTEROCARPACEAE
Dipterocarps

A genus of around seventy species of trees, all native to Indomalaysia, with spirally arranged simple, leathery leaves and resinous bark, leaves, and flowers. They grow up to 66 or 100 ft (20 or 30 m) tall with usually axillary panicles of pendent flowers.

Some species, for example *Dipterocarpus costatus*, are extensively cultivated for their timber, which is widely used for construction or as railway sleepers, resulting in a plethora of common names. Other important species are *D. tuberculatus* from Southeast Asia and *D. zeylanicus* from Sri Lanka. The resins produced by these trees were once commercially exported for use in varnishes.

The huge 20 ft (6 m) high buttresses of *Dipterocarpus dyeri* are asymmetrically thickened and make a planklike outgrowth which provides support for the massive trunk.

Dombeya   STERCULIACEAE
Dombeya

Distributed from Africa to the Mascarenes with many species in Madagascar, this is a large genus of over two hundred and fifty species of monoecious, dioecious, or bisexual evergreen or deciduous shrubs and trees to 66 ft (20 m) tall. The foliage is usually composed of alternate, simple, cordate leaves, and the fragrant flowers, which range in color from white to red or yellow, are held in terminal or axillary clusters.

Dombeyas, with their lush foliage and attractive, scented clusters of flowers, are principally cultivated as ornamental plants: *Dombeya wallichii* is one with deep pink flowers. The hybrid *D.* × *cayeuxii* (*D. burgessiae* × *D. wallichi*), of which there are many forms, is also commonly grown. The species are also exploited locally for fibers.

Dracaena   DRACAENACEAE
Dragon Tree

An Old World genus of about sixty species found in tropical Asia and Africa (extending to the Canary Islands) with just two species found in the Americas: one in Central America, the other in Cuba. Relatively long-lived (rumored to survive for thousands of years but only several hundred are proven), the much-branched stems of *Dracaena* may grow up to over 66 ft (20 m) and are clothed in glossy, smooth, linear leaves.

The resins exuded from several species (for example, *Dracaena cinnabari* and *D. draco*) are the source of "dragons blood," which is used in varnishes. The latter species, the Dragon Tree of the Canary Islands, is alleged to be one of the longest-lived trees and capable of living for over two thousand years. A number of species have become important in the horticultural industry, especially as houseplants in more northern regions on account of their tolerance of low light levels. There are now many colorful cultivars, particularly of *D. fragrans*.

Drysoxylum   MELIACEAE
Australian Mahogany

The eighty species in this genus are distributed from Indomalaysia through New Zealand and Tonga. The species bear alternately arranged leaves and panicles of small flowers growing either directly on the stem or in the leaf-axils.

Drysoxylum are often referred to locally as Satinwood (*D. pettigrewianum*) or as Australian Mahogany (*D. fraserianum*). They are commercially important timber trees in Australia and Malaysia, closely related to the true mahoganies, the *Khaya* of Africa, and the *Swietenia* of the Americas. They are cultivated for their often fragrant wood used in fine carpentry.

Durio   BOMBACACEAE
Durian

A genus of twenty-eight large evergreen trees with buttressed trunks native to the rainforests of Myanmar and Malaysia. Their simple leathery leaves and clusters of small bat-pollinated flowers often appear directly on the stem (cauliferous). The fruit for which they are best known is a green woody capsule covered in spines and up to 10 in (25 cm) diameter and weighing several pounds.

Durio zibethinus from western Malaysia is the best-known species which produces the much sought-after fruit. The fleshy aril which surrounds the seeds smells unpleasant when the fruit is ripe, but tastes delicious, reminiscent of vanilla, caramel, and banana.

Dyera   APOCYNACEAE
Jeluong

A small genus (two or three species) native to the rainforests of Malaysia where the tall, sometimes buttressed trees with simple leaves are an important commercial source of light hardwood, especially *Dyera costulata*. The trunks of *Dyera* were formerly tapped for their milky white latex known as chicle—used in chewing gum—though this source is now largely replaced by commercial synthetic production.

The Dragon Tree, *Dracaena draco*, thrives in the dry brush on Gran Canaria, the largest of the Canary Islands. The tree is extremely slow-growing, taking ten to fifteen years or more to reach 2–3 ft (60–100 cm). Flowering causes the stem to branch and it does so every ten years, creating the characteristic divided crown.

Huge plantations of *Elaeis guineensis*, the commercially important Oil Palm, have replaced the natural cover of rainforest in many areas of Southeast Asia.

Echinopsis   *CACTACEAE*
Tree Cactus

This South American genus of tree-like cacti is not well understood and has between fifty and a hundred species. They range in form from erect, ribbed, columnar branching tree-like plants up to 26 ft (8 m) tall, to shrubby, clump-forming, or prostrate specimens, and may be either spineless or very spiny. Their elongated tubular lateral flowers vary in color and may be diurnal or nocturnal

Echinopsis species are found in cultivation primarily as ornamental plants (e.g. *E. chiloensis*). The fleshy fruits of this species are also edible. The stem of *E. pasacana* is harvested for furniture and fencing.

Elaeis   *PALMAE*
Oil Palm

The fruits of these elegant palms are the most important source of palm oil, used extensively in the manufacture of margarine, soaps, and in the cosmetic industry. These trees are widely grown in the Tropics and have become naturalized in peninsular Malaysia. They grow to 66 ft (20 m) tall with solitary erect stems bearing the persistent leaf bases of old leaves, and a full crown of pinnate leaves up to 13 ft (4 m) in length.

Elaeis are slow-growing monoecious palms with just two species in the genus, one native to tropical America, *E. oleifera*, and the other, *E. guineensis*, from tropical Africa. In economic terms, the latter is the more important species as it is extensively cultivated for the large amount of palm oil yielded by its fruits.

Ensete   *MUSACEAE*
Abyssinian Banana

A small genus of eight species restricted to the Old World Tropics of Asia and Africa. Strictly speaking, the plants are not trees since they never become woody. They are evergreen perennial herbs similar to banana (*Musa*) and belong to the same family, but their proportions are tree-like, potentially growing as tall as 40 ft (12 m). They are monocarpic (flowering once and then dying), though new herbaceous growth will appear from the rhizome once the old flowering stem dies down.

The flowering heads and seeds can be eaten—as are those of *Ensete ventricosum* in Ethiopia—though the plants are generally cultivated as ornamentals, making impressive specimens with banana-like leaves up to 20 ft (6 m) in length.

Eriobotrya   *ROSACEAE*
Loquat

Eriobotrya is made up of some twenty-six species of evergreen trees native to the Himalaya, Malaysia, and east Asia. They grow to 33 ft (10 m) tall with tough, leathery, alternate leaves and small, fragrant, white flowers generally held in terminal panicles densely covered in hairs, and producing clusters of apricot-like fruits up to 1.6 in (4 cm) across.

While some species (and *E. japonica* especially, owing to its tolerance of light frosts), are grown as ornamentals in temperate regions, they are extensively cultivated in sub-tropical and tropical regions for their edible fruits. The slightly acid fruits can be eaten raw or used in pickles or preserves. *Eriobotrya japonica*, native to China and Japan, is the most widespread species in cultivation and there are many hundreds of cultivars in Japan, where it is most commonly grown.

Erythrina   *LEGUMINOSAE*
Coral Tree, Kaffir Boom

Erythrina is a pantropical genus of over one hundred evergreen or deciduous shrubs and trees. They grow to 66 ft (20 m) tall with alternately arranged deeply pinnate foliage and racemes of spectacular, usually red, though sometimes pink, orange, or yellow, flowers.

All produce copious amounts of nectar and as a result many species enjoy symbiotic relationships, for example with humming birds, which act as pollinators in the Americas, and often with colonies of ants, which help protect the trees. The species are grown mostly for ornament, especially *E. crista-galli*, a smallish tree with racemes of dark scarlet flowers. Many species, for example *E. caffra*, have attractively colored red and black seeds which are often used as beads. Species of this genus are also commonly cultivated as shade trees for such crops as coffee, for instance *E. subumbrans* and *E. mitis*.

The flowers of *Grevillea polybotrya* are quite small but occur in brush-shaped clusters of a hundred or more individuals. Winter to early spring is the peak flowering period of the silk oaks. After flowering, thin-walled pods containing the seeds develop.

Eugenia   MYRTACEAE
Pitanga, Brazil Cherry

A large tropical genus (over five hundred species) of evergreen shrubs or trees, which occasionally reach 100 ft (30 m). The leaves are opposite, simple and glossy, and the flowers are usually borne on short stems in lateral racemes. *Eugenia* is predominantly American, though one species is found in Australia, and another in New Guinea. It was formerly united with *Syzygium*, which is its counterpart in the Old World. Many species (for example, *E. dombeyi*) are extensively cultivated for their edible fruits, eaten fresh or made into jellies or preserves. *Eugenia uniflora*, another American species, is also widely grown for its cherry-like fruits, and is frequently found as a hedging plant.

Euphorbia   EUPHORBIACEAE
Tree Euphorbia

A huge genus—around two thousand species—which is distributed throughout the Tropics and temperate regions of the world. Monoecious or dioecious and with a distinctive milky latex, by far the greatest number of species are herbs or small shrubs, though some, for instance *Euphorbia candelabrum*, a tree from Africa, can grow as tall as 66 ft (20 m). Many are succulent plants from dry subtropical regions and are often spiny; these are the African equivalent of the family Cactaceae, found in the Americas. All bear their flowers in a head (or cyathia) surrounded by a whorl of often brightly colored bracts.

Other species of *Euphorbia* that form trees are *E. abyssinica*, which can grow up to 33 ft (10 m) in height, and *E. triucalli*, known as the Finger Tree. Most are grown as ornamental plants, though many are also exploited locally, especially for their latex, which is a potential source of fuel in the case of *E. triucalli*.

Fouquieria   FOUQUIERIACEAE
Ocotillo

Succulent plants native to southwest North America, which range in size from small, short-stemmed succulents to trees up to 66 ft (20 m) tall. Spiny stemmed and bearing simple alternate leaves, which are deciduous in dry conditions, the species are valued for their panicles or racemes of brightly colored showy flowers.

Fouquieria columnaris, native to the Sonora Desert in northwest Mexico, is the tallest of the eleven species with an erect succulent columnar trunk to 66 ft (20 m) and panicles of fragrant yellow flowers. It is one of two *Fouquieria* species commonly seen in cultivation. The other, *F. splendens*, is widely used as hedging material on account of its intertwining spiny stems, which form an impenetrable barrier.

Garcinia   GUTTIFERAE
Mangosteen

A genus of two hundred tropical evergreen shrubs and trees found throughout the Old World Tropics but particularly in Asia and South Africa. They grow to 50 ft (15 m) tall, have opposite, leathery, deep green leaves, and flowers that range in form from solitary to axillary or terminal clusters, and in color from green to white, red, or yellow.

Several species of the genus are cultivated for their edible fruits. *Garcinia mangostana* is extensively grown throughout Malaysia for its large berry-like fruits, though outside its native area cultivation is unproductive. Other species grown for their fruits (and often used in flavorings) include *G. indica*, while others, among them *G. xanthochymus*, an attractive low-growing tree, are tapped for their resins, which are used in the dyeing industry and are planted as screens in landscape schemes.

Grevillea   PROTEACEAE
Silk Oak

Over 260 species make up this genus of evergreen shrubs and trees, the great majority of which (254 species) are endemic to Australia with a few isolated species found in parts of Indonesia and Melanesia. They can grow to heights of 100 ft (30 m), though are usually much smaller, around 10–26 ft (3–8 m), with alternate wavy-edged or deeply lobed leaves, and nectar-rich tubular flowers in terminal panicles.

Grevillea are principally cultivated as ornamentals or used as screening plants, in particular the fast-growing *G. robusta*, which has attractive fern-like foliage and is a popular choice in temperate regions in bedding schemes with its showy clusters of orange, red, or white flowers. This species, and likewise *G. striata*, are also the source of a good timber for fine joinery work.

Guaiacum   ZYGOPHYLLACEAE
Lignum Vitae

A valuable genus of six species of evergreen, resinous shrubs and trees to 33 ft (10 m) tall, all native to dry coastal habitats of tropical America. They have opposite pinnate leaves and usually blue or purple starry flowers, either solitary or in axillary clusters.

Several species, including *Guaiacum officinale* and *G. sanctum*, are exploited for their timber, which is extremely hard but resinous, lending it self-lubricating qualities. It is much used in the manufacture of such items as pulleys and bowls (for bowling), though they are also grown as attractive ornamental plants in warm climates, and are especially useful in maritime areas. The resins extracted from the bark have medicinal properties and were formerly used for a variety of ills.

Guarea *MELIACEAE*
Acajou, West Indian Redwood

Native to tropical Africa and America, this genus of forty species of trees is often used as a mahogany substitute. They grow to 82 ft (25 m) tall with alternate pinnate leaves and panicles of small, often moth-pollinated flowers. Acajous are not widely commercially cultivated, but many species are exploited to some extent where they are found: *Guarea cedrata* and *G. thompsonii* are both harvested for timber in tropical Africa and similarly *G. guidonia* in tropical America, where it is also utilized medicinally.

Haematoxylon *LEGUMINOSAE*
Logwood

The logwoods are a small genus of tropical legumes with just three species—two native to tropical America, one to Namibia in southern Africa. They make spiny shrubs or trees to 26 ft (8 m) tall with pinnate leaves and axillary racemes of yellow flowers, the shrubs sometimes being grown ornamentally in warm regions either as lawn specimens or as spiny hedges.

Haematoxylon campechianum, found in swampy habitats throughout Mexico, the West Indies, and Central America, and *H. brasiletto*, from tropical America, are the two economically important species. Their timber is used for furniture and dyes, and inks are extracted from the dark heartwood, which is in addition the source of haemotoxylin, still used in the preparation of slides for microscope work.

Hevea *EUPHORBIACEAE*
Rubber

An extremely important genus of twelve species of which one in particular, *Hevea brasiliensis*, is the best natural source of rubber, which is extensively used in industry.

The trees have spirally arranged trifoliate leaves and panicles of small fragrant yellow flowers clustered toward the branch tips. *Hevea brasiliensis* can grow up to 66 ft (20 m) tall and is now cultivated as far afield as Malyasia and Sri Lanka. In *Hevea*'s Amazonian home, rubber is collected from widely spaced wild trees. Plantations are impossible there because natural pests build to such levels that they devastate the trees. Cheap rubber became available after plantations were established in the Far East from seed collected in Brazil. Despite the development of synthetic rubber, 40 percent of rubber comes from *Hevea* and ever-increasing volumes are being produced.

Hydnocarpus *FLACOURTIACEAE*
Chaulmoogra

Approximately forty species comprise this genus native to Indomalaysia. They are all trees up to 100 ft (30 m) tall with alternate leathery leaves with serrated edges borne on short-lived twigs, and insignificant flowers either solitary or in axillary clusters, and large globose fruits.

The seeds of several species, among them *Hydnocarpus pentandra*, which occurs throughout Southeast Asia, and *H. castanea* from Myanmar, are the source of chaulmoogra oil, which was once frequently used in dermatological treatments, including leprosy.

Hyphaene *PALMAE*
Doum Palm

This genus of dioecious palms exhibits a variety of forms, from stemless creeping shrubs to arborescent palms up to 33 ft (10 m) tall. The leaves are palmate with the inflorescences, up to 3 ft (1 m) long, arising from the axils of the leaves.

The ten species native to Africa, Madagascar, Arabia, and India are important locally to humans and wildlife. The seeds are thought to be dispersed by grazing animals, while humans also utilize the leaves of such species as *Hyphaene petersiana* for basketweaving. The leaves are also utilized to make mats and ropes, and *H. thebaica*, the Doum or Gingerbread Palm (named for the gingerbread taste of the fruit), is often cultivated as an ornamental.

Much rainforest in Sumatra is now replaced by Rubber tree plantations. *Hevea braziliensis*, one of the most widely planted trees in humid, tropical parts of Southeast Asia, is a major economic crop. The tall, straight-growing trees reach 60 ft (20 m) in eight years.

Jacaranda trees display their distinctive mauve trumpet flowers, which usually appear before the leaves on their bare, gray branches.

Species of *Inga* are cultivated as ornamentals or as shade trees for other crops. Some, including *I. laurifolia*, are harvested for fuelwood or timber. The large (up to 6 in/15 cm) oblong fruits, which may be either densely pubescent or entirely smooth, are edible in other species (for example, *I. feuillei*).

Jacaranda   BIGNONIACEAE

Jacaranda

Important as ornamentals for their striking blooms, this genus has pinnate leaves and abundant blue or purple campanula-like flowers in axillary or terminal racemes. The genus includes some thirty-four species of shrubs and trees up to 100 ft (30 m) tall, all native to the drier parts of tropical America.

Jacaranda mimosifolia is the most commonly cultivated species and grows to 50 ft (15 m) tall with finely divided fern-like foliage: it is clothed in summer in a crown of panicles of fragrant blue flowers. It is widely seen throughout the tropics and subtropics as a street tree. The genus also has some timber value for pulp (for example *J. copaia*), and some medicinal treatments are also extracted from the bark.

Jubaea   PALMAE

Coquito Palm, Chilean Wine Palm

Jubaea is a monotypic genus from the coastal valleys of central Chile. The sole species, *J. chilensis*, is an impressive monoecious palm, which can grow to a height of 82 ft (25 m) tall and has a crown of feathery, pinnate leaves, which can be up to 16 ft (5 m) in length. The inflorescences themselves, which can be over 3 ft (1 m) in length, are composed of many tiny purple flowers followed by yellow fruits.

It is grown as an ornamental, and, because it is able to tolerate relatively cool climates, it is suitable for cultivation outside of its native area. The trees are also felled or tapped for their sap, which produces large quantities of palm honey.

Idesia   FLACOURTIACEAE

Idesia

A monotypic genus that originates from China and Japan. *Idesia* is a deciduous dioecious tree that grows to about 40 ft (12 m) tall. It has alternate, almost heart-shaped leaves and the greenish-yellow, fragrant flowers are produced in pendent panicles. The fruits are held in clusters of many small orange-red berries and often persist after leaf fall.

Idesia polycarpa is cultivated as an ornamental and is greatly prized for its stately habit, fragrant flowers, and abundant brightly colored fruits.

Inga   LEGUMINOSAE

Spanish Oak

Inga comprises around 350 species of shrubs and trees to 130 ft (40 m) tall with alternate pinnate leaves, often with winged petioles, the leaves themselves being deep green and leathery. The usually white flowers are borne in small spikes, sometimes in larger masses, and are an attractive feature. The genus is native to tropical and warm parts of America, and is often found near rivers where the fruits may be fish-dispersed.

Khaya   MELIACEAE

African Mahogany

Seven species of tree native to Africa and Madagascar, where they are used as a local substitute for the closely related true mahoganies, *Swietenia*. Khayas grow up to 130 ft (40 m) tall, and have usually alternately arranged pinnate foliage and clusters of small flowers which can be borne either in the axils of the leaves or directly on the main stem or branches.

All seven *Khaya* species are highly valued for their timber and are of commercial significance. Among the more economically important are *K. grandifolia* and *K. madagascariensis*. Medicinal compounds are also extracted from the bark.

Lagerstroemia   **LYTHRACEAE**
Crape Myrtle

A genus of over fifty species of deciduous tree to 130 ft (40 m) tall, which usually bear opposite elliptical leaves, and pink to white flowers held in loose axillary and terminal panicles. *Lagerstroemia* species (most notably *L. indica* and *L. speciosa*) are widely cultivated as ornamental trees both within and outside their native tropical Asia and Australia, and some are important for timber (*L. hypoleuca* and *L. microcarpa*). *Lagerstroemia indica* is perhaps the most widely grown ornamental, and consequently there is a range of cultivars with a variety of flower color, from mauve to white. The species also provide attractive fall color.

Litchi   **SAPINDACEAE**
Lychee

A single very variable tree species up to 82 ft (25 m) tall comprises this monotypic genus native to tropical China and Malaysia. Cultivated since ancient times, *Litchi chinensis* has three recognized subspecies, only one of which, ssp *philippensis,* is known in the wild; the other two, ssp *javensis* and ssp *chinensis,* only in cultivation.

Occasionally seen as an ornamental, this evergreen species with its spirally arranged pinnate leaves and terminal panicles of whitish flowers is primarily cultivated for its vitamin-rich white, juicy-fleshed fruit. The hard, knobbly shell of the unripe fruit is green, becoming pink or red as it matures.

Now grown as far afield as South Africa and Australia and to a lesser extent in North America, two distinct forms of lychee, a mountain form and a monsoon form (the commercial fruit), are grown. There are also many cultivars currently recognized, bred for better or larger fruit. Most are sold canned in sugar syrup and served as a dessert, but in Chinese cuisine they are often served with fish or meat dishes.

Lithocarpus   **FAGACEAE**
Mempening

A genus of over a hundred species of evergreen trees native to Indomalaysia, but with fossil records from North America, these trees resemble oaks though have erect rather than pendulous male flower spikes. The tropical representatives of one of the most widely cultivated timber families, this genus has, relatively speaking, been so far little exploited.

Tanbark oaks can grow to over 66 ft (20 m), in the case of *Lithocarpus fissus,* with alternate leathery elliptical leaves, usually glossy green above, often gray-white pubescent below, and bearing acorn-like nuts in clusters. Trees of this genus are most closely allied to the genus *Castanopsis.*

Livistonia   **PALMAE**
Livistonia Palm

A genus of twenty-eight attractive fan palms distributed from North Africa to Arabia, Indomalaysia, and Australia. They grow to 82 ft (25 m), with palmate leaves to 6 ft (2 m), and inflorescences that can grow to a similar length. The flowers are yellow and the fruits range in color from green, orange, purple, to black.

Widely cultivated throughout the Tropics and subtropics as ornamentals, these elegant palms may be successfully cultivated in protected spots in more temperate regions. The young buds are sometimes eaten locally, e.g. *Livistonia australis* from eastern Australia.

Lodoicea   **PALMAE**
Double Coconut, Coco de Mer

Lodoicea maldivica, endemic to the Seychelles, is the only member of this genus. Up to 100 ft (30 m) tall and living three hundred or more years, this slow-growing palm is now restricted to a few areas (current distribution owing more to geographic isolation than economic overexploitation) and is rare in cultivation. Dioecious with a solitary stem and palmate leaves, its flowers are large, the males on 6 ft (2 m) long inflorescences, and the females, up to 4 in (10 cm) in diameter, are held on 3 ft (1 m) long spikes.

The species is best known for its fruit, a double coconut up to 20 in (50 cm) in diameter and bilobed, resembling a large wooden heart. The seeds it contains are also up to 20 in (50 cm) long—the largest of any plant—and take many years to develop. The shells of the fruits are used locally as bowls.

Macadamia   **PROTEACEAE**
Macadamia Nut

Twelve evergreen species of shrubs and trees with whorled, entire, or serrated leaves and axillary or terminal panicles of small pink to white flowers, and usually edible nuts, which occur throughout eastern Malaysia, Australia, to New Caledonia, with the majority endemic to eastern Australia.

Long cultivated as attractive ornamental trees in Australia, Macadamias are now commercially produced for their nuts: *Macadamia integrifolia* and, to a lesser extent, *M. tetraphylla* are the most commonly grown species. They form an important crop in other parts of the world, including South Africa, North America, and especially Hawaii, where many cultivars are now known. The nuts are sold dried or shelled and roasted and have a taste similar to hazelnut.

Famous for its giant seeds, *Lodoicea maldivia* is a large fan palm that grows to about 100 ft (30 m) tall.

Mangifera   ANACARDIACEAE
Mango
With up to perhaps sixty species this genus is one of the
most economically important in the Tropics. The Mango
is native to Indomalaysia, with the most important species,
Mangifera indica (an ancient cultigen), originally from
India where many hundreds of cultivars exist. It is now
cultivated pantropically and naturalized in many areas.

Mangifera are large trees with simple alternate foliage
and panicles of small flowers, and many species produce
the sweet, vitamin-rich fruits, among them *M. pajang*
and *M. odorata*, sometimes also cultivated in place of
M. indica. Mangoes are highly esteemed in India and
are eaten raw, or served as garnishes, preserves, and
chutneys. The timber of *M. indica* is also utilized and it is
also sometimes grown as a shade tree for other crops.

Manihot   EUPHORBIACEAE
False Rubber, Cassava
An extremely important genus of almost one hundred
trees shrubs and herbs native to tropical America and
cultivated extensively throughout lowland tropical
regions. Manihot are small trees to no more than 10–16 ft
(3–4 m) with alternate lobed leaves and large flowers
in usually terminal panicles. All possess the white milky
latex characteristic of Euphorbiaceae, which in the case of
this genus contains large amounts of cyanide, rendering
the plants relatively immune to pests.

The most important species, *M. esculenta,* is an
important food crop, once the poisonous cyanide is
removed by squeezing the ground tuber repeatedly in
water and allowing it to evaporate. Many different
cultivars with varying amounts of cyanide exist. *Manihot*
is able to survive on poor soils and is widely grown by
indigenous people of Amazonia, though because it is low
in protein, malnutrition can result where the crop forms a
large part of a diet. Cassava meal or tapioca is commonly
used in soups and puddings and also exploited for a glue-
like substance and alcohol. A form of rubber is also
derived from another species, *M. glaziovii.*

Manilkara   SAPOTACEAE
Chicle, Sapodilla
A pantropical genus of sixty-five species of large (up to
100 ft/30 m) evergreen trees with simple spirally arranged
leaves and axillary flowers either solitary or in small
clusters. Manilkara has is greatest diversity in central and
southern America with thirty species, though it has been
most extensively exploited in the Yucatan area of Mexico,
Belize, and Guatemala. Tapped for the milky resin in its
main stem, *M. budentata* is the source of a nonelastic
rubber used in industry, and *M. zapota* was once used as
the basis of chewing gum. The trees were usually harvested

in the wild every two or three years, a practise dating
back to the Aztec and Mayan civilizations, who were to
some extent responsible for the present distribution of the
species in central America. *Manilkara zapota* is also the
source of an edible plum-like, aromatic fruit. It also
produces a good hard timber (it has been found in many
Mayan ruins), as does *M. hexandra* from India.

Melaleuca   MYRTACEAE
Cajuput Tree
A large genus of 220 species of evergreen shrubs and
trees native to Indomalaysia and the Pacific, and with its
greatest diversity in Australia where over two hundred
species are endemic. *Melaleuca* resembles the genus
Callistemon (to which it is related) and displays simple
crowded, glandular foliage, often papery bark, and showy
flowers with long, conspicuous stamens held in axillary
heads or spikes.

Species such as *M. cajuputi*, which can grow to heights
of 82 ft (25 m), are exploited in their native habitat for a
variety of uses. Cultivated as ornamental specimens, the
bark is also the source of medicinal oils such as cajuput
and niaouli oil (from *M. quinquenervia*), and the trees are
a good source of timber. The common name derives from
the Malay word for white wood.

Melia   MELIACEAE
Pride of India, White Cedar,
Ceylon Mahogany
Three species of deciduous trees to 50 ft (15 m) tall are
included in this genus and widely distributed throughout
the Old World Tropics to Australia. Alternate pinnate
leaves form the backdrop to loose panicles of fragrant
white or lilac flowers, making them attractive choices
as ornamentals. The main species cultivated, *Melia
azederach*, is fast growing and exploited for its timbers
which is much used in construction. It is now widely
naturalized outside its native habitat. The leaves and bark
are also the source of various medicinal compounds and
its yellow fruits are often used as beads.

ABOVE Mango, *Mangifera indica*,
is a tall, tropical tree with a
dense, heavy crown. Its leaves
are coppery, purplish red when
young, maturing to green, and
lance-shaped. The fruits grow
in clusters.

BELOW Flowers of the *Melaleuca*
species are really an
inflorescence formed by a cluster
of flowers. Their petals are small;
the pink and red stamens are
their most conspicuous feature.

Mesua
GUTTIFERAE
Ironwood

Mesua is a genus of some forty species of evergreen tropical trees native to Indomalaysia. They grow to over 33 ft (10 m) with simple, opposite, leathery leaves and large showy, fragrant solitary flowers, held in the leaf-axils. The predominantly grown species, *M. ferrea*, is widely cultivated as the source of an extremely hard wood, hence the common name, used for railway sleepers. It is also often planted on sacred ground in Sri Lanka, India, and Malaya. The flowers have some medicinal properties.

Metrosideros
MYRTACEAE
New Zealand Christmas Tree

The fifty species of *Metrosideros* are shrubs, climbers, and trees, to 33 ft (10 m), distributed throughout eastern Malaysia, New Zealand, the Pacific, and South Africa. They are evergreen, aromatic plants with simple, opposite, glandular leaves and attractive colorful flowers in axillary and sometimes terminal inflorescences.

Grown mainly as ornamental trees for their leathery foliage and attractive flowers, some (*M. polymorpha* and *M. robusta*) provide useful timbers for the construction industry. The best-known ornamental species, both from New Zealand, are the endemic *M. excelsa*, which has a show of crimson flowers at Christmas time (summer in the southern hemisphere), and *M. umbellatus*. The tree species are also sometimes utilized as hedging plants.

Metroxylon
PALMAE
Sago Palm

A genus of five monocarpic palms restricted to eastern Malaysia, which grow to 33 ft (10 m) tall with extremely large (to 23 ft/7 m long) pinnate leaves and equally large inflorescences. The main species exploited is *M. sagu*, the Sago Palm. To extract the sago, trees are felled as soon as the inflorescence appears and the stems are then washed and crushed. When allowed to grow to maturity, the fruits take many years to ripen, and though the main stem dies after flowering, the trees will often produce suckers from the base.

Milicia
MORACEAE
Iroko

A small but important genus of two species from tropical Africa. The trees, to 66 ft (20 m) tall and with a white milky latex, are dioecious with the male flowers in dense spikes and the female flowers forming large globose heads. Occasionally planted as ornamentals, these trees are more commercially exploited for wood. *Milicia excelsa*, known as African Teak, is the source of a strong termite-proof timber widely used for furniture. It is now endangered because of overexploitation.

Moringa
MORINGACEAE
Horseradish Tree

Native to semiarid areas of Africa and Asia, the twelve, deciduous trees of this genus are grown mostly for their ornamental value. They grow to 26 ft (8 m) tall with thick succulent trunks (especially *Moringa ovalifolia*), large spirally arranged pinnate leaves, and long racemes of white or red fragrant flowers.

Moringa oleifera is the most widely exploited species. It is grown as an ornamental in tropical and subtropical regions, and is also of economic value. Its seeds act as water purifiers and yield an edible oil (also valued in the paint and cosmetics industry); likewise its roots are edible.

The bloated white trunk of *Moringa ovalifolia* makes the Horseradish Tree stand out starkly in the landscape, earning it the common name "Ghost Tree." The crown is distinctively gnarled and misshapen.

Musa violascens, a wild Banana. It is not a true tree because the trunk is composed of the fleshy, overlapping bases of the leaves, not wood.

Musa
Banana   MUSACEAE

As with *Ensete* (*see* page 259), this genus of thirty-five tropical, rhizomatous herbs are not strictly trees as they are nonwoody, but they attain tree-like proportions reaching as much as 20 ft (6 m) in height. They bear large simple elliptical leaves in a spiral arrangement and a terminal flower spike. *Musa* is native to tropical Asia, but is now extensively cultivated throughout the Tropics, especially in South America and the Caribbean.

Originally cultivated in Asia in ancient times as fiber plants, the genus is now best known for the production of edible fruits, and banana plantations are now a major economic resource of many tropical American countries. The bananas now exported worldwide are derived from forms of *M. acuminata* and the hybrid *M.* × *paradisiaca*, though other species are eaten locally, such as *M. textilis*, which is also used as a source of fiber.

Plants of this genus are also increasingly seen planted as ornamentals, either in gardens in warmer regions, or as houseplants in more temperate parts.

Musanga
Umbrella Tree   CECROPIACEAE

Musanga, a small genus of two species of evergreen trees, *M. cecropioides* and *M. smithii*, is native to tropical Africa and closely related to *Cecropia* (Trumpet trees), though not harboring ants as is characteristic of that genus. The compound leaves are arranged alternately in terminal rosettes and the small flowers form round heads.

Musanga cecropioides is cultivated as an ornamental

fast-growing tree, reaching 66 ft (20 m), though it is relatively short-lived, lasting perhaps twenty to twenty five years. Both species produce stilt roots and are also harvested for their light timber, which is used in the construction of rafts and similar objects, though it is now largely superseded by the introduction of the related *Cecropia peltata*.

Myristica
Nutmeg   MYRISTICACEAE

An economically important genus of large dioecious evergreen trees reaching 33 ft (10 m), native to Asia and Australia but now cultivated throughout the Tropics. They have alternate simple leaves, often waxy below, and small flowers are in axillary clusters.

Nutmeg and mace are derived from *Myristica fragrans*. The yellow fruit is fleshy and contains the kernel wrapped in the fine network of the waxy red aril, which is the source of mace. The kernel (nutmeg) is ground, and used as a flavoring. The major producers are Indonesia and Grenada in the West Indies. *Myristica fragrans* is also sometimes grown as an ornamental tree in tropical coastal regions.

Myroxylon
Peru Balsam   LEGUMINOSAE

A useful genus of two to three species of resinous evergreen trees which grow to 40 ft (12 m) with alternate, pinnate, glandular leaves, and axillary or terminal racemes of small pea-like flowers. The species are native to tropical America but now naturalized in the Old World Tropics.

Myroxylon balsamum is the source of a sweet balsam used to flavor medicines and ointments; var *pereirae* is the source of Peru balsam, now used in the same way, but it was formerly highly valued for its medicinal properties. It is also the source of a good timber and is occasionally planted as an ornamental in tropical regions.

Myrtus
Myrtles   MYRTACEAE

Restricted to North Africa and the Mediterranean, *Myrtus* is a genus of two evergreen shrubby trees, which can grow to 16 ft (5 m) in height. The species possess opposite, simple, aromatic foliage and solitary white or pink flowers in the leaf-axils.

Naturally found in maquis scrub of the Mediterranean, *Myrtus communis* especially has been long and widely cultivated for its aromatic foliage and the oil extracted from its flowers and fruit, which is used in perfumes. It has many ritual and ceremonial associations. Consequently there are now several recognized varieties and many different cultivars, and the original natural distribution is today unclear. The wood is also utilized for furniture and a tannin is derived from the roots.

Nephelium — SAPINDACEAE
Rambutan

Nephelium is a genus of twenty-two species of evergreen trees to 66 ft (20 m) tall and with alternate, simple or compound leaves, and small insignificant flowers in loose clusters.

Nephelium is native to Indomalaysia and contains the important fruit tree *N. lappaceum*, the Rambutan, which reproduces apomictically (by self-pollination). Its seeds do not germinate in the wild unless they are eaten by monkeys and then excreted. *Nephelium ramboutan-ake* is also cultivated for its edible fruit and many cultivars of both species exist. The pulped seeds are also edible. The genus is closely related to *Litchi*.

Nypa — PALMAE
Nypa Palm

Nypa is a monocarpic palm genus of mangroves from India to the Solomon Islands. The single species, *N. fruticans*, is a monoecious tree, its stem often either subterranean or prostrate. The large-leaved, pinnate fronds extend to 33 ft (10 m) in length with the inflorescences emerging from the leaf-axils. The seeds are sea dispersed, requiring permanent moisture to complete the germination process, which apparently begins prior to release.

Because of its ability to withstand constant immersion at the roots in its native mangrove areas, the tree is sometimes used to help control erosion. Other economic uses include using the leaves for thatching and basket-making, and the inflorescences are tapped for their sap, to be fermented as palm wine.

Ochroma — BOMBACACEAE
Balsa

This genus is composed of single variable species, *Ochroma pyramidalis*, a fast-growing tree to 100 ft (30 m), often with buttressed roots. The leaves are alternate, either simple or palmately lobed, and the large, solitary, whitish yellow flowers, which are up to 5 in (12 cm) in diameter and tubular, are bat-pollinated.

Native to the lowland tropical forests of tropical America, where it is a pioneer tree, the species is generally found in forest clearings where it is harvested for its remarkably light timber (it is the lightest commercial timber available) for use in insulation and model construction.

Ocotea — LAURACEAE
Greenheart

A genus of 350 species of tropical tree ranging from tropical and warm America through tropical Africa, South Africa, and Madagascar, with a single species present in the relict laurel forests of Macaronesia. Most species of *Ocotea*, however, are native to tropical America. The usually evergreen leathery leaves are glandular—as are most parts—and the three-parted flowers are held in racemes.

Ocotea is extensively used as timber: *O. cymbarum* from Brazil has fragrant bark, *O. rubra* is widely exploited in the Americas, while in Africa *O. bullata* is probably the most economically important species.

Opuntia — CACTACEAE
Prickly Pear

A diverse genus of two hundred species, which range in habit from low-growing prostrate forms to shrubs and trees up to 33 ft (10 m) tall (*Opuntia brasiliensis*), though more usually 10–13 ft (3–4 m). The segmented stems of *Opuntia* may be either cylindrical or flattened and are often spiny, though all possess glochids (short, barbed hairs) which can cause severe skin irritation. The usually solitary, large flowers are diurnal and also bear glochids and sometimes spines. The genus has a wide distribution, from southern Canada to the southern tip of South America.

Some species (especially *O. ficus-indica*) are harvested for their edible fruits and spineless forms are often used as a source of forage. The more spiny species may be utilized as fencing. Other cultivated species include *O. cochenillifera*, which is the source of cochineal.

Some species introduced to Australia and South Africa have become invasive (for example *O. aurantiaca*), in grazing land, but are now controlled by moth larvae imported from their native habitat.

The pink/red flowers of *Opuntia fulgida* are displayed at the joint tips or old fruit tips in midsummer. Unlike other *Opuntia* species, *O. fulgida* fruit do not ripen, but remain on the plant and then a new flower and fruit develop upon the old fruit the following year.

Orbigyna
PALMAE
Babassu Palm

Orbigyna is a species of genus of twenty slow-growing palms native to tropical America. They can reach 50 ft (15 m), and have huge pinnate leaves to 26 ft (8 m) in length. The inflorescences, both male and female, arise in the leaf-axils of the lower leaves and may be up to 10 ft (3 m) in length.

Principally found in tropical rainforest the species are exploited for a wide variety of uses, particularly for the valuable oil extracted from the kernels (*O. phalerata* especially), which is used in cosmetics. Many other species possess edible seeds, and the leaves of *O. spectabilis*, among others, are often used for thatching by indigenous peoples.

Oxydendrum
ERICACEAE
Sourwood

Oxydendrum is a monospecific genus native to the southeastern United States. The single species, *O. arboreum*, is a deciduous tree to 82 ft (25 m) tall with attractive fissured bark, and alternate elliptical leaves. The small cylindrical flowers are held in long terminal panicles.

Though relatively slow growing and tender, the Sourwood is cultivated as an ornamental for the panicles of fragrant white flowers that appear in late summer, and for its attractive deep-red fall foliage.

Pachycerus
CACTACEAE
Tree Cactus

The dozen species of tree-like cacti that make up this genus come from Central America. They have erect spiny or spineless stems that can grow to 50 ft (15 m), and tubular diurnal or nocturnal, often woolly flowers and fleshy globose fruits.

Various members of the *Pachycerus* genus are cultivated as ornamentals for their statuesque habit, including *P. pecten-aboriginum* and the similar *P. pringlei*, which form tall branching specimens with large white flowers. Their fruits are edible and the seeds can also be ground for flour.

Palaquium
SAPOTACEAE
Gutta Percha

A genus of over one hundred species found throughout Indomalaysia, Taiwan, and Samoa, all containing the white latex characteristic of the Sapotaceae family. Trees may be 100 ft (30 m) tall with spirally arranged simple leaves and small clusters of scented flowers.

The so-called Garden Cactus, *Pachycerus pringlei*, is a striking feature of the arid landscape in Baja California. It is the world's largest cactus, some having been measured at nearly 70 ft (21 m) tall and weighing up to 25 tons. Flowers appear on the upper tips of the stems and open at night, as they depend on nectar-feeding bats for pollination.

As with other members of the family, *Palaquium* is becoming increasingly important as a timber source. However, the trees are most commonly cultivated as the source of gutta-percha, a whitish rubber-like substance that is derived from the coagulated milky latex of various species but from *P. gutta* in particular. This substance has many properties and was once much exploited for industry—especially as a form of electrical insulation—and also for dental work, where it is still used today.

Pandanus
PANDANACEAE
Screw Pines

Found throughout the Old World Tropics though especially Malaysia, this is an extremely large genus (around seven hundred species) of dioecious evergreen trees that produce conspicuous stilt roots, and may grow up to 66 ft (20 m) tall, as in the case of *Pandanus utilis*. They have a mass of leaves resembling those of the pineapple, and form twisted spirally arranged terminal rosettes, with the lower stems bearing the old leaf-scars. The leaves themselves are usually long and thin and the flowers are terminal spadices.

Screw pines are widely distributed, often in maritime locations where the heavy, cone-like fruits are dispersed by the tides or by sea-dwelling animals such as turtles and crabs. They have a range of uses: the fibrous fruits of *P. julianettii*, for instance, are edible when cooked, and the leaves are commonly used for thatching and basketry. Other uses include the extraction of perfumes from the male spadices, for which *P. fascicularis* is widely cultivated in India.

The binding action of their stilt roots makes *Pandanus* species useful in erosion control. Some species are also seen in cultivation as ornamentals, including *P. veitchii*, which is commonly grown as a houseplant in more temperate regions.

Parkinsonia
LEGUMINOSAE
Jerusalem Thorn

The genus *Parkinsonia* comprises perhaps up to thirty species of usually thorned, evergreen trees native to the drier parts of America, and to northeast and South Africa. They grow to heights of 30 ft (10 m), with green branches and pinnate foliage. Their numerous scented yellow to orange flowers, which appear in spring, are held in short axillary clusters.

Appreciated as graceful ornamental trees, species such as *P. florida* are often found in the wild, following water-courses in the deserts of the southwest United States. Another important species, *P. aculeata*, in addition to being cultivated as an ornamental, is harvested for the fibers from the stem, which are used in the manufacture of paper pulp.

Pereskia

Tree Cactus

Pereskia is a small genus found in the Caribbean and Central and South America. The sixteen species range in form from leafy trees up to 26 ft (8 m) tall to small shrubs and scrambling climbers. Although the stems are not swollen and lack glochids (irritant hairs) the leaves are succulent, and it appears to represent a primitive lineage in the family. The smallish diurnal flowers are usually held in panicles though may also be solitary.

The main cultivated species, *P. aculeata*, is not strictly a tree but a climber to 33 ft (10 m) grown for its edible fruit and its ornamental value. *Pereskia grandiflora*, a tree to over 16 ft (5 m), also produces fleshy edible fruits.

Pericopsis

Afrormosia

Pericopsis is a genus of three species native to tropical Africa and one other, which ranges from Sri Lanka to Micronesia, previously known under the name *Afrormosia*. All have the distinctive pinnate foliage and pea-like flowers characteristic of the Leguminosae family. None is extensively cultivated but some, especially *P. elata* and *P. laxiflora* (also known as False Dalbergia), both from West Africa, are important timber trees.

Persea

Avocado

An economically important genus of two hundred species of evergreen trees and shrubs native to tropical America and Asia. The trees can be up to 66 ft (20 m) tall, and have alternate, entire leaves and small insignificant greenish-white flowers in terminal or axillary panicles.

Cultivated for many thousands of years for their extremely vitamin-rich fruit, known as avocados or avocado pears, the most important species is *Persea americana* from Central America. Many cultivars and races are derived from this species, and various crosses are now widely cultivated in Africa, Israel, and California for export, especially to Europe. Species exploited for their timber include *P. borbonia* and *P. nanmu*.

Phoenix

Date Palm

Phoenix is distributed throughout tropical and warm Asia and Africa, with a single species in Europe (*Phoenix theophrasti*), and one, *P. canariensis*, in the Canary Islands. Seventeen species of dioecious palms to 100 ft (30 m) tall, with solitary erect stems and pinnate leaves to 10 ft (3 m) in length, make up the genus. The inflorescences, which can be up to 10 ft (3 m) long, though usually shorter, are interfoliar and bear the fleshy blue-black fruits for which the genus is best known.

By far the most important species is *P. dactylifera*, cultivated for thousands of years and a significant source of fruit (usually dried and sold as dates). Formerly an important local staple crop in arid areas, the species is now widely commercially grown and there are many cultivars. The leaves are used for thatching and the wood for timber. Some species, such as *P. sylvestris*, are also a source of palm sugar and toddy. *Phoenix canariensis* is widely grown as an ornamental street tree in its native Canary Islands and in southern Europe.

The Date Palm *Phoenix dactylifera* is a handsome tree rising to 100 ft (30 m). It has striking blue/gray fronds which push stiffly outward up to 25 ft (7 m) and are spiny at the base. Its tiny flowers develop among the fronds, each sex on a different tree.

Pimenta

Allspice

Native to the forests of tropical America, the genus *Pimenta* comprises up to five species of tropical tree to 50 ft (15 m tall) with leathery, evergreen, opposite, entire leaves and clusters of flowers in short-stemmed branching inflorescences. Both the leaves and flowers are glandular, containing the aromatic oils typical of members of the Myrtaceae family.

Some species, among them *P. racemosa*, which once were used to flavor bay rum and in scents, have been introduced elsewhere. The spice for which the genus is known is extracted from the unripe fruits of *P. dioica* and is used as a flavoring.

Pistacia   ANACARDIACEAE
Mastic

This genus of nine dioecious shrubs and trees to 33 ft
(10 m) tall is found throughout the Mediterranean region
and Asia as well as in Central America, and the southern
United States. The usually deciduous pinnate leaves are
alternate and the tiny flowers are in short panicles up to
8 in (20 cm) long.

The trees have been cultivated since ancient times for
their many products, including mastic, a gum extracted
from the evergreen *Pistacia lentiscus*, and oils used in
varnishes, and at one time turpentine (*P. terebinthus*).
The seeds are edible; *P. vera* has been grown for its prized
nuts for many years in central and western Asia, and is
now extensively cultivated in the Mediterranean region
and North America.

Plumeria   APOCYNACEAE
Frangipani

Seventeen deciduous shrubs and small trees form this
small tropical American genus. The trees grow to 23 ft
(7 m) tall with swollen branches forming a candelabra
shape, and alternate, entire, lanceolate leaves. The white,
yellow, pink, or (more often) mixed flowers are showy,
tubular, and very fragrant, and borne in terminal clusters,
usually on the bare branches.

Plumeria are widely cultivated as ornamental plants
across the Tropics—especially *P. rubra*, a tallish tree,
tolerant of coastal conditions, the flowers of which, when
produced en masse, are used as offerings in temples. The
bark is reputed to have purgative properties.

Protea punctata grows to 13 ft
(4 m) and has a waterlily-like
flower with bracts that open
wide to display a white/pink
flower in the middle.

Protea   PROTEACEAE
Proteas

Protea comprises over one hundred evergreen shrubs and
small trees native to tropical and South Africa, where the
highest concentration of species occurs, many of them
endemic. The trees do not exceed 20 ft (6 m), and have
alternate, simple, leathery leaves and usually solitary,
terminal inflorecences composed of many large showy
flowers. The flowers are a source of nectar that attracts
many bird and bee pollinators.

Primarily grown as ornamentals, species such as
P. neriifolia and *P. grandiceps*, both from South Africa's
Cape, have brightly colored flowers, which are useful for
drying, and also attractive foliage. The cut heads are very
long-lasting and much favored in the cut-flower trade—
especially those of *P. cynaroides*.

Pterocarpus   LEGUMINOSAE
Padouk, Redwood

A pantropical legume genus of about twenty species of
locally important deciduous timber trees and climbers to
40 ft (12 m) tall. With typically alternate, pinnate leaves
and panicles of attractive pea-like flowers, the species are
also often grown as ornamental and shade trees.

Pterocarpus dalbergioides is extensively used for fine
carpentry work, as is *P. indicus*, which yields a fragrant
timber. Other uses include construction, carving, and also
boatbuilding. Another important species is *P. santalinus,*
used in joinery but also the source of a red dye, widely
used as a mark of caste by Hindus.

Punica   PUNICACEAE
Pomegranate

A small genus of just two species of deciduous shrubs or
small trees to 6 ft (2 m), found from southeastern Europe
to the Himalaya. They have clustered branching,
opposite, crowded entire leaves, and flowers in terminal
or axillary clusters toward the ends of the branches. The
flowers are tubular, fleshy, and brightly colored.

Punica granatum, the Pomegranate, is an ancient
cultigen known as long ago as the Bronze Age and is of
uncertain, possibly Asiatic origin. The fruits have a fleshy
edible pulp surrounding the seeds, which are eaten fresh
or dried and used as an ingredient or condiment. This
pulp is also used to produce the cordial Grenadine. The
ancient Egyptians fermented the fruit into a heady wine.
Sometimes grown as an ornamental, *P. granatum* is
mostly exploited for its fruit, though its bark is used as
a tannin and as a medicinal agent.

The only other species, *P. protopunica,* from the
isolated islands of Socotra in the Arabian Sea, is now
endangered, having been reduced to a very small number
of individuals through overexploitation.

Raphia farinifera is at home on the edges of rivers and lakes in Madagascar and East Africa. It is a spectacular palm, with a trunk 30 ft (10 m) tall and leaves that can grow to 60 ft (20 m). Inflorescences are produced at the top of the trunk

Quassia   SIMAROUBACEAE
Bitterwood

A pantropical genus of forty species of small deciduous tropical trees to 13 or 16 ft (4 or 5 m), with alternate, pinnate or simple leaves, which are often flushed red when young before becoming glossy green. The panicles or racemes of tiny, often brightly colored flowers give rise to multiple fruits, which may become large and woody.

The genus is sometimes planted for its esthetic value, but primarily cultivated for its chemical properties. Various species are exploited as a source of bitters, such as *Quassia amara* and *Q. cedron,* while others, including *Q. indica,* are the source of medicinal oils.

Quillaja   ROSACEAE
Soap Bark Tree

A small genus of just three species of evergreen shrubs or trees growing no taller than 33 ft (10 m), with glossy, leathery leaves, which are alternate and simple. Their large white, rosaceous flowers with purple centers are polygamous.

Native to warm temperate regions of South America, the species are tender, though they are sometimes grown as ornamental specimens for their attractive foliage and flowers. They are best known, however, especially *Quillaja saponaria* from Chile, for the medicinal properties of their inner bark, which is also a source of saponin and was formerly used in soap manufacture.

Raphia   PALMAE
Raffia

A monocarpic palm genus native to tropical Africa with a single species also in tropical America. The twenty-eight species occur in a variety of habitats though rarely in arid areas. They grow to 82 ft (25 m) tall and have pinnate leaves to an impressive 66 ft (20 m)—the largest in the plant kingdom. The inflorescence appears between the leaves and is usually branched, and it may be pendent or erect and tightly clustered.

Raffias are cultivated in their native regions for a variety of uses, principally raffia, a fiber made from the young leaves. The older leaves are a source of wax, and the trees are also utilized for construction purposes. *Raphia farinosa* is perhaps the most widely grown species, while others (*R. hookeri* and *R. palma-pinus*) are exploited for palm wine.

Ravenala   STRELITZIACEAE
Travelers Tree

A single species endemic to secondary rainforests in Madagascar forms this genus. *Ravenala madagascariensis* is often referred to as the Travelers Palm, though it is in fact not related to the palm family. It is a giant tree-like herb up to 52 ft (16 m) tall, forming clumps of palm-like stems with large alternate leaves to 13 ft (4 m) long. The leaves are elliptical and become shredded, which adds to their palm-like appearance.

Both pith and seeds are edible, and the floral bracts and leaf sheaths hold water—hence the common name. The species is now widely planted throughout the Tropics as an ornamental tree.

Rhododendron   ERICACEAE
Rhododendron

A large genus of some 850 species of deciduous and evergreen shrubs and trees native to northern temperate regions, including the Himalaya, Southeast Asia, Malaysia and North America. They have a wide altitudinal range, from lowland tropical rainforest almost up to the treeline at 19,000 ft (5,800 m) in the Himalaya. The simple entire, usually evergreen leaves are alternate and vary greatly in size, color, and texture. The often showy, colorful flowers are held in lateral or terminal racemes.

Rhododendrons are horticulturally extremely important with many hundreds of species in cultivation and over one thousand named cultivars. Some species are invasive, however, including *Rhododendron ponticum,* introduced from southern Europe, which is now an aggressive weed on acid soils in Britain. Apart from an ornamental value, some rhododendrons are harvested for their leaves, which are used as an insect repellant in China (*R. molle*), or as the basis for a tea in North America (*R. tomentosum*).

Ricinus   **EUPHORBIACEAE**
Castor Oil

A monospecific genus native to East and northeast Africa
and the Middle East though now widely naturalized
throughout the Tropics. The single species, *Ricinus
communis*, a small monoecious tree to 13 ft (4 m), has
large alternate, palmately lobed leaves and terminal
panicles of flowers, the female flowers at the base and the
males toward the apex.

Ricinus is often seen as an ornamental bedding plant in
temperate regions, though the species has been grown for
more than 5,000 years in its native regions, largely for the
oils extracted from the seeds. As with other members of
the family, all parts of the plant possess a milky latex, and
the seeds are the source of ricin—a poison. Previously
used in ancient times as a purgative, the seed oils are also
used in a wide variety of products including soaps,
varnishes, and cosmetics.

ABOVE The seed pods
of *Ricinus communis*
are globular, prickly,
and contain three flat
seeds. They explode
when ripe.

LEFT The Royal Palm (*Roystonea
regia*) has a smoothly sculpted
trunk which is swollen at the
base. The canopy tops the
crown shaft—an extension of
the trunk made up by the
overlapping bases of the leaves.

Roystonea   **PALMAE**
Royal Palm

Roystonea comprises up to a dozen species of large (up
to 82 ft/25 m), statuesque palms native to the Caribbean
and northwest South America. The trees are monoecious
with columnar stems and pinnate foliage up to several
feet in length and relatively short-branched inflorescences.
They can be locally dominant in some areas.

Sometimes cultivated as ornamentals—*R. regia* in
particular—royal palms make ideal street trees in tropical
regions with their tall straight stems and noble stature,
but they have other uses too. Some have edible fruits and
the long fronds of their leaves are used for thatching.
Edible palm hearts, with a flavor similar to artichoke,
come from *R. regia* and *R. oleracea*.

Sabal   **PALMAE**
Palmetto

Distributed from the southeast United States to South
America, *Sabal* comprises sixteen species of palms
ranging from stout dwarf species to trees up to 100 ft
(30 m) tall in the case of *S. palmetto*. The palmate leaves
can be between 2 and 10 ft (0.6–3 m) long, and the leaf
bases of old leaves often persist, clothing the erect stems.
The interfoliar inflorescence is branched and may reach
the same length as the leaves, with the branches each
bearing solitary tubular cream flowers.

Occasionally cultivated as ornamental specimens in
tropical regions, the species are widely exploited in their
native regions. The leaf fibers, especially of *S. causiarum*,
are of commercial importance and are used in thatching,
matting, and basketry. *Sabal palmetto* is similarly used
and is also the source of palm cabbage.

Santalum   **SANTALACEAE**
Sandalwood

A widely distributed genus of twenty-five species of
evergreen shrubs and small trees to 10–13 ft (3–4 m),
native to Indomalaysia, Australia, Hawaii, and Juan
Fernandez Island off the coast of Chile. The leaves are
opposite and leathery and the flowers held in panicles.
The genus is semiparasitic on the roots of other plants,
hence often difficult to establish in cultivation.

Santalum has long been exploited, however, for its
fragrant wood and distilled oils used in perfumes and
incense-making. Many species have suffered from being
overexploited, including *S. freycinetianum* in Hawaii,
and one, *S. fernandezianum*, has been extinct since the
beginning of the twentieth century. *Santalum album* is
widely cultivated in India in addition to being harvested
in the wild, and is an important and costly commodity,
highly valued for its hard, light-colored heartwood as
well as its aromatic oils.

Schinus　　　　　　　　　　　　　　　**ANACARDIACEAE**

Pepper Tree

This genus comprises twenty-seven evergreen, usually dioecious, shrubs and elegant, graceful trees up to 50 ft (15 m) tall. The leaves are alternate and variable, ranging from entire simple forms to dentate, and from thin to leathery, depending on the species. The many small flowers are held in branching panicles, often followed by attractive fruits.

　　Schinus is native to tropical America. *Schinus molle* is the most well-known species in cultivation, forming an attractive pendent tree with clusters of pink fruits, and is frequently grown as an ornamental or used as a shade tree. Its seeds may be ground and used as a substitute for pepper. Another commonly cultivated species, *S. trebinthifolius*, is a native of southern South America but now naturalized in Florida, where it can sometimes cause dermatological or respiratory problems. It exhibits a more upright habit than *S. molle*, and bears attractive white fruits in winter.

Senna　　　　　　　　　　　　　　　**LEGUMINOSAE**

Senna

A large and diverse genus composed of over three hundred and fifty herbs, shrubs, and trees up to 130 ft (40 m) tall in the case of *Senna multijuga*, though usually no more than 33 ft (10 m). Species of *Senna* are distributed throughout the Tropics, with a few, —for instance *S. marilandica* (a herb)— extending as far north as Iowa. All possess the typical pinnate foliage of the Leguminosae family and panicles of small pea-like flowers. *Senna* differs from *Cassia* in the shape of the filaments and the absence of bracteoles.

　　Several species of *Senna* are cultivated as ornamentals, while others are highly valued for their medicinal properties such as *S. auriculata*. The Senna of commerce is mostly derived from the pods and leaves of *S. italica* and *S. alexandrina*. *Senna siamea* is cultivated both as an ornamental and as the source of a strong hard timber.

Shorea　　　　　　　　　　　**DIPTEROCARPACEAE**

Meranti, Alan, Balau, Selangan

Shorea is an extremely important genus of over three hundred and fifty species of very large tropical tree up to 230 ft (70 m) tall with alternate simple leaves, small flowers, usually borne in racemes, and the fruit a single-seeded winged nut. This genus dominates the graceful mixed-dipterocarp forests of Southeast Asia. These trees and the forests in which they are found, are a globally important source of hardwood.

　　Many species, among them *S. albida*, *S. curtisii*, *S. Leprosula*, *S. macrophylla*, and *S. ovata*, are widely harvested commercially. The timber is used in the construction industry as veneers or plywood. All species possess resin canals and exude an aromatic resin, dammar, used in varnishes, though this is a minor product in comparison to their enormous value to the timber trade.

Spathodea　　　　　　　　　　　**BIGNONIACEAE**

African Tulip Tree

A monotypic genus from tropical Africa, though, due to widespread cultivation, now widely naturalized elsewhere in the Tropics, especially parts of Asia. It forms a tall buttressed tree up to 66 ft (20 m) with pinnate foliage and spectacular terminal racemes of scarlet, tulip-like tubular flowers.

　　Spathodea campanulata is an attractive tree with deep green foliage and, with maturity, fissured bark and the characteristic buttresses. It is widely planted as a specimen park tree, valued for the shade its large crown provides, and also the beautiful profusion of scarlet flowers, carried over long periods.

Strelitzia　　　　　　　　　　　**STRELITZIACEAE**

Bird of Paradise

Restricted to woody glades and riverbank habitats in South Africa, this is a genus of five species of perennial evergreen herbs sometimes becoming woody with age. Some species (*Strelitzia nicolai*) grow to 33 ft (10 m) tall with large banana-like leaves over 6 ft (2 m) long. The inflorescence is enclosed in axillary spathes from which the spectacular flowers emerge sequentially. The flowers are usually brightly colored and nectar bearing, attracting sunbirds in their native region.

　　Strelitzia are widely cultivated as ornamental plants and also for the cut-flower trade, *S. reginae* being the most commonly cultivated species, though at 3 ft (1 m) tall it is more herb- than tree-like. *Strelitzia nicolai* is the giant of the genus, with white or purplish-white flowers.

The African Tulip Tree, *Spathodea campanulata*, has vivid orange-scarlet flowers lined with yellow which can be 4 in (10 cm) in diameter. They appear in large racemes at the ends of branches. As a few open at a time, the display can last a few months. The leaves are large, up to 20 in (50 cm), pinnate, and ruffled.

Strychnos **STRYCHNACEAE**

Strychnine

Strychnos is large pantropical genus of 190 lianas, shrubs, and trees to 66 ft (20 m) tall, with opposite, rounded or elliptical leaves, sometimes sessile and varying from thin or membraneous to thick and leathery. The small, usually white, yellow, or greenish flowers are held in densely branched axillary or terminal heads.

Rarely cultivated for ornamental value, though occasionally used for timber (*S. potatorum*), the genus is best known as the source of strychnine and other toxic alkaloids. *Strychnos nux-vomica* is the commercial source of strychnine used in poisons. Other species (*S. ignatii*) are used medicinally locally, or, as in the case of *S. toxifera*, as a source of curare, a poison much used by indigenous people in South America.

Swietenia **MELIACEAE**

Mahogany

This genus of three species of large evergreen trees with alternate pinnate foliage and panicles of tiny flowers is renowned for its hardwood timber. Specimens grow up to 130 ft (40 m) tall in the tropical rainforests of Central and South America.

Once extensively exploited for their fine timber used in construction and shipbuilding, wild populations of Mahogany have been extensively reduced, with many of the larger trees felled, leaving isolated individuals and trees of inferior quality. *Swietenia mahogani* is the most widely used species, populations of which continue to be logged today. The two others—*S. humilis* and *S. macrophylla*—have similar uses and are now cultivated in plantations.

Syzyigium **MYRTACEAE**

Clove

A huge genus (over one thousand species are recognized) of evergreen shrubs and trees up to 150 ft (45 m) native to the Old World Tropics. The leaves are opposite and glandular, and the often colorful small flowers held in terminal or axillary panicles.

The species are widely cultivated as ornamental trees and for their edible fruits, especially *Syzyigium jambos,* known locally as "rose apple," and *S. aqueum*, known as "water rose apple." The red flowers of *S. aromaticum*, an evergreen tree to 66 ft (20 m), are the principal source of cloves, which are the sundried flower buds. *Syzyigium aromaticum* has been cultivated since ancient times (the Chinese used cloves well before the Christian era for their medicinal and culinary properties) and is now grown all over the Tropics. Currently, Zanzibar, Madagascar, and the Caribbean are the principal producers of this aromatic spice.

Tabebuia **BIGNONIACEAE**

Poui

A genus of some one hundred species of trees to 100 ft (30 m) from tropical America with opposite, simple or digitate leaves and panicles of tubular fragrant flowers. Equally prized for their timber and ornamental value, some, including *Tabebuia chrysantha*, an important coastal species, are resistant to salt spray.

Trees of this genus are the source of an extremely long-lasting and durable timber for which they are much exploited (e.g. *T. guayacan*). Others, among them *T. serratifolia* and *T. rosea*, provide valuable timber and are also cultivated for their ornamental value.

Tamarindus **LEGUMINOSAE**

Tamarind

Now naturalized across the Tropics, the single species of this genus, *Tamarindus indicus,* is an ancient cultigen possibly of tropical African origin. Bearing typical pinnate foliage, this evergreen tree reaches a height of 82 ft (25 m) and produces pendent racemes of up to a dozen yellow and red fragrant flowers, and thin, curved brown pods (fruits) 4–6 in (10–15 cm) long, containing an edible bitter-sweet pulp with a few hard seeds.

On account of its many uses, the Tamarind has long been cultivated. All parts except the roots have medicinal properties and are exploited throughout its current range. The fleshy pulp surrounding the seeds is rich in vitamins and is used in preserves, spice mixtures, drinks, and condiments. The species is also cultivated as an ornamental shade tree and harvested for its timber.

ABOVE The illegal logging of Mahogany growing wild in rainforests is a major factor behind the dwindling world stocks of this much-prized hardwood species.

BELOW *Tabebuia rosea* has a profusion of rosy trumpet flowers borne in short terminal clusters.

Tectona
VERBENACEAE

Teak

Tectona is a small but economically highly important genus of four deciduous trees to 130 ft (40 m) tall, with large entire leaves opposite in pairs, or in threes or more, those on the lateral branches up to 28 × 12 in (70 × 30 cm). The tiny insignificant flowers are held in terminal or axillary panicles to 12 in (30 cm).

Distributed across Southeast Asia and Malaysia, the most significant species is *T. grandis,* which yields a valuable source of timber much utilized in shipbuilding and general construction as well as furniture-making. The green timber is so dense and heavy that it sinks in water—consequently the trees are often ring barked and left to dry out prior to being felled.

Terminalia
COMBRETACEAE

Myrobalan

A pantropical genus comprising some hundred and fifty trees and shrubs with characteristic spirally arranged, large-leaved foliage, often clustered toward the ends of the branches. The trees are widely cultivated as a source of timber (*Terminalia alata,* Indian Laurel), and for tannins and dyes (*T. bellirica* and *T. chebula, myrobalan*). They are also cultivated for shade and as street trees. *Terminalia catappa* (the Indian Almond) is often planted as an ornamental tree. It is salt tolerant and has become naturalized in many instances; it also provides a source of food in the form of an edible nut.

The genus commonly occurs in savanna areas though some species are found in tropical rainforests. *Terminalia amazonica* in the forests of Central America can grow to form a large, buttressed tree, up to 165 ft (50 m) tall.

Theobroma
STERCULIACEAE

Cocoa

A genus of some twenty species of trees to 33 ft (10 m) with large alternate entire leaves, and small flowers either borne in the axils of the leaves or directly on the trunk.

Theobroma is native to lowland tropical America, though the most commonly cultivated species, *T. cacao,* an evergreen tree, is now also widely cultivated throughout the Tropics for the seeds, which are used to make chocolate. Cocoa is a nutritious food with a high energy value and has been cultivated since ancient times. Apparently, it was introduced to Europe by Sir Hans Sloane (1660–1753), who first encountered it in Jamaica, describing it as an "unpalatable drink." Milk chocolate was invented in the nineteenth century, when there was a glut of milk.

Cocoa is now a commercial crop of major economic significance, and the seeds—and the chocolate produced from them—contain many stimulating alkaloids, including caffeine and theobromine. Other species used in the chocolate industry, albeit to a lesser degree, include *T. bicolor, T. angustifolium,* and *T. grandiflorum.*

Toona
MELIACEAE

Australian or Chinese Cedar

Toona is a small genus found from Indomalaysia to Australia, and formerly included in the genus *Cedrela,* which is confined to the Americas. The four or five species are evergreen or deciduous trees to 66 ft (20 m) with attractive bark and pinnate foliage and loose panicles of fragrant flowers.

Toona are important timber trees where they occur, especially *T. ciliata* (Australian Cedar) and *T. sinensis* (Chinese Cedar). Both are used extensively for furniture and construction and also (*T. sinensis* in particular) as a shade tree for coffee crops or as a street tree.

The buttressed Pittier tree (*Terminalia chiriquensis*) is a forest species found in Central and South America. It can reach heights of over 115 ft (35 m).

Trachycarpus   **PALMAE**
Windmill Palm

A palm genus of four or more species of solitary-stemmed, usually dioecious palms to 66 ft (20 m) tall, native to the Himalayan region of subtropical Asia, where they are found in montane oak forest up to 8,200 ft (2,500 m). The leaves are palmate and the branched inflorescences interfoliar.

Trachycarpus is largely cultivated for its ornamental value; one species, *T. fortunei,* is hardy and can withstand relatively severe frosts, and several cultivars exist. They are of limited economic potential, though are cultivated locally for a fiber made from the leaf bases used to make brooms, cord, and similar items. The leaves are also utilized, as are the edible flowers.

Xanthorrhoea   **XANTHORRHOEACEAE**
Grass Trees

The twenty-eight species of this genus, all endemic to Australia, are slow-growing, long-lived evergreen plants, becoming tree-like with succulent stems, which become woody with age. Their grass-like leaves are up to 3 ft (1 m) long, clustered in terminal tufts, and the small white flowers are grouped in striking white spikes borne on long stalks.

Xanthorrhoea have a subtropical arid origin, and thus an esthetic value in desert or semiarid landscapes. However, they are more generally grown for their resins (used in varnishes) which are produced at the bases of old leaves as they are discarded. They are fire-tolerant, and in many cases fire stimulates flowering, which may otherwise be delayed for up to two hundred years in the case of *X. preissii,* though other species flower much more frequently.

Yucca   **AGAVACEAE**
Joshua Tree

Yucca are thick-stemmed plants ranging from evergreen perennial herbs to small shrubs or trees to 33 ft (10 m). The thirty species are found in the southern United States, Mexico, and the Caribbean. All generally have apical rosettes of spirally arranged strap-like leaves, which are

often toothed or spine tipped. The campanulate, fragrant flowers are moth-pollinated and held in dense, erect spikes in the leaf-axils.

Joshua trees make striking ornamental plants, especially *Y. gloriosa.* Many species are also used for the fibers derived from their leaves, among them *Y. brevifolia,* a fast-growing species from the southwest United States. Some species, for instance *Y. elephantipes,* are utilized as a fuelwood, and various others are exploited for their edible fruits or for use in the cosmetics industry.

Zanthoxylum   **RUTACEAE**
Prickly Ash, Satinwood

Zanthoxylum is a pantropical genus of 250 species of deciduous or evergreen spiny trees to 66 ft (20 m) tall, with alternate pinnate leaves and small, usually greenish-yellow or white flowers borne in axillary or terminal panicles, often appearing before the leaves in the deciduous species—in *Z. americanum,* for example.

The trees have aromatic leaves and bark and are sometimes cultivated as ornamentals. However, they are far better known for the medicinal properties of the bark, which contains various alkaloids. The fruits are also harvested and sold as spices (*Z. acanthopodium*), while other species, including *Z. flavum* and *Z. gillettii,* are the source of good-quality timbers.

Ziziphus   **RHAMNACEAE**
Jujube

Occurring throughout the Tropics and subtropics, this is a genus of eighty-six deciduous or evergreen shrubs and trees to 33 ft (10 m), with one species, *Ziziphus jujuba,* reaching into Europe, its huge range being from China to the Mediterranean. Trees of this genus have alternate foliage, and the leaves have thorns at the base of their stalks. The yellow flowers are held in axillary clusters, which ultimately produce the globose fleshy fruits.

Widely exploited throughout their range, many species have edible fruits the size of olives, including *Z. jujuba,* of which there are many cultivars, and *Z. lotus,* which may be eaten fresh, cooked, or dried. Large jujubes, exported from the Far East, are known as "red dates." Other species (*Z. chloroxylon*) are harvested for their timber, or have medicinal properties (*Z. spinosa*).

ABOVE *Yucca brevifolia*, the Joshua Tree, is forked when middle aged, with two dense crowns. It is a slow-growing tree, reaching 25 ft (8 m) tall and 15 ft (4.5 m) wide.

LEFT *Xanthorrhoea* are very slow growing but they are also very long lived. Grass Trees can survive for up to six hundred years. Their stems can reach 3 ft (1 m) tall and their bladelike leaves are just as long.

Further Reading

BAILEY, L.H. (revised 1949). *Manual of Cultivated Plants*. The Macmillan Company, New York.

BAILEY, L.H. & BAILEY, E.Z. ET AL. (1977) *Hortus Third*. Macmillan Publishing Co. Inc., New York; Collier-Macmillan, London.

BEAN, W.J. (8th edn, 1970–1976). *Trees and Shrubs Hardy in the British Isles* (vols 1–3). John Murray, London.

BLACKALL, W.E. (rev. & ed. R.J. Grieve, 1954, 1956). *How to Know Western Australian Wild Flowers*. The University of Western Australia Press, Nedlands, Western Australia.

BOSE, T.K. ET AL. (1988). *Trees of the World Vol I*. Regional Plant Resource Centre, Orissa.

CARR, J.D. (1966). *The South African Acacias*. Conservation Press (Pty) Ltd, Johannesburg, London, Manzini.

CHITTENDEN, F.J. (ed.) (2nd edn, 1956–1969). *Dictionary of Gardening*. Clarendon Press, Oxford.

DALLIMORE, W. & JACKSON, A.B. (4th edn rev. R.G. Harrison). *A Handbook of Coniferae & Ginkgoaceae*. Edward Arnold, London.

DAVIS, P.H. & CULLEN, J. (2nd edn, 1979). *The Identification of Flowering Plant Families*. Cambridge University Press, London, New York, Melbourne.

DIRR, M.A. (1997) *Dirr's Hardy Trees and Shrubs*. Timber Press, Portland.

DIRR, M.A. (2002) *Dirr's Trees and Shrubs for Warm Climates*. Timber Press,

DYER, R.A. (1975). *The Genera of South African Plants* Pretoria.

ENGLER, A. & PRANTL, K. (eds) (2nd edn, 1926, vol. 13). *Die Natürlichen Pflanzenfamilien*. Wilhelm Engelmann, Leipzig.

ENGLER, A. ET AL. (12th edn, 1954, 1964). *Syllabus der Pflanzenfamilien*. Bros Borntraeger, Berlin.

EXELL, A.W. ET AL. (1960–1978). *Flora Zambesiaca*. Crown Agents for Overseas Governments & Administration, London.

GAUSSEN, H. (1943–1968) *Les Gymnosperms, Actuelles et Fossiles*. Toulouse.

HEYWOOD, V.H. (ed.) (1993). *Flowering Plants of the World*. Oxford University Press, New York.

Hillier's Colour Dictionary of Trees & Shrubs (2nd edn, 1993). David & Charles, Newton Abbot.

JOHNSON, H. (rev. edn, 1993). *The International Book of Trees*. Mitchell Beazley, London.

KOMORAOV, V.L. (ed.) *Flora of the USSR* (vol. IX, 1939, vol. X, 1941). Moscow, Leningrad. English trans. Israel Program for Scientific Translation.

KRÜSSMAN, G. (2nd edn, 1960) *Die Nadelgehölze*. Paul Parey, Berlin, Hamburg.

KRÜSSMAN, G. (1985) *Manual of Cultivated Conifers*. Timber Press, Portland.

LITTLE, E.L. *National Audubon Society Field Guide to North American Trees: Western Region* (1994), *Eastern Region* (1996). Alfred A. Knopf, New York.

MABBERLEY, D.J. (2nd edn, 1997). *The Plant-Book: A Portable Dictionary of Vascular Plants*. Cambridge University Press, Cambridge, New York.

MITCHELL, A.F. (1972). *Conifers in the British Isles*. HMSO, London.

MITCHELL, A.F. (1974). *A Field Guide to the Trees of Britain & Northern Europe*. Collins, London.

MOORE, D. AND WHITE, J. (eds) (2003). *Cassell's Trees of Britain & Northern Europe*. Cassells, London.

OHURI, J. (1965). *Flora of Japan*. Smithsonian Institute, Washington, D.C. Portland.

PERRY, F. (1972). *Flowers of the World*. Hamlyn, London, New York, Sydney, Toronto.

POLUNIN, O. & EVERARD, B. (1976). *Trees & Bushes of Europe*. Oxford University Press, London, New York, Toronto.

REHDER, A. (2nd edn, 1940). *Manual of Cultivated Trees & Shrubs Hardy in North America*. Macmillan Publishing Co. Inc., New York.

SCHNEIDER, C.K. (1904–1912). *Illustriertes Handbuch der Laubholzkunde*. Gustav Fischer, Jena.

STERNBERG, G. (2004) *Native Trees for North American Landscapes*. Timber Press, Portland.

TUTIN, T.G. & HEYWOOD, V.H. (eds) (1964–1980). *Flora Europea*. Cambridge University Press, Cambridge, New York, Melbourne.

VAN GELDESEN, D.M. & VAN HOEY SMITH, J.R.P. (1996) *Conifers. The Illustrated Encyclopedia*. Timber Press, Portland.

WILLIS, J.C. (8th edn by H.K. Airy Shaw, 1973). *A Dictionary of Flowering Plants*. Cambridge University Press, Cambridge, New York, Melbourne.

Picture Credits

Glossary

ABAXIAL On the side facing away from the stem or axis.

ACHENE A small, dry, single-seeded fruit that does not split open to release its seeds.

ACICULAR Needle-like (*see* leaf shapes, page 19).

ACUMINATE Narrowing gradually by somewhat concave edges to a point (*see* leaf tips, page 18).

ACUTE Tapering by straight or slightly convex edges to a point (*see* leaf tips, page 18).

ADNATE Joined or attached to; eg stamens attached to petals.

ADPRESSED = APPRESSED Pressed closely to the axis and pointing to the shoot tip.

ALBEDO The whitish, spongy layer lying between the outer skin (flavedo) and juicy segments of Citrus fruits.

ALTERNATE Arranged with one leaf at each node of the stem (*see* leaf arrangement, page 18).

AMPLEXICAUL With leaf bases clasping the stem (*see* leaf arrangement, page 18).

ANASTOMOSIS Joining by cross connections to form a network.

ANDROECIUM The male reproductive organs of a flower; the stamens.

ANGIOSPERM A flowering plant— one that produces seeds enclosed in an ovary; broadleaves, palms and palm-like species are angiosperms. (*See also* Flower, Ovule, Seed.)

ANTHER Terminal part of a stamen, usually borne on a stalk and developing to contain pollen within the pollen sacs (*see* page 20).

APICULATE With a short, sharp, often flexible point (*see* leaf tips, page 18).

APOPHYSIS (of cones) The exposed outer surface of the ovuliferous-scale.

ARBORESCENT Tree-like in size and appearance.

ARIL (adj arillate) Fleshy outgrowth either from the hilum or funicle of a seed or from the stem, as in yews.

ARISTATE Tapering to a sharp point (*see* leaf tips, page 18).

AURICLE (adj auriculate) Small ear-like projection at the base.

AWL-SHAPED Narrow, triangular, flat, stiff, sharp-pointed, usually less than 13 mm (0.5 in) long.

AWN A stiff, bristle-like extension of an organ.

AXIL The upper angle formed by the union of a leaf with the stem.

AXILLARY An organ such as a bud, flower, or inflorescence, in the axil of a leaf.

BERRY Fleshy fruit without a stony layer. Usually contains many seeds.

BIPINNATE A pinnate leaf with the primary leaflets themselves divided in a pinnate manner; cf pinnate (*see* leaf shapes, page 19).

BISEXUAL Male and female reproductive organs in a single flower.

BRACT A modified leaf, often scale-like.

BRACTEOLE A small leaf-like organ, occuring along the length of a flower stalk, between a true bract and the calyx.

BRACT-SCALE (of cones) A modified leaf which subtends the ovuliferous-scale to which it may be fused to form a single scale (*see* cone structure, page 20).

BROADLEAVED TREE Any tree in the subclass Dicotyledonae of the class Angiospermae (flowering plants).

BULLATE Blistered or puckered.

CADUCOUS Falling off easily or prematurely.

CALYX Collective term for all the sepals of a flower (*see* page 20).

CAMBIUM A layer of cells which occurs within stem and roots and divides to produce either secondary vascular tissues (vascular cambium) or cork (cork cambium).

CAPITATE Head-like.

CAPITULUM An inflorescence consisting of a head of closely-packed stalkless flowers.

CAPSULE A dry fruit which normally splits open to release its seeds.

CARPEL One of the flower's female reproductive organs, comprising an ovary and a stigma, and containing one or more ovules (*see* page 20).

CATKIN A hanging cluster of unisexual flowers.

CHROMOSOMES Thread-like strands of DNA which occur in the nucleus of living cells and carry the units of heredity—the genes. Normal cells contain two sets of chromosomes, one derived from each parent.

CILIATE With protruding hairs at the margin (*see* leaf margins, page 18).

CLADODE Flattened stem that assumes the form and function of a leaf.

CLAVATE Club-shaped.

CLONE A group of plants that have arisen by vegetative reproduction from a single parent, and which therefore all have identical genetic composition.

COMPOUND With the leaf blade divided into separate segments (leaflets).

CONCOLOROUS Of uniform color.

CONDUPLICATE Folded longitudinally upward or downward along the axis so that the ventral or dorsal sides face each other.

CONE-SCALE (of conifers) General term for the elements that make up a female cone and subsequently the fruiting cone, that is the bract-scale, ovuliferous-scale or the product of the fusion of these two. In the mature cone the term cone-scale is applied to the main contributor to the structure of the cone (*see* cone structure, page 20).

CONE = STROBILUS The reproductive structures of conifers and their allies. Female cones are formed of either alternating ovuliferous-scales in the axils of bract-scales or these scale-pairs are fused to form a series of cone-scales. The ovuliferous- or cone-scales bear naked on their surfaces ovules which contain the eggs. After pollination and fertilization the scales become woody, less often fleshy, the whole structure forming the characteristic fruiting or mature cone which bears the seeds on the surface of the scales. Male cones consist of clusters of pollen sacs and are short-lived after pollen dispersal (*see* page 20).

CONIDIAL A stage in the life cycle of certain fungi in which sexual spores (conidia) are produced.

CONNATE Joined or attached to; said of similar organs fused during formation, such as petals.

CONVOLUTE Rolled together.

CORALLOID Much-branched.

CORDATE Heart-shaped (*see* leaf shapes, page 19).

COROLLA All the petals of a flower.

CORYMB (adj corymbose) A rounded or flat-topped inflorescence like a raceme but the flower stalks are longer on the outside so that the flowers are at about the same level.

COTYLEDON The first leaf, or pair of leaves, of an embryo within the seed. In conifers there are more than two cotyledons for each embryo.

CRENATE (of leaf margins) Shallowly round-toothed, indentations no more than $1/16$ of the distance to the midrib (*see* leaf margins, page 18).

CRENULATE Very shallowly round-toothed, indentations no more than $1/16$ of the distance to the midrib.

CRYPTOGAM A general term applied to plants that do not produce seeds.

CULTIVAR (abbreviation cv) Cultivated variety. A taxonomic rank used to denote a variety that is known only in horticultural cultivation. Cultivar names are nonlatinized and in living languages; typographically distinguished in a non-italic typeface, with a capital initial letter and enclosed in single quotation marks, for example *Betula pendula* 'Fastigiata.'

CUNEATE With the base gradually tapering (*see* leaf shapes, page 19).

CUPULE Cup-like structure surrounding some fruits.

CUSPIDATE With an abrupt, rigid, apical point (*see* leaf tips, page 18).

CV Abbreviation for cultivar.

CYME (adj cymose) An inflorescence in which each terminal growing point produces a flower, with subsequent flowers produced from a lateral growing point, so that the oldest flowers are at the apex, or center if flat.

CZ Climate zone, see page 39.

DECURRENT With the leaf base continuing along the stem (*see* leaf arrangement, page 18).

DECUSSATE Arranged in opposite pairs on the stem, with each pair at 90° to the preceding pair.

DEHISCENT Opening to shed pollen or seeds.

DELTOID Triangular (*see* leaf shapes, page 19).

DENTATE (of leaf margins) Toothed, with the teeth pointing at right angles to the midrib (*see* leaf margins, page 18).

DENTICULATE (of leaf margins) Minutely toothed (dentate).

DICOTYLEDON One of two subclasses of angiosperms which contains the broadleaved trees; a plant whose embryo has two cotyledons; cf monocotyledon.

DIGITATE With leaflets arranged as the fingers of a hand; palmate (*see* leaf shapes, page 19).

DIMORPHIC Having two different shapes and/or sizes within the same species.

DIOECIOUS Having male and female flowers or cones borne on separate plants; cf monoecious.

DIPLOID Having in the nucleus of its cells two sets of chromosomes, one from each parent.

DISCOID Orbicular with convex faces; disc-like.

DISCOLOROUS Not the same color throughout.

DISSECTED Cut into segments.

DISTICHOUS Arranged in two vertical rows.

DIURNAL Daily.

DORSAL Upper.

DRUPE A fleshy fruit containing one or more seeds, each surrounded by a stony layer.

ECOTONE The band of vegetation which forms a boundary between two major vegetation types, as between forest and grassland.

ELLIPTIC Oval-shaped with the widest axis at the midpoint (*see* leaf shapes, page 19).

EMARGINATE With a shallow notch at the apex (*see* leaf tips, page 18).

ENDEMIC A species or population which is either restricted to a special habitat and/or a very limited geographical range.

ENDOCARP The innermost layer of the fruit surrounding the seed.

ENDODERMIS A cylinder of cells surrounding the vascular bundle of a root. All substances passing in or out of the vascular cylinder must

pass through the center of these cells, not between them.

ENSIFORM Sword-shaped (*see* leaf shapes, page 19).

ENTIRE (of leaf margins) Without incisions or indentations (*see* leaf margins, page 18).

EPICALYX A ring of bracts below an inflorescence.

EPICORMIC (of shoots) Developing from dormant lateral buds on the trunk which have become active, for example due to damage.

EPIDERMIS The outer protective, usually single-celled, layer of many plant organs, particularly leaves and herbaceous stems.

EPIGYNOUS (of flowers) With the sepals, petals and stamens inserted near the top of the ovary.

EPIMATIUM (of conifers) The fleshy covering of some seeds.

EPIPHYTE Living on another plant but not dependent on it for nutrition.

EXCURRENT (of veins) Projecting beyond the lamina of a leaf.

EXFOLIATING Cracked or splitting off in flakes or scales.

EXSERTED Protruding.

FALCATE Sickle-shaped (*see* leaf shapes, page 19).

FASCICLE A cluster or bundle.

FASTIGIATE (fastigate) Erect, many branches parallel to the main stem.

FEMALE CONE (of conifers) A cone on the scales of which the female sex organs (the ovules) are borne (*see* cone structure, page 20).

FEMALE FLOWER A flower containing functional carpels but no fertile stamens.

FILAMENT The stalk of an anther (*see* page 20 for representations of half flowers).

FILIFORM Thread-like.

FIMBRIATE (of margins) Fringed, usually with hairs.

FLAVEDO The outer, thin, colored and fragrant skin of Citrus fruits.

FLOWER The structure concerned with sexual reproduction in angiosperms—broadleaves and mono-cotyledonous trees (page 20 shows representations of half flowers).

FOLLICLE A dry fruit which splits open along one side only.

FORMA OR FORM A taxonomic division ranking below variety and used to distinguish plants with trivial differences.

FRUIT Strictly the ripened ovary of a seed plant and its contents. Loosely the structure containing ripe seeds.

FUNICLE The stalk of an ovule.

GENUS A taxonomic rank grouping together more or less closely related plants. The genus title is the first word of the species binomial. A genus may be divided into subgenera, sections, and series, in descending order of hierarchy.

GEOPHYTE A plant that survives from growing season to growing season by means of dormant underground buds, as in bulbs.

GLABRESCENT Becoming devoid of hairs.

GLABROUS Without hairs or projections.

GLAUCOUS With a waxy, grayish-blue bloom.

GLOBOSE Spherical; rounded.

GYMNOSPERM A seed plant in which the seeds are not enclosed in an ovary; conifers are the most familiar example.

GYNOECIUM The female reproductive organs of a flower, comprising one or more free or fused carpels.

HAPLOID Having within the nucleus of its cells only one complete set of chromosomes, as in the gametes or sex cells.

HARDY Able to withstand extreme conditions, usually of cold.

HASTATE Shaped like an arrow-head with the basal lobes outturned (*see* leaf shapes, page 19).

HEAD A cluster of sessile or short-stalked flowers.

HILUM The scar left behind on a seed after separation from the stalk.

HISPID Covered with very long stiff hairs.

HYBRID The offspring of two plants of different taxa, most often species.

HYDATHODE Gland that exudes water.

HYPANTHIUM Cup-shaped enlargement of the floral receptacle or the bases of the floral parts, which often enlarges and surrounds the fruits, eg the fleshy tissue in rose-hips.

HYPODERM(IS) A layer of thickened cells which lies immediately below the epidermis.

HYPOGYNOUS (of flowers) With sepals, petals and stamens attached to the receptacle or axis, below and free from the ovary.

IMBRICATE (of sepals and petals) Overlapping; cf valvate.

IMPARIPINNATE (of pinnate leaves) With an odd terminal leaflet; cf paripinnate.

INCISED Margins deeply and sharply cut (*see* leaf margins, page 18).

INDEFINITE (of flower parts) Of a number large enough to make a precise count difficult.

INFLORESCENCE Any arrangement of more than one flower.

INSERTED Growing from another organ.

INTROGRESSION Transfer of genetic material from one population to another by hybridization followed by backcrossing.

INTRORSE Directed and opening inward toward the center, as in the opening of anthers to shed pollen.

INVOLUCRE A whorl of bracts below an inflorescence.

IRREGULAR (of flowers) Not regular (*see* page 20).

LACERATE (of leaf margins) Irregularly cut.

LACINIATE Deeply cut into narrow ribbon-like projections that may be lobed (*see* leaf margins, page 18).

LAMINA The thin flat blade of a leaf.

LANCEOLATE Narrow with tapering ends (*see* leaf shapes, page 19).

LEAFLET Separate segment of a compound leaf.

LENTICEL A pore through the bark which allows gaseous exchange.

LIANE (liana or vine) A climbing annual or perennial plant with an elongated twining stem.

LIGNOTUBER A woody tuber (swollen under-ground root or stem).

LINEAR Elongated, with parallel sides (*see* leaf shapes, page 19).

LOBE (of flowers) A rounded segment of the corolla and/or calyx.

LOBED (of leaf margins) With large round-toothed incisions.

LOCULE The chamber or cavity of an ovary or anther.

LOCULICIDAL (of fruits) Splitting open longitudinally along the midrib of each segment of the wall.

LONG SHOOT (of conifers) An elongated shoot produced by rapid annual growth.

MALE CONE The male reproductive structure of conifers. Each male cone is a series of modified leaves (microsporophylls) on the under surface of which are pollen sacs (microsporangia) within which the pollen grains develop. Male cones often cluster together into groups.

MALE FLOWER A flower containing functional stamens, but no carpels.

MATURE CONE A woody or fleshy cone containing mature seeds.

MEGASPOROPHYLL (of conifers) The modified leaf which bears the ovules.

MESIC With adequate or high moisture availability or needs.

MESOPHYLL Internal tissues of a leaf that are concerned with photosynthesis; also, term used to describe leaves of size 2025 mm^2 to 18,222 mm^2—the range for most leaves from temperate broadleaves.

MICROPHYLLOUS Small, up to 2025 mm^2, often found on xerophytic plants; cf. nanophyll.

MICROSPORANGIA Structure in which microspores (pollen grains) develop.

MICROSPOROPHYLL (of conifers) The modified leaf on the surface of which the microsporangia develop.

MIDRIB The central supporting strand of a leaf.

MONOCARPIC Fruiting only once and then dying.

MONOCOTYLEDON One of two subclasses of angiosperms, which contains the palms amongst others; a plant whose embryo has one cotyledon; cf dicotyledon.

MONOECIOUS Having separate male and female flowers on the same plant; cf dioecious.

MONOPODIAL With a single main axis from which laterals arise.

MONOTYPIC A genus or family containing a single species.

MUCRO A short sharp point formed by the extension of the midrib.

MUCRONATE Terminated by an abrupt short, sharp point (*see* leaf tips, page 18).

NAKED Not enclosed by scales or other coverings such as petals.

NANOPHYLL Very small leaves with an area not exceeding 225 mm^2.

NEEDLE An elongated slender, needle-like leaf usually over 5 cm (2 in) long.

NUMEROUS Usually meaning more than 10; cf indefinite.

NUT A dry, single-seeded and indehiscent fruit with a woody wall.

OBCONIC Inversely conical.

OBCORDATE Inversely heart-shaped with the notch at the apex (*see* leaf shapes, page 19).

OBLANCEOLATE Lanceolate with the apex broader than the base (*see* leaf shapes, page 19).

OBLATE Globose, wider than long.

OBLIGATE Only able to live in one way, as with obligate parasites, ie plants that can only survive as parasites.

OBLIQUE With unequal bases (*see* leaf shapes, page 19).

OBLONG Longer than broad, with the sides more or less parallel for most of their length (*see* leaf shapes, page 19).

OBOVATE Having the shape of an egg with the narrow end below the middle; inversely ovate (*see* leaf shapes, page 19).

OBTUSE With the tip bluntly rounded (*see* leaf tips, page 18).

OPERCULUM A lid.

OPPOSITE Occurring in pairs on opposite sides of the stem (*see* leaf arrangement, page 18).

ORBICULAR More or less circular (*see* leaf shapes, page 19).

OVARY The hollow basal region of a carpel, containing one or more ovules and surmounted by the style(s) and stigma(s). It is made up of one or more carpels which may fuse together to form one or more chambers (*see* page 20).

OVATE Having the shape of an egg with the narrow end above the middle (*see* leaf shapes, page 19).

OVOID Egg-shaped.

OVULE The female reproductive structure that contains the egg cell. The ovule develops into the seed after fertilization. In gymnosperms, ovules lie naked on the ovuliferous-scale; in angiosperms they are enclosed in an ovary (*see* page 20).

OVULIFEROUS-SCALES (of cones) Highly modified lateral branches of the female cone that arise in the axils of bract-scales and bear the naked ovules. May be woody or fleshy and in some cases fuse with the bract-scales to form a single scale (*see* cone structure, page 20).

PALMATE More than three segments or leaflets arising from a single point (*see* leaf shapes, page 19).

PALMATIFID Cut in a palmate fashion, about half-way to the base (*see* leaf shapes, page 19).

PALMATISECT Cut in palmate fashion, usually more than halfway to the base (*see* leaf shapes, page 19).

PANICLE A branched inflorescence of stalked flowers.

PARIPINNATE (of pinnate leaves) Without a terminal leaflet.

PECTINATE Arranged like the teeth of a comb (*see* leaf shapes, page 19).

PEDATE Palmately-lobed with the outer leaflets or lobes again divided or cleft (*see* leaf shapes, page 19).

PEDICEL The stalk of a single flower (page 20 shows representations of half flowers).

PEDUNCLE The stalk of an inflorescence.

PEG (of conifers) A short lateral stem-projection on which a leaf is produced and which persists after leaf fall.

PELTATE (of leaves and scales) More or less circular and flat with the stalk inserted in the middle (*see* leaf shapes, page 19).

PENDULOUS Hanging loosely or freely.

PENNINERVED With veins extending parallel to each other from the midrib to the edge.

PERFOLIATE Stalkless with the leaf bases enclosing the stem so that the latter appears to pass through the leaf center (*see* page 18).

PERIANTH The floral envelope whose segments are usually divisible into an outer whorl (calyx) of sepals, and an inner whorl (corolla) of petals. Segments of either or both whorls may fuse to form a tube.

PERICYCLE A cylinder of tissue lying immediately inside the endodermis of a root.

PERIDERM The outer protective layer of woody organs; it includes the cork, cork cambium and phelloderm.

PERIGYNOUS (of flowers) Having the stamens, corolla and calyx inserted around the ovary, their bases often forming a disk.

PERULES Scales enclosing a bud; bud-scales.

PETAL A sterile often highly colored segment of the flower; one of the units of the corolla (see page 20).

PETALOID Petal-like.

PETIOLATE With a leaf stalk (petiole) (*see* leaf arrangement, page 18).

PETIOLE Leaf stalk.

PHYLLOCLADE A flattened stem resembling and functioning as a leaf.

PHYLLOMORPHS Young shoots that are spray-like and flattened.

PHYSIOGNOMY The general appearance of a community by which it is recognized.

PINNA The primary division of a fern leaf.

PINNATE Compound, with the leaflets in pairs on opposite sides of the midrib; cf imparipinnate, paripinnate (*see* leaf shapes, page 19).

PINNATIFID Cut pinnately to about half-way to the midrib (*see* leaf shapes, page 19).

PINNATISECT Pinnately divided, but not quite as far as the midrib (*see* leaf shapes, page 19).

PLICATE Folded as a fan.

PODZOL Soil profile with a distinct layer of humus overlying a zone of pale leached soil then a zone that contains the leached particles. Typically developed on well-drained soil with cool climate and high rainfall.

POLLEN Collective name for the pollen grains.

POLLEN SAC Male reproductive body within which pollen is produced.

POLYGAMOUS Having separate male, female and bisexual flowers on the same plant.

POME A fleshy false fruit the main flesh comprising the swollen receptacle, as in the apple.

PUBERULENT Covered in fine hairs.

PUBESCENT Covered in soft, short hairs.

PULVINUS A swelling at the base of a leaflet or leaf stalk, concerned with movement in response to a stimulus.

PUNCTATE Shallowly dotted or pitted, often with glands.

PYRIFORM Pear-shaped.

RACEME An inflorescence consisting of a main axis bearing single flowers alternately or spirally on stalks of about equal length. The apical growing point continues to be active so there is usually no terminal flower and the youngest branches or flowers are nearest the apex.

RACEMOSE Arranged like a raceme; in general any inflorescence capable of indefinite growth.

RECEPTACLE The tip of the pedicel or cone stalk to which the organs of the flower or cone are attached (page 20 shows representations of half flowers).

REGULAR (of flowers) Radially symmetrical (*see* page 20).

RENIFORM Kidney-shaped (*see* leaf shapes, page 19).

RESIN CANAL Space or channel within an organ lined with secreting cells and filled with resinous material.

RETICULATE With the surface marked with a system of ridges.

RETUSE With the leaf-tip very slightly notched (*see* leaf tips, page 18).

REVOLUTE Margins rolled under.

RHOMBOID Diamond-shaped with the widest axis at the midpoint.

ROTATE Wheel-shaped.

RUGOSE Covered with coarse, netted lines.

RUNCINATE Coarsely toothed or incised, with the teeth pointing toward the base (*see* leaf margins, page 18).

SAGITTATE Shaped like an arrowhead (*see* leaf shapes, page 19).

SAMARA A dry fruit in which the wall is extended to form a flattened membrane or wing.

SAPROPHYTE A plant that obtains its nutrients from organic remains of plants and animals.

SCALE A small, membranous or sometimes stiff, reduced leaf.

SCALE LEAF (of conifers) A small, adpressed leaf with overlapping margins.

SCION (of grafts) The part inserted into the stock.

SCLEROPHYLLOUS Adapted to dry conditions, such as hard, stiff, tough leaves.

SECTION A subdivision of a genus ranking between subgenus and series.

SEED Unit of sexual reproduction developed from a fertilized ovule, which either lies naked on the ovuliferous-scale as in gymnosperms (including conifers) or is enclosed in fruit as in angiosperms (including broadleaves and palms).

'SENSU LATO' In a broad sense.

'SENSU RESTRICTO' (sensu stricto) In a narrow or strict sense.

SEPAL A floral leaf or individual segment of the calyx of a flower, usually green (page 20 shows representations of half flowers).

SEPTATE Divided into chambers by walls.

SEPTICIDAL (of fruits) Splitting open longitudinally along the chamber walls so that the carpels are separated.

SEPTUM A wall between chambers.

SERAL One stage in the succession toward a climax vegetation.

SERIATE Arranged in a row.

SERIES A subdivision of genus ranking below section.

SERRATE Saw-toothed, with sharp, ascending teeth (*see* leaf margins, page 18).

SERRULATE Minutely serrate (*see* leaf margins, page 18).

SESSILE Without a stalk (*see* leaf arrangement, page 18).

SHEATHING With a sheath that encases the stem (*see* leaf arrangement, page 18).

SHORT SHOOT (of conifers) A very short lateral shoot which grows slowly if at all and bears the leaves.

SHRUB A perennial woody plant with well-developed side-branches that appear near the base, so that there is no trunk. They are less than 10 m (30 ft) high.

SIMPLE Not divided into leaflets.

SINUATE (of leaf margins) With shallow and smooth indentations (*see* leaf margins, page 18).

SOMATIC All parts of the plant except the gametes or gamete mother cells.

SP Abbreviation for species (singular).

SPATHULATE Spoon-shaped (*see* leaf shapes, page 19).

SPECIES The basic unit of classification. Species are grouped into genera and variations may be broken down into subspecies, variety and forma (form) in descending order of hierarchy. A species name consists of two units (binomial): the genus title and specific epithet, both italicized and only the initial letter of the genus part capitalized, for example *Betula pendula*.

SPINOSE Spiny.

SPINY With spine-tipped lobes (*see* leaf margins, page 18).

SPOROPHYLL A modified leaf which bears reproductive organs.

SPP Abbreviation for species (plural).

SSP Abbreviation for subspecies.

STAMEN The male reproductive organ of a flower. It consists of a bilobed anther, usually borne on a stalk (filament) (*see* half flowers, page 20).

STAMINODE A sterile, or reduced, stamen.

STERILE Not involved in reproduction; not bearing sex organs.

STIGMA The receptive part of the female reproductive organs on which the pollen grains germinate; the apex of a carpel. (page 20 shows representations of half flowers).

STIPEL (adj stipelate) Leafy or scale-like appendage at the base of a leaflet stalk.

STIPULE (adj stipulate) A leafy appendage, often paired, and usually at the base of the leaf stalk (*see* leaf arrangement, page 18).

STOLONIFEROUS Producing stolons—shoots that root at the tip and produce new plants.

STOMATA Pores that occur in large numbers in the epidermis of plants, particularly leaves, and through which gaseous exchange takes place.

STOMATAL BANDS Areas of leaves that have a high density of stomata (pores) and thus appear paler or a yellowish color.

STRIATE With longitudinal lines.

STYLE The elongated part of a carpel or ovary bearing the stigma at its apex (*see* page 20).

SUBGENUS Subdivision of a genus ranking between genus and section.

SUBGLOBOSE Almost globose (round or spherical).

SUBSPECIES A taxonomic division ranking between species and variety. It is often used to denote a geographical variation of a species.

SUBULATE Very narrowly triangular.

SULCATE With longitudinal grooves.

SYMPODIAL Without a main stem or axis but with a number of more or less equal laterals.

SYNCARP A multiple fleshy fruit.

SYNONYM Said of a name once applied but now rejected in favor of the correct one.

TAXON Any taxonomic group, as a species, genus, family etc.

TELEUTOSPORE A thick-walled, overwintering spore produced by rust fungi.

TERETE Cylindrical.

TERMINAL Situated at the apex.

TOMENTOSE Covered in dense, interwoven hairs (trichomes).

TRANSFUSION TISSUE (of conifer leaves) A zone of tissue lying on either side of the vascular bundle.

TRICHOME A hair.

TRIFID Divided into three parts or lobes.

TRIFOLIOLATE With three leaflets (*see* leaf shapes, page 19).

TRIQUETROUS Three-angled with the sides usually concave.

TRUNCATE Tip cut straight across.

TUBE The cylindrical part of a corolla and/or calyx.

TUBERCLE A rounded often warty swelling or protuberance.

TURBINATE Top-shaped.

UMBEL A flat-topped inflorescence with the flower stalks arising from a common point.

UMBO (of cones) A projection on the apophysis of the cone-scale; it may bear a spine or prickle.

UNDULATE (of leaf margins) With shallow inden-tations and wavy in the vertical plane (*see* leaf margins, page 18).

UNIFOLIOLATE With a single leaflet that has a stalk distinct from the entire leaf stalk.

UNISEXUAL Of one sex.

URCEOLATE Urn-shaped.

VALVATE Touching at the edges but not overlapping.

VARIETY Taxonomic division ranking between subspecies and forma, although in the past often used as the major subdivision of a species. Such taxa are named by adding the italicized variety name, preceded by var, to the parent species name, for example *Pinus ponderosa* var *arizonica*. Once used to designate variants of horti-cultural origin or importance, but "cultivar" should now be applied, though many names of horticultural origin still reflect the historical use of the variety rank.

VASCULAR STRANDS Bundles of tissue which conduct water and nutrients around the plant; veins of a leaf.

VENTRAL Anterior or in front; uppermost; nearest to the axis.

VERNAL (of flowers) Opening in the spring.

VILLOUS Covered by long, soft, interwoven hairs.

VISCID Sticky or glutinous.

VIVIPOROUS (of seeds) Germinating before becoming detached from the parent.

XEROMORPHIC Having characteristics which are adaptations to conserve water and so withstand extreme dry conditions.

Index of Common Names

Page numbers in *italic* type refer to artwork: numbers in **bold** type refer to photographs.

Index of Latin Names

Page numbers in *italic* type refer to artwork: numbers in **bold** type refer to photographs.